New York

THE ROUGH GUIDE

KU-441-725

Rough Guide Credits

Text Editor:	Jack Holland
Series Editor:	Mark Ellingham
Editorial:	Martin Dunford, John Fisher, Jonathan Buckley, Greg Ward, Jules Brown, Graham Parker, Jo Mead, Samantha Cook
Production:	Susanne Hillen, Andy Hilliard, Gail Jammy, Vivien Antwi, Alan Spicer
Cartography:	Melissa Flack
Publicity:	Richard Trillo
Finance:	Celia Crowley, Simon Carloss
Administration:	Tania Hummel

Acknowledgements

Thanks on this new edition go to everyone at the Rough Guides office, especially Gail Jammy for editorial suggestions and improvements way beyond the call of duty and Melissa Flack for making map specification seem so easy. We'd also like to thank, in no particular order, Daniela Marino of the State of New York Division of Tourism, Syd Lazarus, Robert Fisher, Dorothy Vaghela, Roy Videen, Lola Lenzo, Bridget Bouch, Greg Ward, Hank. S. Fried, Margaret Doyle for proofreading, Donald Suggs, Phil Cheeseman, the multi-talented Darren Colby, Mog Greenwood, Sally-Ann Whittaker for cash and crusts and Claire Sharp for nooz scanning.

Many thanks also to those who **wrote in** with comments on, and corrections to, previous editions: please keep writing!

Simon Urwin, Dixon Adams, Beth Conchard, Trevor Gordon, Gordon Harper, Cindy Taylor, Tim Perry, Simon Branch, Jamie "Dipso" Brown, Tessa Mooij, Michael Francis, Brian Nugent, Tom Towey, Jennifer Peck, Michael Feinberg, Paula & Steve from Highbury Hill, Jenny Radford, J. Mayle, Ben Andrews, Kate Gunning, George Shanks, John from Leek, Mahala Mehmet, Peter Simmons, Eileen E. Green, Sara Dickinson, Vivienne Conley, Steve Lynch, Sheril Pollard, Gerard van Veen, Andy Cooper, Mantz Yorke, Grace Hodge, (especially) Dr Terence Ingram, Mike and Marilyn Miller, Laura Drazin Boyes, Eveline Thevenard, David McClelland, Penny Geary, R.G. Bowden, David Smith, Jane Lawrence, Hugh Duffy, A.E.M Oijen, Marion Butcher, Alexandre F. Stotz, A.E. Egerton, Brian Anderson, Sylvia Woods, Albert Hoffmann, Igor Pashutinski, Annette Grey, Adrienne Banks, Peter Morris, Damien Rea, Joyce Gold, Jackie Weinstein, Olga Happenin, Peter Smith, Helen Hill, the folks at the Mission, John Davies, Pablo Ramirez, Petri Pajulahti, Richard Connaughton, Yale Alexander, Rory Houston, Robin Katz, Jon Melnick, Ken Scudder, Henrietta O' Connor, Mark Flannagan, Jay Dixon, David Nicholls, Sarah Howell, David Smith, Andrew T. Irving, Bob Smith, Jon Lee, J. Jerrard Dinn, Millie Bastha, R. Audifredi, Andrew Bone and Cynthia Arnolds.

This fourth edition published and reprinted 1994 by Rough Guides Ltd, 1 Mercer Street, London WC2H 9QJ.

Distributed by the Penguin Group:

Penguin Books Ltd, 27 Wrights Lane, London W8 5TZ
Penguin Books USA Inc., 375 Hudson Street, New York 10014, USA
Penguin Books Australia Ltd, 487 Maroondah Highway, PO Box 257, Ringwood, Victoria 3134, Australia
Penguin Books Canada Ltd, 10 Alcorn Avenue, Toronto, Ontario, Canada M4V 1E4
Penguin Books (NZ) Ltd, 182–190 Wairau Road, Auckland 10, New Zealand

Originally published in the UK by Harrap Columbus Ltd.
Previous edition published in the United States and Canada as *The Real Guide New York*.

Printed in the United Kingdom by Cox & Wyman Ltd (Reading).
Typography and **original design** by Jonathan Dear and The Crowd Roars.
Illustrations throughout by Edward Briant.

British Library Cataloguing in Publication Data
A catalogue record for this book is available from the British Library.
ISBN 1-85828-058-3

New York

THE ROUGH GUIDE

Written and researched by

Martin Dunford and Jack Holland

With additional contributions by

Celia Woolfrey, June Joseph and Jeanne Muchnick

THE ROUGH GUIDES

Contents

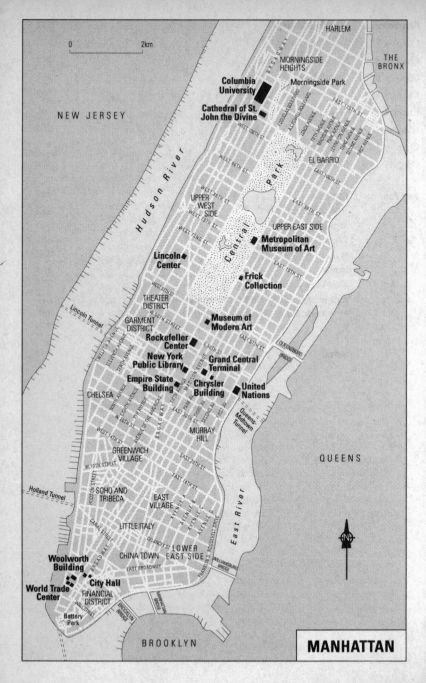

Introduction

New York City is the most beguiling place there is. You may not think so at first – for the city is admittedly mad, the epitome in many ways of all that is wrong (and really drastically wrong) in modern America. But spend even a week here and it happens – the pace, the adrenalin takes hold and the shock gives way to myth. Walking through the city streets *is* an experience, the buildings like icons to the modern age, to the excitement and violence of change and above all to the power of money. And despite all the hype, the movie-image sentimentalism, Manhattan – the central island and the city's real core – has massive romance: whether it's the flickering lights of the midtown skyscrapers as you speed across the Queensboro bridge, the 4am half-life in Greenwich Village, or just wasting the morning on the Staten Island ferry. You really would have to be made of stone not to be moved by it all.

None of which is to suggest that New York is a conventionally pleasing city. Take a walk in **Manhattan** beside Central Park, past the city's richest apartments and keep walking, and within a dozen or so blocks you find yourself in the burnt-out degradation of the lower reaches of Harlem. The shock could hardly be more extreme. The city is constantly like that – nowhere in the Western world are there so many derelicts alongside so much glaring wealth. And the problems – racism, the drug trade, homelessness – are increasing. For many, New York is a city on the brink, home to some of the world's most classic and vivid cases of urban neglect. Whether you seek it or not, it's hard to not to become aware of this very quickly: indeed, in a perverse way, it's these tangible and potent contrasts that give New York much of its excitement.

But the city also has more straightforward pleasures. There are the different **ethnic neighbourhoods** of Lower Manhattan, from Chinatown to the Jewish Lower East Side or – ever diminishing – Little Italy, or among the arts and gay concentrations of SoHo and TriBeCa, Greenwich and East Village. There is the **architecture** (the whole city reads like an illustrated history of modern design) of corporate Midtown Manhattan and the more residential Upper East and West Side districts. And there is the **art**, to some unrivalled, which affords weeks of wandering in the Metropolitan and Modern Art Museums and countless smaller collections.

All of which is just the background. For to enjoy and experience New York the greatest draw of all, whether you're resident or visitor, is in the action. You can **eat** anything, cooked in any style; **drink** in any kind of company; sit through any amount of (or simply continuous) **movies**. The established arts – **dance, theatre, music** – are superbly catered for, and though the contemporary **music scene** is nowhere as vital or original as in London, New York's **clubs** are varied and exciting, if rarely inexpensive. And for the avid consumer, the choice is vast, almost numbingly exhaustive in this heartland of the great capitalist dream.

Costs, climate and when to go

Perhaps your biggest single problem in New York is going to be **money**, or rather how to hold on to what you have, although the exchange rate for foreign visitors is fairly good these days – around $1.50 to the pound sterling at time of writing – and the city is cheaper than it has been for some time. **Accommodation** will be your biggest day-to-day expense, with rock-bottom double hotel rooms in Manhattan costing up to $100 a night and even a basic YMCA bed going for well over $30 – though there are a few hostel options that work out cheaper. The **bottom line** for staying alive – *after this* – is around $25 a day, a figure which will of course skyrocket the more you dine out and party, although it is possible to eat out both well and inexpensively. There are bargain **restaurants** – see Chapter 8, *Drinking and Eating*, for listings – where you'll be well fed for as little as $10, while the all-American breakfast will set you up for the day and ubiquitous delis and pizza places provide the cheapest snacks for just a couple of dollars. Foreign visitors, however, should note that in restaurants of all kinds you're expected to tip no less than fifteen percent. **Transport** costs also mount up fast, with flat fares of over a dollar for any Manhattan bus or subway journey – passes and season tickets don't exist.

New York's **climate** ranges from the stickily hot and humid in mid-summer to well below freezing in January: winter and high summer (most people claim the city is unbearable in July and August) are much the worst time you could come. Spring is gentle, if unpredictable, and usually wet, while autumn is perhaps the best season: come at either time and you'll find it easier to get things done and the people more welcoming. Bring warm coats, woollies and thermal underwear in January – and wellies, stout hats and ear-muffs to combat the blizzards – and t-shirts, shorts and the like if you arrive in July. Whatever time of year you come, dress in layers: buildings tend to be absurdly over-heated during the winter months and air-conditioned to the point of iciness in summer. Also bring comfortable shoes or trainers – you're going to be doing a lot of walking.

Average New York Temperatures

	Jan	Feb	Mar	April	May	June	July	Aug	Sept	Oct	Nov	Dec
Max °F	39	40	48	61	71	81	85	83	77	67	54	41
Max °C	4	5	8	16	21	27	29	28	25	19	12	5
Min °F	26	27	34	44	53	63	68	66	60	51	41	30
Min °C	-3	-3	1	6	11	17	18	19	16	10	5	-1

For a full and up-to-the-minute rundown on weather conditions in NYC phone ☎976-1212.

Basics

Getting there from Britain and Ireland

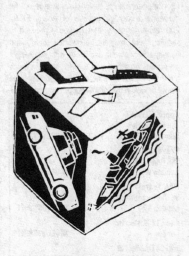

Unless you're in no hurry and can afford the QE2, the only way to get to New York from Britain and Ireland is **to fly**. There's a wide range of airlines that service the London–New York route, making competition intense and the choice of tickets and fares at times bewildering. For the best current offers, it pays to shop around, either checking the travel ads in the Sunday papers – and, in London, *Time Out* and the *Evening Standard* – or by consulting one of the agents detailed below. Above all, you should treat our comments as a general guide only, one that's likely to have undergone at least subtle alterations by the time you read it.

From London

Flights tend to **leave** London in the morning or afternoon and **arrive** in New York in the after-noon or early evening; flying time is seven to eight hours. Coming back, most flights depart in the evening to arrive in London early next morn-ing; flying time, due to the prevailing winds, is a shorter six to seven hours.

Fares and airlines

Fares vary according to season, availability and the current level of inter-airline competition. **Standby deals** are few and far between, and don't give great savings: in general you're better off with an **Apex** ticket. The conditions on these are pretty standard whoever you fly with – seats must be booked 21 days or more in advance, and you must stay for a minimum of seven nights; tickets are normally valid for up to six months. Prices, too, don't vary a great deal from one airline to another: with the majority of the airlines, low-season midweek rates start at £400–500 return, rising to £500–600 during the spring season, and over £600 in high season. Some airlines also do a less expensive, **Super-Apex** ticket, which can be up to £100 cheaper than an ordinary Apex but often must be booked thirty days in advance and is only valid for up to 21 days; usually, it's also non-refundable or changeable. With all flights, weekend rates tend to be £30–50 more expen-sive than those in the week.

Whenever you're travelling, the competition between carriers is such that it's always worth phoning the **airlines** direct to check on **current deals** they may be offering, which will often be at rates vastly undercutting even the Apex fares. Most of the airlines who fly from London to New York have departures at least once daily, some-times more, especially in high season. All of the airlines listed overleaf fly direct except *Northwest*, with whom you have to stop off in Boston. *Virgin Atlantic* are normally cheaper than most of the other carriers (as are, in general, *Continental*), and their in-flight service and entertainment is far and away the best of any of the transatlantic carriers – overall they offer an incomparably better deal. *Virgin* have a broad spread of fares, ranging from extra-cheap bookable seats off season, when prices come down to as low as £200 return, through late-savers, which you must book no more than seven days before departure, to ordi-nary Apex and Super-Apex tickets for £350–600 depending on season.

Agents and charter flights

For an overview of the various offers, and unofficially discounted tickets, go straight to an **agent** who specialises in low-cost flights (we've listed some below), who – especially if you're under 26 or a student – may be able to knock up to fifty percent off the fares quoted by the airlines, regularly bringing prices down to as low as £200 return. You can also pick up cut-price seats on charter flights through a number of **specialist agents** – excellent value at £300–380 return, particularly if you're travelling from elsewhere in Britain, although they tend to be limited to the summer season. Their brochures are available in most high street travel agents, or contact them direct at the addresses given below.

For details on how to reach Manhattan from the various airports, see *Points of Arrival*, p.14.

Courier flights

If you're on a really tight budget it's worth trying to fly as a **courier**. Most of the major courier firms offer opportunities to travel cheaply in return for delivering a package, at rates of around £150–200 return. Normally, though, you're required to sacrifice your baggage allowance (only hand baggage is allowed) and fit in with some tight restrictions on when you travel – stays of much more than a fortnight are rare. For addresses see below or look in the Yellow Pages.

Airline addresses in Britain

Air India
17–18 New Bond St
London W1   ☎ 071/493 4050

American Airlines
15 Berkeley St
London W1   ☎ 081/572 5555

British Airways
156 Regent St
London W1   ☎ 081/897 4000

Continental Airlines
Beulah Court, Albert Rd,
Horley
Surrey RH6 7HZ   ☎ 0800/776464

El Al
185 Regent St
London W1   ☎ 071/439 2564

Kuwait Airways
16–20 Baker St
London W1   ☎ 071/486 6666

Northwest Airlines
8–9 Berkeley St
London W1   ☎ 0293/561000

United Airlines
193 Piccadilly
London W1   ☎ 081/990 9900

Virgin Atlantic
Sussex House, High St
Crawley
West Sussex RH10 1BZ   ☎ 0293/747747

Low-Cost flight agents

Campus Travel
52 Grosvenor Gardens
London SW1   ☎ 071/730 2021
and many other branches around the country.

Council Travel
28a Poland St
London W1V 3DB   ☎ 071/437 7767

Travel Cuts
295 Regent St
London W1   ☎ 071/637 3161

STA Travel
86 Old Brompton Rd
London SW7   ☎ 071/937-9971

and 117 Euston Rd
London N1   ☎ 071/937 9921

and 25 Queens Rd
Bristol BS8 1QE   ☎ 0272/294399

and 38 Sidney St
Cambridge CB2 3HX   ☎ 0223/66966

Specialist US flight agents

Globespan
PO Box 149   ☎ 041/332 6600 or
Glasgow G2 3EJ   0293-541541

Jetsave
Sussex House, London Rd
East Grinstead
W Sussex RH19 1LD   ☎ 0342/322771

North American Travel Club
38 Hurstpierpoint
W Sussex BN6 9RG   ☎ 0273/835095

Unijet
"Sandrocks", Rocky Lane
Haywards Heath
W Sussex   ☎ 0444/458181

Courier firms

Inflight /Polo Express   ☎ 081/759 5383
TNT Skypack   ☎ 071/351 0300

From elsewhere in Britain

You'll find that choices are few as regards flying direct from anywhere else in Britain. Some *British Airways* flights from London (usually Gatwick) stop off in **Manchester**, and you can normally pick these up for the same rates as from London. *British Airways* also fly from Glasgow around three times a week as do *Northwest*, whose flight (via Boston) stops off in Glasgow three times a week.

From Ireland

Aer Lingus, 41 Upper O'Connell St, Dublin 1 (☎01/377 777 or ☎01/370191), fly daily direct to New York at a cost of around IR£400 for an Apex ticket. *USIT*, Aston Quay, O'Connell Bridge, Dublin 2 (☎01/778117), often have cheaper deals, especially for those under 26 or students.

From Europe

Flying from other parts of Europe, your best bet is to contact *Nouvelles Frontières*, who often have cheap deals out of Paris and Brussels. Their offices can be found at 66 boulevard Saint-Michel, Paris (☎46.34.55.30), and 21 rue de La Violette (Grand Place), Brussels (☎02/511 8013). There's also a London office at 1–2 Hanover St, W1 (☎071/629 7772).

Inclusive tours

All-in deals – flights plus hotel accommodation in New York City – can be a good idea if you're only planning a short stay. Costs are around £390 per person for return flight plus three nights in a middle-range midtown hotel. Among many operators are *Virgin Holidays*, Sussex House, High St, Crawley, West Sussex RH10 1BZ (☎0293/775511); *Thomson*, Greater London House, Hampstead Rd, London NW1 7SD (☎071/387 6534); *Poundstretcher*, Atlantic House, Hazelwick Ave, Three Bridges, Crawley, W Sussex RH10 1NP (☎0293/518022); and *Travelscene*, 94 Baker St, London W1M 2HD (☎071/935 1025) – all of whose brochures are in high street travel agents.

If you plan to explore upstate, **fly-drive** programmes are worth looking into. *Northwest Flydrive*, PO Box 45, Bexhill-on-Sea, East Sussex TN40 1PY (☎0424/224400) offer excellent deals for not much on top of an ordinary Apex fare, as do *Poundstretcher* and some of the specialist American agents (addresses on p.41). You could also try either *Renown Holidays*, 19 Connaught St, London W2 2AY (☎071/723 6689), or *Destination USA*, 1a Martindale Rd, Hounslow West, Middx TW4 7EW (☎081/891 3131).

Getting there from Australia and New Zealand

Qantas, Continental, United and *Air New Zealand* fly the **Sydney–LA/Melbourne–LA** route. The **Apex** fare in the high season is around Aus$1435 round trip, with a New York add-on fare of US$200. The same airlines, except for *Qantas*, fly from **Auckland** New Zealand to LA: **Apex** return trip fares are around NZ$2300 in the high season; domestic supplements to New York as above. For the best bargain fares, try an agent like **STA**, 1a Lee St, Railway Square, Sydney 2000 (☎2/212 1255) and, in New Zealand, **STS**, 10 High St, PO Box 4156, Auckland (☎9/399723). See the phone book for other branches in other cities.

Airlines and Agents in Australasia

Air New Zealand
Air New Zealand House
Queen St, Auckland ☎09/357-3000

Anywhere Travel
345 Anzac Parade, Kingsford
Sydney ☎02/663-0411

Brisbane Discount Travel
360 Queen St, Brisbane ☎07/229-9211

British Airways
64 Castlereagh St
Sydney, NSW ☎02/258-3300

Dilworth Building
Queen St/Customs St
Auckland ☎09/367-7500

Budget Travel
PO Box 505, Auckland ☎09/309-4313

Flight Centres
Circular Quay, Sydney ☎02/241-2422
Bourke St, Melbourne ☎03/650-2899
205–225 Queen St, Auckland ☎09/309-6171
152 Hereford St, Christchurch ☎03/379-7145
50–52 Willis St, Wellington ☎04/472-8101

Northwest
309 Kent St, Level 13
Sydney NSW ☎02/290-4455

Passport Travel
320b Glenferrie Rd, Malvern
Melbourne ☎03/824-7183

Qantas
Qantas International Centre,
International Square
Sydney, NSW ☎02/236-3636

STA Travel
209 King St, New Town
Sydney, NSW 2000 ☎02/519-9866
256 Flinders St, Melbourne ☎03/347-4711
10 High St, Auckland ☎09/309-9723
233 Cuba St, Wellington ☎04/385-0561
223 High St, Christchurch ☎03/799-098

Thai International Airways
Kensington Swan Building
22 Fanshawe St, Auckland ☎09/377-0268

Topdeck Travel
45 Grenfell St, Adelaide ☎08/410-1110

Tymtro Travel
Wallaceway Shopping Centre
Chatswood, Sydney ☎02/411-1222

United
5th Floor, 10 Barrack St
Sydney NSW ☎02/237-8888
7 City Rd, Auckland ☎09/379-3800

Getting there from the United States and Canada

For information on how to reach Manhattan from the airports, along with full details of each of the bus and train stations at which you're likely to arrive, see *Points of Arrival*, p.14.

By air

New York is a hub of most North American air traffic so not surprisingly **flying** is the fastest, and usually the cheapest, way of getting there. **Shuttles** from the nearby centres of **Washington DC** and **Boston** will set you back about $290 round trip, $150 one way, though from any point beyond, the cost is much more dependent on passenger volume than distance. As an example, bargain-basement one ways from the West Coast hover around $160, while the least expensive flight from Miami, half the distance, is about $150 during the same season. Prices fluctuate wildly depending on the time of year and whether there's a price war on, but historically you've been able to count on paying up to $190 one way in summer or around Christmas from California, or a slightly more advantageous $350 for a round-trip ticket. Regular fares – ie those booked fourteen days in advance with a major airline – cost around $450 to $500.

The **main carriers** to call (there's little point in going through an agent initially; check newspaper ads instead) are *Air Canada, American, Delta,* *United, TWA,* and *USAir.* There is usually a discount on flying late at night on the so-called "red-eye" flights and when staying over a Saturday night; fares tend to be uniform across the industry, whether there's a price war on or not, so the difference will be in service, not cost.

Airports

New York has three **airports**: **La Guardia**, in Queens about eight miles from Manhattan, **John F. Kennedy (JFK International)**, also in Queens but fifteen miles out, and **Newark** in New Jersey, sixteen miles away on the other side of the Hudson River. La Guardia tends to handle the majority of domestic flights. Any flight continuing internationally will go through JFK; many of the cut-rate services are required to land at Newark, though this is only slightly less convenient.

By train

For those heading to New York City from within the same radius as the shuttle flights noted above, travel **by train** is a viable alternative, though not likely to be any cheaper. The best services are along the New England–New York–Washington DC *Metroliner* corridor; round-trip fares from Washington or Boston are around $90. There are also two daily trains linking Montreal with New York, and one each day with Toronto.

Although in theory it's possible to haul yourself **long-distance** from the West Coast, the Midwest, or the South, it's a slow trip (three-plus days from California). One-way tickets will be downright expensive as well, but full-fare tickets do allow **stopoffs** and round-trip fares are often competitive. Current examples, both available only by booking well in advance, are the "All

Council Travel in the US
Head Office
205 E 42nd St
New York, NY 10017 ☎212/661-1450

Emery Village, 1561 N Decatur Rd
Atlanta, GA 30307 ☎404/377-9997

2000 Guadalupe St, Suite 6
Austin, TX 78705 ☎512/472-4931

2486 Channing Way
Berkeley, CA 94704 ☎510/848-8604

729 Boylston St, Suite 201
Boston, MA 02116 ☎617/266-1926

1138 13th St ☎303/447-8101/
Boulder, CO 80302 905-5777

1384 Massachusetts Ave,
Suite 206
Cambridge, MA 02138 ☎617/497-1497

1153 N Dearborn St
Chicago, IL 60610 ☎312/951-0585

1093 Broxton Ave, Suite 220
Los Angeles, CA 90024 ☎310/208-3551

6363 Charles St
New Orleans, LA 70118 ☎504/866-1767

198 W 4th St
New York, NY 10011 ☎212/254-2525

895 Amsterdam Ave
New York, NY 10025 ☎212/666-4177

715 SW Morrison, Suite 600
Portland, OR 97205 ☎503/228-1900

171 Angell St, Suite 212
Providence, RI 02906 ☎401/331-5810

530 Bush St, Suite 700
San Francisco, CA 94108 ☎415/421-3473

1314 Northeast 43rd St, Suite 210
Seattle, WA 98105 ☎206/632-2448

1210 Potomac St, NW
Washington, DC 20007 ☎202/337-6464

STA Travel in the US
273 Newbury St
Boston, MA 02116 ☎617/266-6014

914 Westwood Blvd
Los Angeles, CA 90024 ☎310/824-1574

48 E 11th St
New York, NY 10003 ☎212/477-7166

166 Geary St, Suite 702
San Francisco, CA 94108 ☎415/391-8407

Travel Cuts in Canada
Head Office
87 College St
Toronto, Ontario M5T 1P7 ☎416/979-2406

12304 Jasper Ave
Edmonton T5N 3K5 ☎403/488-8487

6139 South St
Halifax B3H 4J2 ☎902/424-7027

Université McGill
3480 rue McTavish
Montréal H3A 1X9 ☎514/398-0647

1613 rue St Denis
Montréal H2X 3K3 ☎514/843-8511

1 Stewart St, Suite 203
Ottawa K1N 6H7 ☎613/238-8222

96 Gerrard St E
Toronto M5B 1G7 ☎416/977-0441

1516 Duranleau St
Granville Island
Vancouver V6H 3S4 ☎604/689-2887

Student Union Building
University of British Columbia
Vancouver V6T 1W5 ☎604/822-6890

University Centre
University of Manitoba
Winnipeg R3T 2N2 ☎204/269-9530

Nouvelles Frontières
12 E 33rd St
New York, NY 10016 ☎212/779-0600

1001 Sherbrook East, Suite 720
Montréal H2L 1L3 ☎514/526-8444

Aboard" fare that gives a cross-country round trip with three stops for $339. A standard one-way fare is around $325.

Amtrak has realised that it can't compete with the airlines on the long-distance runs, so it has intelligently divided the US into several regions and offers extremely advantageous fares for travel within each **zone**; for a flat rate of a hundred-plus dollars you usually get unrestricted travel within the region for a couple of weeks, a month for somewhat more. If you're going to be doing a lot of visiting along the eastern seaboard, using New York as a base, it makes good sense to inquire about these specials. In New York City the information and reservations number is ☎1-800/USA RAIL. VIA *Rail Canada* (☎204/949-1830 or ☎1-800/561-8630) may offer something advantageous other than a straight fare from Quebec or Ontario; from elsewhere in Canada people usually fly in.

All *Amtrak* services, including trains from Canada, **arrive** at Penn Station, 33rd Street and Seventh Avenue; only local Metro North commuter trains use Grand Central Station at 42nd Street and Park Avenue.

By bus

This is the most time-consuming and least comfortable mode of travel and, by the time you've kept yourself alive on the trip, is rarely the most economical. To add insult to injury, simple tickets are no longer the bargains they once were. *Greyhound* runs special deals occasionally, with round-trip fares across the country starting at $70, but remember that even the shorter, more bearable trips cost only about $10 less than the train. In New York you'll arrive by bus at the **Port Authority Bus Terminal**, Eighth Avenue and 42nd Street.

Green Tortoise

The alternative to Bus Hell is the famous, slightly counter-cultural *Green Tortoise* service, connecting **California** to **New York** and **Boston** a dozen times a year between May and September. Their buses are comfortable and congenial, with tape-deck systems, ample mattresses to sack out on, and – usually – a very interesting mix of people. The 10-day trip costs $249 (food $61 extra) and is actually a mini-tour, serpentining through various beauty spots of America, with plenty of stops for hiking, river-rafting, and hot springs. There's also a fourteen-day trip for $389 plus $81 for food.

Two routes are offered: a **northern one** via Reno, Idaho, Montana, Wyoming, South Dakota, Minnesota, Chicago, Indiana and Pennsylvania; and a **southern one**, via Los Angeles, the Mojave Desert, Arizona, New Mexico (plus Juarez), the Rio Grande country of Texas, New Orleans, and Appalachia. Round-trip itineraries are somewhat different so you wouldn't get bored doing it two ways. They also run trips between Seattle and Los Angeles ($30 more for Pacific Northwest passengers going to New York), through the western national parks, to the highlights of California, to Alaska, and Baja.

Driveaways

Potentially the cheapest legitimate way of getting to New York, not counting hitching, is to arrange for a **driveaway**, in which you deliver a car cross

Branches of Green Tortoise in the US and Canada

Main Office
PO Box 24459
San Francisco
CA 94124   ☎ 415/285-1441

Seat Reservation Numbers:

Vancouver	☎ 604/732-5153
Seattle	☎ 206/324-7433
Portland	☎ 503/224-0310
Eugene	☎ 503/937-3603
San Francisco	☎ 415/821-0803
Santa Cruz	☎ 408/462-6437
Santa Barbara	☎ 805/569-1884
Los Angeles	☎ 213/392-1990
New York	☎ 212/431-3348
Boston	☎ 617/265-8533

From other points outside California: ☎ 800/227-4766

country for someone who, out of laziness or other good reasons, won't do it themselves. Look in your local Yellow Pages under "Automobile Transporters and Driveaway Companies".

The usual requirements stipulate that you have to be over 21, have a valid driver's licence (and sometimes a clean record printout from your local DMV), and have between $100 and $200 and/or a credit card handy as a deposit (which raises the question of why you're not flying if you have that kind of cash or plastic handy . . .).

The deposit is refundable on arrival and theoretically there's nothing to pay on the way except gas – and motel overnights. But keep in mind that while it's accepted that you may want to see a bit of the country on the way, there are generally tight delivery deadlines – four to seven days is the norm – and if you're late without good reason you'll forfeit the deposit.

Inclusive tours

Many operators run **all-inclusive vacations**, combining plane tickets and hotel accommodation with (for example) sightseeing, wining and dining, or admission to Broadway shows. Even if the "package" aspect doesn't thrill you to pieces, these deals can still be more convenient and sometimes even more economical than arranging the same thing yourself, providing you don't mind losing a little flexibility. With such a vast range of these packages available, it's impossible to give an overview – major travel agents will have brochures detailing what's on offer.

Entry requirements for foreign visitors

Visas

To enter the US for less than ninety days, British citizens need a **full UK passport** (not a British Visitor's Passport) and a **visa waiver form**, which can be provided either by travel agents, the airline during check in, or on the plane, and must be presented to immigration on arrival. The same visa waiver form can be used by citizens of most European countries, provided their passports are up to date, although citizens of Eire, Australia and New Zealand must have a **non-immigrant visitor's visa** before arriving. To obtain a visa, fill in the application form available at most travel agents and send it with a full passport to the nearest US embassy or consulate. Visas are not

---

US embassy and consulates in Canada

Embassy:
100 Wellington St
Ottawa
Ontario K1P 5T1   ☎ 613/238-5335

Consulates:
Suite 1050, 615 Macleod Trail
Calgary   ☎ 403/266-8962

Suite 910, Cogswell Tower
Scotia Square
Halifax   ☎ 902/429-2480

Complex Desjardins, South Tower
Montréal   ☎ 514/281-1468

2 Place Terrace Dufferin
Québec City   ☎ 418/692-2095

360 University Ave
Toronto   ☎ 416/595-1700

1095 West Pender St
Vancouver   ☎ 604/685-4311

US embassies and consulates elsewhere

Australia
Moonhah Place
Canberra   ☎ 62/270 5000

Denmark
Dag Hammerskjöld Allé 24
2100 Copenhagen   ☎ 31/ 42 31 44

Ireland
42 Elgin Rd, Ballsbridge
Dublin   ☎ 01/687122

Netherlands
Museumplein 19
Amsterdam   ☎ 020/310 9209

New Zealand
29 Fitzherbert Terrace, Thorndon
Wellington   ☎ 4/722 068

Norway
Drammensveien 18
Oslo   ☎ 22 44 85 50

Sweden
Strandvägan 101
Stockholm   ☎ 08/783 5300

UK
5 Upper Grosvenor St
London W1   ☎ 071/499 9000

3 Regent Terrace
Edinburgh EH7 5BW   ☎ 031/556 8315

Queens House, 14 Queen St
Belfast BT1 6EQ   ☎ 0232/328239

*For the addresses of **foreign consulates** in New York, see p.49.*

issued to convicted criminals and anybody who owns up to being a communist, fascist, or drug dealer. You'll need to give precise dates of your trip and declare that you're not intending to live or work in the US (if you are intending to do either of these things, see p.46).

Immigration control

During the flight, you'll be handed an **immigration form** (and a customs declaration form: see below), which must be filled out and, after landing, given up at immigration control. On the form you must give details of where you are staying on your first night (if you don't know write "touring") and the date you intend to **leave** the US. Part of the form will be attached to your passport, where it must stay until you leave, when an immigration or airline official will detach it.

In addition to the form, the officer will be interested in how you intend to support yourself during your stay. Particularly if you're intending to stay for more than a couple of weeks, you may be asked to show a return ticket and ample means of support: about $300–400 per week is considered sufficient, so it's wise to have a stash of travellers' cheques and credit cards to flash (bring all you can muster even if you don't intend to use them). If you're **staying with friends**, you'll need to provide their address and phone number, which may be checked if the officer sees fit to do so. If you've written "touring" on the immigration form, you'll be asked where you intend to spend your first night. Saying "a hotel" or "a hostel" and giving a broad indication that you know how to find one should suffice.

There are, of course, ways to bend the rules slightly. One popular method is to borrow enough money to get into the country, afterwards returning it using an international money order. It's sad but true to say that you stand the best chance of a problem-free entry if you happen to be English-speaking, white, well-dressed, sober, and polite to the officials. Remember, too, that the reason for all this red tape is that the land of plenty is terrified by the idea of foreigners coming to look for work there – so even if you are thinking of doing this, on no account say so.

Customs

Customs officers will relieve you of your customs declaration and ask if you have any fresh foods. If you say "yes" you'll have to hand them over and probably won't get them back, certainly not in the case of meat or fruit; say "no" and they might decide to check your baggage anyway. You'll also be asked if you've visited a farm in the last month: if you have, you could well lose your shoes. The **duty-free allowance** if you're over 17 is 200 cigarettes and 100 cigars, and, if you're over 21, a litre of spirits.

As well as foods and anything agricultural, it's also prohibited to carry into the country any articles from Vietnam, North Korea, Kampuchea or Cuba, obscene publications, lottery tickets, chocolate liqueurs or Pre-Columbian architecture. Anyone caught carrying drugs into the country will not only face prosecution but be entered in the records as an undesirable, and probably denied entry for all time.

Extensions and leaving

The date stamped on the form in your passport is the **latest** you're legally entitled to stay. Leaving a few days after may not matter, especially if you're heading home, but more than a week or so can result in a protracted – and generally unpleasant – interrogation from officials: it's been known for immigration control to question overstayers just long enough to miss their flights. Additionally, you may well find that you are denied entry to the US in the future, and that your American hosts and/or employers face legal proceedings.

If you do want to stay on, the best option is to get an extension *before* your time is up. It's likely you'll run into a blank wall of officialdom and a firm statement that the only way you can get an extension is by leaving the country and returning. However, you can try going to the **US Immigration and Naturalization Service**, 26 Federal Plaza, New York (Mon–Fri 7.30am–4.45pm; ☎206-6500), and applying for an *Issuance or Extension of Permit to Re-Enter the USA*. They will automatically assume that you are working illegally, so it's up to you to dissuade them and furnish convincing proof that you can support yourself financially. Taking along an upstanding US citizen to vouch for you is a good idea. You'll also need to think up a good reason to explain why you didn't allow the extra time initially: well-worn but effective excuses include saying your money lasted longer than you planned, or that your parents/husband/wife have decided to come over for a while. Should you need a further extension, apply for it at a different office, and keep your fingers crossed.

Health and insurance

Coming from Europe, you don't require any inoculations to enter the States. What you do need is **insurance**, as medical bills for the simplest accident can be astronomical – and there's no way they can be escaped.

Health

If you need to see a **doctor**, lists can be found in the Yellow Pages under "Clinics" or "Physicians and Surgeons". The British Consulate (845 Third Ave; ☎745-0200) also has selected names, or there's a 24-hr home referral service known as "Doctors on Call" (☎718/238-2100). A basic consultancy fee is $75 before you start talking, and medicines (US "medications") don't come cheap either; keep receipts for all you spend and claim off your insurance when you return.

Minor ailments can be remedied at a **drugstore**. These sell a fabulous array of lotions and potions designed to allay the fears of the most neurotic New Yorkers, but foreign visitors should bear in mind that many pills available over the counter at home are by prescription only here (for example, most codeine-based painkillers) and brand names can be confusing. If in doubt, ask at a **pharmacy**, where prescription drugs are dispensed (for addresses see Chapter 14).

Should you be in an **accident**, don't worry about dying on the sidewalk – medical services will pick you up and charge later. For more minor accidents, there are **casualty departments** (called "emergency rooms"), open 24 hours, at

the following Manhattan hospitals: *Bellevue Hospital* at First Avenue and East 29th Street (☎561-4141); *St Vincent's Hospital*, Seventh Ave at 11th St (☎790-7997); *New York Hospital*, E 70th St at York Ave (☎746-5454); *Mount Sinai Hospital*, Madison Ave at 100th St (☎241-7171). For emergency **dental treatment**, the number to ring is ☎679-3966 (after 8pm ☎679-4712).

New York has gained infamy as one of America's cities worst affected by **AIDS**: it's certainly a major health problem here, and the statistics are alarming, so whatever your sexual preference you should most certainly bring condoms if you intend to have penetrative sex.

Insurance

Though not compulsory, **travel insurance** is *essential* for **foreign travellers**. The US has no national health system, and you can lose an arm and a leg (so to speak) having even minor medical treatment. Insurance policies can be bought through any high street travel agent or insurance broker, though the cheapest are generally *Endsleigh*, who charge around £35 for three weeks to cover life, limb and luggage (with a 25 percent reduction if you choose to forego luggage insurance). Their forms are available from most youth/student travel offices (though their policies are open to all), or direct from 97–107 Southampton Row, London WC1 (☎071/436 4451). Another good option in Britain is *Touropa*, 52 Grosvenor Gardens, London SW1W 0NP (☎071/730 2101). Elsewhere in the world, get in touch with your nearest *STA* or *Travel Cuts* office (addresses on p.8). On all policies, read the small print to ensure the cover includes a sensible amount for medical expenses – this should be at least £1,000,000, which will cover the cost of an air ambulance to fly you home in the event of serious injury or hospitalisation.

American travellers should find that their **health insurance** should cover any charges or costs; if you don't have any you can get adequate coverage either from a travel agent's insurance plan or from specialist travel insurance companies such as *The Travelers*. If you are unable to use a phone or if the practitioner requires immediate payment, save all the **forms** to support a claim for subsequent reimbursal. Remember also that time limits may apply when making claims after the fact, so promptness in contacting your insurer is highly advisable. Few, if any, American health insurance plans cover against **theft** while travelling, but most **renter's or homeowner's insurance** policies will cover you for up to $500 while on the road.

Most insurance policies for foreigners cover your money and personal possessions against **theft**. If you have anything stolen report it to the nearest police station (for the address of this phone ☎ 374-5000) and don't forget to make a note of their precinct number. They will issue you with a reference number to pass on to your insurance company – not the full statement that insurance people usually require. Don't worry about this; your company won't be surprised.

Points of arrival

Airports

Two **international airports** serve New York: **Newark** (☎908/961-2000) in New Jersey for some *Virgin* and *Continental Airlines* arrivals, and **John F. Kennedy (JFK)** (☎718/656-4520) in Queens for all other airlines. **La Guardia** airport (☎718/533-3400), also in Queens, handles **domestic flights**.

Wherever you arrive, the cheapest and most straightforward way into Manhattan is by **bus**. The two Manhattan **bus terminals**, used by all airport buses, are Grand Central Station and the Port Authority Bus Terminal. For most hotels, **Grand Central** (at Park Ave and 42nd St; ☎532-4900) is the more convenient: well poised for taxis to midtown Manhattan and with a subway station if you're heading towards the east of the city. Bear in mind, also, that some of the larger midtown hotels – the Marriot Marquis, Hilton, etc – operate a free shuttle service to Grand Central. The **Port Authority Terminal**, on Eighth Ave and 42nd St (☎564-8484), isn't as good a bet for Manhattan (there's a lot of humping luggage from bus to street) though you may find it handier if you're heading for the west side of the city (via the A train), out to New Jersey (by bus) or on to other parts of America by train from the nearby Pennsylvania station.

Taxis are the easiest option if you are in a group or are arriving at an antisocial hour, but are otherwise an unnecessary expense; reckon on paying $20 from La Guardia, $30 plus from JFK, $40 or more from Newark – and you'll be responsible for paying the turnpike tolls, an additional $4. **Car and minibus services** (limos or minibuses that are booked by phone rather than hailed) can also be costly *from* the airports, but

when leaving Manhattan (again especially as a group or in the early hours) may be a viable alternative. Prices are around $12 per person to La Guardia, $15 to JFK, $18 to Newark, but check with the company first. Any hotel will book a car for you, or there are listings in the Yellow Pages. Failing that, call *Gray Line Air Shuttles* on ☎757-6840. Finally, for those with money to throw around, a **helicopter ride** (around $65 plus tax), will deposit you within minutes at the East Side heliport (34th Street and First Ave); call ☎1-800/645-3494 for more details.

JFK

Carey Buses Coaches leave JFK for Manhattan every thirty minutes between 6am and midnight; in the other direction they run from Grand Central Station and Port Authority Bus Terminal every twenty to thirty minutes between 5am and 1am. Journeys take from 45 to 75 minutes, depending on time of day and traffic conditions; the fare is $11 one-way. Details: ☎718/632-0500.

JFK Express bus/subway link There are a number of bus/subway links between JFK and Manhattan, all – at just the price of a subway token ($1.25) – much cheaper than a scheduled bus or taxi. The only one that's really any use on arrival, though, is the shuttle bus link which runs every ten minutes from each of the JFK terminals to Howard Beach station on the A line of the subway system, from where trains leave every twenty minutes (6am–1am), stopping at lower and midtown Manhattan subway stations. The journey time is at least an hour to central Manhattan. You can get further info on ☎718/330-1234.

When you come to **leave**, remember that JFK is large and very spread out: if your terminal is last on the bus route (like *British Airways*) you should allow a further fifteen minutes or so to get there.

Airlines offices in New York City

Air Canada	☎ 1-800/776-3000
1166 Sixth Ave	or ☎ 869-8840
Aer Lingus	
122 E 42nd St	☎ 557-1110
Air India	
400 Park Ave	☎ 751-6200
American	
100 E 42nd St	☎ 1-800/433-7300
British Airways	
530 Fifth Ave	☎ 1-800/247-9297
Continental Airlines	
One World Trade Center	
Airline Lobby	☎ 319-9494

El Al	domestic	☎ 1-800/225-2525
850 Third Ave	international	☎ 1-800/447-4747
Kuwait Airways		
405 Park Ave		☎ 308-5454
Northwest Airlines		
347 Fifth Ave		☎ 736-1220
TWA		
1 E 59th St		
and all over the city		☎ 290-2121
United		
100 E 42nd St		☎ 1-800/241-6522
Virgin Atlantic		
96 Morton St		☎ 242-1330

Newark

Olympia Trails Airport Express Buses leave for Manhattan every twenty minutes (6.15am–midnight), stopping at the World Trade Center and Grand Central and Penn stations. The journey takes twenty to forty minutes depending on the traffic; fare $7. Details: ☎ 201/964-6233, ☎ 908/354-3330 or ☎ 718/622-7700.

New Jersey Transit Buses run to the Port Authority Terminal every fifteen to thirty minutes (24hr). Journey time thirty to forty minutes; fare $7. Details: ☎ 201/762-5100.

PATH Rapid Transit The cheapest option, though not by much, involving taking a shuttle Airlink bus to Newark's Penn Station, where PATH trains run to stations in Manhattan; fare is $4 for the bus, $1 for PATH.

La Guardia

Carey Buses leave every twenty to thirty minutes for Grand Central (6.45am–midnight) and Port Authority (6.45am–midnight). Journey time thirty to sixty minutes; fares for both services are $8.50 one-way. Details: ☎ 718/632-0500.

JFK to La Guardia

Carey Buses There's a non-stop service that links JFK and La Guardia airports between 6.30am and 11pm. Buses leave every thirty minutes and take 45–75 minutes; the fare is $9.50 one way.

Rock-bottom alternatives

For those whose stay has left them financially embarrassed, there are a couple of cheaper alternative routes out from the city to JFK and La Guardia – though not really to Newark. They're real last resorts, however, and not options you'd want to consider for getting into New York City after an eight-hour flight.

For **JFK**, the best thing to do is to take the JFK subway/bus link (see above). Failing that, take the **E** train to the Union Turnpike-Kew Gardens station and then catch the **Q10** green bus (every ten minutes) to the airport: this will cost $1.25 for the subway, $1.25 for the bus and takes around ninety minutes. To get to **La Guardia**, take the **7** train to Roosevelt Ave-Jackson Heights stop and a **Q33** bus to the airport: total $2.50. For **Newark**, your only real hope is the PATH train and bus link from Manhattan (see above), though this doesn't save much on the price of the regular bus ticket.

Arriving by bus or train

If you're coming to New York by **Greyhound bus**, you'll arrive at the Port Authority Bus Terminal (see above). By **train**, you'll come in at either **Grand Central** or **Penn Station**. Grand Central takes arrivals from the Hudson Valley, the North and West US and Canada. Penn serves Long Island and New Jersey. Trains from Boston, Chicago, Washington and Florida arrive at either station.

City transport

The subway

The **New York subway** is dirty, noisy, intimidating and initially incomprehensible. But it's also the fastest and most efficient method of getting from A to B throughout Manhattan and the boroughs, which means that sooner or later you'll have to use it. Here are the basics. . .

• Broadly speaking, **train routes** run uptown or downtown, following the great avenues and targetting in on the downtown financial district; crosstown routes are limited.

• Trains and their routes are identified by a **number** or **letter**. Though the subway is open 24 hours a day, some routes operate at certain times of day only.

• There are two types of train: **expresses**, which stop only at major stations, and **locals**, which stop at every station. If your destination is an express stop, the quickest way to get there is to change from local to express at the first express station, either by walking across the platform or taking the stairs to another level.

• Any subway journey costs a **flat fare of $1.25** (rumoured to be going up to $1.50 soon), bought in the form of a **subway token** from a token booth. There's no discount for buying several, but stocking up means less queuing, and they can be used for buses too. The best way to do this is to ask for a "ten-pack", which costs $12.50. If you're nowhere near a subway station and need tokens for the bus, you can buy them from any branch of *McDonalds*.

• **Subway maps** can in theory be obtained from token booths (at any subway station – though many run out), or, more reliably, from the concourse office at Grand Central or NYU information Center at W 4th St and Washington Square; as a stopgap there's a map on pp.18–21. Study it before you set out – there are few on the platforms, and knowing your route will make travel much easier, and prevent the appearance of the "Tourist – Please Mug" sign that hangs around the neck of those who peer at maps on trains. If you're starting to panic or are lost, phone ☎718/330-1234 and state your destination: they'll tell you the most direct route by subway or bus.

• **A special treat** is to stand right at the front next to the driver's cabin and watch stations hurtle by and rats fleeing along the track: the A train from 125th to 59th is best for this.

Lines, directions

Perhaps the main source of confusion is the multiplicity of **line/train names**. The line names on the subway map will be recognised by most people, but the old line names (the IRT, the IND and the BMT) are still very much in use, as are popular "direction names". Just to give one example: the West Side IRT, Broadway Local, Seventh Avenue Local and Number 1 train are all the same thing.

The main lines and directions, however, are:

• **IRT** (Interborough Rapid Transport). Runs north and south on the west and east sides of Manhattan. Trains **#1 (local)**, **#2** and **#3** follow Broadway and Seventh Avenue on the west side; **#4**, **#5** and **#6 (local)** follow Lexington Avenue on the east side. Train **#7** runs from Grand Central out to Corona and Flushing in Queens.

• **Grand Central–Times Square Shuttle**. Connects the east and west sides of the IRT by going along 42nd Street.

• **L**. Connects the east and west sides of the IRT at 14th Street.

• **A and C (local)**. Follow Eighth Avenue through midtown Manhattan and cut through lower Manhattan to connect with Brooklyn.

• **N and R (local)**. Follow Broadway through Manhattan connecting with Brooklyn and Queens.

Safety on the subway

Everyone has different views on safety, and everyone, too, has their horror stories. Many are exaggerated – and the subway definitely feels more dangerous than it actually is – but it's as well to follow a few established rules:

• **At night** always try to use the **centre cars**, as they are more crowded, and while you're waiting, keep to the area marked in **yellow** where you can be seen by the booth attendants (more subway crime occurs on the platform than in the trains).

• **By day** the whole train is theoretically safe, but *don't* go into empty carriages if you can help it.

• If you do find yourself in an **empty or near empty car**, move into a fuller one at the next station.

• Keep an eye on **bags** at all times, especially when sitting/standing **near the doors**, a favourite snatching spot.

Buses

New York's bus system is a lot simpler than the subway, and a lot more frequent; you can also see where you're going and hop off when you pass anything interesting. Its one disadvantage is that it can be extremely slow – in peak hours almost down to walking pace.

Bus maps, like subway maps, can be obtained from the main concourse of Grand Central. Again, we've printed a small-size one to tide you over.

A quick glance at the **routes** will reveal that they run along all the avenues and across major streets. There are three **types of bus**: **regular**, which stop every two or three blocks arriving at five- to ten-minute intervals; **limited stop**, which travel the same routes though stopping at only about a quarter of the regular stops; and **express**, which stop hardly anywhere, shuttling commuters in and out of the suburbs for a $4 fare payable in tokens that can be bought from eleven downtown Manhattan stations. In addition, you'll find small private buses running in from New Jersey.

Bus and subway information ☎ 718/330-1234 (daily 6am–9pm).
Lost and Found ☎ 330-4484.

Bus stops are marked by yellow curbstones and signs indicating bus routes, times (rarely accurate) and intersections. Buses **display their number, origin and destination** up front. If a bus arrives that isn't going the whole way to your intended destination ask for a **transfer** when boarding: this enables you to change to another service (or from an uptown/downtown bus to a crosstown bus) within one hour of the ticket's issue, a facility designed so that a single fare lets you make any one-way trip in Manhattan. It's always worth asking for a transfer when you get on a bus, just in case.

Anywhere in Manhattan the **fare** is $1.25, payable on entry with either a subway token (the most convenient way) or with the correct change – the driver won't give you any, nor accept pennies or dollar bills.

Taxis

Taxis are worth considering if you're in a hurry or a group, or if it's late at night.

There are two types: **medallion cabs**, immediately recognisable by their yellow paintwork and medallion up top, and **gypsy cabs**, unlicensed, uninsured operators who tout for business where the tourists arrive. Avoid gypsy cabs like the plague as they're rip-off merchants – their main hunting grounds are outside Grand Central and the East Side Airline Terminal on East 38th Street and First Avenue.

Up to **four people** can travel in an ordinary medallion cab, **five** in the chunky, old-fashioned *checker* cab – though these are thin on the ground these days. **Fares** are $1.50 for the first eighth of a mile, 25¢ for each fifth of a mile thereafter. Basic charges rise by 50¢ after 8pm and all day Sundays, and by 100 percent if you're rich or foolish enough to take a cab outside New York City limits (eg to Newark airport). Trips off Manhattan can additionally incur toll fees (which the driver either asks you for at the time or pays and charges at the end of the trip).

The **tip** should be ten to twenty percent of the fare; you'll get a dirty look (if not a nasty comment) if you offer less. Also likely to cause a problem is **change**: drivers don't like splitting anything bigger than a $10 bill, and anything bigger than a $20 will produce invective.

Before you hail a cab, it's always a good idea to work out exactly where you're going and if possible the quickest route there, since New

THE NEW YORK SUBWAY: NORTH

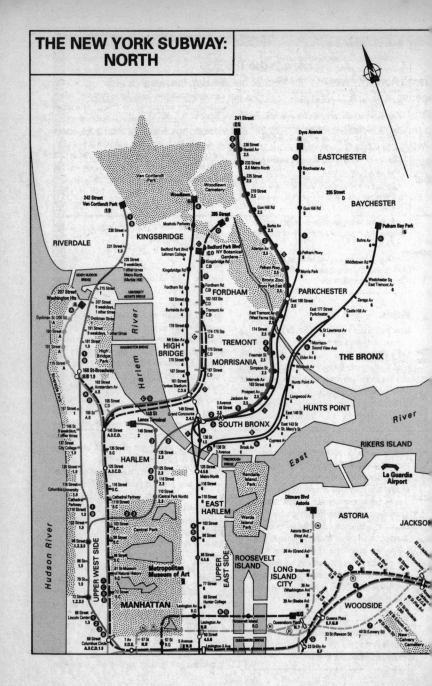

How to Use This Map

Transit Authority services operates 24 hours a day, but not all routes operate at all times. Train identification letters or numbers below station names on this map show the basic, seven-day-a-week service from 6 AM to midnight. A heavy letter or number at a station indicates that the route always operates and always stops at the station between 6 AM and midnight (**N.R S 1.2 7 9**). A light letter or number indicates that the route either does not operate at all times or sometimes skips the station

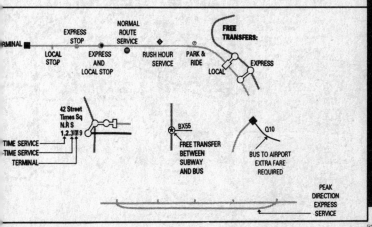

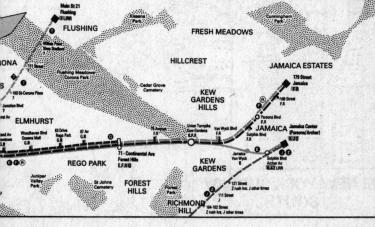

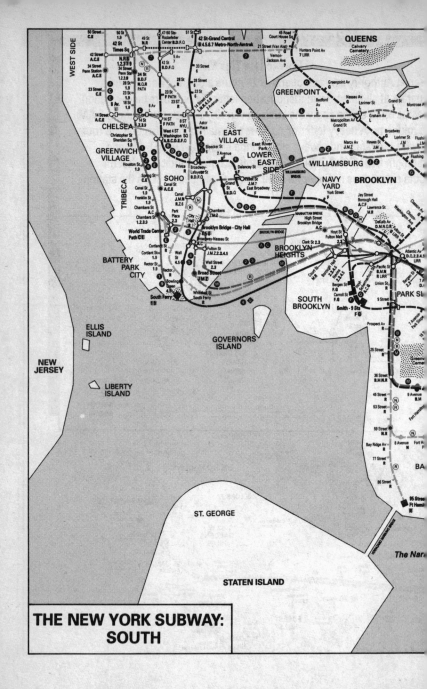

THE NEW YORK SUBWAY:
SOUTH

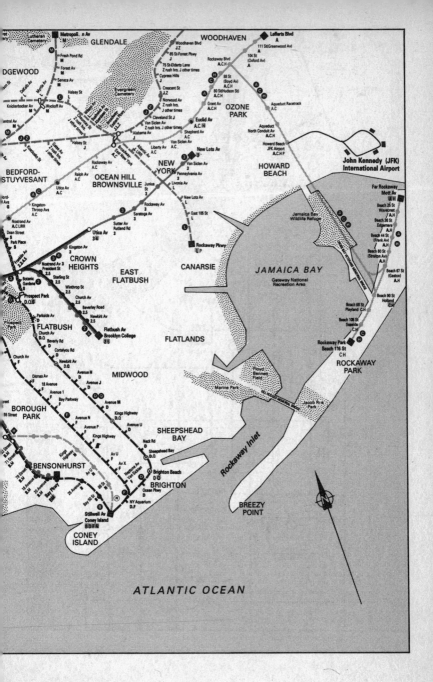

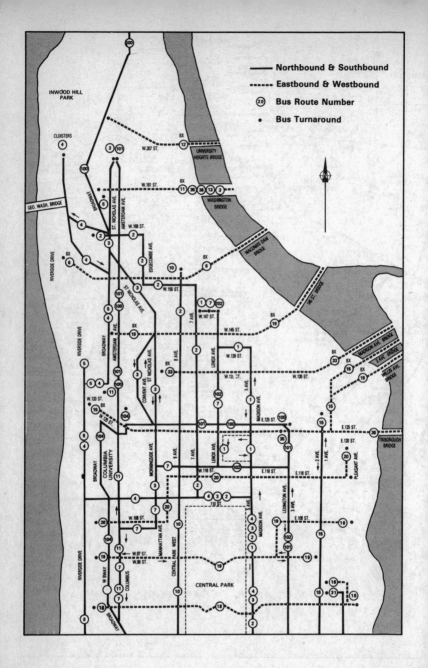

Northbound & Southbound

Eastbound & Westbound

20 Bus Route Number

• Bus Turnaround

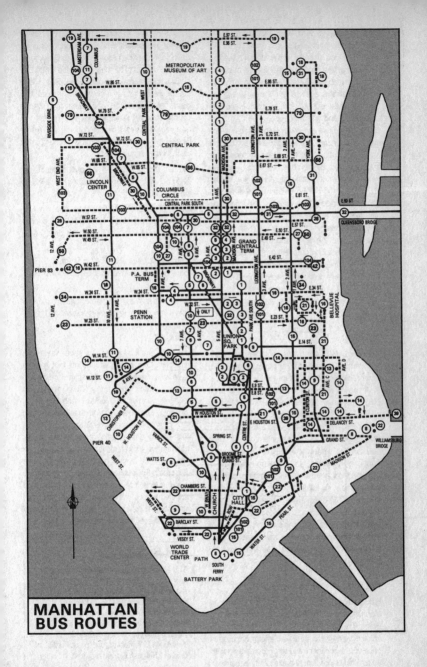

MANHATTAN
BUS ROUTES

York taxi drivers don't have The Knowledge of their London equivalents and often speak little English. If you feel the driver doesn't seem to know your destination, don't hesitate to point it out on a map. An illuminated sign on top of the taxi indicates its availability; if the small lights on the side of the sign are lit, it means the cab is on radio call – and won't pick you up.

Officially there are certain **regulations** governing taxi operators. A driver can ask your destination only when you're seated – and must transport you (within the city limits), however undesirable your destination. Also, if you request it, a driver must pick up or drop off other passengers, open or close the windows, and stop smoking (they can also ask you to stop). If you have any **problems** with a driver get the licence number from the right-hand side of the dashboard, or medallion number from the rooftop sign or on the print-out receipt for the fare, and phone the *NYC Taxis and Limousine Commission* on ☎840-4577. Should you leave something in a cab try the commission's **lost and found office** – ☎840-4735.

Driving

In a word, don't. Car hire is expensive and parking almost laughably so. Far better to keep your American driving fantasies to upstate excursions.

If you do need to drive, though, bear in mind NYC's particular **driving rules**, which include compulsory seat belts for those in front, a 35-mph speed limit within the city, and a breathalyser – the *alcotest* – to weed out drunken drivers. When you can find somewhere to **park** don't do so in front of a fire hydrant, and check on which side of the street it's permitted: this alternates daily on many streets, so follow the signs or the crowds. Private parking is expensive, extremely so at peak periods, but it makes sense to leave your car somewhere legitimate: if it's towed away you'll need to liberate it from the **car pound** (☎971-0770): expect to pay around $150 and waste the best part of a day.

Cycling

Pulling away from the lights on a bike in Manhattan can mean a replay of the Monaco Grand Prix, and it's just about as dangerous. To enjoy it – and it can be a viable form of transport once you're confident enough – do as the locals and go for all possible hireable safety equipment:

pads, a helmet, goggles and a whistle to move straying pedestrians. When you stop, be sure to chain your machine to something totally immovable if you'd like it to be there when you return.

Bike **hire** starts at about $6 an hour, $25 a day (more for racing models). You'll need two pieces of ID (passport and credit card) and a deposit (usually $100, though some firms will take your credit card details instead). The Yellow Pages have full listings of firms but among good value, central suppliers are:

Bikes in the Park, Loeb Boathouse, Central Park (☎517-2233). The best place to hire bikes to tour the park.

Metro Bicycles, 1311 Lexington Ave (☎427-4450); 546 Sixth Ave (☎255-5100); and other branches in Manhattan. One of the city's largest bike stores.

Midtown Bicycles, 360 W 47th St (☎581-4500). Corner of Ninth Avenue, useful for the West Side.

Metro Bicycles Store, 231 W 96th St (☎663-7531). Upper West Side store, again handy for Central Park. Open seven days a week.

Walking

Few cities equal New York for sheer street-level stimulation, and getting around **on foot** is often the most exciting – and exhausting – method of exploring. Count on around fifteen minutes to walk ten north-south blocks – rather more at rush hour. And keep in mind that however you plan your wanderings you're going to spend much of your time slogging it out on the streets. **Footwear** is important (trainers are good for spring/summer; winter needs something more waterproof). So is **safety**: a lot more people are injured in New York carelessly crossing the road than are mugged. Pedestrian crossings don't give you automatic right of way unless the *WALK* sign is on – and even then be prudent.

Rollerblading

This is used by some as a speedy way to get about the city, though, if you're not proficient, the streets of Manhattan aren't really the place to learn. Get some practice in Central Park though, and you're away. Rollerblades can be rented at *The Spot Downtown*, 19 E 7th St (☎477-7590) for $25 a day, Saturday to Tuesday, $15 Wednesday to Friday. Credit card or $150 cash deposit required.

Information, maps and tours

You can send away for information before you leave from the *United States Travel and Tourist Administration*, who hold a good stock of free maps, booklets and glossy bumph on each region of America, especially New York. Their London office has no walk-in facilities, but you can write to USTTA, PO Box 1EN, London W1A 1EN for an information pack.

Once in New York, the best place to head for all kinds of information is the **New York Convention and Visitors Bureau** at 2 Columbus Circle (Mon–Fri 9am–6pm, Sat & Sun 10am–6pm;

☎397-8222), with additional smaller offices open during the summer months at 47th St and Broadway (daily, 11.30am–7pm) and 52nd St and Seventh Ave (daily, 10.30am–6pm). They have up-to-date leaflets on what's going on arts-wise and otherwise, bus and subway maps, and information on hotels and accommodation – though they can't actually book anything for you. Their high-gloss *Big Apple Guide* is good too, though the kind of information it gives – on restaurants, hotels and sights – is also available in the many kinds of free magazines and guidettes like *Where*, *Broadway*, *Key* and *City Guide*, which you can pick up all over the city. These appear in hotel foyers and the like and include complete (if superficial) rundowns on what's on in the arts, eating out and shops, and a host of ads that might just point you in the right direction.

The state-run *I Love New York* organisation also has a good stock of free booklets and maps. They have an office at 1515 Broadway, New York City, NY 10036 (☎827-6251) and 1 Commerce Plaza, Albany, NY 12245 (☎518/474-4116). Much of their information concentrates on New York State, including a comprehensive state-wide map and a glossy guide to each region of the state, but they do have specifically New York City-orientated information too, not least restaurant and hotel lists, and maps.

USTTA offices

Note that only in Australia and the Netherlands do USTTA have proper offices: elsewhere your first contact should be the embassy/consulate at the address or phone number given below.

Britain
PO Box 1EN
London W1A 1EN
No walk-in facilities: address for information pack only.

Northern Ireland & Ireland
US Consulate, Queen's House
14 Queen St
Belfast BT1 6EQ ☎0232/328239

Netherlands
Museumplein 19
Amsterdam ☎20/622-9500

Sweden
American Embassy
101 Strandvagen
Stockholm ☎8/783 5350

Norway
Drammensveien 18
Oslo ☎2/244 8550

Denmark
Dag Hammarskjölds Alle 2
2100 Copenhagen ☎1/1423144

Australia
Suite 6106, MLC Centre
King & Castlereagh Sts
NSW 2000 Sydney ☎612/233 4666

We reckon our maps of the city should be fine for most purposes; **commercial maps**, like the *Rand McNally* plan of the city and all five boroughs ($2.95), fill in the gaps. Others include the tiny shiny-finished *Streetwise* maps – neatly laid out and not expensive at around $4.95–$5.95 from most bookshops – or *Fodor's Flashmaps*, a book of different New York maps for $7.95. If you're after a map of one of the individual Outer Boroughs, try those produced by *Geographia* at $2.95, again on sale in bookshops – or, for Brooklyn, the free plan doled out by the borough's information booth at Cadman Plaza West. A good **map shop**, if you have trouble finding any of these, is the *Complete Traveller*; see Chapter 14 for the details.

Tours

One way of getting a hold on New York is simply to climb up to the **observation deck** of one of its tallest buildings, most obviously the Empire State Building or World Trade Center. Of the two, the Empire State's position in the heart of Manhattan gives it the edge; see the guide for more details. Or you can enjoy the view of Lower Manhattan for free by simply walking across the **Brooklyn Bridge**. However, if you want more detailed background than this, or you have a specific interest in the city, there are all kinds of **tours** you can join, taking in the city from just about every angle and by just about every means of transport available.

Bus tours

Apart from equipping yourself with a decent map, perhaps the most obvious way of orientating yourself to the city is to take a **bus tour** – something that's extremely popular, though frankly you'll find yourself swept around so quickly as to scarcely see anything. In recent years *Gray Line* have cornered the market in bus tours, with everything from two-hour jaunts to day-long trips. They have two terminals in midtown Manhattan: on Eighth Avenue between 53rd and 54th streets (☎397-2600), and at 166 West 46th St (☎354-5122). Half-day tours, taking in the main sights of Manhattan, go for around $27, while a full day costs $39, bookable through any travel agent. *Gray Line* also run a **trolley service**: for $15 you can hop on and off wherever you like, as many times as you like. There are sixteen stops dotted between the lowermost tip of Manhattan and Central Park. The trolley operates every half-hour from 8.30am to 7.30pm.

An alternative to the *Gray Line* trolley is the **Manhattan Neighborhood Trolley**, a refurbished trolley bus which between April and October runs daily from noon to 6pm around Lower Manhattan below Canal Street, taking in the major sights of the Financial District and around, Chinatown and Little Italy and the Lower East Side. The bus starts at the South Street Seaport, and for the price of a $3.50 ticket you can get off when and where you like all day. There's a guide on board, and reservations are not required. For more details – and a timetable – call ☎677-7268.

Helicopter tours

If you have the money, a better and certainly a more exciting option is to take a look at the city from the air, by catching a ride on a **helicopter**. This is expensive, but is an experience you won't easily forget. *Island Helicopter*, at the far eastern end of East 34th St (☎683-4575), and *Liberty Helicopter Tours*, at the western end of 30th St, near the Jacob Javits Convention Center (☎465-8905), offer flights from $40 upwards. You can't book a place, but the helicopters take off throughout the day, seven days a week; just go down and stand in line – and bear in mind that in high season you may have quite a wait. One decision to make is whether to go by day or night; after doing one, you'll probably want to do the other.

Tours on water

Cheaper, if not nearly as breathtaking, is the **Circle Line Ferry** (☎563-3200), which sails all the way around Manhattan from Pier 83 at the far west end of 42nd St between March and December. This is probably the most popular way of seeing the island first-off, at least on a fine day, taking in everything from the classic soaring views of Lower Manhattan to the bleaker stretches of Harlem and the industrially blighted Bronx, and complete with a live wise-cracking commentary and on-board bar. It runs roughly twice a day in low season, almost hourly in midsummer, and the three-hour voyage costs $16 (children under 12 $8). The two-hour evening cruise is superb in summer.

Two further alternatives for seeing the city from the water are the **Seaport Line**, Pier 16 at the South Street Seaport (☎800/552-2626 or ☎233-4800), which for $12 spends ninety minutes cruising around Lower Manhattan and the outlying islands, or for those rather less flush the regular **Staten Island ferry** (☎718/390-5253), whose 45-minute journey to the city's remotest borough costs just 50¢ and lays on an equally staggering panorama.

Walking tours

Walking tours, which allow you to get to know a specific part of Manhattan or the Outer Boroughs, are another matter. Usually led by experts, the range is considerable – some are general city strolls, others (like those of the Brooklyn Historical Society) devoted to one particular area. Detailed below are some of the most interesting: note that they don't all operate year-round, the more esoteric only setting up for a couple of outings at specific times of year. If you're interested, phone ahead for the full schedules.

Art Tours of Manhattan (☎609/921-2647). Much the best people to go with if you're interested in first-hand accounts of the city's art scene, establishment and fringe. The custom-designed tours include the galleries of SoHo, 57th Street and Madison Avenue, as well as "hospitality" visits to an artist's studio, all guided by qualified – and entertaining – art historians. All this individual attention doesn't come cheap: tours for up to four people cost $225.

Bronx County Historical Society, 3309 Bainbridge Ave, Bronx (☎718/881-8900). According to its fans, there really is enough in the Bronx to warrant neighbourhood tours, ranging from strolls through suburban Riverdale to furtive hikes across the desolate wastes of the South Bronx. Excellent value at about $5 per person, though the least frequent of any of the tours listed here.

Brooklyn Historical Society, 128 Pierrepont St, Brooklyn (☎718/624-0890). Walking tours of Brooklyn neighbourhoods like Brooklyn Heights itself, Park Slope, Greenpoint and plenty more. Cost around $12, reservations necessary.

Central Park The *Urban Rangers* (☎427-4040) run a varied selection of free educational walks throughout the year, highlighting the many facets of the park.

Harlem Gospel and Jazz Tours, 1457 Broadway (☎302-2594). Various tours of Harlem, ranging from Sunday morning visits to a Baptist church, to night-time affairs taking in dinner and a club. Professionally run and excellent value, with prices starting at $27 per person.

Joyce Gold, 141 W 17th St (☎242-5762). Sunday tours of Manhattan neighbourhoods by an informed local author and historian: $12 per person. Choose from fifteen different routes which cover the city's history from the earliest days, including a special tour of Ellis Island ($18).

Lower East Side Tenement Museum, 97 Orchard St (☎431-0233). This museum organises Sunday walking tours of the Lower East Side; prices around $12.

Municipal Arts Society, 457 Madison Ave (☎439-1049 or ☎935-3960). As the name implies, principally tours with an architectural or cultural slant, but no less enjoyable to the layperson for all that. Regular trips around Harlem, the Upper West Side and other neighbourhoods, as well as "hard hat" jaunts around construction sites for the *really* committed, and free (donations requested) Wednesday lunchtime tours – at 12.30pm – of Grand Central Station. Most other tours start at 11am, last for ninety minutes and cost $10.

Museum of the City of New York, Fifth Ave at 103rd St (☎534-1672). Sunday walking tours between March and October, again around New York neighbourhoods, downtown, midtown and in Brooklyn. Prices around $15.

The 92nd Street Y, 1395 Lexington Ave (☎415-5600 or ☎415-5599). None better, offering a mixed bag of walking tours ranging from straight explorations of specific New York neighbourhoods (like Park Slope in Brooklyn or Harlem) to art tours, walking tours of political New York or a pre-dawn visit to the city's wholesale meat and fish markets. Average costs are $12–20 per person, and the commentary is erudite and informative. Look out, too, for the Y's day excursions by bus to accessible parts of upstate New York, and their specialised location talks led by well-known writers and artists. All in all, an excellent and useful organisation, whose brochure is well worth getting hold of.

The Penny Sightseeing Company, 1565 Park Ave (☎410-0080). A black-run tour company that specialises in tours of Harlem, claiming to give an "honest view of Harlem as it is". Walking tours run on Tuesdays, Thursdays and Saturdays at 11am and cost $18; reservations are needed a day in advance. They also offer Harlem Gospel Tours that take in the rousing spiritual singing of a Baptist service: Sundays at 10.30am, reservations a day in advance, cost $20.

Prospect Park Environmental Center, Tennis House, Prospect Park, Brooklyn (☎718/788-8500). Their sporadic "Take-Out Noshing Tours" ($30) take you around several of Brooklyn's distinct neighbourhoods giving a flavour of the area via visits to exceptional ethnic take-out food places and delis. They also run ecology boat tours around Jamaica Bay ($25) and walking tours ($6) – with a different theme each season – with an emphasis on the built as well as the natural environment. Every Sunday they run a free one-hour tour of Prospect Park – phone for a schedule and details of other tours.

Queens Historical Society, 143–35 37th Ave, Flushing, Queens (☎718/939-0647). No actual walking tours as such, but if you write to them enclosing an SAE they'll send a free do-it-yourself walking tour of "historic" Flushing. Can you resist?

River to River Downtown Tours, 375 South End Ave (☎321-2823). Individual and small group tours of Lower Manhattan by New York aficionado Ruth Alscher-Green. Individual prices are $35, or $50 for two people, for a unique two-hour tour spiced with gossip and anecdotal titbits.

Sidewalks of New York, PO Box 1660, Cathedral Station, NY 10025 (☎517-0201). Quirkily designed walking tours covering all aspects of the city, from famous murder sites to celebrity homes. Cost $10 per person, by appointment only.

The Media

Newspapers and magazines

The Nineties have so far not been good to the New York print media, and the days are gone when New York could support twenty different **daily newspapers**. Today, only four remain, and all of these – the broadsheet *New York Times* (50¢) and tabloids *Daily News* (40¢), *New York Post* (40¢) and *Newsday* (35¢) – are in various stages of disrepair, mainly due to decades of cynical and poor management and union abuses and restrictive practices. The decline of the city's tabloids, especially, has been a sad sight to witness. In July 1993 the *New York Post* almost closed down after a succession of owners and a deal in which the staff accepted a pay cut of twenty percent to try and recover debts of some $25 million. Only by bending the federal anti-trust laws was the paper's future secured. In 1990, the *Daily News* became embroiled in a dispute that saw the circulation of the paper drop by two-thirds, as it was blacked by newsstands and sold by homeless hawkers on the subway.

The New York Times is an American institution: it prides itself on being the "paper of record" and is the closest thing America's got to a quality national paper. It has solid, sometimes stolid international coverage, and places much emphasis on its news analysis, though its coverage of issues closer to home is much thinner, and few New Yorkers turn to the *Times* for purely local news. Each weekday there's a special section, such as a special sports section on Monday and a good weekend section on Friday. The Sunday edition ($1.50), available from early Saturday night over most of the city, is a thumping bundle of newsprint divided into eight or nine different supplements that could take you the whole day to read – though much of it is made up of advertisements.

Both the *Post* and the *Daily News* concentrate on local news, usually screamed out in banner headlines. Pre-strike, the **Daily News** was far and away the better of the two, renowned as a picture newspaper but with a fresh, energetic – and serious – style that put its British equivalents to shame, with intelligent features and many racy headlines, most famous of which was their succinct summary of the President's attitude to

New York during the crisis of the mid-1970s: "FORD TO CITY – DROP DEAD". Five months after the strike began, the paper's owners, the *Chicago Tribune*, paid Robert Maxwell $60 million to take the paper (with all its pension and severance liabilities) off its hands, and the unions agreed to return to work. However, crippled by enormous debts and having lost most of its star writers, the general feeling was that "New York's Hometown Newspaper", as it likes to call itself, was about to go down the pan. After Maxwell's death one Mortimer Zuckerman stepped in as the new owner but, despite the cloud hanging over the *Post* (see below), the *Daily News* is still far from back on the rails.

The **New York Post** is the city's oldest newspaper, started in 1801 by Alexander Hamilton, though it's been in decline for the last twenty years. Known for its solid city news reporting, not to mention consistent conservative-slanted sermonising, it's perhaps renowned most for its sensational approach to stories: "HEADLESS WOMAN FOUND IN TOPLESS BAR" was one of its more memorable headlines from the 1980s. The *Post* came close to ceasing publication after a sorry series of long-running wrangles that came to a head when real-estate broker Abraham Hirschfeld attempted a takeover of the paper early in 1993. The *Post* devoted four extraordinary issues to villifying Hirschfeld, dishing the dirt on his business affairs. This had the desired effect, and he backed off, letting News International mogul Rupert Murdoch into the bidding: his company ran the paper from March 1993, but ran into problems concerning his ownership of other areas of the media. But rather than force the *Post* into bankruptcy, the laws governing media monopolies were relaxed in Murdoch's favour – though how long News International can prop up the ailing *Post* is moot.

Newsday is essentially a Long Island newspaper which in recent years has attempted to corner part of the New York tabloid market, scoring some success with its strong Outer Boroughs coverage. Despite a rather ugly design, the paper is good on New York and international news, and is generally reckoned to have the city's best sports section (it even has a regular cricket column).

The other New York-based daily newspaper is **The Wall Street Journal** (75¢), in fact a national financial paper that also has strong national and international news coverage – despite an old-fashioned design that eschews the use of photographs. The USA's only other national daily newspaper is the ailing **USA Today** (50¢), a colour broadsheet that places its emphasis on weather and news roundups rather than in-depth reporting – all in all an exceptionally dull read. It was the original model for the British tabloid *Today*, and you'll see it on sale throughout New York – though less often read.

The weeklies and monthlies

Of the **weekly papers**, the **Village Voice** (Wednesdays, $1) is the most widely read, mainly for its comprehensive arts coverage and investigative features. Originating in Greenwich Village, it made its name as a youthful, intelligent, vaguely left journal – the nearest the city ever got to "alternative" journalism. After a brief flirtation in the 1980s with Rupert Murdoch's News International group, the paper is now owned by pet-food mogul Leonard Stern and, although it has grown a little mainstream over the last decade or so, it's still a good read – and much the best pointer to what's on around town.

The other leading weekly, the glossier **New York** magazine ($2.95), has more comprehensive listings and is more of an entertainment journal than the harder-hitting *Voice*. Look out also for the free weekly paper, **NY Press**, which has news and listings covering all aspects of city life, and, of course, the long-established **New Yorker** ($1.95). With a brief to rid the magazine of its conservative, fuddy-duddy image Tina Brown caused ructions when she was appointed editor of the *New Yorker*. Brown has taken the magazine back to its smart, sophisticated, irreverent and urbane roots of the 1930s; the theatre and gallery reviews remain the best available. The monthly **Details** ($2) is a high fashion glossy, good for getting the lowdown on the latest nightspots – and nightpeople – while the late Andy Warhol's **Interview** ($2.95) is, as the name suggests, mainly given over to interviews, as well as fashion. Perhaps the best, certainly the wackiest, most downtown-orientated alternative to the *Voice* is **The Paper** ($2.95), a monthly which carries witty and well-written rundowns on New York City nightlife, restaurants and all the current news and gossip.

British and European publications

British and European newspapers are widely available throughout the city, usually the day after publication – except for the *Financial Times* which is printed (via satellite) in the US and sold on most newsstands. If you're after a specific paper, or **magazines**, a number of outlets are worth trying: *The Magazine Store*, 30 Lincoln Plaza, at 63rd St and Broadway (☎246-4766), where you can also pick up most UK periodicals; *Hotalings*, 142 W 42nd (☎840-1868); the kiosks on 42nd St between Fifth and Sixth avenues; or *Nico's*, on the corner of Sixth Avenue and 11th St (☎255-9175) one of the best sources in the city of general and specialist magazines, with a huge worldwide stock.

Television

American TV is bad and there's too much of it. The two dozen (plus) stations do come up with a gem once in a while, but to catch it you'll have to sit through an awful lot of crap – not to mention frequent and clumsy commercial breaks. At some time in the city though, you're almost bound to allow curiosity to get the better of you, so we've included a brief guide to the dial and the two varieties – broadcast and cable TV.

The best way to fathom out **what's on and when** is to buy *TV Guide* (89¢), or check the day's newspapers listings – the *New York Times* has the most comprehensive.

Broadcast TV

Broadcast TV offers a choice of eleven channels in NYC, and you'll be able to get at least these in almost all hotel rooms. Perhaps the most noticeable aspect of American broadcast TV is the amount of scheduled **news** shown every even-

Broadcast TV channels
2 WCBS (CBS)
4 WNBC (NBC)
5 WNYW (Fox)
7 WABC (ABC)
9 WWOR (Independent)
11 WPIX (Independent)
13 WNET (PBS)
25 WNYE (Educational)
31 WNYC (PBS)
41 UNIVISION (Spanish language)
47 WNJU (Spanish language)

ing, though you can still find yourself uninformed,
since most of the news is local and as much
time is devoted to sport and weather as to truly
national news stories. The only decent, truly
national news coverage is at 6.30pm on ABC,
CBS and NBC. *Sixty Minutes* (CBS, Sunday at
7pm) is probably the best news analysis show
and an American institution, with top quality
investigative reporting. *Nightline* (ABC, 11.30pm
Monday to Friday), anchored by leading journalist
Ted Koppel, is also worth catching, a decent
forum for debate of the major stories that day.

As for **entertainment**, *Saturday Night Live*
(NBC, Saturday 11.30pm), though not the *tour de
force* it was in the 1970s when it launched the
careers of Dan Ackroyd, Eddie Murphy and John
Belushi, is also worth watching if you happen to
be indoors, as is *Living Color* (Fox, Sunday 8pm),
an erratic and often very funny comedy show
directed by and starring the leading Black
American talent, Keenan Ivory Wayans.

Channels 13 and 31 are **PBS** (Public
Broadcasting Service), and on a different planet
from the other stations as far as quality is
concerned, showing drama, documentaries and
educational programmes alongside the best that
British TV has to export. Watch out for
Masterpiece Theater, introduced with avuncular
condescension by Alastair Cooke.

Cable TV

In many hotels **cable TV** is also available; the
number of channels received depends on how
much the subscriber pays. As with broadcast TV,
you'll find quite a bit of trash; but high quality
programming does exist. There are various movie
channels, including **HBO** (Home Box Office), which

has repeated schedules of recently released and
popular movies; endless sports channels – the
Sports Channel shows British Division 1 football
games on Monday afternoons; and again plenty
of news. **CNN** (Cable News Network), already well
known in Europe, offers round-the-clock news; **C-
SPAN** does much the same but concentrates on
news from the Congress and Supreme Court,
including live sessions from both, as well as the
British House of Commons. On a lighter note, **MTV**
(Music Television) – also known in Europe these
days – offers a thoroughly addictive, mindless mix
of rock/pop/new wave videos, concerts and interviews; **Channel J** is the channel to tune to for late-
night sex shows – though this last may well be
curtailed by new cable viewing regulations.
Manhattan Cable TV on channel 35 offers a
public access slot that provides – amidst much
dross – some of the most bizzare viewing on the
planet as the city's most deranged weirdos exercise their right to twenty minutes' air time.

Radio

The **FM** dial is crammed with local stations of
highly varying quality and content. If you possess
a Walkman radio bring it, as skipping through the
channels is a pleasure. Stations are constantly
chopping and changing formats, opening up and
closing down. **AM** stations aren't nearly so interesting, with just a few good talk shows amid a
sea of belting rock and lobotomised easy listen-
ing. The *New York Times* has complete listings.

Incidentally, if all this American noise is getting
on top of you it's possible to tune into the **BBC
World Service** on the 49 metre short wave band,
or just the World Service news, broadcast on
public stations like WPBX on Long Island.

FM radio stations

WPLJ (95.5) Pop/rock/etc. One of many stations that focus (with numbing repetition) on the top forty hits.

WRKS (98.7) Calls itself KISS 98FM. Aggressively poppy and urban.

WHTZ (100.3) Top forty station.

WBLS (107.5) Soul and black pop, and, on Friday and Saturday nights, two hours of rap, house and great dance music.

WQXR (96.3) Commercial classical station so staid it makes Britain's Radio 3 look bold and innovative.

WNYC (93.9) Adventurous classical music and the best morning news programme – 6–8.30am.

WNCN (104.3) Reliable end-of-the-dial classical station.

WKCR (89.9) Excellent jazz.

WBAI (99.5) Non-profit-making independent radio station with an intelligent variety of features.

WXRK (92.3) Famous New Yorker Howard Stern insults and delights.

AM radio stations

WOR (710) Worth dipping into for its interviews.

WINS (1010) All news.

WCBS (880) All news.

WNYC (820) Good quality local talk station that uses regular news reports and programmes from National Public Radio (NPR) in Washington, including Morning Edition every weekday and Weekend Edition on Sat and Sun, 8–10am.

Money and banks

Travellers' cheques and credit cards

The best way to take the bulk of your money to New York is in **travellers' cheques. In Britain** you can buy them over the counter at any bank – at a cost of one percent of the amount ordered – and a fast-increasing number of building societies (who generally waive the charge provided you maintain a certain balance in your account). The most universally recognised cheques in the US are *American Express* travellers' cheques, available in Britain from Lloyds and The Royal Bank of Scotland, and, to a lesser extent, *Visa* travellers' cheques, from the TSB, Co-Op, Yorkshire and Barclays Banks. *Thomas Cook* travellers' cheques (sold at all their

major agents) come a clear third in terms of recognition in American banks and shops. Always buy **dollar cheques** rather than sterling, since most banks stateside will look askance at anything that doesn't firmly insist on calling itself a dollar.

The advantage of the better-known cheques is that they can be used as cash in very many shops, restaurants and garages (don't be put off by a "No Checks" sign in the window as this refers to personal cheques). You'll get your change in dollars, and for this reason remember to order a good number of $10 and $20 cheques: few places like to hand over all their spare change in return for a cheque. Additionally, almost all 24-hour Korean greengrocer/delis will cash small cheques – a lifesaver if you run out of cash at 4am.

Credit cards

If you have a **Visa**, **Mastercard** (known elsewhere as **Access**), **Diners Club**, **Discover**, or **American Express** card you really *shouldn't* leave home without it. Almost all stores, most restaurants, and many services will take some kind of plastic. In addition, hotels and car rental companies will ask for a card either to establish your credit-worthiness or as security, or both. Even in these dark days for credit buying, some people still get funny about cash.

Money: a note for foreign travellers

Regular upheaval in the world money markets causes the relative value of the **US dollar** against the currencies of the rest of the world to vary considerably. Generally speaking, one **pound sterling** will buy between $1.45 and $1.90; one **Canadian dollar** is worth between 76¢ and $1; one **Australian dollar** is worth between 67¢ and 88¢; and one **New Zealand dollar** is worth between 55¢ and 72¢.

Bills and coins

US currency comes in **bills** worth $1, $5, $10, $20, $50 and $100, plus various larger (and rarer) denominations. Confusingly, all are the same size and same green colour, making it necessary to check each bill carefully. The dollar is made up of 100 cents in **coins** of 1 cent (known as a **penny**), 5 cents (a **nickel**), 10 cents (a **dime**) and 25 cents (a **quarter**). Very occasionally you might come across **JFK half-dollars** (50¢), **Susan B. Anthony dollar coins**, or a **two-dollar bill**. Change (quarters are the most useful) is needed for buses, vending machines and telephones, so always carry plenty.

For the record (and for fans of American historical figures) a $1 bill has a portrait of Washington; $5 Lincoln; $10 Hamilton; $20 Jackson; $50 Grant; $100 Franklin.

Numbers to ring for lost credit cards or travellers' cheques

American Express Cards: 1-800/528-4800
Cheques: 1-800/221-7282

Diners Club 1-800/525-9135

Mastercard (Access) 1-800/826-2181

Thomas Cook 1-800/223-9920

Visa Cards: 1-800/336-8472
Cheques: 1-800/227-6811

With *Mastercard* or *Visa* it is also possible to **withdraw cash** at any bank displaying relevant stickers, or from appropriate automatic teller machines (**ATMs**). *Diners Club* cards can be used to cash personal cheques at *Citibank* branches. *American Express* cards can only get cash, or buy travellers' cheques, at *American Express* offices (check the Yellow Pages) or from the travellers' cheque dispensers at most major airports. Most **Canadian** credit cards issued by hometown banks will be honoured in the US.

Thanks to relaxation in interstate banking restrictions, American holders of ATM cards from out of state are likely to discover that their cards work in the machines of select New York banks (check with your bank before you leave home). Not only is this method of financing safer, but at around only a dollar per transaction it's economical as well.

Most major credit cards issued by **foreign banks** are accepted in the US, as well as cash-dispensing cards linked to international networks such as *Cirrus* and *Plus* – though it's important to check the latest details with your credit card company before departing, as otherwise the machine may simply gobble up your plastic friend. Overseas visitors should also bear in mind that fluctuating exchange rates may result in spending more (or less) than expected when the item eventually shows up on a statement.

Each of the two main ATM networks operates a toll-free line to let customers know the location of the nearest ATM:

Plus System ☎ 1-800/THE PLUS

Cirrus ☎ 1-800/4CIRRUS

Banks and exchange

Banking hours are usually Monday–Friday 9am–3/3.30pm, with certain banks staying open later on Thursdays or Fridays. Major banks such as *CitiBank* and *Chemical Bank* will exchange travellers' cheques and currency at a standard rate. Outside banking hours, you're dependent on a limited number of private exchange offices in Manhattan (listed below), as well as offices at the international airports. All will change travellers' cheques and exchange currency, although they may offer disadvantageous rates and/or commission charges, the cost of which it's wise to find out first.

Emergencies

All else has failed. You're broke and 3500 miles from home. Before you jump off the Brooklyn Bridge, weigh up the alternatives . . .

• Arrange for someone to transfer cash from any branch of **Thomas Cook's** in Britain to *Thomas Cook* in Manhattan at 630 Fifth Ave (Mon–Fri 9am–5pm; ☎755-9780); in Times Square at 48th St and Broadway (daily 11am–7pm; ☎265-6049); and at the International Arrivals Building, JFK Airport (daily, 8am–9.30pm; ☎718/656-8444). This takes 24–48 hours and costs around $25. For details of other *Thomas Cook* office locations and helpful advice on cash transfers, phone ☎883-0400.

• **Transfer money** from your bank account. Find a bank that has connections with your own (whether it handles credit cards associated with

Exchange offices

The following offices are all open outside banking hours, and handle wire transfers and money orders as well as straightforward transactions.

Chequepoint, 551 Madison Ave at 55th St (Mon–Fri 8am–6pm, Sat & Sun 10am–6pm; ☎1-800/544-9898 and ☎980-6443).

Freeport Money Exchange, 132 W 45th St; 49 W 57th St (Mon–Fri 9am–6pm, Sat & Sun 10am–5pm; ☎1-800/223-6776 and ☎ 223-1200).

People's Foreign Exchange, 500 Fifth Ave and 109 Lafayette St (both daily 8am–8pm; ☎391-5270).

Piano Money Transfer Corp, 645 Fifth Ave at 51st St (Mon–Fri 9am–5pm; ☎1-800/554-5613 or ☎909-9458).

Harold Reuter, Met Life Building, Third Floor East, Room 332, 200 Park Ave (Mon–Fri 8am–4pm; ☎1-800/258-0456 ☎661-0826).

British banks is a good guide) and phone, fax or telegraph your bank to telex the money to the specified New York bank. This will take 48 hours at least and costs at least $20. Alternatively, your bank can wire the money to *Thomas Cook*'s HQ in Peterborough, England (☎0733/63200), where it will be transferred to *Cook*'s office in New York. This will cost £25 for transactions up to £1000.

• If there's time, get someone to buy an **international money order** and send it through the post. The commission is low but you'll have to rely on international airmail service (allow at least seven days from London).

• Should you have literally no cash nor access to any, the alternatives include **selling blood**, **working illegally** (see "Staying On") or throwing yourself at the mercy of the **British Embassy** (845 Third Ave; ☎745-0200), who might (very begrudgingly) repatriate you but will never, repeat never, lend money.

Communications: telephones and the post

The New York **telephone system** is reliable though expensive, especially when dialling long distance. Payphones, no matter how graffitied or otherwise unpromising, invariably work, though the **postal system** doesn't quite match the efficiencies European visitors may expect.

Phone calls

Public telephones invariably work and are easily found – on street corners, in hotel lobbies, bars, restaurants – and they take 25¢, 10¢ and 5¢ coins. The cost of a **local call** – ie one within the 212 area code covering Manhattan – is 25¢ for the first three minutes and a further 10¢ for each additional three minutes. When necessary, a voice will tell you to pay more.

More expensive are **long-distance calls** (ie to the Outer Broughs, or pricier still, the rest of the USA), for which you'll need plenty of change. If you still owe money at the end of the call, the phone will ring immediately and you'll be asked

---

Squeaks and blips

If it's your first time in the USA, the various tones used by the phone system need a little explanation. The **dialling tone** is a low, continuous rasp or a single low drone; the **ringing tone** a long nasal squark with short gaps; the **engaged (busy) tone** a series of rapid blips; **number unobtainable** is a single high-pitched squeak.

---

for the outstanding amount (if you don't cough up, the person you've been calling will get the bill). Long-distance calls are far cheaper if made between 6pm and 8am, and calls from **private phones** are always much cheaper than those from public phones.

Making telephone calls from **hotel rooms** is usually more expensive than from a payphone (and there are usually payphones in hotel lobbies). On the other hand, some budget hotels offer free local calls from rooms – ask when you check in. An increasing number of phones accept **credit cards** – simply swipe the card through the slot and dial. Another way to avoid the necessity of carrying copious quantities of change everywhere is to obtain an **AT&T charge card** (information on ☎1-800/874-4000 ext 359), for which you have to have an American credit card.

Any number with **800** in place of the area code is "toll free", which means it costs nothing to dial. Many national firms, government agencies, enquiry numbers, hotel and car hire reservations have a central toll-free number. To find it look in the Yellow Pages or dial ☎1-800/555-1212 for toll-free directory enquiries. Some numbers, such as ☎1-800/AIR RIDE to get info on transport to the city's airports, employ letters on the push button phones as part of their "number".

Yellow Pages

Unbelievably useful (if hardly the sort of things you'll want to lug around) are the Manhattan **White** and **Yellow Page phone books** – the first an alphabetical list of private numbers and businesses (with the **Blue Pages** containing government agencies at the end), the second detailing every consumer-orientated business and service in the city, listing delicatessens, grocers, liquor stores, pharmacies, physicians and surgeons by location, and restaurants by location and cuisine. It's also handy for finding bike and car hire firms – and just about anything legal that can be paid for. Look for it in most bars, hotel rooms and lobbies and the larger post offices.

Area codes around Manhattan

Bronx, Brooklyn, Queens and Staten Island (1) **718**

Long Island (1) **516**

New Jersey (north) (1) **201**or **908**

New Jersey (south) (1) **609**

To phone into Manhattan from these areas or anywhere else (1) **212**

Service numbers

Emergencies **911** for police, ambulance and fire

Operator **0**

Directory Enquiries **411** (Manhattan)

1 555-1212 (local)

1 + (area code) + 555-1212 (numbers in other area codes)

For other **useful telephone numbers** – to find out the time, weather, etc – see p.51

International telephone calls

International calls can be dialled direct from private or (more expensively) public phones. You can get assistance from the international operator (☎00), who may also interrupt every three minutes asking for more money, and call

you back for any money still owed immediately after you hang up; if you don't pay, it will be charged to the person you called.

One alternative is to make a **collect call** (to "reverse the charges") by dialling ☎1-800/445-5667, which will connect you with an operator in Britain. The **cheapest rates** for international calls to Europe are between 6pm and 7am, when a direct-dialled call will cost $5.20 for the first minute, plus 71¢ for each subsequent minute. In **Britain**, it's possible to obtain a free **BT Chargecard** (☎0800/800 838), using which all calls from overseas can be charged to your quarterly domestic account; from Florida, you contact the British operator via AT&T, and your call is charged at standard payphone rates.

The telephone code to dial **TO the US** from the outside world (excluding Canada) is 1.

To make international calls **FROM the US**, dial 011 followed by the country code:

Australia 61
Denmark 45
Germany 49
Ireland 353
Netherlands 31
New Zealand 64
Sweden 46
United Kingdom 44

Area codes

Normally, **telephone numbers** are in the form of ☎123/456-7890. The first three digits are the **area code** and are needed only when dialling a different area. In New York City, the **212** code covers Manhattan; phoning within this area, simply dial the seven-figure number. Outside the area – long distance or to the Outer Boroughs of Brooklyn, The Bronx, Queens or Staten Island dial **1** first, then the **area code** and **number**.

Where we've given phone numbers for areas outside Manhattan, you'll find codes are included. To check codes elsewhere, consult the phone book or call the operator (see box above).

Letters and poste restante

In terms of efficiency the New York (and American) **postal service** comes a very poor second to its phone system. Even within Manhattan mail can take a few days to arrive, and a letter to LA might take a week – and that's airmail. Services to Europe take anything between five and ten days, and sending mail abroad by

surface post consigns it to anywhere from four to eight weeks' disappearance.

Letters

Ordinary mail **within the US** costs 29¢ for letters weighing up to an ounce; addresses must include the sender's address and the **zip code**: without the code, letters can end up terminally lost, and certainly delayed. If you're unsure of a Manhattan zip use the guide in the front pages of the phone book or phone ☎967-8585; elsewhere ask for the relevant zip directory at the post office.

For **airmail** services to Europe, **postcards** go cheapest (40¢), aerograms are slightly more expensive (45¢), while **letters** proper are costlier still once you've passed the half-ounce minimum (50¢). You can buy **stamps** in shops, some supermarkets and delis, and from (usually non-functioning) vending machines, though these cost around three times the face value. The best place is, unsurprisingly, a post office: these are open Monday–Friday 9am–5pm, Saturday 9am–noon, and there are a lot around. In Manhattan, the

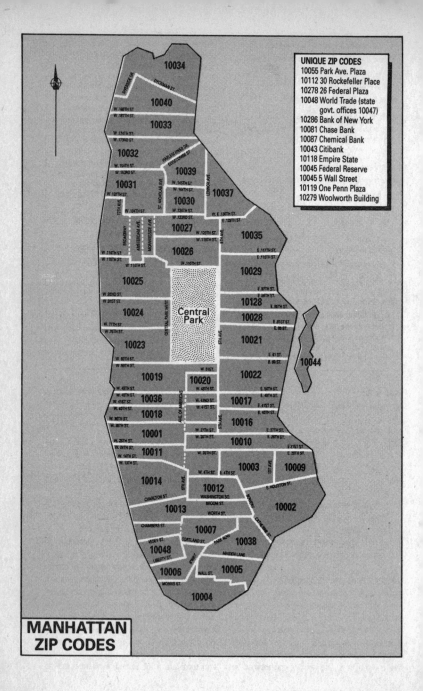

UNIQUE ZIP CODES
10055 Park Ave. Plaza
10112 30 Rockefeller Place
10278 26 Federal Plaza
10048 World Trade (state govt. offices 10047)
10286 Bank of New York
10081 Chase Bank
10087 Chemical Bank
10043 Citibank
10118 Empire State
10045 Federal Reserve
10045 5 Wall Street
10119 One Penn Plaza
10279 Woolworth Building

MANHATTAN ZIP CODES

Manhattan post offices	
JAF Building, 421 Eighth Ave, NY 10001.	Grand Central, 450 Lexington Ave, NY 10017.
Knickerbocker, 128 E Broadway, NY 10002.	Midtown, 221 W 38th St, NY 10018.
Cooper, 93 Fourth Ave, NY 10003.	Radio City, 322 W 52nd St, NY 10019.
Bowling Green, 25 Broadway, NY 10004.	Rockefeller Center, 610 Fifth Ave, NY 10020.
Wall Street, 73 Pine St, NY 10005.	Lenox Hill, 217 E 70th St, NY 10021.
Church, 90 Church St, NY 10007.	FD Roosevelt, 909 Third Ave, NY 10022.
Peter Stuyvesant, 432 E 14th St, NY 10009.	Ansonia, 211 W 61st St, NY 10023.
Madison Square, 149 E 23rd St, NY 10010.	Planetarium, 127 W 83rd St, NY 10024.
Old Chelsea, 217 W 18th St, NY 10011.	Cathedral, 215 W 104th St, NY 10025.
Prince, 103 Prince St, NY 10012.	Morningside, 232 W 116th St, NY 10026.
Canal Street, 350 Canal St, NY 10013.	Manhattanville, 365 W 125th St, NY 10027.
Village, 201 Varick St, NY 10014.	Gracie, 229 E 85th St, NY 10028.
Murray Hill, 115 E 34th St, NY 10016.	Times Square, 340 W 42nd St, NY 10036.
	Yorkville, 1591 Third Ave, NY 10128.
	Peck Slip, 1 Peck Slip, NY 10038.

main **General Post Office** at Eighth Avenue between W 31st and W 33rd streets is open Monday–Saturday round-the-clock for important services. Letters posted from here or other larger post offices seem to arrive soonest, whereas the blue bin-like **mail boxes** on street corners tend to take a while.

Parcels

US mail regulations concerning **parcels** are decidedly complicated: post offices are highly specific in the type of container that must be used and won't allow it to be sealed with sticky tape. Buy one of their boxes and study the post office instructions before you start – turn up with a parcel that breaks the rules and you'll be curtly sent away. Parcels are delivered surface unless you specify airmail and either service costs more the further the destination and the larger and heavier the parcel. To send anything abroad you need a Customs Declaration Form, again available at the post office.

Telegrams

To send a **telegram** (US *cable*) you'll want not a post office but a telegraph company office, addresses of which can be found in the Yellow Pages. With a credit card you can simply phone up (☎1-800/325-6000 or ☎1-800/835-4723) and dictate. Prices for international telegrams are marginally cheaper than the shortest possible phone call. For domestic telegrams ask for a **mailgram**, which will be delivered to any address the following morning.

Poste restante

To send – or receive – something **poste restante**, have it addressed to the General Post Office, 421 Eighth Ave, NY 10001. Americans use the phrase "c/o General Delivery" after the name of the addressee – though simply writing "Poste Restante" is unlikely to confuse anyone. To collect letters you'll need two forms of ID (passport, credit card and driving licence form the holy trinity of identification). Mail will be kept for thirty days before being returned to sender – so make sure there's a return address on the envelope. **Receiving mail at someone else's address**, be sure your correspondent puts c/o on the envelope, since without that you risk your mail being returned to sender by an over-zealous post deliverer.

Police and trouble

The **City Police** (aka "New York's Finest") are for the most part approachable, helpful and over-worked. This means that asking directions gets a friendly response, reporting a theft a weary "Whaddya want me to do about it?". Each locality has a station, numbered at a **precinct**; to find out which is the nearest phone ☎374-5000. In **emergencies** phone ☎911 or use one of the outdoor posts that give you a direct line to the emergency services. Out of the city you may have to tangle with the **State Police**, who operate the Highway Patrol – and do so quite ruthlessly.

Irrespective of how dangerous New York really is, it *feels* dangerous. Perhaps more than any other city in the world, a sense of nervy self-preservation is rife here: people make studied efforts to avoid eye contact, and any unusual behaviour clears a space immediately: the atmosphere of impending violence is sometimes sniffable.

The reality is somewhat different. There *is* a great deal of crime in New York, some of it violent. But over seven million people live in the city and as far as per capita crime rates go, Boston is more dangerous, as are Phoenix, Dallas, Washington, Atlanta and half a dozen other cities. New York's tension doesn't automatically mean violence: as with any big city, anywhere, the main thing is to walk with confidence and to be aware of the few places and/or times that you really should avoid. Though crime can and does happen day and night it's unlikely you'll be robbed outside the Rockefeller Center at midday; Times Square at midnight is a different matter. Throughout the guide we've outlined places where you should be careful and those few best avoided altogether, but really it's a case of using your common sense; it doesn't take long to figure out that you're some-where unsavoury.

It is of course the murders that make the headlines: reassure yourself that ninety percent of victims are known to their killers, which is to say most killings are personal disputes rather than random attacks. More real a problem – and the subject of obsessive conversation among New Yorkers – is **street crime**, especially **mugging**. It's impossible to give hard and fast rules on what to do should you meet up with a mugger: whether to run or scream or fight depends on you and the situation. Most New Yorkers would hand over the money every time, and that's probably what you should do – indeed, keeping a spare $20 or so as "mugger's money", lest your attacker turn nasty at finding empty pockets, is common practice.

Of course the best tactic is to **avoid being mugged** and there are a few simple points of mental preparation worth taking: *don't* flash money, jewellery or your Oyster Rolex around; *don't* peer at your map (or this book) at every street corner thereby announcing that you're a lost stranger; even if you are terrified or drunk (or both) *don't* appear so; *never* walk down a dark side street, especially one you can't see the end of; and in the early hours stick to the roadside edge of the pavement so if approached it's easier to run into the road and attract the attention that muggers hate.

If **the worst** happens and your assailant is toting a gun or (more likely) a knife, play it calmly. Remember that he (for this is generally a male pursuit) is probably almost as scared as you and just as jumpy; keep still, don't make any sudden movements – and do what he says. When he has run off hail a cab and ask to be taken to the nearest police station: taxis rarely charge for this, but if they do the police are supposed to pay. Don't stand around on the street in a shocked condition – this is inviting more trouble. At the stations you'll get sympathy and little else; file the theft and take the reference (see "Insurance and Health") to claim your insurance back home.

Victim Services

If you are unlucky enough to be mugged, the city's **Victim Services** phoneline (☎577-7777) offers both telephone and one-to-one counselling for anyone who has suffered a crime against their person.

Women's New York: problems and contacts

Newcomers to the city, whether male or female, face the fact that New York is a huge, over-whelming and potentially violent place. On a first visit, it will probably take a few days mentally to adjust to the city and its culture, and this is the time when you'll be feeling (and appearing) at your most vulnerable. Affecting an attitude of knowing where you're going (even if you don't) protects you from trouble, as will some basic tips in survival psychology.

The first – and fundamental – step is to avoid being seen as an easy target: female New Yorkers project a tough, streetwise image through their body language and dress, even when they're all glammed up and ready to party. If this play-acting sounds exhausting, the pay-off is that there's nothing unusual in women travell-ing alone or with other women in the city, so you won't be the focus of attention that you might be in other parts of the world. People grav-itate to New York from the rest of America whether to study, further their careers or just hang out – so it's easy to move around, make friends and plug into New York's networks. Also on the positive side, the women's movement of the 1960s and 1970s has had a much more dynamic effect in New York (indeed throughout East and West Coast America) than in Europe. Women are much more visible in business, poli-tics and the professions, and the attitudes around can equally well be more progressive and sophisticated – even if it's the negative that first and most powerfully catches your attention.

Feeling safe

It must be safe to travel around New York; American women do it all the time. So runs the thinking, but New York does throw up unique and definite problems for women – and especially for women travelling alone and just getting to know this city. If you feel and look like a visitor, not quite knowing which direction to ride the subway, for instance, it's little comfort to know that New York women routinely use it on their own and late in the evening. What follows are a few points to bear in mind when beginning your explorations of the city: if they duplicate, in part, the comments on "Trouble" (opposite), no apologies.

The truth is you're more likely to feel unsafe than be unsafe – something that can lead to problems in itself, for part of the technique in surviving (and enjoying) New York is to look as if you know what you're doing and where you're going. Maintain the facade and you should find a lot of the aggravation fades away, though bear in mind that for Americans subtle hints aren't the order of the day: if someone's bugging you, let them know your feelings loudly and firmly. Some women carry whistles, gas and sprays, which, while pretty useless in the event of real trouble, can lend confidence and ward off creeps.

Harassment in the city is certainly worse for women than men – and it can be a lot scarier. But it's not always that different, at least in intent. You're far, far less likely to be raped than you are **mugged**. For a few ground rules on lessening chances of mugging, see "Trouble", but above all be wary about any display of wealth in the wrong place – if you wear jewellery (or a flash-looking watch) think about where you're walking before setting out for the day. If you are being **followed**, step off the sidewalk and into the streets as attackers hate the open. Never let yourself be pushed into a building or alley and never turn off down an unlit, empty-looking street. If you're unsure about the area where you're staying, don't hold back asking other women's advice. They'll tell you when they walk and when they take a bus so as to avoid walk-ing more than a block; which bars and parks they feel free to walk in with confidence; and what times they don't go anywhere without a cab. Listen to this advice and merge it into your own experience. However, don't avoid parts of the city just through hearsay – you might miss out on what's most of interest – and learn to expect Manhattanites to sound alarmist ... it's part of the culture.

If you don't have much money, **accommodation** is important: it can be very unnerving to end up in a hotel with a bottom-of-the-heap clientele. Make sure that you have a hotel lobby that's well lit, the door locks on your room are secure and the night porters seem reliable. If you feel uneasy, move. If you're staying for a couple of weeks or more, you might try one of the city's women-only long-term residences; for addresses of these, see "Staying On".

Crisis/support centres

There are competent and solid support systems for women in **crisis**, or in need of **medical** or **emotional** support. At the following you can be assured of finding skilled, compassionate staff.

The Saint Mark's Women's Health Collective, 9 Second Ave (☎228-7482). One of the foundations of the New York lesbian community, offering general medical, chiropractic, acupuncture and gynecological services, as well as counselling, massage and nutritional info at sliding scale prices.

Women's Care Clinic, 235 E 67th St at Second Ave, 2nd floor, room 204 (☎734-5700). Handles all women's health needs for reasonable fees.

Women's Healthline, (☎230-1111). Provides a broad range of infomation on women's health problems (such as birth control, abortion, sexually transmitted diseases) and can refer callers to specific hospitals and medical practices.

Identity House, PO Box 572, Old Chelsea Station (☎243-8181). Psychological assistance and counselling.

Sex Crimes Hotline (☎267-7273 or ☎267-RAPE). Staffed by specially trained female detectives of the New York City Police Department, who will take your statement and conduct an investigation, referring you to counselling organisations if you wish. If you don't want to go to the police, then **Victims of Violent Assault Assistance** at Bellevue Hospital Center, First Ave and 27th St (☎561-3755), provides free emergency medical treatment and follow-up counselling and referral. See also details of the **Victim Services phoneline** on p.40.

Other feminist contacts

Three Lives, 154 W 10th St at Waverly Place (☎741-2069). A store with a good selection of books by and for women. Try also *A Different Light*, 548 Hudson St (☎989-4850). Aside from books, you'll be able to pick up *Sappho's Isle*, the city's monthly feminist newspaper – a good read and reasonably comprehensive for feminist/lesbian events, readings, dances and gatherings.

Barnard College Women's Center, Barnard College, 117th St and Broadway (☎854-2067). Clearing house for information on women's organisations, studies, conferences, events, etc. They also maintain an extensive library collection of books, articles and periodicals.

National Organisation for Women, 9th Floor, 15 W 18th St (☎807-0721). The largest feminist organisation in the US – active in abortion and lesbian rights and ERA agitation.

More Fire! Productions Apt 16, 63rd E 7th St (☎533-7667); **WOW** (Women's One World Theatre), 59 E 4th St (☎460-8067). Feminist theatre groups. If you're interested, WOW welcome visits (and foreign contacts).

Ceres, 584 Broadway (☎226-4725). Art gallery run by an all-women cooperative. Exhibits mainly – though not exclusively – women's work.

Women's Health Action and Mobilization (WHAM), PO Box 733, NY 10009 (☎713-5966). Militant activist organisation focusing on reproductive rights, which (among other things) provides women with escorts when there are anti-choice harassers at women's health clinics. Meets weekly.

Women's Action Coalition (WAC). High-profile direct action network specialising in emergency demos ("zaps"). Concerns include political, health, social, economic, cultural and other issues affecting women's lives. Meets Tuesdays at 7pm at PS41, W 11th St between Fifth and Sixth avenues.

> *See also the lesbian listings in* "Gay and lesbian New York" *opposite, and the women's/lesbian bars and clubs fully detailed in* Chapter 8.

Gay and lesbian New York

Gay refugees from all over America and the world come to New York, and it's estimated that around twenty percent of New Yorkers (or at least Manhattanites) are lesbian or gay. The passage of the Gay Rights Bill has contributed to the high visibility of gay men and women in the community: NY's State Governor and Mayor, its City Council President and Controller, and the Manhattan Borough President all employ full-time liaison officers to gay and lesbian groups. So too does the Health Department in the midst of the horrifying AIDS epidemic – a major problem which has further politicised an already outspoken community.

Greenwich Village is the traditional and most established gay neighbourhood and it's here that you'll find most of the action – bars and nightclubs, bookshops, businesses, theatre, arts and contact/support groups. The East Village, too, has a growing scene, especially for younger, more politically active gays and lesbians. Other promising locales include the East 20s and 30s, Chelsea, and the Upper West Side.

You'll find all bars and nightclubs detailed in Chapters 8 and 9 respectively: what follows are the more community/resource kind of listings. If you need to supplement these (and obviously space forbids a comprehensive New York gay guide) get the Gayellow Pages ($11.95), available from any of the bookshops below. For up-to-the-minute info, check also Homo Xtra (HX), New York's provocative free listings mag for gay men, or Sappho's Isle, a free monthly lesbian/feminist newssheet. Both, along with the more national The Advocate ($3.95), are available from many newsstands or from one of the bookshops below.

Lesbian and gay resources

Centres
Gay and Lesbian Visitors' Center, 135 W 20th St (☎1-800/395-2315 or ☎463-9030). Offers a full travel service for lesbian and gay visitors to New York City, including hotel reservations, tours, tickets and entertainment info.

Lesbian and Gay Community Services Center, 208 W 13th St (☎627-1398). Occupying a

run-down high school, this has only been in existence since 1985, but has already provided meeting space for more than fifty organisations ranging from Gay Alcoholics Anonymous to a group for gay advertising executives. In addition to the numerous groups which have activities going all the time – from sports to political lobbying – the Center itself sponsors regular dances and other social events. Call to see what's happening.

Health and well-being
Community Health Project, 208 W 13th St, 2nd floor (☎675-3559). Low-priced gay clinic which can either treat or refer you.

Identity House, 544 Sixth Ave (☎243-8181). Coming-out groups and counselling.

Lambda Legal Defence and Education Fund, 666 Broadway, 12th floor (☎995-8585). Legal referrals, publications, speakers and newsletter.

New York Area Bisexual Network (☎459-4784). Support groups, discussions, social events and other activities.

SAGE: Senior Action in a Gay Environment, 208 W 13th St (☎741-2247). Advice and numerous activities for gay seniors.

Bookshops
The Oscar Wilde Memorial Bookshop, 15 Christopher St between Sixth and Seventh Avenues (☎255-8097). The first gay bookshop in America. Unbeatable.

A Different Light, 548 Hudson St (☎989-4850). Excellent selections of gay and lesbian publications. Open late throughout the week, and often hosts booksigning parties and readings.

Judith's Room, 681 Washington St (Tues–Sun noon–8 or 9pm; ☎727-7330). Sells "books for women and their friends" and has readings and discussions.

Arts and media
There's always a fair amount of gay theatre (and some TV) going on in New York: check the listings in Outweek and The Village Voice.

HOT An annual celebration of gay culture, featuring theatre, dance, performance art and music created by lesbian and gay artists. HOT usually takes place in July and August: for details, contact Dixon Place, 258 Bowery (☎219-3088 or ☎477-5171).

Lesbian and Gay Film Festival. Runs throughout June; details on ☎343-2702.

Leslie-Loman Gay Art Foundation, 127 Prince St (☎673-7007). The foundation maintains an archive and permanent collection, with galleries open to the public from September to June.

The Barry Z Show. An hourly show each Tuesday and Friday at 8.30pm on Manhattan Cable TV (channel 35), repeated on broadcast channels 38, 44 and 54 on Thursdays at 11.30pm.

The Gay Show and **Outlook**. Alternate weeks on WBAI 99.5FM, Sunday 7–8pm. Both programmes are for and about the gay and lesbian communities.

Accommodation

A couple of suggestions if you're looking for a place to rest your head that is specifically friendly to gay and lesbians, as well as being handy for the Village. Both hotels welcome straight guests.

Chelsea Pines Inn, 317 West 14th St (☎929-1023). Well-priced hotel housed in an old brownstone on the Greenwich Village/Chelsea borders that offers clean, comfortable, attractively furnished rooms for $55–85 a double. Best to book in advance.

Incentra Village House, 32 Eighth Ave between 12th and Jane streets (☎206-0007). Twelve-room town house, some rooms with open fireplace, most with kitchenette. $89 for one person, $99 for two, with $10 supplement and a two-night minimum stay at weekends.

Religion

There are numerous gay religious organisations in New York:

Beth Simchat Torah (☎929-9498). A gay synagogue at 57 Bethune St.

Dignity (☎818-1309). Catholic liturgy and social each Saturday at 8pm at a church community centre.

Metropolitan Community Church (☎242-1212). Protestant.

Exclusively for women

Lesbian Switchboard (Mon–Fri 6–10pm; ☎741-2610). Because no lesbian organisations receive any centralised funding, the community relies on the commitment of small groups of volunteers. One such group is the Switchboard – *the* place to phone for information on events, happenings and contacts in the New York community.

Astraea, 666 Broadway, #520 (☎529-8021). National lesbian action foundation offering information and networking service.

National Organisation for Women (NOW), 15 W 18th St, 9th floor (☎ 807-0721). Committed to supporting lesbian rights in national legislation.

Lesbian Herstory Archives (☎718/768-3953 for an appointment). Celebrated and unmissable.

Women Who Dare (WWD), 227 Palisade Ave, Yonkers, NY 10703 (☎212/439-1065 or ☎914/965-3112). Women-only travel agent organising weekend getaways and holidays.

See also "Women's New York"; p.41.

Exclusively for men

Gay Switchboard (daily noon–midnight; ☎777-1800). Help and what's-on information.

Gay Rap WBAI 99.5FM Wednesdays 9–10pm. Weekly programme for and about the gay male community.

Gay Roomate Service, 133 W 72nd St, Suite 504 (by appointment only; ☎580-7696). Mon–Fri 11.30am–7.30pm. $100 registration fee (no fee to list your apartment).

Disabled access in the city

Depending on what you're used to at home, New York City either suffers or benefits from the fact that it has had recent, wide-ranging disabled access regulations imposed on an aggressively disabled-unfriendly system. Thus while wheelchair users in particular benefit from the vast amount of money spent on public buildings such as museums (which have all had special ramps and lifts added), travellers with less visible disabilities, or those wishing to use the public transport system, will be confronted with difficulties.

Getting around

Getting around the **subway** is impossible without someone to help you, and extremely difficult at most stations even then. Only the old (and increasingly rare) checker **cabs** tend to be big enough for wheelchairs, and many cab drivers are unwilling to stop for anyone who looks likely to cause them problems. **Buses** are better, since the modern ones are fitted with a lowering platform which considerably eases getting on and off, and drivers are obliged to – and generally do – help out. Further information on New York City for disabled people can be had from the *Center for the Handicapped*, 52 Chambers Street, Office 206 (☎566-3913).

Useful literature

The **New York Division of Tourism**, 1 Commercial Plaza, Albany, NY 12245 (☎1-800/355-5697 or ☎518/474-4116) publishes the *I Love New York Travel and Adventure Guide* which rates the accessibility of buildings and sites throughout the city. The **New York State Parks Department's** *Guide to New York State Parks* does a similar job outside New York City. It's available from the department at Empire State Plaza, Albany, NY 12238 (☎518/474-0456).

Staying on

Nobody ever says it's easy to **live and work** in New York City, New Yorkers especially – most of whom, when you broach the subject of prolonged residence, will talk obsessively about their jobs and salaries (assuming they have them), and where they live, or will live, or won't be living any more. Which should give you some idea of the nature of the competition for a good apartment address – definable to the street by most natives, in terms of money, social status and mobility.

As a **foreigner**, you naturally start at a disadvantage, at least as far as contacts go. If you have an English accent it may help, but don't count too heavily on it. The British Consulate claims that each year an alarming number of Britons wind up in New York City in need of shelter, sustenance and sympathy. Both work and rooms, however, *are* there, if you've got the energy, imagination or plain foolhardiness to pursue them. Below are the basic ground rules and those matters of bureaucracy which, even if you choose to ignore them, you should certainly be aware of.

Legal (and illegal) work: information for foreigners

For **extended, legal stays** in the US it helps if you have relatives (parents, or children over 21) who can sponsor you. Alternatively, a firm offer of work from a US company or, less promisingly, an individual, will do. Armed with a letter specifying this you can apply for a **special working visa**, from any American embassy or consulate abroad (see "Red Tape") *before* you set off for the States.

There are a whole range of these visas, depending on your skills, projected length of stay, etc – but with a couple of exceptions they're extremely hard to get. The easiest tend to be for academic posts or other jobs (in the computer field, for instance) which the US feels it particularly needs to fill. For **students** (and occasionally non-students) there are a limited number of *Exchange Visitor Programmes* (EVPs), for which participants are given a *J-1 visa* that entitles them to accept paid summer employment and to apply for a **social security number** (an identification for tax purposes which virtually no American citizen is without). Most J-1 visas are issued for positions in American summer camps through schemes like *BUNAC* (information on this from their offices at 16 Bowling Green Lane, London, EC1R OBD; ☎071/ 251 3472).

Should all this seem too far-fetched, you could, like thousands of others each year, forget regulations completely and hunt out **work on your own**. To do this you'll have to pound the streets, check the noticeboards (see the "Directory" on p.49) and the media, and, most likely, lie about your social security number to satisfy your prospective boss. If you're already in New York and decide you want to stay and work, this will most likely be your only choice: employment visas can't realistically be obtained in the city. Be advised, though, that for anyone with only a standard tourist visa, *any* kind of work is **totally illegal**. If you're caught, you could be liable for deportation, and your employer for a $10,000 fine – something which has made employers much more wary of taking on casual labour.

Of more immediate concern, for **temporary workers**, is the business of finding out exactly what people do in New York – and how you can fit in. For ideas (and positions) check the employment want ads in *The New York Times* and *Village Voice* and in the plethora of smaller, freebie neighbourhood tabloids available throughout the city.

Possibilities obviously depend on your own personal skills and inventiveness, but among the more general or obvious you might look at some of the following suggestions:

• **Restaurant work**. With over 25,000 restaurants in the city, this is perhaps the best bet, waiting tables, dishwashing or even cooking, though restaurateurs are much more wary than they were about taking someone on who doesn't have (or who has obviously made up) a social security number; jobs are no longer assured in this field. Experience helps, as does dropping by in person since most restaurants won't deal with you over the phone. And don't forget about **tending bar** in one (or more) of the city's thousands of watering holes: as in the restaurant biz, tips can be good.

• **Child-care, house-cleaning, dog-walking**. New Yorkers frequently advertise these tasks on notices posted in supermarkets and corner drugstores, healthfood shops, bus shelters, and on university and college bulletin boards.

• **Telemarketing/market research**. Often not too choosy about whom they employ – and sometimes impressed (especially the market research people) with very English English.

• **Music teacher**. If you can teach guitar, saxophone or keyboards there's lots of scope among wannabe band members in the East Village.

• **Painting and decorating**. Hard work but good rates. Some agencies offer this kind of work – or you can hunt privately through friends.

• **Foreign language lessons**. If you've a language or two try advertising it on a noticeboard or in the *Voice*, etc. Rates can be good.

• **Artist's model**. Pass your name and a contact number around to the various independent studios or artist hang-outs in SoHo or TriBeCa. Or try to reach the model booking directors at the art schools themselves.

• **Nightclub bouncer**. For those with physique – and a liking for the hours.

• **Blood donation**. A final, if slightly desperate, option for quick emergency cash. Check Yellow Pages for agencies or hospitals.

Whatever you do (or try to do), proceed with caution. Be selective, if you can. And don't enter into any sweatshop or slave labour type set-up if you're at all suspicious.

Finding an apartment or long-stay room

If work can be hard to find, wait till you start **apartment hunting**. Costs are outrageous. A one-room **Manhattan** flat with bathroom and kitchenette in a reasonably safe neighbourhood can rent for upwards of $1000 a month, and even in traditionally undesirable parts of the city – the Lower East Side being the most recent and extreme example – gentrification (and property rentals) are proceeding apace. More and more, unless you have established New York friends (or intend to make some fast), the options are being restricted to commuting in from the Outer Boroughs, or even further afield, from Jersey City, say, or Hoboken. It's a fact that the further you get from Manhattan, the lower the rent . . ..

The best **source** for actually hearing about an apartment or apartment room is, as anywhere, word of mouth. On the media front keep an eye on the ads in the *Voice*, *The New York Times*, *New York Magazine* and other publications; and if you're reading this before setting out for New York consider advertising yourself, particularly if you've a flat in London to exchange. Try the **commercial and campus noticeboards**, too, where you might secure a **temporary flat-sit** or a **sublet** while the regular tenant is away.

Some of the city's many universities and colleges also provide **holiday vacancies**, especially in the summertime. For instance, *Barnard College* (Columbia University, 3009 Broadway, NY 10027; ☎854-8021) offers a variety of dormitory facilities to students, interns and associates of the college from the end of May through mid-August for under $500 a month: write well in advance as they're "selective" about who gets a room. During a similar period *New York University* has several hundred shared dorm rooms going for a fixed weekly rate supplemented by meal plans.

Less satisfactory, perhaps, but a common fallback option are **long-stay hotels**. A number of these cater specifically for **single women on long stays**: *Allerton House*, 130 E 57th St, NY 10022 (☎753-8841), the *Martha Washington Hotel*, 30 E 30th St, NY 10016 (☎689-1900), *Webster Apartments*, 419 W 34th St NY 10001 (☎967-9000), *Parkside Evangeline Residence*, 18 Gramercy Park South (☎677-6200), and *Katherine House*, 118 W 13th St (☎242-6566). The last two are much the nicest, though each usually has a long waiting list – call ahead. Others, open to both women and men, include: the *West Side Y*, 5 W 63rd St, NY 10023 (☎787-4400); the *International Student Hospice*, 154 E 33rd St, NY 10016 (☎228-7470/4689) – students only for $25 a night; the *Chelsea Center*, 511 W 20th St, NY 10011 (☎243-4922) – $18–

20 a head including breakfast; and the *International Student Center*, 38 W 88th St, NY 10024 (☎787-7706) – just $12 per person. At most of these, prices vary depending on the facilities available; though bear in mind that most of the cheaper hotels offer reduced weekly rates. Contact the respective reservations managers for full details.

Another, less likely source is **Travelers' Aid** (☎944-0013). Although they mostly deal with crime victims and (US) travellers stranded without funds, they may refer you to low-budget (or even free) temporary accommodation. The **New York Convention and Visitors Bureau** (2 Columbus Circle; ☎397-8222) can also be worth a call. They dole out a leaflet listing all reduced hotel rates.

Just possibly, you might also find it to your advantage to resort to one of the city's several **roommate finding agencies**. Oldest and most reliable of these is *Roommate Finders*, 250 W 57th St (☎489-6860), a non-discriminatory but discriminating company. If you use one of the other agencies – and the *Voice* carries all their names, numbers and descriptions – make sure you read the contract before any money changes hands or papers are signed.

Lastly, for the really organised, other viable accommodation alternatives include **homesteading, co-op** and **mutual housing associations**. These revolve around low-rent group occupation and renovation of often abandoned, city-owned buildings. It's the group element – and the commitment that entails – that mark this system as different from squatting. Each individual tenant contributes the particular skills at his or her disposal, as well as monthly dues that collectively support normal operating, maintenance and repair costs. Various agencies designed to assist and protect co-op groups and tenant associations have sprung up, providing legal assistance, rehabilitation and repair loan pools, architectural services, tool lending and so on: all very urban grass roots, community-orientated stuff. As for getting involved: in the words of one young British homesteader it's a matter of "being in the street and seeing what's happening". Sound advice in any case, but for more direct information call the *TIL (Tenant Interim Lease) Programme* (☎240-5666) or phone the *Urban Homestead Assistance Board* (40 Prince St, NY 10013; (☎226-4119) and enquire about *Self-Help Work Consumer Cooperative*. And good luck.

Directory

AIRPORT TAX This is invariably included in the price of your ticket.

BRING . . . Films, toiletries, cosmetics, razor-blades, all of which work out more expensive in the States. And don't forget your credit card(s) – you'll be considered barely human without it.

BUY . . . Good things to take home to Britain, especially with a decent exchange rate, include baseball caps – from street corner stalls for $6–10; basketball shoes – *Converse All-Star* originals cost two-thirds the British price; American Levis – available in cuts and styles you can't get in the UK, and cheaper; and trainers – also half as much as in the UK. Any photographic equipment or electrical goods will be much cheaper, but make sure the voltages match (see below).

COCKROACHES To other Americans New York is known as "Roach City", and no wonder. The creatures infest every apartment or hotel, however luxurious, and it's no good imagining that a $300-a-night suite will ensure you're free of the things. It won't. Latest invention to deal with the problem is a spray said to render all roaches sterile.

CONSULATES *Australia,* 630 Fifth Ave (☎245-4000); *Canada,* 1251 Sixth Ave (☎768-2400); *Denmark,* 825 Third Ave (☎223-4545); *Ireland,* 515 Madison Ave (☎319-2555); *Netherlands,* 1 Rockefeller Plaza (☎246-1429); *Sweden,* 1 Dag Hammerskjöld Plaza (☎751-5900); *United Kingdom,* 845 Third Ave (☎745-0200).

CONTRACEPTION Condoms are available in all pharmacies and delis. If you're on the pill it's obviously best to bring a supply with you; should you run out, or need advice on other aspects of contraception, abortion or related matters, contact *Planned Parenthood,* 380 Second Ave (☎677-6474) or *The Women's Healthline* (☎230-1111).

DATES Written the other way round to what Europeans are used to. For example, 4.1.87 is not the 4th of January but the 1st of April.

DOGS Dog shit on the sidewalk is much less of a problem than it was, since it's now illegal not to clear up after your mutt. This law is firmly enforced, and wherever you go in the city you'll see conscientious dog owners scraping up after their pets with makeshift cardboard shovels and dumping the evidence in the nearest litter bin. So if you're doing your New York friend a favour and walking the dog, you know what to do.

DRUGS Though cannabis is now decriminalised in a few American states – Alaska for example – it's most definitely not in New York and if you're caught with any you'll incur at least a $100 fine. Harder drugs are, of course, illegal too and so best avoided. If anyone offers you a "nickel bag" in the street, they're not selling sweeties (probably not even selling drugs), but touting a $5 deal of a hard drug – possibly crack, a refined form of cocaine which is highly addictive, and as well as stewing brains it can also make the user extremely violent and aggressive. The urgent whispers of the traders around Washington Square and many other parts of the city of "Sens, sens" are short for sensamilia (a particular type of marijuana) – though again whether that's what you'd actually end up with if you handed over any money is debatable.

ELECTRIC CURRENT 110V AC with two-pronged, rather primitive plugs. Unless they're dual voltage, all British appliances will need a voltage converter as well as a plug adapter.

EMERGENCIES For Police, Fire or Ambulance dial ☎911.

FLOORS In the States, the ground floor is known as the first floor, the first floor the second . . . so if someone you know lives on the third floor you only have to walk up two flights of stairs.

HOMELESSNESS Partly simply due to the lack of affordable accommodation, partly to a policy a few years back of releasing long-term mental patients into the community without any real policy of community care, you will be struck by the number of people living on the streets in New York – a population which is ever-growing.

ID Carry some at all times, as there are any number of occasions on which you may be asked to show it. Two pieces of ID are preferable and one should have a photo – passport and credit card are the best bets.

LAUNDRY Hotels do it but charge the earth. You're much better off going to an ordinary launderette (here called a *laundromat*) or dry cleaners, both of which you'll find plenty of in the Yellow Pages under "Laundries". Remember also that the YMCAs have coin-op washing machines.

LEFT LUGGAGE The most likely place to dump your stuff is Grand Central Station (42nd St and Park Ave; ☎340-2555), where the luggage department is open Monday–Friday 7am–8pm, Saturday & Sunday 10am–6pm, and charges $1 an item, $2 for a rucksack, $3 for a bike.

LIBRARIES The real heavyweight is the central reference section of the New York Public Library on Fifth Ave at 42nd St, see p.113. However, as the name suggests, while this is a great place to work and its stock of books is one of the best in America and indeed the world, you can't actually take books home at the end of the day. To do this you need to go to a branch of the NYC Public Library (for a full list ask in the reference library) and produce proof of residence in the city.

LOST PROPERTY Things lost on buses or on the subway: *NYC Transit Authority*, at the 34th Street/ Eighth Avenue Station on the A, C and E line; Mon–Wed & Fri 8am–noon; Thurs 11am–6.45pm; (☎718/330-4484). Things lost on *Amtrak*: Penn Station (☎630-7389). Things lost in a cab: *Taxi & Limousine Commission Lost Property Information Dept.*, 211 W 41st St (☎840-4735). Otherwise, the nearest police station, particularly if you think items may have been stolen.

NOTICEBOARDS For contacts, casual work, articles for sale, etc it's hard to beat the noticeboard just inside the doorway of the *Village Voice* office at 842 Broadway (near Union Square). Otherwise there are numerous noticeboards up at Columbia University, or in the Loeb Student Centre of NYU on Washington Square.

MEASUREMENTS AND SIZES The US has yet to go metric and measurements of length are for the moment in inches, feet, yards and miles, of weight in ounces, pounds and tons. Liquid measures are slightly more confusing in that an imperial pint is roughly equivalent to 1.25 American pints, and an American gallon thus only equal to about four-fifths of an imperial one. Clothing and shoe sizes are easier: women's garment sizes are always two figures less than they would be in Britain. Thus, a British size 12 will be a size 10 in the States, a size 14 a size 12. To calculate shoe sizes in America, simply add 1 to your British size – thus, if you're normally size 8 you'll need a size 9 shoe in New York. See Chapter 14 *Shops and Markets..*

PUBLIC HOLIDAYS You'll find most offices, some stores and certain museums closed on the following days: January 1; *Martin Luther King's Birthday* (third Monday in January); *Presidents' Day* (third Monday in February); *Memorial Day* (last Monday in May); *Independence Day* (July 4); *Labor Day* (first Monday in September); *Columbus Day* (second Monday in October); *Veterans Day* (November 11); *Thanksgiving* (third Thursday in November); *Christmas Day* (December 25). Also, New York's numerous parades mean that on certain days – *Washington's Birthday, St Patrick's Day, Easter Sunday,* and *Columbus Day* – much of Fifth Avenue is closed altogether.

PUBLIC INFORMATION Phone ☎978-5602 for help with anything connected with local government services in New York City.

SUBWAY GRAFFITI Once a major feature of the New York cityscape, there's been a campaign against subway graffiti over recent years that has left trains looking much cleaner; indeed most of the trains are now no more graffitied than those of any other major capital. Whether this is a good or bad thing, it certainly means subway stations are less colourful, though one thing is certain – most New Yorkers hated the graffiti and are glad to see the back of it.

SWIMMING POOLS See Chapter 11, *Sport and outdoor activities.*

TAMPONS Available in all pharmacies, department stores and, most cheaply, from branches of *Duane Reed* (see Chapter 14).

TAX Within New York City you'll pay an 8.25 percent sales tax on top of marked prices on just about everything but the very barest of essentials, a measure brought in to help alleviate the city's 1975 economic crisis, and one which stuck.

TIME Five hours behind Britain, three hours ahead of West Coast America.

TELEPHONE SERVICES AND HELPLINES AIDS Hotline (☎718/485-8111 – 24 hours); Alcoholics Anonymous (☎683-3900); Drugs Anonymous (☎874-0700); Crime Victims Hotline (☎577-7777 – 24 hours); Events (☎360-1333); Herpes Hotline (☎213-6150); Missing Persons Bureau (☎374-6913); Parking Information (☎566-4121); Restaurants (☎540-DINE); Road conditions (☎964-2110); Samaritans (☎673-3000); Sex Crimes Hotline (☎267-7273); Sleep (☎439-2992); Time (☎976-1616); VD Hotline (☎427-5120); Wake-up call (☎540-4444); Weather (☎976-1212); What's On Stage (☎768-1818).

TERMINALS AND TRANSPORT INFORMATION Grand Central Terminal, 42nd St and Park Ave (☎532-4900); Amtrak (☎1-800/872-7245 and ☎582-6875); For services from Pennsylvania Station, 31st–33rd Streets and Seventh-Eighth Avenues, call either New Jersey Transit (☎201/762-5100) or Long Island Railroad (☎718/217-5477); Port Authority Bus Terminal, 41st St and Eighth Ave (☎564-8484); George Washington Bridge Bus Terminal, W 179th St and Broadway (☎564-1114); Greyhound bus office (☎971-6363).

TIPPING It won't be long before you realise that tipping, in a restaurant, bar, taxi cab, hotel lobby or toilet, is a part of life in the States – and that anyone who doesn't join in is considered "cheap": the ultimate American insult. There's not really any way around this, and in most cases you'll find that it's easier to simply cough up the minimum (double the tax) than brave the withering gaze of the staff, or worse, the horror-struck looks of your American friends. The secret is to save as much cash as possible by refusing all offers of help in public places – ie carry your own bags up to your room, open all doors yourself, and most importantly, never accept handouts of aftershave or perfume in posh washrooms.

TOILETS Don't really exist as such, and bars and restaurants like to put casual users off with forbidding signs like "Restrooms for patrons only". This can be overcome with the right degree of boldness and lack of care for appearances – and if you're desperate you're not going to be that worried anyway. Among centrally located places

you can steal into without feeling too guilty are the glossy Grand Hyatt Hotel; the Trump Tower, where there are public loos on the Garden level; the Waldorf Astoria, where the Ladies is sumptuous in the extreme; the New York Public Library at 42nd St and Fifth Ave; and the Lincoln Center's Avery Fisher Hall and Library, both of which have several bathrooms. Barney's, Macy's and Bloomingdales stores and most museums also have accessible and clean restrooms.

TRAVEL AGENTS Council Travel, America's principal student/youth travel organisation, have an office at 205 E 42nd St (☎661-1450) and deal in airline and other tickets, inclusive tours, car rental, international student cards, guidebooks and work camps. Bear in mind, though, that Greyhound passes, etc are better value if you purchase them before you leave. Other agents you might try are STA Travel, 48 E 11th St (☎477-7166); Nouvelles Frontières, 12 E 33rd St (☎779-0600); Whole World Travel, Room 103, Ferris Booth Hall, Columbia University, 116th St and Broadway (part of STA: ☎854-2224).

TURKISH BATHS Tenth Street Turkish Baths, 268 E 10th St (☎674-9250). Manhattan's longest-established Turkish bath, where you can use the steam rooms and pool for just $15; a massage is $20 extra.

WHAT'S ON Any number of ways to pick up information. These include popping into the Convention and Visitors Bureau (see p.25) who have up-to-date leaflets; buying New York magazine, the New Yorker or Village Voice; or getting hold of one of several free weekly magazines you find in hotels (Key, Where and Broadway are three) or the free weekly papers Critics' Choice (a New York Times' digest) and the New York Press. If your appetite for absolutely fresh data still isn't sated, phone ☎360-1333 for a rundown of the day's special events.

WORSHIP There are regular services and masses at the following churches and synagogues. Anglican (Episcopal): Cathedral of St John the Divine, Amsterdam Ave at 112th St (☎316-7400); St Bartholomew's, 109 E 50th St (☎751-1616); Trinity Church, Broadway and Wall St (☎602-0800). Catholic: St Patrick's Cathedral, Fifth Ave at 50th St (☎753-2261). Jewish: Temple Emanu-el, Fifth Ave at 65th St (☎744-1400). Unitarian: Church of all Souls, Lexington Ave at 80th St (☎535-5530).

The City

Chapter 1

Introducing the City

New York City comprises the central island of Manhattan along with four outer boroughs – Brooklyn, Queens, the Bronx and Staten Island.

Manhattan, to many, is New York. Certainly, whatever your interest in the city, it's here that you'll spend most time, and, unless you have friends elsewhere, are likely to stay. Understanding the intricacies of Manhattan's layout, and above all getting some grasp of its subway and transport system (for which see *Basics*), should be your first priority. If at all possible, try to master at least some of the following before arrival – if needs be on the flight over.

Manhattan orientation

In this guide, we've divided Manhattan into chapters that broadly split the island into three sections, **Lower**, **Midtown** and **Upper Manhattan**. Each of these chunks covers a large area and will require several days at least of wandering even if you intend taking in just the salient parts of what there is to see. And as mentioned above, you'll need to have at least a basic knowledge of New York's public transport system in order to get around what are often distances too long to tackle on foot.

Lower Manhattan

Lower Manhattan, the oldest part of the island, contains New York's **Financial District** in breezy proximity to the harbour; as well as containing the attractions of Wall Street, it forms the springboard for trips out to **Ellis Island's Immigration Museum** and the **Statue of Liberty**. Heading north, past the twin icons of the **World Trade Center** and **Woolworth Building**, you reach the municipal buildings of the **Civic Center** which form a prelude to the fast gentrifying if still rather bleak area of **TriBeCa**, which in turn runs into the chic and lively streets of **SoHo**, an area known for its art businesses and cast-iron architecture. **Chinatown** is Lower Manhattan's most homo-

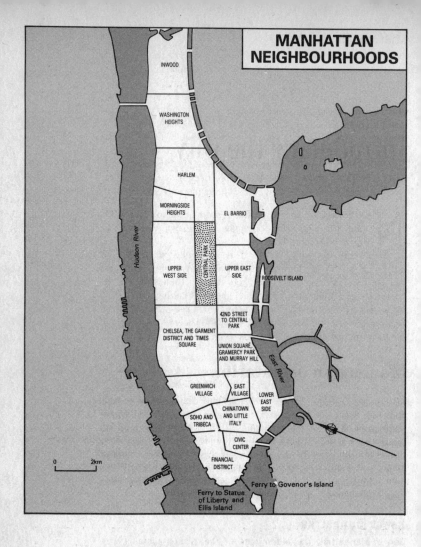

MANHATTAN
NEIGHBOURHOODS

INWOOD

WASHINGTON
HEIGHTS

HARLEM

MORNINGSIDE
HEIGHTS

EL BARRIO

Hudson River

UPPER
WEST SIDE

CENTRAL PARK

UPPER EAST
SIDE

ROOSEVELT ISLAND

42ND STREET
TO CENTRAL
PARK

CHELSEA, THE GARMENT
DISTRICT AND TIMES
SQUARE

UNION SQUARE,
GRAMERCY PARK
AND MURRAY HILL

East River

GREENWICH
VILLAGE

EAST
VILLAGE

LOWER
EAST
SIDE

CHINATOWN
AND LITTLE
ITALY

SOHO AND
TRIBECA

CIVIC
CENTER

FINANCIAL
DISTRICT

0   2km

Ferry to Govenor's Island

Ferry to Statue
of Liberty and
Ellis Island

geneous ethnic area, great for Chinese food and ethnic shopping;
nearby **Little Italy**, on the other hand, has few traces of the once
strong immigrant presence. **Greenwich Village**, originally famous
as a hang-out for artists and writers, then as a focus of 1960s radicalism, is today much tamer, though its restaurants and clubs still
buzz with activity: you need to head to the **East Village** or the
Lower East Side to find an earthier mix of low-income residential
buildings, scattered with some of the city's more intriguing shops
and low-life bars and clubs.

Midtown Manhattan

Starting with the scruffy streets of **Chelsea** and the once grand area around Union and Madison squares, **Midtown Manhattan** rises like a switchback to a crescendo of some of the world's greatest skyscrapers. First and most famous of these is the **Empire State Building**, marking the beginning of a district of stunning architecture that straddles **Fifth Avenue** and runs east to west along 42nd Street. Most of the city's hotels are in Midtown, and when you're not eyeballing buildings like **Rockefeller Center** and the **Chrysler** and **Seagram buildings**, there are numerous museums – most notably the **Museum of Modern Art** – to take in. Yet, in the midst of all this high-rise glamour, dishevelled areas around **Times Square** and west of **Broadway** are reminders that much of the city still lives on the breadline.

Upper Manhattan

Upper Manhattan, an area we've taken to run from 57th Street to the northern tip of the island, has at its core **Central Park**, one of the best urban open spaces anywhere, now restored to its erstwhile glory after decades of mistreatment. Flanking the western side of the park, the **Upper West Side** is mostly residential, punctuated with **Lincoln Center**, Manhattan's temple to the performing arts, and some of the city's better restaurants. The eastern side of the park, the **Upper East Side**, is decidedly grander, the nineteenth-century millionaires' mansions now transformed into a string of classic museums – the **Frick Collection**, **Metropolitan Museum** and **Guggenheim** among them – collectively known as **Museum Mile**. North of the park is **Harlem**, for years the black neighbourhood of the city and one synonymous with Afro-American culture. Part of Harlem north of the Upper East Side is known as El Barrio, with a strong Latino culture. On Harlem's southwestern border, **Columbia University** inevitably brings a strong student presence – and budget cafés – to Upper Manhattan. Continuing north, **Washington Heights** and **Inwood** hold little to tempt you, save the **Cloisters**, a nineteenth-century display of medieval Europe's finest art and architecture.

Manhattan's layout

Despite its grid-pattern arrangement, **Manhattan** can seem a wearyingly complicated place to get around: blocks of streets and avenues, apparently straightforward on the map, can be uniquely confusing on foot and the psychedelic squiggles of the subway map impenetrably arcane. Don't let subways and buses overawe you, though, as with a little know-how you'll find them efficient and fast. And if you're at all unsure, just ask – New Yorkers are the most helpful and accurate of direction givers and have seemingly infinite interest in initiating visitors into the great mysteries of their city.

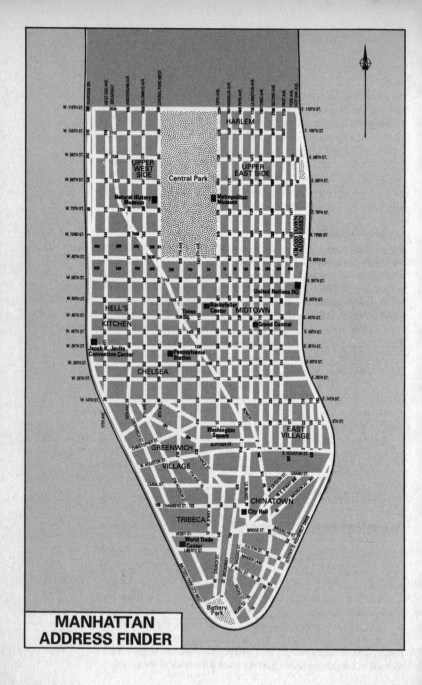

MANHATTAN
ADDRESS FINDER

From north to south **the island** of Manhattan is about thirteen miles long and from east to west around two miles wide. Whatever is north of where you're standing is **uptown**, whatever south **downtown**; east or west is **crosstown**. As far as **districts** go, there are three major divisions:

• **Downtown** (below 14th St).

• **Midtown** (from 14th St up as far as Central Park).

• **Upper Manhattan** (north of Central Park).

The **southern (downtown) part of Manhattan** was first to be settled, which means that its streets have names and that they're somewhat randomly arranged. **Uptown, above Houston Street on the east side, 14th Street on the west**, the streets are numbered and follow a strict grid pattern. The numbers of these streets increase as you move north. Downtown, the main **points of reference** are buildings: the World Trade Center and Woolworth Building are unmistakable landmarks. Uptown, just look out for the big north–south **avenues**. **Fifth Avenue**, the greatest of these, cuts along the east side of Central Park and serves as a dividing line between east streets (the "**East Side**") and west streets ("**the West Side**"). **House numbers** increase as you walk away from either side of Fifth Avenue; numbers on avenues increase as you move north.

Addresses

Locations are easily pinpointed by giving the nearest intersection of avenue and street: the Chrysler Building, for example, is at Lexington Avenue and 42nd Street – "Lex and 42nd" in conversational shorthand. If you know the number of an address on an avenue it's possible to work out fairly precisely where the building is by referring to the plan of Manhattan printed opposite. If you ask directions, the unit of distance always quoted is the **block**, the rectangle of land marked out by the lattice of streets and avenues. As they're rectangles, remember that walking east–west blocks will take about three times longer than the same number of north–south blocks.

When **cycling, driving or looking for a bus**, it's useful to know that traffic on **odd**-numbered streets runs from east to west, on **even**-numbered streets from west to east, and in both directions on major crosstown streets. Apart from Park, Broadway and 11th (which are two-way), avenues run in alternate directions.

Chapter 2

Lower Manhattan

L ower Manhattan harbours its extremes in close proximity. For some it's the most spectacular, most glamorous skyline in the world, for others a run-down and seedy home. But whatever your final perspective, it is undeniably archetypal New York: an area that encompasses Greenwich Village and the East Village, Chinatown and Little Italy, and, at the skyscraper heart of things, the startling corporate identity of the Financial District.

As a prelude to neighbourhood wanderings, the **Statue of Liberty** provides an obvious focus, not so much for the vaunted symbol (though this is hard to ignore) as for the views of southern Manhattan. This lower part of the island begins with the shoreline **Financial District** – Wall Street at its centre – and then drifts, within half a mile, into the first of the city's ethnic districts. **Chinatown** is still solidly a community (often Chinese-speaking only) and seemingly oblivious of nearby real estate wealth. It's part of the city worth getting to know, not least for very cheap lunchtime food. **Little Italy**, adjacent, is in contrast a warning of New York's irresistible tide – a quarter now largely overrun by slick cafés and restaurants.

Over to the west, quite different again in population and feel, are **SoHo** and **TriBeCa**, one-time industrial areas, now up-and-coming residential blocks and home to Manhattan's (and the world's) art scene. Further north, a less radical shift, are traditionally politicised/literary **Greenwich Village** (touristy now but fun) and the **East Village**, which has taken on much of Greenwich's alternative/arts/political mantle. All of which makes for enjoyable and rewarding walking and café browsing. Walk beyond, though, into the **Lower East Side**, and the riches fade fast – New York's very real poverty quite unhidden and not a little threatening.

The Harbour Islands

The tip of Manhattan island and the enclosing shores of New Jersey, Staten Island and Brooklyn form the broad expanse of **New York harbour**, one of the finest natural harbours in the world and one of the things that persuaded the first immigrants to establish their first settlement here several centuries ago. It's an almost landlocked body of water, divided into the Upper and Lower Bay, some hundred miles square in total and stretching as far as the Verrazano Narrows – the narrow neck of land between Staten Island and Long Island. It's possible to appreciate it by simply gazing out from the promenade on Battery Park. But to get a proper sense of New York's specialness, and to get the best views of the classic skyline, you should really take to the water. You can do this by taking a trip on the Staten Island Ferry, though the islands in the bay, notably the Statue of Liberty and Ellis Island, provide far more compelling targets for a trip.

The Harbour Islands

For details of the Staten Island ferry, see p.186.

Practicalities

Ferries, run by *Circle Line*, go to both the Statue of Liberty and Ellis Island and leave from the pier in Battery Park, every half-hour in summer roughly between 9.15am and 3.30pm during the week, 4.30pm at weekends. The fare is $6 for the full round trip, half-price for children (tickets from Castle Clinton). If you took the last ferry it wouldn't be possible see both islands, so it's best to try and leave as early as possible, thereby avoiding the queues (which can be long in high season, especially at weekends) and giving yourself enough time to explore both islands properly: Liberty Island needs a good couple of hours, and if the weather's fine and there aren't too many people, it can be a pleasant place to spend an afternoon; Ellis Island, too, demands two hours at least if you want to see everything. There are no admission fees for either Ellis Island or the Statue of Liberty.

The Statue of Liberty

Of all the many symbols of America, none has proved more enduring or evocative than the **Statue of Liberty**. This giant figure, torch in hand and clutching a stone tablet, has for a century acted as a kind of figurehead for the American Dream, and it's a measure of the global power of the United States that there is today probably no more immediately recognisable profile in existence. It's worth remembering, also, that the statue is – for Americans at least – a potent reminder that the USA is a land of immigrants: it was New York harbour where the first big waves of European immigrants arrived, their ships entering through the Verrazano Narrows to round the bend of the bay and catch a first glimpse of "Liberty Enlightening the World" – for them the end of their journey into the unknown and symbolic beginning of a new life. Now, although only the very wealthy can afford to arrive here by sea these days, and a would-be immigrant's first (and possibly last) view of the States is more likely to be the customs check at JFK Airport, Liberty remains – notwithstanding US foreign policy – a stirring sight, Emma Lazarus's poem, written originally to raise funds for the statue's base, no less quotable than when it was written . . .

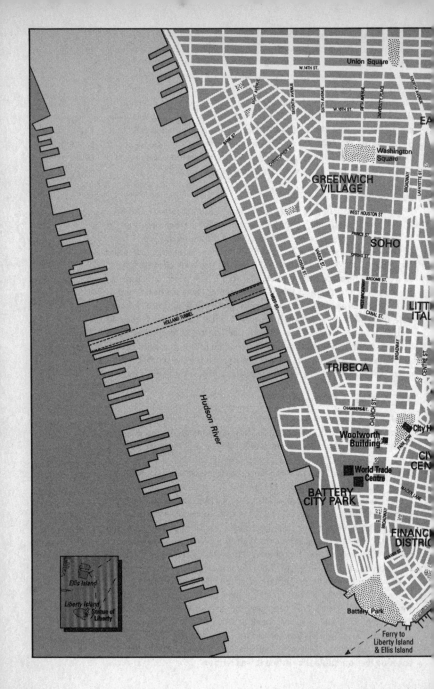

Union Square

W.14TH ST.

W.10TH ST.

EIGHTH AVENUE

SEVENTH AVENUE

SIXTH AVENUE

FIFTH AVENUE

UNIVERSITY PLACE

FOURTH AVENUE

EA

BANK ST.

CHRISTOPHER ST.

Washington
Square

GREENWICH
VILLAGE

BROADWAY

LAFAYETTE ST.

WEST HOUSTON ST

PRINCE ST.

SOHO

HUDSON ST.

VARICK ST.

SPRING ST.

BROOME ST.

GREENE ST.

LITT
ITAL

CANAL ST.

HOLLAND TUNNEL

BROADWAY

CENTRE ST.

WEST STREET

TRIBECA

Hudson River

CHAMBERS ST.

CHURCH ST.

City H

Woolworth
Building

WEST STREET

WEST BROADWAY

World Trade
Centre

BATTERY
CITY PARK

BROADWAY

CIVI
CEN

MAIDEN LANE

FINANCI
DISTRIC

Battery Park

Ellis Island

Liberty Island
Statue of
Liberty

Ferry to
Liberty Island
& Ellis Island

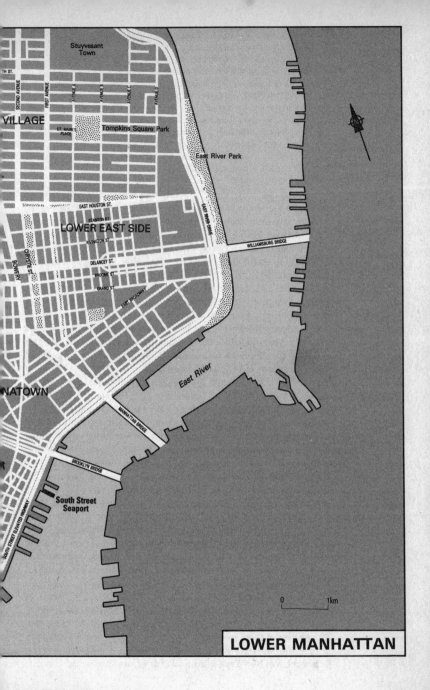

Stuyvesant Town

SECOND AVENUE
FIRST AVENUE
AVENUE A
AVENUE B
AVENUE C
AVENUE D

TH ST.

VILLAGE

ST. MARK'S PLACE

Tompkins Square Park

East River Park

EAST HOUSTON ST.

STANTON ST.

LOWER EAST SIDE

RIVINGTON ST.

BOWERY
CHRYSTIE ST.

DELANCEY ST.

BROOME ST.

GRAND ST.

EAST BROADWAY

EAST RIVER DRIVE

WILLIAMSBURG BRIDGE

East River

NATOWN

MANHATTAN BRIDGE

BROOKLYN BRIDGE

SOUTH STREET / FDR HIGHWAY

South Street
Seaport

0   1km

LOWER MANHATTAN

The Harbour Islands

Here at our sea-washed, sunset gates shall stand
A mighty woman with a torch, whose flame
Is the imprisoned lightning, and her name
Mother of Exiles. From her beacon-hand
Glows world-wide welcome; her mild eyes command
The air-bridged harbour that twin cities frame.
'Keep ancient lands, your storied pomp!' cries she
With silent lips. 'Give me your tired, your poor,
Your huddled masses yearning to breathe free,
The wretched refuse to your teeming shore.
Send these, the homeless, tempest-tost to me,
I lift my lamp beside the golden door.

The statue, which depicts Liberty throwing off her shackles and holding a beacon to light the world, was the creation of the French sculptor Frédéric Auguste Bartholdi, crafted a hundred years after the American Revolution in recognition of fraternity between the French and American people (though it's fair to add that Bartholdi originally intended the statue for Alexandria in Egypt). Bartholdi built Liberty in Paris between 1874 and 1884, starting with a terra-cotta model and enlarging it through four successive versions to its present size, a construction of thin copper sheets bolted together and supported by an iron framework designed by Gustave Eiffel. The arm carrying the torch was exhibited in Madison Square Park for seven years, but the whole statue wasn't officially accepted on behalf of the American people until 1884, after which it was taken apart, crated up and shipped to New York.

It was to be another two years before it could be properly unveiled: money had to be collected to fund the construction of the base, and for some reason Americans were unwilling – or unable – to dip into their pockets. Only through the campaigning efforts of newspaper magnate Joseph Pulitzer, a keen supporter of the statue, did it all come together in the end. Richard Morris Hunt built a pedestal around the existing star-shaped Fort Wood, and Liberty was formally dedicated by President Cleveland on October 28, 1886, in a flag-waving shindig that has never really stopped. The statue was closed a few years back for extensive renovation once more paid for by a fervently patriotic public – but now the whole thing is accessible again, opened in July 1986 with more back-patting ceremonial to commemorate the statue's centennial. Fifteen million people descended on Manhattan for the celebrations, well over half a million of them piling into Central Park to hear a special Liberty performance by the New York Philharmonic.

You can today climb steps up to the crown, though the torch, to which there is a cramped stairway, is sadly to remain closed to the public. Don't be surprised if there's an hour-long queue to ascend, though even if there is, Liberty Park's views of the Lower Manhattan skyline, the twin towers of the World Trade Center lording it over the jutting teeth of New York's financial quarter, are spectacular enough.

Ellis Island

Just across the water, and just a few minutes on by ferry, sits **Ellis Island**, the first stop for over twelve million immigrants hoping to settle in the USA. The island, originally known as Gibbet Island by the English (who used it for punishing unfortunate pirates), became an immigration station in 1894, in order to cope with the massive influx of mostly southern and eastern European immigrants. It remained open until 1954, when it was abandoned and left to fall into atmospheric ruin.

The immigration process

Up until the 1850s there was no official immigration process in New York. Then, the upsurge of Irish, German and Scandinavian immigrants, escaping the great famines of 1846 and failed revolutions of 1848, forced authorities to open an immigration centre at Castle Clinton in Battery Park. By the 1880s widespread hardship in eastern and southern Europe, the pogroms in Russia, and the massive economic failure in southern Italy forced thousands to flee the continent. At the same time, America was experiencing the first successes of its Industrial Revolution and more and more people started to move to the cities from the country. Ellis Island opened in 1894, just as America came out of a depression and began to assert itself as a world power. News spread through Europe of what the New World could offer and immigrants left in their thousands.

The immigrants who arrived at Ellis Island were all steerage-class passengers; richer immigrants were processed at their leisure on board ship. The scenes on the island were horribly confused: most families arrived hungry, filthy and penniless, rarely speaking English and invariably overawed by the beckoning metropolis across the water. Con men preyed from all sides, stealing their baggage as it was checked and offering rip-off exchange rates for whatever money they had managed to bring. Each family was split up, men sent to one area, women and children to another, while a series of checks took place to weed out the undesirables and the infirm. The latter were taken to the second floor, the Registry Room, where doctors would check for "loathsome and contagious diseases" as well as signs of insanity. Those who failed medical tests were marked with a white cross on their backs and either sent to the hospital or put back on the boat. Steamship carriers had an obligation to return any immigrants not accepted to their original port, though according to official records only two percent were ever rejected, and many of those jumped into the sea and tried to swim to Manhattan rather than face going home. There was also a legal test, which checked nationality and, very important, political affiliations. The majority of the immigrants were processed in a matter of hours and then headed either to New Jersey and trains to the West, or into New York City to settle in one of the rapidly expanding ethnic neighbourhoods.

The Museum of Immigration

By the time of its closure, Ellis Island was a formidable complex. The first building burnt down in 1897, the present one was built in 1903, and there were various additions built in the ensuing years – hospitals, outhouses and the like, usually on bits of landfill that were added to the island in an attempt to contend with the swelling numbers passing through. The buildings were derelict until the mid-1980s, since when the main, four-turretted central building has been completely renovated, reopening in 1990 as the **Museum of Immigration**. This is an ambitious museum, and tries hard to recapture some of the spirit of the place, with films and tapes documenting the celebration of America as the immigrant nation, although you can't help but feel that it might have been more memorable before the authorities got their hands on the place.

Nonetheless some 100 million Americans can trace their roots back through Ellis Island, and for them especially it must be an engaging display. The huge vaulted Registry Room has been left bare, with just a couple of inspectors' desks and American flags, and gives on to a series of interview rooms and white-tiled corridors that also have been left suitably institutional, more reminiscent of a prison or mental institution than a stepping stone to liberty. Each is illustrated by the recorded voices of those who passed through Ellis Island recalling their experience, along with photographs, thoughtful and informative explanatory text, and small artefacts – train timetables and familiar items brought from home. There are descriptions of arrival and the subsequent interviews, examples of questions asked and medical tests given; there are also evocative photographs of the building before it was restored, along with items rescued from the building and rooms devoted to the peak years of immigration; on the top floor one of the dormitories, used by those kept overnight for further examination, has been left almost intact.

Outside, the place has an eerie, unfinished feel, heightened by the derelict shell of what was once the centre's hospital. On the fortified spurs of the island, names of immigrant families who passed through the building over the years are engraved in copper; paid for by a minimum donation of $100 from their descendants, this "American Immigrant Wall of Honor" helped fund the restoration.

Governor's Island

The last of the three small islands which lie just south of Manhattan, **Governor's Island** is home to the US Coast Guard and only visitable one day each month: call ☎668-3402 for exact times. In summer free tours are run and it makes for a close-by escape from the city if you've an hour or two to spare. "Nowhere in New York is more pastoral", Jan Morris wrote of the island in *The Great Port*. Sights include a handful of colonial and nineteenth-century houses, and Fort Jay and Castle Williams – the former put up in 1789 by zealous and ever-vigilant revolutionary volunteers. Otherwise it's once again the views of downtown Manhattan that steal the show: more impressive than ever from the peaceful, almost villagey environment of the island.

The Financial District

The skyline of Manhattan's **Financial District** is the one you see in all the movies – dramatic skyscrapers pushed into the narrow southern tip of the island and framed by the monumental elegance of the Brooklyn Bridge. Heart of the nation's wheeler-dealing, this is where Manhattan (and indeed America) began – though precious few leftovers of those days remain, shunted out by big business eager to boost corporate image with headquarters in the right places. Like the City of London, the Financial District has a nine-to-five existence: don't go expecting life outside of these times or at weekends.

The Stock Exchange and the Wall Street Crash

The Dutch arrived here first, building a wooden wall at the edge of their small settlement as protection from pro-British settlers to the north. Hence the narrow canyon of today's **Wall Street** gained its name, and it's here, behind the thin neoclassical mask of the **New York Stock Exchange**, that the purse strings of the capitalist world are pulled. From the **Visitors' Gallery** (Mon–Fri 9.15am–4pm; free) the exchange floor appears a mêlée of brokers and buyers, all scrambling for the elusive fractional cent on which to make a megabuck. Sit through the glib introductory film, though, and the hectic scurrying and constantly moving hieroglyphs of the stock prices make more sense. Along with the film, there's a small exhibition on the history of the Exchange – notably quiet on the more spectacular cock-ups. The most disastrous, the notorious "Black Tuesday" of 1929, is mentioned almost in passing, perhaps because it was so obviously caused by the greed and short-sightedness of the money men themselves. In those days shares could be bought "on margin", which meant the buyer needed to pay only a small part of their total cost, borrowing the rest using the shares as security. This worked fine so long as the market kept rising – share dividends came in to pay off the loans, investors' money bought more shares. But it was, as Alistair Cooke put it, "a mountain of credit on a molehill of actual money", and only a small scare was needed to start the avalanche. When the market slackened punters had to find more cash to service their debts and make up for the fall in value of their stocks, which they did by selling off shares cheaply. A panicked chain reaction began, and on October 24 sixteen million shares were traded; five days later the whole Exchange collapsed as $125 million was wiped off stock values. Fortunes disappeared overnight: millions lost their life savings, banks, businesses and industries shut their doors, unemployment spiralled helplessly. The Great Depression

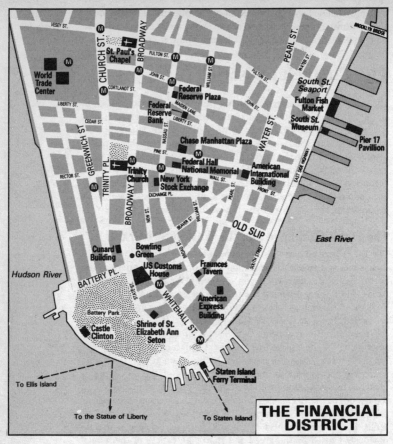

THE FINANCIAL DISTRICT

began. It says much for the safety nets that today surround the market's operations that the equally tumultuous crash of October 1987 caused comparatively negligible reverberations.

Federal Hall and Trinity Church

The **Federal Hall National Memorial**, at Wall Street's canyon-like head, can't help but look a little foolish, a Doric temple that woke up one morning and found itself surrounded by skyscrapers. The building was once the Customs House, later a bank, but the exhibition inside (Mon–Fri 9am–5pm; free) relates the headier days of 1789 when George Washington was sworn in as America's first president from a balcony on this site. It was a showy affair for a great if rather pompous man: "I fear we may have exchanged George III for George I", commented one senator observing Washington's affectations. The documents and models of the event repay a wander, as does the daintily rotunded hall. Washington's statue stands, very properly, on the steps.

At Wall Street's other end, **Trinity Church** (guided tours at 2pm, daily) waits darkly in the wings, an ironic onlooker to the street's dealings. There's been a church here since the end of the seventeenth century, but this one in knobbly neo-Gothic went up in 1846, and for fifty years was the city's tallest building, a reminder of just how recently high-rise Manhattan has sprung up. It's got much of the air of an English church (Richard Upjohn, its architect, came from Dorset), especially in the sheltered **graveyard**, resting place of early Manhattanites and lunching office workers. A search round the old tombstones rewards with such luminaries as first Secretary to the Treasury Alexander Hamilton.

Around Wall Street

Trinity Church is an oddity amid its office-block neighbours, several of which are worth nosing into. **One Wall Street**, immediately opposite the church, is among the best, with an Art Deco lobby in sumptuous red and gold that naggingly suggests a bankers' bordello. East down Wall Street, the **Morgan Guaranty Trust Building**, at no. 23, bears the scars of a weird happening of 1920. On September 16 a horse-drawn cart pulled up outside and its driver jumped off and disappeared down a side street. A few seconds later the cart blew up in a devastating explosion, knocking out windows half a mile away. Thirty-three people were killed and hundreds injured, but the explosion remains unexplained. One theory holds that it was a premeditated attack on Morgan and his vast financial empire; another that the cart belonged to an explosives company and was illegally travelling through the city. Curiously, or perhaps deliberately, the pockmark scars on the building's wall have never been healed.

The most impressive leftover of the confident days before the Wall Street Crash is the old **Cunard Building** at 25 Broadway, whose marble walls and high dome housed the steamship's booking office – hence the elaborate, whimsical murals of sea travel and nautical gods splashed all around. As the large liners gave way to jet travel, Cunard could no longer afford such an extravagant shop window. Its sorry fate today is to house a post office, one that's been fitted out with little feeling for the exuberant space it occupies.

Bowling Green and around

Broadway comes to a gentle end at the **Bowling Green**, an oval of turf used for the game by eighteenth-century colonial Brits on a lease of "one peppercorn per year". The encircling iron fence is an original of 1771, though the crowns that once topped the stakes were removed in later revolutionary fervour, as was a statue of George III, to be melted down and put to more practical use in cannonballs. Earlier still the green was the site of one of Manhattan's more

From Fall 1994,
the Customs
House will
contain the
Museum of the
American
Indian; see
p.223.

memorable business deals, when Peter Minuit, first director general of the Dutch colony of New Amsterdam, bought the whole island from the Indians for a handful of baubles worth 60 guilders (about $25): but the other side of the story, the bit you never hear, was that these Indians didn't actually own the island; no doubt both parties went home smiling. Today the green is a spot for office people picnicking in the shadow of Cass Gilbert's **US Customs House**, which forms a grandiose plug to the south. With its back firmly to the sea the Customs House is a heroic monument to New York the port; four statues at the front represent the four continents (sculpted by Daniel Chester French, who also created the Lincoln Memorial in Washington, DC) and the twelve near the top personify the world's commercial centres, all fixed in homage to the maritime market. Inside, on the rotunda, are some rumbustious murals by Reginald Marsh, celebrating the activities of New York's harbourside.

Battery Park and Castle Clinton

Beyond the Customs House, Lower Manhattan lets out its breath in **Battery Park**, a bright and breezy space with **Castle Clinton** at one side. Before landfill closed the gap this nineteenth-century fort was an island, protecting Manhattan's southern tip – the battery of cannon providing its name. Later it found new life as a prestigious concert venue – in 1850 the enterprising P.T. Barnum threw a hugely hyped concert by soprano Jenny Lind, the "Swedish Nightingale", with tickets at $225 a throw – before doing service (pre-Ellis Island) as the drop-off point for arriving immigrants. Today the squat castle isn't that interesting, though if you're curious it's open daily (9am–5pm); bear in mind that it's also the place to buy ferry tickets to the Statue of Liberty and Ellis Island.

South of Castle Clinton stands the **East Coast Memorial**, a series of granite slabs inscribed with the names of all the American seamen who were killed in World War II. Fittingly, it looks out across New York harbour, and this stretch has tremendous views out to the Statue of Liberty and Ellis Island.

Back on State Street a dapper Georgian facade identifies the **Shrine of Elizabeth Ann Seton**, the first native-born American to be canonised. St Elizabeth lived here briefly before moving to found a religious community in Maryland. The shrine – small, hushed and illustrated by pious and tearful pictures of the saint's life – is one of a few old houses that have survived the modern onslaught. On the corner of Pearl and Broad streets is another, **Fraunces Tavern**, set dramatically against a backdrop of skyscrapers. The three-storey Georgian brick house has been almost totally reconstructed to mimic the day of the incident that ensured its survival: on December 4, 1783, the British conclusively beaten, a weeping George Washington took leave of his assembled officers, intent on returning to rural life in Virginia: "I am not only retiring from all public employments," he wrote, "but am retiring within myself" – with hindsight a hasty statement as six years later he was to return as the new nation's President. The second floor re-creates the simple colonial dining room where this took place – all probably as genuine as the relics of Washington's teeth and hair in the adjacent museum. Admission is Mon–Fri, 10am–4pm, Sun noon–5pm; free Mon–Fri 10am–noon, other times $2.50, $1 students.

Along Water Street

Turn a corner by the tavern and you're on **Water Street**, in its southern reaches a thinned-out agglomeration of skyscrapers developed in the early 1960s when the powers-that-were took it into their heads that Manhattan's business was stagnating because of lack of room for growth and so tore down the Victorian brownstones and warehouses that lined the waterfront. They thus missed a vital chance to let the old give context to the new, and if you stand on the barren plaza of the **American Express Building** at 2 New York Plaza, you're a long way from feeling anything other than windswept and alone. But not all of Water Street's development is quite so faceless: turn east down Old Slip and a pocket-size palazzo that was once the **First Precinct Police Station** slots good-naturedly into the narrow strip, a cheerful throwback to a different era. A little to the south, off Water Street, is the **Vietnam Veterans' Memorial**, an ugly assembly of glass blocks etched with troops' letters home. While these are sad and occasionally moving, the memorial is unpleasantly shabby, reminiscent of an ill-kempt municipal toilet.

Cross Water Street, take the next left to Pine Street and you'll find one of Manhattan's most joyful skyscrapers. In 1916 the authorities became worried that the massive buildings looming up around town would shield light from the streets, turning the lower and midtown areas into grim passages between soaring monoliths. The result of their fears was the first *zoning ordinance*, which ruled that a building's total floor space couldn't be any more than twelve times the area of its site. This led to the "setback" style of skyscraper, and the **American International Building** at 70 Pine Street is the ultimate wedge of Art Deco wedding cake: light, zestful and with one of the best Deco interiors. As with other lobbies, no one minds you going in, and recent demolitions mean you can get a good view of the whole building – which might have been almost as well known as the Empire State or Chrysler had it been more visible. Almost opposite, I. M. Pei's grid-iron **88 Pine Street** stands coolly formal in white, a self-confident and self-contained modern descendant.

Around the South Street Seaport

At the eastern end of Fulton Street the **South Street Seaport** comes girded with the sort of praise and publicity that generally augurs a commercial bland-out. In fact it's a likeable project that's attempting to preserve one of Lower Manhattan's few surviving historic industrial areas. A fair slice of commercial gentrification was needed to woo developers, but the presence of a working fish market has kept things real in a way that should be a lesson for the likes of London's Covent Garden.

For a hundred years this stretch of the waterside was New York's sailship port: it began when Robert Fulton started a ferry service from here to Brooklyn and left his name on the street and then its market. The harbour lapped up the trade brought by the opening of the Erie Canal, and, by the end of the nineteenth century, was sending cargo ships on regular runs to California, Japan and Liverpool. Trade eventually moved elsewhere, though, and the blocks of warehouses and ship's chandlers, gradually and secretively being bought up by property speculators, were left to rot. Their rescue – by a historical monument order – was probably only just in time.

Regular guided tours of the Seaport run from the Visitors' Center at 207 Water Street, but the best place to start looking round is the market's so-called **Museum Block**, an assembly of upmarket shops hidden behind Water Street's hotchpotch of Greek Revival and Italianate facades. Adjacent is the **New Fulton Market**, which, despite outward appearances, went up in 1983. Essentially it's a food emporium, and if the prices aren't bargain basement they're certainly within reach, especially for the eclectic variety of fast food on the second floor, the best bet for a cut-price lunch. Across the way the cleaned-up **Schermerhorn Row** has the "English" *North Star Pub* at one end and the pricey *Sloppy Louie's* restaurant around the corner.

The Fish Market and South Street Seaport Museum

The elevated East Side Highway forms a suitably grimy gateway to the **Fulton Fish Market**, a tatty building that wears its eighty years as the city's wholesale outlet with no pretensions. If you can manage it, the time to be here is around 5am (organised tours run each first and third Thursday; $10, reservations needed – ☎669-9416) when buyers' lorries park up beneath the highway to collect the catches, the air reeks of salt and scale and there's lots of nasty things to step in. But it's invigorating stuff, a twilight world that probably won't be around that much longer – the adjacent **Pier 17 Pavilion**, a hypercomplex of restaurants and shops, could be one nail in its coffin.

For more places to eat around the Seaport, see Chapter 8, Drinking and Eating.

Next door, around piers 15 and 16, is the **South Street Seaport Museum** (daily 10am–5pm; $6 admission includes all tours, films and visits), a collection of nimble sailships and chubby ferries slowly being refitted to former glories. In the summer, the schooner *Pioneer* will coast you round the harbour for an additional consideration, though unless sailing is your passion it's better to skip the ships; more fun to freeload at the outdoor **jazz concerts** on Friday and Saturday evenings (8pm throughout July and August).

The Brooklyn Bridge

From just about anywhere in the seaport you can see one of New York's most celebrated delights, the **Brooklyn Bridge**. This is now just one of several spans across the East River – and the Gothic slabs of the bridge's gateways are dwarfed by lower Manhattan's skyscrapers. But in its day the Brooklyn Bridge was a technological quantum leap: it towered over the low brick structures around and for twenty years was the world's largest suspension bridge, the first to use steel cables and for many more the longest single span. To New Yorkers it was an object of awe, the massively concrete symbol of the Great American Dream: "All modern New York, heroic New York, started with the Brooklyn Bridge," wrote Kenneth Clark, and indeed its meeting of art and function, of romantic Gothic and daring practicality, became a sort of spiritual model for the next generation's skyscrapers.

It didn't go up without difficulties. John Augustus Roebling, its architect and engineer, crushed his foot taking measurements for the piers and died of gangrene three weeks later; his son Washington took over only to be crippled by the bends from working in an insecure underwater caisson, and subsequently directed the work from his sick bed overlooking the site. Twenty workers died during the construction and, a week after the opening day in 1883, twelve people were crushed to death in a panicked rush on the bridge's footway. Despite this (and innumerable suicides), New Yorkers still look to the bridge with affection: for the 1983 centennial it was festooned with decorations – "Happy Birthday Brooklyn Bridge" ran the signs – and the city organised a party, replete with shiploads of fireworks.

*For more on
Brooklyn see
Chapter 5, The
Outer Boroughs.*

Whether the bridge has a similar effect on you or not, the view from it is undeniably spectacular. Walk across, near sunset if possible, from City Hall Park and don't look back till you're midway: the Financial District's giants clutter shoulder to shoulder through the spidery latticework, the East River pulses below and cars scream to and from Brooklyn. It's a glimpse of the 1980s metropolis, and on no account to be missed.

The Federal Reserve Bank

Back on the island, Fulton Street arcs right across Lower Manhattan with **Maiden Lane** as its southern parallel, an august and anonymous rollercoaster of finance houses, with **Nassau Street** linking the two in a downbeat precinct of discount goods and fast food. Where Nassau and Maiden Lane meet, Johnson and Burgee's toybox castle of **Federal Reserve Plaza** resounds like a witless joke over the original **Federal Reserve Bank**, whose fortressy walls supplied their postmodernist idea. While the loggia of the plaza isn't all bad, the Federal Reserve Plaza proved to be one of Philip Johnson's last projects with John Burgee: he split with the architect soon after, leaving Burgee broke and in the architectural wilderness.

There's good reason for the Reserve Bank proper's iron-barred exterior: stashed eighty feet below the street are most of the "free" world's **gold reserves** – 11,000 tonnes of them, occasionally shifted from vault to vault as wars break out or international debts are settled. It is possible – but tricky – to tour the piles of gleaming bricks; write to the Public Information Department, Federal Reserve Bank, 33 Liberty Street, NY 10045 or phone ☎720-6130 at least a week ahead, as tickets have to be posted. Upstairs, dirty money and counterfeit currency are weeded out of circulation as automated checkers shuffle dollar bills like unending packs of cards. Assistants wheelbarrow loads of cash around ("How much there?" I asked one: "$8.5 million", he replied) and, as you'd imagine, the security is just like in the movies.

Around the Federal Reserve Bank

When you've unboggled your mind of high finance's gold you can see some of its glitter at **One Chase Manhattan Plaza** immediately to the south on Pine Street. Prestigious New York headquarters of the bank, its boxy International-style tower was the first in Lower Manhattan and brought downtown the concept of the plaza, an open forecourt at the entrance. Unfortunately Chase Manhattan's plaza has all the soul and charm of a car park, and even Dubuffet's *Four Trees* sculpture can't get things going.

Continue to the end of Cedar Street and you'll find the **Marine Midland Bank** at 140 Broadway, a smaller, more successful tower by the same design team, with a tiptoeing sculpture by Isamu Noguchi. More sculpture worth catching lies behind Chase Manhattan Plaza on **Louise Nevelson Plaza**. Here a clutch of Nevelson's works lie like a mass of shrapnel on an island of land: a striking ploy of sculpture that works well within the urban environment.

Go back down Liberty Street to Church Street and at **One Liberty Plaza** stands the **US Steel Building**, a threatening black mass all the more offensive since the famed **Singer Building** was demolished to make way for it. Ernest Flagg's 1908 construction was one of the most delicate on the New York skyline, a graceful Renaissance-style tower of metal and glass destroyed in 1968 and replaced with what has justly been called a "gloomy, cadaverous hulk".

The World Trade Center

Wherever you are in Lower Manhattan, two buildings dominate the landscape. Critics say the twin Ronson lighters of the **World Trade Center towers** don't relate to their surroundings and aren't especially pleasing in design – and spirited down to a tenth of their size they certainly wouldn't get a second glance. But the fact is they're *big*, undeniably and frighteningly so, and a walk across the plaza in summer months (closed in winter as icicles falling from the towers can kill) can make your head reel.

Perhaps the idea of so huge a project similarly affected the judgement of the Port Authority of New York and New Jersey, the Center's chief financier, which for several years found itself expensively stuck with two half-empty white elephants – which were quickly surpassed as the world's tallest building by the Sears Tower in Chicago. Now the Center, whose towers are the best part of a five-building development, is full and successful, and the building has become one of the emblems of the city itself. With courage, a trip to the 107th floor **observation deck** of Two World Trade Center (daily 9.30am–9.30pm; $4) gives a mind-blowing view from a height of 1350 feet – over a quarter of a mile. From the open-air rooftop promenade (closed during bad weather) the silent panorama is more dramatic still: everything in New York is below you, including the planes gliding into the airports. Even Jersey City looks exciting. As you timidly edge your way around, ponder the fact that one Philippe Petit once walked a tightrope between the two towers: nerve indeed. Best time to ascend is towards sunset when the tourist crowds thin and Manhattan slowly turns itself into the most spectacular light show this side of the Apocalypse.

The various restaurants and cafés in the World Trade Center – including the renowned Windows on the World *– are closed for renovation until early 1994.*

The bombing of the World Trade Center

On February 26, 1993, the World Trade Center complex was rocked by an **explosive device** left in one of the underground car parks; six people were killed and over a thousand injured. For a moment, the nightmare scenario of the destruction of one of the world's largest office buildings seemed possible, but apart from some minor structural damage, the building held fast. The evacuation of over 50,000 office workers was swiftly and safely carried out, and the biggest headache for the companies in the Trade Center was the fact that the towers were closed for weeks while structural examinations took place. Blame for the bomb fell upon an Arab terrorist group led by the radical Muslim cleric Shaikh Omar Abdel-Rahman, though their involvement has still conclusively to be proved.

St Paul's Chapel

Straight across from the World Trade Center on Vesey Street and Broadway, **St Paul's Chapel** comes from a very different order of things. It's the oldest church in Manhattan, dating from 1766 – eighty years earlier than Trinity Church and almost prehistoric by New York standards. The church's architect was from London – St Martin-in-the-Fields was his model – though his building seems quite American in feel, an unfussy eighteenth-century space of soap bar blues and pinks. George Washington worshipped here and his pew, zealously treasured, is much on show.

Battery Park City

The hole dug for the foundations of the World Trade Center's towers threw up a million cubic yards of earth and rock which were dumped into the Hudson to form the 23-acre base of **Battery Park City**. This, more than anything else, will change the character of the Financial District, with more office blocks and luxury apartments designed to turn the area into a place where the fortunate few can live as well as work. Originally, ten percent of the housing was to be set aside for low-income groups, but with the recession of the 1970s that plan was scrapped: now the city has promised to invest just under half of the $1 billion it will receive in profits back into housing schemes for the poor.

Architecturally, though, the park is one of the better events of recent years: traditional themes are picked up throughout, and the whole scheme has a loose conformity that echoes much of the rest of Manhattan. Even before completion it was being lauded as the new Rockefeller Center. Using Rector Park as a starting point, wandering through the gloomy Wintergarden (which often hosts lunch-hour concerts in its huge indoor arboretum) and Dow Jones lobby provides a more sober view. A little piece of suburbia tacked onto the edge of the island and seemingly out of place with the rest of the city, Battery Park City has few shops, even fewer restaurants and no traffic (one of its main selling points), and seems lost in some 1980s vision of a futuristic urban dream.

City Hall Park and the Civic Center

Broadway and Park Row form the apex of **City Hall Park**, a noisy, pigeon-splattered triangle of green with the **Woolworth Building** as a venerable and much venerated onlooker. Some think this is New York's definitive skyscraper, and it's hard to disagree – money, ornament and prestige mingle in Cass Gilbert's 1913 "Cathedral of Commerce", whose soaring, graceful lines are fringed with Gothic decoration more for fun than any portentous allusion: if the World Trade Center towers railroad you into wonder by sheer size, then the Woolworth charms with good nature, and the famous lobby is one of the musts of the city. Frank Woolworth made his fortune from his "five and dime" stores – everything cost either 5¢ or 10¢, strictly no credit. True to his philosophy he paid cash for his skyscraper, and the whimsical reliefs at each corner of the lobby show him doing just that, counting out the money in nickels and dimes. Facing him in caricature are the architect (medievally clutching a model of his building), renting agent and builder. Within, vaulted ceilings ooze honey-gold mosaics and even the mailboxes are magnificent. The whole building has a well-humoured panache more or less extinct in today's architecture – have a look at the Citibank next door to see what recent years have come up with.

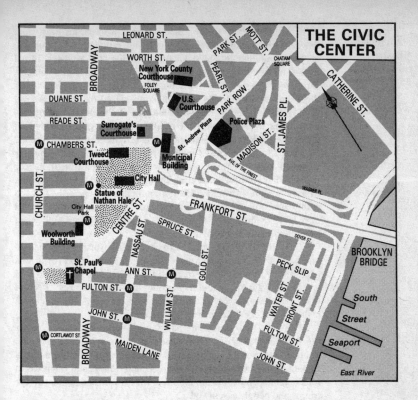

The Civic Center

At the top of the park, marking the beginning of the **Civic Center**
and its incoherent jumble of municipal offices and courts, stands
City Hall (Mon–Fri 10am–4pm). Finished in 1812 to a good-looking
design that's a marriage of French Chateau and American Georgian,
its first sorry moment of fame came in 1865 when Abraham
Lincoln's body lay in state for 120,000 New Yorkers to file past.
Later, after the city's 1927 feting of the returned aviator Charles
Lindbergh, it became the traditional finishing point for Broadway
tickertape parades given for triumphant baseball stars, astronauts,
and, more recently, returned Iranian hostages. Inside it's an elegant
meeting of arrogance and authority, with the sweeping spiral staircase delivering you to the precise geometry of the **Governor's
Room** and the self-important rooms that formerly contained the
Board of Estimates Chamber.

The Tweed Courthouse

If City Hall is the acceptable face of municipal bureaucracy, the
Tweed Courthouse behind is a reminder of a seamier underbelly of

corruption. William Marcy "Boss" Tweed worked his way from nowhere to become chairman of the Democratic Central Committee at Tammany Hall in 1856, and by a series of adroit and illegal moves manipulated the city's revenues through his own and his supporters' pockets. He consolidated his position by registering thousands of immigrants as Democrats in return for a low-level welfare system, and by hand-outs and pay-offs to the queues of critics waiting to be bought. For a while Tweed's grip strangled all dissent (even over the budget for the courthouse itself, which rolled up from $3 million to $12 million, possibly because one carpenter was paid $360,747 for a month's work, a plasterer $2,870,464 for nine) until a political cartoonist, Thomas Nast, and the editor of the *New York Times* (who'd refused a half-million dollar bribe to keep quiet) turned public opinion against him. With suitable irony Tweed died in 1878 in Ludlow Street jail – a prison he'd had built when Commissioner of Public Works.

City Hall Park is dotted with statues of worthier characters, number one in whose pantheon is **Nathan Hale**. In 1776 he was captured by the British and hanged for spying, but not before he'd spat out his gloriously and memorably famous last words: "I regret that I only have but one life to lose for my country." These, and his over-swashbuckled statue, are his epitaph.

The same year and same place saw George Washington order the first reading of the **Declaration of Independence** in the city. Thomas Jefferson's eloquent, stirring statement of the new nation's rights had just been adopted by the Second Continental Congress in Philadelphia, and it no doubt fired the hearts and minds of the troops and people assembled.

> We hold these truths to be self-evident, that all men are created equal, that they are endowed by their creator with certain unalienable rights, that among these are Life, Liberty and the pursuit of Happiness; that to secure these rights Governments are instituted among Men, deriving their just powers from the consent of the governed; that whenever any form of Government becomes destructive of these ends, it is the Right of the People to alter or abolish it, and to institute new Government . . .

The Municipal Building and around

Back on Center Street the **Municipal Building** stands like an oversized chest of drawers, its shoulders straddling Chambers Street in an attempt to embrace or engulf City Hall. Atop, an extravagant pile of columns and pinnacles signals a frivolous conclusion to a no-nonsense building. Walk through and you reach **Police Plaza**, a concrete space with the russet-hued **Police Headquarters** at one end and a rusty-coloured sculpture at its centre. One side of the plaza runs down past the anachronistic neo-Georgian church of St Andrews to the glum-grey **Foley Square** where, with some pomp, reside the United States and New York County **courthouses**, grand though underwhelming buildings after what has preceded. The County Court is the more interesting and accessible (Mon–Fri 9am–5pm), its rotunda decorated with storybook WPA murals illustrating the history of justice. If there's time take a look too at the Art Deco **Criminal Courts Building** (known as "The Tombs" from a funereal Egyptian-style building that once stood on this site) on Center Street and the unapologetically modern **Family Court** across the way; but by and large civic dignity begins to fade north of here, as ramshackle electrical shops mark the edge of **Chinatown**.

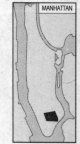

City Hall
Park and the
Civic Center

For more on the
WPA project,
see p.378.

Chinatown and Little Italy

With close on 100,000 residents (about half of New York's Chinese population), seven Chinese newspapers, around 150 restaurants and over 300 garment factories, **Chinatown** is unique in that it's Manhattan's only truly thriving ethnic neighbourhood, over recent years pushing its boundaries north across Canal Street into Little Italy, and sprawling east as far as the nether fringes of the Lower East Side.

On the face of things Chinatown is prosperous – a "model slum", some have called it – with the lowest crime rate, highest employment and least juvenile delinquency of any city district. Walk through its crowded streets at any time of day, and every shop is doing a brisk and businesslike trade: restaurant after restaurant booming, displays of shiny squids, clawing crabs and clambering bucketfuls of lobster, and all manner of exotic green vegetables, give this part of the city the feel of a land of plenty. The reason why lies with the Chinese themselves, who, even here, in the very core of downtown Manhattan, have been careful to preserve their own way of dealing with things, keeping affairs close to the bond of the family and allowing few intrusions into what is a still insular culture. The one time of the year when Chinatown bursts onto the New York scene is during the Chinese New Year **festival** in January or February (see Chapter 12, *Parades and Festivals*), when a giant dragon runs down Mott Street to the accompaniment of firecrackers, and the gutters run with ceremonial dyes.

Chinese immigration

The Chinese began to arrive in the mid-nineteenth century, following in the wake of a trickle of Irish and Italians. Most had previously worked out west, building railways and digging gold mines, and few intended to stay: their idea was simply to make a nest-egg and retire to a life of leisure with their families (99 percent were men) back in China. Some, a few hundred perhaps, did go back, but on the whole the big money took rather longer to accumulate than expected, and so Chinatown as a permanent settlement began. Which is not to say

Chinatown
and Little
Italy

that they were welcomed by the authorities. The Mafia-style Tong
Wars, towards the end of the nineteenth century, made the quarter's
violence notorious, and in 1882 the government passed an act
forbidding entry for ten years to any further Chinese workers.

After the 1965 Immigration Act did away with the 1924
"National Origins" provision, a large number of new immigrants
started arriving, many of whom were women. Within a few years the
massive male majority had been displaced. At this time, Chinatown
businessmen started to take advantage of the declining midtown
garment business and made use of a new, large and unskilled female
workforce: they opened extensive garment factories and paid below
minimum wages, which in turn enforced long hours. At the same
time, many small restaurants opened up, spurred in part by the
early 1970s western interest in Chinese food. Many of the working
women had no time to cook, and frequented these restaurants to
take food home for their families – hence the growth (and cheap-
ness) of the restaurants. With the interest of the Wall Street crowd
came fancier restaurants, more money and greater investment in the
area, which soon attracted more Asian money from overseas. Soon,
Chinatown had an internal economy unlike any other new immigrant neighbourhood in New York. Recently the community has
swollen once again, with immigrants from Hong Kong anticipating
the colony's uncertain future as it passes into the hands of the
Chinese in 1997.

Today, beneath the neighbourhood's blithely prosperous
facade, sharp practices apparently continue to flourish, with traditional extortion, protection rackets and non-union sweatshops. But
the community is so concerned with being cloistered that you'd
need long residence to detect any hint of it. And any kind of
unpleasantness is certainly not directed towards the customer or
tourist.

Around Chinatown

All of which is in any case academic, at least for most New Yorkers,
who come to Chinatown not to get the lowdown on the Chinese but
to eat. Nowhere in this city can you eat so well, and so much, for so
little. **Mott Street** is the area's main thoroughfare and along with
the streets around – Canal, Pell, Bayard, Doyers and Bowery – hosts
a positive glut of restaurants, tea and rice shops and grocers. The
different groups (all with different dialects) each tend to cluster in
various sections of Chinatown: Fukienese on Division Street,
Burmese Chinese on Henry Street, Chinese from Taiwan on Centre
Street and the Vietnamese on East Broadway. The food is dotted all
over; Cantonese cuisine predominates, but there are also many
restaurants that specialise in the spicier Szechuan and Hunan
cuisines, along with Fukien, Soochow and the spicy Chowchou
dishes. Anywhere you care to walk into is likely to be good, but if

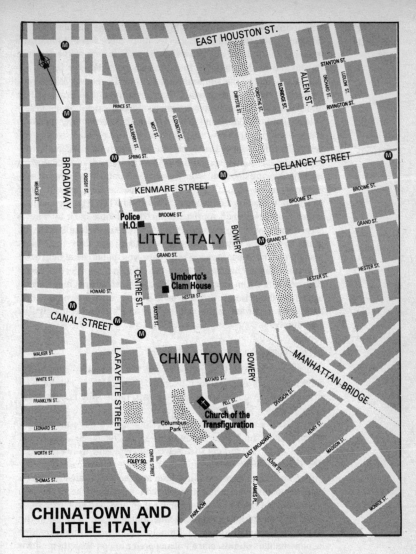

CHINATOWN AND LITTLE ITALY

you're looking for specific recommendations (especially for lunchtime *dim sum*), some of the best are detailed in Chapter 8, *Drinking and Eating*.

The lure of Chinatown lies largely in this – eating and wandering amid the exotica of the food and goods shops, and absorbing the neighbourhood's vigorous streetlife – though there are a few interesting routes if you want to set structure to your explorations. Mott Street, again, is the obvious starting point, and you may want to

You need to study the glossary of Chinese food terms on p.254 before eating in Chinatown.

detour from here to Mulberry Street, which runs parallel, and its flanking **Columbus Park**. Back on Mott there's the **Chinatown Museum** (see Chapter 6, *Museums and Galleries*) at the far end, on the site of the district's first Chinese shop. Further up, a rare building predates the Chinese intake, the early nineteenth-century **Church of the Transfiguration**; right from here the corner of Pell and Doyers streets was once known as "Bloody Angle" for its miserable reputation as dumping ground for dead bodies during the Tong Wars. Though rather less sinister now, it's still no place to linger – and really, once you've made this circuit (or at least a rough approximation of it), you've seen more or less all there is of Chinatown's nucleus. Moving on, stroll over **Bowery** and wander the streets leading down to the housing projects that flank the East River, most of which are nowadays indigenous Chinese and where you'll encounter rather more local than tourist traffic. Then double back by way of East Broadway or Henry Street to where the **Manhattan Bridge**, its grand Beaux Arts entrance slightly ridiculous these days, mounts its assault on the East River. From here you could head north up Chrystie Street, which forms the nominal border between Chinatown and the Lower East Side, or west down Canal Street, back into the turmoil of Chinatown and the area known as Little Italy, long regarded as the hub of the city's considerable Italian community.

Little Italy

While many New Yorkers refuse to admit it, and many guidebooks continue to witter on about little old signoras and elderly men sitting on street corners sipping espresso, **Little Italy** is light years away from the solid ethnic enclave of old. It is also a lot smaller than it was, and the area settled by New York's huge nineteenth-century influx of Italian immigrants – who (like their Jewish and Chinese counterparts) cut themselves off clannishly to re-create the Old Country – is encroached upon a little more each year by Chinatown. Few Italians still live here and the restaurants (of which there are plenty) tend to have valet-parking and high prices. In fact, it is this quantity of restaurants, more than anything else, that gives Little Italy away: go to the city's true Italian areas, Belmont in the Bronx or Carroll Gardens in Brooklyn, and you'll find very few genuine Italian eateries, since Italians prefer to consume their native food at home. It's significant, too, that when Martin Scorsese came to make *Mean Streets* – though the film was about Little Italy – it was in Belmont that he decided to shoot it.

But that's not to advise missing out on Little Italy altogether. Some original delis and bakeries do survive, and there are still plenty of places to indulge yourself with a cappuccino and pricey pastry, not least *Ferrara's* on Grand Street, the oldest and most popular, with a vibrant street-life in summer. If you're here in

September the **Festa di San Gennaro** is a wild, tacky and typically Italian splurge to celebrate the saint's day, when Italians from all over the city turn up and **Mulberry Street**, Little Italy's main strip, is transformed by street stalls and numerous Italian fast-snack outlets. Of the **restaurants**, *Umberto's Clam House* on Mulberry Street remains most famed, not for the food but for the fact that it was the scene of a vicious gangland murder in 1972, when Joe "Crazy Joey" Gallo was shot dead while celebrating his birthday with his wife and daughter. Gallo, a big noise keen to protect his business interests in Brooklyn and as provenly ruthless as the rest of them, was alleged to have offended a rival family and so paid the price: the bullet holes from the slaying are still visible in the windows.

For a full listing on Umberto's *and* Little Italy's *other restaurants, see* Chapter 8, Drinking and Eating.

Slightly west of here, at the corner of Center and Broome streets and in striking counterpoint to the clandestine lawlessness of the Italian underworld, the old **Police Headquarters** rears grandiosely out of the gloom, a palatial neoclassical confection meant to cow would-be criminals into obedience with a high-rise dome and lavish ornamentation. The police headquarters long since moved to a bland modern building in the Civic Center, and the overbearing palace has been converted into upmarket condominiums – a sure sign of the times. Walk beyond Broadway and you're already in **SoHo**, like Chinatown a booming district bursting its borders from the further side of Broadway.

SoHo and TriBeCa

Since the mid-1960s, **SoHo**, the grid of streets that runs *So*uth of *Hou*ston Street, has meant art. Squashed between the Financial District and, further north, Greenwich Village, it had long been a raggy wasteland land of manufacturers and wholesalers, but as the Village declined in hipness, SoHo was suddenly "in". Its loft spaces were ideal for cheap-rental studios, and galleries quickly attracted the city's art crowd, while boutique and restaurant hangers-on converted the ground floors. Like the Village, gentrification quickly followed – most of the artists left, the galleries stayed – and what remains is a mix of chi-chi antique, art and clothes shops, earthy industry and high living. Today a loft in SoHo means money (and lots of it) but no amount of gloss can cover up SoHo's quintessential appearance, its dark alleys of paint-peeled factories fronted by some of the best cast-iron facades in America, and indeed, the world.

Exploring SoHo

Houston Street (pronounced *How*ston rather than *Hew*ston) marks the top of SoHo's trellis of streets, any exploration of which necessarily means criss-crossing and doubling back. **Greene Street** is as good a place to start as any, highlighted all along by the cast-iron

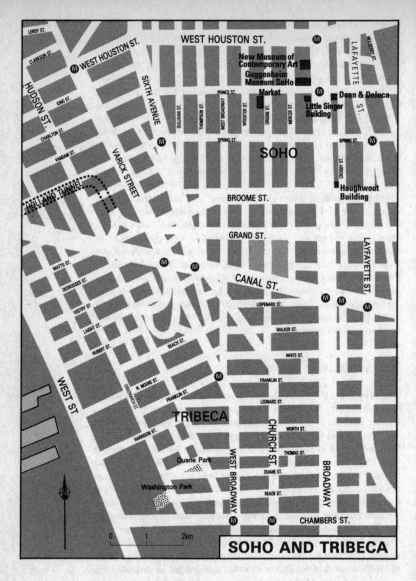

SOHO AND TRIBECA

facades that, in part if not in whole, saved SoHo from the bulldozers. Their origins are nineteenth century, a time when the quarter fringed New York's liveliest street, Broadway marking a fashionable run of hotels, shops and theatres, and the streets to the west a seamier backdrop of industrial and red light areas cheerfully known as "Hell's Hundred Acres".

Cast-iron architecture

The technique of **cast-iron architecture** was utilised simply as a way of assembling buildings quickly and cheaply, with iron beams rather than heavy walls carrying the weight of the floors. The result was the removal of load-bearing walls, greater space for windows, and, most noticeably, remarkably decorative facades. Almost any style or whim could be cast in iron and pinned to a building, and architects indulged themselves in Baroque balustrades, forests of Renaissance columns and all the effusion of the French Second Empire to glorify SoHo's sweatshops. Have a look at **72–76 Greene Street**, a neat extravagance whose Corinthian portico stretches the whole five storeys, all in painted metal, and at the strongly composed elaborations of its sister building at no. **28–30**. These are the best, but from Broome to Canal Street most of the fronts on Greene Street's west side are either real (or mock) cast iron. Ironically, what began as an engineering trait turned into a purely decorative one as stone copies of cast iron (you'd need a magnet to tell the real from the replicas) came into fashion. At the northeast corner of Broome Street and Broadway the magnificent **Haughwout Building** is perhaps the ultimate in the cast-iron genre. Rhythmically repeated motifs of colonnaded arches are framed behind taller columns in a thin sliver of a Venetian palace – and it's the first building ever to boast a steam-powered Otis elevator. In 1904 Ernest Flagg took the possibilities of cast iron to their conclusion in his **"Little Singer" Building** at 561 Broadway (at Prince Street), a design whose use of wide window frames points the way to the glass curtain wall of the 1950s.

Markets and galleries

SoHo celebrates all this architecture in Richard Haas's smirky **mural** at 114 Prince Street (corner of Greene Street), also the venue of one of SoHo's affordable **markets** (there's another at the meeting of Spring and Wooster streets). Many, probably most, of the clothes and antique shops around are beyond reasonable budgets, though the junkier bric-a-brac places may provide a bargain – search around Wooster and Thompson streets, and see Chapter 14, *Shops and Markets*, for details.

For something slightly less contemporary, visit the Guggenheim SoHo, p.218.

What you'll find in the innumerable **galleries** is similarly overpriced but makes for fascinating browsing, with just about every variety of contemporary artistic expression on view. No one minds you looking in for a while, and doing this is also a sure way of bumping into the more visible eccentrics of the area. Most of the galleries are concentrated on **West Broadway**, in a patch that fancies itself as an alternative Madison Avenue (though certainly not a lower priced one any longer). They're generally open from Labor Day to Memorial Day Tuesday–Saturday 10/11am–6pm, Saturdays being most lively; for listings of galleries (and details of gallery tours) see Chapter 6, *Museums and Galleries*, and pick up a copy of the *Art Now Guide* from (almost) any gallery. For a view of recent art outside the confines of SoHo, drop in on the **New Museum of Contemporary Art** at 583 Broadway between Prince and Houston streets (again, see Chapter 6).

Loosely speaking, SoHo's diversions get grottier as you drop south. Here, SoHo hits **Canal Street**, which links the Holland Tunnel with the Manhattan Bridge and forms a main thoroughfare between New Jersey and Brooklyn. This is SoHo's open bazaar, brash shop fronts loaded with fake Cartiers, dismembered torsos of electrical gear, books, cameras, records, and recently a budding pornographic video business that's been inherited from the sanitised Times Square district. Most people come here for the clothes places like the *Canal Jean Co.* at 504 Broadway between Spring and Broome streets and a host of others – but the army surplus and discarded technology stores crave most attention. Like the signs say it's all "as seen" – mainly trash, but good affordable fun. As TriBeCa to the south skips up the social ladder it's reckoned that Canal Street will be "cleaned up", which will be a pity.

TriBeCa

TriBeCa, the *Tri*angle *Be*low *Ca*nal Street, has caught the fall-out of SoHo artists, and retains a lived-in, worked-in feel. Less a triangle than a crumpled rectangle – the area bounded by Canal and Chambers streets, Broadway and the Hudson – it takes in spacious industrial buildings whose upper layers sprout plants and cats behind tidy glazing, the apartments of TriBeCa's new gentry. Like "SoHo" the name TriBeCa was a 1960s invention to label the newly found scramble of warehouses that became such popular residential quarters. Bought while still abandoned, these apartments and lofts still resemble the former sweatshops they replaced, with clothes-hanging rails still running through the rooms; today they're approaching SoHo in status and price, and it's only a matter of time before TriBeCa becomes just another piece of juicy real estate.

Best place to get a feel of TriBeCa's old and new is **Duane Park** between Hudson and Greenwich streets, a tiny wedge of green trapped by old depots of egg and cheese distributors and new smart residential apartments, with the World Trade Center and Woolworth and Municipal buildings peering over their shoulders. A block or two away, with less character but more space, there is also **Washington Park**, one of the few downtown patches you can stretch out on unintimidated, looking up to views of the World Trade Center and Woolworth Building.

At night TriBeCa seems completely deserted, save for the sound of footsteps echoing off the cobbled streets and against the cast-iron buildings for which the area is famous. TriBeCa used to shut when the Wall Street crowd went home, but the growth of Battery Park City has brought some smart restaurants into the neighbourhood, while some of the traditional after-work bars now stay open much later. One notable newcomer at 375 Greenwich is the **TriBeCa Film Center**, a film production company owned by, among others, Robert De Niro, and accompanied by his ground-floor restaurant, the *TriBeCa Grill*, whose clientele often includes well-known names and faces from the film world.

Greenwich Village

If you're a New Yorker, it's fashionable to dismiss **Greenwich Village** (or "the Village" as it's most widely known). There's so much more happening in SoHo, people say; the East Village is *sooo* much more funky and real; TriBeCa will soon be where it's at; or further uptown there's the Upper West Side. . .. And it's true that while the Bohemian image of Greenwich Village endures well enough if you don't actually live in New York, it's a tag that has long since ceased to hold genuine currency. The only writers that can afford to live here nowadays are copywriters, the only actors those that are starring regularly on Broadway, and as for politics – the average Village resident long since dismissed them for the more serious pursuit of making money. Greenwich Village is firmly for those who have Arrived. Not that the Village is no longer exciting: to a great extent the neighbourhood still sports the attractions that brought people here in the first place. It's quiet, residential, but with a busy street-life that lasts later than in any other part of the city; there are more restaurants per head than anywhere else, and bars, while never cheap, clutter every corner. If interesting people no longer live in the Village, they do hang out here – Washington Square is a hub of aimless activity throughout the year – and as long as you have no illusions about the "alternativeness" of the place there are few better initiations into the city's life, especially at night.

Places to eat and drink in the Village are listed in Chapter 8.

Greenwich Village grew up as a rural retreat from the early and frenetic nucleus of New York City, first becoming sought after during the yellow fever epidemic of 1822 as a refuge from the infected streets downtown. When the fever was at its height the idea was mooted of moving the entire city centre here. It was spared that dubious fate, and left to grow into a wealthy residential neighbourhood that sprouted elegant Federal and Greek Revival terraces and lured some of the city's highest society names. Later, once the rich had moved uptown and built themselves a palace or two on Fifth Avenue, these large houses were to prove a fertile hunting ground for struggling artists and intellectuals on the lookout for cheap rents, and by the turn of the century Greenwich Village was well on its way to becoming New York's Left Bank. Of early Village characters, one Mabel Dodge was perhaps most influential. Wealthy and radical, she threw parties for the literary and political cognoscenti – parties to which everyone hoped, sooner or later, to be invited. Just about all of the well-known names who lived here during the first

The Village Voice, New York City's premier listings/ comment/ investigative magazine, began life as a chronicler of Greenwich Village nightlife in the 1960s .

two decades of the century spent some time at her house on Fifth Avenue, a little north of Washington Square. Emma Goldman discussed anarchism with Margaret Sanger, Conrad Aiken and T.S. Eliot dropped in from time to time, and John Reed – who went on to write *Ten Days That Shook the World*, the official record of the Russian Revolution – was a frequent guest.

Washington Square and around

Best way to see the Village is to walk, and much the best place to start is its natural centre, **Washington Square**, commemorated as a novel title by Henry James and haunted by most of the Village's illustrious past names. It is not an elegant-looking place – too large to be a square, too small to be a park, and not helped by the shacky toilet structures that group around its concreted centre. But it does retain its northern edging of redbrick rowhouses – the "solid, honourable dwellings" of Henry James's novel – and, more imposingly, Stanford White's famous **Triumphal Arch**, built in 1892 to commemorate the centenary of George Washington's inauguration as President. James wouldn't, however, recognise the south side of the square now: only the fussy **Judson Memorial Church** stands out amid a messy blend of modern architecture, its interior given over these days to a mixture of theatre and local focus for a wide array of community-based programmes.

Most importantly, though, Washington Square remains the symbolic heart of the Village and its radicalism – so much so that when Robert Moses, that tarmacker of great chunks of New York City, wanted to plough a four-lane motorway through the centre of the square there was a storm of protest which resulted not only in the stopping of the road but also the banning of all traffic from the park, then used as a turnaround point by buses. And that's how it has stayed ever since, notwithstanding some battles in the 1960s when the authorities decided to purge the park of folk singers and nearly had a riot on their hands. You may find it a little threatening at times, particularly after dark when gangs of youths cluster intimidatingly at the junctions of its many paths. But, frankly, nothing's likely to happen to you (this is Greenwich Village after all, not the Lower East Side) and if things look hazardous it's just as easy to walk around. And, as soon as the weather gets warm, the park becomes sports field, dance floor, drug den and social club, boiling over with life as frisbees fly, skateboards flip and "boom boxes" crash through the urgent cries of dope peddlers and the studied patrols of police cars. Times like this there's no better square in the city.

Exploring Washington Square

Eugene O'Neill, probably the Village's most acclaimed resident, lived (and wrote *The Iceman Cometh*) at 38 Washington Square South and consumed vast quantities of ale at **The Golden Swan**

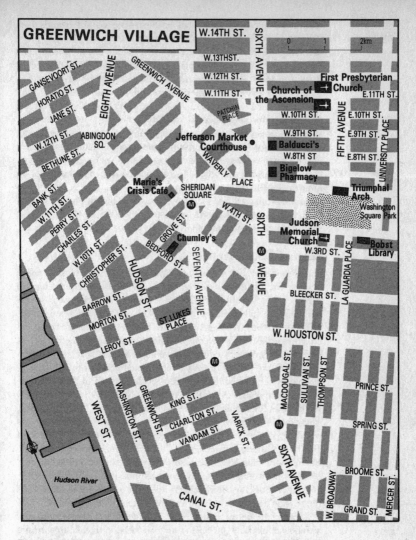

W.14TH ST.

W.13TH ST.

W.12TH ST.

W.11TH ST.

SIXTH AVENUE

EIGHTH AVENUE

GREENWICH AVENUE

GANSEVOORT ST.

HORATIO ST.

JANE ST.

W.12TH ST.

ABINGDON SQ.

BETHUNE ST.

BANK ST.

W.11TH ST.

PERRY ST.

CHARLES ST.

W.10TH ST.

CHRISTOPHER ST.

BARROW ST.

MORTON ST.

LEROY ST.

HUDSON ST.

BEDFORD ST.

GROVE ST.

ST. LUKES PLACE

SEVENTH AVENUE

WASHINGTON ST.

GREENWICH ST.

WEST ST.

KING ST.

CHARLTON ST.

VANDAM ST.

VARICK ST.

CANAL ST.

Hudson River

PATCHIN PLACE

Jefferson Market Courthouse

WAVERLY PLACE

Marie's Crisis Café

SHERIDAN SQUARE

W.4TH ST.

Chumley's

SIXTH AVENUE

BLEECKER ST.

W. HOUSTON ST.

MACDOUGAL ST.

SULLIVAN ST.

THOMPSON ST.

LA GUARDIA PLACE

SIXTH AVENUE

W. BROADWAY

BROOME ST.

GRAND ST.

MERCER ST.

PRINCE ST.

SPRING ST.

Church of the Ascension

First Presbyterian Church

E.11TH ST.

W.10TH ST.

E.10TH ST.

W.9TH ST.

E.9TH ST.

Balducci's

W.8TH ST

E.8TH ST.

Bigelow Pharmacy

FIFTH AVENUE

UNIVERSITY PLACE

Triumphal Arch

Washington Square Park

Judson Memorial Church

W.3RD ST.

Bobst Library

0   1   2km

Bar, which once stood on the corner of Sixth Avenue and West 4th Street. *The Golden Swan* (variously called The Hell Hole, Bucket of Blood and other enticing nicknames) was best known in O'Neill's day for the dubious morals of its clientele, a gang of Irish hoodlums known as the Hudson Dusters. O'Neill was great pals with this lot, and drew many of his characters from the personalities in this bar. It was nearby, also, that he got his first dramatic break, with a company called the Provincetown Players who, on the advice of John Reed, had moved down here from Massachusetts and set up shop on Macdougal Street, in a theatre which still stands (see "Theatre" in Chapter 10, *Performing Arts and Film*). Follow **Macdougal Street** south, pausing for a detour down Minetta Lane (once one of the city's most prodigious slums) and you hit **Bleecker Street** – Main Street, Greenwich Village in many ways, with a greater concentration of shops, bars, people and restaurants than any other Village thoroughfare. This junction is also the area's best-known meeting-place, a vibrant corner with mock-European sidewalk cafés that have been literary hang-outs since the beginning of this century. The **Café Figaro**, made famous by the Beat writers in the 1950s, is always thronged throughout the day: far from cheap though still worth the price of a cappuccino to people-watch for an hour or so. Afterwards, you can follow Bleecker Street one of two ways – **east** toward the solid towers of Washington Square Village, built with typical disregard for history by NYU in 1958, or **west** right through the hubbub of Greenwich Village life.

West of Sixth Avenue

Sixth Avenue itself is mainly tawdry shops and plastic eating houses, but just the other side, across Father Demo Square and up Bleecker Street (until the 1970s an Italian open marketplace on this stretch, and still lined by a few Italian stores) are some of the Village's prettiest residential streets. Turn left on **Leroy Street** and cross over Seventh Avenue, where, confusingly, Leroy Street becomes St Luke's Place for a block. The houses here, dating from the 1850s, are among the city's most graceful, one of them (recognisable by the two lamps of honour at the bottom of the steps) the ex-residence of **Jimmy Walker**, mayor of New York in the Twenties. Walker was for a time the most popular of mayors, a big-spending, wise-cracking man who gave up his work as a songwriter for the world of politics and lived an extravagant lifestyle that rarely kept him out of the gossip columns. Nothing if not shrewd, at a time when America had never been so prosperous, he for a time reflected people's most glamorous, big-living aspirations. He was, however, no match for the hard times to come, and once the 1930s Depression had taken hold he lost touch and – with it – office.

South of Leroy Street, the Village fades slowly into the warehouse districts of SoHo and TriBeCa, a bleak area where nothing much stirs outside working hours and the buildings are an odd mixture of Federal terraces juxtaposed against grubby-grey rolldown-entranced packing houses. There's a neatly preserved **row** from the 1820s on Charlton Street; the area just to its north, **Richmond Hill**, was George Washington's headquarters during the Revolution, later the home of Aaron Burr and John Jacob Astor. But those apart, you may just as well continue on up to Morton Street, which curves tranquilly round to Seventh Avenue a block north of St Luke's Place.

Around Bedford Street

Connecting with Seventh Avenue, **Bedford Street**, with Barrow and
Commerce streets nearby, is one of the quietest and most desirable
Village addresses. Edna St Vincent Millay, the young poet and
playwright who did much work with the Provincetown Playhouse,
lived at no. 75.5 – said to be the narrowest house in the city, nine
feet wide and topped with a tiny gable. Another superlative: the
clapboard structure next door claims fame as the oldest house in
the Village, built in 1799 but much renovated since and probably
worth a considerable fortune now.

Further up Bedford Street, past the former speakeasy
Chumley's (see Chapter 8, *Drinking and Eating*), recognisable
only by the metal grille on its door, is **Grove Street**. There, if you've
time, peer into one of the neighbourhood's most typical and
secluded little mews, **Grove Court**. Back on Seventh Avenue look
out for **Marie's Crisis Café** (see "Gay and lesbian bars" in *Drinking
and Eating*), now a gay bar but once home to Thomas Paine,
English by birth but perhaps *the* most important and radical thinker
of the American revolutionary era, and from whose *Crisis Papers*
the café takes its name. Paine was significantly involved in the
Revolution, though afterwards regarded with suspicion by the
government, especially after his active support for the French
Revolution. By the time of his death here, in 1809, he had been
condemned as an atheist and stripped of citizenship of the country
he helped found. Grove Street meets Seventh Avenue at one of the
Village's busiest junctions, **Sheridan Square** – not in fact a square
at all unless you count Christopher Park's slim strip of green, but
simply a wide and hazardous meeting (the Mousetrap, some call it)
of several busy streets.

Christopher Street

Christopher Street, main artery of the west Village, leads off from
here – traditional heartland of the city's gay community. The Square
was named after one General Sheridan, cavalry commander in the
Civil War, and holds a pompous-looking statue to his memory, but
it's better known as scene of one of the worst and bloodiest of New
York's Draft Riots, when a marauding mob assembled here in 1863
and attacked members of the black community. It's said that if it
hadn't been for the protestations of local people they would have
strung them up and worse; as it was they made off after sating the
worst of their blood-lust.

Not dissimilar scenes occurred in 1969 when the gay community
wasn't quite as established as it is now. The violence on this occasion
was down to the police, who raided the **Stonewall gay bar** and
started ejecting its occupants – for the local gay community the latest
in a long line of petty harassments from the police. Spontaneously
they decided to do something about it: word went round the other

*For more on
gay New York
see* Basics.

bars in the area, and before long the *Stonewall* was surrounded, resulting in a siege which lasted the best part of an hour and ended with several arrests and a number of injured policemen. Though hardly a victory for their rights, it was the first time that gay men had stood up *en masse* to the persecutions of the police, and as such represents a turning point in their struggle, formally instigating the Gay Rights movement and remembered still by the annual **Gay Pride march** (held on the last Sunday in June). Nowadays, too, the gay community is much more a part of Greenwich Village life, indeed for most the Village would seem odd without it, and from here down to the Hudson is a tight-knit enclave – focusing on Christopher Street – of bars, restaurants and bookshops used specifically, but not exclusively, by gay men. The scene on the Hudson itself, along and around West Street and the river piers, is considerably raunchier, and only for the really committed or curious (native New Yorkers, gay ones included, warn against going there at all), but this far east things crack off with the accent less on sex, more on a camp kind of humour. Among the more accessible gay bars, if you're strolling this quarter, are *The Monster* on Sheridan Square itself, *Marie's Crisis* on Grove Street (see previous page), and *Ty's*, further west on Christopher Street; for full gay listings, see "Gay and lesbian bars" in Chapter 8, *Drinking and Eating*.

North of Washington Square

At the eastern end of Christopher Street is another of those car-buzzing, life-risking Village junctions where Sixth Avenue is met by **Greenwich Avenue**, one of the neighbourhood's major shopping streets. Hover for a while at the romantic Gothic bulk of the **Jefferson Market Courthouse**, voted fifth most beautiful building in America in 1885, and built with all the characteristic vigour of the age. It hasn't actually served as a courthouse for forty-odd years now; indeed at one time – like so many buildings in this city – it was branded for demolition. It was saved thanks to the efforts of a few determined Villagers, and now lives out its days as the local library. Walk around behind for a better look, perhaps pondering for a moment on the fact that the adjacent well-tended allotment was, until 1974, the **Women's House of Detention**, a prison known for its abysmal conditions and numbering among its inmates Angela Davis. Look out, also, for **Patchin Place**, a tiny mews whose neat grey terraces are yet another Village literary landmark, home to e e cummings for many years and at various times also to John Masefield, the ubiquitous Dreiser and O'Neill, and John Reed (who wrote *Ten Days that Shook the World* here).

Across the road, **Balducci's** forms a downtown alternative to its uptown deli rival, *Zabar's*, its stomach-tingling smells pricey but hard to resist. Nearby, **Bigelow's Pharmacy** is possibly the city's oldest chemist and apparently little changed; and, south a block and

left, **West 8th Street** is an occasionally rewarding strip of brash
shoe shops and cut-price clothes stores. Up **West 10th Street** are
some of the best preserved early nineteenth-century town houses in
the Village, and one of particular interest at **no. 18**. The facade of
this house, which juts anglewise into the street, had to be rebuilt
after the terrorist Weathermen had been using the house as a bomb
factory and one of their devices exploded. Three of the group were
killed in the blast, but two others escaped and remained on the run
until just a few years ago.

For anyone not yet sated on architecture, a couple of imposing
churches are to be found by following 10th Street down as far as the
Fifth Avenue stretch of the Village, where the neighbourhood's low-
slung residential streets give on to some eminently desirable apartment blocks. On the corner stands the nineteenth-century **Church
of the Ascension**, a small, light church built by Richard Upjohn (the
Trinity Church architect), later redecorated by Stanford White and
currently appealing desperately for funds to complete a much-
needed restoration. Inside is a gracefully toned La Farge altarpiece
and some fine stained glass but otherwise, unless the refurbishment
is over, much of what you'll glimpse will be covered in brickdust
and scaffolding. A block away, Joseph Wells's bulky, chocolatey-
brown Gothic revival **First Presbyterian Church** is decidedly less
attractive than Upjohn's structure, less soaring, heavier, and in
every way more sober, with a tower said to have been modelled on
the one at Magdalen College Oxford. To look inside, you need to
enter through the discreetly added Church House (ring the bell for
attention if the door's locked). Afterwards you're just a few steps
away from the pin-neat prettiness of **Washington Mews**.

The East Village

The **East Village** is quite different in look, feel and tempo to its
western counterpart, Greenwich Village. Once, like the Lower East
Side proper which it abuts, a refuge of immigrants and always a
solidly working-class area, it became home to New York's non-
conformist fringe in the earlier part of this century when, disen-
chanted and impoverished by rising rents and encroaching tourism,
they left the city's traditional Bohemia and set up house here. Today
the differences persist: where Greenwich Village is the home of Off-
Broadway, the East Village plays stage to Off-Off, and rents, while
rising fast as the district becomes trendier and more sanitised, are
about a third of what you'll pay further west.

The East Village has seen its share of famous artists, politicos
and literati: W. H. Auden lived at 77 St Mark's Place, the neighbourhood's main street, and from the same building the Communist
Journal *Novy Mir* was run, numbering among its more historic
contributors Leon Trotsky, who lived for a brief time in New York.

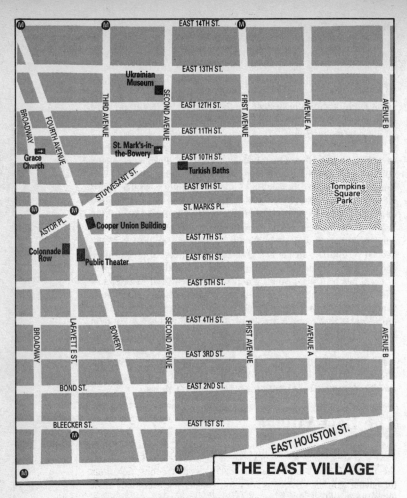

THE EAST VILLAGE

Much later the East Village became the New York haunt of the Beats – Kerouac, Burroughs, Ginsberg *et al.*, who, when not jumping trains across the rest of the country, would get together at Alan Ginsberg's house on East 7th Street for declamatory poetry readings and drunken shareouts of experience. Later, Andy Warhol debuted the Velvet Underground; the Fillmore East played host to just about every band you've ever heard of – and forgotten about; and, more recently, Richard Hell noisily proclaimed himself the inventor of punk rock. Perhaps inevitably, a lot has changed over the last decade or so. Escalating rents have forced many people out, and the East Village isn't the hotbed of dissidence and creativity it once was. But St Mark's Place is still one of downtown Manhattan's more vibrant strips, even if the thrift shops and panhandlers and political hustlers have given way to a range of ritzy boutiques selling punk chic, and the area remains one of the city's most exciting enclaves.

Around Cooper Square

To explore the East Village best use **St Mark's Place** as a base and branch out from there. Start at the western, more peopled end, between Second and Third avenues, where radical bookstores compete for space with offbeat clothiers, and, just beyond, young self-proclaimed priests of funky Manhattan chic mill around sucking on pizzas or gazing lazily at the mildewed items for sale at the unofficial flea market across the road on **Cooper Square**, a busy crossroads formed by the intersection of the Bowery, Third Avenue and Lafayette Street. This is dominated by the seven-storey brownstone mass of the **Cooper Union Building**, erected in 1859 by a wealthy industrialist as a college for the poor, and the first New York structure to be hung on a frame of iron girders. It's best known as the place where, in 1860, Abraham Lincoln wowed an audience of top New Yorkers with his so-called "might makes right" speech, in which he boldly criticised the pro-slavery policies of the southern states and helped propel himself to the White House later that year. For all its history, however, the Cooper Union remains a working college, with a well-respected architecture school, and it has recently and sensitively been restored to nineteenth-century glory with a statue of the benevolent Cooper just in front.

Astor Place and around

Just beyond, feeding through to Broadway, is **Astor Place**, named after John Jacob Astor and, for a very brief few years, just before high society moved west to Washington Square, one of the city's most desirable neighbourhoods. In the 1830s Lafayette Street in particular was home to the city's wealthiest names, not least John Jacob, one of New York's most hideously greedy tycoons, notorious for having won his enormous fortune by deceiving everybody right up to the President. When old and sick in his house here – no mean affair by all accounts but long since destroyed – it's said that although so weak he could accept no nourishment except a mother's milk, and so fat he had to be tossed up and down in a blanket for exercise, his greed for money was such that he lay and dispatched servants daily to collect his rents. The Astor Place **subway station**, bang in the middle of the junction, discreetly remembers the man on the platforms, its coloured reliefs of beavers recalling Astor's first big killings – in the fur trade.

Today it's hard to believe this was once the home of money and influence, though. **Lafayette Street** is an undistinguished sort of thoroughfare, steering a grimy route through the no-man's land between the East Village, and, further down, SoHo, and all that's left to hint that this might once have been more than a down-at-heel gathering of industrial buildings is **Colonnade Row**, a terrace of four monumental houses, now home to the Colonnade Theater. Opposite, the stocky brownstone and brick building is the late Joseph Papp's **Public Theater**, something of a legend as forerunner of Off-Broadway theatre, and original venue of hit musicals like *Hair* and *A Chorus Line* and for years run by the man who pioneered Shakespeare in the Park (see "Theatre" in Chapter 10, *Performing Arts and Film*). From the Public Theater you can either follow Lafayette Street down to Chinatown, or cut down Astor Place and turn right into Broadway. Two minutes away, the **corner of Washington Place and Greene Street** is significant. It was here in 1911 that one of the city's most notorious sweatshops burned to the ground, killing 125 women workers and spurring the state to institute laws forcing employers to take account of their workers' safety. Even now, though, there are sweatshops in New York in which safety conditions are probably little better. Back on Broadway, look north and the lacy marble of **Grace Church** fills a bend in the street, built and designed in 1846 by James Renwick (of St Patrick's Cathedral fame) in a delicate neo-Gothic style. Dark and aisled, with a flattened, web-vaulted ceiling, it's one of the city's most successful churches – and, in many ways, one of its most secretive escapes.

Heading east

Walk east from here, cross back over Third Avenue and you come to another, quite different church – **St Mark's-in-the-Bowery**, a box-like structure originally built in 1799 but with a neoclassical portico added half a century later. In the 1950s the Beat poets gave readings here, and it remains an important literary rendezvous with regular readings and music recitals, as well as a traditional gathering point for the city's down-and-outs, desperately hanging on to their can collections (passport to a frugal meal that night), or slumped half-dead on drugs.

Cross Second Avenue, on this stretch lined with Polish and Ukranian restaurants, and you're on **10th Street**, formerly the heart of the East Village art scene though nowadays very quiet, most of the galleries having moved to SoHo or further uptown; as yet no new centre has emerged as a focus for avant-garde, relatively affordable art. Follow 10th Street east, past the old redbrick **Tenth Street Turkish Baths**, its steam and massage services active back into the last century, and you will reach Avenue A, Tompkins Square, and what is in effect the eastern fringe of the East Village.

For details of the Tenth Street Turkish Baths, see "Directory" in Basics.

Tompkins Square Park

Tompkins Square Park isn't one of the city's most inviting spaces, but has long acted as focus for the Lower East Side/East Village community and has a reputation as the city's centre for political demonstrations and home of radical thought. It was here in 1874 that the police massacred a crowd of workers protesting against unemployment, and here too in the 1960s that protests were organised and made themselves heard. The late Yippie leader Abbie Hoffman lived nearby, and residents like him, along with many incidents in the square and down St Mark's Place (which joins the square on its western side), have given the East Village its maverick name.

A few years back Tompkins Square Park became the focus of dissent against the gentrification of the East Village and Lower East Side. From the mid-1980s, large chunks of real estate were bought up, renovated and turned into condominiums or co-ops for the new professional classes, much to the derision of the old squatters and new activists. Until the early 1990s the Square was more or less a shantytown (known locally as "Tent City") for the homeless, who slept on benches or under makeshift shelters on the patches of green between the paths. In the winter, only the really hardy or really desperate lived here, but when the weather got warmer the numbers swelled, as activists, anarchists and all manner of statement-makers descended upon the former army barracks from around the country, hoping to rekindle the spirit of 1988. This was the year of the Tompkins Square **riots**, when in August massive demonstrations led to the police, badge numbers covered up and night-sticks drawn, attempting to clear the park of people. In the ensuing battle, many demonstrators were hurt, including a large number of bystanders, and in the investigation that followed the police were heavily criticised for the violence that had occurred.

One of the few things to see on the Square is a small **relief** just inside the brick enclosure on the northern side, which shows a woman and child gazing forlornly out to sea. It's a commemoration of a disaster of 1904, when the local community, then mostly made up of German immigrants, was decimated by the sinking of a cruise ship, the *General Slocum*, in Long Island Sound, with the death of around a thousand people.

The Lower East Side

I don't wanna be buried in Puerto Rico
I don't wanna rest in Long Island cemetery
I wanna be near the stabbing shooting
gambling fighting and unnatural dying
and new birth crying
So please when I die . . .
Keep me nearby
Take my ashes and scatter them thru out
the Lower East Side . . .

Miguel Piñero *A Lower East Side Poem*

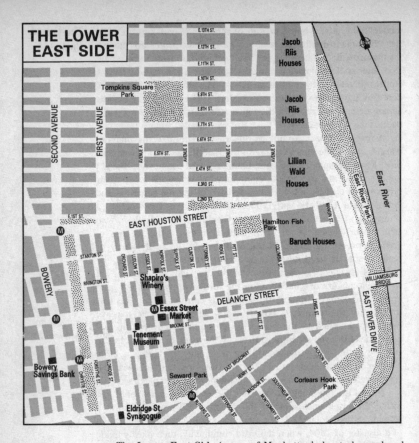

THE LOWER EAST SIDE

The **Lower East Side** is one of Manhattan's least changed and most unalluring downtown neighbourhoods, a little-known quarter which began life towards the end of the last century as an insular slum for over half a million Jewish immigrants. They came here from eastern Europe via Ellis Island, refugees in search of a better life, scratching out a living in a free-for-all of crowded, sweatshop competition. Since then the area has become considerably depopulated, and the slum-dwellers are now largely Puerto Rican rather than Jewish; but otherwise, at least on the surface, little has visibly changed.

The area's lank brick tenements, ribbed with blackened fire escapes and housing rundown bargain basements, must have seemed a bleak kind of destiny for those who arrived here, crammed into a district which daily became more densely populated, and where low standards of hygiene and abysmal housing made disease rife and life expectancy horribly low. It was conditions like these which spurred local residents like Jacob Riis and, later, Stephen Crane to record the plight of the city's immigrants in their writings and photographs, thereby spawning not only a whole school of realistic writing but also some notable social reforms. Not for nothing – and not without some degree of success – did the Lower East Side become known as a neighbourhood where political battles were fought. Today the Lower East Side splits neatly into two distinct parts. **South of East Houston Street** is the most respectable: wholesomely seedy and much of it still firmly Jewish. **North of East Houston** is part trendy Bohemia, abutting the East Village, but for the rest predominantly ruined and derelict, its houses either boarded up or serving as slum residences for the local Puerto Rican population.

South of Houston

This is the most explorable part of the Lower East Side – and the more rewarding. In the streets south of Houston, Jewish immigrants indelibly stamped their character, with their own shops, delis, restaurants, synagogues and, latterly, community centres. Even now, with a broader ethnic mix, it feels uniquely Jewish and a place apart from the rest of Manhattan – geographically isolated, too, set out on the island's heel and served by few subway stations. If outsiders come here at all it's for the **bargain shopping**. You can get just about anything at cut-price in the stores down here: clothes on Orchard Street, lamps and shades on the Bowery, ties and shirts on Allen Street, underwear and hosiery on Grand Street, textiles on Eldridge. And, whatever you're buying, people will if necessary still haggle down to the last cent. The time to come is Sunday morning, for the **Orchard Street Market**, when you'll catch the vibrancy of the Lower East Side at its best. Weekdays the stores are still there, and they're open, most of them, but far fewer people come to shop and the streets can have a forbidding, desolate feel, though the **Lower East Side Tenement Museum**, at 97 Orchard Street, is much the best place to get the lowdown on the neighbourhood's immigrant past – and present.

For details on shopping see Chapter 14.

Around East Broadway

East Broadway used to be the Jewish Lower East Side's hub, though this is now almost exclusively Chinese. For the old feel of the quarter – where the synagogues remain active (many in the north of the area have become churches for the Puerto Ricans) – best explore north of here, starting with **Canal Street. The Eldridge Street Synagogue** is worth a look, in its day one of the neighbourhood's grandest, though now the main doors of its formidable facade have been sealed shut and only the basement left for the sporadic get-togethers of a much-dwindled congregation. Carry on up Eldridge Street, though, and there is a little more activity: **Grand Street**, particularly, is lined with shops like the **Kossars Bakery**, at no. 367, whose hot fresh *bialys* are hard to resist.

Grand leads east, through housing projects to the messy **East River Park** – not one of the city's most attractive open spaces. Halfway down is the **Church of St Mary**, with elderly Jewish couples sitting on the benches outside, watching the world go by. The church bills itself as the oldest neo-Gothic building (1832) in the city, a dignified claim somewhat diminished by the sign adjacent, advertising the church's current crowd-puller of weekend bingo sessions.

Essex Street and around

Essex Street, north from here, leads to **Delancey**, horizontal axis of the Jewish Lower East Side, and to the **Williamsburg Bridge** – adopted as a shelter by New York's homeless, clustered below around oil drums, emerging occasionally to browbeat a motorist into risking their makeshift car washes. Either side of Delancey sprawls the **Essex Street Covered Market**, worth a quick peep, with *Ratner's Dairy Restaurant*, one of the Lower East Side's most famous dairy restaurants, across the road. Further up on Essex is the exotic culinary experience of *Bernstein's* – believe it or not, a kosher Chinese eatery. For more on Jewish food in the Lower East Side – and elsewhere in New York – see Chapter 8, *Drinking and Eating*.

The atmosphere changes abruptly east of Essex Street. Here the inhabitants are mainly Latino, comprising largely Puerto Ricans, but with a fair smattering of immigrants from other Latin and South American countries. Most of the Jews got richer long ago and moved into middle-income housing further uptown or in the other boroughs, and there's little love lost between those who remain and the new inhabitants.

Today, much of the area east of Essex has lost the traditional Sunday bustle of Jewish market shopping and has been replaced by the Saturday afternoon Spanish chatter of the new residents shopping for records, cheap clothes and electrical goods. **Clinton Street**, a mass of cheap Latino retailers, restaurants and travel agents, is in many ways the central thoroughfare of the Puerto Rican Lower East Side. Otherwise, if you are here on a Sunday, check out the free wine tours and tastings at **Schapiro's Winery** at 124 Rivington Street (daily 11am–4pm, on the hour), the neighbourhood's – and probably the city's – only kosher wine and spirits warehouse where wine is made on the premises. Afterwards, head over to **Orchard Street**, again best on a Sunday when most of it becomes pedestrianised and filled with stalls selling off designer togs for hefty discounts. The rooms above the stores here used to house sweatshops, clothes factories so called since whatever the weather a stove had to be kept warm all the time for pressing the clothes when completed. The (reformed) garment industry moved uptown ages ago, but the buildings are little more salubrious now, slummy apartments at the end of dank unlit hallways occupied by poor, again mainly Latino, families.

At the top end of Orchard, East Houston Street forms the northern border of this part of the Lower East Side. The area just below East Houston Street has in recent years become a very desirable place to live for those hoping to escape the rising rents of the East Village while keeping in with the Village scene. Bars such as the *Ludlow Street Café* and *Max Fish*, both on Ludlow Street, have helped expand the allure of the East Village arts and social scene south of Houston. But, as with all things fashionable in New York, they may well soon have upped and gone elsewhere.

The Bowery

Walk east from here and it's for the most part burnt-out tenements interspersed with a scattering of Spanish-style grocery stores; to the west things aren't much better. **Bowery** spears north out of Chinatown as far as Cooper Square on the edge of the East Village. This wide thoroughfare has gone through many changes over the years: it took its name from "Bouwerie", the Dutch word for farm, when it was the city's main agricultural supplier; later, in the closing decades of the last century, it was flanked by music halls, theatres, hotels and middle-market restaurants, drawing people from all parts of Manhattan. Currently it's a skid row for the city's drunk and derelict, flanked by a long and demoralising line of boarded-up shops and SRO hotels near which few New Yorkers venture of their own accord. If you do, it may be intimidating and uneasy, but rarely dangerous – the people who crash down here are mostly long past acts of physical violence. The one – bizarre – focus, certainly a must for any Lower East Side wanderings, is the **Bowery Savings Bank** on the corner of Grand Street. Designed by Stanford White in 1894, it rises out of the neighbourhood's debris like a god, much as its sister bank on 42nd Street, a shrine to the virtue of saving money. Inside, the original carved cheque writing stands are still in place, and the coffered ceiling, together with White's great gilded fake marble columns, couldn't create a more potent feeling of security. An inscription above the door as you exit leaves you in no doubt: "Your financial welfare is the business of this bank." Quite so, but back on the Bowery, stepping over the drunks and avoiding the panhandlers, you can't help pondering what went wrong.

Single Room Occupancy – SRO – hotels are those used as hostels for the city's down-and-outs.

North of Houston

Cross East Houston Street and the Lower East Side takes on another different mantle, veering from downbeat (but trendy) Tompkins Square and the East Village to, further east and in marked contrast, what ranks as one of the most serious and unchecked pieces of urban blight in Manhattan. Here the island bulges out beyond the city's grid structure, the extra avenues being named A to D, and the area, by its devotees, **Alphabet City** (*Loisada* to the Puerto Ricans). Until a very few years ago, this was

The Lower East Side

a notoriously unsafe corner of town, run by drug pushers and the hoodlums that controlled them. People told of cars queuing up for fixes in the street, and the terraces here were well-known safe-houses for the brisk heroin trade. All of this was brought to a halt in 1983 with "Operation Pressure Point", a massive police campaign to clean up the area and make it a place where people would want to live. This has to some extent been achieved, with crime figures radically down, although appearances remain much the same: the people who live here are poor Puerto Ricans; their houses, what's left of them, bombed-out shells amid fields of flattened rubble, next to which gangs of homeless have erected makeshift shelters. Half the houses aren't lived in at all, and many are plastered with graffiti protesting their misuse ("Property of the People of the Lower East Side", some say). Come down here and you'll certainly get hassled, but – during the day at least – you're unlikely to be mugged. And it's worth a quick circuit around this part of the Lower East Side just to see how bad things can get through lack of effective city money or control. Oddly enough it's also the best illustration of the absurdity of the Manhattan housing issue: here there is astounding poverty, filth, even danger. Yet the area is in the process of a huge gentrification, and its apartments, though they may be next to some rat-infested ruin, are going for ever-rocketing rents.

For details of bars and restaurants in the area, see Chapter 8, Drinking and Eating.

Walking down Avenue A away from the park and toward Houston Street, there are, however, a number of good bars and restaurants, such as *Benny's Burrito* (4th Street and A), *Sophie's* (5th Street and A), and *Joe's* (6th Street between A and B). As you head east from A, the mood is far less relaxed. Avenue C is also known as "Avenue Loisaida" and is far less studenty and youthful than Avenue A and other points west. At Second Street and Avenue B, the **Gas Station** is a bizarre outdoor art gallery of customised junk – spray-painted telephone booths, chairs made out of fire hydrants, all very East Village. Also check out the *Nuyorican Poets' Café*, 236 East Third Street. Further over, past Avenue D, are the East River housing projects, a good bet if you are a drug dealer but not recommended for the sensible tourist.

Chapter 3

Midtown Manhattan

Y ou're likely to spend a fair amount of time in **Midtown Manhattan**. It's here most of the city's hotels are situated, here too that you'll arrive – at Penn or Grand Central Station, or the Port Authority. And the area is in many ways the city's centre. Cutting through its heart is **Fifth Avenue**, New York's most glamorous (and most expensive) street, with the theatre strip of **Broadway**, an increasingly disreputable neighbour, just to its west.

The character of midtown undergoes a rapid and radical transformation depending on which side of Fifth you find yourself. **East** are the corporate businesses, a skyward wave that creates Manhattan's rollercoaster appearance. If you've any interest in architecture (or simply sensation) you'll want to stroll this sector, looking in and up at such delights as the **Chrysler**, **Citicorp** and **Seagram buildings** and the magnificent **Rockefeller Center**. **Fifth Avenue** itself, and its fashion-orientated counterpart, **Madison**, should be experienced too, if only to take measure of how much wealth a large number of Americans have accrued. And of course this is also a major museum strip, with the **Museum of Modern Art** and a host of lesser collections grouped together on **53rd Street** (see the individual museum accounts in Chapter 6 for more on these).

West of Fifth Avenue, and in particular west of Broadway, the area takes a dive – both in status and interest. The **theatre districts** are a natural entertainment focus, though these days more than a little sleazy, notwithstanding the fact that **Times Square,** the traditional centre of sex shows and petty crime, has recently undergone a multimillion-dollar cleanup. **The Garment District** has a certain throwback interest as a nineteenth-century foil to the corporate skyscrapers across the way – and a startling nearby landmark in the **Empire State Building**. But the residential districts are frankly dull: **Chelsea** is long established but downbeat; **Clinton**, further up the west side, is gentrifying slowly but is still rough down by the West Side Highway; and **Murray Hill**, on the other side of town, has little to offer beyond some semi-elegant brownstones.

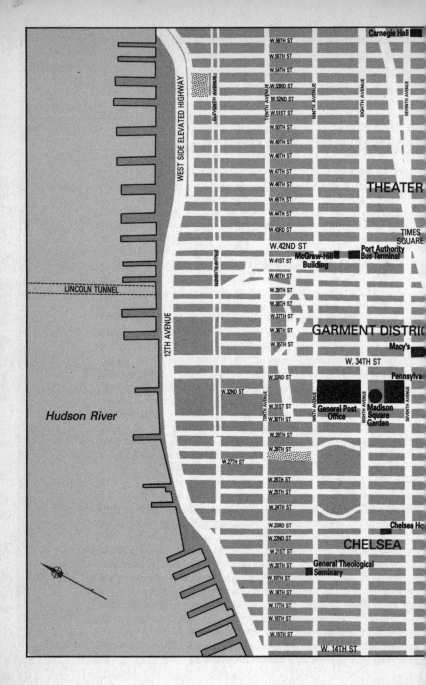

Carnegie Hall

WEST SIDE ELEVATED HIGHWAY

W. 56TH ST
W. 56TH ST
W. 54TH ST
W. 53RD ST
W. 52ND ST
W. 51ST ST
W. 50TH ST
W. 49TH ST
W. 48TH ST
W. 47TH ST
W. 46TH ST
W. 45TH ST
W. 44TH ST
W. 43RD ST
W. 42ND ST
W. 41ST ST
W. 40TH ST
W. 39TH ST
W. 38TH ST
W. 37TH ST
W. 36TH ST
W. 35TH ST
W. 34TH ST
W. 33RD ST
W. 32ND ST
W. 31ST ST
W. 30TH ST
W. 29TH ST
W. 28TH ST
W. 27TH ST
W. 26TH ST
W. 25TH ST
W. 24TH ST
W. 23RD ST
W. 22ND ST
W. 21ST ST
W. 20TH ST
W. 19TH ST
W. 18TH ST
W. 17TH ST
W. 16TH ST
W. 15TH ST
W. 14TH ST

ELEVENTH AVENUE
TENTH AVENUE
NINTH AVENUE
EIGHTH AVENUE
SEVENTH AVENUE
TWELFTH AVENUE
12TH AVENUE

LINCOLN TUNNEL

Hudson River

THEATER

TIMES
SQUARE

McGraw-Hill
Building

Port Authority
Bus Terminal

GARMENT DISTRIC

Macy's

Pennsylva

General Post
Office

Madison
Square
Garden

Chelsea Ho

CHELSEA

General Theological
Seminary

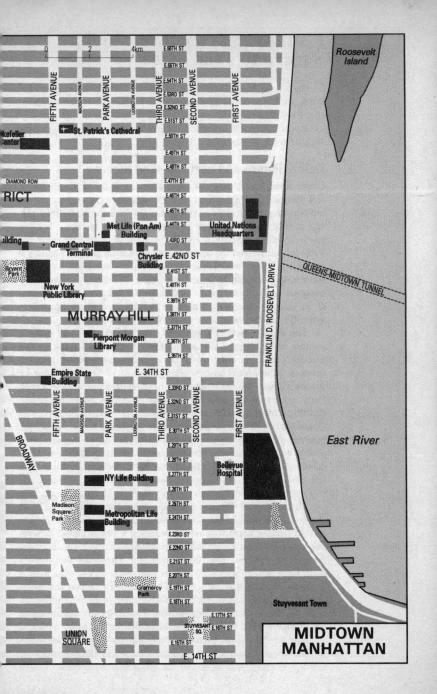

MIDTOWN MANHATTAN

MANHATTAN

Fifth Avenue and East: Union Square to 42nd Street

Downtown Manhattan ends with 14th Street, which slices across the island from the housing projects of the east side to the cut-price shops and eventually the meat-packing warehouses on the banks of the Hudson River. In the middle, where Broadway, Fourth and Park avenues meet, is Union Square.

Union Square and north to 42nd Street

Union Square was once the elegant centre of the city's theatrical and shopping scene, but was better known more recently as gathering-point for political demonstrations. Up until the mid-1980s this was a seedy haunt of dope pushing and street violence, but it's much more inviting now, the spill of shallow steps enticing you in to stroll the paths, feed the squirrels, and gaze at its array of statuary – something no one would have dared do a few years back. As for the statues, they include an equestrian figure of George Washington, a Lafayette by Bartholdi (more famous for the Statue of Liberty), and, at the centre of the park, a massive flagstaff base whose bas-reliefs symbolise the forces of Good and Evil in the Revolution.

The square itself is flanked by some good cafés and quite a mixture of buildings, not least the **American Savings Bank** on the eastern edge, of which only the grandiose columned exterior survives. The pedimented building just south of here is the former Tammany Hall, the once notorious headquarters of the Democratic Party, decorated with a Native American headdress, while the narrow building almost opposite was Andy Warhol's original Factory. The **Consolidated Edison** structure, off the southeast corner, the headquarters of the company responsible for providing the city with energy and those famous steaming sewer access holes, is, with its campanile, an odd premonition of the Metropolitan Life Building a few blocks further north. Inside, there's a museum devoted to the city's power supplies through the ages – strictly for energy buffs.

The stretch of **Broadway** north of here was known once as "Ladies' Mile" for its fancy stores and boutiques (*Lord & Taylor* started trading here), but notwithstanding a few sculpted facades and curvy lintels, it's now hard to imagine as an upmarket shopping mall. Turn right on East 20th Street for **Theodore Roosevelt's birthplace** at number 28 (Wed–Sun 9am–5pm; $1) – or at least a reconstruction of it: a rather grim brownstone mansion that's not terribly exciting, just a few rooms with their original furnishings, some of Teddy's hunting trophies and a small gallery documenting the President's life, viewable on an obligatory guided tour.

Past here Manhattan's clutter breaks into the ordered open space of **Gramercy Park**, a former swamp reclaimed in 1831. Residential London in spirit, this is one of the city's best squares, its centre

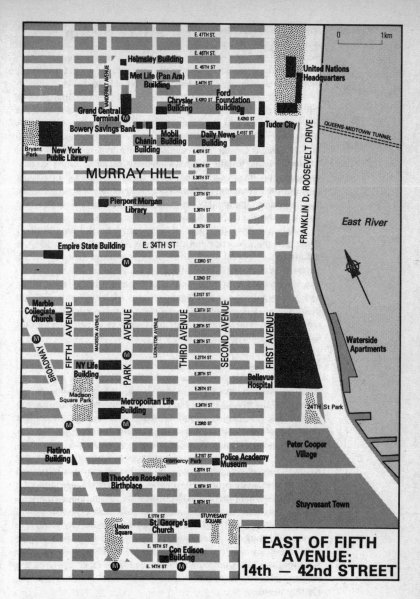

EAST OF FIFTH
AVENUE:
14th — 42nd STREET

clean, tidily planted and, most noticeably, completely empty for
much of the day – principally because the only people who can gain
access are those rich or fortunate enough to live here. To the east
Peter Cooper Village and **Stuyvesant Town** are perhaps the city's
most successful examples of dense-packed urban housing, their tall,

angled apartment blocks siding peaceful tree-lined walkways. It's worth knowing, though, that this is private not public housing, and the owners, Metropolitan Life, were accused of operating a colour-bar when the projects first opened. Certainly, the contrast with the immigrant slums a little way downtown isn't hard to detect.

A block over, the land that makes up **Stuyvesant Square** was a gift to the city from its governor and, like Gramercy Park, the park space in the middle was modelled on the squares of London's Bloomsbury. Though partially framed by the buildings of **Beth Israel Medical Center** and cut down the middle by the bustle of Second Avenue, it still retains something of its secluded quality, especially on the western side. Here there's a smatter of elegant terrace, the strangely colonial-looking **Friends' Meeting House**, and, next door, the weighty brownstone **Church of St George** – best known as the place where financier J.P. Morgan used to worship.

Lexington Avenue begins its long journey north from Gramercy Park, past the lumbering **69th Regiment Armory** – site in 1913 of the notorious Armory Show which brought modern art to New York for the first time (see "Twentieth-century American art" in *Contexts*) – to Manhattan's most condensed ethnic enclave, **Little India**. Blink, and you might miss this altogether: most of New York's 100,000 Indians live in Queens and their only trace here is a handful of restaurants and fast-food places – far outnumbered by those down on East 6th Street – and a pocket of sweet and spice stores.

Madison Square

Broadway and Fifth Avenue meet at **Madison Square**, by day a maelstrom of dodging cars and cabs, buses and pedestrians but, mainly because of the quality of the buildings and the clever park-space in the middle, possessing a monumentality and neat seclusion that Union Square has long since lost. The **Flatiron Building**, set cheekily on a triangular plot of land on the square's southern side, is another famed city building, one that evokes images of Edwardian New York. Its thin tapered structure creates unusual wind currents at ground level, and years ago policemen were posted to prevent men gathering to watch the wind raise the skirts of women passing on 23rd Street. The cry they gave to warn off voyeurs – "23 Skidoo!" – has passed into the language. It's hard to believe that this was the city's first true skyscraper, hung on a steel frame in 1902 with its full twenty storeys dwarfing all the other structures around. Not for long though: the **Metropolitan Life Company** soon erected their clock tower on the eastern side of the square which, height-wise at least, put the Flatiron to shame.

Next door is the corinthian-columned marble facade of the **Appellate Division** of the New York State Supreme Court, resolutely righteous with its statues of Justice, Wisdom and Peace turning their weary backs on the ugly black glass New York Life Annexe behind. The grand structure behind that, the **New York Life**

Building proper, was the work of Cass Gilbert, creator of the Woolworth Tower downtown. It went up in 1928 on the site of the original **Madison Square Garden** – renowned scene of drunken and debauched revels of high and Broadway society. This was the heart of the theatre district in those days and the place where the Garden's architect, **Stanford White**, was murdered by Harry Thaw. White, a partner in the illustrious architectural team of McKim, Mead and White, who designed many of the city's great Beaux Arts buildings, such as the General Post Office, the old Penn Station, and Columbia University, was something of a rake by all accounts, with a reputation for womanising and fast living. His affair with Thaw's wife Evelyn Nesbit, a Broadway showgirl, had been well publicised – even to the extent that the naked statue of the goddess Diana on the top of the building was said to have been modelled on her. Millionaire Thaw was so humiliated by this that one night he burst into the roof garden, found White, surrounded as usual by doting women and admirers, and shot him through the head. Thaw was carted away to spend the rest of his life in mental institutions, and his wife's show business career took a tumble: she resorted to drugs and prostitution somewhere in Central America.

So ended one of Madison Square's more dramatic episodes. Madison Square Garden has moved twice since then, first to a site on Eighth Avenue and 50th Street, finally to its present location in a hideous drum-shaped eyesore on the corner of 32nd Street and Seventh Avenue. There is, however, one reminder of the time when this was New York's theatreland – the **Episcopal Church of the Transfiguration** just off Fifth Avenue on 29th Street. This, a dinky rusticated church set back from the street, brown brick and topped with copper roofs, has since 1870 been the traditional place of worship of showbiz people. It was tagged with the name "The Little Church Around the Corner" after a devout but understanding priest from a nearby church had refused to marry a theatrical couple and sent them here. It's an intimate building, furnished throughout in warm wood and with the figures of famous actors (most notably Edwin Booth as Hamlet) memorialised in the stained glass.

The Empire State Building

Further up Fifth Avenue is New York's prime **shopping territory**, home to most of the city's heavyweight department stores. *Macy's* is just a short stroll away on Herald Square; filling the space between 38th and 39th streets are the lavish headquarters of *Lord & Taylor* (see Chapter 14, *Shops and Markets*). The **Empire State Building** – overshadowing by far the lure of such consumer items – occupies what has always been a prime site. Before it appeared this was home to the first Waldorf Astoria Hotel, built by William Waldorf Astor as a ruse to humiliate his formidable aunt, Caroline Schemmerhorn, into moving uptown. The hotel opened in 1893 and immediately became a focus for the city's rich – in an era, the "Gay

Skyscrapers

Along with Chicago and Hong Kong, Manhattan is one of the best places in the world in which to see **skyscrapers**, its puckered, almost medieval skyline of towers the city's most familiar and striking image. In fact there are only two main clusters of skyscrapers, but they set the tone for the city – the Financial District, where the combination of narrow streets and tall buildings forms slender, lightless canyons, and midtown Manhattan, where the big skyscrapers, flanking the wide central avenues between the thirties and the sixties, have long competed for height and prestige.

The term "skyscraper" was coined in 1890 by one John J. Flinn, describing the evolving style of building in turn-of-the-century Chicago, since when the two cities have always been battling to produce the tallest building. It's uncertain which city actually built the first real skyscraper, but the first generally recognised instance in New York was the Flatiron Building on Madison Square, designed in 1902, not least for the obvious way its triangular shape made the most of the new iron-frame technique of construction that had made such structures possible. A few years later, in 1913, New York clinched the title of the world's tallest building with the sixty-storey Woolworth Building on Broadway, later going on to produce such landmarks as the Chrysler and Empire State buildings, and, more recently, the World Trade Center – though the latter's status as world's tallest building has since been usurped by Chicago's Sears Tower.

Styles have changed over the years, and have perhaps been most influenced by the stringency of the city's zoning laws, which early in the century placed restrictions on the types of building permitted. At first skyscrapers were sheer vertical monsters, maximising the floor space possible from any given site but with no regard to how this affected the neighbouring buildings, which more often than not were thrown into shade by the new arrival. In order to stop this happening the city authorities invented the concept of "air rights", putting a restriction on how high a building could be before it had to be set back from its base. This forced skyscrapers to be designed in a series of steps – a law most elegantly adhered to by the Empire State Building, which has no less than ten steps in all, but it's a pattern you will see repeated all over the city.

Due to the pressure on space in Manhattan's narrow confines, and the price of real estate, which makes speculatively building office blocks potentially so lucrative, the skyscrapers continue to rise, and it's always possible to see some slowly rising steel frame somewhere in the city. Traditionally the workers who brave the heights to work on the skyscrapers, lifting the girders into place and bolting them together, often bent into impossible positions, squatting or balancing on thin planks, are Native Americans, due to their unusual agility and remarkable head for heights. They still make up forty percent of such workers in New York, and even eighty floors up don't wear any kind of safety harness, claiming it restricts their movements too much.

As for the future, there seems to be almost no limit to the heights that are envisaged, the most notable plan being Donald Trump's bid to reclaim the tallest-building title for New York with a new structure on the Upper West Side well over a hundred storeys high. Whether or not this comes off, it's certain that even in times of recession skyscrapers remain the "machines for making money" that Le Corbusier originally claimed they were.

Nineties", when "Meet me at the Waldorf" was the catchphrase to conjure with.* However, though the reputation of the Waldorf – at least for its prices – endures to this day, it didn't remain in its initial premises for very long, moving in 1929 to its current Art Deco home on Park Avenue.

Few would dispute the elegance of what took its place. The Empire State Building remains easily the most potent and evocative symbol of New York, and has done since its completion in 1931 – well under budget and after just two years in the making. Soon after, King Kong clung to it and distressed squealing damsels while grabbing at passing planes; in 1945 a plane crashed into the building's 79th storey; and most recently two Englishmen parachuted from its summit to the ground, only to be carted off by the NY police department for disturbing the peace. Its 102 storeys and 1472 feet – toe to TV mast – make it the world's third tallest building, but the height is deceptive, rising in stately tiers with steady panache. Inside, its basement serves as an underground marbled shopping precinct, lined with newsstands, beauty parlours, cafés, even a post office, and is finished everywhere with delicate Deco touches. After wandering around you can visit the *Guinness World of Records Exhibition* – though, frankly, you'd be better advised to save your money for the assault on the top of the tower.

The first lift, alarmingly old and rickety if you've previously zoomed to the top of the World Trade Center, takes you to the 86th floor, summit of the building before the radio and TV mast was added. The views from the outside walkways here are as stunning as you'd expect – better than those from the World Trade Center since Manhattan spreads on all sides. On a clear day visibility is up to eighty miles, but given the city's pollution, on most it's more likely to be between ten and twenty. If you're feeling brave, and can stand the queues for the small single lift, go up to the Empire State's last reachable zenith, a small cylinder at the foot of the TV mast which was added as part of a harebrained scheme to erect a mooring post for airships – a plan subsequently abandoned after some local VIPs almost got swept away by the wind. You can't go outside and the extra sixteen storeys don't really add a great deal to the view, but you will have been to the top (daily 9.30am–midnight; $3.50).

Murray Hill

Back down to earth, Fifth Avenue carves its way up the island. East down 34th Street lies **Murray Hill**, a tenuously tagged residential

---

*It was the consort of Mrs Schemmerhorn Astor, Ward Macallister, who coined the label "The Four Hundred" to describe this lot. "There are only about four hundred people in fashionable New York society," he asserted. "If you go outside that number you strike people who are either not at ease in a ballroom or else make other people not at ease. See the point?"

area of statuesque canopy-fronted apartment buildings, but with little apart from its WASPish anonymity to mark it out from the rest of midtown Manhattan. Like Chelsea further west, it lacks any real centre, any sense of community, and unless you work, live or are staying in Murray Hill, there's little reason to go there at all; indeed you're more likely to pass through without even realising it. Its boundaries are indistinct, but lie somewhere between Fifth Avenue and Third and, very roughly, 32nd to 40th streets, where begins the rather brasher commercialism of the midtown office block district.

When Madison Avenue was on a par with Fifth as *the* place to live, Murray Hill came to be dominated by the **Morgan family**, the crusty old financier J.P. and his offspring, who at one time owned a clutch of property here. Morgan junior lived in the **brownstone** on the corner of 37th Street and Madison (now headquarters of the American Lutheran Church), his father in a house which was later pulled down to make way for an extension to his **library** next door, the mock but tastefully simple Roman villa that still stands and is commonly mistaken for the old man's house. (If you've read the book or seen the film *Ragtime*, you'll remember that Coalhouse Walker made this fundamental mistake when attempting to hold Pierpont Morgan hostage.) In fact, Morgan would simply come here to languish amongst the art treasures he had bought up wholesale on his trips to Europe: manuscripts, paintings, prints and furniture. Here during a crisis of confidence in the city's banking system in 1907, he entertained New York's richest and most influential men night after night until they agreed to put up the money to save what could have been the entire country from bankruptcy, giving up $30 million himself as an act of good faith. You can visit the library's splendid interior and priceless collection; see Chapter 6, *Museums and Galleries*.

As you continue up Madison Avenue the influence of the Morgans rears its head again in the shape (or at least the name) of **Morgan's Hotel** between 37th and 38th streets – the last word in ostentatious discretion, not even bothering to proclaim its presence with the vulgarity of a sign. Look in on its elegant bar for a drink if you've got the cash, and for details on how much it costs to sleep here, see Chapter 7.

East 42nd Street

After Morgan's you've more or less exhausted Murray Hill, so follow 38th Street back to Fifth Avenue and turn north. Before long you're standing on the corner of **42nd Street**, one of the few streets in the world to have an entire musical named after it. With good reason too, for you *can* do anything on 42nd Street, highbrow or low, and it's also home to some of the city's most characteristic buildings, ranging from great Beaux Arts palaces like Grand Central Station to vulgar charge-card traps like the Grand Hyatt Hotel.

The New York Public Library

The New York Public Library (Central Research Library) on the corner of 42nd and Fifth is the first notable building on 42nd Street's eastern reaches: Beaux Arts in style and faced with white marble, its steps act as a meeting point and general hang-out for pockets of people throughout the year. To tour the library either walk around yourself or take one of the **tours** (Mon–Sat at 11am & 2pm) which are free, last an hour and give a good all-round picture of the building. The main thing to see is the large coffered Reading Room at the back of the building. Trotsky worked here on and off during his brief sojourn in New York just prior to the 1917 Revolution, introduced to the place by his friend Bukharin, who was bowled over by a library you could use so late in the evening. The opening times are considerably less impressive now, but the library still boasts a collection among the five largest in the world, stored in eight levels beneath this room, which alone covers half an acre. And while Trotsky may have been, with hindsight, a far less prestigious customer than Karl Marx, the computerised technology, with which you can find a book and have it delivered in a matter of minutes, makes the reading room of London's British Library seem primitive by comparison.

Grand Central Station

Back outside, push through the crush crossing Fifth Avenue and walk east down Manhattan's most congested stretch to where Park Avenue lifts off the ground at Pershing Square to weave its way around the solid bulk of **Grand Central Station**. This, for its day, was a masterful piece of urban planning: after the electrification of the railways made it possible to reroute trains underground, the rail lanes behind the existing station were sold off to developers and the profits went towards the building of a new terminal – constructed around a basic iron frame but clothed with a Beaux Arts skin. Since then Grand Central has taken on an almost mythical significance, and though with the insidious eating away of the country's rail network its major traffic is now mainly commuters speeding out no further than Westchester County, it remains in essence what it was in the nineteenth century – symbolic gateway to an undiscovered continent.

You can either explore Grand Central on your own or take one of the free **tours** run by the Municipal Arts Society (see *Basics*); these leave from under the Kodak billboard every Wednesday at 12.30pm and are excellent. But for the efforts of a few dedicated New Yorkers (and, strangely enough, Jackie Onassis, whose voice was no doubt a godsend) Grand Central wouldn't be here at all, or at least it would be much uglified. For it was only deemed a National Landmark in 1978, after the railroad's plan to cap the whole lot with an office tower was quashed. The most spectacular aspect of the building is its size, now cowed by the soaring airplane wing of

Fifth Avenue
and East:
Union
Square to
42nd Street

the Pan Am building behind but still no less impressive in the main station **concourse**. This is one of the world's finest and most imposing open spaces, 470 feet long and 150 feet high, the barrel-vaulted ceiling speckled like a Baroque church with a painted representation of the winter night sky, its 2500 stars shown back to front: "As God would have seen them", the painter is reputed to have remarked. It's a pity about the broad advertising hoardings, which can't help but obscure the enormous windows, but stand in the middle and you realise that Grand Central represents a time when stations were seen as appropriately dwarfing preludes to great cities. "A city within a city", as it has been called.

For the best view of the concourse climb up to the catwalks which span the sixty-feet-high windows on the Vanderbilt Avenue side; then explore the terminal's more esoteric reaches: places like the **Tennis Club** on the third floor, which used to be a CBS studio but now punts out court-time for a membership fee of several thousand dollars a year; and the **Oyster Bar** in the vaulted bowels of the station – one of the city's most highly regarded seafood restaurants, serving something like a dozen varieties of oyster and cram-packed every lunchtime with the midtown office crowd. Just outside is something that explains why the Oyster Bar's babble is not solely the result of the big-mouthed business people who eat there: you can stand on opposite sides of any of the vaulted spaces and hold a conversation just by whispering, an acoustic fluke that makes this the loudest eatery in town.

The Chrysler Building

Across the street, the **Bowery Savings Bank** echoes Grand Central's grandeur – like its sister branch downtown, extravagantly lauding the twin shibboleths of sound investment and savings. A Roman-style basilica, it has a floor paved with mosaics, the columns are each fashioned from a different kind of marble, and, if you take a look at the elevator doors (through a door on the right) you'll see bronze bas-reliefs of bank employees hard at various tasks. But then, this kind of lavish expenditure is typical of the buildings on this stretch of 42nd Street, which is full of lobbies worth popping inside for a glimpse as you're passing. The **Grand Hyatt Hotel** back on the north side of the street is a notable one, if nothing else probably the best example in the city of all that is truly vulgar about contemporary American interior design, its slushing waterfalls, lurking palms and gliding escalators representing plush-carpeted bad taste at its most meretricious.

The **Chrysler Building**, across Lexington Avenue, is a different story, dating from a time (1930) when architects carried off prestige with grace and style. This was for a fleeting moment the world's tallest building – until it was usurped by the Empire State in 1931 – and since the rediscovery of Art Deco a decade or so ago has become easily Manhattan's best loved, its car-motif friezes, jutting gargoyles and arched stainless steel pinnacle giving the solemn midtown skyline a welcome touch of fun. Its designer, William Van Alen, indulged in a feud with an erstwhile partner who was designing a building at 40 Wall Street at the same time. Each were determined to have the higher skyscraper: Alen secretly built a stainless steel spire *inside* the Chrysler's crown; when 40 Wall Street was finally topped out a few feet higher than the Chrysler, Alen popped the 185-foot spire out through the top of the building, and won the day.

Chrysler moved out some time ago, and for a while the building was left to degenerate by a company that didn't wholly appreciate its spirited silliness, but now a new owner has pledged to keep it lovingly intact. The **lobby**, once a car showroom, is for the moment all you can see (there's no observation deck), but that's enough in itself, with opulently inlaid elevators, walls covered in African marble and on the ceiling a realistic, if rather faded, study of work and endeavour, showing aeroplanes, machines and brawny builders who worked on the tower.

Around the Chrysler Building

Flanking each side of Lexington Avenue on the southern side of 42nd Street are two more buildings worthy of a studied walk past. The **Chanin Building** on the right is another Art Deco monument, cut with terracotta carvings of leaves, tendrils and sea creatures. More interestingly, the design on the outside of the weighty **Mobil Building** across the way is deliberately folded so as to be cleaned automatically by the movement of the wind.

East of here, beyond the deceptively modern headquarters of the **New York Daily News**, whose foyer holds blown-up prints of the paper's more memorable front pages, including the famous summary of the President's attitude to New York during the municipal fiscal crisis of the mid-1970s: "FORD TO CITY – DROP DEAD". Despite huge financial problems over recent years – including a spell under the ownership of Robert Maxwell – the paper lumbers on, and though many of its best writers have left, it still manages a style and quality that puts British tabloids to shame.

East of here, beyond the *Daily News* building, 42nd Street grows more tranquil. And on the left, between Second and First avenues, is one of the city's most peaceful spaces of all – the **Ford Foundation Building**.

Built in 1967, this was the first of the atriums that are now commonplace across Manhattan, and is probably the best. Structurally, it's a giant greenhouse, gracefully supported by soaring granite columns and edged with two walls of offices from which workers can look down onto a sub-tropical garden which changes naturally with the seasons. This was one of the first attempts at creating a "natural" environment, and it's astonishingly quiet: 42nd Street is no more than a murmur outside, and all you can hear is the burble of water, the echo of voices and the clipped crack of feet on the brick walkways, mingled with the ripe smell of the atrium's considerable vegetation: all in all making for one of the great architectural experiences of New York City.

East to the United Nations Building

At the east end of 42nd Street, steps lead up to **Tudor City**, which rises behind a tree-filled parklet and with its coats of arms, leaded glass and neat neighbourhood shops is the very picture of self-contained dowager respectability. Trip down the steps from here and you're plum opposite the building of the **United Nations**, which rose up after the last war on the site of what was once known as Turtle Bay. Some see the United Nations complex as one of the major sights of New York; others, usually those who've been there, are not so complimentary. For whatever the symbolism of the UN there can be few buildings that are quite so dull to walk round. What's more, the self-congratulatory nature of the (obligatory) guided tours can't – in the face of years of UN impotence in war and hunger zones the world over – help but grate a little.

For the determined, the complex consists of three main buildings – the thin glass-curtained slab of the **Secretariat**, the sweeping curve of the **General Assembly Building**, and, just between, the low-rise connecting **Conference Wing**. It went up immediately after World War II and was finished in 1963, the product of a suitably international team of architects which included Le Corbusier – though he pulled out before the building was completed. Daily **tours** leave from the monumental General Assembly lobby (First Avenue at 46th Street; tours leave every half hour, 9.15am–4.45pm; $6.50, students $4.50; ☎963-7713) and take in the main conference chambers of the UN and its constituent parts, foremost of which is the General Assembly Chamber itself, expanded a few years back to accommodate up to 179 members' delegations (though there are at present only 159). It's impressive certainly, but can't help but seem wasted on a body that only meets for a few months each year. Other council chambers, situated in the Conference Building, include the Security Council Chamber, the Economic and Social Council and the Trusteeship Council.

Once you've been whisked around all these, with the odd stop for examples of the many artefacts that have been donated to the UN by its various member states – rugs, paintings, sculptures, and so on – the tour is more or less over, and will leave you in the basement of the General Assembly Building, where a couple of **shops** sell ethnic items from around the world and a **post office** will flog you a UN postage stamp to prove that you've been here – though bear in mind it's only valid on mail posted from the UN. You might also want to try the **restaurant** here, which serves a varied lunch buffet each day with dishes from different United Nations member countries.

The West Side: Chelsea, the Garment District and Times Square

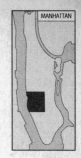

Few visitors bother with Chelsea and the Garment District, the two areas that fill the land between 14th and 42nd streets. Chelsea is a low-built, surly, seedy grid of tenements and row houses of so mixed a character as to be almost characterless. To the north, the Garment District muscles in between Sixth and Eighth avenues on 34th to 42nd streets taking in the dual monsters of Penn Station and Madison Square Garden. The majority of people who come here do so for a specific reason – to catch a train or bus, to watch wrestling or to work in factories, and it's only a wedge of stores beween Herald and Greeley squares that attract the out-of-towner.

Chelsea

Chelsea took shape in 1830 when its owner, Charles Clarke Moore, laid out his land for sale in broad lots. Enough remains to indicate Chelsea's middle-class suburban origins, though in fact the area never quite made it onto the shortlist of desirable places to be. Stuck between Fifth Avenue and Hell's Kitchen and caught between the ritziness of the one and the poverty of the other, Manhattan's chic residential focus leapfrogged Chelsea to the East 40s and 50s. These days the dreary facades quickly establish Chelsea's atmosphere of rundown residentialism; the grid plan seems too wide, the streets too bare to encourage you to linger.

But that's not to say Chelsea doesn't have its moments. Moore donated an island of land to the **General Theological Seminary** on Chelsea Square at 20th Street and Ninth Avenue, an assembly of ivy-clad gothicisms seemingly dropped in from rural Oxfordshire. It's possible to explore inside – the entrance is via the modern building on Ninth Avenue – but the countrified feel is what makes it special, not any particular architectural feature.

The Chelsea Hotel

During the nineteenth century this area, especially West 23rd Street, was a centre of New York's theatre district before it moved uptown. Nothing remains of the theatres now, but the hotel which put up all the actors, writers and Bohemian hangers-on remains a New York landmark. The **Chelsea Hotel** has been undisputed watering-hole of the city's harder-up literati for decades: Mark Twain and Tennessee Williams lived here and Brendan Behan and Dylan Thomas staggered in and out during their New York visits. Thomas Wolfe assembled *You Can't Go Home Again* from thousands of pages of manuscript he had stacked in his room, and in 1951 Jack Kerouac, armed with a specially adapted typewriter (and a lot of

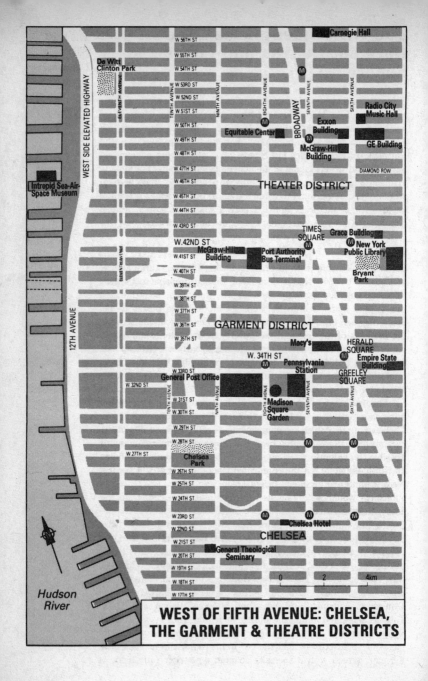

WEST OF FIFTH AVENUE: CHELSEA, THE GARMENT & THEATRE DISTRICTS

Benzedrine) typed the first draft of *On the Road* non-stop on to a 120-foot roll of paper. William Burroughs (in a presumably more relaxed state) completed *The Naked Lunch* here, and Arthur C. Clarke, Arthur Miller and Paul Bowles all had rooms.

In the 1960s the *Chelsea* took off again when Andy Warhol and his doomed protégés Edie Sedgwick and Candy Darling walled up here and made the film *Chelsea Girls* in (sort of) homage; Nico, Hendrix, Zappa, Pink Floyd and various members of the Dead passed through, Bob Dylan wrote songs in and about it, and more recently, Sid Vicious stabbed Nancy Spungen to death in their suite, a few months before his own pathetic life ended with an overdose of heroin. On a more cheerful note, the hotel inspired Joni Mitchell to write her song *Chelsea Morning* – a song that twanged the heart-strings of the young Bill and Hilary Clinton, who named their daughter after it (though there's no record of Chelsea ever having stayed in her eponymous hotel).

With a pedigree like this it's easy to forget the hotel itself, which has a down-at-heel Edwardian grandeur all of its own and, incidentally, is an affordable place to stay and an interesting one in which to drink; see Chapter 7, *Accommodation*.

East Chelsea

Sixth Avenue forms Chelsea's eastern perimeter, with the city's largest **antiques market** taking place at weekends in an open-air car park at the junction with 26th Street: open till 6pm, it's possible to find bargains amid the piles of overpriced junk (see Chapter 14, *Shops and Markets*). The area around 28th Street is also Manhattan's **Flower Market**: not really a market as such, more the warehouses where potted plants and cut flowers are stored before brightening offices and atriums across the city. Nothing marks the strip, and you come across it by chance, the greenery bursting out of drab blocks, blooms spangling shopfronts and providing a welcome touch of life to an otherwise dull neighbourhood. For the record, West 28th Street was the original **Tin Pan Alley**, where music publishers would peddle songs to artists and producers from the nearby theatres. When the theatres moved, so did the publishers.

Greeley Square and the Garment District

A few streets north, Sixth Avenue collides with Broadway at **Greeley Square**, an overblown name for what is a trashy triangle celebrating Horace Greeley, founder of the **Tribune** newspaper. Perhaps he deserves better: known for his rallying call to the youth of the nineteenth century to explore the continent ("Go West, young man!"), he also supported the rights of women and trade unions, commissioned a weekly column from Karl Marx and denounced slavery and capital punishment. His paper no longer exists (though one of its descendants is the bored traveller's last resort, the *International*

The West
Side:
Chelsea, the
Garment
District and
Times
Square

Herald Tribune) and the square named after him is one of those bits of Manhattan that looks ready to disintegrate at any moment.

Across the way is **Macy's**, the all-American superstore. Until the mid-1970s *Macy's* contented itself by being the world's largest store (which it remains); then, in response to the needs of the maturing Yuppie (and *Bloomingdale's* success) it went fashionably and safely upmarket, somewhere in the realm of *Harrods* and *Heal's*. Like all great stores it's worth exploring – there's an amazing food emporium plus a reconstruction of P. J. Clarke's bar in the basement – though leave all forms of spending power at home. Nearby, the thoroughly unlikeable eight floors of the **A & S Plaza** attempt to add a little gloss to the street scene though, inside at least, they can't hold a candle to *Macy's*.

In 1993 Macy's sailed close to bankruptcy – something unthinkable to most New Yorkers.

The Garment District
In a way this part of Broadway is the shopfront to the **Garment District**, a loosely defined pool between 34th and 42nd streets and Sixth and Eighth avenues. From this patch three-quarters of all the women's and children's clothes in America are made, though you'd never believe it: outlets are strictly wholesale with no need to woo customers, and the only clues to the industry inside are the racks of clothes shunted around on the street and occasional skips of offcuts that give the area its look of an open-air jumble sale.

Around Madison Square Garden
The Garment District is something to see in passing: the unmissable landmark in this part of town is the **Pennsylvania Station** and **Madison Square Garden** complex, a combined box and drum structure that swallows up millions of commuters in its train station below and accommodates the *Knicks* basketball and *Rangers* hockey teams (along with their fans) up top. There's nothing memorable about Penn Station: its subterranean levels seem to have all the grime and just about everything else that's wrong with the subway, and to add insult to injury the original Penn Station, demolished to make way for this, is now hailed as a lost masterpiece. One of McKim, Mead and White's greatest designs, it reworked the ideas of the Roman Baths of Caracalla to awesome effect: "Through it one entered the city like a god . . .. One scuttles in now like a rat," mourned an observer. A whimsical reminder of the old days is the **Penta Hotel** on the corner of Seventh Avenue and 33rd Street: a main venue for Glenn Miller and other big swing bands of the 1940s, it keeps the phone number that made it famous – 736-5000: under the old system PENNsylvania 6-5000, title of Miller's affectionate hit.

For details on how to get tickets for Knicks *and* Rangers *games, see p.311.*

Immediately behind Penn Station the **General Post Office** is a McKim, Mead and White structure that survived, a relic from an era when municipal pride was all about making statements – though to say that the Post Office is monumental in the grandest manner still seems to underplay it. The old joke is that it had to be this big to fit in the sonorous inscription above the columns – "Neither snow nor rain nor heat nor gloom of night stays these couriers from the swift completion of their appointed rounds" – a claim about as believable as the official one that the Manhattan postal district handles more mail than Britain, France and Belgium combined. The Post Office moved out of the building in 1993, and plans are afoot to utilise the building as a **new entrance** to Penn Station. Many New Yorkers see this as some sort of expiation for the destruction of the original station: whether the scheme will come to anything, time will tell, but the plans for the new entrance – a massive steel arch filling the centre of the Post Office – are certainly spectacular.

The **Port Authority Terminal Building** at 40th Street and Eighth Avenue is another sink for the area: a Dantesque version of a British concrete-and-glass bus station. Buses strain, waiting to escape the city to all points in America, and though initially confusing it's efficiently run. *Greyhound* leave from here, as do regional services out to the boroughs and (should you arrive in the early hours) it's a remarkably safe place, station staff keeping the winos and weirdos in check.

Herald Square to 42nd Street

Back to Broadway, and **Herald Square** faces Greeley Square in a headlong replay of the battles between the *Herald* newspaper and its arch rival Horace Greeley's *Tribune*. During the 1890s this was the **Tenderloin** area, dance halls, brothels and rough bars thriving beside the elevated railway that ran up Sixth Avenue. When the *Herald* arrived in 1895 it gave the square a new name and dignity, but it's perhaps best remembered as the square George M. Cohan said Hello to in the famous song. These days it wouldn't fire anyone to sing about it, saved only from unkempt sleaziness by *Macy's* on the corner below.

Cross **42nd Street** and you find Broadway at its worst. The excitement and *élan* of the street's eastern section are gone, and all that's left is a clutch of squalid sex shops and porno cinemas. Neither do things improve if you turn west: 42nd Street here is a sordid corner of prostitution and petty vice you'll do better to skip altogether – and that goes for much of Eighth Avenue north of 42nd. For years local residents and businesses have lobbied for the neighbourhood to be cleaned up, and with the recent attempts to sanitise Times Square it looks as though the days of the porn shops may be numbered. Unfortunately, market forces dictate that these shops won't disappear, but relocate – they've already begun to turn up on West Canal Street and in the Village, much to the alarm of the locals. For the moment, though, it's best to head straight on along 42nd Street, where at number 330 is the **McGraw-Hill Building**, a greeny-blue radiator that architects raved over: "proto-jukebox modern", Vincent Scully called it. The lobby should be seen.

For full practical details on the Port Authority Terminal, see p.14.

The West
Side:
Chelsea, the
Garment
District and
Times
Square

Clinton – aka "Hell's Kitchen"

Ninth Avenue makes amends of sorts for Eighth's unsavouriness with a long slash of ethnic delis and greengrocers of all kinds that come into their own in May when the **Ninth Avenue Food Festival** (see Chapter 12, *Parades and Festivals*) closes the run between 34th and 57th streets. This stretch down to the Hudson was once known as **Hell's Kitchen**, a descriptive name for one of New York's poorest and most violent areas. Impoverished Irish immigrants settled here, quickly followed by Greeks, Italians and Latinos: by the end of the nineteenth century the tenements were the most over-crowded in the world, gangs roamed the rubbish-filled streets, and disease and infant mortality were rife. (It wasn't until 1867 that the city officially prohibited the indigenous herds of **pigs** that brushed with the gentry of Broadway and acted as a primitive method of removing the human waste that was dumped on the streets at night.) With the Tenement Housing Act of 1901 things started to get better, and since then the old tenements have been flattened and the area renamed as **Clinton** to hide its past. In 1977 **Manhattan Plaza** went up on 42nd and 43rd streets between Ninth and Tenth, in an attempt to draw the monied classes into the area. But prices were high and takers few for apartments irreparably sullied by nearby Times Square, and in a fit of innovation the buildings were let to actors, artists and the like who could prove a low income and would enhance the theatre district's "creative feel". Welfare families, needless to say, were deemed not to provide the right "class". Now Hell's Kitchen is gradually gentrifying against a background of raggy, multi-ethnic neighbourhoods, at its centre safe enough, but west of Ninth Avenue in the 40s and 50s bombed out and intimidat-ing – a prelude to the out-and-out sleaze of the bars on the West Side Highway. There's no reason to go there, especially not at night, but if you do, take care.

Times Square

Eventually Broadway runs into **Times Square**, a pinched strip that in its excess and brashness was for years a distillation of the city itself. Centre of the Great White Way, it's been much cleaned up recently, and it seems that its days as a venue of lurid enticements to sex shows alongside theatres only a touch more reputable are finally over. Traditionally, Times Square was the place where out-of-towners supplied easy pickings for petty criminals, drug dealers and women working as prostitutes. You were more likely to be hassled here than anywhere in the city, and as the decline continued the municipal authorities were forced into action, slapping compulsory purchase orders on whole blocks and spending billions of dollars to tear out the diseased heart of the square. Now almost all of the peep shows and sex shops have gone, replaced by a massive new office block development and safely sanitised cinemas and electrical shops. (Under the leasing conditions imposed by the city, businesses renting these offices have to allow neon signs and illuminated billboards on their walls – an attempt to retain the traditional feel of the square.) Much of the danger and a lot of the feel have gone, but you should still be careful in the streets off the square, though there's too much going on when the theatres empty to make street crime viable: at other times beware – and keep to the main drag.

Like Greeley and Herald squares, Times Square took its name from a newspaper connection when the *New York Times* built offices here in 1904. While the *Herald* and *Tribune* fought each other in ever more vicious circulation battles, the *NYT* took the sober middle ground under the banner "All the news that's fit to print", a policy that enabled the paper to survive and become one of the country's most respected liberal voices. **Times Tower**, the slim chip at the square's southern end, was its original headquarters, with the newspaper being printed on underground presses beneath the tower, where they could easily be bundled onto the subway for distribution around the city. Today, though, the paper itself has long since crept off round a corner to 43rd Street, and most of the printing goes on in New Jersey. Dotted around Times Tower are some of Broadway's great theatres (see "Theatre" in Chapter 10, *The Performing Arts and Film*) – and it's these last that add flavour to the scene: the clock-and-globe topped **Paramount Theater Building** at 1501 Broadway, between 43rd and 44th streets, is a favourite, and the **Lyceum**, **Shubert** and **Lyric** each have their original facades. It's the nifty canvas and frame stand of the **TKTS**, the cut-price ticket shop, that immediately catches the eye though, selling tickets for shows that no one could otherwise afford. A lifelike statue of Broadway's doyen **George M. Cohan** looks on – though if you've ever seen the film *Yankee Doodle Dandy* it's impossible to think of him other than as a swaggering Jimmy Cagney. Last word on the scene to Henry Miller from *Tropic of Capricorn*:

> *It's only a stretch of a few blocks from Times Square to Fiftieth Street, and when one says Broadway that's all that's really meant and it's really nothing, just a chicken run and a lousy one at that, but even at seven in the evening when everyone's rushing for a table there's a sort of electric crackle in the air and your hair stands on end like an antennae and if you're receptive you not only get every bash and flicker but you get the statistical itch, the quid pro quo of the interactive, interstitial, ectoplasmic quantum of bodies jostling in space like the stars which compose the Milky Way, only this is the Gay White Way, the top of the world with no roof and not even a crack or a hole under your feet to fall through and say it's a lie. The absolute impersonality of it brings you to a pitch of warm human delirium which makes you run forward like a blind nag and wag your delirious ears.*

The West
Side:
Chelsea, the
Garment
District and
Times
Square

The West Fifties

The West 50s between Sixth and Eighth avenues are emphatically tourist territory. Edged by Central Park in the north and the Theater District to the south, and with Fifth Avenue and Rockefeller Center in easy striking distance, the area has been invaded by overpriced restaurants and cheapo souvenir shops: should you want to stock up on *I Love New York* underwear, this could be the place.

One sight worth searching out is the **Equitable Center** at 757 Seventh Avenue. The building itself is dapper if not a little self-important, with **Roy Lichtenstein**'s 68-foot *Mural with Blue Brush Stroke* poking you in the eye as you enter: best of all, look out for **Thomas Hart Benton**'s *America Today* murals (in the left-hand corridor), which dynamically and magnificently portray ordinary American life in the days before the Depression.

Carnegie Hall and the Russian Tea Room

Otherwise **Carnegie Hall**, an overblown and fussy warehouse-like venue for opera and concert at 154 West 57th Street, is the thing to see (Tchaikovsky conducted the programme on opening night and Mahler, Rachmaninov, Toscanini, Frank Sinatra and Judy Garland played here), and though it's dropped down a league since Lincoln Center opened, the superb acoustics still ensure full houses most of the year. If you don't fancy or can't afford a performance, sneak in through the stage door on 56th Street for a look – no one minds as long as there's not a rehearsal in progress. Alternatively, tours are held on Mondays, Tuesdays and Thursdays at 11.30am, 2pm and 3pm; $6, $5 students; ☎903-9790 for more details.

A few doors down at no. 150, the **Russian Tea Room** (see Chapter 8, *Drinking and Eating*) is one of those places to see and be seen at, ever popular with in-names from the entertainment business. Reservations are needed for lunch and dinner, but to get an idea of the sumptuous red and gold interior, its totally un-Russian atmosphere and its astronomical prices, just order a sandwich.

Sixth Avenue

Sixth Avenue is properly named Avenue of the Americas, though no New Yorker ever calls it this: guidebooks and maps labour the convention, but the only manifestation of the tag are lamppost flags of Central and South American countries which serve as useful land-marks. If nothing else Sixth's distinction is its width, a result of the elevated railway that once ran along here, now replaced by the Sixth Avenue subway. In its day the Sixth Avenue "El" marked the border-line between respectability to the east and dodgier areas to the west, and in a way it's still a dividing line separating the glamorous strips of Fifth, Madison and Park avenues and the less salubrious western districts.

Around Bryant Park

Running north from Herald Square, **Bryant Park** is the first open space, once again named after a newspaper editor – William Cullen Bryant of the erstwhile *New York Post*, also famed as a poet and instigator of Central Park. Recently the park benefited from a civic cleanup, and nowadays secondhand bookstalls have replaced the former dope dealers. This is for the good, as Bryant Park is by design attractive – a bit straitlaced and formal perhaps, but more welcoming than many small parks. From here you can't miss the **Grace Building** which swoops down on 42nd Street, breaking the rules by stepping out of line with its neighbours, though with a showiness that rings rather hollow – and which, in any case, is less well finished than its twin, the Solow Building, on West 57th Street. Much more approachable is the **American Radiator Building** (now the American Standard Building) on West 40th, its black Gothic tower topped with honey-coloured terracotta that lights up to resemble a glowing coal – appropriate enough for the headquarters of a heating company.

Diamond Row

One of the best things about New York City is the small hidden pockets abruptly discovered when you least expect them. West 47th Street between Fifth and Sixth is a perfect example: this is **Diamond Row**, a short strip of shops chock-full with wildly expensive stones and jewellery, managed by ultra-Orthodox Hasidic Jews who seem only to exist in the confines of the street. Maybe they are what gives the street its workaday feel – Diamond Row seems more like the Garment District than Fifth Avenue, and the conversations you overhear on the street or in the nearby delicatessens are memorably Jewish. The Hasidim are followers of a mystical sect of Judaism – the name means "Pious Ones" – and traditionally wear beards, sidelocks and dark, old-fashioned suits. A large contingent live in Williamsburg and Crown Heights in Brooklyn.

Around the Rockefeller Extension

By the time it reaches midtown Manhattan, Sixth Avenue has become a dazzling showcase of corporate wealth. True, there's little of the ground-floor glitter of Fifth or the razzmatazz of Broadway, but what *is* here, and in a way what defines the stretch from 47th to 51st streets, is the **Rockefeller Center Extension**. Following the earlier **Time & Life Building** at 50th Street, three near-identical blocks went up in the 1970s, and if they don't have the romance of their predecessor they at least possess some of its monumentality. Backing on to Rockefeller Center proper, by day and especially by night, the repeated statement of each block comes over with some power, giving the wide path of Sixth Avenue much of its visual excitement. At street level things can be just as interesting: the broad sidewalks allow pedlars of food and handbills, street musicians, mimics and actors to do their thing.

The West
Side:
Chelsea, the
Garment
District and
Times
Square

Across the avenue at 49th Street **Radio City Music Hall** has far greater rewards (for a description see p.129). Keep an eye open too for the **CBS Building** on the corner of 52nd Street: dark and inscrutable, this has been compared to the monolith from the film *2001* and, like it or not, it certainly forces a mysterious presence on this segment of Sixth Avenue.

The rack of streets below Central Park are home to some of the most opulent hotels, shops and apartments in America, which means you spend a lot of time gawping at windows and gasping at prices. Best place to do both is along **57th Street**, where antiquarian bookstores and galleries crowd alongside the dyspeptic wealth of *Van Cleef and Arpels* (jewellery) and *Bergdorf Goodman* (jewellery and just about every other fashion that big money can buy). 57th Street has also recently overtaken SoHo as *the* centre for upmarket art sales, and galleries here are noticeably snootier than their downtown relations, often requiring an appointment for viewing. A couple that usually don't are the **Marlborough Gallery** (2nd floor, 40 West 57th), specialising in famous names both American and European, and the **Kennedy Gallery** (same building, 5th floor), which deals in nineteenth-century and twentieth-century American painting.

MANHATTAN

Fifth Avenue and East: 42nd Street to Central Park

Fifth Avenue bowls ahead from 42nd Street with all the confidence of the material world. It's been a great strip for as long as New York has been a great city, and its name is an automatic image of wealth and opulence. Here that image is very real: all that considers itself suave and cosmopolitan ends up on Fifth, and the shops showcase New York's most opulent and conspicuous consumerism. That the shopping is beyond the power of most people needn't put you off, for Fifth rewards with some of the city's best architecture: the boutiques and stores are just the icing on the cake.

Fifth Avenue

In its lower reaches Fifth Avenue isn't really as alluring as the streets off. The only eye-catcher is the **Manufacturers Hanover Trust Bank** on the southwest corner of 43rd, an early glass 'n' gloss box that teasingly displays its safe to passers-by, a reaction against the fortress palaces of earlier banks. Around the next corner, West 44th Street contains three New York institutions. The Georgian-style **Harvard Club** at no. 27, easily spotted of an evening by the paparazzi hanging about outside, has interiors so lavish that lesser mortals aren't allowed to enter. But it's still possible to enjoy the **New York Yacht Club**, its playfully eccentric exterior of bay windows moulded as ships' sterns, and with waves and dolphins

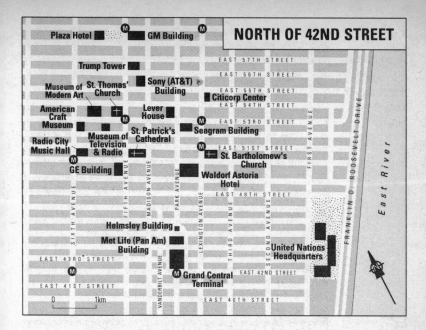

Plaza Hotel GM Building

Trump Tower

Museum of St. Thomas' Sony (AT&T)
Modern Art Church Building
Citicorp Center

American Lever
Craft House
Museum Museum of St. Patrick's Seagram Building
Radio City Television Cathedral
Music Hall & Radio St. Bartholomew's
Church
GE Building Waldorf Astoria
Hotel

Helmsley Building

Met Life (Pan Am)
Building United Nations
Headquarters

Grand Central
Terminal

EAST 57TH STREET
EAST 56TH STREET
EAST 55TH STREET
EAST 54TH STREET
EAST 53RD STREET
EAST 51ST STREET
EAST 48TH STREET
EAST 43RD STREET
EAST 41ST STREET
EAST 42ND STREET
EAST 40TH STREET

FIFTH AVENUE
MADISON AVENUE
PARK AVENUE
LEXINGTON AVENUE
THIRD AVENUE
SECOND AVENUE
FIRST AVENUE
FRANKLIN D. ROOSEVELT DRIVE
VANDERBILT AVENUE
SIXTH AVENUE

East River

0   1km

completing the effect of tipsy Beaux Arts fun. For years this was
home of the Americas Cup, a yachting trophy first won by the
schooner *America* in 1851 and held here (indeed bolted to the
table) until lost to the Australians amid much loss of face in 1984.
Now though, for the time being at least, it's back in its place.

"Dammit, it was the twenties and we had to be smarty." So said
Dorothy Parker of the group known as the Round Table who hung
out at the **Algonquin Hotel** at no. 59 and gave it a name as *the*
place for literary visitors to New York – a name which still to some
extent endures. The Round Table used to meet regularly here, a
kind of American-style Bloomsbury group of the city's sharpest-
tongued wits which had a reputation for being as egotistical as it
was exclusive. Times have changed considerably, but over the years
the *Algonquin* has continued to attract a steady stream of famous
guests, most of them with some kind of literary bent, not least Noel
Coward (whose table someone will point out to you if you ask
nicely), Bernard Shaw, Irving Berlin and Boris Karloff. The bar is
one of the most civilised in town.

West 47th Street, or Diamond Row (for an account of which,
see p.125), is another surprise off Fifth Avenue, but the first building to strike out at street level is the facade of what was once
Charles Scribner & Son's bookstore at 597 Fifth Avenue. Today
occupied by a branch of *Brentano's* bookstore, the black and gold
iron-and-glass storefront that seems to have fallen from an

*Practical
details of the
Algonquin can
be found in
Chapter 7,
Accommo-
dation.*

Edwardian engraving has been given historic landmark status. If you're looking to browse through bargain books, **Barnes & Noble** across the Avenue offers no frills but good value.

Rockefeller Center

Central to this stretch of Fifth is a complex of buildings that, more than any other in the city, succeeds in being utterly self-contained and at the same time in complete agreement with its surroundings. Built between 1932 and 1940 by John D. Rockefeller, son of the oil magnate, **Rockefeller Center** is one of the finest pieces of urban planning anywhere: office space with cafés, a theatre, underground concourses and rooftop gardens work together with an intelligence and grace rare in any building then or now. It's a combination that shows every other city-centre shopping mall the way, leaving you thinking that Cyril Connolly's snide description – "that sinister Stonehenge of Economic Man" – was way off the mark.

You're lured into the center from Fifth Avenue down the gentle slope of the **Channel Gardens** (so named because they divide La Maison Française and the British Empire Building) to the **GE Building** (formerly the RCA Building, but renamed when General Electric took it over a few years ago), focus of the center. Rising 850 feet, its monumental lines match the scale of Manhattan itself, though softened by symmetrical setbacks to prevent an overpowering expanse of wall. At its foot the **Lower Plaza** holds a sunken restaurant in the summer months, linked visually to the downward flow of the building by Paul Manship's sparkling *Prometheus*; in winter it becomes an ice rink, giving skaters a chance to show off their skills to passing shoppers. More ponderously, a panel on the eastern side relates John D. Rockefeller's priggish credo in gold and black.

Inside, the GE Building is no less impressive. In the lobby José Maria Sert's murals, *American Progress* and *Time*, are faded but eagerly in tune with the 1930's Deco ambience – presumably more so than the original paintings by Diego Rivera, which were removed by John D.'s son Nelson when the artist refused to scrap a panel glorifying Lenin. A leaflet available from the lobby desk details a **self-guided tour** of the center, and while you can't reach the building's summit, a cocktail in *The Rainbow Room* restaurant on the 65th floor (see p.271) gives you Manhattan's best skyscraper view, especially at night, when helicopters hang like fireflies over the Financial District, and Central Park glitters to the north.

*For more on
how to get
tickets for TV
show
recordings, see
p.31.*

Among the many offices in the GE Building are the **NBC Studios**, and it's possible to tour these (one-hour tours leave regularly, daily 9.30am–4.30pm, reservations from the desk in the GE foyer first; $8; arrive as early as possible as tours fill fast; ☎664-4000, though if you're an American TV freak you'll do better to pick up a (free) ticket for a **show recording** from the mezzanine lobby or out on the street. The most popular tickets evaporate before 9am.

Radio City Music Hall

Just northwest of Rockefeller Center, at Sixth Avenue and 50th Street, is the **Radio City Music Hall**, an Art Deco jewel box that represents the last word in 1930s luxury. The staircase is regally resplendent with the world's largest chandeliers, the murals from the men's toilets are now in the Museum of Modern Art, and the huge auditorium looks like an extravagant scalloped shell or a vast sunset: "Art Deco's true shrine", as Paul Goldberger rightly called it. Believe it or not Radio City was nearly demolished in 1970: the outcry this caused left it designated a national landmark. To explore, take a tour from the lobby (Mon–Sat 10.15am–4.45pm, Sun 11.15am–4.45pm; $8; ☎632-4041).

North towards Central Park

A further bit of sumptuous Deco is the **International Building** on Fifth Avenue, whose black marble and gold leaf give the lobby a sleek, classy feel dramatised by the ritz of escalators and the view across Lee Lawrie's bronze *Atlas* out to **St Patrick's Cathedral**. Designed by James Renwick and completed in 1888, St Patrick's sits bone-white in the sullied streets and seems the result of a painstaking academic tour of the Gothic cathedrals of Europe – perfect in detail, lifeless in spirit. There's something wrong too in the way the cathedral slots ever-so-neatly into Manhattan's grid pattern; on the plus side, the Gothic details are perfect and the cathedral is certainly striking – and made all the more so by the backing of the sunglass-black **Olympic Tower**, whose exclusive apartments house notables like Jackie Onassis when she's in town.

North of 52nd Street, Fifth Avenue's ground floors quickly shift from airline offices to all-out glitz, with *Cartier*, *Gucci* and *Tiffany's* among many gilt-edged names. The window shopping is fine, but beware assistants, who seem to flip between the crawlingly obsequious and the downright rude according to how much they think you're worth. This isn't the case at **Steuben Glass**, 715 Fifth Avenue at 56th Street, a showcase of delicate glass and crystalware perfectly displayed; nor at **Nat Sherman's** at 711, tobacconist to the stars and purveyor of some lethal smokes (see Chapter 14 for fuller listings).

Just when you thought all the glitter had gone about as far as it could, you reach the **Trump Tower** at 57th Street, whose outrageously over-the-top atrium is just short of repellent – perhaps in tune with those who frequent the glamorous designer shops here. Perfumed air, polished marble panelling and a five-storey waterfall are calculated to knock you senseless with expensive "good" taste: as it is even some of the security people look faintly embarrassed. But the building is clever, a neat little outdoor garden is squeezed high in a corner, and each of the 230 apartments above the atrium gets views in three directions. Donald Trump, the property developer all New York liberals love to hate, lives here, along with other worthies of the hyper-rich in-crowd.

The antidote to all this is **F.A.O. Schwartz**, a block north at 745 Fifth Avenue at 58th Street, a colossal emporium of children's toys. Fight the kids off and there's some great stuff to play with – once again, the best money can buy. Across 58th Street Fifth Avenue broadens to Grand Army Plaza and the fringes of **Central Park**.

Madison, Park and Lexington avenues

If there is a stretch that is immediately and unmistakably New York it is the area that runs east from Fifth Avenue in the 40s and 50s. The great avenues of Madison, Park, Lexington and Third reach their richest heights as the skyscrapers line up in neck-cricking vistas, the streets choke with yellow cabs and office workers, and Con Edison vents belch steam from old heating systems. More than anything else it's buildings that define this part of town, the majority of them housing anonymous corporations and supplying excitement to the skyline in a 1960s build-em-high glass-box bonanza. Others, like the new AT&T headquarters and Citicorp Center, don't play the game; and enough remains from the pre-box days to keep variety.

Madison Avenue

Madison Avenue shadows Fifth with some of its sweep but less of the excitement. A few good stores sit behind the scenes here, like *Brooks Brothers*, on the corner of East 44th Street, traditional clothiers to the Ivy League and inventors of the button-down collar, but Madison doesn't have quite the prestige of Fifth or Park. Between 50th and 51st streets the **Villard Houses** merit a serious walk past, a replay of an Italian palazzo (one that didn't quite make it to Fifth Avenue) by McKim, Mead and White. The houses have been surgically incorporated into the Helmsley Palace Hotel and the interiors polished up to their original splendour.

Madison's most interesting buildings come in a four-block strip above 53rd Street: **Paley Park**, on the north side of East 53rd between Madison and Fifth, is a tiny vest-pocket park complete with mini-waterfall. Around the corner the **Continental Illinois Center** looks like a cross beween a space rocket and a grain silo. But it's the **Sony Building** between 55th and 56th streets that grabbed all the headlines. Another Johnson-Burgee collaboration, it followed the postmodernist theory of eclectic borrowing from historical styles: a Modernist skyscraper sandwiched between a Chippendale top and a Renaissance base – the idea being to quote from great public buildings and simultaneously return to the fantasy of the early part of this century. The building has its fans – especially for the lobby which contains Evelyn Longman's sculpture *The Spirit of Communication*, removed from the old AT&T headquarters down-town – but in the main the tower doesn't work, and it's unlikely to stand the test of time. Perhaps Johnson should have followed the advice of his teacher, Mies Van der Rohe: "It's better to build a good

The Sony Building was originally the HQ of telephone company AT&T; you'll occasionally hear it referred to as "the AT&T Building".

building than an original one." More info is on hand from the lobby attendants.

Less flamboyantly, the **IBM Building** next door at 590 Madison has a stylish enclosed plaza of plants, water and tinkling classical music, achieving the effect the Trump Tower aimed for and missed, and scoring much higher in the user-friendly stakes than the AT&T. Across 57th Street, as the first of Madison's boutiques appear, the **Fuller Building** is worth catching – black and white Art Deco, with a fine entrance and tiled floor.

Park Avenue

"Where wealth is so swollen that it almost bursts", wrote Collinson Owen of **Park Avenue** in 1929, and things aren't much changed: corporate headquarters jostle for prominence in a triumphal procession to capitalism, pushed apart by Park's broad avenue that once carried railtracks. Whatever your feelings it's one of the city's most awesome sights. Looking south, everything progresses to the high altar of the **New York Central Building** (now rechristened the Helmsley Building), a delicate, energetic construction with a lewdly excessive Rococo lobby. In its day it formed a skilled punctuation mark to the avenue, but had its thunder stolen in 1963 by the **Pan Am Building** that looms behind. Bauhaus guru Walter Gropius had a hand in designing this, and the critical consensus is that he should have done better. Headquarters of the international airline, the building has a profile meant to suggest an aircraft wing, and the blue-grey mass certainly adds drama to the cityscape, though whatever success the Pan Am scores it robs Park Avenue of the views south it deserves and needs, sealing 44th Street and drawing much of the vigour from the buildings all about. Another black mark was the rooftop helipad, closed in the 1970s after a helicopter undercarriage collapsed shortly after landing, causing a rotor to sheer off and kill four passengers who had just got off, as well as injuring several people on the ground.

Despite Park Avenue's power, an individual look at most of the skyscrapers reveals the familiar glass box, and the first few buildings to stand out do so exactly because that's what they're not. Wherever you placed the solid mass of the **Waldorf Astoria Hotel** (between 49th and 50th) it would hold its own, a resplendent statement of Art Deco elegance. If you're tempted, it's a smidgen cheaper than the comparable competition, with double rooms between $200 and $300. Crouching behind, **St Bartholomew's Church** is a low-slung Byzantine hybrid that by contrast adds immeasurably to the street, giving the lumbering skyscrapers a much-needed sense of scale. As you'd imagine, every so often property developers wave a huge cheque under the church fathers' noses for the land rights: so far they've managed to resist. The spikey-topped **General Electric Building** behind seems like a wild extension of the church, its slender shaft rising to a meshed crown of

In spring 1993, following Pan Am's bankruptcy, the building was renamed the MetLife Building after its new owners.

abstract sparks and lightning strokes that symbolises the radio waves used by its original occupier, RCA. The lobby (entrance at 570 Lexington) is yet another Deco delight.

Amongst all this it's difficult at first to see the originality of the **Seagram Building** between 52nd and 53rd streets. Designed by Mies Van der Rohe with Philip Johnson and built in 1958, this was the seminal curtain-wall skyscraper, the floors supported internally, allowing a skin of smoky glass and whisky-bronze metal (Seagram are distillers), now weathered to a dull black. In keeping with the era's vision, every interior detail down to the fixtures and lettering on the mailboxes was specially designed. It was the supreme example of Modernist reason, deceptively simple and cleverly detailed, and its opening caused a wave of approval. The plaza, an open fore-court designed to set the building apart from its neighbours and display it to advantage, was such a success as a public space that the city revised the zoning laws to encourage other high-rise build-ers to supply plazas. The result was the windswept anti-people places now found all over down- and midtown Manhattan, and a lot of pallid Mies copies, boxes that alienated many from "faceless" modern architecture.

Across Park Avenue McKim, Mead and White's **Racquet and Squash Club** seems like a Classical continuation of the Seagram Plaza. More interesting is the **Lever House** across the way between 53rd and 54th, the building that set the Modernist ball rolling on Park Avenue in 1952. Then, the two right-angled slabs that form a steel and glass bookend seemed revolutionary compared to the traditional buildings that surrounded it. Nowadays it's overlooked and not a little dingy.

Lexington Avenue and east

Lexington Avenue is always active, especially around the mid-40s, where commuters swarm around Grand Central and a well-placed post office on the corner of 50th Street. Just as the Chrysler Building dominates these lower stretches, the chisel-topped **Citicorp Center** (between 53rd and 54th streets) has taken the north end as its domain. Finished in 1979, the graph-paper design sheathed in aluminium is architecture become mathematics, and the building is now one of Manhattan's most conspicuous landmarks. The slanted roof was designed to house solar panels and provide power, but the idea was ahead of the technology and Citicorp had to content them-selves with adopting the distinctive top as a corporate logo. The atrium of stores known as The Market is also one of the city's best, with inexpensive food (try a *Healthwork's* salad) and live music at 6–8pm Saturdays, noon on Sundays. A more likeable meeting of commerce, culture and friendly mall you couldn't hope to find.

Hiding under the Center's skirts is **St Peter's**, a tiny church built to replace one originally demolished to make way for the Citicorp. Part of the deal was that the church had to stand out from the center

– which explains the granite material. Thoroughly modern inside, it's worth peering in for sculptor Louise Nevelson's *Erol Beaker Chapel*, venue for Wednesday lunchtime jazz concerts, and a church hall-cum-theatre with a reputation of being one of the city's most innovative.

The Citicorp provided a spur for the development of Third Avenue, though things really took off when the old elevated railway that ran here was dismantled in 1955. Until then Third had been a strip of earthy bars and rundown tenements, in effect a border to the more salubrious midtown district. After the Citicorp gave it an "official" stamp of approval, office blocks sprouted, revitalising the flagging fortunes of midtown Manhattan in the late 1970s. The best section is between 44th and 50th streets – look out for the sheer marble monument of the **Wang Building** between 48th and 49th, whose cross-patterns reveal the structure within.

All this office space hasn't totally removed interest from the street (there are a few good bars here, notably *P. J. Clarke's* at 55th, a New York institution – see Chapter 8, *Drinking and Eating*), but most life, especially at night-time, seems to have shifted across to **Second Avenue** – on the whole lower, quieter, more residential and with any number of singles/Irish bars to crawl between. The area from Third to the East River in the upper 40s is known as **Turtle Bay**, and there's a scattering of brownstones alongside chirpier shops and industry that disappear as you head north. Of course the UN Headquarters Building (see p.116) has had a knock-on effect, producing buildings like **1 UN Plaza** at 44th and First, a futuristic chess piece of a hotel that takes its design hints from the UN Building itself. Inside, its marbled, chrome lobby is about as uninviting as any other modern American luxury hotel. Should this be your cup of tea, a double room will set you back a few hundred dollars; if not, just pray that all New York hotels don't end up like this.

First Avenue has a certain raggy looseness that's a relief after the concrete claustrophobia of midtown, and **Beekman Place** (49th–51st streets between First Avenue and the river) is quieter still, a beguiling enclave of garbled styles. Similar, though not quite as intimate, is **Sutton Place**, a long stretch running from 53rd to 59th between First and the river. Originally built for the lordly Morgans and Vanderbilts in 1875, Sutton increases in elegance as you move north and, for today's crème de la crème, **Riverview Terrace** (off 58th Street) is a (very) private enclave of five brownstones. The Secretary-General of the UN has a place here and the locals are choosy who they let in: disgraced former President Richard Nixon was refused on the grounds he would be a security risk.

Chapter 4

Upper Manhattan

U pper Manhattan begins above 57th Street, the corporate wealth of Midtown giving way abruptly to the smug residentialism of the Upper East and West sides. **Central Park** lies in between, the city's back garden, where people come to play and jog or, in the summer months, just stay sane, escaping midtown's crowds in one of the most intelligent pieces of urban landscaping ever.

The **Upper East Side** is at its most opulent in the mansions of **Fifth** and **Madison avenues**, today taken over by the **Metropolitan** and other of the city's great museums in what has become known as **Museum Mile**. For the rest it's in part an elegant, mind-your-own-business residential area, a scattering of historical attractions towards its periphery, with to the north, still more or less identifiable, the old German neighbourhood of **Yorkville** – the only concession to ethnic presence.

The **Upper West Side** is a lot less refined, though it does have one building – **Lincoln Center** – that carries considerable cachet, hosting New York's most prestigious arts performances. It is again predominantly residential, well heeled on its southern fringe, especially along stretches of Columbus Avenue, though considerably less so as you move north. At its top end, marked at the edge by the monolithic **Cathedral of St John the Divine**, is **Morningside Heights**, an area that is the last gasp of Manhattan's wealth before the decayed streets of **Harlem** and – much further east – its Latino counterpart **El Barrio**. Further north is **Inwood** and the city's least expected museum, the medieval arts collection of **The Cloisters** – for which see Chapter 6, *Museums and Galleries*.

Central Park

"All radiant in the magic atmosphere of art and taste." So enthused *Harper's* magazine on the opening of **Central Park** in 1876, and though it's hard to be quite so jubilant about the place today, few New Yorkers could imagine life without it. For whether you're into jogging, baseball, boating, botany or just plain walking, or even if you rarely go near the place, there's no question that it's Central Park which makes New York a just-about-bearable place to live. For many people here, it's their only contact with nature: they know it's spring because Central Park is turning green; winter must be coming when the trees start losing their leaves. Certainly, life without it would be a lot more unhinged.

Some history

Central Park came close to never happening at all. It was the poet and newspaper editor, William Cullen Bryant, who had the idea for an open public space back in 1844, and he spent seven years trying to persuade city hall to carry it out, while developers leaned heavily on the authorities not to give up any valuable land. But eventually the city agreed and an 840-acre space north of the city limits was set aside, a desolate swampy area then occupied by a shantytown of squatters. The two architects commissioned to design the landscape, Frederick Olmsted and Calvert Vaux, planned to create a rural paradise, a complete illusion of the countryside bang in the heart of Manhattan, which even then was growing at a fantastic rate. They also saw their scheme as a leveller, a democratic park where all would contribute "to the greater happiness of each . . . rich and poor, young and old, Jew and Gentile".

The park was finished in 1876 and opened with such publicity that Olmsted and Vaux were soon in demand as park architects all over the States. Locally they went on to design the Riverside and Morningside parks in Manhattan, and Prospect Park in Brooklyn. Working alone, Olmsted laid out the campuses of Berkeley and Stanford in California, and had a major hand in that most televised of American artificial landscapes – Capitol Hill in Washington DC.

Today, in spite of the advent of motorised traffic, the sense of disorderly nature Olmsted and Vaux intended largely survives, with cars and buses cutting through the park in sheltered canyons originally meant for horse-drawn carriages. The skyline, however, has changed, buildings thrusting their way into view and detracting from the park's original pastoral intention. Worse still are Robert Moses' alterations, which turned large stretches of landscaped open space into asphalted playground. Lately, too, the success of Central Park has in a way been its downfall, for as the crowds have become thicker, so the park has become more difficult to keep up to scratch; its lawns have become muddied, the gardens weary-looking and patchy, and the quieter reaches, which the two architects imagined a haven of peace and solitude, sites of muggings and attacks on women. To their credit, the city authorities have mounted a determined assault on all these evils, renovating large portions, upping the park's policing, and greenifying it at the expense of the softball fields and basketball nets. But it will be some time before Central Park is looking anything like its best.

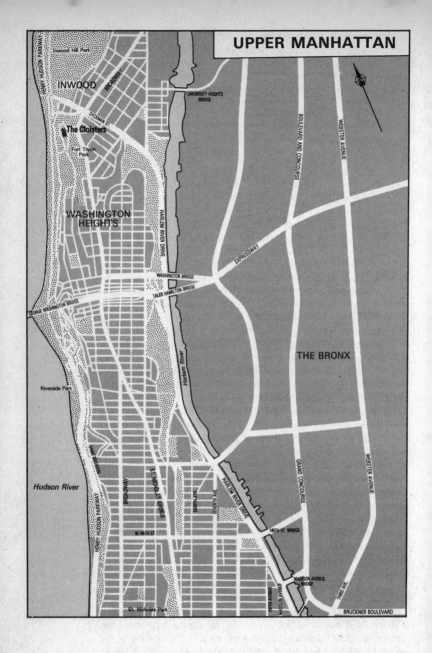

UPPER MANHATTAN

Inwood Hill Park

INWOOD

HENRY HUDSON PARKWAY

BROADWAY

DYCKMAN ST.

The Cloisters

Fort Tryon Park

UNIVERSITY HEIGHTS BRIDGE

WASHINGTON HEIGHTS

HARLEM RIVER DRIVE

BOULEVARD AND CONCOURSE

WEBSTER AVENUE

EXPRESSWAY

WASHINGTON BRIDGE

ALEX. HAMILTON BRIDGE

GEORGE WASHINGTON BRIDGE

Harlem River

THE BRONX

Riverside Park

RIVERSIDE DRIVE

Hudson River

HENRY HUDSON PARKWAY

BROADWAY

ST. NICHOLAS AVENUE

EIGHTH AVE.

SEVENTH AVE.

HARLEM RIVER DRIVE

GRAND CONCOURSE

WEBSTER AVENUE

W. 145TH ST

145TH ST. BRIDGE

MADISON AVENUE BRIDGE

THIRD AVE.

PARK AVENUE

MADISON AVENUE

St. Nicholas Park

BRUCKNER BOULEVARD

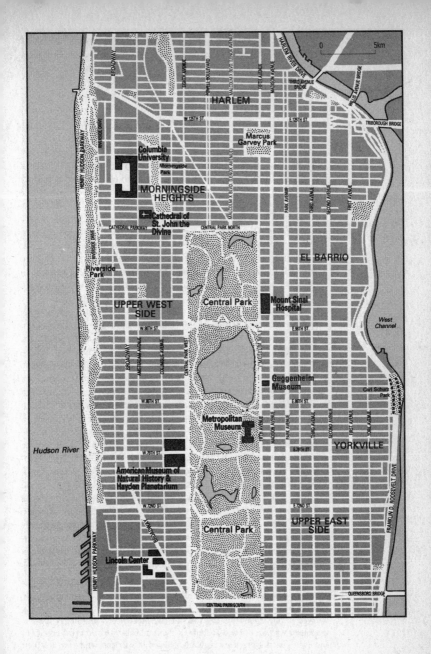

There's not really much else to say: the attractions of Central Park depend on the time of year, and the thing to do is explore it for yourself – and check out possible events at the Visitors' Center (see below).

Getting around in the park

Much the best way is to hire a **bicycle** from either the *Loeb Boathouse* or *Metro Bicycles* (Lexington at 88th Street – see p.24). Both charge around $6 an hour plus deposit, a much better deal than the famed (and extortionate) **buggy rides** (about $25 for a half-hour's trot*; bargain with the drivers and establish price and tip first). **On foot**, there's little chance of getting lost since one glance at the skyline should provide the clue to where you are. To know exactly, just find the nearest lamppost: the first two figures signify the number of the nearest street. As for **trouble**, should you run into anything serious best give up all you've got and make a dash for it. You should be all right during the day, though always be careful. After dark it's verging on suicidal to enter on foot, so if you want to look at the buildings of Central Park West lit up, à la Woody Allen's *Manhattan*, best fork out for a buggy.

The park divides easily in two: the area south of the reservoir, and the rest; most things of interest lie in the south. Entering here from Grand Army Plaza, the **Pond** lies to your left and to your right Central Park **Zoo** (April–Oct Mon–Fri 10am–5pm, Sat & Sun 10am–5.30pm; Nov–March Mon–Sun 10am–4.30pm; $1). The zoo, whose collection is based on three climatic regions – the Tropic Zone, the Temperate Territory and the Polar Circle – tries to keep caging to a minimum and the animals as close to the viewer as possible. It's an exciting and successful philosophy, and kids will love it.

First point to head for (unless you fancy a game of chess at the **Chess and Checkers Pavilion**) is the **Dairy**, a kind of dolly-Gothic ranch building originally intended to provide milk for nursing mothers and now the park's **Visitors' Center** (Tues–Sun 11am–4pm), giving out free leaflets and maps, selling books and putting on sporadic exhibitions. There are two routes beyond. The first skirts the southern fringe of **Sheep's Meadow** past the **Carousel** (which kids can ride on for a pittance) to **Tavern on the Green**, actually planned as a sheep enclosure but now one of the city's most exclusive – and expensive – restaurants. The second, and more obvious, is north up the **Mall**, the park's most formal stretch, flanked by statues

---

*Before you consider taking one of these "romantic" rides around the park, bear in mind that there's a vocal opposition group to the practice being allowed at all. Opponents say that the incompetence of the buggy drivers, combined with an offhand attitude to their animals, leads to great cruelty to the horses used. Horses are regularly maimed in accidents with cars, and their owners are lax about shodding horses with the correct shoe for constant use on the pavement – which leads to early laming.

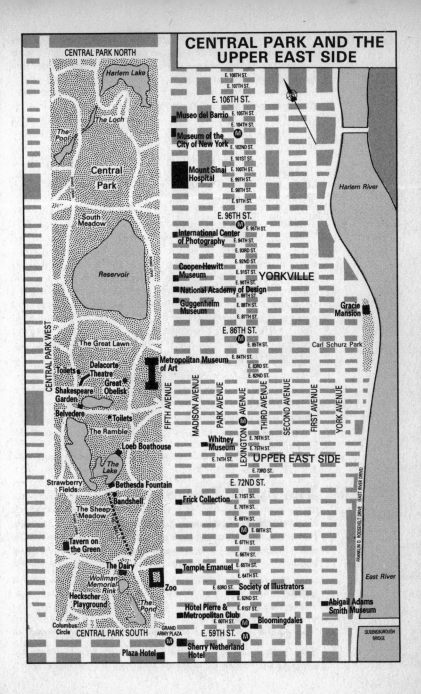

CENTRAL PARK AND THE UPPER EAST SIDE

CENTRAL PARK NORTH

Harlem Lake

The Loch

The Pool

Central Park

South Meadow

Reservoir

The Great Lawn

Delacorte Theatre

Great Obelisk

Shakespeare Garden

Belvedere

Toilets

The Ramble

Loeb Boathouse

The Lake

Strawberry Fields

Bethesda Fountain

Bandshell

The Sheep Meadow

Tavern on the Green

The Dairy

Wollman Memorial Rink

Heckscher Playground

The Pond

Columbus Circle

CENTRAL PARK SOUTH

GRAND ARMY PLAZA

Plaza Hotel

Toilets

CENTRAL PARK WEST

E. 108TH ST.
E. 107TH ST.
E. 106TH ST.
E. 105TH ST.

Museo del Barrio

E. 104TH ST.

Museum of the City of New York

E. 102ND ST.
E. 101ST ST.
E. 100TH ST.

Mount Sinai Hospital

E. 99TH ST.
E. 98TH ST.
E. 97TH ST.

E. 96TH ST.
E. 95TH ST.

International Center of Photography

E. 94TH ST.
E. 93RD ST.
E. 92ND ST.

Cooper-Hewitt Museum

E. 91ST ST.
E. 90TH ST.

National Academy of Design

E. 89TH ST.

Guggenheim Museum

E. 88TH ST.
E. 87TH ST.

E. 86TH ST.
E. 85TH ST.
E. 84TH ST.

Metropolitan Museum of Art

E. 83RD ST.
E. 82ND ST.

FIFTH AVENUE

MADISON AVENUE

PARK AVENUE

LEXINGTON AVENUE

THIRD AVENUE

SECOND AVENUE

FIRST AVENUE

YORK AVENUE

YORKVILLE

Harlem River

Gracie Mansion

Carl Schurz Park

Whitney Museum

E. 76TH ST.
E. 75TH ST.
E. 74TH ST.
E. 73RD ST.

UPPER EAST SIDE

E. 72ND ST.

Frick Collection

E. 71ST ST.
E. 70TH ST.
E. 69TH ST.
E. 68TH ST.
E. 67TH ST.
E. 66TH ST.
E. 65TH ST.

Temple Emanuel

E. 64TH ST.
E. 63RD ST.

Society of Illustrators

E. 62ND ST.
E. 61ST ST.

Hotel Pierre & Metropolitan Club

E. 60TH ST.

Bloomingdales

E. 59TH ST.

Sherry Netherland Hotel

Abigail Adams Smith Museum

East River

FRANKLIN D. ROOSEVELT DRIVE (EAST RIVER DRIVE)

QUEENSBOROUGH BRIDGE

of an ecstatic-looking Robert Burns and a pensive Walter Scott, to the **Bandshell**, and, beyond that, to the terrace and sculpted birds and animals of the **Bethesda Fountain**. To your left, **Cherry Hill Fountain** provided a turnaround point for carriages, and has deliberately excellent views of the **Lake**, which sprawls a gnarled finger from here across the heart of Central Park. **Strawberry Fields** is just west of here, opposite the home of Yoko Ono in the Dakota Building on Central Park West. This is nothing special in itself, but is invariably crowded with those here to remember John Lennon (see p.148).

To go out on the lake, **hire a boat** from the **Loeb Boathouse** on the eastern bank (April–Oct daily 9am–5pm; $20 deposit, $10 per hour); or cross the water by the elegant cast-iron **Bow Bridge** and delve into the wild woods of **The Ramble**. Take care, though, as The Ramble provides notorious cover for muggers and rapists. On the other side, **Belvedere Castle** is a mock medieval citadel recently renovated, giving views over the northern half of the park and mounting small exhibitions. Just below, the **Shakespeare Garden** holds, they say, every species of plant or flower mentioned in the Bard's plays, and the **Delacorte Theater** is venue for the annual *Shakespeare in the Park* festival. Across the **Great Lawn** stand **Cleopatra's Needle** (from the Heliopolis in Egypt and 3000 years old) and the **Metropolitan Museum** (see Chapter 6, *Museums and Galleries*). Otherwise there's little beyond here – only the reservoir and, in the park's most northerly reaches, the **Conservatory Garden**. If you're planning on walking all the way to Harlem, this is a possible route.

Monthly Park Information ☎860-1809

Daily Park Information ☎794-6564

Urban Park Rangers ☎427-4040 (activities information); ☎860-1351 (emergencies)

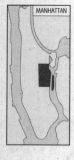

The Upper East Side

A two-square-mile grid, scored with the great avenues of Madison, Park and Lexington, the **Upper East Side**'s defining characteristic is wealth – as you'll at once appreciate if you've seen one of the many Woody Allen movies set here. It's the **west** of this area that sets this tone; **east** of Lexington Avenue was until recently a working-class district of modest houses, though not surprisingly gentrification is quickly changing its character.

The west East Side – Fifth and Madison avenues

Fifth Avenue has been the haughty patrician face of Manhattan since the opening of Central Park attracted the Carnegies, Astors

and Whitneys to migrate north and build fashionable residences on
the strip alongside. Gazing out over the park, most went up when
neoclassicism was the rage, and hence the original buildings – those
that survive – are cluttered with columns and Classical statues. A
great deal of what you see, though, is third or fourth generation
building: through the latter part of the nineteenth century, fanciful
mansions would be built at vast expense, to last only ten or fifteen
years before being demolished for even wilder extravagances.
Rocketing land values made the chance of selling at vast profit
irresistible.

Grand Army Plaza is the introduction to all this, an oval at the
junction of Central Park South and Fifth Avenue that marks the division between Fifth as a shopping district and residential boulevard.
It's one of the city's most dramatic open spaces, flanked by the
extended chateau of the Plaza Hotel, with the darkened swoop of
the Solow Building behind. Across the plaza, no one has a good
word to say for the General Motors Building or its sunken fore-
court, especially since a much-admired hotel, the Savoy, was demolished to make way for it a few years back. Two more hotels, the
high-necked Sherry Netherland and Pierre, luxuriate nearby,
mocked by the size of General Motors' marble-clad monolith. Many
of the rooms here have permanent guests – and they're not on
welfare.

When J.P. Morgan and his pals arrived on the social scene in
the 1890s, established society cocked a snook at the "new money"
by closing its downtown clubs on Morgan and anyone else it considered infra dig. Morgan's response was the time-honoured all-
American one: he commissioned Stanford White to design him his
own club, bigger, better and grander than all the rest – and so the
Metropolitan Club at 1 East 60th Street was born, an exuberant
confection with a marvellously over-the-top gateway. Just the thing
for arriving robber barons. On the corner of 65th Street America's
largest reform synagogue, the Temple Emanuel, strikes a more
sober aspect, a brooding Romanesque-Byzantine cavern that
manages to be bigger inside than it seems out. The interior melts
away into mysterious darkness, making you feel very small indeed.

East 65th and most streets of the East 60s are typical Upper
East Side, a trim mix of small apartment houses which, not as valuable or coveted as the mansions on the avenues, escaped demolition
as land prices escalated. Even so they've always been salubrious
places to live: 45–49 East 65th was commissioned by Sara Delano
Roosevelt as a handy townhouse for her son Franklin, no. 142
belonged to Richard Nixon, and no. 115 is the US headquarters of
the PLO. Quite a neighbourhood.

Museum Mile and beyond
Fifth Avenue's wall continues with Henry Clay Frick's house at 70th
Street, marginally less ostentatious than its neighbours and now the

tranquil home of the **Frick Collection**, one of the city's musts. This
is the first of many prestigious museums that gives this stretch its
name of "Museum Mile". Along the avenue (or just off it) are the
Whitney (modern American art), the **National Academy of Design**,
the **Metropolitan Museum** (New York's British Museum and
National Gallery rolled into one), the **Guggenheim Collection**
(twentieth-century painting housed in Frank Lloyd Wright's helter-
skelter mustard pot), the **Cooper-Hewitt Museum of Design**, the
International Center of Photography and, pushing further north,
the **Museum of the City of New York**. Enough to be going on with
for a week at least; for listings see Chapter 6.

Take away Fifth Avenue's museums and a resplendent though
fairly bloodless strip remains. **Madison Avenue**, especially above
62nd Street, is totally different, lined with top-notch designer
clothes shops whose doors are kept locked, with security cameras
to check you over before entry. **Park Avenue** is less developed and
less extravagant yet still as stolidly comfortable – medium-rise
apartment blocks in anonymous dark brick with a little ornament at
ground level to prove the worth of their owners. The occasional
building stands out, like the self-glorifying **Colonial Club** at 62nd
Street, but the best feature is the view as Park Avenue coasts down
to the New York Central and Pan Am buildings. Another landmark is
the **Seventh Regiment Armory** between 66th and 67th streets, a
Lego fortress bedecked with fairy-tale crenellations – yet just a little
sinister all the same. It's the venue for a winter antiques fair each
January, a good opportunity to gawp at the enormous drill hall
inside, one that drew complaints from the locals not so long ago
when it was used as a temporary shelter for the homeless.

The eastern East Side: Yorkville

Lexington Avenue is Madison without the class, firmly **eastern
East Side**. As the west became richer, property developers rushed
to slick up real estate in the east, seldom with total success.
Subsequently, apartment blocks have been repartitioned to cater to
the growing demand for single accommodation. Much of the East
60s and 70s now house lone, young, upwardly mobile professionals
wanting to play it safe with a conservatively modish address, as the
number of singles bars on Second and Third avenues gives away.

Yorkville

It's left to **Yorkville**, a German-Hungarian neighbourhood that spills
out from 77th to 96th streets between Lexington and the East River,
to try and supply character. Much of New York's German community arrived after the failed revolution of 1848–9, to be quickly
assimilated into the area around Tompkins Square before the opening of the Elevated Railway forced a move uptown in the 1870s. The
community here is greatly depleted, but the four- or five-block

stretch south of 86th Street still has traditional German delicatessens like **Schaller and Weber** (1654 Second Avenue between 84th
and 85th streets) or **Bremen House** (218–220 East 86th between
Second and Third avenues). Try also the baroque cakes and pastries
at **Café Geiger** (206 East 86th) or a meal at **Ideal** (238 East 82nd
between Second and Third avenues).

86th Street runs into a park named after **Carl Schurz**, a German
immigrant who rose to fame as Secretary of the Interior under
President John Quincy Adams and as editor of *Harper's Weekly*.
It's a model park, a breathing space for elderly German speakers
and East Siders escaping their postage-stamp apartments. The FDR
Drive cuts beneath, giving uninterrupted views across the river to
Queens and the confluence of dangerous currents where the Harlem
River, Long Island Sound and Harbour meet – not for nothing
known as **Hell Gate**.

One of the reasons Schurz Park lacks the all-too-usual park
weirdos is the high-profile security that surrounds **Gracie Mansion**
at 88th Street nearby. Roughly contemporary with the Morris-Jumel
Mansion (see "Washington Heights", p.160), it has been much cut
about over the years to end up as the official residence of the mayor
of New York City – though "mansion" is a bit overblown for what is
a rather cramped clapboard cottage. The mansion is open for walk-
round **tours**, usually on Wednesday, though you need to book in
advance (☎570-4751).

Across from the park and just below Gracie Mansion is
Henderson Place, a set of old servants' quarters now transformed
into luxury cottages. Built in 1882 by John Henderson, a fur
importer and real estate developer, the small Queen Anne-style
wooden and brick dwellings were constructed to provide close and
convenient housing for servants working in the palatial old East End
Avenue mansions, most of which have now been torn down. The
servants' quarters now represent some of the most sought-after real
estate in the city, offering the space, quiet and privacy that much of
the city's housing lacks.

North of 86th Street, the mood begins to change rapidly as the
bright turquoise facade of the diagonal housing projects on 97th and
First signal the change as the streets become busier with the
offshoots of **El Barrio**, the best-known part of New York's ever-
expanding Latino community. Further west, the elevated tracks of
the #4, #5 and #6 Bronx-bound trains surface at Park and 96th,
signalling the end of Park Avenue's old money dominance, while
both Madison and Fifth retain their grandeur for only a few blocks
more.

The streets south of Yorkville are again residential, mostly high-
rise apartment blocks of zero interest, in the main with little to lure
you. On the southern perimeter, **Bloomingdale's** at 59th and Third
is the celebrated, definitive American store for clothes and accessories, skilfully aiming its wares at the stylish and affluent (see

Chapter 14, *Shops and Markets*). And nearby, at 421 East 61st Street between York and First Avenue, is the **Abigail Adams Smith Museum** (Mon–Fri noon–4pm, Sun 1–5pm; $2), another of those eighteenth-century buildings that managed to survive by the skin of its teeth. This wasn't the actual home of Abigail Adams, daughter of President John Quincy Adams, just its stables, restored with Federal-period propriety by the Colonial Dames of America as the dwelling house it became. In late years the Smith family fell on hard times, and there are interesting knick-knacks from that era, including the simple dress poor Abigail had to make for herself. The contents are more engaging than the house itself and there's an odd sort of pull if you're lucky enough to be guided around by a chattily urbane Colonial Dame.

The house is hemmed in by decidedly unhistoric buildings and overlooked by the **Queensboro Bridge**, which may stir memories as the 59th Street bridge of Simon and Garfunkel's *Feeling Groovy* or from the title credits of TV's *Taxi*. An intense profusion of clanging steelwork, it's utterly unlike the suspension bridges that elsewhere lace Manhattan to the boroughs; "My God, it's a blacksmith's shop!" was architect Henry Hornbostel's comment when he first saw the finished item in 1909.

Roosevelt Island

To get a view of the bridge, best way over is on the **aerial tramway** that connects with **Roosevelt Island** across the water. For a $1.40 token the trip is worth it in itself – and if you feel like exploring, Roosevelt Island rewards with some imaginative housing and eerie views. On paper this should long have been an ideal residential spot, but its history as "Welfare Island", a gloomy quarantine block of jail, poorhouse, lunatic asylum and smallpox hospital, for years put it out of bounds to Manhattanites. The stigma only started to disappear in the 1970s when Johnson and Burgee's masterplan spawned the Eastview, Westwood, Island House and Rivercross housing areas. The grim ruins remain – the octagonal **tower** at the island's north end is the insane asylum (it briefly housed Mae West after an unpalatably lewd performance in 1927) and to the south the **Smallpox Hospital** stands as a ghostly Gothic shell; currently both are off limits awaiting restoration. Roosevelt Island seems far away from New York City, a sort of post-Manhattan purgatory before the borough of Queens. Crossing back over the bridge gives a spine-tingling panorama of the city, the one Nick Carraway described in F. Scott Fitzgerald's *The Great Gatsby*:

> *Over the great bridge, with the sunlight through the girders making a constant flicker upon the moving cars, with the city rising up across the river in white heaps and sugar lumps all built with a wish out of non-olfactory money. The city seen from the Queensboro Bridge is always the city seen for the*

first time, in its wild promise of all the mystery and the
beauty in the world . . . "Anything can happen now that we've
slid over this bridge" I thought; "anything at all . . .".

The Upper
East Side

The Upper West Side and Morningside Heights

North of 59th Street, paralleling the spread of Central Park,
midtown Manhattan's tawdry west side becomes decidedly less
commercial, less showy and, after the Lincoln Center, fades into a
residential area of mixed and multiple charms. This is the **Upper
West Side**, these days one of the city's most desirable addresses,
though unlike its counterpart to the east of the park a neighbourhood whose typical resident would be hard to pin down. The Upper
West Side is an odd mixture of districts and faces: there's no short-
age of money, as one glance at the statuesque apartment blocks of
Central Park West will testify, but this exists alongside slum areas
that, while they have been pushed north, have been little affected by
any shifts in status.

First some **orientation**. The Upper West Side proper stretches
west from Central Park as far as the Hudson River, and north from
the bottom end of the park to Columbia University and Morningside
Heights. Its main artery is Broadway, and generally speaking the
further you get away from here, to the east or west, the wealthier
things become, until you reach either Central Park West or
Riverside Drive. Sandwiched between these most prestigious of
Manhattan addresses are enclaves of public housing, SRO hotels
and downbeat street hustle that increase the further north you go,
until, on Amsterdam Avenue and Columbus Avenue in the 100s
(streets that in the blocks around the 70s have become irreparably
yuppified), you're walking through solid and very poor Latino neighbourhoods. These different lifestyles and incomes do co-exist – and
for the most part happily. Give it a few years though, a handful
more gourmet grocers, Japanese restaurants, sidewalk cafés, book
and antique stores, and the Upper West Side may look quite
different.

To explore, best start at **Columbus Circle**, an odd cast of buildings grouped around a roundabout at the Central Park's southwest
corner. Christopher Columbus stands uncomfortably atop a column
in the centre, and at the southern end, the city's Department of
Cultural Affairs has recently found a home in a structure which,
when it went up in 1965, was said to resemble a Persian brothel.
From here the **NY Conventions and Visitors Bureau** gives advice
and dispenses free leaflets, city, bus and subway maps seven days a
week (Mon–Fri 9am–6pm, weekends 10am–6pm), while upstairs is
venue for exhibitions of local and community art.

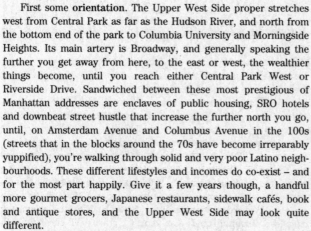

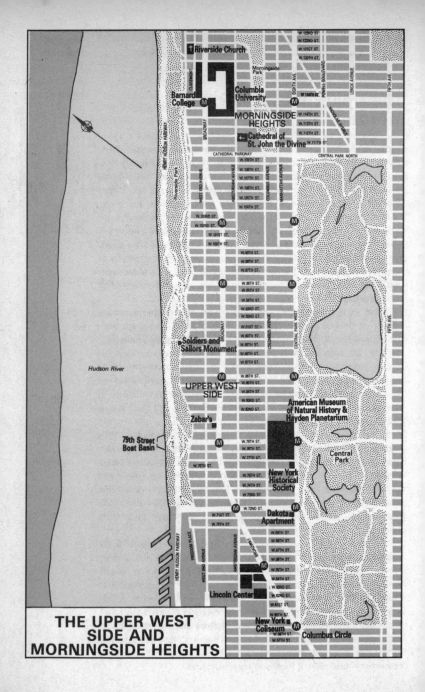

Riverside Church

Morningside Park

Columbia University

Barnard College

MORNINGSIDE HEIGHTS

Cathedral of St. John the Divine

CENTRAL PARK NORTH

CATHEDRAL PARKWAY

W.109TH ST.
W.108TH ST.
W.107TH ST.
W.106TH ST.
W.105TH ST.
W.104TH ST.

W.103RD ST.
W.102ND ST.
W.101ST ST.
W.100TH ST.

W.99TH ST.
W.98TH ST.
W.97TH ST.
W.96TH ST.
W.95TH ST.
W.94TH ST.
W.93RD ST.
W.92ND ST.
W.91ST ST.
W.90TH ST.
W.89TH ST.
W.88TH ST.
W.87TH ST.
W.86TH ST.
W.85TH ST.
W.84TH ST.
W.83RD ST.
W.82ND ST.

Soldiers and Sailors Monument

UPPER WEST SIDE

American Museum of Natural History & Hayden Planetarium

Central Park

Hudson River

Zabar's

79th Street Boat Basin

W.79TH ST.
W.78TH ST.
W.77TH ST.
W.76TH ST.
W.75TH ST.
W.74TH ST.
W.73RD ST.

New York Historical Society

W.72ND ST.
W.71ST ST.
W.70TH ST.

Dakota Apartment

W.69TH ST.
W.68TH ST.
W.67TH ST.
W.66TH ST.
W.65TH ST.
W.64TH ST.
W.63RD ST.
W.62ND ST.
W.61ST ST.

Lincoln Center

New York Coliseum

W.60TH ST.
W.59TH ST.
W.58TH ST.
W.57TH ST.

Columbus Circle

W.123RD ST.
W.122ND ST.
W.121ST ST.
W.120TH ST.

LENOX AVENUE

FIFTH AVENUE

W.116TH ST.

W.114TH ST.
W.113TH ST.
W.112TH ST.
W.111TH ST.

EIGHTH AVE.

POWELL BOULEVARD

MANIDA AVENUE

AMSTERDAM AVENUE

COLUMBUS AVENUE

MANHATTAN AVENUE

CENTRAL PARK WEST

BROADWAY

WEST 3RD AVENUE

Riverside Park

CLAREMONT

EAST HUDSON PARKWAY

HENRY HUDSON PARKWAY

FREEDOM PLACE

WEST END AVENUE

AMSTERDAM AVENUE

BROADWAY

THE UPPER WEST
SIDE AND
MORNINGSIDE HEIGHTS

Lincoln Center

Broadway sheers north from the circle to **Lincoln Plaza** and, on the left, the **Lincoln Center for the Performing Arts**, a marble assembly of buildings put up in the early 1960s on the site of some of the city's most rancid slums. Home to the Metropolitan Opera and the New York Philharmonic, as well as a host of other smaller companies, this is worth seeing even if you're not into catching a performance, and the best way to do it is to go on an **organised tour**. These leave roughly every hour on the hour between 10am and 5pm each day, and take in the main part of the Center at a cost of $7.75 for an hour-long tour. Be warned that they can get very booked up; best phone ahead (☎769-7020 or ☎875-5350) to be sure of a place.

The New York State Theater and Avery Fisher Hall

The complex itself pulls you in by way of its neat central plaza and fountain, which focuses on the grand classical forms of the Opera House. Of the three principal halls, Philip Johnson's **New York State Theater** on the left is most imposing, at least inside, its foyer serried with balconies embellished by delicately worked bronze grilles, and with a ceiling finished in gold leaf. Johnson also had a hand in the **Avery Fisher Hall** opposite; he was called in to refashion the interior after its acoustics were found to be below par. The seating space here, though, has none of the magnificence of his glittery horseshoe-shaped auditorium across the way, and the most exciting thing about Avery Fisher Hall is its foyer, dominated by a huge hanging sculpture by Richard Lippold, whose distinctive style you may recognise from an atrium or two downtown.

The Metropolitan Opera House

The **Metropolitan Opera House** (aka "the Met") is by contrast overdone, its staircases designed for the gliding evening wear of the city's élite. Behind each of the high windows hang **murals** by Marc Chagall. The artist wanted stained glass, but it was felt these wouldn't last long in an area still less than reverential towards the arts, so paintings were hung behind square-paned glass to give a similar effect. These days they're covered for part of the day to protect them from the morning sun; the rest of the time they're best viewed from the plaza outside. The left-hand one, *Le Triomphe de la Musique*, is cast with a variety of well-known performers, landmarks snipped from the New York skyline and a portrait of Sir Rudolph Bing, the man who ran the Met for more than three decades – here garbed as a gypsy. The other mural, *Les Sources de la Musique*, is reminiscent of Chagall's renowned Met production of *The Magic Flute*: the god of music strums a lyre while a Tree of Life, Verdi and Wagner all float down the Hudson River. As for performances, you'll find full details of what you can listen to and how to do it in Chapter 10, *The Performing Arts and Film*.

The rest...

Each side of the Met broadens into two further piazzas, one centring on the **Guggenheim Bowl** where you can catch free summer lunch-time concerts, the other faced by the **Vivian Beaumont** and the **Mitzi E. Newhouse Theaters**. This latter square is mostly taken up by a pool, around which Manhattan office workers munch their lunch: while mid-pond reclines a lazy Henry Moore figure, given counter-point at the edge by a spidery sculpture by Alexander Calder.

Whatever people say about the whys and wherefores of Lincoln Center, there can be little doubt of its impact on an area which before the 1960s was one of the city's most pitiful urban disasters. (It was here that the film of *West Side Story* was shot in 1960.) As well as creating an arts centre, the Lincoln scheme was an exercise in urban renewal, a grand plan intended to make this part of the Upper West Side a truly desirable neighbourhood – which has succeeded remarkably well, even if in typical New York style it has in effect replaced a poor ghetto with a rich one and dumped the slum dwellers further uptown. Up from Lincoln Plaza roads lead all ways, Broadway curving off north and Ninth Avenue becoming the increasingly sought-after **Columbus Avenue**. Not so long ago this too was run-down; now its shops are being upgraded and its restaurants – and there are plenty, especially between the 60s and 80s – battle it out for the upwardly mobile custom of the local residents.

Central Park West – and John Lennon

A block east from Columbus Avenue, however, has always been well off – and as long as the monumental apartment blocks that line **Central Park West** continue to stand the area will remain so. Stroll down West 67th Street past the **Hotel des Artistes**, one-time Manhattan address of the likes of Noel Coward, Isadora Duncan and Alexander Woollcott, and do a left, following Central Park West as far as the junction of 72nd Street. More huge apartment blocks loom here, first the **Majestic**, yellow-brick and rectangular and topped with commanding twin towers; then, more famously, the **Dakota Building**, a grandiose German Renaissance-style mansion built in the late nineteenth century to persuade wealthy New Yorkers that life in an apartment block could be just as luxurious as in a private house. Over the years there have been few residents here not publicly known in some way: big-time tenants included Lauren Bacall and Leonard Bernstein, and not so long ago the build-ing was used as the setting for Polanski's film *Rosemary's Baby*.

The Death of John Lennon

Most people, however, now know the Dakota Building as the former home of **John Lennon** – and (still) of his wife Yoko Ono, who owns a number of the apartments. It was outside the Dakota, on the night of December 8, 1980, that Lennon was murdered – shot by a man who professed to be one of his greatest admirers.

His murderer, Mark David Chapman, had been hanging around outside the building all day, clutching a copy of his hero's latest album, *Double Fantasy*, and accosting Lennon for his autograph – which he got. This was nothing unusual in itself – fans often used to loiter outside and hustle for a glimpse of Lennon – but Chapman was still there when the couple returned from a late-night recording session, and pumped five bullets into Lennon as he walked through the Dakota's 72nd Street entrance. Lennon was picked up by the doorman and rushed to hospital in a taxi, but he died on the way from a massive loss of blood. A distraught Yoko issued a statement immediately: "John loved and prayed for the human race. Please do the same for him."

Why Chapman did this to John Lennon no one really knows; suffice to say his obsession with the man had obviously unhinged him. Fans may want to light a stick of incense for Lennon across the road in **Strawberry Fields**, a section of Central Park which has been restored and maintained in his memory through an endowment by Yoko Ono; trees and shrubs were donated by a number of countries as a gesture towards world peace. The gardens are pretty enough, if unspectacular, and it would take a hard-bitten sceptic not to be a little bit moved by the *Imagine* mosaic on the pathway and Yoko's handwritten note inviting passers-by to pay their respects.

Nearby museums

Afterwards, keep on north up Central Park West, past the dull grey Beaux Arts slab of the **New York Historical Society**, which has a permanent museum (see Chapter 6 *Museums and Galleries*), and left by the **American Museum of Natural History**. Said to be the largest museum of any kind in the world, this fills four blocks with its bulk, a strange architectural mélange of heavy neoclassical and rustic Romanesque styles, that was built in several stages, the first by Calvert Vaux and Jacob Wrey Mould in 1872. For a full account of the museum and its exhibits, see Chapter 6, *Museums and Galleries*.

West to the Hudson

South of here West 72nd Street leads west to Broadway, where several streets meet in a busy, hustly riot of fast-food joints and downgrade bars. This is officially named **Verdi Square**; unofficially, and rather more accurately, it's known as Needle Park (as in the movie "Panic in . . ."), some say after the thin strip of gardens, others, less naively, because of its former function as a smack users' playground.

A short walk further west brings you down to the Hudson River and West Side Highway, where you can see the old **Penn Railroad**

Yards, abandoned for close on two decades, though now earmarked for a new luxury housing project. Local residents, scared of yet another new influx of people into an already crowded and increasingly gentrified neighbourhood, whipped up a storm of protest over this, but the plan currently looks set to go ahead regardless. North from here, weaving its way up the western fringe of Manhattan island is **Riverside Drive**, the Upper West Side's second best address after Central Park West and flanked by palatial townhouses and multi-storey apartment blocks put up in the early part of this century by those not quite rich enough to compete with the folks down on Fifth Avenue. **Riverside Park**, following for fifty blocks or so, provides a gentle break before the traffic hum of the Henry Hudson Parkway, landscaped in 1873 by Frederick Olmsted of Central Park fame.

A few blocks away, through the park and down the steps under the road, is a place few people know about: the **79th Street Boat Basin**, where a couple of hundred Manhattanites live on the water. It's one of the city's most peaceful locations, and while the views across to New Jersey aren't exactly awesome, they're a tonic after the congestion of Manhattan proper. Across the canyon of West End Avenue, turn left at the junction of Broadway and 79th Street. Crossing 80th Street, the first thing you notice is another area landmark, **Zabar's** – the Upper West Side's principal and best gourmet shop. Here you can find more or less anything connected with food, the ground floor given over to things edible, the first to cooking implements and kitchenware, a collection which, in the obscurity of some of its items, must be unrivalled anywhere. What yuppie kitchen, for example, could do without a duck press?

The northern reaches

To the north, the Upper West Side gets rapidly more seedy, merging into poor black and Latino neighbourhoods where people hang out listlessly on street corners, hassling for small change. The transformation is sudden, but like so many districts of New York it's not entirely complete, and even here stately apartment blocks rub shoulders with SRO hotels, and always the spiky towers of the luxury **Eldorado Building** on Central Park West peak tantalisingly over the skyline.

The Cathedral Church of St John the Divine

A little further up, the **Cathedral Church of St John the Divine** rises out of the burned-out tenements, dumped cars and hustlers of the southern fringes of Harlem with a sure, solid kind of majesty – far from finished but already one of New York's main tourist hotspots, and on the itinerary of a steady stream of coach parties throughout the season. The church was begun in 1892, to a Romanesque design that with a change of architect became French

Gothic. Work progressed quickly but stopped with the outbreak of war in 1939 and has only resumed recently, fraught with funding difficulties and hard questioning by people who consider that, in such an impoverished area of the city, the money might be better spent on something of more obvious benefit. That said, St John's is very much a community church, housing a soup kitchen and shelter for the homeless, studios for graphics and sculpture, a gymnasium, and (still to be built under the choir) an amphitheatre for the production of drama and concerts. And the building work itself is being undertaken by local blacks trained by English stonemasons. Progress is long and slow: still only two-thirds of the cathedral is finished, and completion isn't due until around 2050 – even assuming it goes on uninterrupted. But if this happens it will be the largest cathedral structure in the world, its floor space – at 600 feet long and at the transepts 320 feet wide – big enough to swallow both the cathedrals of Notre Dame and Chartres whole, or, as tour guides are at pains to point out, two full-size American football fields.

Walking the length of the nave, these figures seem much more than just another piece of American braggery. Though the cathedral appears a lot more finished here, it's not until you reach the crossing, where the naked stone has still to be encased in the milk-white marble of the choir, that you realise how far it is from completion. Here too you can see the welding of the two styles, particularly in the choir which rises from a heavy arcade of Romanesque columns to high, light Gothic vaulting, the dome of the crossing to be replaced by a tall and delicate Gothic spire. For some idea of how the cathedral as a whole will look, glance in on the gift shop, housed, for the moment, in the north transept, where there's a scale model of the projected design. Afterwards, take a stroll out into the cathedral yard and workshop, in which you can watch Harlem's apprentice masons tapping away at the stone blocks of the future – and finished – cathedral.

Columbia University and Morningside Heights

West out of the church towards Broadway is fringed by cheap restaurants, bars and secondhand bookshops. No. 2911, between 113th and 114th streets, is the **West End Café**, hang-out of Kerouac, Ginsberg and the Beats in the 1950s; "one of those nondescript places," wrote Joyce Johnson, "before the era of white walls and potted ferns and imitation Tiffany lamps, that for some reason always made the best hangouts." It's little changed, and still serves the student crowd from the nearby university.

Columbia University and around
Columbia University, whose campus fills seven blocks between Amsterdam and Broadway, is one of the most prestigious academic institutions in the country, ranking with the other Ivy League

colleges of the northeast and boasting a set of precincts laid out by McKim, Mead and White in grand Beaux Arts style. Of the buildings, the domed and colonnaded Low Memorial Library stands centre-stage at the top of a wide flight of stone steps, focus for demos during the Vietnam war. Guided **tours** leave regularly Monday to Friday from the information office on the corner of 116th Street and Broadway. For sustenance and great views of Manhattan, eat in the restaurant on the top floor of the Butler Library.

Across the road **Barnard College** is no less pastoral in feel, but was until relatively recently, when Columbia removed their men-only policy, the place where women had to study for their degrees. Just beyond, **Riverside Church** has a graceful French Gothic Revival tower, loosely modelled on Chartres and like St John's turned over to a mixture of community centre and administrative activities for the surrounding parish. Take the lift to the 20th floor and ascend the steps around the carillon for some classic spreads of Manhattan's jaggy skyline, New Jersey and the hills beyond – and the rest of the city well into the Bronx and Queens. Take a look too at the church, whose open and restrained interior (apart from the apse, which is positively sticky with Gothic ornament) is in stark contrast to the darkened mystery of St John the Divine.

Around the corner from the church is **Grant's Tomb**, a grubby, Greek-style memorial plastered with graffiti and surrounded by bizarre, reptilian, mosaic-covered benches. The Grant in question is General Ulysses S., Yankee Civil War hero and miserable failure as US President in the latter years of the nineteenth century. Perhaps not surprisingly, this memorial concentrates on the general's military successes rather than his term in the White House, the sarcophagi holding the general and his wife grandiosely based on that of Napoleon in Paris.

This area is known as **Morningside Heights**, buffer zone for Harlem sprawling forbiddingly below, and with an academic, almost provincial air lent by its abundance of colleges and some swanky properties on Riverside and Morningside drives. **Morningside Park** was landscaped in 1887 by Frederick Olmsted, but it's never been especially appealing and is today a refuge of muggers and the dispossessed. If it's light it's quite feasible to walk north into Harlem; after dark you'd best turn south for the downtown crowds.

Harlem, Hamilton Heights and the North

Harlem is the side of Manhattan that few visitors bother to see. Home of a declined and still declining black community, its name is synonymous with racial tension and urban decay, languishing under the bad reputation gained from riots of the 1940s, 1950s and 1960s. Yet Harlem is more a focus of black consciousness and

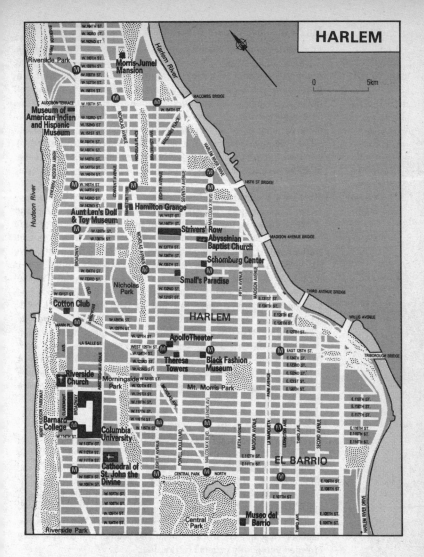

HARLEM

0   5km

Riverside Park

Morris-Jumel
Mansion

Harlem River

MACOMBS BRIDGE

Museum of
American Indian
and Hispanic
Museum

AUDOBON TERRACE

W. 156TH ST.

W. 154TH ST.

145TH ST BRIDGE

Hudson River

Aunt Len's Doll
& Toy Museum

Hamilton Grange

Strivers' Row

MADISON AVENUE BRIDGE

Abyssinian
Baptist Church

Schomburg Center

Nicholas
Park

Small's Paradise

THIRD AVENUE BRIDGE

WILLIS AVENUE

HARLEM

Cotton Club

ApolloTheater

EAST 125TH ST.

TRIBOROUGH BRIDGE

Riverside
Church

Theresa
Towers

Black Fashion
Museum

Morningside
Park

Mt. Morris Park

Barnard
College

Columbia
University

EL BARRIO

Cathedral of
St. John the
Divine

CENTRAL PARK   NORTH

Central
Park

Museo del
Barrio

HARLEM RIVER DRIVE

Riverside Park

culture than out-and-out ghetto. And, perhaps because of its near-
total lack of support from federal and municipal funds (one example
– there is no public high school here, the kids have to be shipped
out), Harlem has formed a self-reliant and inward-looking community. For many downtown Manhattanites, white and black, 125th
Street is a physical and mental border not willingly crossed: but to
understand New York, its problems and its strengths, it is necessary
to understand – and explore – Harlem.

Harlem – hints and history

Practically speaking, Harlem's **sights** are too spread out to amble between. You'll do best to make several trips, preferably using one of the **guided tours** available (see "Information, Maps and Tours" in *Basics*) to get acquainted with the area. Harlem's **problems** of poverty, unemployment and attendant crime mean that foreign visitors, especially whites, can be soft targets for trouble. Though it's unlikely you'll be in any danger during the daytime, 125th Street, 145th Street, Convent and Lenox avenues (Malcolm X. Boulevard) and East 116th Street in Spanish Harlem are the places you're *least* likely be hassled – at night stick to the clubs only.

*Lenox Avenue
has been
officially
renamed
Malcolm X.
Boulevard –
but it's still
known by the
old name.*

Harlem's beginnings

As the name suggests, it was the Dutch who founded the settlement of Nieuw Haarlem, naming it after a town in Holland. Until the mid-nineteenth century this was farmland, but when the New York and Harlem railroad linked the area with Lower Manhattan it attracted the richer immigrant families (mainly German Jews from the Lower East Side) to build elegant and fashionable brownstones in the steadily developing suburb. When work began on the IRT Lenox line later in the century, property speculators were quick to build good-quality homes in the expectation of seeing Harlem repeat the success of the Upper West Side. They were too quick and too ambitious, for by the time the IRT line opened most of the buildings were still empty, their would-be takers uneasy at moving so far north. A black real estate agent saw his chance, bought the empty houses cheaply and rented them to blacks from the run-down, midtown districts.

The black community

Very quickly Harlem became black, while remaining home to a mix of cultural and social communities: the western areas along **Convent Avenue** and **Sugar Hill** were for years the patch of the middle classes, and preserve traces of a well-to-do past. In the east the bulge between Park Avenue and the East River became **Spanish Harlem**, now largely peopled by Puerto Ricans and more properly called El Barrio – "the Neighbourhood". In between live the descendants of West Indian, African, Cuban and Haitian immigrants, often crowded into poorly maintained housing.

This cramping together of dissimilar cultures has long caused tensions and problems not easily understood by downtown bureaucracy. Dotted around Harlem are buildings and projects that attest to an uneasy municipal conscience, which have not in any real sense solved the problems of unemployment and urban decay. Sometimes, amid the boarded-up shopfronts and vacant lots, it's hard to believe you're but a mile or two away from the cosily patrician Upper East Side.

The 1920s and 1930s

But there was a brief period when Harlem enjoyed a golden age. In the 1920s whites began to notice the explosion of black culture that had occurred here: jazz musicians like Duke Ellington, Count Basie and Cab Calloway played in nightspots like the Cotton Club, Savoy Ballroom, Apollo Theater and Small's Paradise; the drink flowed as if prohibition had never been heard of and the sophisticated set drove up to Harlem's speakeasies after downtown had gone to bed. Maybe because these revellers never stayed longer than the last drink, they and history seldom recall the poverty then rife in Harlem, the harshness of scraping a living even before the Depression finally put paid to the revels of the few and decline drove middle-class blacks out of Harlem. One of the most evocative voices heard in the clubs those days was of Ethel Waters, who sang in the Sugar Cane Club:

> *Rent man waitin' for his forty dollars,*
> *Ain't got me but a dime and some bad news.*
> *Bartender give me a bracer, double beer chaser,*
> *Cause I got the low-down, mean, rent man blues.*

Harlem today

And today? As midtown real estate prices continue to rocket, new interest is being shown in sprucing up Harlem's residential dereliction. Unlike in many "ghettos", the basic quality of the nineteenth-century houses here is excellent and ripe for renovation: what unsettles black activists is that 65 percent of the property in Harlem is owned by the City of New York, which assumed control after houses were abandoned by their owners. Mindful of historical precedent the downtown developers are viewed with suspicion, and renovation is seen as a chance to attract young middle-class whites to the area and so signal the end of a black community that has won strength through long adversity. Others think that the arrival of whites would be a trickle at most, given the expense of renovation; and that integration in itself would be no bad thing. For Harlem, the future remains undecided . . ..

Around Harlem

125th Street between Broadway and Fifth Avenue is the working centre of Harlem, a flattened, shell-shocked expanse spiked with the occasional skyscraper. The subway throws you up here and the **New York State Office Building** on the corner of Seventh Avenue provides a looming modern landmark: commissioned after the last serious riots in 1968, it was intended to show the state's commitment to the support of the community, though really it's an intrusion on the earthy goings-on of 125th Street. Walk a little west from here and you reach the **Apollo Theater** at no. 253. Not much from the outside, it was right into the 1960s the centre of black entertainment in New York City and northeastern America: almost all the great figures of jazz and blues played here along with singers, comedians and dancers. Since then it's served as a warehouse, movie theatre and radio station, and in its latest incarnation is the venue for a weekly TV show, "Late Night at the Apollo". Across the way at 125th and Seventh Avenue the Theresa Towers office block was until the 1960s the **Theresa Hotel**. Fidel Castro was once a guest here, shunning midtown luxury in a popular political gesture.

125th Street rolls energetically eastwards: turn right at Lenox Avenue (officially named Malcolm X. Boulevard, though known locally by both names) and you enter the **Mount Morris Park Historical District** and at 201 Lenox the **Mount Oliphet Church**, an American version of a Roman version of what they thought a Greek temple looked like, and one of literally hundreds of religious buildings dotted around Harlem. The sombre, bulky **St Martin's** at the southeast corner of Lenox Avenue and 122nd Street is among them, and both have been fortunate in avoiding falling into decay as church and community declined. Elsewhere the Mount Morris Park Historic District comprises some lovely **row houses** that went up in the speculative boom of the 1890s: take a look at the block on **Lenox Avenue** between 120th and 121st streets or the Romanesque **Mount Morris Park West** for the best. When, a few years back, the city held a lottery to sell a dozen abandoned houses on Mount Morris Park there was an immediate outcry from the local people, who considered one of the prime slices of Harlem was being raffled off to faceless downtown concerns. A compromise was reached that ensured each prospective buyer who lived in Harlem would be entered three times, guaranteeing a 50-50 chance of a win. For these twelve houses, 2500 applications were received – which is hardly surprising. Looking at Mount Morris Park West you can't help but feel that it too will go the way of Greenwich Village and the Lower East Side – the quality of building is so good, the pressures on Manhattan so great, it seems just a matter of time.

The former Mount Morris Park is now **Marcus Garvey Park**, taking its name from the black leader of the 1920s, and altogether a decidedly odd urban space. Craggy peaks block off views, meaning you never get an idea of the square as a unity, and the jutting outcrops contradict the precise lines of the houses around. At the top an elegant octagonal fire tower of 1856 is a unique example of the early warning devices once found throughout the city. Spiral your way to the top for a great view.

Powell Boulevard

Seventh Avenue becomes **Adam Clayton Powell Jr. Boulevard** above 110th Street, a broad sweep pushing north between low-built houses that for once in Manhattan allow the sky to break through. Since its conception Powell Boulevard has been Harlem's main concourse, and it's not difficult to imagine the propriety the shops and side streets had in their late nineteenth-century heyday, though now they're a chain of graffiti-splattered walls and storefronts punctuated with demolished lots. At 135th Street and Powell Boulevard the new **Small's Paradise** is also a reminder of that era, taking its cue from the famous club of the 1920s where monied downtowners, gangsters and bootleggers mingled with Small's dancing waiters to the sounds of jazz. The tradition is kept up in Friday and Saturday night jams and concerts; no cover and no minimum mean you can afford the car service back home – ☎234-6330 for more details of this and who's on. When here during the day it's worth checking out the **Schomburg Center for Research in Black Culture** at 515 Malcolm X. Boulevard at 135th Street (Mon–Wed noon–8pm, Fri–Sat 10am–6pm; ☎491-2200) for its exhibitions on the history of black culture in the US: see Chapter 6, *Museums and Galleries*.

The Reverend Adam Clayton Powell Jr.

A few streets north at 132 West 138th Street is yet another church – though this one, the **Abyssinian Baptist Church**, is special not because it's architecturally interesting, but because of its long-time minister, the **Reverend Adam Clayton Powell Jr.** In the 1930s Powell was instrumental in forcing the mostly white-owned, white-workforce shops and stores of Harlem to begin employing the blacks who ensured their economic survival. Later he became the first black on the city council, then New York's first black representative at Congress – a career which came to an embittered end in 1967, when amid strong rumours of the misuse of public funds he was excluded from Congress by majority vote. This failed to diminish his standing in Harlem, where voters twice re-elected him before his death in 1972. In the church there's a small **museum** to Powell's life, the scandal of course unmentioned, but a more fitting memorial is the boulevard that today bears his name.

Gospel tours and Strivers' Row

The Abyssinian Baptist Church is also famed for its revival-style Sunday morning **services** and a gospel choir of gut-busting vivacity. Usually all are welcome to join in, though it's discreet to phone ahead (☎862-7474). An alternative, and a viable one, is to join the Penny Sightseeing Company's **Harlem Gospel Tour** (Thurs 10am and Sun 10.30am; $17, reservations at least two days in advance from the address in "Information, Maps and Tours" in *Basics*).

These days no one is going to make grandiose claims for Powell Boulevard, but cross over to 138th Street between Powell and Eighth Avenue (aka Frederick Douglass Boulevard) and you're in what many consider the finest, most articulate block of row houses in Manhattan – **Strivers' Row**. Commissioned during the 1890s housing boom, this takes in designs by three sets of architects – the best McKim, Mead and White's north side of 139th, a dignified Renaissance-derived strip that's an amalgam of simplicity and elegance. Within the burgeoning black community of the turn of the century this came to be *the* desirable place for ambitious profession-als to reside – hence its nickname. Maybe it's an indication of Harlem's future that despite the presence of Strivers' Row there's been no knock-on effect on the wasteland all around; if streets like these can't trigger redevelopment, cynics argue, then what can?

El Barrio

From Park Avenue to the East River is Spanish Harlem or **El Barrio**, dipping down as far as East 96th Street to collide head on with the affluence of the Upper East Side. The centre of a large Puerto Rican community, it is quite different from Harlem – the streets are dirtier, the atmosphere more intimidating. El Barrio was originally a working-class Italian neighbourhood (a small pocket of Italian fami-lies survives around 116th Street and First Avenue) and the quality of building here was nowhere as good as that immediately to the west. In the early 1950s the American government offered Puerto Ricans incentives to emigrate to the US under a policy known as "Operation Bootstrap" (so-named in the theory that the scheme would help pull Puerto Rico up "by the straps of its boots" by reduc-ing its overpopulation problem). But the occupants have had little opportunity to evolve Latino culture in any meaningful or noticeable way, and the only space where cultural roots are in evidence is **La Marqueta** on Park Avenue between 111th and 116th Streets, a five-block street market of tropical fruit and veg, sinister-looking meats and much shouting; brush up your Spanish and watch your change. To get some background on the whole scene **El Museo del Barrio** at Fifth Avenue and 104th Street (see Chapter 6, *Museums and Galleries* is a showcase of Latin American art and culture.

Hamilton Heights

The further uptown you venture, the less like New York it seems. Much of Harlem's western edge is taken up by the area known as **Hamilton Heights**, like Morningside Heights to the south a mixed bag of campus, rubbishy streets and slender parks on a bluff above Harlem. Just one stretch, the **Hamilton Heights Historic District** that runs down Convent Avenue to City College, pulls Hamilton Heights up from the ranks of the untidily mediocre. Years ago the black professionals who made it up here and to Sugar Hill a little further north could glance down on lesser Harlemites with disdain: it's still a firmly bourgeois residential area – and one of the most attractive uptown.

But even if this mood of shabbiness around a well-heeled neigh-bourhood is to your liking, there's little in the way of specific sights. The 135th Street St Nicholas subway is as good a place to start as any, for up the hill and round the corner is Convent Avenue, containing the Heights' single historic lure – the house of Alexander Hamilton, **Hamilton Grange**.

Alexander Hamilton

Alexander Hamilton's life is as fascinating as it was flamboyant. An early supporter of the Revolution, his enthusiasm quickly brought him to the attention of George Washington, and he became the general's aide-de-camp, later founding the Bank of New York and becoming first Secretary to the Treasury. Hamilton's headlong tackling of problems made him enemies as well as friends: alienating Republican populists led to a clash with their leader Thomas Jefferson, and when Jefferson won the Presidency in 1801, Hamilton was left out in the political cold. Temporarily abandoning politics, he moved away from the city to his grange here (or rather near here – the house was moved in 1889) to tend his plantation and conduct a memorably sustained and vicious feud with one **Aaron Burr**, who had beaten Hamilton's father-in-law to a seat in the Senate and then set up the Bank of Manhattan as a direct rival to the Bank of New York. After a few years as Vice-President under Jefferson, Burr ran for the governorship of New York; Hamilton strenuously opposed his candidature and after an exchange of extraordinarily bitter letters, the two men fought a duel in Weehawken, New Jersey, roughly where today's Lincoln Tunnel emerges. Hamilton's eldest son had been killed in a duel on the same field a few years earlier, which may explain why, when pistols were drawn, Hamilton honourably discharged his into the air. Burr, evidently made of lesser stuff, aimed carefully and fatally wounded Hamilton. So died "the most restless, impatient, artful, indefatigable and unprincipled intriguer in the United States", as President John Adams described him; you'll find his portrait on the back of a $10 note.

All of which is a lot more exciting than the **house** he lived in at 287 Convent Avenue (at 142nd Street, daily 9am–5pm; free), a Federal-style mansion today uncomfortably transplanted between a fiercely Romanesque church and an apartment block. It's probably only worth dropping in if visiting the wonderful **Aunt Len's Doll and Toy Museum** nearby – for which you'll need an appointment; see Chapter 6, *Museums and Galleries*.

Don't miss Aunt Len's Museum – *it's one of the most enjoyable in town.*

Convent Avenue and City College

If you've just wandered up from Harlem, **Convent Avenue** comes as something of a surprise. Its secluded, blossom-lined streets have a garden suburb prettiness that's spangled with Gothic, French and Italian Renaissance hints in the happily eclectic houses of the 1890s. Running south, the feathery span of the **Shepard Archway** announces **City College**, a rustic-feeling campus of Collegiate Gothic halls built from grey Manhattan schist dug up during the excavations for the IRT subway line and mantled with white terracotta fripperies. Founded in 1905, City College made no charge for tuition, so becoming the seat of higher learning for many of New York's poor, and though free education came to an end in the

1970s, 75 percent of the students still come from minority backgrounds to enjoy a campus that's as warmly intimate as Columbia is
grandiose.

Washington Heights

The change from Convent Avenue to Broadway is almost as abrupt
as it is up from Harlem. Broadway here is a once-smart, now raggy
sweep that slowly rises to the northernmost part of Manhattan
island, **Washington Heights**. Even from Morningside or Hamilton
Heights the haul up is a long one: but the first two good stopoffs are
both easily reached from the #1 train to 157th and Broadway or the
A to 155th or 163rd. **Audubon Terrace** at 155th and Broadway is
an Acropolis in a cul-de-sac, a weird, clumsy nineteenth-century
attempt to deify 155th Street with museums dolled up as Beaux Arts
temples. Easily the best of these is the **Museum of the American
Indian**, but as you might expect from something so far from the
centre of town, it's little known and little visited. For a full account
of each museum, see Chapter 6, *Museums and Galleries*.

The Morris–Jumel Mansion

Within walking distance the **Morris–Jumel Mansion** (160th Street
between Amsterdam and Edgecombe avenues, Tues–Sun 10am–
4pm; $2) is another uptown surprise: cornered in its garden, the
mansion somehow survived the destruction all around, and today is
one of the more successful house museums, its proud Georgian
outlines faced with a later Federal portico. Inside, the mansion's
rooms reveal some of its engaging history: built as a rural retreat in
1765 by Colonel Roger Morris, it was briefly Washington's headquarters before falling into the hands of the British. A leaflet
describes the rooms and their historical connections, but curiously
omits much of the later history. Wealthy wine merchant Stephen
Jumel bought the derelict mansion in 1801 and refurbished it for his
wife Eliza, formerly a prostitute and his mistress. New York society
didn't take to such a past, but when Jumel died in 1832, Eliza still
married ex-Vice President Aaron Burr – she for his connections, he
for her money. Burr was 78 when they married, 20 years older than
Eliza: the marriage lasted for six months before old Burr upped and
left, to die on the day of their divorce. Eliza battled on to the age of
91, and on the top floor of the house you'll find her obituary, a
magnificently fictionalised account of a "scandalous" life.

From most western stretches of Washington Heights you get a
glimpse of the **George Washington Bridge** that links Manhattan to
New Jersey, and it's arguable that the feeder road to the bridge
splits two distinct areas: below is bleakly run-down, the biggest area
of crack-selling in the city, mainly to New Jersey residents making
good use of the bridge; above the streets relax in smaller, more
diverse ethnic neighbourhoods of old-time Jews, Greeks, Central

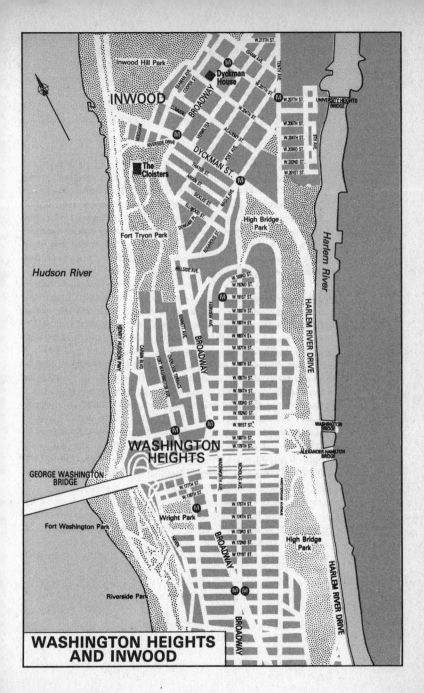

WASHINGTON HEIGHTS
AND INWOOD

Europeans and especially Irish, though a major Latino community has recently built up. A skilful, dazzling sketch high above the Hudson, the bridge skims across the channel in massive metalwork and graceful lines, a natural successor to the Brooklyn Bridge. "Here, finally, steel architecture seems to laugh," said Le Corbusier of the 1931 construction. To appreciate what he meant, grit your teeth and walk – midtown Manhattan hangs like a visible promise in the distance.

The Cloisters Museum and Inwood

What most visitors pass through Washington Heights to see, though, is **The Cloisters**, the Metropolitan Museum's collection of medieval art housed in a Frankenstein's monster of a castle in **Fort Tryon Park**. Unequivocally, this is a must (see Chapter 6, *Museums and Galleries* for persuasion), and should you plump for riding up on the subway you'll find an additional reward in the park itself, cleverly landscaped by Frederick Law Olmsted and a comfortable place to get lost for half an hour or so.

Fort Tryon Park joins Inwood Park by the Hudson River, and despite the presence of the Henry Hudson Parkway running underneath, it is possible to walk across Dyckman Street and into Inwood Park. The path up the side of the river gives a beautiful view of New Jersey, surprisingly hilly and wooded this far upstream. Keep walking and you will reach the very tip of Manhattan, an area known as *Spuyten Duyvil*, "the spitting devil" in Dutch, nowadays Columbia University's Athletic Stadium. Inwood Park itself is wild and rambling, often confusing and a little threatening if you get lost. It was once the stamping ground for Indian cave dwellers, but unfortunately, the site of their original settlement is now buried under the Henry Hudson Parkway. Inwood's single tourist attraction is the **Dyckman House** (4881 Broadway at 204th Street, Tues–Sun, 11am–5pm; free), an eighteenth-century Dutch farmhouse restored with period bits and bobs; pleasant enough, but hardly worth the journey.

Chapter 5

The Outer Boroughs

anhattan is a hard act to follow, and the four **Outer Boroughs** – **Brooklyn**, **Queens**, **The Bronx** and **Staten Island** – inevitably pale in comparison. They lack the excitement (and the mass money) of Manhattan's architecture; with a few honourable exceptions they don't have museums to compare with the Met or MoMA, nor galleries like SoHo's; and their life, essentially residential, is less obviously dynamic.

So why step off the island? The answer, perhaps, if you've just a few days in NYC, is "don't" – or at least only do so for the fun of returning on the **Staten Island Ferry**. But if you're staying longer, you will probably be more receptive to the boroughs' attractions, not least among them the chance to escape the sometimes stifling environment of Manhattan. And there are definite, if modest, attractions. **Brooklyn** offers the beautiful **Prospect Park**, salubrious **Brooklyn Heights** and, for addicts of run-down seaside resorts, **Coney Island**. **Queens**, scarcely ever visited by outsiders, has the bustling Greek community of **Astoria**. As for **Staten Island**, the ferry is its own justification. Whether you choose to take a look at the fourth borough, **The Bronx**, is a more ambivalent exercise. The area is ordinarily residential at its north end but the south, as any number of New York stories will attest, is Hard Territory, as desolate and bleak an urban landscape as you'll find anywhere.

Brooklyn

THE OUTER BOROUGHS

Duh poor guy! Say, I've got to laugh, at dat, when I t'ink about him! Maybe he's found out by now dat he'll neveh live long enough to know the whole of Brooklyn. It'd take a guy a lifetime to know Brooklyn t'roo an' t'roo. An' even den, you wouldn't know it at all.

               Thomas Wolfe *Only the Dead Know Brooklyn*

"The Great Mistake". So New York writer Pete Hamill summed up the 1898 annexation of his borough, and in a way, that's how

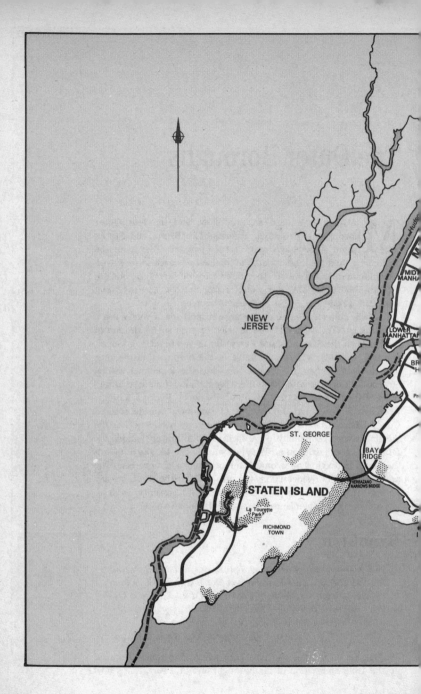

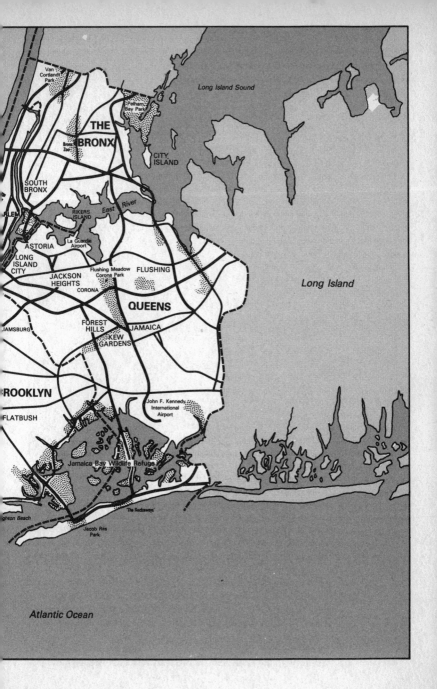

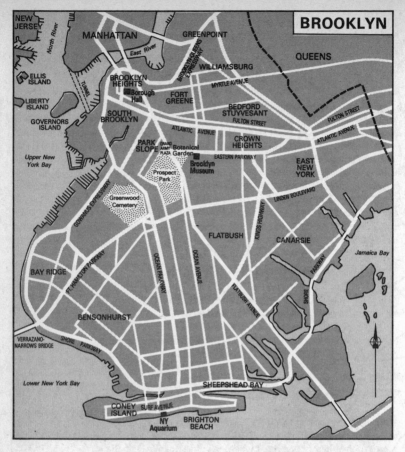

BROOKLYN

most Brooklynites feel even today, traditionally seeing themselves as **Brooklyn** residents first, inhabitants of New York City a poor second. Though always the underdog to Manhattan, Brooklyn has a firm and individual identity, a definite feel which is embodied in a mass of urban folklore. The Brooklyn Dodgers, the accent, Woody Allen, Mel Brooks, Barbra Streisand: all, in one way or another, are unmistakably Brooklyn – and all to some degree sum up this most diverse of New York City's boroughs.

If it were still a separate city Brooklyn would be fourth largest in the United States, but until as recently as the early 1800s it was no more than a group of loosely connected towns and villages existing relatively autonomously from already thriving Manhattan across the water. It was with the arrival of Robert Fulton's steamship service, linking the two, that Brooklyn began to take on its present form, starting with the establishment of a leafy retreat at Brooklyn Heights.

What really changed the borough was the opening of the Brooklyn Bridge, and thereafter development began to spread deeper inland, as housing was needed for the increasingly large workforce necessary to service a more commercialised Manhattan. By the turn of the century, Brooklyn was fully established as part of New York City, and its fate as Manhattan's perennial kid brother was sealed.

Brooklyn Heights is the most obvious – and justly the most visited – district, but that's as far as most people get. Yet there are other neighbourhoods which are at least as picturesque, and in a way a lot more real. **Park Slope**, for example, has some of the city's best preserved brownstones, and Calvert and Vaux's **Prospect Park** is for many an improvement on their more famous bit of landscaping in Manhattan; **Coney Island** and **Brighton Beach** are worth the subway ride for their unique atmospheres if not as beach resorts; and the **Brooklyn Museum** has a collection which can compete with anything on Manhattan. Basically, treat Brooklyn not as a suburb but as a separate city, and you begin to appreciate it.

Downtown Brooklyn: Brooklyn Heights, Atlantic Avenue and south

Brooklyn Heights is one of New York City's most beautiful and wealthy neighbourhoods, and as such it has little in common with the rest of the borough. From the early eighteenth century on, bankers and financiers from Wall Street could live amongst its peace and exclusivity and imagine themselves far from the tumult of Manhattan, but still close enough to gaze across to the monied spires. Today the Heights are not far different, the original brownstones being assured protection back in 1965 when the Heights was made the first member of the New York Historical District scheme. Walking down the tree-lined streets, with their perfectly preserved terraces and air of civilised calm, it's not hard to see why people want to live here. That is, though, give or take a handful of churches, all there is to see: students of urban architecture could have a field day, but for the rest of us there's little to do beyond wander and breathe in the neighbourhood's peace.

Arriving from the Brooklyn Bridge

Assuming you're walking from Manhattan (and it really is the best way, for the views if nothing else), the Brooklyn Bridge is the most obvious place to begin a tour of the district. At its far end you'll find yourself in what's called the **Fulton Ferry District**. This, hard under the glowering shadow of the Watchtower (world headquarters of the Jehovah's Witness organisation), was where Robert Fulton's ferry used to put in, and during the nineteenth century it grew into Brooklyn's first and most prosperous industrial neighbourhood. With the coming of the bridge it fell into decline, but now is on the way up again: its ageing buildings are being slowly tarted up as loft spaces, and, down on the ferry slip itself, a couple of barges-cum restaurants – *Bargemusic* and the *River Café* entice die-hard Manhattanites across the bridge by night.

Camden Plaza West leads off beneath the elevated highway: follow this for a little way and a right up Henry Street will take you into the oldest part of Brooklyn Heights proper. Middagh Street holds the neighbourhood's oldest house, number 24, dating from 1829 and built in the wooden Federal style – dubbed "gingerbread" because of its elaborately carved details. On the next street up, Orange, stands the **Plymouth Church of the Pilgrims**, a simple church that went up in the mid-nineteenth century and became the preaching base of **Henry Ward Beecher**, under whom it grew to be one of the country's most talked-about churches. Beecher – liberal, abolitionist, campaigner for women's rights – was a great orator: he held mock slave auctions here and used the money to buy slaves' freedom, and toured the country persuading the rich to give to charitable institutions. This brought the famous to his church, and Horace Greeley, Mark Twain, even Abraham Lincoln, all worshipped here on more than one occasion. Sadly, though, Henry Ward remains less known outside New York than his wife, Harriet Beecher Stowe, author of *Uncle Tom's Cabin*, since his later years were marred by an adultery scandal of which he was acquitted but never finally cleared in public esteem. The church is kept locked most of the time, so the only chance you'll get to see its barn-like interior is when there's a service on. No great loss.

The Esplanade and Pierrepoint Street

Clark Street leads down to the river and **the Esplanade** (called "The Promenade" by the locals), home of such as Norman Mailer (he lives in one of the creeper-hung palaces here) and with fine views of Lower Manhattan across the water. East is **Pierrepoint Street**, one of the Heights' main arteries and studded with delightful – and fantastic – brownstones. On the corner of Henry Street the **Herman Behr House** is a chunky Romanesque Revival mansion which has been, successively, a hotel, brothel, Franciscan monastery (it was the brothers who added the horrific canopy) and currently private apartments. Further down Pierrepoint, look in if you can on the **Church of the Saviour**, notable for its exquisite neo-Gothic interior, and, across the road, the **Brooklyn Historical Society**, who present regular exhibits on the borough's social history. The society's walking tours of the Heights also leave from here (see "Information, Maps and Tours" in *Basics*).

Montague Street and around

Head west, and you're on **Montague Street**, Brooklyn Heights' lively main thoroughfare, lined with bars and restaurants and, surprisingly for such an exclusive district, with a workaday atmosphere that makes it one of New York's most pleasant thoroughfares. At the far

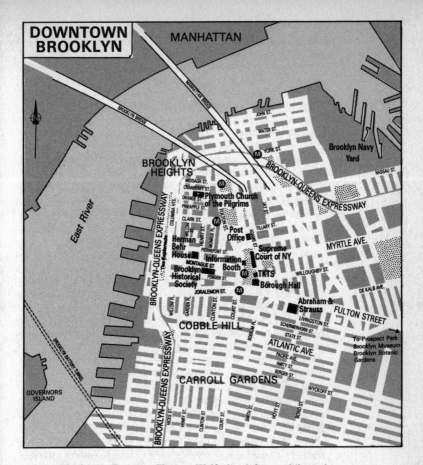

MANHATTAN

MANHATTAN BRIDGE

BROOKLYN BRIDGE

JOHN ST.

WATER ST.

YORK ST.

Brooklyn Navy
Yard

NASSAU ST.

BROOKLYN-QUEENS EXPRESSWAY

BROOKLYN
HEIGHTS

East River

COLUMBIA HTS.

MIDDAGH ST.

CRANBERRY ST.

ORANGE ST.

Plymouth Church
of the Pilgrims

PINEAPPLE ST.

CLARK ST.

HENRY ST.

MONROE ST.

MYRTLE AVE.

BROOKLYN-QUEENS EXPRESSWAY

The Esplanade

Herman
Behr
House

Post
Office

TILLARY ST.

PIERREPONT ST.

Supreme
Court of NY

MONTAGUE ST.

Information
Booth

WILLOUGHBY ST.

Brooklyn
Historical
Society

PEMSEN ST.

TKTS

Borough Hall

DE KALB AVE.

JORALEMON ST.

Abraham &
Strauss

FULTON STREET

WILLOW ST.

GARDEN PL.

CLINTON ST.

COURT ST.

LIVINGSTON ST.

COBBLE HILL

DEGRAW PL.

SCHERMERHORN ST.

STATE ST.

ATLANTIC AVE.

To Prospect Park
Brooklyn Museum
Brooklyn Botanic
Gardens

PACIFIC AVE.

AMITY ST.

BERGEN ST.

BROOKLYN-QUEENS EXPRESSWAY

CARROLL GARDENS

WYCKOFF ST.

HICKS ST.

HENRY ST.

CLINTON ST.

COURT ST.

SMITH ST.

HOYT ST.

BOND ST.

BROOKLYN BATTERY TUNNEL

GOVERNORS
ISLAND

end, on **Montague Terrace**, Thomas Wolfe lived for a while and wrote *Of Time and the River*. South of here are a couple of neat mews, **Grace Court Alley** and **Hunts Lane**, not unlike those off Washington Square in Manhattan, and just below, **Joralemon Street**, traditionally a street of artisans rather than brokers and consequently holding houses decidedly less grand. The far end of Montague is known as "Bank Row" – downtown Brooklyn's business centre – and leads on to what is in effect the borough's Civic Center, the end of the residential Heights signalled by the tall Art Deco blocks of Court Street. Across the road the sober Greek-style **Borough Hall** is topped with a cupola-ed belfry; to its left there's the massive **State Supreme Court** and Romanesque **post office**, next to which stands a bronze of Henry Ward Beecher. There's little to linger for, and the buildings are ugly, but stop off at the **Information Booth/TKTS Office** just in front for a map and Brooklyn information pack – if they have any left.

Beyond the civic grandeur **Fulton Street** leads east, principal shopping street for the borough as a whole and here pedestrianised into a characterless shopping mall. There's another TKTS office, plentiful mainstream shops, and **Gage & Tollner**, Brooklyn's most famous restaurant that serves seafood and steaks in a setting determinedly left unchanged. If you can afford it – and the food doesn't come cheap – there are worse places to break for lunch.

Atlantic Avenue

South of Brooklyn Heights is **Atlantic Avenue**, which runs from the East River all the way to Queens and is for a short stretch centre to New York's Middle Eastern minority. There are some fine and reasonably priced Yemeni and Lebanese restaurants here and a good sprinkling of Middle Eastern grocers and bakeries. Try the **Damascus Bakery** for pitta bread, and the **Sahadi Importing Co.** at no. 187 for nuts, dried fruit, halva and the like; and see Chapter 8, *Drinking and Eating* for listings of the best restaurants.

Cobble Hill

Crossing Atlantic Avenue, Cobble Hill, Carroll Gardens and Boerum Hill, along with the old wharfing community of Red Hook, make up the area better known as South Brooklyn, a piece of land that juts out into Upper New York Bay. Of these three small districts (which adopted their historical names back in the 1960s to engender a sense of community spirit) **Cobble Hill** is most elegant, its main streets – Congress, Warren and Amity – a mixture of solid brownstones and colourful redbrick terraces, most of which have long been a haven of the professional classes. Really, the attraction is just in strolling the streets, but there are a couple of features you may want to base your walk around: Jenny Jerome, later Lady Randolph Churchill and mother of Winston, was born at **197 Amity Street** in a house now disfigured by aluminium windows and a modern rustic facing; and **Warren Place** is worth a quick peek for a tiny alley of workers' cottages from the late nineteenth century – a shelter of quiet just a stone's throw from the thunder of the Brooklyn–Queens Expressway.

Carroll Gardens

Cobble Hill stops at De Graw Street, where the mood changes and the strong Italian community of **Carroll Gardens** begins. Originally a middle- and upper-class community of many nationalities, South Brooklyn was invaded by a massive influx of Italian dockworking immigrants who came in the early 1900s and settled in the area named after Charles Carroll, the only Roman Catholic signee of the Declaration of Independence. Today, it remains staunchly Italian and is the first stop for many new Italian immigrants. **Court Street** is the main thoroughfare, lined with ubiquitous pizzerias, Italian pastry shops and seafood restaurants. It's very family oriented, lower middle class and far removed from the more famous Little Italy. The most bizzare sight in Carroll Gardens is the large number of religious shrines and statues that decorate the large gardens that give the neighbourhood its name.

Red Hook

South of Carroll Street, the streets become distinctly seedy, with the elevated section of the Gowanus Expressway marking the beginning of **Red Hook**, an old Irish and Italian community of dockworkers now largely idle, following the demise of New York's docking industry. Most of the original immigrant groups left in the 1950s and 1960s as the growing automisation of the docking industry left Red Hook behind (vividly portrayed in the film and the notorious novel *Last Exit to Brooklyn*), most ships choosing instead to dock at modern facilities in New Jersey, where ships could be unloaded much more quickly – and cheaply. A small Italian contingent remains here and shares the now cheap housing with African-Americans and Latinos, many of whom live in the infamous Red Hook housing projects. While definitely not to be recommended for casual sightseeing, Red Hook is a testament to the ruthlessness of New York's development – one of the communities that helped build the city, and that has been left behind in its wake.

Red Hook is separated from the further reaches of Brooklyn by the old Gowanus Canal, and only overcome by the elevated section of the F train, which rises out of the ground at Carroll Street, heading to Park Slope and ultimately Coney Island.

Boerum Hill

To the east of Cobble Hill, and south of Atlantic Avenue, is **Boerum Hill**, scruffier and less architecturally impressive than its neighbours and home to Italian- and Irish-descended families, and most recently a large Latino community. It's they who bring salsa music and dancing to the stoops of the neighbourhood brownstones, and single room storefront social clubs are a common sight on Smith Street. Smith Street is also the site of one of Boerum Hill's gaudier attractions, the pastille green and silver of **J. Michaels Department Store** on the corner of Smith and Warren streets, a severe break with the more sober Greek Revival and Italianate Boerum Hill architecture.

Central Brooklyn: Fort Greene, Bedford-Stuyvesant, Crown Heights and Park Slope

Just to the east of downtown Brooklyn sits **Fort Greene**, named after Nathaniel Greene, a prominent general in the American Revolution, and long established as a strong multiracial community. Easily navigated by keeping an eye on the Williamsburg Savings Bank, Brooklyn's tallest building, Fort Greene also boasts America's oldest performing arts centre at 30 Lafayette Avenue, the **Brooklyn Academy of Music** – BAM to its friends and one of the borough's most cherished institutions, playing host over the years to a glittering – and innovative – array of names.

At the northern tip of the neighbourhood lies the **Brooklyn Naval Yard**, once one of the main means of employment for Brooklyn workers, now a rather less impressive industrial park. Officially commissioned in 1801, it reached its peak in World War II, when over 70,000 men and women worked day and night building such famous battleships as the *Iowa*, *New Jersey* and *Arizona*. The *USS Missouri* is still in use today. While Fort Greene remains strongly African-American in its make-up, gentrification is creeping into the neighbourhood and real estate values are increasing rapidly. At the moment the mix of neighbourhood families and young professionals gives the area a pleasant feel: *Spike's Joint*, the movie merchandise and clothes store of film director and Fort Greene native Spike Lee, is at 1 South Elliot Place (☎718/802-1000), and for somewhere to eat, try the soul food at *Harper Valley* on Fulton Street near Greene Avenue.

Bedford-Stuyvesant

Immediately east of Fort Greene is **Bedford-Stuyvesant**, originally one of the most elegant neighbourhoods in the city, today one of the most badly neglected. Originally two separate areas, populated by both blacks and whites, the opening of the Brooklyn Bridge and later the construction of the A train brought a massive influx of African-Americans into the area. This led to increased hostility between the two groups, which in turn led to fighting. In the 1940s the white population left, and took with them funding for many important community services. This was the start of the decline of Bed-Stuy, as it has become colloquially known, and though the area has suffered the all-too-usual problems of inner city neglect and drug dealing, today the African-American community here, the largest in the country, is desperately trying to stop Bed-Stuy's rot and take advantage of an architectural legacy of some of the best Romanesque Revival brownstones in the city.

Brownsville

Bedford-Stuyvesant's eastern neighbours of Bushwick, East New York, Brownsville and East Flatbush have a similar story of generational ethnic development. In the early part of this century, **Brownsville** was notable in being a hotbed for prominent anarchists, Bolsheviks and other political free thinkers. Emma Lazarus, author of the spirited inscription on the Statue of Liberty, lived here, and in 1916, with over 150 prospective clients waiting outside its doors, the first birth control clinic in America opened here – only to be raided and closed nine days later by the vice squad and its founder, Margaret Sanger, imprisoned for thirty days as a "public nuisance".

Williamsburg

North of Bedford-Stuyvesant and Fort Greene is **Williamsburg**, home of the huge landmark **Williamsburg Savings Bank** and immediately recognisable because of the large numbers of **Hasidic Jews** who live there. The men, dressed in black with long *payess* (curls) hanging from under their hats, have been a common sight since the Williamsburg Bridge linked the area to the Lower East Side in 1903. Many of the Jews from that neighbourhood left for the better conditions in Williamsburg, and during World War II a further settlement of Hasidim, mainly from the ultra-orthodox Satmar sect, established Williamsburg as a Jewish centre. At about the same time a large number of Puerto Ricans began to arrive here, and the two communities have coexisted in a state of strained tolerance ever since. Tensions boiled over in November 1990, with Latino residents accusing the police of favouritism toward the Jewish community. This was denied by the local 90th Precinct, but Jewish anger at the arrest of a Hasidic man on molestation charges brought over 300 Hasidim to the police station in late October, and a riot almost erupted.

The best place to start exploring Williamsburg is on **Lee Avenue**, the main shopping street, or the more residential **Bedford Avenue** that runs parallel. On either you'll see manifestations of the neighbourhood's Orthodox Jewish character: *Glatt Kosher* delicatessens line the streets, signs are written in Hebrew, and the distinctive dress of the men especially gives the area the feel of being a throwback to some *mitteleuropa* town of the nineteenth century. If you do make it here, drop by the **Domsey Warehouse** at the end of South 9th Street for some of the cheapest clothes in the city: search long enough through the piles of coats and dresses and you're bound to find a bargain.

Crown Heights and Prospect Park

Fulton Street and Atlantic Avenue separate Bedford-Stuyvesant from **Crown Heights**, New York's largest West Indian neighbourhood, which bursts into life with an enormous carnival each Labor Day.

More interesting, though, is the route up Flatbush Avenue to **Grand Army Plaza**. This is where Brooklyn really asserts itself as a city in its own right – pure classicism, with the traffic being funelled around the central open space. It was laid out by Calvert and Vaux in the late nineteenth century, who designed it as a dramatic approach to their newly completed Prospect Park just behind. The triumphal **Soldiers and Sailors' Memorial Arch**, which you can climb (spring and autumn weekends only), was added thirty years later and topped with a fiery sculpture of Victory in tribute to the triumph of the north in the Civil War. On the far side of the square the creamy smooth **Brooklyn Public Library** continues the heroic theme, its facade smothered with stirring declarations to its function as fountain of knowledge, and with an entrance showing the borough's home-grown poet, Walt Whitman. Behind, there's the **Brooklyn Museum** and the **Brooklyn Children's Museum** (see Chapter 6, *Museums and Galleries* and the **Brooklyn Botanic Garden** (April–Sept Tues–Fri 8am–6pm, Sat & Sun 10am–4pm; Oct–March Tues–Fri 8am–4.30pm, Sat & Sun 10am–4.30pm).

The Botanic Garden is one of the most enticing park spaces in the city, smaller and more immediately likeable than its more celebrated rival in the Bronx, and making for a relaxing place to unwind after a couple of hours in the museum. Sumptuous but not over-planted, it sports a Rose Garden, Japanese Garden, a Shakespeare Garden (laid out with plants mentioned in the bard's plays) and some delightful lawns draped with weeping willows and beds of flowering shrubs. There's also a conservatory housing, among other things, the country's largest collection of bonsais.

The Botanic Garden is about as far away from Manhattan's bustle as it's possible to get, but if you can tear yourself away there's also **Prospect Park** itself. Energised by their success with Central Park, Olmsted and Vaux landscaped this in the early 1890s, completing it just as the finishing touches were being put to Grand Army Plaza outside. In a way it's better than Central Park, having more effectively managed to retain its pastoral quality, and though there have been encroachments over the years – tennis courts, a zoo – it remains for the most part remarkably bucolic in feel. Focal points include the **Lefferts Homestead**, an eighteenth-century colonial farmhouse shifted here some time ago and now open for tours from Wednesday to Sunday, the **Zoo** (though it's no better and no less cruel than Central Park zoo) and the lake in the southern half. The **boathouse** has maps and information on events in the park (dance, drama and music are performed in the bandshell most summer weekends) or you can pick up all kinds of park information on ☎ 718/788-0055.

Park Slope – and a note on Bensonhurst

The western exits of Prospect Park leave you on the fringes of **Park Slope**, with some of New York's best preserved brownstones and, in an area currently building itself up as a serious rival to Brooklyn Heights, some of the city's fastest-soaring property prices. Main streets are **Seventh** and **Fifth avenues**, both of which share new shops for the recent incomers and old-established stores in almost equal proportion – though of the two Fifth is more downmarket, still supporting a solid Hispanic community.

Walk down Fifth Avenue, across the Prospect Expressway, and you reach **Greenwood Cemetery**: larger even than Prospect Park and very much the place to be buried in the last century if you could afford to lash out on an appropriately flashy headstone – or better still mausoleum. Among the names buried here Horace Greeley, politician and campaigning newspaper editor, lies relatively unpretentiously on a hill; William Marcy "Boss" Tweed, nineteenth-century Democratic chief and scoundrel, slumbers deep in the wilds; and the Steinway family, of piano fame, have their very own 119-room mausoleum. Look out also for the tomb of one John Matthews, who made a fortune out of carbonated drinks and had himself a memorial carved with birds and animals, some fierce-looking gargoyles, and (rather immodestly) scenes from his own life. You can stroll around the cemetery and find all this for yourself; or take a **guided tour** (see "Information, Maps and Tours" in *Basics*).

Bensonhurst, to the south of Greenwood Cemetery, merits a mention not for being a predominantly Italian area but for an incident that underlines the racism found in certain outlying parts of the city. In August 1989, Yusef Hawkins, a black boy of sixteen, wandered into the neighbourhood looking to buy a bike. Surrounded by a gang of youths and mistaken for someone else, he was beaten and finally shot to death because he was black. The incident brought to the surface racial tensions that had long been suppressed, and split the city in two. Rightly or wrongly, Bensonhurst will long be associated with racism in New York City.

Coney Island and Brighton Beach

Coney Island, reachable direct from Manhattan on the B, D, F or N subway lines, was for years where generations of working-class New Yorkers came to relax, at its height visited by 100,000 people a day who idled away their weekends in an extended party of beach-lounging, hot dogs, candy floss and strolls down the boardwalk. By the 1950s, however, the resort was past its best, and now, although plenty of people still flock here when the weather's fine, the good-time, carefree atmosphere is long gone. Coney Island is today one of Brooklyn's – and New York's – poorest districts, predominantly Hispanic and with a pervasive atmosphere of menace through which even the police travel in groups of three. The amusement park is peeling and run-down, until recently the boardwalk was cracked and broken, and *Nathan's*, Coney Island's once legendary and unique hot dog stand, now has franchises all over the city. But if you like run-down seaside resorts, there's no better place on earth.

The main street is **Surf Avenue**, above which run the gaudy subway trains on their way back to Manhattan. Weekdays here are a depressing sight – gangs of youths hanging about outside bars and souvenir-hung arcades that, whatever the weather, emit cringingly inappropriate fairground music. The **beach** at least is beautiful, a broad clean swathe of golden sand, and it's not difficult to see what once made people come here. But the rusty Meccano sprawl of the amusement park is an unwelcoming backdrop, and on hot weekends it's hard to find a space even now; dedicated bathers would be better off making for Long Island.

Brighton Beach

Further along, **Brighton Beach**, or "Little Odessa", is home to the country's largest community of Russian emigrés, around 20,000 in all, who arrived in the 1970s following a relaxation of emigration restrictions on Soviet citizens entering the US. There's also a long-established and now largely elderly Jewish population. It's a livelier neighbourhood than Coney Island, more prosperous, less defeated. But out of season the boardwalk, lined with melancholy elderly Slavs, can seem just as sad.

Things cheer up on **Brighton Beach Avenue**, the neighbourhood high street which runs underneath the el in a hotchpotch of foodshops and appetising restaurants. Russian souvenirs are everywhere, and any number of grocers offer a range of possibilities for lunch – maybe some caviar or smoked fish from *International Food* at no. 249, as a topping to some heavy black bread. Or there's *Mrs Stahl's Knishes* on the corner of Brighton Beach and Coney Island Avenue, a remnant from more firmly Jewish days. **Sit-down food** is also readily available, though you'd be better off waiting until evening as it's then the restaurants really hot up, becoming a near parody of a rowdy Russian night out with loud live music, much glass clinking and the frenzied knocking back of vodka. All very definitely worth a trip: see "The Outer Boroughs" in Chapter 8, *Drinking and Eating*.

Next stop on the D or Q subway line from Brighton Beach is **Sheepshead Bay**: not a place to swim from (although you can swim from Manhattan Beach, a short walk away). At night the Bay is lively, especially along the main drag, **Emmons Avenue**, where the bars and restaurants along the waterside make it a pleasant place to wander, especially of an afternoon or evening.

THE OUTER BOROUGHS

The Bronx

The Bronx. There's no other part of New York about which people are so ready to roll out their latest and most gruesome horror stories. For this, the city's northernmost borough, represents in its decaying reaches one of the most severe examples of urban deprivation you're ever likely to see. But whatever they tell you in Manhattan, however many Bronx jokes you hear, it's not as unequivocally bleak as people would have you think. In fact, it's really only the South Bronx and a few isolated pockets which are in any way dangerous, and for the most part you can treat it much as you would any other part of New York.

The Bronx developed – and has since declined – more quickly than any other part of the city. First settled in the seventeenth century by a Swedish landowner named Jonas Bronk, like Brooklyn it only became part of the city proper at the turn of the last century. From 1900 onwards things moved fast, and the Bronx became one

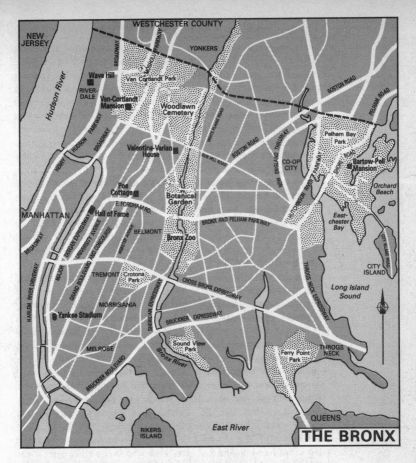

of the most sought-after parts of the city in which to live, its main
thoroughfare, **Grand Concourse**, becoming edged with increasingly
luxurious Art Deco apartment blocks – many of which, though
greatly run-down, still stand today. This avenue runs the length of
the borough, and many places of interest lie on it or reasonably
close by. Most people travel up for the **Zoo**, or bypass the greater
part of the borough altogether for **Orchard Beach** or **City Island**.
Other places besides these are worth seeing: the grotesqueries of
Woodlawn Cemetery and smug **Riverdale** in the north; the **New
York Botanical Gardens** – large enough to seem a really tangible
escape from the city; and even the **South Bronx**, probably best
experienced only as a passing cityscape from the relative comfort of
the subway train. This is easy to do, as the subway travels above
ground after leaving Manhattan, cutting directly through the worst
of the South Bronx decimation.

THE OUTER BOROUGHS   1 7 7

Yankee Stadium and the South Bronx

First stop the subway makes after leaving Manhattan is at **Yankee Stadium**, home to the New York Yankees baseball team and holding some of the best facilities for the sport in the country. The Yankees played in north Harlem before moving here in 1923, a move that was in part due to their most famous player ever, George Herman "Babe" Ruth, who joined the team in the spring of 1920 and went on to command a place in the team for the next fifteen years. It was the star quality of Babe Ruth, the original Bronx Bomber (as the team is now known), that helped pull in the cash to build the current stadium, which for a while was known as the "House that Ruth Built". Inside, Babe Ruth, Joe di Maggio and a host of other baseball heroes are enshrined by statues, but unless coming to watch a game (or, on occasion, be blessed – in 1965 and 1979 popes said mass here to over 50,000 New Yorkers), there's little reason to visit. (See Chapter 11, *Sport and Outdoor Activities*, for details.)

The South Bronx

North and west stretches the awful wasteland of the **South Bronx**, first part of the borough to become properly urbanised but now scarred by huge squares of rubble, levelled apartments sprawling between gaunt-eyed tenements, and with streets dotted with huddled groups of young blacks and Hispanics. The sense of hope-lessness is overwhelming, and without a massive injection of money, and some encouragement to businesses and the white middle classes (all of which have long since moved way up- or downtown) to come back with their cash, there are no signs that the South Bronx will ever get back on its feet. Carter promised to do some-thing about this and did nothing, and Reagan's withdrawal of employment support made things even worse. This is the place where a city's dispossessed have been shovelled up, dumped, and left to rot – and no one, not even those who live in other parts of the Bronx, would seem to care. Somehow, the South Bronx jokes you heard back in Manhattan fall a little flat when you experience the neighbourhood for yourself.

Through all this, if you are on foot, **Grand Concourse** still manages to shine with some level of sanity. Stray either side, however, and you're getting into areas which most people – not all alarmists by any means – would consider dangerous. The Concourse itself contains the ever-busy **Bronx Supreme Court House**, where part of *The Bonfire of the Vanities* was filmed, and further along at 1040 Grand Concourse and East 165th Street, the **Bronx Museum of Art** (Wed–Fri 10am–5pm, Sat–Sun 1–6pm; $3; $2 students) with changing displays of temporary exhibits, many orientated towards the Bronx. Carry on, and the junction with Fordham Road marks the beginning of the South Bronx's main shopping districts. Here on East Fordham and West Fordham Road are the main department

stores and the focus of Saturday afternoon shopping. Fordham Road
boasts every fast-food franchise imaginable, complete with the
necessary quota of homeboys checking out the territory. They
would stand out were it not for the hundreds of families, street
vendors and barbecued-shrimp sellers that also vie for space on the
crowded pavement. If you're seriously interested in seeing what the
rest of the South Bronx looks like, a trip on the elevated #4 train
down to Yankee Stadium gives a good view of the decimation – and
will reinforce your wish to stay on the train.

Central Bronx: Belmont, the Zoo and the Botanical Gardens

Beyond 180th Street the Bronx improves radically. Turn north up
Arthur Avenue and you're in **Belmont**, a strange mixture of tenements and clapboard houses that is home to by far the largest
segment of New York's Italian community. It's a small area,
bordered to the east by the Zoo and the west by Third Avenue, and
with 187th Street as its axis. And it's far enough away from
Manhattan for the Italians to keep it their own. Few tourists come
here but if you're on your way to the zoo, amble through to see its
pungent grocery stores and pork butchers, cafés and sweet-smelling
bakeries. There's also no better part of the Bronx if you want to **eat**:
choose from swanky *Mario's* (where Al Pacino shot the double-
crossing policeman in *The Godfather*) or the pizzas at *Ann &
Tony's*, both on Arthur Avenue. (See Chapter 8, *Drinking and
Eating*, for more details.)

The Bronx Zoo and New York Botanical Gardens

Follow 187th to the end and you're on the edge of the park which
holds **Bronx Zoo** (daily 10am–5pm, Sundays and holidays 10am–
5.30pm; Fri–Mon $4.75, rest of the time a donation is sufficient),
accessible either by its main gate on Fordham Road or by a second
entrance on Bronx Park South. This last is the entrance to use if you
come directly here by subway (East Tremont Avenue stop).

The zoo is probably the only reason many New Yorkers from
outside the borough ever visit the Bronx. Even if you don't like
zoos, it's as good a one as any: the largest urban zoo in the United
States, and one of the first to realise that animals both looked and
felt better out in the open – something done artfully through a
variety of simulated natural habitats. Visit in summer to appreciate
it at its best (in winter a surprising number of the animals are still
caged): one of the most interesting parts is the Wild Asia exhibit, an
almost forty-acre wilderness through which tigers, elephants and
deer roam relatively freely, viewable from a monorail train ($1.25) –
though this is only open from May to October. Look in also on the
World of Darkness (a re-creation of night, holding nocturnal
species) and a simulation of a Himalayan mountain area, with

endangered species like the giant panda and snow leopard. All in all a good focus for a day trip to the Bronx.

Across the road from the zoo's main entrance is the back turnstile of the **New York Botanical Gardens** (Tues–Sun 10am–5pm, last admission 4pm), which in their southernmost reaches are as wild as anything you're likely to see upstate. Further north near the main entrance (Pelham Parkway subway) are more cultivated stretches and the Enid A. Haupt Conservatory, where you'll find eleven galleries of palms, ferns, cacti and orchids in an airy iron-framed building of 1902. This costs $2.50, however, and unless you're especially keen is just as good from the outside. The gardens themselves are enormous enough to wander around for hours; you can get hold of a guide from the shop in the Museum Building.

The Poe Cottage

Leave the gardens by their main entrance and walk west and you come eventually to Grand Concourse and the **Poe Cottage**. This tiny white clapboard anachronism in the midst of the Bronx's bustle was Edgar Allen Poe's home for the last three years of his life, though it was only moved here recently when threatened with demolition. Poe came here in 1846 with his wife Virginia and her mother; Virginia suffered from tuberculosis and he thought the country air would do her good. Never a particularly stable character and dogged by problems, Poe was rarely happy in the cottage: he didn't write a great deal (only the short, touching poem, "Annabel Lee"), there was never enough money, and his wife's condition declined until she eventually died, leaving Poe with a distraught mother-in-law and a series of literary ambitions that never seemed to come off. He left the cottage for the last time in 1849 to seal the backing for his longest-running dream – his own literary magazine – but got entangled in the election furore in Baltimore, disappeared, and was eventually found weak and delirious in the street, dying in hospital a few days later. What actually happened no one knows, and the house, with its few meagre furnishings spread thinly through half a dozen rooms, tells you little more about the man (Wed–Fri 9am–5pm, Sat 10am–4pm, Sun 1pm–5pm; $1).

North Bronx

The **North Bronx** is the topmost fringe of New York City, and if anyone actually makes it up here it's to see the **Woodlawn Cemetery** (subway Woodlawn), which is worth a stroll around if only to see how money doesn't necessarily buy good taste. This has for many years been the top people's cemetery, and like Greenwood in Brooklyn (see pp.174–75) brags some tombs and mausoleums which are memorable mainly for their hideousness. It's a huge place but there are some tombs which stand out: one Oliver Hazard

Belmont, financier and horse dealer, lies in a dripping Gothic fantasy near the entrance, modelled on the resting place of Leonardo da Vinci in Amboise, France; F.W. Woolworth has himself an Egyptian palace guarded by sphinxes; while Jay Gould, not most people's favourite banker when he was alive, takes it easy in a Greek-style temple. And that's not all. Pick up a guide from the office at the entrance and you can discover all kinds of famous names and disgusting mausolea.

Van Cortlandt Park

West of the cemetery lies **Van Cortlandt Park**, forested and hilly (dangerous say some) and used in winter by skiers and tobogganists. Apart from the sheer pleasure of hiking through its woods, the best thing here is the **Van Cortlandt Mansion**, nestled in its south-west corner not far from the subway station. This is an authentically restored Georgian building, very pretty, and with its rough-hewn grey stone really rather rustic. During the Revolutionary wars it changed hands a number of times, and was used as an operations headquarters by both the British and the Patriots. On the hills above, George Washington had fires lit to dupe the British into thinking that he was still here (he was in fact long gone) and it was in this house he slept before heading his victory march into Manhattan in 1783. Nowadays most of the rooms are open to the public and kept up by the Society of Colonial Dames of America (Mon–Sat 10am–5pm, Sun noon–5pm; $2).

Riverdale

Immediately west rise the monied heights of **Riverdale** – one of the most desirable neighbourhoods in the city, and so far from the South Bronx in feel and income it might as well be on the moon. Venture up if you wish, but there's not a lot to see save **Wave Hill**, a small country estate donated to the city a couple of decades back and which in previous years was briefly home to Mark Twain and, later, Teddy Roosevelt. The grounds are botanical gardens, the nineteenth-century mansion a forum for temporary art installations, concerts and workshops: a great idea, but a pity it couldn't have been in one of the parts of the city that needed it much more badly (daily 10am–5.30pm; greenhouses 10am–noon & 2–4pm; $2, students $1).

City Island

At the other side of the Bronx **Pelham Bay Park** gives onto **Orchard Beach** and, linked by a short causeway, **City Island**. This, reachable by taking subway #6 to the end and a Bx12 bus, is something of an oddity in this part of town: a small fishing village whose main street is lined with fish and seafood restaurants and whose harbour is crammed with visiting yachtspeople. That it's so hard to get to is probably just as well . . ..

THE OUTER BOROUGHS

Queens

Of New York City's four outer boroughs, **Queens**, named after the wife of Charles II, is the most consistently ignored. Even Staten Island, across the water and barely considered part of the city at all, has something to offer, even if it's only the ferry that takes you there. But Queens, despite being considerably more accessible than Staten Island, a great deal larger than Brooklyn, and immeasurably safer than the Bronx, simply lacks enough cachet to make it a desirable place to live. People who live in Queens, the thinking seems to run, are either excruciatingly dull or can't afford to live anywhere else.

Assuming you're still reading, it's worth pointing out that Queens isn't in fact so terrible. Just that architecturally it's more semi-detached suburbia than tenements and brownstones, there are for the moment fewer immigrant areas than in Brooklyn or the Bronx, and if Queens has any historic buildings they tend to be clapboard. Do, however, check out Greek **Astoria**, both for its restaurants and foodstores and the film studios; **Jackson Heights**, which has the city's largest concentration of South Americans; and **Kew Gardens** and **Forest Hills**, which have any amount of yuppie chic.

Astoria and around

Bleak industrial **Long Island City** is most people's first view of Queens: it's through here that the subway train cuts above ground after crossing over from Manhattan. Unless it's a weekend and you fancy browsing through the **Queens Plaza Flea Market** on the corner of Queens and Northern Boulevard, or the **Isamu Noguchi museum** (see Chapter 6), there's no point in getting off as there's nothing to see. This might change, as Long Island City is on the verge of being colonised by artists escaping extortionate Manhattan rents and taking over the disused loft spaces here. But it's not exactly SoHo yet, and for the present it's **Astoria** that makes it worth crossing the river, one of Queens' original communities and famous for two things: film making and the fact that it's the largest single concentration of Greeks outside Greece itself (Melbourne included). Until the **movie industry** moved out to the West Coast in the early 1930s Astoria was the cinematic capital of the world. Paramount had their studios here until the lure of Hollywood's reliable weather left Astoria empty and disused by all except the US Army – which was how it remained until recently when Hollywood's stranglehold on the industry weakened. The new studios here now rank as the country's fourth largest and, encouraged by the success of films like *The Wiz*, *Ragtime* and others where the bulk of the filming was done in New York, are set for a major expansion. They're not open to the public at present but you can visit the **Museum of the Moving Image** in the old Paramount complex at 34–31 35th Street, near Broadway, where there's an excellent display of posters, stills, sets and equipment

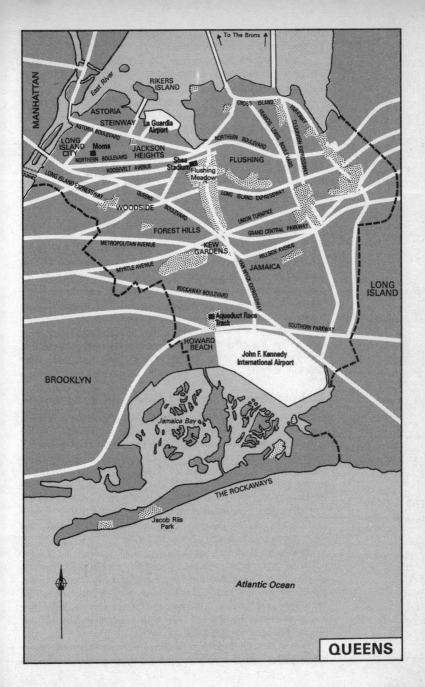

both from Astoria's golden age and more recent times. See Chapter 6 for opening times and a full description.

Greek Astoria stretches from Ditmars Boulevard in the north right down to Broadway, and from 31st across to Steinway Street. Between 80,000 and 100,000 Greeks live here (together with a substantial community of Italians) and the evidence is on display in a sizable quantity of **restaurants and patisseries** that repay a closer look. There's not a great deal else to see, but check out our restaurant listings in Chapter 8 before you write the area off.

Steinway

East of Astoria lies **Steinway**, a district that was bought up by the piano manufacturers and used as housing for their workers. These were mainly Germans and the area had for a time a distinctly Teutonic feel, but the community has long since gone, and apart from the **piano factory** (☎718/721-2600 for visits) there's little to keep you. Next door the noise-trap of **La Guardia Airport** handles domestic flights to and from the city. If you're lucky, you may find yourself travelling through the **Marine Air Terminal**, built in the early 1930s for the huge flying boats that took off from the lake outside. A small exhibit details the history of this stylish building, whose best feature is the mural depicting the history of flight, uncovered recently after being declared "Socialist" and painted over in the early 1950s. Just offshore, **Riker's Island** holds the city's largest and most overcrowded prison. Not surprisingly, this isn't NYC's most appealing corner.

For full details of La Guardia Airport, see "Points of Arrival" in Basics.

Jackson Heights, Flushing, Forest Hills and beyond

Next door to Steinway is the South American enclave of **Jackson Heights**, a small and largely self-contained community of 150,000 or so Colombians, half as many Ecuadorians and a good number of Argentinians and other South American peoples. The neighbourhood first turned Hispanic in the 1960s, when huge influxes of people came over – many illegally – to find work and escape from the poverty and uncertain politics of their own countries, and it's now the largest South American contingent in the States. Tighter immigration controls, however, have radically cut the intake, and the community here is now more or less static.

Eating-wise, there's no better part of Queens for exotic, unknown and varied cuisines. Roosevelt Avenue and, running parallel, 37th Avenue between 82nd Street and Junction Boulevard are focus for the district, and along both streets you'll find Argentinian steakhouses, Colombian restaurants, and pungent coffee houses and bakeries stacked high with bread and pastries. See Chapter 8 for restaurant listings.

East of Jackson Heights you hit **Corona**, its subway yards ringed by menacing barbed wire and patrolled by dogs to deter graffiti artists. A few steps away is **Shea Stadium**, home of the New York Mets. The Beatles too, played here in 1965 (at that point far more successfully than the Mets – who have since, however, won two world series), and the stadium, presumably in anticipation of further such events, has recently been upgraded with a giant video screen. For details on the Mets and when they play, see Chapter 11, *Sport and Outdoor Activities*.

Shea went up as part of the 1964 World Fair, held in adjoining **Flushing Meadow Park**. This is now the site of the US Tennis Open Championships each summer, and boasts around thirty courts and seating for well over 25,000 people (again see Chapter 11). The other side of the park, **Flushing** is a rather dull middle-income suburb which has picked up the tag "birthplace of religious freedom in America" for its role as secret Quaker meeting place during the seventeenth century, when anyone who wasn't a Calvinist was persecuted by the Dutch.

The Quakers met in the **Bowne House** which still stands, officially the oldest house in the city and open to the public on selected days of the week. It's a short walk from the Bowne Street subway station and if you're in Flushing you may just as well take a look. But be warned that the enthusiasm of the volunteers who show you around is not always mirrored by the excitement of the displays, which in the main consist of the drab furniture used over the years by the Bowne family; and, as symbolic centrepiece, the kitchen where the Quaker meetings took place. Outside stands **Kingsland House**, shifted here from its original site about a mile away and reputedly the first house in Flushing to release its slaves. All this and more is detailed in the Queens Historical Society's do-it-yourself walking tour of "Historic Flushing", for details of which see "Information, Maps and Tours" in *Basics*. Or go to their headquarters in the Kingsland House itself.

Forest Hills and Jamaica Bay

On the other side of Flushing Meadow Park – and a long walk or a bus ride from Flushing – **Forest Hills** is perhaps choicest of Queens neighbourhoods, home to Geraldine Ferraro and the West Side Tennis Club. This is snooty, a high-income suburb with a strong Jewish component, spectacularly pricey housing and a high street (Austin) of designer clothes shops and chi-chi restaurants. Priciest bit of all is **Forest Hills Gardens**, a mock Tudor village that is interesting not for what it is but for what it might have been, since it was built originally as housing for the urban poor until the rich grabbed it for themselves. Another "planned" neighbourhood, **Kew Gardens**, to the south, was at the turn of the century a watering hole popular with ageing New Yorkers, complete with hotels, lakes and a whole tourist infrastructure. All that has gone now but Kew remains, in a leafy and dignified kind of way, one of Queens' most visually enticing districts.

Just beyond is the city's other airport, **JFK International**, with to its right the wild, island-dotted indent of **Jamaica Bay** – now an official wildlife refuge where you can observe around 300 varieties of birds, for free, seven days a week. Partly enclosing the bay, the narrowing spit of **The Rockaways** is the largest beach area in the country, stretching for ten miles back towards Brooklyn – most of it strollable by the boardwalk. At the far end **Jacob Riis Park** offers another beach and assorted facilities, with **nude bathing** tolerated (if not officially allowed) in the eastern corner, haunt of predominantly gay naturists.

THE OUTER BOROUGHS

Staten Island

Until about twenty five years ago **Staten Island**, the common name for what's officially Richmond County, was isolated – getting to it meant a ferry trip or long ride through New Jersey, and daily commuting into town was almost an eccentricity. Staten Islanders enjoyed an insular, self-contained life in the state's least populous borough, and the stretch of water to Manhattan marked a cultural as much as physical divide. In 1964 the opening of the Verrazano Narrows Bridge changed things; upwardly mobile Brooklynites found cheap property on the island and swarmed over the bridge to buy their parcel of suburbia. And today Staten Island has swollen into tightly packed residential neighbourhoods amid the rambling greenery, endless backwaters of tidy look-don't-touch homes.

But most don't even see as much as this. Nine out of ten tourists who take the Staten Island ferry drool over the view and on arriving promptly turn back to Manhattan. What they miss are a couple of museums and a nerve-soothing break from the city, but that's about it: a few other bits and bobs lie scattered around but none are worth going out of the way for; thankfully either or both of the two museums repay the inland excursion.

The ferry, the Jacques Marchais Center and Richmondstown Restoration

The **Staten Island ferry** sails around the clock with half-hourly departures between 9.30am and 4pm, and is famed as New York's best bargain: for 50¢ (return) wide-angled views of the city and Liberty are yours, becoming more spectacular as you retreat. By the time you arrive Manhattan's skyline stands mirage-like, filtered through the haze as the romantic, heroic city of a thousand and one posters. The Staten Island ferry terminal quickly dispels any romance: it's a dirty, disreputable sort of place, which serves as a mini-training ground for winos on their way to the Bowery. But if you're exploring the island it's easy enough to escape to the adjoining bus station and catch the #74 (connects with ferry so have

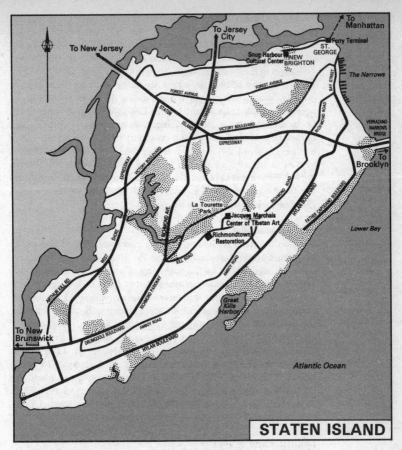

STATEN ISLAND

change or a token ready as they're unavailable at the terminal)
which cuts down and across to the two central museums. Along the
way the **Verrazano Narrows Bridge** flashes its minimalist message
across the entry to the bay, a slender, beautiful span that was (until
the Humber Bridge opened) the world's longest at 4260 feet – so
long that the tops of the towers are 4cm out of parallel to allow for
the curvature of the earth.

The Jacques Marchais Center of Tibetan Art
In the middle of Staten Island's residential heartland the **Jacques
Marchais Center of Tibetan Art** (May–Sept Wed–Sun 1–5pm; April,
Oct, Nov, Fri–Sun 1–5pm; $3; ☎718/987-3478 for additional
summer hours) is an unlikely find; the bus drivers don't know it's
there, so ask to be let off at Lighthouse Avenue, walk up the hill and
it's on the right at number 338. Jacques Marchais was the alias of

Jacqueline Kleber, a New York art dealer who reckoned she'd get on better with a French name. She did, and combined with the advantages of a rich husband, used her wealth to indulge her passion for Tibetan art. Eventually she assembled the largest collection in the Western world, reproducing a *gompah* or Buddhist temple on the hillside in which to house it. Even if you know nothing about such things the exhibition is small enough to be accessible, with magnificent bronze Bodhisattvas, fearsome deities in union with each other, musical instruments, costumes and decorations from the mysterious world of Tibet. Give it time – after a while the air of the temple and its gardens is heady. Best time to visit is in the first or second week of October when the Tibetan harvest festival takes place: Tibetan monks in saffron robes perform the traditional ceremonies, and Tibetan food and crafts are sold. Phone ahead for the exact date.

The Richmondstown Restoration

Back on the main Richmond Road, a short walk brings you to the **Richmondstown Restoration** (Wed–Fri 10am–5pm, Sat & Sun 1–5pm; $2, students $1.50), a gathering of a dozen or so old houses and miscellaneous buildings transplanted from their original sites and grafted on to the eighteenth-century village of Richmond. Starting from the **Historical Museum**, half-hourly tours negotiate the best of these – including the **Voorlezer's House**, oldest elementary school in the country, a picture-book **general store**, and the lovely, atmospheric **Guyon-Lake-Tyson House** of 1740. What brings it to life are the craftspeople using old techniques to weave cloth and fire kilns – in the summer conducted tours stop and the becostumed workers fill you in on the facts. It's all carried off to picturesque and ungimmicky effect in rustic surroundings: difficult to believe you're just twelve miles from downtown Manhattan.

Landfills and oil spills

To New Yorkers from other boroughs, Staten Island is mainly terra incognita. Ask most what they know of the smallest New York borough and you get the reply "garbage" – the reason being that ninety percent of New York's **rubbish** – some 100,000 tons *a week* – is dumped in Staten Island's Fresh Kills landfill. This is the largest landfill in the world, holding 2400 million cubic feet of refuse (for lovers of useless facts, that's twenty-five times the size of the Great Pyramid at Giza), and it's a claim to fame over which Staten Islanders feel strong resentment, not only because of environmental concern, but also because of the financial implications. They consider themselves as paying high taxes, only to be used by the city as a cheap rubbish dump. There's been much talk of Staten Island seceding from the city – something that may well be a popular cause on the Island, but which stands little chance of acceptance anywhere else. New York would lose a large amount in tax revenue from the many commuters who live on the Island, and would have to pay considerably more to dispose of its garbage.

A further reason Staten Islanders have become concerned over their environment has been the number of recent **oil spills**. The Island lies next to New Jersey's Perth Amboy, one of the largest refining centres in America and where spills are almost commonplace. These have continually polluted the Arthur Kill, once a favourite spot for local fishermen. Now, it's joked, the Kill produces the only crude cod liver oil in the US.

St Georges

For the committed explorer the up-and-coming area of **St Georges** (near the ferry terminal), is slightly more mixed than the firmly middle-income families further inland. Good antique shops abound: try the **Edgewater Hall Antique Center**, a bank that's been refurbished as a shopping mall. About a mile and a half away in New Brighton is the Greek Revival pile of the **Snug Harbour Cultural Center** – former home for retired sailors that now houses the galleries and studios of the island's swelling artists' community. In summer the Metropolitan Opera and New York Philharmonic give concerts here – good music in intimate outdoor surroundings – and each weekend there are guided tours of the Center and nearby **Botanical Gardens** (March–Nov 2pm; free; ☎ 718/273-8200 for more info).

Chapter 6

Museums and Galleries

New York is not a city that lacks visual stimulation – and you may find there's enough on the streets without having to contemplate walking inside a museum. But you should at least be aware of what you're missing. For in the big two Manhattan museums – the **Metropolitan** and **Museum of Modern Art** – there are few aspects of Western art left untapped. The Metropolitan, in particular, is exhaustive (mercilessly so, if you try to take in too much too quickly), with arguably the world's finest collection of European art as well as superlative displays of everything from African artefacts to medieval sculpture. The Museum of Modern Art (MoMA) takes over where the Met leaves off, emphasising exactly why (and how) New York has become art capital of the world.

The shops of the larger museums are the best places to buy inexpensive cards, prints and posters. See Chapter 14, Shops and Markets.

Among the other **major museums**, you'll find exciting collections of modern art and invariably excellent temporary shows at the **Whitney** and **Guggenheim**, a wide array of seventeenth- and eighteenth-century paintings at the **Frick**, and – amid unexpectedly pastoral scenes – a glorious display of medieval art out at **The Cloisters** in Fort Tryon. All of which should, if time permits, be seen. So too, depending on personal interests and tastes, should some of the minor **museums**, often quirkily devoted to some otherwise total obscurity.

Free museums

The following museums are **free** at the stated times:

Tuesday Guggenheim (5–8pm pay what you wish), International Center of Photography (5–8pm), Cooper-Hewitt (5–9pm), Museum of American Folk Art (5.30–8pm).

Thursday Whitney (6–8pm), Museum of Modern Art (5–9pm pay what you wish).

Opening hours

Opening hours don't fall into any fixed patterns: many museums close on Mondays (and national holidays), opening into the early evening one or two nights a week. **Admission charges** are often

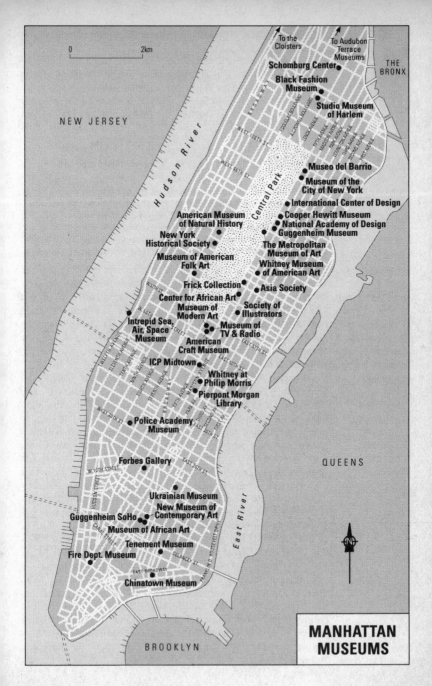

0   2km

To the
Cloisters

To Audubon
Terrace
Museums

THE
BRONX

NEW JERSEY

Schomburg Center

Black Fashion
Museum

Studio Museum
of Harlem

Hudson River

BROADWAY

WEST 110TH ST.

WEST 86TH ST.

Central Park

Museo del Barrio

Museum of the
City of New York

International Center of Design

Cooper Hewitt Museum
National Academy of Design
Guggenheim Museum

American Museum
of Natural History

New York
Historical Society

Museum of American
Folk Art

W.57TH ST.

W. 50TH

STREET

The Metropolitan
Museum of Art

Whitney Museum
of American Art

Frick Collection

Asia Society

Center for African Art

Museum of
Modern Art

Society of
Illustrators

Intrepid Sea,
Air, Space
Museum

Museum of
TV & Radio

EAST 57TH ST.

American
Craft Museum

EAST 50TH ST.

ICP Midtown

Whitney at
Philip Morris

Pierpont Morgan
Library

Police Academy
Museum

WEST 20TH ST.

Forbes Gallery

EAST 10TH ST.

W. 10TH STREET

HUDSON STREET

Ukrainian Museum

New Museum of
Contemporary Art

Guggenheim SoHo

Museum of African Art

CANAL STREET

Tenement Museum

Fire Dept. Museum

DELANCEY ST.

EAST BROADWAY

FRANKLIN D. ROOSEVELT DRIVE

East River

QUEENS

Chinatown Museum

N

MANHATTAN
MUSEUMS

BROOKLYN

high, occasionally softened for those with student ID cards, but happily, certain museums are free or much reduced one evening a week. Otherwise you'll commonly find the "voluntary donation" system in operation. This in theory means you're allowed to give as little or as much as you like to get in (hence enabling museums to keep their charitable status); in practice you'll need to be pretty hard-headed to give any less than the (not particularly low) recommended minimum.

The Metropolitan Museum of Art

Fifth Ave at 82nd St. Subway #4, #5 or #6 to 86th St–Lexington Ave. Tues–Thurs & Sun 9.30am–5.15pm, Fri & Sat 9.30am–8.45pm, closed Mon. Recorded info ☎535-7710 or ☎879-5500. Admission by voluntary donation, suggested $6, $3 for students (includes admission to the Cloisters on the same day). Free conducted tours, "Highlights of the Met", daily; also highly detailed tours of specific galleries; recorded tours of the major collections $3.75.

The Met, as it's usually known, is the foremost museum in America. Its galleries take in over three-and-a-half million works of art and span the arts and cultures not just of America and Europe (though these are the most famous collections) but also of China, Africa, the Far East, and the Classical and Islamic worlds. Any kind of overview of the museum is out of the question: it demands many and specific visits, or, at least, self-imposed limits.

Broadly, the Met breaks down into five **major collections**: *European Painting, American Painting, Medieval Art, "Primitive" Art* and *Egyptian Antiquities*. You'll find the highlights of these detailed below. Keep in mind, however, that there is much, much more for which space forbids anything other than a passing mention. Among the **"lesser" Met collections** are *Greek and Roman galleries* (second only to those in Athens), *Islamic art* (possibly the largest display anywhere in the world), a *Far Eastern gallery* (with a reconstruction of a Chinese garden, assembled by experts from the People's Republic), *Arms and Armor Galleries* (the largest and most important in the western hemisphere), a *Musical Instrument Collection* (the world's oldest piano, of course, included) and what would, anywhere else, be seen as essential *Twentieth-Century Art galleries* (Picasso's *Portrait of Gertrude Stein* and Pollock's *Parsiphaë* are just two standouts).

Initial orientation, despite the problem of size, is not too hard. There is just one main entrance and once within you find yourself in the **Great Hall**, a deftly lit neoclassical cavern where you can consult plans, check tours and pick up info on the Met's excellent lecture listings. Directly ahead is the **Grand Staircase** and what is for many visitors the single greatest attraction – the European Painting galleries.

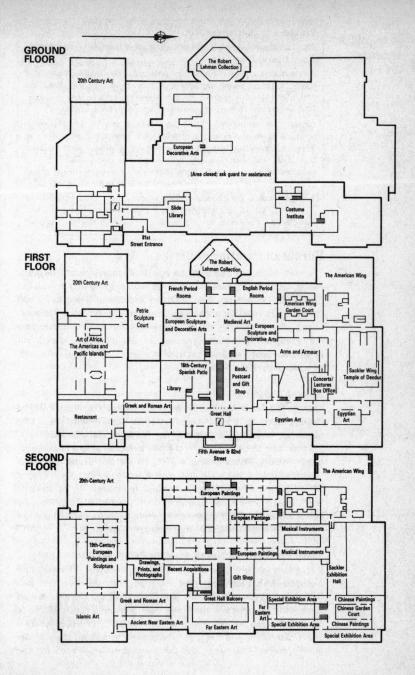

GROUND FLOOR

20th Century Art

The Robert Lehman Collection

European Decorative Arts

(Area closed; ask guard for assistance)

Slide Library

Costume Institute

81st Street Entrance

FIRST FLOOR

20th Century Art

The Robert Lehman Collection

The American Wing

French Period Rooms

English Period Rooms

Petrie Sculpture Court

American Wing Garden Court

European Sculpture and Decorative Arts

Medieval Art

European Sculpture and Decorative Arts

Art of Africa, The Americas and Pacific Islands

Arms and Armour

16th-Century Spanish Patio

Book, Postcard and Gift Shop

Concerts/ Lectures Box Office

Sackler Wing Temple of Dendur

Library

Greek and Roman Art

Restaurant

Great Hall

Egyptian Art

Egyptian Art

Fifth Avenue & 82nd Street

SECOND FLOOR

20th-Century Art

The American Wing

European Paintings

European Paintings

19th-Century European Paintings and Sculpture

Musical Instruments

European Paintings

Musical Instruments

Drawings, Prints, and Photographs

Recent Acquisitions

Gift Shop

Sackler Exhibition Hall

Greek and Roman Art

Great Hall Balcony

Special Exhibition Area

Chinese Paintings

Islamic Art

Far Eastern Art

Chinese Garden Court

Ancient Near Eastern Art

Far Eastern Art

Special Exhibition Area

Chinese Paintings

Special Exhibition Area

MUSEUMS AND GALLERIES

193

The
Metropolitan
Museum of
Art

Problems in visiting the Met

There are three main **problems** in visiting, other than the obvious frustrations of size and time:

Scheduling. Certain collections are open only on a rotating basis, so if you're intent on seeing anything less than obvious, phone ahead first (☎535-7710). (This rotating schedule affects galleries only on Tuesdays, Wednesdays and Thursdays; opening on other days are not affected.)

Layout. The second difficulty is the piecemeal way the Met has developed. Its nineteenth-century multimillionaire benefactors were often as intent on advertising their own taste as on setting America on the cultural high road, and their bequests often stipulated distinct and **separate galleries** for their donations. If you're interested in one particular period or movement of art you won't necessarily find it all in the same place.

Reorganisation. The museum is in the process of reorganising the layout of some of the painting galleries, which means that the order in which we've listed the paintings may not necessarily be that in which they appear.

European Painting galleries

The Met's European Painting galleries divide in two parts. The initial rooms start with a scattering of Italian works, move into a small but fine English collection, then Northern and Italian Renaissance and (probably the most significant) seventeenth-century Dutch. The nineteenth-century galleries follow and are dominated by a tremendous core group of Impressionist painting. Ideally, try to take in each half in separate bouts, separated at least by a break in the museum's café: these are large collections.

English Painting

Though the Met's **English Gallery** is essentially a prelude to the major collections, it's an unusually brilliant and elegant one. At its heart are a group of portraits by **William Gainsborough** and **Thomas Lawrence**, the two great English portrait artists of the eighteenth century. Gainsborough's *Mrs. Grace Dalrymple Elliott* is typical of his portrait style – an almost feathery lightness softening the monumental pose. Lawrence is best represented by his likeable and virtuoso study of *Elizabeth Farren*, painted at the precocious age of 21, and by *The Calmady Children*, a much-engraved portrait that was the artist's own favourite among his works.

Early Flemish and Netherlandish Painting

Beyond, a drop back in time, are the **Early Flemish and Netherlandish Paintings**, precursors of both the Northern and Italian Renaissance. Inevitably the first paintings are by **Jan van Eyck**, who is generally attributed with beginning the tradition of North European realism. There are two definitely accepted works – *The Crucifixion* and *The Last Judgement* – painted early in the artist's career and much like the miniatures he painted for the

Turin-Milan Hours; bright, realistic and full of expressive (and horrific) detail. *The Annunciation* nearby is probably by Jan too; its perspective is tidily if not totally accurately drawn, the Romanesque right-hand side of the portal and the Gothic left symbolising the transition from Old Testament to New.

There's more allusion to things Gothic in **Rogier van der Weyden**'s *Christ Appearing to His Mother*, the apocryphal visit surrounded by tiny statuary depicting Christ's earlier and Mary's later life. It's one of the most beautiful of all van der Weyden's works, quite different in feel to van Eyck with a warmth of design and feeling replacing the former's hard draughtsman's clarity. This development is continued through the third great Northern Gothic painter, **Gerhard David**, as is the vogue for setting religious scenes in Low Countries settings. The background to David's exquisite *Virgin and Child with Four Angels* is medieval Bruges; in *The Rest on the Flight to Egypt* landscape features are added to by Low Country genre scenes. **Bruegel**'s *Harvesters*, one of the Met's most reproduced pictures, and part of the series of twelve paintings that included his (Christmas card familiar) *Hunters in the Snow*, shows how these innovations were assimilated.

Spanish and Italian Painting

Cutting left at this point brings you to the **Spanish Paintings** and the very different landscape of **El Greco**'s *View of Toledo*. This extraordinary picture – all brooding intensity as the skies seem about to swallow up the ghost-like town – is perhaps the best of his works anywhere in the world. Beside it is his *Portrait of a Cardinal*, and there is also **Velazquez**'s *Portrait of Juan de Parej* – "All the rest are art, this alone is truth," remarked a critic of the piercing, sombre portrait when it was first exhibited.

The **Italian Renaissance** is less spectacularly represented but there's a worthy selection from the various Italian schools, including an early *Madonna and Child Enthroned with Saints* by **Raphael**, a late **Botticelli**, the crisply linear *Three Miracles of Saint Zenobius*, and **Fra Filippo Lippi**'s *Madonna and Child Enthroned with Two Angels*. Among the **Mannerists**, best of the Italian collections, is **Bronzino**'s *Portrait of a Young Man*. Turning right from the main galleries takes you to a smaller series of religious paintings: **Michele de Verona**'s handsome *Madonna and Child with the Infant John the Baptist*, very much in the fifteenth-century Italian tradition with a marmoreal surface bathed in soft light. Look out for **Crivelli**'s *Pietá* and **Mantegna**'s rigid and sculptural *Adoration of the Shepherds*.

Dutch Painting

With the **Benjamin Altman Collection**, here cleverly jigsawed into the main gallery, a small number of Dutch works, including **Memling**'s *Tommaso Portinari and his Wife* and a *Mystical Marriage of St Catherine*, prelude the main **Dutch Paintings** section. This, dominated by the major works of Rembrandt, Vermeer and Hals, is the culmination of the main European galleries – and arguably the finest single group of paintings in the museum.

Vermeer, genius of the domestic interior, is represented by five works. *Young Woman with a Water Jug*, which hints at themes of purity and temperance, is a perfect example of his skill in composition and tonal gradation, combined with an uncannily naturalistic sense of lighting. *A Girl Asleep* is deeper in its composition – or at least appears to be, the rich fabric separating the foreground from the rooms beyond. Vermeer often used this trick, and you see it again in *Allegory of the Faith*, where the drawn curtain presents the tableau and separates the viewer from the lesson presented. Most haunting of all is the great *Portrait of a Young Woman*, displaying the artist at his most complex and the Met at its most fortunate.

Vermeer's pictures show the domestic harmony of seventeenth-century Holland. **Hals**'s early paintings reveal its exuberance. In *Merrymakers at Shrovetide* the figures explode out from the canvas in an abundance of gesture and richness. *Young Man and a Woman*, painted five years later, shows a more subdued use of colour (though not vitality). As do the individual portraits, with their capturing of fleeting, telling pointers: step back from his *Portrait of a Man* or *Claes Kuyst Van Voorhout* and the seemingly slapdash strokes melt into a bravura statement of spirit.

The best of **Rembrandt**'s works here are also portraits. There is a beautiful painting of his common-law wife, *Hendrike Stoffjels*, painted three years before her early death – a blow that marked a further decline in the artist's fortunes. In 1660 he went bankrupt, and the superb *Self-Portrait* of that year shows the self-examination he brought to later works. A comparison between the flamboyant 1632 *Portrait of a Lady* and the warmer, later *Lady with a Pink* reveals his maturing genius.

In addition to these big three names, the Dutch rooms also display a good scattering of their contemporaries, most memorably **Pieter de Hooch**, whose *Two Men and a Woman in a Courtyard of a House* is his acknowledged masterpiece, with its perfect arrangement of line, form and colour. At the same time as de Hooch was painting peaceful courtyards and Vermeer lacemakers and lute players, **Adrian Brouwer** was turning his eye to the seamier side of Dutch life. When he wasn't drunk or in prison he came up with works like *The Smokers*, typical of his tavern scenes. Traditionally *The Smokers* is a portrait of Brouwer and his drinking pals – he's the one in the foreground, in case you hadn't guessed.

The Nineteenth-Century Galleries

A suite of twenty rooms opened in September 1993 displays a startling array of **Impressionist and Post-Impressionist** art and nineteenth-century European sculpture. The new gallery is in Beaux Arts style, with decorated detail adapted from designs made for the Metropolitan Museum by architects McKim, Mead and White early this century.

Impressionist Painting

The **Manet gallery** is the largest of the rooms and serves as a focal point, flanked by galleries devoted to Courbet, Degas and the Barbizon School. To the west are rooms of Impressionist and Post-Impressionist paintings, as well as works from the recently donated Annenberg Collection. The display, fittingly, centres around **Edouard Manet**, the Impressionist movement's most influential precursor yet in his early style, contrasting light and shadow with modulated shades of black, firmly linked in tradition with Hals, Velazquez and Goya. The *Spanish Dancer*, an accomplished example of this style and heritage, was well received on Manet's debut at the Paris Salon in 1861. Within a few years, though, he was shocking the same establishment with *Olympia*, *Le Déjuner sur l'Herbe* and the striking *Woman with a Parrot* – the same woman, incidentally, modelled for all three paintings. Later his style shifted again as he adopted the Impressionist lightness of handling and interest in perception. He worked for a time with Renoir and Monet, a period of which *Boating* is typical, a celebration of the middle classes at play.

Claude Monet, who was influenced by Manet's early style before Impressionism, was one of the movement's most prolific painters. He returned again and again to a single subject to produce a series of images capturing different nuances of light or atmosphere. Three superb examples – *Rouen Cathedral*, *The Houses of Parliament from the Thames* and *Poplars* – show the beginnings of his final phase of near-abstract Impressionism.

Cézanne's technique was very different. He laboured long to achieve a painstaking analysis of form and colour, something clear in the *Landscape of Marseilles*. Of his few portraits, the jarring, almost Cubist angles and spaces of *Mme Cézanne in a Red Dress* seem years ahead of their time. Take a look too at *The Card Players*, whose dynamic triangular structure thrusts out, yet retains the quiet concentration of the moment. **Renoir** is perhaps the best represented among the remaining Impressionists, though his most important work here dates from 1878, when he began to move away from the mainstream techniques he'd learned working with Monet. *Mme Charpentier and her Children* is a likeable enough piece, whose affectionate if unsearching tone manages to sidestep the sugariness that affected his later work. Better, or at least more real, is his *Waitress at Duval's Restaurant*.

Post-Impressionist Painting

The Post-Impressionists, logically enough, follow, with **Gauguin**'s masterly *Ia Orana Maria*. The title, the archangel Gabriel's first words to Mary at the Annunciation, is the key to the work: the scene was a staple of the Renaissance; here it is transferred to a wholly different culture in an attempt to unfold the dense symbolic meaning, and perhaps also to voice the artist's feeling for the native South Sea islanders, whose cause he championed. *Two Tahitian Women* hangs adjacent, a portrait of his lover Tehura – skilful, studied simplicity.

Toulouse-Lautrec delighted in painting the world Gauguin went to Tahiti to escape. *The Sofa* is one of a series of sketches he made in Paris brothels. The artist's deformity distanced him from society, and he identified with the life of the prostitutes in his sketches – he also hated posed modelling, which made the bored women awaiting clients an ideal subject.

Courbet and **Degas**, too, are well represented. Courbet especially, with examples of every phase and period of his career, including *Young Ladies from the Village*, a virtual manifesto of his idea of realism, and *Woman with a Parrot*, a superbly erotic and exotic work, and one that gave Manet the idea for his work of the same name. Degas constantly returned to the subject of dancers, and there are studies in just about every medium from pastels to sculpture. Unlike the Impressionists, Degas subordinated what he saw to what he believed, and his *Dancers Practising* shows this – the painting is about structure, alluded to in the way the dancer on the right picks up the form of the watering can used to lay the dust in the studio. Also here is a vaguely macabre casting of his *Little Dancer*, complete with real tutu, bodice and shoes.

All of which is little more than the surface of the galleries. There's also work by **Van Gogh**, **Rousseau** and **Seurat**, paintings from the **Barbizon School**, sculpture by **Rodin** and a peripheral gallery of paintings that express the official taste of the nineteenth century.

The Lehman Pavilion

The Lehman Pavilion was tacked on to the rear of the Met in 1975 to house the collection of Robert Lehman, millionaire banker and art collector. It breaks from the Met's usual sober arrangement of rectangular floor plans: rooms are laid out beside a brilliantly lit atrium, some in re-creation of Lehman's own home.

More importantly, Lehman's enthusiasms fill the gaps in the Met's account of **Italian Renaissance** painting. This was his passion, and the heart of the collection centres around a small **Botticelli** *Annunciation*, an exquisite celebration of the Florentine discovery of perspective. From the Venetian school comes a sculptural *Madonna and Child* by **Giovanni Bellini** and two unaffected portraits by **Jacometto Veneziano**, as well as an unusual *Expulsion from Paradise* by the Sienese **Giovanni di Paolo**, in which an angel gently ushers Adam and Eve from Eden, while a Byzantine God points to their place of banishment.

Left of this core collection are works from the **Northern Renaissance**, highlighted by a trio of paintings by Memling, Holbein and Petrus Christus. **Christus**'s untypically large canvas of *St Elegius*, patron saint of goldsmiths, shows an Eyckian attention to detail in its depiction of the saint's jewels and precious stones – a genre insight into the work of the fifteenth-century goldsmith. **Memling**, working around thirty years later, used a lighter palette to achieve the delicate serenity of his *Annunciation*, in which cool colours and a gentle portrayal of Mary and her attendant angels illuminate the Flemish interior. **Hans Holbein the Younger**'s *Portrait of Erasmus of Rotterdam* was one of three he painted in 1523 that established his reputation as a portraitist. Elsewhere in the Lehman wing – and you could visit the Met rewardingly by limiting yourself just to these halls – are works by artists as diverse as El Greco, Ingres (the luminescent *Princesse de Broglie*) and Ter Bosch. But one painting that really stands out is **Rembrandt**'s *Portrait of Gerard de Lairesse*: by all accounts de Lairesse was disliked for his luxurious tastes and unpleasant character, but mainly for his face – which had been ravaged by congenital syphilis.

As the Lehman wing moves towards the **nineteenth century and twentieth century** it loses authority, but there are minor works by major artists, including Renoir, Van Gogh, Gauguin, Cézanne and Matisse. Have a look at **Suzanne Valadon**'s *Reclining Nude*: Valadon is largely ignored today, and is best known as a model for Toulouse-Lautrec, Renoir and Degas (who encouraged her to become a painter in her own right). But her boldly coloured canvases show her originality and also her influence on her son, **Maurice Utrillo**, whom she taught to paint as an attempt to wean him off the drink and drugs that were his downfall. Utrillo's *Rue Ravignon* here stands besides his mother's painting.

Twentieth Century art

Housed over two floors in the Lila Acheson Wallace Wing, the Met's **twentieth-century collection** is an enjoyable compact group of paintings, and fascinating viewing if you have an interest in the period. The first floor has a chronological installation of American and European art from **1905 to 1940**, with paintings such as **Charles Demuth**'s *The Figure Five in Gold*, and **Picasso**'s *Portrait of Gertrude Stein* alongside works by Klee, Matisse, Braques and Klimt. There's also a small design collection here, with changing pieces of furniture, ceramics and (just about anything else) from the Met's collection.

The second floor contains European and American painting from **1945 on**: **Pollock**'s masterly *Autumn Rhythm (Number 30)*, **Thomas Hart Benton**'s rural idyll of *July Hay*, **R.B. Kitaj**'s *John Ford on His Deathbed*, a dream-like painting of the director of western movies, and **Andy Warhol**'s final *Self-Portrait*, along with works by Max Beckmann, Roy Lichtenstein (*Painting Since 1945*) and Gilbert and George. On top of the Wallace wing is the **Cantor Roof Garden**, open in summer months to display contemporary sculpture against the dramatic backdrop of the New York skyline.

The American wing

The American wing comes nearest to being a museum in its own right, and as an introduction to the development of fine and decorative art in America it's hard to fault.

Galleries – and most immediately a series of **furnished historical rooms** – take off from the **Charles Engelhard Court**, a shrubby, restful sculpture garden enclosed at the lower end by the *Facade of the United States Bank*, lifted from Wall Street. Stepping through the facade would drop you in the **Federal period rooms** and the restrained neoclassical elegance of the late eighteenth century. If you're approaching this section of the Met fresh, however, better to start at the third floor and work down to see the rooms in chronological order. You begin with the **early Colonial period**, represented most evocatively in the Hart room of around 1674, and end with **Frank Lloyd Wright's** *Room from the Little House, Minneapolis*, originally windowed on all four sides, in key with Wright's concept of minimising interior-exterior division. On the second-floor balcony, an elegant accompaniment to all of this, be sure not to miss the iridescent Favrile glass of **Louis Comfort Tiffany** – Art Nouveau at its best.

The collection of American paintings

The collection of American paintings begins on the second floor with **eighteenth-century** works by **Benjamin West**, an artist who worked in London and taught or influenced almost all American painters of his day. *The Triumph of Love* is typical of his neoclassical, allegorical works. More heroics come with **John Trumbull**, one of West's pupils, in *Sortie made by the Garrison of Gibraltar* and the fully blown Romanticism of *Washington Crossing the Delaware* by **Emanuel Leutzes**. This last shows Washington escaping across the river in the winter of 1776, historically and geographically inaccurate but nonetheless a national icon.

Early in the **nineteenth century**, American painters gained the confidence to move away from themes solely European. **William Sidney Mount** depicted genre scenes on his native Long Island, often with a sly political angle – as with *Cider Makers* and *The Bet* – and the painters of the **Hudson Valley School** apotheosised that landscape in their vast lyrical canvases. **Thomas Cole**, the school's doyen, is represented by *The Oxbow*, his pupil **Frederick Church** by an immense *Heart of the Andes* – combining the grand sweep of the mountains with minutely depicted flora. **Albert Bierstadt** and

S.R. Gifford continued to concentrate on the American west – their respective works *The Rocky Mountains, Lander's Peak* and *Kauterskill Falls* have a near-visionary idyllism, bound to a belief that the westward development of the country was a manifestation of divine will.

Winslow Homer is allowed a gallery to himself – fittingly for a painter who was to influence greatly the late nineteenth-century artistic scene in America. Homer began his career illustrating the day-to-day realities of the Civil War – there's a good selection here that shows the tedium and sadness of those years – and a sense of recording detail carried over into his late, quasi-Impressionistic studies of seascapes. *Northeaster* is one of the finest of these, close to Courbet in its strength of composition and colour.

The mezzanine below brings the Met's account of American art into the **twentieth century**. Some of the initial portraiture here tends to the sugary, but **J.W. Alexander's** *Repose* deftly hits the mark – a simple, striking use of line and light with a sumptuous feel and more than a hint of eroticism. By way of contrast, there's **Thomas Eakin's** subdued, almost ghostly *Max Schmitt in a Single Scull*, and **William Merritt Chase's** *For the Little One*, an Impressionist study of his wife sewing. Chase studied in Europe and it was there that he painted his *Portrait of Whistler*. **Whistler** returned the compliment but destroyed the work on seeing Chase's (quite truthful) depiction of himself as a dandified fop – and in a teasing style that mimicked his own. Whatever Whistler's conceits, though, his portraits are adept: witness the *Arrangement in Flesh Colour and Black: Portrait of Theodore Duret* nearby.

The reputation of **John Singer Sargent** has suffered its ups and downs over the years – he now seems to be coming back into fashion. There is certainly a virtuosity in his large portraits, like that of *Mr and Mrs I. N. Phelps Stokes*, the couple purposefully elongated as if to emphasise their aristocratic characters. *Padre Sebastiano* is a smaller, more personal response. The *Portrait of Madam X* (Mme Pierre Gautreau, a notorious Parisian beauty) was one of the most famous pictures of its day: exhibited at the 1884 Paris salon, it was considered so improper that Sargent had to leave Paris for London. "I suppose it's the best thing I've done," he said wearily on selling it to the Met a few years later.

Medieval art

You could – in theory at least – move straight on to the **medieval galleries** from the American wing. But this would be heavy-going – and in any case you'd be missing out on a carefully planned approach.

This is the **corridor** leading in from the Great Hall, an entrance gallery that displays the sumptuous **Byzantine metalwork and jewellery** that J.P. Morgan donated to the museum in its early days.

At its end is the main **sculpture hall**, piled high with religious statuary and carvings (a tremendous *St Nicholas Saving Three Boys in the Brine Tub*) and split with a *reja* (altar screen) from Valladolid Cathedral.

Right from here the **medieval treasury** has an all-embracing – and magnificent – display of objects religious, liturgical and secular. And beyond are the **Jack and Belle Linski Galleries**: Flemish, Florentine and Venetian painting, porcelain and bronzes.

Dotted throughout the medieval galleries are later **period rooms**, panelled Tudor bedrooms and Robert Adam fancies from England, florid Rococo boudoirs and salons from France, and an entire Renaissance patio from Velez Blanco in Spain. It's all a bit much, leaving you with the feeling that Morgan and his robber baron colleagues would probably have shipped over Versailles if they could have laid their hands on it.

The Egyptian collection

"A chronological panorama of ancient Egypt's art, history and culture", boasts the blurb to the Egyptian collection, and the display is certainly lavish. Brightly efficient corridors steer you through the treasures of the digs of the 1920s and 1930s, art and artefacts from the prehistoric to Byzantine periods of Egyptian culture.

The **statuary** are the most immediately striking of the exhibits, though after a while it's the smaller **sculptural** pieces that hold the attention longest. Figures like *Merti and his Wife* were modelled as portraits, but often carvings were made in the belief that a person's *Ka* or life force would continue to exist in an idealised model after their death. There's a beautifully crafted example in the *Carving of Senebi* in gallery 8; what was probably Senebi's tomb is displayed nearby. Also in this room is the dazzling collection of *Princess Sithathorunet's jewellery*, a pinnacle in Egyptian decorative art from around 1830 BC; the *Models of Mekutra's House* (around 1198 BC); and the radiant *Fragmentary Head of a Queen*, sensuously carved in polished yellow jasper.

The Temple of Dendur

At the end of all this sits the **Temple of Dendur**, housed in a vast airy gallery designed to give hints and symbols of its original site on the banks of the Nile. Built by the Emperor Augustus in 15 BC as an attempt to placate a local chieftain, the temple was moved here as a gift of the Egyptian people during the construction of the Aswan High dam – it would otherwise have been drowned. Sadly the gallery, rather than suggest the empty expanses of the Nile, dwarfs what is essentially an unremarkable building, one that might be more engaging if you could explore inside. The temple needs a helping hand, and gets it at night, illuminated on a corner of Central Park with at least some of the mystery that's missing during the day.

The Michael C. Rockefeller Wing

Son of Governor Nelson Rockefeller, Michael C. Rockefeller disappeared during a trip to West New Guinea in 1961. The Rockefeller Wing stands as a memorial to him, including many of his finds alongside the Met's comprehensive collection of art from Africa, the Pacific Islands and the Americas. It's a superb gallery, the muted, reassuring decoration throwing the "Primitive" Art exhibits into sharp and often frightening focus. You don't need much knowledge of "Primitive" cultures to feel the intensity of the work here: the blackened reliquary heads from Gabon once contained the skulls of a family's ancestors and issued magical protection; the elegant spared lines of terracotta heads from Ghana put you in mind of Modigliani portraits, and the rich geometry of the South American jewellery and ornaments too seems often startlingly contemporary.

Other collections

The Met's **other collections** include the **Costume Institute**, which shows rotating exhibitions from its collection of more than 60,000 costumes and accessories dating from the fifteenth century to the present day. The expanding **Department of Photographs** has been busily acquiring work, and now commands a collection to rival that of the Museum of Modern Art. In summer months, **contemporary sculpture** adorns the museum's open-air **roof garden**, set against the spectacular backdrop of the New York skyline.

The Museum of Modern Art

11 W 53rd St. Subway E or F to Fifth Ave–53rd St. Fri–Tues 11am–6pm, Thurs 11am–9pm, closed Wed; $7.50, students $4.50, Thurs 5–9pm pay what you wish.

Instigated in 1929, moved to its present permanent home ten years later, and in the mid-1980s extensively updated in a steel pipe and glass renovation that doubled its gallery space, **The Museum of Modern Art** (plain MoMA to the initiated) offers probably the finest and most complete account of late nineteenth- and twentieth-century art you're likely to find. Basically, if you're in New York for any length of time and you want to catch some museums, MoMA has to be top of the list of places not to miss.

The museum's layout

The MoMA building is designed to guide you as effortlessly and easily as possible into the collections – and, with ultra-modern glass-enclosed landings and gliding escalators, it's an enjoyable place just to walk inside. On the **first floor** you'll find the usual pairing of restaurant and shop, as well as a video room and film theatre

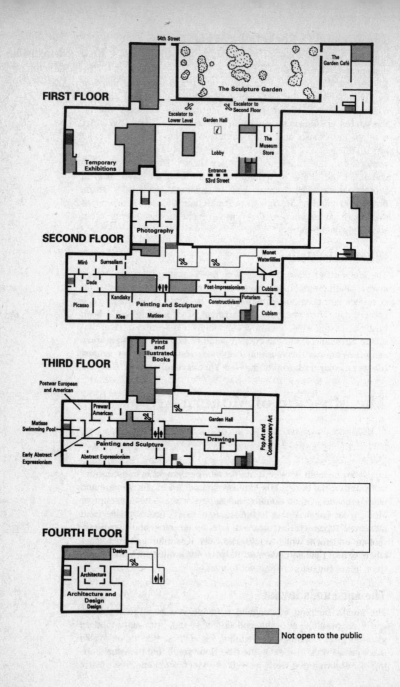

FIRST FLOOR

54th Street

The Sculpture Garden

The Garden Café

Escalator to Lower Level

Escalator to Second Floor

Garden Hall

i

Lobby

The Museum Store

Temporary Exhibitions

Entrance
53rd Street

SECOND FLOOR

Photography

Monet Waterlilies

Miró   Surrealism

Dada

Post-Impressionism   Cubism

Kandisky

Picasso   Painting and Sculpture   Constructivism   Futurism

Klee   Matisse   Cubism

THIRD FLOOR

Prints and Illustrated Books

Postwar European and American

Prewar American

Garden Hall

Matisse Swimming Pool

Pop Art and Contemporary Art

Drawings

Early Abstract Expressionism

Painting and Sculpture

Abstract Expressionism

FOURTH FLOOR

Design

Architecture

Architecture and Design Design

Not open to the public

(pick up a leaflet for a rundown on what's currently showing), and, outside, a **sculpture garden** holding scattered works in rotation by the likes of Rodin and Matisse, alongside artefacts like an example of the curvy Art Nouveau Paris metro sign. The museum proper begins upstairs, with the second and third floors devoted to the main **painting and sculpture galleries**, the fourth to **architecture and design**, and it's these, on the whole, that most people come to see. The roster of artists and major movements in these is, in the main, fairly constant. However, apart from a few key works, paintings are changed regularly, and some of the pieces we've commented on below won't necessarily be up when you visit – though there will usually be something by the same artist in its place.

In addition to the three main sections, the museum also has galleries devoted to **photographs**, **prints** and **drawings**, all of which give rotating displays of the museum's collections. The photographs, in particular, are marvellous – one of the finest, most eclectic collections around and a vivid evocation of twentieth-century America, from the dramatic landscapes of Ansel Adams to Stieglitz's dynamic views of New York and the revealing portraits of Man Ray.

Second floor: painting and sculpture

Once you reach the second floor, **Cézanne**'s *Bather* of 1885, alongside other works by him, pulls you inside, leading on towards further **Post-Impressionists** – principally works by **Gauguin**, **Seurat**, and, most famously, **Van Gogh,** represented by *Starry Night*. In the third room are paintings by the Belgian James Ensor, by Redon and Bonnard, along with Rousseau's *The Dream*, painted in 1910, leading through to galleries given over to works by the major Cubist painters, including a scatter of works by **Picasso** and **Braque**; and, most notably, Picasso's *Demoiselles d'Avignon of 1907*, a jagged, sharp, and, for its time, revolutionary clash of tones and planes which some hold to be the heralder (and initial arbiter) of Cubist principles – though **Derain**'s *Bathers* in the previous room may have equal claim to the title.

A room off to the left from this first Cubist gallery holds **Monet**'s *Water Lilies*, enormous, stirring attempts to abstract colour and form which cover well over half their gallery's space, their swirling jades, pinks and purples making it faintly like sitting in a giant aquarium. Otherwise continue straight through to the right to view some more **Cubist** canvases, later works mainly, taking in work by Leger, Picasso's *Three Women at the Spring* (1921), and *Three Musicians* from the same year, hung opposite Leger's jokier evocation of the same subject, painted in 1944.

Rooms encapsulating entire periods and movements follow, cursory glances but with a staggering quality of material. There are paintings by **Chagall**; **Kirchner**'s *Dresden* and *Berlin* street scenes are the focus of a gallery devoted to the glaring realities of the **German Expressionists**; while the whirring abstractions of **Boccioni** are the mainstay of a room devoted to the **Futurists'** paeans to the industrial age. A further room takes in the work of **De Stijl**, principally **Mondrian**, following the artist's development from early limp Cubist pieces to later works like *Broadway Boogie Woogie*. This, painted in 1940 after he had moved to New York, reflects his love of jazz music – its short, sharp stabs of colour conveying an almost physical rhythm.

Beyond here (past a staircase leading up to the next painting and sculpture floor), **Matisse** has a large room to himself, including many of the works that made the world-wide tour of his paintings such a success in 1991–93. MoMA's collection centres on the *Dancers* of 1909, taking in other lesser-known works like his pudgy series of *Heads of Jeanette*, where straight Impressionism becomes, in the final head, no more than a series of disfiguring lines and lumps. Look out, also, for the *Red Studio*, a depiction of Matisse's studio in France in which all perspective is resolved in shades of rusty red, and, if it's hung (which it's often not), *Le Bateau*. When this was first exhibited, MoMA had it hanging upside down for 47 days before noticing the mistake.

The next gallery holds paintings by **Klee**, some swirling canvases by **Kandinsky**, the smooth shapes of **Brancusi**'s sculpture, leading through to late works by **Braque** and **Picasso**: *Night Fishing at Antibes*; the *Seated Bather*; and the *Charnel House* – like *Guernica*, which used to hang here before it was removed to Spain's Prado, an angry protest against the horrors of war.

In contrast, a room on, are the brooding skies of **de Chirico**; a room containing works by **Miro**, notably his hilarious *Dutch Interior*, 1928; and a handful of dreamlike paintings by **Dali**, **Magritte** – *The Menaced Assassin* – **Delvaux** – *Phases of the Moon* – and **Balthus**: illogical scenes but disturbing in their clarity and undercurrents of eroticism. In Balthus's *The Living Room* the static poses of the adolescent girls and carefully positioned guitar hint at notions of sexual awakening; while his rather odd portrait of Derain, painted in 1936, shows the anxious artist in front of a half-dressed young girl.

Third floor: painting and sculpture

The second painting and sculpture gallery continues chronologically, and, perhaps inevitably, with a more American slant – **Andrew Wyeth**'s *Christina's World*, one of the best known of all modern American paintings, is often hung here, usually along with a couple of typically gloomy canvases by **Edward Hopper** – *House by the Railroad* and *New York Movie*: potent and atmospheric pieces which give a bleak account of modern American life. Contrast these with **Sheeler**'s *American Landscape*: "the industrial landscape

pastoralised", a critic noted, and almost toytown in its neat vision of
industrialisation, in which nothing moves and all gleams neat and
clean.

More abstract pieces follow: early Jackson Pollocks, **Gorky**'s
Miro-like doodles, some neat satires by **Dubuffet** and, at the end of
the room, the anguished scream of **Bacon**'s *No.7 from 8 Studies
for a Portrait*. What many come here for, however, is to see the
later paintings of the artists of the **New York School** – large-scale
canvases meant to be viewed from a distance, as here, in large airy
rooms. The paintings of **Pollock** and **de Kooning** – wild, and in
Pollock's case textured, patterns with no clear beginning or end –
mingle with the more ordered efforts of the Colour Field artists and
the later works of artists like **Matisse** and **Miro**. Matisse's work here
is mainly paper cutouts, most striking the bold blue shapes of his
Swimming Pool which the ageing artist made to decorate the walls
of his apartment in Nice. The work of the so-called **Colour Field
artists** is more vivid but emphasises the importance of colour in a
similar way – their paintings, in **Barnett Newman**'s words, "drained
of impediments of memory, association, nostalgia, legend, myth,
and what have you": in short without anything but pure colour, as in
Newman's own *Vir Heroicus Sublimus*, sheer red and huge against
the wall; in the radiating, almost humming blocks of colour of the
paintings of **Mark Rothko**; and, perhaps most palpably, in the sheer
black canvases of **Ad Reinhardt**. Robert Motherwell's *Elegy to the
Spanish Republic*, one of a series of more than a hundred such
paintings, is slightly different: colour is less important, and the
broad splashes of black are meant to hint at the rituals of the
corrida, the shapes roughly reminiscent of the testicles displayed at
the finale of a bullfight.

The last of the painting and sculpture rooms is in part made up
of donations by Philip Johnson – **Pop Art** mainly, including **Jasper
Johns**' *Flag*, a well-known piece in which the Stars and Stripes is
painted on to newsprint, transforming America's most potent
symbol into little more than an arrangement of shapes and colours.
You might also see work by **Robert Rauschenberg** and **Claes
Oldenburg**, though these galleries are also regularly given over to
contemporary work from the museum's collection.

Fourth floor: architecture and design

Architecture and design is, after painting and sculpture, MoMA's
most important concern. The galleries on the fourth floor take in
models and original drawings by the architects of key modern buildings – **Frank Lloyd Wright**'s *Falling Water*, projects by **Le
Corbusier** and **Mies van der Rohe**. Further aspects of modern
design are traced through the swollen glasswork of **Tiffany**,
Guimard's flowery Art Nouveau furniture and, in addition to a
couple of **Rietveld** chairs, a Rietveld sideboard which looks as if it

The Museum of Modern Art

could do with a spot of Rietveld paint. There are also **chairs and other furniture** designed by Mies van der Rohe, Alvar Alto and Henri van den Velde, some of which have been more successful examples of applied design than others. Look out, too – indeed you can't miss them – for the oversized items at the top of the escalator, notably a green Bell helicopter from 1945, poised delicately in the open space of the landing.

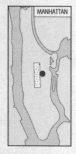

The Guggenheim Museum

Fifth Ave at 89th St. Subway #4, #5 or #6 to 86th St. Fri–Weds 10am–8pm; closed Thurs; $7, students $4; Tuesdays 5–8pm pay what you wish.

The Guggenheim SoHo has annually changing exhibits from the main gallery; see p.218.

Multistorey car park or upturned beehive? Whatever you think of the **Guggenheim Museum**, it's the building which steals the show. Frank Lloyd Wright's purpose-built structure, sixteen years in the making, caused a storm of controversy when it was unveiled in 1959, bearing little relation to the statuesque apartment blocks of this most genteel part of Fifth Avenue. Reactions, though Wright didn't live long enough to hear many, ranged from disgusted disbelief to critical praise and acclaim. And even now, though the years have given the building a certain respectability, no one seems to have quite made up their mind, as the furore over the museum's **extension** proved. From 1990 to summer 1992 the museum was closed, undergoing a $60 million facelift of the original Lloyd Wright building that opened the whole space to the public for the first time. Pokey offices, storage rooms and bits of chicken wire were all removed to expose the uplifting interior spaces so that the public could experience the whole spiral of the central rotunda from top to bottom. This, along with the cleverly added extension, has added the sort of tall, straight-walled flat floored galleries that the Guggenheim so desperately needed. Today, the consensus is that the building is now a better museum and better work of architecture.

Some Guggenheim history

Solomon R. Guggenheim was one of America's richest men, his mines extracting silver and copper – and a healthy profit – all over the USA. Like other nineteenth-century American capitalists the only problem for Guggenheim was what to spend his vast wealth on, so he started collecting Old Masters – a hobby he continued half-heartedly until the 1920s, when various sorties to Europe brought him into contact with the most avant-garde and influential of European art circles. Abstraction in art was then considered little more than a fad but Guggenheim, always a man with an eye for a sound investment, started to collect modern paintings with fervour, buying up wholesale the work of Kandinsky, adding items by Chagall, Gleizes, Léger and others, and exhibiting them to a bemused American public in his suite of rooms in the Plaza Hotel. In 1976 the collector Justin K. Thannhauser bequeathed masterworks by Cézanne, Degas, Gaugin, Manet, Toulouse-Lautrec, Van Gogh and Picasso, among others, to the museum. The Guggenheim's collection of American Minimalist art from the 1960s is particularly rich too.

The collection

It's these works, added to with special purchases and the odd dona-tion, which form the nucleus of the permanent collection, and, between the extension and the rotunda, a significant part of the museum's collection will always be displayed. There are also regu-larly exhibitions based on aspects of the collection, picking up themes from the various styles and periods – which means there's little you can say about the Guggenheim without predicting what's going to be on show. Even so, it's the space itself which dominates – "one of the greatest rooms erected in the twentieth century", wrote Philip Johnson, and quite rightly: even if you hate the sight of the place from the outside it's hard not to be impressed by the tiers of cream concrete opening up above like the ribs of some giant convector fan as you go in. Most of the temporary exhibits are shown in the circular galleries, and the best way of seeing them is to zip straight to the top of the building (by way of the crescent-shaped lifts) and saunter down the gentle slope. On the way, two galleries offer a representative sample of the Guggenheim's **permanent collection**: the first, in the **new extension**, giving a quick glance at the Cubists, Chagall and, most completely, Kandinsky; the other, the **Thannhauser Galleries**, in the restored small rotunda, offering a collection of Post-Impressionist and early Modern masterpieces which is at the core of the museum's holdings. Highpoints here are a handful of late nineteenth-century paintings, not least the exqui-site Degas *Dancers* and other Post-Impressionists, Van Gogh's *Mountains at St Remy* and some sensitive early Picassos.

The Frick Collection

1 E 70th St. Subway #6 to 68th St–Lexington Ave. Tues–Sat 10am–6pm, Sun 1–6pm, closed Mon; $3, students $1.50. Audio-visual installation tells Henry Clay Frick's story, details the mansion and its collection at a quar-ter past each hour between 11.15am and 4.15pm. Concerts of classical music are also held each month: pick up a leaflet for details.

Some history

Housed in the former mansion of Henry Clay Frick, the **Frick Collection** is perhaps the most enjoyable of the big New York galleries, made up of the art treasures hoarded by Frick during his years as probably the most ruthless of New York's robber barons.

Vicious, uncompromising and anti-union, Frick broke strikes with state troopers and was hated enough to narrowly survive a number of assassination attempts. However, the legacy of his self-aggrandisement – he spent millions on the best of Europe's art treasures – is a superb collection of works, and as good a glimpse of the sumptuous life enjoyed by New York's big industrialists as you'll find.

First opened in the mid-1930s, the museum has been kept largely as it would have looked when the Fricks were living there. It's in dubious taste for the most part, much of the furniture heavy eighteenth-century French, but the nice thing about it – and many people rank the Frick as their favourite New York gallery because of this – is that it strives hard to be as unlike a museum as possible. Ropes are kept to a minimum, and even in the most sumptuously decorated rooms there are plenty of chairs you can freely sink into. When weary, you can take refuge in the central closed courtyard, whose abundant greenery, fountains and marble are arranged with a classical attention to order, and whose echoey serenity you'd be hard pushed to find anywhere else in the city.

The collection

The **collection** itself was acquired under the direction of Joseph Duveen, notorious – and not entirely trustworthy – adviser to the city's richest and most ignorant. For Frick, however, he seems to have picked out the cream of Europe's post-World War I private art hoards, even if the opening ensemble of the **Boucher Room** is not to twentieth-century tastes, decorated with succulent representations of the arts and sciences. Next along, the **Dining Room** is more reserved, its Reynoldses and Hogarths overshadowed by the one non-portrait in the room, **Gainsborough**'s *St James's Park*: a subtly moving promenade under an arch of luxuriant trees – "Watteau far outdone", wrote a critic at the time. Outside there's more lusty French painting (Boucher again) and, in the next room, **Fragonard**'s *Progress of Love* series, which was painted for Madame du Barry in 1771 – and rejected by her soon after.

Better paintings follow, not least of them **Bellini**'s *St Francis*, which suggests his vision of Christ by means of pervading light, a bent tree and an enraptured stare. **El Greco**'s *St Jerome*, above the fireplace, reproachfully surveys the riches all around, and looks out to the South Hall, where hangs one of Boucher's very intimate depictions of his naked wife – loaded with meaning – and an early **Vermeer**, *Officer and Laughing Girl*: similarly suggestive, and full of lewd allusions to forthcoming sex. In the opposite direction, the Library holds a number of British works, most notably one of **Constable**'s *Salisbury Cathedral* series, and in the North Hall hangs an engaging and sensitive portrait of the *Comtesse de Haussonville* by **Ingres**.

The West Gallery

But it's the **West Gallery**, beyond here, that's the Frick's major draw, and which holds some of its finest paintings. Two **Turners**, views of Cologne and Dieppe, hang opposite each other, both a blaze of orange and creamy tones; **Van Dyck** pitches in with a couple of uncharacteristically informal portraits of Frans Snyders and his wife – two paintings only reunited when Frick purchased them; and across the room **Frans Hals** reveals himself in a boozy and rare self-portrait. **Rembrandt**, too, is represented by a set of piercing self-portraits, and (although serious doubt has recently been thrown on its authenticity) the enigmatic *Polish Rider* – more fantasy-piece than portrait.

At the far end of the West Gallery **Whistler** shares the Oval Room with **Houdon's** *Diana*, his portrait of fellow-artist *Rose Corder* posed to the point where she would have to faint before Whistler would stop painting. Past here, the East Gallery holds more paintings still, but more interesting is the tiny room on the other side of the West Gallery. This houses an exquisite set of Limoges enamels, mainly sixteenth century, as well as a collection of small-scale paintings that includes a *Virgin and Child* by **Jan van Eyck** – one of the artist's very last works, and among the rare few to have reached America.

The Whitney Museum of American Art

945 Madison Ave at 75th St. Subway #6 to 77th St–Lexington Ave. Closed Mon and Thurs; Tues 1–8pm, Wed–Sun 11am–6pm, Sun noon–6pm; $6, students with ID $4; free for all Thurs 6–8pm. Excellent – and free – gallery talks take place Wed–Sun; times vary from week to week – phone ☎570-3652 for details.

A grey-faced Brutalist arsenal designed by Marcel Breuer, the Whitney's oblique windows and cantilevered floors have an intimidating and suspiciously institutional air. Within, however, all such impressions are quickly dispelled. This is some of the best gallery space in the city and the perfect forum for the works that it owns – one of the pre-eminent collections of twentieth-century American art. It is also a superb exhibition locale and, like the Guggenheim, devotes much of its time and rooms to this end. The majority of Whitney exhibitions are given over to retrospectives and debuts of lesser-known themes – Ed Keinholz and sculpture of the New York School are a couple of recent examples. Every other year, though, there is an exhibition of a wholly different nature – the **Whitney biennial** – designed to give a provocative overview of what's happening in contemporary American art. It is often panned by critics but always packed with visitors; catch it if you can between March and June on odd-numbered years.

The permanent collection

Gertrude Vanderbilt Whitney founded the collection in 1930 around works by Hopper, Thomas Hart Benton, George Bellows and other living painters. Currently the gallery owns over 10,000 pieces of painting, sculpture and photography by artists as diverse as Calder, Nevelson, O'Keefe, de Kooning, Rauschenburg, Le Witt and Nam June Paik. The **Highlights of the Permanent Collection**, a somewhat arbitrary pick of the Whitney's best, are arranged by both chronology and theme. The works form a superb introduction to twentieth-century American art, best evaluated with the help of the gallery talks, designed to explain and locate the paintings and sculptures in their various movements.

Gertrude Whitney's taste tended towards **Realism**, and the paintings often tie in with the expectations of the genre. **George Bellows**' *Dempsey and Firpo*, though, is a sort of Neo-Mannerist view of a boxing match, full of movement and flesh – "I don't know anything about boxing; I'm just painting two guys trying to kill each other", said Bellows.

The collection is particularly strong on **Edward Hopper** (his works were bequeathed to the museum) and several of his best paintings are here: *Early Sun Morning* is typical, a bleak urban landscape, uneasily tense in its lighting and rejection of topical detail. The street could be anywhere (in fact it's Seventh Avenue) and, for Hopper, becomes universal.

As if to balance the figurative works that formed the nucleus of the collection, more recent purchases include much **abstraction**. **Marsden Hartley's** *Painting Number 5* is a strident, overwhelmed work, painted in the memory of a German officer friend killed in the early days of the Great War. **Georgia O'Keefe** called it "a brass band in a closet", and certainly her own work is gentler, though with its darkness: *Abstraction* was suggested by the noises of cattle being driven to the local slaughterhouse. Have a look too at O'Keefe's flower paintings: verging on abstraction but hinting at deeper organic forms.

Featuring particularly strongly are the **Abstract Expressionists**, with great works by high priests **Pollock** and **De Kooning**, leading on to **Rothko** and the **Colour Field painters** – though you need a sharp eye to discern any colour in **Ad Reinhard's** *Black Painting*. In a different direction, **Warhol**, **Johns** and **Oldenburg** each subvert the meanings of their images. Warhol's silkscreened *Coke Bottles* fade into motif, Jasper Johns' celebrated *Three Flags* once again erases the emblem of patriotism, replacing it with ambiguity, and Claes Oldenburg's lighter-hearted *Soft Sculptures*, squidgy loos and melting motors, fall into line with his declaration, "I'm into art that doesn't sit on its ass in a museum." Finally, don't – you can't – miss **Ed Keinholz's** *The Wait*, perhaps the best macabre joke in town.

The Philip Morris Building collection

Situated in the atrium of the Philip Morris Building at 120 Park Ave
at 42nd St (subway #4, #5 or #6 to Grand Central–42nd St), this
has two sections: a small **Picture Gallery** (Mon–Sat 11am–6pm,
Thurs 11am–7.30pm; free; gallery talks Mon, Wed and Fri 7pm)
with changing exhibitions on just about any (modern) theme you
care to mention; and a **Sculpture Court** (Mon–Sat 7.30am–9.30pm,
Sun 11am–7pm; free) festooned with works. A great idea and a
much better place to wait for a train than Grand Central across the
road.

The Cloisters

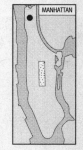

*Fort Tryon Park. Subway 190th St–Washington Ave; also hourly direct
shuttle coach from Metropolitan Museum, June, July & Aug, Fri & Sat; $5.
Museum open March–Oct Tues–Sun 9.30am–5.15pm. Nov–Feb Tues–Sun
9.30am–4.45pm, closed Mon. Suggested donation $6; $3 students
(includes admission to Metropolitan Museum on same day). Free tours
Tues–Thurs 3pm.*

High above the Hudson in Fort Tryon Park, **The Cloisters** stands
like some misplaced Renaissance palazzo-cum-monastery. Which
was presumably the desired effect. For this was the folly of collectors George Barnard and John D. Rockefeller, who in turn spent the
early years of this century shipping over the best of medieval
Europe that was going: Romanesque chapels and Gothic halls,
transplanted brick by brick and now housing the best part of the
Metropolitan Museum's **medieval collection**. If you're familiar with
the type of buildings that have been cannibalised, then the place
can't help but feel something of a Frankenstein's monster, an
assemblage of parts to make a distorted whole. Nevertheless it is all
undeniably well carried off, not without atmosphere, and in detail
superb.

The collection

The best approach – from the 190th Street subway – is directly
across the park; Rockefeller thoughtfully bought up the land on the
other side of the river so as not to spoil the views. Starting from the
entrance hall, working anti-clockwise lays out the collection in a
loosely chronological order. First off is the simple monumentality of
the **Romanesque Hall** made up from French remnants and the frescoed Spanish **Fuentiduena Chapel**, both thirteenth century and
immediately inducing a reverential hush. They corner on perhaps
the prettiest of the four sets of cloisters here, those from **St
Guilhelm**, strong and busily carved capitals from thirteenth-century
France. More or less contemporary, and again from France, is the
nearby **Langon Chapel**, attractive enough in itself and enhanced by

The Cloisters   a twelfth-century **ciborium** that manages to be formal and graceful in just the right proportions, and protects an emotive **Virgin and Child** beneath.

At the centre of the museum is the **Cuxa cloister**, from the twelfth-century Benedictine monastery of Saint Michel de Cuxa near Prades in the French Pyrenees; its capitals are brilliant peasant art, many carved with weird, self-devouring grotesque creatures. Pastiche additions to the scene are the gardens, planted with fragrant, almost overpowering, herbs and flowers and (bizarrely in keeping) piped plainsong.

The museum's smaller **sculpture** is equally impressive. In the **Early Gothic Hall** are a number of carved figures, one a memorably tender and refined **Virgin and Child**, carved in England in the four-teenth century, probably for veneration at a private altar. The collection of **tapestries** is special, too, including a rare surviving Gothic work showing the **Nine Heroes**. The heroes, popular figures of the ballads of the Middle Ages, comprise three pagans (Hector, Alexander, Julius Caesar), three Hebrews (David, Joshua, Judus Macabeas) and three Christians (Arthur, Charlemagne, Godfrey of Bouillon). Five of the nine are here, clothed in the garb of the day (around 1385) against a rich backdrop. The **Unicorn Tapestries**, in the succeeding room, are even more spectacular – brilliantly alive with colour, observation and Christian symbolism.

Most of the Met's medieval painting is to be found downtown, but one important exception here is **Campin's** *Merode Altarpiece*. Housed in its own antechamber, this triptych depicts the Annunciation scene in a typical bourgeois Flemish interior of the day. On the left the donors gaze timidly on through an open door, to the right St Joseph works in his carpenter's shop; St Joseph was mocked in the literature of the day, which might account for his rather ridiculous appearance – making a mousetrap, a symbol of the way the Devil traps souls. Through the windows behind life goes on in a fifteenth-century market square, perhaps Campin's native Tournai.

With the ground floor, you move into Gothic architecture – or at least into a pseudo-Gothic chapel, built around the monumental **sarcophagus of Ermengol VII**, with its whole phalanx of family and clerics carved around to send him off. Two further cloisters are here to explore, along with an amazing downstairs **Treasury**. This is crammed with items but two can easily be singled out: the **Belles Heures de Jean, Duc de Berry**, perhaps the greatest of all medieval Books of Hours, executed by the Limburg Brothers with dazzling genre miniatures of seasonal life; and the twelfth-century **altar cross** from Bury St Edmunds in England, a mass of tiny expressive characters from Biblical stories. Finally, hunt out a minute **rosary bead** from sixteenth-century Flanders: with a representation of the Passion inside, it seems barely possible it could have been carved by hand.

The American Museum of Natural History/Hayden Planetarium

Central Park West at 79th St. Subway C to 81st St–Central Park West. Sun–Thurs 10am–5.45pm; Fri and Sat 10am–8.45pm; suggested donation $4, Planetarium $5.

According to the *Guinness Book of Records*, this is the largest museum in the world bar none, and once you've paced the length of its ageing exhibition hall and witnessed a fair number of its 34 million exhibits, you'll know it. Which is basically to say be selective: anthropologists could have a field day here, but for anyone else a highly discriminating couple of hours should be ample.

The main entrance on Central Park West is the one to make for, leaving you well placed for a loop of the more interesting halls on the first floor: principally intelligently mounted artefacts from Asia and Africa, backed up with informal commentary and lent atmosphere with drums and ethnic music. These are sandwiched between dusty dioramas of the two continents' mammals. Upstairs the wilting dinosaurs on the fourth floor are currently out of sight, as all six galleries are being refurbished. Two will open in April 1994, two more in April 1995 and the rest in 1996. Until then, check out the Hall of Meteorites instead: well laid-out and including some strikingly beautiful crystals – not least the *Star of India*, the largest blue sapphire ever found; or head for the *NatureMax* theatre, with the biggest viewing screen in NYC, presenting IMAX films.

The Hayden Planetarium

The museum's astronomy department is installed in the adjacent **Hayden Planetarium** (Mon–Fri 12.30–4.45pm, Sat 10am–5.45pm, Sun noon–5.45pm) – accessible from the first floor of the Natural History Museum or from a separate entrance on 81st Street. Here you can view a variety of astronomical displays and gadgetry, hear Henry Fonda, Walter Kronkite and assorted celebrities relate an impassioned tale of space endeavour, or watch a soporifically dull history of the universe (narrator Vincent Price) in the theatre. All of which are cloyingly dull – and, again, primarily directed at children. You may instead prefer to fork out for the planetarium's **laser light shows**, held on Friday and Saturday evenings to provide visuals and sound for teenage stoners to freak out to their favourite Led Zep or Floyd tracks.

Minor museums

While you could fill weeks wandering through New York's great museums listed earlier in this chapter, the city is awash with smaller museums, and the collections are so varied as to have something to

*For details of
museums
specifically for
kids, see
Chapter 13,
Kids' New York.*

interests everyone. On a highly selective basis, highlights must include the **Pierpont Morgan Library**, the **International Center for Photography**, the **Museum of the American Indian** (a neglected wonder of the city), the **Jewish Museum** (benefiting from a recent refit), a clutch of first-rate **ethnic museums** and, for anyone less than enamoured with current New York TV screens, the public archives of the **Museum of Broadcasting**.

Art and visuals

Alternative Museum
594 Broadway, between Houston and Prince sts. Subway N or R to Prince St. Tues–Sat 11am–6pm, closed mid-Aug–mid-Sept; suggested donation $3.

Temporary exhibitions of contemporary art, emphasising international developments. Well organised and adventurous, with displays supplemented by regular musical events and poetry readings. For information pick up their calendar, or give them a call – ☎966-4444.

Asia Society Gallery
725 Park Ave at 70th St. Subway #6 to 68th St–Lexington Ave. Thurs and Sat 11am–6pm, Fri 11am–8pm; $2, students $1; Fri evening free.

Small permanent display of the Rockefeller collection of Asian art. Worth the admission fee if the accompanying temporary exhibition looks promising. Asia House also holds interesting performances/lectures/films/free events: ☎517-ASIA for details.

Bronx Museum of the Arts
1040 Grand Concourse, corner of 165th St, the Bronx. Subway #4 to 161st St–Grand Concourse. Wed–Fri 10am–5pm, Sat & Sun 1–6pm; suggested donation $3, students $2.

Contemporary American art, none of any great note, plus changing exhibitions of Bronx-based artists.

The Brooklyn Museum
200 Eastern Parkway, Brooklyn. Subway #2 or #3 to Eastern Parkway–Brooklyn Museum. Weds–Sun 10am–5pm; $4, students $2. The museum's Gift Shop sells genuine ethnic items from around the world at reasonable prices.

When Judy Chicago's *Dinner Party* was exhibited here back in the early 1980s, the Brooklyn Museum had people queuing all the way round the block. Since then it's reverted to its former, little-visited status: a museum good in its own right but doomed to stand perpetually in the shadow of the Met. Which is a pity, for it's a likeable place, and – together with a visit to the adjacent Botanical Garden, not to mention Prospect Park, just beyond – a good reason for forsaking Manhattan for an afternoon.

It does, however, need considerable selectivity, for in terms of size
this is most certainly a major museum, with five floors stacked with
exhibits. The highlights, depending on your personal interests, are
likely to include the **ethnographic department** on the ground floor,
containing arts and applied arts from Oceania and the Americas, **the
Classical and Egyptian antiquities** on the second floor, and the
excellent and evocative **American period rooms** on the fourth floor,
which includes interiors and houses removed intact from elsewhere
in Brooklyn, decorated with period furniture and other features. Be
sure, too, to look in on the **American and European picture galleries** on the top storey. Here there are lots of eighteenth-century
portraits, including one of George Washington by Gilbert Stuart;
bucolic canvases by William Sidney Mount, alongside the heavily
romantic paintings of the Hudson River School, not least the Catskill
scenes of Thomas Cole and Frederick Church and Albert Bierstadt's
Storm in the Rocky Mountains – a vast painting which established
his reputation as a landscape artist. Later galleries display later paintings, notably by Eastman Johnson and John Singer Sargent, especially Johnson's curious *Not at Home*, leading right up to twentieth-
century work by Charles Sheeler and Georgia O'Keefe. There's also a
handful of works by European artists – Degas, Cézanne, Toulouse-
Lautrec, Monet, Dufy, among others – though not including anything
approaching their best work.

Fashion Moda
*2803 Third Ave at 147th St. Subway #2 or #5 to Third Ave–149th St.
Tues–Sat 2–7pm; free.*
"Fashion Moda is impossible to define because by definition we
have no definition." Which goes some way to explaining what you're
likely to see here: anarchic and always surprising temporary exposi-
tions of art that are a positive attempt to break with the at times
chic safety of the Manhattan art scene. Its siting in the worst of the
South Bronx's urban decay is deliberately intimidating, but if you
can get someone to drop you on the doorstep, Fashion Moda's exhibitions rarely fail to entertain.

Forbes Galleries
*62 Fifth Ave at 12th St. Subway #4, #5 or #6 to Union Square, or F to
14th St–Sixth Ave. Tues, Wed, Fri & Sat, 10am–4pm; free.*
The world's largest collection of Fabergé Easter eggs, along with
500 toys boats and 12,000 toy soldiers – among the late Malcolm
Forbes's favourite playthings.

Grey Art Gallery
*33 Washington Place. Subway R to 8th St. Hours vary, but broadly Tues,
Thurs and Fri 11am–6.30pm, Wed 11am–8.30pm, Sat 11am–5pm; free.*
This, the gallery of NYU's art department, displays two outstanding
collections: the **New York University art collection**, known

particularly for its American painting from the 1940s onwards, and prints by Picasso, Miró and Matisse; and the **Abbey Weed Grey Collection of Contemporary Asian and Middle Eastern Art**.

Guggenheim Museum SoHo

575 Broadway at Prince St. Subway N or R to Prince Street. Sun, Mon and Weds 11am–6pm; Thurs Sat 11am–10pm; $5, students $3; two-day pass for both uptown and SoHo Guggenheims $10, students $6.

By renting three floors of a loft building in the heart of SoHo, the Guggenheim is the first major museum to move downtown to where New York's contemporary art scene really happens. The site provides space for exhibitions for older rather than contemporary art, providing an historical context for the new and helping break down the traditional barrier between uptown museums and downtown artists. Annually hanging exhibitions of major works from the Guggenheim's collection take place in a series of all-white galleries, and it's certainly worth dropping by to see what's on.

International Center of Photography

1130 Fifth Ave at 94th St. Subway #6 to 96th St–Lexington Ave. Tues 11am–8pm, Wed–Fri 11am–6pm, Sat–Sun 11am–6pm; $4, students $2.50. Free on Tues after 5pm.

Founded and directed by Cornell Capa, brother of Robert, the ICP exhibits photography in all its aspects. The Center's permanent collection features most of the greats – Cartier-Bresson, Adams, Kertesz, Eugene Smith – and there are often three temporary shows on at any given time. At least one of these is bound to be worthwhile, often featuring the city's most exciting avant-garde and experimental work. Overall, an excellent adjunct to MoMA's static collection.

ICP Midtown

77 W 45th St (International Paper Plaza). Subway B, D or F to 47th–50th St-Rockefeller Center. Hours and admission prices as ICP above; no free entry Tuesdays.

Smaller, changing exhibitions of photographs from the main collection.

Isamu Noguchi Garden Museum

32–37 Vernon Boulevard, Long Island City, Queens. Weekend shuttle bus from Asia Society every hour on the half-hour 11.30am–3.30pm, $5 roundtrip; call ☎718/204-7088 for more info. Museum open April–Nov Wed, Sat and Sun 11am–6pm; suggested donation $4, students $2.

A comprehensive collection containing over 250 stone metal and wood sculptures, on the site of the studio of **Isamu Noguchi** (1904–88). Noguchi was born in Japan and came to the US at the age of 14, later studying under Brancusi in Paris. His sculpture and designs for gardens can be seen throughout America: if you admire his work, then the collection here will knock you out.

Museum of the Moving Image

*35th Ave at 36th St, Astoria, Queens. Subway R to Steinway St. Tues–Fri
noon–4pm, Sat & Sun noon–6pm; $5, students $2.50; film and exhibition
information ☎ 718/784-0077.*

Relatively new exhibition on film, TV and video, housed in part of
the once-again functioning Astoria Studios, which are used by
Woody Allen and the Cosby Show among others. Part of the
museum is given over to temporary exhibitions – the ground floor
and second floor — while the first floor holds a permanent exhibition devoted to the development of the media through the ages.
Along with posters and wonderfully kitsch movie souvenirs from the
1930s and 1940s are screenings designed to explain the technical
development of an art form that, to millions around the world,
defined America. You can listen in to directors explaining sequences
from famous movies; watch fun short films made up of well-known
clips; add your own sound effects to movies; and view original sets
and costumes. There's also a wonderful, mock-Egyptian pastiche of
a 1920s movie theatre designed specially for the museum and actually used for showings of kids' movies and TV classics. Excellent
and enthralling, though a shame it couldn't have been larger. See
also "Astoria" in Chapter 5, *The Outer Boroughs*.

National Academy of Design

*1083 Fifth Ave at 89th St. Subway #4, #5 or #6 to 86th St–Lexington Ave.
Wed–Sun noon–5pm, Fri till 8pm; $3.50, students $2.*

Samuel Morse founded the National Academy of Design along the
lines of London's Royal Academy, and though 1083 Fifth Avenue is
nothing so grand as Burlington House, similarities remain: a school
of fine art, exclusive membership and regular exhibitions which, as
you'd imagine, are usually (though not exclusively) American.
There's a tradition that academicians and academics give a work of
art on their election here: associates a self-portrait, academicians a
"mature work". One hundred and fifty years' worth of these pictures
are now held by the Academy and form the mainstay of the
Selection from the Permanent Collection – varied throughout the
year but always with a strong slant towards portraiture.

   Icing on the cake is the building itself: a faintly snooty Beaux Arts
townhouse donated to the academy by the husband of sculptor Anna
Hyatt Huntingdon; her *Diana* gets pride of place below the cheerful
rotunda.

New Museum of Contemporary Art

*583 Broadway between Prince and Houston sts. Subway N or R to Prince
St, or #6 to Spring St. Wed, Thurs, Sun noon–6pm, Fri–Sat noon–8pm,
Sun noon–6pm; $3.50, students and artists $2.50.*

Regularly changing exhibitions by contemporary American and
international artists. Offbeat, eclectic and worth checking out, the
New Museum will mount sometimes risky exhibitions that other

museums are unable – or unwilling – to show. Its SoHo-centre library (Weds–Fri noon–6pm; free access, but appointments preferred) claims to be the only library in the world devoted entirely to contemporary art criticism and theory. Pick up the museum's calendar for details on current and forthcoming exhibits and lectures.

The Pierpont Morgan Library

29 E 36th St. Subway #6 to 33rd St–Park Ave. Tues–Sat 10.30am–5pm, Sun 1–5pm, closed Sun in July & Aug; pay what you wish, suggested $5, students $3.

Built by McKim, Mead and White for J. Pierpont Morgan in 1917, this gracious Italian-style nest, feathered with the fruits of the financier's magpie-ish trips to Europe, is one of New York's best small museums – though many of the exhibits are changed regularly so it's difficult to say precisely what you'll see.

The focal points are two main rooms, access to which is along a corridor usually lined with a fine assortment of **Rembrandt prints**. The first room you come to, the **West Room**, served as Morgan's study and has been left much as it was when he worked here, with a carved sixteenth-century Italian ceiling, a couple of paintings by Memling and Perugino, and, among the few items contemporary with the building, a desk custom-carved to a design by McKim. There's a portrait of J.P's father over the fifteenth-century Florentine fireplace, and a portrait of J.P. Junior on the far wall, swathed in the academic finery of an honorary Cambridge degree conferred in 1919. Through a domed and pillared hallway from here lies the **East Room** or library, a sumptuous three-tiered cocoon of rare books, autograph musical manuscripts and various trinkets culled from European households and churches. In a changing exhibit, there are original manuscripts by Mahler (the museum holds the world's largest collection of his work); a Gutenburg Bible from 1455 (one of 11 surviving); the only complete copy of Thomas Malory's *Morte d'Arthur*; as well as literary manuscripts of everyone from the letters of Vasari and George Washington to works by Keats and Dickens. All in all a fascinating display.

Roerich Museum

319 W 107th St. Subway #1 to 110th St–Broadway. Tues–Sun 2–5pm; free.

Nicolas Roerich was a Russian artist who lived in India, was influenced by Indian mysticism, and produced strikingly original paintings. A small, weird, and virtually unknown collection.

Society of Illustrators' Museum

128 East 63rd St. Subway #4, #5 or #6 to 59th St–Lexington Ave. Mon–Fri 10am–5pm, Tues 10am–8pm; free.

Changing selections from the Society's permanent collection of illustrations – wartime propaganda to slick contemporary adverts, with all manner of cartoons and drawings between. The exhibitions centre on theme or illustrator – designed primarily for aficionados but always accessible, well mounted and topical.

Museum of Television and Radio

25 W 52nd St. Subway E or F to Fifth Ave–53rd St. Tues–Sat noon–5pm; suggested $4, $3 students. Tues noon–8pm; pay what you wish. Phone ☎621-6600 for details of lectures by artists and directors.

An archive of American TV and radio broadcasts, unusually accessible to the public, whose excellent card reference system allows you to trace 1950s comedies, old newsreels and other oddities. Be warned, though, that there are only a couple of dozen video consoles and someone before you may well be getting down to a day's worth of "I Love Lucy". Arrive, if possible, at opening.

City history

Fraunces Tavern

54 Pearl St. Subway #4 or #5 to Bowling Green. Mon–Fri 10am–4.45pm, Sun noon–4pm; free Mon–Fri 10am–noon, other times $2.50, students $1.

Odds and sods from the Revolutionary era likeably housed in an historic building; see "The Financial District" in Chapter 2, *Lower Manhattan*.

Museum of Bronx History

3266 Bainbridge Ave, the Bronx. Subway D to 205th St–Bainbridge Ave. Mon–Fri 9am–5pm by appointment, Sat 10am–4pm, Sun 1–5pm; $1.

Bronx-related artefacts from Indian times to the Depression.

Museum of the City of New York

Fifth Ave at 103rd St. Subway #6 to 103rd St–Lexington Ave. Weds–Sat 10am–5pm, Sun 1–5pm; suggested donation $5, students $3.

Spaciously housed in a purpose-built neo-Georgian mansion on the fringes of Spanish Harlem, this gives a competent if unexciting rundown on the history of the city from Dutch times to the present day. Paintings, furniture and a slide show – plus the museum runs Sunday walking tours of New York neighbourhoods (see "Information, Maps and Tours" in *Basics*).

Museum of Immigration

Ellis Island: access by Circle Line Statue of Liberty Ferry from Battery Park. Ferry ($6) runs daily 9.30am–5.30pm in summer, 9.30am–5pm in winter, though you need to be on the 3pm ferry at the latest to be able to see the museum. Entry to museum is free.

Artefacts, photographs, maps and ethnic music tell the story of the immigrants who passed through Ellis Island on their way to settle throughout America. See Chapter 2, *Lower Manhattan*.

Minor Museums

New York City Transit Exhibit

Old subway entrance at Schermerhorn St and Boerum Place, Brooklyn. Nearest subway Borough Hall. Tues–Fri 10am–4pm, Sat–Sun 11am–4pm; $3.

Subway cars from the turn of the century, artefacts and ephemera connected with the world's largest underground railway. Cheap and engaging, even for non-enthusiasts, and made all the better by being housed in a disused subway station.

The New York Historical Society

Central Park West at 77th St. Subway #1 to 79th St. Tues–Sun 10am–5pm; closed till Fall 1994 for refurbishing.

More a museum of American than New York history, but another venue well worth keeping an eye on, after it reopens, for its temporary exhibitions, and with a permanent collection that repays a visit in its own right. Focus of this are the paintings of **James Audubon**, the Harlem artist and naturalist who specialised in lovingly detailed watercolours of birds – all very similar, and unless you're a keen ornithologist, not exactly attention-grabbing. Other galleries hold a broad sweep of **nineteenth-century American painting**: principally portraiture (a slobbish Aaron Burr, the picture of Alexander Hamilton that found its way on to the $10 bill) and Hudson River School landscapes (among them Thomas Cole's famed and fanatically pompous *Course of Empire* series). More rewarding is the glittering display of **Tiffany glass**, providing an excellent all-round view of Louis Tiffany's attempts "to provide good art for American homes". On a more historical note, and for a small additional fee, you can look round the museum **library**, which boasts such diverse items as the original Louisiana Purchase document and the correspondence between Aaron Burr and Alexander Hamilton that led up to their duel (see p.159). An interesting museum, and often overlooked.

Police Academy Museum

235 E 20th St. Subway #6 to 23rd St–Park Ave. Mon–Fri 9am–2pm by appointment only (☎477-9753); free.

A collection of memorabilia of the New York Police Department, the largest and oldest in the country. It's used to inculcate reverence for the force in young cadets, and just about merits itself to anyone not wildly interested in law and order. Really, it's not about crime or punishment so much as the personal effects of New York's Finest: night sticks, uniforms, photos and the like. There's a copper badge of 1845 as worn by the sergeants of the day, earning them the sticking nickname of "coppers". If you're into firepower, search out the tommy gun in a violin case – original gangster issue.

Queens Museum

Flushing Meadows–Corona Park. Subway #7 to Willets Point–Shea Stadium. Tues–Fri 10am–5pm, Sun noon–5pm; $3, students $1.50.

Primarily worth the trip for its one and only permanent item, which should be back on display by late 1994, after its most recent updating: an 18,000-square-foot model of the five boroughs of New York City, spectacularly lit, constantly remodelled and originally conceived for the 1964 World's Fair by Robert Moses. Great fun if you know the city, and useful orientation if you don't. The zoo here has an aviary in one of Buckminster Fuller's geodesic domes.

Community and ethnic

Museum of African Art
593 Broadway. Subway N or R to Prince St. Weds–Sun 11am–6pm, Fri & Sat 11am–8pm; $3, students $1.50.

Changing exhibitions of the best of traditional African art. An eye-opener compared to the static/junk collections that are usually found.

The Museum of the American Indian
Audubon Terrace, 3753 Broadway at 155th St (but see note below). Subway #1 to 157th St–Broadway. Tues–Sat 10am–5pm, Sun 1–5pm. $3, students $2.

Way the finest of the Audubon Terrace collections, this languishes up in Harlem almost totally ignored. When a few of its prize exhibits were shown downtown for a couple of weeks, more people went to look than turned up at the museum that year. Don't follow this pattern, for you'll miss out on a superb and fascinating assemblage of daily artefacts from almost every tribe native to the Americas. This might sound a little overpowering, but the display is skilful and backed up with an intelligent range of informational aids. Highlights include assorted scalps, the personal knick-knacks of Sitting Bull and Geronimo, shrunken human figures from Ecuador and some amazing Inuit scrimshaw. There's also a reasonably priced museum shop selling various authentic items. At the end of 1994, the core of the collection will be moved to the US Customs House on the Bowling Green in Lower Manhattan (see Chapter 2); the remainder of the exhibits will go to the Smithsonian Institute in Washington D.C..

Museo del Barrio
1230 Fifth Ave at 104th St. Subway #6 to 103rd St. Wed–Sun 11am–5pm; suggested donation $2, students $1. Following renovation during 1994, the Museo will reopen with a grand 25th anniversary exhibition.

Literally "the neighbourhood museum", this place was founded in the 1960s by a group of Puerto Ricans from Spanish Harlem who wanted to educate their children and remind them of their roots. Now, although the emphasis remains largely Puerto Rican, the museum has come to embrace the whole of Latin America, with five major loan exhibits of painting, photographs and crafts each year. Supplementary events include talks, summer concerts and kids' puppet theatre – all free.

Minor Museums

Chinatown Museum
8 Mott St. Subway N or R to Canal St. Mon–Sat 10am–6pm, closed Sun.

A hoard of Chinese costumes, Buddhas and religious accoutrements located at the end of a sleazy amusement arcade (which itself includes a devastatingly cruel contraption caging a "live, dancing chicken"). A neat stop-off on any tour of Chinatown were it not for the fact that it's open only to groups of eight or more.

The Hall of Chinese History
246 Bowery, between Prince & Houston streets. Open for groups only, by appointment on ☎962-3634.

Life-size terracotta warriors and horses of the Qin dynasty are the high spot of this collection of Chinese art across the ages.

Hispanic Museum
Audubon Terrace (see Museum of the American Indian, p.223). Tues–Sat 10am–4.30pm, Sun 1–4pm; free.

Inevitably this is overshadowed by the adjacent Museum of the American Indian (until it relocates), but it's worth sticking your nose round the door of the Hispanic for the chocolatey terracotta interior, a scattering of Spanish masters, and, best of all, the joyful *Murals of Spain* by Joaquin Sorolla y Bastida. The library of 100,000 books is a major centre for research in art, history and literature (Tues–Fri 1–4.15pm and Sat 10am–4.15pm).

Schomburg Center for Research in Black Culture
515 Malcolm X. Boulevard at 135th St. Subway #2 or #3 to 125th St–Lenox Ave. Mon–Wed noon–8pm, Fri–Sat 10am–6pm, Sun 1–5pm; free.

Thought-provoking exhibitions of documents, art, photos and sculpture that detail the history of blacks in the US. The five million items in its collections make the Center the world's pre-eminent research facility for the study of black history and culture.

Jewish Museum
1109 Fifth Ave at 92nd St. Subway #4, #5 or #6 to 92nd St. Sun–Thurs 11am–5.45pm, Tues till 8pm; $6, students $4; Tues after 5pm pay what you wish.

The Jewish Museum reopened in 1993 following a major refurbishment and expansion that made it the largest museum of Judaica outside Israel. Its centrepiece is the permanent exhibition on the Jewish experience – the basic ideas, values and culture developed over 4000 years. More vibrant and exciting, however, are the changing exhibitions on the ground floor, which feature major international artists, and the children's "hands-on" area on the fourth floor.

Studio Museum of Harlem
144 W 125th St. Subway #2 or #3 to 125th St–Lenox Ave. Wed–Fri 10am–5pm, Sat & Sun 1–6pm; $3.

Exhibitions of contemporary (and often local) art, photography and sculpture.

Lower East Side Tenement Museum

97 Orchard St. Subway F to Delancey St–Essex St. Tues–Fri 11am–4pm, Sun 10am–5pm; suggested donation $3. The museum also organises Sunday walking tours of the Lower East Side, usually starting between noon and 2pm. Call ☎431-0233 for a programme.

Housed in a former tenement building, this museum aims to present a complete picture of immigrant history in New York, especially Lower Manhattan, through a variety of changing temporary exhibitions on its ground floor. The two galleries show photos and community-based exhibits (importantly not just concentrating on the Jewish history of the area), while the upstairs rooms have been preserved more or less as they were when the house was occupied by numerous immigrant families earlier this century. This part is currently closed to the public, but there are plans to develop it as a "living history" display, with people occupying the evocatively decayed rooms – unlived in since the 1930s – in authentic costume. An earnest and sympathetic attempt to document the immigrant experience – well worth a visit if you're in the area.

Ukrainian Museum

203 Second Ave. Subway #4, #5 or #6 to Astor Place. Wed–Sun 1–5pm; $1, students 50¢.

Situated in the heart of the Ukrainian East Village, there's little to entice outsiders into this small collection. On two tiny floors, it divides itself between recounting the history of immigration to the US from the Ukraine, and showing (more interestingly) some ethnic items from the Ukraine itself. Look out for the hand-painted Easter eggs or *pysanky* – a craft that's still practiced today because, according to Ukrainian folklore, when production ceases the world will end.

Crafts, fashion and design

American Craft Museum

40 W 53rd St. Subway E or F to Fifth Ave–53rd St. Wed–Sun 10am–5pm, Tues 10am–8pm; $3.50, students $1.50, free Tues 5–8pm.

A showcase of modern crafts as chosen by the American Craft Council. Bright, brash and good fun.

Museum of American Folk Art

Columbus Ave at 66th St. Tues–Sun 11.30am–7.30pm; suggested donation $2.

Changing exhibitions of traditional handicrafts with the emphasis on the domestic; could be just the place if the splendours the Met offers aren't your cup of tea.

Black Fashion Museum

155 W 126th St. Subway #2 or #3 to 125th St–Lenox Ave. Mon–Fri noon–
8pm; phone ☎666-1320 for an appointment; suggested donation $1.50,
students $1.

It's on the premise that the contribution of the black fashion designers has gone largely unrecognised that the Black Fashion Museum
organises its exhibits, a wide variety of costumes designed and made
by blacks from the eighteenth century on. The second floor has a
quirky group of robes and gowns, including a slave dress of finely
stitched cotton and Mary Todd Lincoln's velvet inaugural gown
designed by Elizabeth Keckley, a freed slave. The museum's situation
up on Lenox Avenue, sadly, makes for specialist interest only.

Cooper-Hewitt Museum

2 E 91st St. Subway #4, #5 or #6 to 86th St–Lexington Ave. Tues 10am–
9pm, Wed–Sat 10am–5pm, Sun noon–5pm; $3, students $1.50, free Tues
5–9pm.

When he decided to build at what was then the unfashionable end of
Fifth Avenue, millionaire industrialist Andrew Carnegie asked for
"the most modest, plainest and most roomy house in New York".
And that's nearly what he got – a series of wood-panelled boxes too
decorative to be plain, too large to be modest. But they provide
good gallery space today for the Cooper-Hewitt collection of design,
shown off here in three floors of changing exhibitions. Themes vary
so check what's on first – the Cooper-Hewitt is as good as its exhibitions, which tend to be excellent.

Commercial galleries

Art, and especially contemporary art, is big in New York: a fact
reflected in the number and variety of **private galleries**: there are
roughly 500 art galleries in NYC, the majority in SoHo, and as many
as 90,000 artists living in and around the city. Even if you have no
intention of buying, many of these galleries are well worth seeing,
as are some of the **alternative spaces**, run on a non-profit basis and
hence less commercial than mainstream galleries.

Broadly galleries fall into three main areas: along **Madison
Avenue** in the 60s and 70s for antique works and the occasional
(minor) old master; **57th Street** between Sixth and Park avenues
for contemporary big names; and **SoHo** for whatever is currently
fashionable (until a couple of years ago the East Village scene held
much of the more exciting – and cheaper – work, but sadly it's
pretty well dead today). A few of the more exclusive places are
invitation only, though one of the best ways to see the galleries is
with *Art Tours of Manhattan* (see "Information, Maps and Tours"
in *Basics*), who run excellent and informed (though pricey)
conducted tours.

Below are listed some of the more interesting options in the main Manhattan locations. Opening times are roughly Tuesday–Saturday 11am–6pm, and the best time to gallery-hop, especially in SoHo, is a Saturday, or wherever you spy an opening. These are identifiable by the crowds and are generally free for those with enough bluff..

SoHo galleries

A.I.R. Gallery, 63 Crosby St ☎966-0799. Women's co-op exhibiting work by members and others.

The Drawing Center, 35 Wooster St ☎219-2166. Specialises in oversized painting/sculpture/construction.

Dyansen Gallery, 122 Spring St ☎226-3384. Contemporary painting and sculpture, plus an Erté sculpture collection.

Edward Thorp, 103 Prince St ☎431-6880. Mainstream figurative painting.

Jay Gorney Modern Art, 100 Greene St ☎966-8545. Hosts many group shows.

John Weber, 3rd floor, 142 Greene St ☎966-6115. Conceptual, Minimal and highly unusual works, including those by Sol LeWitt and younger, similarly inspired, artists.

Leo Castelli, 2nd floor, 420 West Broadway ☎431-5160. One of the original dealer/collectors, instrumental in aiding the careers of Rauschenberg and Warhol. Big names at big prices. His two other galleries are at 578 Broadway (between Houston and Prince sts; ☎431-6279) and 65 Thompson St (between Spring and Broome sts; ☎219-2219).

Louis Meisel, 141 Prince St ☎677-1340. The place to find out what Abstract Illusionism looks like. Meisel claims to have invented the term, along with Photorealism, also well in evidence here.

Louvet, 130 Prince St ☎925-9205. Always worth a look for its innovative installations.

Mary Boone, 420 and 417 Broadway ☎431-1818. Leo Castelli's protégé, specialising in up-and-coming European and American artists.

Michael Russ's Studio Furuique, 32 Watts St ☎274-9654. Mixed media environment exhibits: "future fish, giant recycle bugs, and flies, bottle people and organic furniture".

O.K. Harris, 383 West Broadway ☎431-3600. A lively, unpredictable gallery run by Ivan Karp, champion of Super-realism. One of the first SoHo galleries.

Paula Cooper, 155 Wooster St ☎674-0766. Minimal and Abstract works, and much more.

Sonnabend, 3rd floor, 420 West Broadway ☎966-6160. Across-the-board painting, photography and video.

Commercial Galleries

Sperone Westwater, 2nd floor, 142 Greene St ☎431-3685. Flashy European and American painting.

Vorpal, 411 West Broadway ☎334-3939. Chiefly the tiresome conundrums of Max Escher's prints.

Galleries elsewhere

Blum-Helman, 20 W 57th St ☎245-2888. Blum-Helman mounted the first Andy Warhol exhibition and have since gone on to promote both new and existing American art.

Jordan Volpe Gallery, 958 Madison Ave ☎570-9500. Specialities include the American Arts and Crafts movement, the furniture of Gustav Stickel, Rookwood Pottery and Louis Tiffany lamps.

M. Knoedler, 19 E 70th St ☎794-0550. Very highly reputed gallery specialising in European Old Masters and some of the best-known twentieth-century American artists.

Marlborough Gallery, 40 W 57th St ☎541-4900. Another internationally renowned gallery that shows some of the best British and American artists.

Nature Morte, 204 E 10th St ☎420-9544. One of the few survivors of the pretty much defunct East Village scene.

Robert Miller, 41 E 57th St ☎980-5454. Twentieth-century American art.

Pace Gallery, 32 E 57th St ☎421-3292. Well-known gallery that holds a large stock of modern American artworks.

Alternative spaces

The galleries listed above are part of a system designed to channel artists' work through the gallery spaces and, eventually, into the hands of the collector. While initial acceptance by a major gallery is an important rite of passage for an up-and-coming artist, it shouldn't be forgotten that the gallery system's philosophy is centred on making money – sometimes a great deal of money – for the owners. For an artist's work to be uncommercial is perhaps even more damning than to be socially, politically, even aesthetically unacceptable. The galleries below, often referred to as **alternative spaces**, provide a forum for the kind of risky and not commercially viable art (such as installations) that commercial galleries may not be able to afford to show. The recession of the 1990s has given the alternative space a new lease of life, and those mentioned here are at the cutting edge of new art in the city.

Artists' Space, 223 W Broadway (between Franklin and White sts) ☎226-3970. One of the most respected alternative spaces, with frequently changing exhibits – usually on a theme – film screenings, video art and installations, and events. Their *Artists' File* is a computerised slide registry of over 2500 New York State artists, and can be scanned free of charge.

The Broken Kilometer, 393 West Broadway (between Spring and Broome) ☎431-3789. Adventurous new work – painting, graphics, sculpture and installations – in a remarkable gallery space filled with metal piping.

Clocktower, 108 Leonard St (between Broadway and Lafayette) ☎233-1096. Temporary exhibitions and an annual studio programme in which artists work in the studio space within the clocktower. When this is happening, you're allowed to wander round and talk to the artists about their work.

DIA Art Foundation, administrative offices 107 Franklin St ☎431-3789. Non-profit organisation which commissions and exhibits work by new artists in three galleries: the *New York Earth Room*, the *Broken Kilometer* and the *DIA Center for the Arts*. New York's major alternative art organisation.

DIA Center for the Arts, 548 W 22nd St (between 10th and 11th aves) ☎431-3789. The foundation's largest gallery space shows year-long exhibitions of work by artists such as Joseph Beuys, Robert Ryman and Kids of Survival.

New York Earth Room, 141 Wooster St (between Prince and Houston) ☎431-3789. An incredible gallery, filled, as literally as the name suggests, with masses of earth. Changing exhibitions, installations and performances by contemporary artists.

PS1, 46-01 21st St in Long Island City, Queens ☎718/784-2084. Part of the same organisation (the Institute for Art and Urban Resources) as *Clocktower*, and based in an old schoolhouse. *Meeting*, a stunning installation by artist James Turrell, is the highlight of the collection.

PS122, 150 First Avenue ☎228-4249. Non-profit gallery space open September to June which specialises in showing emerging artists.

White Columns, 154 Christopher St, 2nd floor ☎924-4212. Curator Bill Arning has a finger on the pulse of what's happening in the NYC art world. The gallery has a more responsible attitude than many, and is very influential for emerging artists. Check out the changing group shows, open Weds–Sun noon–6pm.

New York Listings

Chapter 7

Accommodation

Accommodation in New York City is a major cost. The only way to cut it radically is to utilise every contact you have – however tenuous – in the city and the Tri-State area. Spend some of your time on a floor or two and suddenly the city, cost-wise at least, isn't all that different from any other. All that the recommendations below can do is cut a few corners . . and steer you towards the better value places and the more interesting locations.

There aren't many alternatives at the **cheap** end of the market. The choice is between a room in a **YMCA/YWCA** (a Y, as they're known), the official New York YHA **youth hostel**, or one of a number of student-orientated long-stay hostels. The latter are the cheapest, with dormitory rooms for as little as $12 a night, though they are distinctly a last resort. The YMCAs charge around $50 a double, while the official YHA hostel has dorm beds for $23 with breakfast.

Bed and breakfast is an increasingly popular (and inexpensive) option, staying in a New Yorker's spare room or, better still, subletting an apartment. Normally arranged through an agency, rates run at an average of about $70 a double, per night, $80 a night for a studio apartment.

Hotels, which do not normally include breakfast, also start at around $70 a double, though at this end of the scale they are rarely too enticing. If you want a place you won't dread going back to each evening, count on $90 and up, and even then be selective in where you choose; mid-range prices are around

$140 for a double room. When you've established the price, you'll need to add on **taxes**, and these can come as a nasty shock – see p.236 for details.

Whether you decide to plump for a hostel or hotel, **booking ahead** is very strongly advised. At certain times of the year – Christmas and early summer particularly – you're likely to find *everything* (and we mean this) chock-a-block full. You can book a room yourself, by phoning direct to the hotel (☎0101/212 before the listed number if you're dialling from Britain), or by going through a specialist **travel agent** – which can sometimes work out cheaper (see "Getting There" in *Basics* for addresses). Bear in mind, too, the possibilities of all-in flight and hotel package holidays, again detailed under "Getting There". There are also **booking services**, such as *Meegan's* and *Express Reservations*, that reserve rooms at no extra charge. CRS (Central Reservation Service) offers discounts on normal prices, as does *The*

Booking services

CRS ☎ 1-800/950-0232; fax 305/274-1357.

The Room Exchange 450 Seventh Ave NY 10123 ☎ 760-1000.

Meegan's ☎ 718/995-9292; from outside the city ☎ 1-800/221-1235.

Express Reservations ☎ 1-800/356-1123.

Accommodations Express ☎ 609/645-8688.

Accommodation

Room Exchange, though you may find, particularly at peak periods, that most of their budget accommodation has gone.

Hostels

Chelsea Center Hostel, 511 W 20th St ☎243-4922. Small, clean and safe private downtown hostel, with prices from $18 in winter, $20 in summer. A useful alternative for downtown, though you'll need to book two or three weeks in advance in high season. Dorms sleep between six and sixteen, and facilities include a safe for valuables and summer barbecues on the garden courtyard.

International House of New York, 500 Riverside Drive, NY 10027 ☎316-8400. Large, well-equipped hostel with good, clean accommodation. Singles with shared bathroom cost $25, dropping to $18 for stays of a fortnight or more, suites for two to four people cost $74–94. Hotel standard guest rooms with private bathroom go for $58 per night. Though anyone can stay here, stays of a month or longer require you to have student ID or intern status. The hostel is open year-round; the only disadvantage is that the sequestered two-building site is way uptown. Write or phone for reservations.

International House – Sugar Hill, 722 St Nicholas Ave, NY 10031 ☎926-7030. Noisy but adequate dorm accommodation in a friendly, well-run hostel on the border of Harlem and Washington Heights. $12 per night, no curfew, no chores and no lock-out during the day. Take the A or D train to 145th Street – the hostel is just across the road.

International Student Center, 38 W 88th St ☎787-7706. New York's bottom line, little more than a few grubby, roach-ridden dorms sleeping twelve to fourteen. Rates are around $12 a bed, and there are kitchen facilities and a lounge with TV. Phoning ahead is advised, and keeping an eye on your belongings essential (the dorms don't go in for the luxury of lockers for your gear, but you can leave valuables at the front desk).

International Youth Hostel, 891 Amsterdam Ave at 103rd St ☎932-2300.

For details of long-stay residences, particularly ones geared specifically to women, see "Staying On" in *Basics*.

The most decent cost-cutting alternative to the YMCAs, with dormitory-style beds for $20 per night (on-the-spot IYHA membership is $25), and facilities including a restaurant, travel shop and theatre. Though large (480 beds) there's a good chance it'll be heavily booked, so phone well in advance.

YMCAs

Vanderbilt YMCA, 224 E 47th St ☎755-2410. Smaller and quieter than the hostels mentioned above, and neatly placed in midtown Manhattan, just five minutes' walk from Grand Central Station. Inexpensive restaurant, swimming pool, gym and launderette. Singles $45, doubles $55.

De Hirsch Residence at the 92nd Street Y, 1395 Lexington Ave between 91st and 92nd sts ☎415-5650. If you're planning to stay for a week or more, the De Hirsch Residence is a relaxing alternative. Single or shared bright study-bedrooms cost $245 and $175 per week respectively, a little more for rooms with air conditioning. Cooking and laundry facilities are available on each floor, along with shared bathroom facilities. The 92nd Street Y is renowned for its poetry and music events (to which residents get a discount), along with a host of other social activities, not least some of the best walking tours in the city – see "Information, Maps and Tours" in *Basics*.

Newark YMWCA, 600 Broad St, Newark, New Jersey 07102 ☎201/624-8900. Worth considering as a major cost-cutting option if you don't mind not being based in Manhattan. The Newark YMWCA is basic, but has a gym and swimming pool and costs $25 per person per night, $85 per week. The building is ten minutes' walk from Newark's Penn Station, where frequent PATH and NJ Transit trains run into Manhattan for $1. It's also reasonably close to the airport.

Camping

You won't save a great deal on any of the above options by **camping**. All of the campsites that could conceivably serve New York City are situated so far out as to make travel in and out a major cost. For the dedicated, though, these are the most accessible.

Battle Row Campground, Claremont Rd, Old Bethpage, Long Island ☎516/293-7120. The nearest site to the city – a short way up Long Island. You'll need either your own vehicle or a taxi to reach Manhattan as public transport is virtually non-existent. Site is open April to November; cost is $7 per tent.

Hecksher State Park Campground, East Islip, Long Island ☎516/581-2100. Beautiful situation and easier to reach than Battle Row – from Penn Station take the Long Island Railroad to Great River Station. Open mid-May to mid-September; prices around $11 for a tent and up to six people. Campers must be over 21.

Bed and breakfast

Bed and breakfast has taken off in a big way in America of late, particularly in New York where Manhattanites need all the cash possible to find their astronomical rent money. For the visitor, it can be a good way of staying bang in the centre of Manhattan at a reasonably affordable price. Don't expect to socialise with your temporary landlord/lady – chances are you'll have a self-contained room and hardly see them – and don't go looking for street signs or adverts; all rooms – except for a few out in Brooklyn which advertise individually (see below) – are let out via the following official **agencies**.

Colby International, 139 Round Hey, Liverpool L28 1RG England ☎051-220 5848. If you want guaranteed B&B accommodation, Colby International are without doubt your best bet – and they can fix up accommodation from the UK. Excellent-value double rooms start at $70 a night, studios from a mere $90: book at least a fortnight ahead to be sure of a room in high season, though it's worth trying for last-minute reservations.

Bed and Breakfast in Manhattan, PO Box 533 NYC, NY 10150-0533 ☎472-2528. The ex-casting director head of this agency really knows her hosts, and will match you up with the place and people where you'll be most comfortable. Rooms in a hosted apartment cost between $60 and $90 a night; unhosted places go for between $90 and $250 a night; an unusual option are the semi-hosted places (a private floor in a townhouse, for example) where you have plenty of space and privacy but there are hosts on hand for advice if you need it.

Bed and Breakfast Network of New York, Suite 602, 134 W 32nd St, NY 10001 ☎645-8134, 8am–6pm Mon–Fri. Growing network with hosted singles for around $60, doubles $80–90; prices for unhosted accommodation are slightly more, running to luxury multi-bedded apartments for $300. Weekly rates also available. For an assured booking write at least a month in advance, though short-notice reservations are possible by phone.

City Lights Bed & Breakfast, PO Box 20355, Cherokee Station, New York NY 10028 ☎737-7049. Around 400 carefully screened B&Bs on its books, with many of the hosts involved in theatre and the arts. Hosted singles run from $60–75, doubles from $75–95. Unhosted accommodation costs from $95 to $300 per night depending on whether it's a studio or four-bedroom apartment. Minimum stay two nights.

Urban Ventures, PO Box 426, New York NY 10024. Personal callers welcome at Suite 1412, 38 W 32nd St ☎594-5650. The first and largest registry in the city. Their budget double rooms go for $65 upwards, "comfort range" rooms (with private bath) from about $80. If you wish, you can rent an entire apartment minus hosts from $95 a night. No minimum stay, and you can book up until the last minute.

New World Bed & Breakfast, Suite 711, 150 Fifth Avenue, New York NY 10011 ☎675-5600. Budget hosted singles $50–60, doubles $65–70; budget unhosted studios $70–80. Larger places with more facilities slightly pricier.

Accommodation

Accommodation

Brooklyn B&Bs

Foy House, 819 Carroll Street, Brooklyn NY 11215 ☎718/636-1492. Beautiful 1894 brownstone in Park Slope, with rooms for $79, $89 and $109.

Bed & Breakfast on the Park ☎718/499-6115. A few minutes' walk from Prospect Park, with rooms in the $150 range.

Hotels

Most of New York's hotels tend to be in midtown Manhattan – which is as good a **location** as any. You'll find only a handful downtown. The **selections** below cover the range from the cheapest to New York's most luxurious, the latter a small and select grouping of really special places for which it's worth paying over the odds. Our alphabetical listings approximately follow the geography of the *Guide* chapters; for an overview of where to find a listed hotel, see the map on pp.238–39.

Taxes and other hidden costs

Taxes levied by New York City and State will add considerably to the quoted price of a hotel room. For rooms under $100 add 14.25% New York State sales tax, then the New York City hotel sales tax of 6%, then a further $2 "occupancy tax" on top of that. Suddenly your $99 room has jumped up to $122. For rooms costing over $100 the news is even worse: here you need to add 19.25% State tax – plus the 6% City tax and the $2. The price codes at the end of each of the following listings represent the price of a double room *inclusive* of all taxes: remember that prices advertised anywhere in New York *never* include tax.

On top of this you'll need to fork out around $5 for **breakfast** (a figure that can

swell alarmingly the more upmarket the hotel); it's a better idea to pop round the corner to the nearest diner and fill up on a breakfast special for half the price. **Tipping** too will absorb at least some of your cash: unless you firmly refuse, a bell hop will grab your bags when you check in and expect $5 for carrying them to your room. Other rip-offs to catch the unwary are luxuriously stocked minibars, with booze and chocolate goodies at astronomical prices, and hotel shops that sell basic necessities at three times the street price.

Discounts and special deals

With almost any hotel room it's possible to **cut costs** slightly if you can fill a double with three or even four people. This is normal practice in the US and managements rarely mind providing an extra bed or two for an extra $20 or so. If you're staying long enough, you may also be able to pay a special **weekly rate**, maybe getting one night in seven for free. Some hotels, particularly those that see tourists as a major part of their revenue, also lay on special **weekend discounts** if

How taxes add to room costs			
Basic room cost	$99	$150	$250
NY State sales tax	14.25%	19.25%	19.25%
NY City sales tax	6%	6%	6%
Occupancy tax	$2	$2	$2
Total	**$121.88**	**$191.60**	**$318**

Hotels by price

The following lists hotels in groups **by price**: with the exception of the suites in the last group, prices are for the cheapest double room per night, and include all taxes.

Inexpensive: ①–⑤ Below $100 per night

Aberdeen	Malibu Studios	President
Allerton House	Mansfield	Remington
American	Martha Washington	Riverside Tower
Best Western Broadway	(women only)	Roger Williams
Carlton Arms	New York Bed &	Rossoff's
Chelsea Esplanade	Breakfast	Stamford
Excelsior	Off SoHo Suites	Webster (women only)
Herald Square	Penn Plaza	Wollcott
Iroquois	Portland Square	

Moderate: ⑥–⑦ $101–180 per night

Ameritania	Gramercy Park	Roger Smith
Barbizon	Helmsley Windsor	Roosevelt
Beacon	Howard	Salisbury
Best Western Woodward	Johnson Plaza	San Carlos
Beverly	Jolly Madison Towers	San Moritz on the Park
Carlton	Journey's End	Southgate Tower
Chatwal Inn on 45th	Lexington	Wales
Chelsea Inn	Milburn	Washington Square
Comfort Inn	Novotel	Wentworth
Days Inn	Pickwick Arms	West Park
Edison	Radisson Empire	Windham
Elysee	Ramada Hotel	
Gorham	Pennsylvania	

Expensive ⑧ $181–250 per night

Algonquin	Marriott Marquis	Plaza 50
Holiday Inn Downtown	Paramount	Wellington
Marriott Financial Center		

Very Expensive ⑨ Over $250 per night

Beekman Tower	Lyden House	Shelburne Murray Hill
Box Tree	Macklowe	Sherry Netherland
Doral Park Avenue	Mark	Surrey
Dorset	Michelangelo	Tudor
Drake	Millenium	Waldorf
Essex House	Pierre	Warwick
Lowell	Royalton	

you stay two nights or more, bringing prices down by as much as a third. One good thing: almost all US hotels, even the grottiest, have **TVs** in their rooms as a matter of course – so if you've spent all your money on a bed for the night you can always curl up in front of David Letterman . . .

For full hotel listings and prices, consult the New York Convention and Visitors Bureau leaflet, *Hotels in New York City*, available from one of their offices, or,

25. Edison
26. Elysée
27. Esplanade
28. Essex House
29. Excelsior
30. Gramercy Park
31. Helmsley Windsor
32. Holiday Inn Downtown
33. Howard Johnson Plaza
34. International House of New York
35. International House – Sugar Hill
36. International Student Center
37. International Youth Hostel
38. Iroquois
39. Jolly Madison Towers
40. Journey's End
41. Lexington
42. Loews
43. Lowell
44. Lyden House
45. Macklowe
46. Malibu Studios
47. Mansfield
48. Mark
49. Marriott Financial Center
50. Marriott Marquis
51. Martha Washington
52. Mayflower
53. Michelangelo
54. Milburn
55. Milford Plaza
56. Millenium
57. Morgans
58. New York Bed and Breakfast
59. Novotel
60. Off SoHo Suites

MANHATTAN HOTELS

61. Paramount
62. Penn Plaza
63. Pickwick Arms
64. Pierre
65. Plaza
66. Plaza 50
67. Portland Square
68. Radisson Empire
69. Ramada Hotel Pennsylvania
70. Remington
71. Riverside Tower
72. Roger Smith
73. Roger Williams
74. Roosevelt
75. Rossoff's
76. Royalton
77. Salisbury
78. San Carlos
79. Shelburne Murray Hill
80. Sherry Netherland
81. Southgate Tower
82. St Moritz on the Park
83. Stanford
84. Surrey
85. The Tudor
86. Vanderbilt YMCA
87. Waldorf-Astoria
88. Wales
89. Warwick
90. Washington Square
91. Webster Apartments
92. Wellington
93. Wentworth
94. Westpark
95. Wolcott
96. Wyndham

1. Aberdeen
2. Algonquin
3. Allerton House
4. Ameritania
5. Barbizon
6. Beacon
7. Beekman Tower
8. Best Western President
9. Best Western Woodward
10. Beverly
11. Box Tree
12. Broadway American
13. Carlton
14. Carlton Arms
15. Chatwal Inn
16. Chelsea
17. Chelsea Center Hostel
18. Chelsea Inn
19. Comfort Inn
20. Days Inn
21. De Hirsch Residence
22. Doral Park Avenue
23. Dorset
24. Drake

→ To Hotels 49, 56

→ To Hotel 60

Accommodation

For details of hotels sympathetic to gay and lesbian travellers, see "Gay and Lesbian New York" in Basics.

before you leave Britain, from the *USTTA* (see "Information, Maps and Tours" in *Basics*).

Lower Manhattan

Holiday Inn Downtown, 138 Lafayette St, NY 10013 at corner of Howard St ☎966-8898. An idiosyncratic member of the well-known chain, in the heart of Chinatown. The cheaper weekend rates make this a possible base for exploring the area, though the rooms themselves are small for the highish price. ⑧

Marriott Financial Center, 85 West St, NY 10006 ☎385-4900. Doubles at ⑥ make this civilised business hotel with superb views of the World Trade Center, the Hudson and New York harbour affordable at weekends. Weekdays are a different story, but the high rates (⑨) are well worth it. Service is excellent.

Millenium, 55 Church St, NY 10007 ☎693-2001. Opened in Spring 1992, Hotel Millenium was designed for style-conscious business people on expense accounts – but again, lower weekend rates make it worth consideration. Relax in the sky-lit swimming pool overlooking St Paul's Chapel, enjoy your cocktail at the bar overlooking the World Trade Center Plaza, or eat in the two, not overly expensive, restaurants. Rooms are luxurious: ask for one with a view (unforgettable) of the Brooklyn Bridge. ⑨, dropping to ⑧ at weekends.

Off SoHo Suites, 11 Rivington St, NY 10002 ☎979-9808. These small, apartment-style suites are well located, on the border of Little Italy and the Lower East Side. The cheapest prices for the area (even more economical if four are sharing) include fully equipped kitchen, VCR, and use of laundry and fitness room. This part of town can be a little tense – you may want to make use of the hotel's discount cab service at night. ⑤, suites for four ⑥

Washington Square, 103 Waverley Place, NY 10011 ☎777-9515. Bang in the heart of Greenwich Village, and a stone's throw from the NYU campus. Don't be deceived by the posh-looking lobby – the rooms

are what you'd expect for the price, and the staff are surly. ⑥

Midtown Manhattan east: Union Square to 42nd Street

Carlton, 22 E 29th St, NY 10016 ☎532-4100. A very well-priced, nicely moder-nised hotel in a Beaux Arts building. There are two plusses: you're in the safe residential area of Murray Hill, and you also get room and valet service, not often associated with hotels in this price bracket. ⑦

Carlton Arms, 160 E 25th St, NY 10010 ☎684-8337. A strong contender for the city's latest Bohemian hang-out, with eclectic interior decor by would-be artists, very few comforts, and a clientele made up of Europeans, down-at-heel artists and longstay guests. People either love it or hate it – so check it out before you commit yourself to staying. ④, cheaper rooms without bathroom.

Doral Park Avenue, 70 Park Ave at 38th St, NY 10016 ☎637-7050. A multimillion-dollar restoration has turned the *Doral Park Avenue* into one of the snazziest deluxe hotels, with re-creations of classical friezes and frescoes and original designs for light-ing and furnishings. Service is excellent. ⑧

Gramercy Park, 2 Lexington Ave, NY I0010 ☎475-4320. Pleasant enough hotel located next to the only private park in the city (residents get a key to the gate) and popular with Europeans. There are smoking and non-smoking rooms (you really know when you're in one of the former) and a mixture of newly reno-vated and tatty rooms. ⑦; weekends ⑥

Jolly Madison Towers, Madison Ave at 38th St, NY 10016 ☎685-3700. The lobby and Whaler Bar are looking very dated these days, but the rooms are rest-ful, clean and fairly spacious. Among the facilities is an Oriental health spa with whirlpool bath and sauna. ⑥

Journey's End, 3 E 40th St, NY 10016 ☎447-1500. This is a motel-style hotel, owned by a Canadian chain with very low weekend rates ($88+tax for a double). If you're here on business, the PC/FAX dataports, desks and same-day valet service will come in handy. Rooms are bright and well-furnished, and there's a very comfortable lounge and restaurant on the premises. ⑦

Martha Washington, 30 E 30th St, NY 10016 ☎689-1900. A women-only hotel with very low room rates, but a character that's a little on the depressing side. There's a choice of single or double rooms, with or without bathrooms. Singles without bathroom cost $35, singles with bath $54, doubles without bathroom $50, doubles with bath $69. Weekly rates $140–136 (all prices without tax).

Morgans, 237 Madison Ave, NY 10016 ☎686-0300. Created by the instigators of *Studio 54* and the *Palladium* nightclub, this is self-consciously – and quite successfully - one of the chicest doss-houses in town. Discreet furnishings are by Andre Putnam, good-looking young staff clothed in Klein and Armani. These days the stars stay at the *Royalton*, but those wanting to keep a low profile – like Julia Roberts or Sean Penn – still frequent the place, able as they are to slip in and out unnoticed. The black-white-grey decor is starting to look to self-consciously 1980s and hence a little passé, but you do get a jacuzzi, a great stereo system and cable TV in your room. ⑧

Roger Williams, 28 E 31st St, NY 10016 ☎684-7500. A good choice for families or friends travelling together on a budget. Rooms in this Murray Hill ex-apartment building have kitchenettes (two-burner gas stove, sink, refrigerator and cabinet), simple furnishings, and colour cable TV. There's a 24-hour deli-salad bar on the same block, and the friendly staff will provide a "Kitchen Kit" of kettle, pots and pans, plastic crockery and tea, coffee, sugar and salt as well as a copy of their 12-page guide to the area called *Herald Square/Murray Hill Tips*. ④ and ⑤; triples ⑤, quads ⑥

Shelburne Murray Hill, 303 Lexington Ave, NY 10016 ☎689-5200. Another reliable Manhattan East suite hotel, in the poshest part of Murray Hill. The outstanding features are the Secret Harbor Bistro with dishes of the day chalked up above

the bar, and the stunning open-air penthouse roof garden. ⑧, suites ⑧–⑨

The Tudor, 304 E 42nd St, NY 10017 ☎986-8800. One of the more stylish hotels close to Grand Central Station, in the unique residential area built in the 1920s and known as Tudor City. Rooms are deluxe, with mini-bar, cable and in-room movies, hair dryer and opulent marble bathrooms. There's a fitness room and sauna too. Service is excellent. ⑧/⑨

Midtown Manhattan west: Chelsea and Times Square to 57th Street

Aberdeen, 17 W 32nd St, NY 10001 ☎736-1600. Rather spartan rooms, but in a good location just off Fifth Avenue. Complimentary continental breakfast is served in the lobby, under chandeliers. ⑤

Algonquin, 59 W 44th St, NY 10036 ☎840-6800. New York's classic literary hang-out, as created by Dorothy Parker and her associates and perpetuated by Noel Coward, Bernard Shaw, Irving Berlin and most names subsequent (see p.127). Decor remains little changed except in the bedrooms which have all been refurbished to good effect. Prices compare very well with many much more mundane "moderate" places. ⑧

Ameritania, 230 W 54th St, NY 10019 ☎247-5000. Opened in 1992 and very good value at ⑤ for a double room if you mention *Rough Guides*; normal rates ⑥–⑦. Even at the higher price this is the best value of the city's inexpensive hotels: you get a brand new, well-furnished room with marble bathroom, cable TV, individual climate control and a cocktail bar, restaurant and pizza parlour off the high-tech, neon-lit lobby.

Best Western President, 234 W 48th St, NY 10036 ☎246-8800. This solid, reasonably priced hotel is a member of the Indian-owned Chatwal chain, offering small, recently renovated rooms and free continental breakfast. ⑤–⑦

Best Western Woodward, 219 W 55th St ☎247-2000. Recently renovated and handy for the Museum of Modern Art, the reasonable rates include continental breakfast. ⑥

Accommodation

Price categories:
① *under $30*
② *$30–45*
③ *$46–60*
④ *$61–80*
⑤ *$81–100*
⑥ *$101–130*
⑦ *$131–180*
⑧ *$181–250*
⑨ *over $250*

Accommodation

Chatwal Inn on 45th, 132 W 45th St, NY 10036 ☎921-7600. Located on the edge of the theatre district, the *Chatwal* nevertheless manages to be an oasis of calm. Suites are very spacious and can easily accommodate four people; decor is in restful Queen Anne and Federal styles. There's also a laundry, and continental breakfast is included in the price. ⑥

Chelsea, 222 W 23rd St, NY 10011 ☎243-3700. One of New York's most noted landmarks, both for its ageing neo-Gothic building and, more importantly, its long list of alumni, from Dylan Thomas to Bob Dylan and Leonard Cohen, to Sid Vicious, doomed punk icon, and his girlfriend Nancy (see p.117 for the full cast). It's still something of a haunt of musicians and art-school types, though these days it's as much an apartment building as a hotel with its majority of guests being semi-permanent. The older rooms are to be avoided. Ask instead for a renovated room with polished wood floors, log-burning fireplaces, and plenty of space to cram a few extra friends into. ⑤

Chelsea Inn, 46 W 17th St, NY 10011 ☎645-8989. Nicely situated in the heart of Chelsea, not too far from the Village, and with a choice of guest rooms, studios and suites, most equipped with kitchenettes. ⑤ with bath shared with one other guest room; studio with bathroom ⑥

Comfort Inn, 42 W 35th St, NY 10001 ☎947-0200. The best thing about the *Comfort Inn* is the free hot coffee, Danish pastries and newspapers they give you in the elegant lobby each morning. It's a solid, good-value place to stay but the management can be very unhelpful – you won't be able to see a room before you hand over your cash, for example. ⑥; triples ⑦

Days Inn, 790 Eighth Ave, between W 48th and W 49th sts, NY 10019 ☎581-7000. A rooftop pool open during the summer months is the main attraction of this slightly characterless chain hotel (formerly a *Ramada Inn*). Still, rooms are in good condition (the hotel was last renovated at the end of the 1980s), and the rates are reasonable. ⑦

Dorset, 30 West 54th St, NY 10019 ☎247-7300. The *Dorset's* inexpensive weekend rates make it very popular with groups, who sometimes pack out the lobby and restaurant. Rooms are very large, have recently been redecorated, and in some cases overlook the Museum of Modern Art sculpture park. ⑨

Edison, 228 W 47th, NY 10036 ☎840-5000. The most striking thing about the 1000-room *Edison* is its beautifully restored Art Deco lobby, re-creating the original from 1931. Ask for a refurbished room if possible – the older-style bedrooms have seen better days. ⑥

Gorham, 136 W 55th St, NY 10019 ☎245-1800. Excellent value midtown hotel, handy for Central Park and with jacuzzis, cable TV and self-service kitchen in every room. One of the bargains in this part of town. ⑦

Herald Square, 19 W 31st St, NY 10001 ☎279-4017. Home of the original *Life Magazine*, and with Philip Martiny's sculptured cherub known as *Winged Life* still presiding over the doorway of this Beaux Arts building. That's where the ornamentation stops – inside, the hotel has few frills, but rooms are fine for the price. ④; triples and quads ⑤

Howard Johnson Plaza, Eighth Ave at 52nd St, NY 10019 ☎581-4100. Not the usual bland, chain hotel you might have expected, the 300-room hotel offers very well-decorated rooms, space to spread out, and a piano bar and restaurant. ⑦

Iroquois, 49 W 44th St, NY 10036 ☎840-3080. The rooms are better than the lobby suggests – they're well furnished with plush carpets. This is a family-run hotel (some of the family are more helpful than others), and its low rates make it popular with UN delegates. ⑤

Macklowe, 145 W 44th St, NY 10036 ☎768-4400. Black marble and wall-to-ceiling artworks dominate the *Macklowe's* lobby; the sleek lines continue in the beautiful off-white bedrooms. This is the place to come for an intimate after-theatre supper, if you decide against the high (but justifiable) room rates. ⑨

Mansfield, 12 W 44th St, NY 10036 ☎944-6050. The real-value alternative to both the nearby *Algonquin* and the *Royalton*, with better-than-average rooms for the price with such luxuries as thermo-vapour whirlpools and steambaths. The deli off the lobby will make up snacks for you, or there's a steakhouse on the premises. ⑤; triples and quads ⑥

Marriott Marquis, 1535 Broadway, NY 10036 ☎398-1900. The hotel as fantasy palace: even if you can't afford to stay here it's worth dropping by to gawp at the split-level atrium and to ride the glass elevators to NY's only revolving restaurant. ⑧

Michelangelo, 152 W 51st St, NY 10019 ☎765-1900. An Italian chain took over last year and created a palazzo on Broadway, with acres of marble, and no expenses spared in the luxurious and super-large rooms. In terms of decor you have a choice: rooms are in Art Deco, Empire or Country French styles. At weekends and special holidays (New Year's Eve and Valentine's Day for example), prices drop. ⑧–⑨

Milford Plaza, 270 W 45th St, NY 10036 ☎869-3600. Rooms are tiny and the atmosphere is impersonal, but hoardes of theatre-goers still flock here for the "Lullabuy (sic) of Broadway" deals. ⑦

Novotel, 226 W 52nd St, NY 10019 ☎315-0100. Chain hotel large enough to offer a decent range of facilities, while small enough to avoid anonymity. The decor is sophisticated, the food good, as you would expect from a French-owned establishment, and the hotel offers special rooms for the disabled. ⑦

Paramount, 235 W 46th St, NY 10036 ☎764-5500. A former budget hotel renovated by the *Morgans/Royalton* crew and now not surprisingly one of the hippest places in town to stay, popular with a pop and media crowd, who come to enjoy an interior designed by Philippe Starck and be waited on by sleek young things. Doubles aren't as pricey as you'd think, and they sport prints of Vermeer's *Lacemaker* as headboards along with VCRs and designer bathrooms. The branch of *Dean and DeLuca* off the lobby, the *Whiskey Bar* and the newly opened *Brasserie des Theatres* are busy and fun. ⑧

Penn Plaza, 215 W 34th St, NY 10001 ☎947-5050. A cheap hotel in a slightly sleazy location opposite Penn Station. The prices make it worth thinking about for a night or two's stay, and the rooms are decent enough. There's also a private second-floor lobby lounge for guests' use as a respite from Seventh Avenue. ③ without bath; ⑤ with bath; both include breakfast.

Portland Square, 132 W 47th St, NY 10036 ☎382-0600. A theatre hotel since 1904, and former home to Jimmy Cagney and other members of Broadway casts. The *Portland* has a few more comforts than its sister hotel in Herald Square, but is still a budget operation, good for a few nights' sleep but not for hanging out in. Doubles ⑤; triples and quads ⑥

Ramada Hotel Pennsylvania, 401 Seventh Ave, NY 10001 ☎736-5000. Boasting the same telephone number since 1917 (the Pennsylvania six five thousand of the Glenn Miller song), this is now the world's largest Ramada hotel. It's located across from Madison Square Garden, and offers every possible convenience, though you can't help thinking it looked better when it was a good old-fashioned hotel. ⑦

Remington, 129 W 46th St, NY 10036 ☎221-2600. A very tacky, but spotless, hotel right in the heart of things. Service is brusque and efficient; all rooms have air-conditioning, cable TV and a telephone. ④ without bath; with bath ⑤; triples and quads ⑥

Roosevelt, 45 W 45th St, NY 10017 ☎661-9600. The *Roosevelt*'s heyday was in the Railway Age, when its proximity to Grand Central Station meant that thousands of travellers came to stay. In a bid to win new business the hotel is smartening itself up, starting with a vast neoclassical lobby, and the good-size rooms are an excellent deal, especially at the weekend rates. ⑦; weekends ⑥

Accommodation

Price categories:
① *under $30*
② *$30–45*
③ *$46–60*
④ *$61–80*
⑤ *$81–100*
⑥ *$101–130*
⑦ *$131–180*
⑧ *$181–250*
⑨ *over $250*

Accommodation

Rossoff's, 147 W 43rd St, NY 10036 ☎869-1212. A decent, inexpensive hotel on a theatre-lined street (one or two buildings are boarded up, making it intimidating at times). The rooms were revamped in 1991 and are a very good deal for the price. Each has colour TV and telephone; there's also a second-floor sitting area and helpful staff. ④; triples and quads ⑤

Royalton, 44 W 44th St, NY 10036 ☎869-4400. Owned by the same management as the *Paramount*, the Royalton attempts to capture the market for the discerning style-person, with more interiors designed by Philippe Starck. It aims to be the *Algonquin* of the 1990s, and is as much a power-lunch venue for NYC's media and publishing set as a place to stay. ⑨

Salisbury, 123 W 57th St, NY 10019 ☎246-1300. Good service and large rooms with kitchenettes are the *Salisbury's* main attraction. The hotel's *Terrace Café* doesn't have a liquor licence, but you can drink over the road at the famous *Russian Tea Room*. ⑦; weekends ⑥ including breakfast

Stanford, 43 W 32nd St, NY 10001 ☎563-1480. Clean, inexpensive hotel on the block known as "Little Korea". As well as the basic hotel facilities the *Stanford* offers room service and valet laundry, an American café in the lobby and good Korean cuisine in the very relaxing surroundings of the *Gam Mee Ok* restaurant. ⑥

Southgate Tower, 371 Seventh Ave NY 10001 ☎563-1800. A member of the excellent Manhattan East Suites chain, *Southgate Tower* is way over on the western edge of midtown, but popular with those headed for the Javits Convention Center. The least expensive options here are the guest rooms with refrigerator. If you're here for a week or two it's well worth staying in one of the big, fully equipped suites with kitchen. ⑦

Warwick, 65 W 54th St, NY 10019 ☎247-2700. Stars of the 1950s and 1960s – including Cary Grant, Rock

Hudson, The Beatles, Elvis Presley and JFK – stayed at the *Warwick* as a matter of course. Although the hotel's lost its show-business cachet now, it's an exceptionally spacious, pleasant place to stay, from the elegant lobby and Italian restaurant, to the apartment-sized rooms with views of Sixth Avenue. ⑨

Webster Apartments, 419 W 34th St, NY 10001 ☎967-9000, ☎1-800/242-7909. One of the nicer women-only residences with some unusual extras considering the price: several lounges with piano or stereo, a leafy private garden and plant-filled roof terrace. Rooms are all singles, with shared bathrooms on each floor. Only drawback is the unexciting location. (Single $35 per night including breakfast; weekly rate $120–165 depending on salary, includes two meals a day; all prices before taxes.)

Wellington, Seventh Ave at 55th St, NY 10019 ☎247-3900. The *Wellington's* gleaming, mirror-clad lobby is the result of recent renovations and similar attention has been paid to the rooms. Many have kitchenettes, and family rooms offer two bathrooms. Close to Carnegie Hall and handy for Lincoln Center, the hotel's a fair price for this stretch of town. ⑥

Wentworth, 59 W 46th St, NY 10036 ☎719-2300. Hard by Diamond Row and a stone's throw from Rockefeller Center. This budget hotel has out-of-date decor and is very worn around the edges, but all rooms come with private bath, cable TV and telephone, and there's a garden. ⑤

Wolcott, 4 W 31st St, NY 10001 ☎268-2900. A surprisingly relaxing budget hotel, with a gilded, ornamented lobby and more than adequate rooms. People travelling alone will benefit from the economical single rate; if you're travelling with friends ask for the triple and quad room prices. A very good deal. ③ without bath; ④ with bath

Upper Manhattan: the East Side: E 48th St to E 86th St

Allerton House, 130 E 57th St, NY 10022 ☎753-8841. Well located in a busy East Side shopping district, Allerton House offers tiny single rooms (with or without private bath) to women only. There's also a roof-top terrace, bar and laundry, and gym facilities nearby. They could do with some less creepy male staff. ④, singles at $35+tax.

Barbizon, 140 E 63rd St, NY 10021 ☎838-5700. Pleasant, recently renovated hotel with bar and restaurant, and good views from the terrace suites. Located three blocks from *Bloomingdales*. ⑥; discounts at weekends.

Beekman Tower, 3 Mitchell Place (49th St and First Ave), NY 10017 ☎355-7300. A member of the same group as *Lyden House*, this is a snootier suite hotel. Suites are of a similar size and high standard, however, and the Art Deco top floor *Top of the Towers* restaurant offers superb East Side views. ⑨

Beverly, 125 E 50th St, NY 10022 ☎753-2700. Nicely furnished, comfortable rooms in an otherwise slightly run-down looking building. Laundry and valet service, safe deposit boxes, room service, a steak-house, concierge and 24-hour pharmacy are some of the many extras. ⑦

Box Tree, 250 E 49th St, NY 10017 ☎758-8320. Twenty elegant rooms and suites fill two adjoining brownstones and make one of New York's more eccentric lodgings. The Egyptian-, Chinese- and Japanese-style rooms have fur throws on the beds, great lighting and ornament and decoration everywhere. A $100 dining credit towards a meal in the excellent *Box Tree Restaurant* is included in the room rate. Worth it for a splurge. ⑨

Drake, 440 Park Ave at 56th St, NY 10022 ☎421-0900. A first-class hotel, and member of the Swissotel chain, with bustling cocktail bar and superb French restaurant. This used to be an apartment building, so the rooms are large. ⑨

Elysee, 60 E 54th St, NY 10022 ☎753-1066. The *Elysee* was until recently famed for its eccentric, theatrical style, but sadly enthusiastic new management have refurbished the whole place in the best possible taste. You have to pay more for the large rooms but this

is still a fine place to stay, and close to Fifth Avenue. ⑦

Essex House, 160 Central Park South, NY 10019 ☎247-0300. A beautiful hotel for a special occasion, *Essex House* has been restored by new Japanese owners to its original Art Deco splendour. The best rooms have spectacular Central Park views. Despite the excellent service the atmosphere is not at all formal or hushed. ⑨, dropping to ⑧ at weekends.

Lexington, Lexington Ave at E 48th St, NY 10017 ☎755-6963. This large, elegantly renovated old hotel successfully gathers a very good Chinese restaurant, Western-style nightclub ("A shot of country with a splash of rock n' roll"), and refined north-Italian restaurant under one roof. The rooms are small and unexciting but the winter citysaver rate of ⑤ for a double is exceptional for this high-quality accommodation. ⑦

Loews, 569 Lexington Ave at E 51st St, NY 10022 ☎752-7000. There's a Deco-esque theme throughout the *Loews* New York, from the beautiful circular *Lobby Bar* and *Lexington Avenue Grill* to the very well-decorated guest rooms. The weekend rates (⑥) make this an even better deal. ⑧

Lowell, 28 E 63rd St, NY 10021 ☎838-1400. Madonna loved to work out so much when she stayed here (so it's said) that the *Lowell* built a Gym Suite, with fitness machines for the use of that room alone. Then Roseanne and Tom Arnold stayed in it and now you can too, for just $680, plus taxes. Along with the room you get great views of New York, a wood-burning fireplace and tons of posh seclusion. ⑨

Lyden House, 320 E 53rd St, NY 10022 ☎888-6070. One of the friendliest of the Manhattan East chain, where even the smallest suites are apartment-sized by New York standards and could sleep four (second two adults at $20+tax per person per night). All suites have eat-in kitchens and have the luxury of a maid to do the dishes. September to Christmas is the busiest time, so rates are negotiable the rest of the year. ⑧

Accommodation

Price categories:
① *under $30*
② *$30–45*
③ *$46–60*
④ *$61–80*
⑤ *$81–100*
⑥ *$101–130*
⑦ *$131–180*
⑧ *$181–250*
⑨ *over $250*

Accommodation

*Price
categories:*

① *under $30*
② *$30–45*
③ *$46–60*
④ *$61–80*
⑤ *$81–100*
⑥ *$101–130*
⑦ *$131–180*
⑧ *$181–250*
⑨ *over $250*

Mark, Madison Ave at E 77th St, NY 10021 ☎744-4300. One of a handful of NYC's hotels which really does live up to its claims of sophistication and elegance. A recent renovation has kitted the lobby out with Biedermeier furniture and sleek Italian torchieres. In the guest rooms, restaurant, and invitingly dark *Mark's Bar* there's a similar emphasis on the best of everything. ⑨

Pickwick Arms, 230 E 51st St, NY 10022 ☎355-0300. A thoroughly pleasant budget hotel, and for the price, one of the best deals you'll get in this part of midtown. All 400 rooms are air-conditioned, with cable TV, direct-dial phones and room service. The *Pickwick's* open-air roof deck with stunning views and *Torremolino's* restaurant are added attractions. ⑥

Pierre, 795 Fifth Ave, NY 10021 ☎838-8000. The *Pierre* has consistently retained its reputation as one of New York's top hotels and is certainly luxurious. It was Salvador Dali's favourite place to stay in the city, but the only surreal aspects today are the prices. If these prohibit a stay, take afternoon tea in the gloriously frescoed Rotunda, or experience a power-breakfast in the *Café Pierre*. ⑨

Plaza, 768 Fifth Ave, NY 10019 ☎759-3000. The last word in New York luxury, at least by reputation, and worth the money for the fine old pseudo-French chateau building if nothing else. Doubles start at $250 and run to $15,000 for a speciality suite, and that's before taxes. A place to stay if someone else is paying. ⑨

Plaza 50, 155 East 50th St, NY 10022 ☎751-5710. A suite hotel with guest rooms as well as studio, one-, two- and three-bedroom suites, particularly good for business travellers. The *Plaza 50* also offers concierge, valet and room service. ⑧

Roger Smith, 501 Lexington Ave, NY 10017 ☎755-1400. One of the best midtown hotels with very helpful service, individually decorated roons, a great restaurant which doubles as a jazz bar, and artworks and sculpture on display in the public areas. Breakfast is included in the price, along with a refrigerator and coffee maker in most rooms and VCRs with 2000 videos available from the hotel's library. Popular with bands, and guests who like the arty ambience. ⑧; weekends ⑦

San Carlos, 150 E 50th St, NY 10022 ☎755-1800. The *San Carlos* is well-located in the East 50s near plenty of bars and restaurants, and the large rooms all have fully equipped kitchenettes. This is a useful stand-by when everything else is booked solid. ⑦

Sherry Netherland, 781 Fifth Ave, NY 10022 ☎355-2800. The place to rent a whole floor and live in permanently, if a large sum of money ever comes your way. Many of the *Sherry Netherland's* guests already do this, and the service is geared to satisfying their every whim. Room service is by renowned restaurateur Harry Cipriani. ⑨

St Moritz on the Park, 50 Central Park South, NY 10019 ☎755-5800. If you'd like a view of Central Park but you don't want to pay the $300–400 a night room rates of the other hotels round here, then this is the place for you. The catch is that the rooms are tiny, so enjoy the views and then spend time in the *Sidewalk Café*, piano bar or *Rumpelmayer's Ice Cream Parlour* on the premises. ⑦

Surrey, 20 E 76th St, NY 10021 ☎288-3700. A genteel east Manhattan suite-hotel, in the heart of the "Museum Mile". ⑨; weekends ⑧

Waldorf-Astoria, 301 Park Ave at E 50th St, NY 10022 ☎355-3000. One of the great names among New York hotels, and newly restored to its 1930s glory, making it a wonderful place to stay if you can afford it or someone else is paying. ⑨

Wales, 1295 Madison Ave, NY 10128 ☎876-6000. Almost in Spanish Harlem, though very definitely Upper East Side in feel. Excellent prices for the high standard of accommodation: the original oak mouldings and mantles have been lovingly restored, and tea, cookies and classical music are served up every after-noon in the parlour. ⑦

Upper Manhattan: the West Side

Beacon, 2130 Broadway at 75th St, NY 10023 ☎787-1100. A pleasantly buzzing hotel with generously sized rooms, high ceilings, deep closets, colour cable TV and fully equipped kitchenettes. *Zabar's*, NYC's famous gourmet deli, is conveniently situated across the road. ⑥

Broadway American, 2178 Broadway, NY 10024 ☎362-1100. A budget hotel decorated in minimalist Art Deco style with shared kitchen and laundry facilities on each floor. Cheapest doubles are those with shared bathrooms. ⑤

Esplanade, 305 West End Ave, NY 10023 ☎874-5000. A good choice if you want to stay in a quieter residential area within reach of midtown's attractions. Considering the low prices, decor is surprisingly smart. ⑤

Excelsior, 45 W 81st St ☎362-9200. Old-fashioned hotel situated across from the Natural History Museum in the heart of the liveliest stretch of the Columbus Avenue scene. All the rooms are a decent size, but the suites in particular (⑥) would be good for four sharing. ⑤

Helmsley Windsor, 100 W 58th St, NY 10019 ☎265-2100. Enjoy coffee on the house each morning in the richly decorated, wood-panelled lobby. Like the other Helmsley hotels, the *Windsor* has a pleasantly old-fashioned air, with plenty of useful extras in the rooms. Central Park is a short walk away. ⑦

Malibu Studios, 2688 Broadway at W 103rd St, NY 10025 ☎222-2954. Probably the best-value budget accommodation in the city. A fair step from the heart of things up at the Morningside Heights end of the Upper West Side, but adjacent to the 103rd St stop on the #1 subway line, and within walking distance of plenty of restaurants and nightlife due to the nearby presence of Columbia University. Prices, all before taxes, are $35 for a single room ($50 with bath), $50 for a double ($60 with bath). Mention the *Rough Guides* and pay for 3 nights or more up front, and the rate goes down to $29.50 for a single without bath. Friendly management too, who will help get you discount tickets for the city's best music clubs if you ask. ③

Mayflower, 15 Central Park West at 61st St, NY 10023 ☎265-0060. A slightly down at heel but very comfortable hotel a few steps from Central Park and Lincoln Center. It's so close to the latter, in fact, that performers and musicians are often to be seen in the hotel's very good *Conservatory Café*. ⑦

Milburn, 242 W 76th St ☎362-1006. Welcoming and well-situated hotel which has recently been renovated in very gracious style. There are a few double rooms as well as large two-room suites with fully equipped kitchens. Practical extras are in-room safes, laundry and maid service. ⑥

New York Bed and Breakfast, 134 W 119th St ☎666-0559. Lovely old brownstone with nice double rooms going very cheaply. The only drawback is the location, way uptown in El Barrio. ③

Radisson Empire, 44 W 63rd St, NY 10023. A lavishly renovated member of the Radisson chain, the *Empire* will suit music lovers − not only is it opposite the Metropolitan Opera House and Lincoln Center, but also each (box-sized) room comes equipped with excellent CD player/tape deck and VCR. ⑦

Riverside Tower, 80 Riverside Drive, NY 10024 ☎877-5200. The area's alternative budget accommodation, this time in a quiet, residential part of the Upper West Side. Restaurants and bars are just a few blocks away, which is just as well as the rooms are not designed to make you want to spend much time in them. They are decent and clean though, with telephone and TV, and views of the Hudson River. It's worth noting that the triples and quads work out at around $25 per person, per night. ④

Westpark, 308 W 58th St, NY 10019 ☎246-6440. The *Westpark's* best rooms look out over Columbus Circle and the southwestern corner of Central Park. The rooms were more recently decorated than the public areas, which have a slightly seedy air, but it's a good choice overall. There's no restaurant on the premises,

Accommodation

Accommodation

but plenty of places to eat in the streets around. ⑥

Wyndham, 42 W 58th St, NY 10019 ☎753-3500. The *Wyndham*'s large rooms and suites vary enormously in terms of decor and it's the kind of place where the hotel's devotees – many of whom are Broadway actors and actresses – request their favourite each time they stay. All the rooms are homely, though, and the place feels more like an apartment building than a hotel. ⑦

Chapter 8

Drinking and Eating

There isn't anything you can't **eat** in New York. The city has more restaurants per head than anywhere else in the States, and New Yorkers not only eat out often but take their food incredibly seriously, devoting long hours of discussion to the study of different cuisines, new dishes and new restaurants – which can find themselves received with all the fervour of a second coming. As you stroll through the heavenly odours that emanate from the city's delis, bagel shops, Chinese restaurants and popcorn palaces, it's hard not to work up an appetite.

As for **drinking**, the basic American bar can be enjoyably like the ones you've seen on TV – a few cigar-smoking drunks propping up the counter, with a wise-cracking, philosophising barman. This is, however, only one sort of bar you'll come across, and there are many different kinds, ranging from ordinary neighbourhood locals, sometimes Irish and invariably pretty much male-only territory, to larger, designer hang-outs that are often the last word in Manhattan fashion.

Budget food: breakfast, lunch and snacks

The cheapest place to eat any kind of meal, wherever you are in New York, is a **coffee shop** or a **diner**. For some reason, these are invariably run by Greeks (thus explaining why the standard takeout coffee cup is decorated with a picture of the Parthenon), and they serve filling breakfasts, burgers, sandwiches and basic American fare from a usually enormous menu, which often includes good-value lunchtime specials, either at formica-topped tables or at stools set around a counter. Prices are around $6 for a heavily garnished burger and fries, $8 or so for anything more elaborate, making coffee shops in general the best option for a fill-ing lunch on a budget – though, brightly lit and fairly basic, they're not really places you'd want to eat dinner.

Breakfast

Although most hotels serve a breakfast of some kind, it works out much less expensive to go out to a coffee shop for the first meal of the day. Most coffee shops do special deals up until 11am, allowing you to eat and drink until you're full for under $5. Figuring high on **breakfast menus** are sausages (spicier than British ones) and bacon (streaky, cut very thin and fried to a crisp), along with eggs, waffles and pancakes – the latter thick and heavy, and served with a smothering of honey or maple syrup. Be prepared to be interro-gated as to how you want your eggs, and be ready to snap back with an answer – breakfast may be taken seriously in the States but it is never taken slowly. Basically, "sunny side up" means fried unturned, "over" means flipped over and done on both sides, and "over easy" turned for a few seconds only. **Breakfast specials**, served in most diners, usually means eggs (fried or scrambled), home fries (chunky potatoes fried with onions) or french fries, toast, juice and coffee for an all-in price.

Drinking and Eating

Lunch and snacks

Aside from coffee shops, most **restaurants** in New York open at lunchtime, when you tend to get the better deals, either because there's a set menu or because prices are simply cheaper.

Some of the best lunchtime deals can be had in **Chinatown**, where you can get a massive plate of meat with noodles or rice for around $5 or less, or, if you're feeling a little more adventurous, feast at a *dim sum* restaurant for $7–8. *Dim sum* (literally "your heart's delight") consists of small dishes that you choose from a moving trolley and pay for at the end, according to the empty dishes in front of you. For the inexperienced (and *dim sum* is not recommended to vegetarians) there's an element of chance, since Chinatown waiters tend not to speak English and the dishes themselves are often unrecognisable until the first bite. But duckwebs aside, it's mostly pretty accessible fare (see the lists on p.254 for some of the standards).

Another option for lunch – and one that's not just limited to Manhattan – is to get a **sandwich "to go"** (ie takeaway) from a **deli**. Once again, be prepared for a quick-fire question-and-answer session with the assistant, who will not only ask which kind of bread you want – white, whole wheat, rye or french (in which case ask for a "hero" or a "sub") – but also whether you want "mayo" (mayonnaise), lettuce or anything else. Deli sandwiches are custom-built and constrained only by your imagination, so bear in mind the size of the thing you're creating; if you hear them say "full house" it means you've ordered everything. You can expect to pay around $5 for a sandwich, but it is almost a meal in itself.

For **quick snacks**, many delis also do ready-cooked hot meals. City **vendors** (most concentrated on lower/midtown Manhattan) sell hot dogs, pretzels and knishes, or for around $1.50 you can get a slice of **pizza** (*Ray's* is the most widespread and reliable New York City chain). Additionally, there are of course the regular and familiar **burger chains**, such as (in descending order of quality) *Wendy's*,

Burger King and *McDonald's*, as well as a host of other fast-food franchises that haven't yet made it across the Atlantic.

Bar food and bargains

Just about every American **bar** serves food of one kind or another, and you'll find a substantial – and inevitable – cross-over between our "Bars" and "Budget eats" sections. Even in the lowliest bar there's a good chance they'll cook you at least a burger or a plate of potato skins, and many places offer a full menu, particularly the more upmarket Irish hangouts. Though bars open late (see p.258), their kitchens are usually closed by midnight.

In the **ritzier bars** – basically in Manhattan – there are almost invariably hot **hors d'oeuvres**, laid out between 5pm and 7pm Monday to Friday. For the price of a single drink (it won't be cheap) you can stuff yourself silly on pasta, seafood, chilli or whatever. Remember, though, that the more you look like an office-person (it's for them, after all, that the hors d'oeuvres are put out) the easier you'll blend in with the free-loading crowds. Some places even demand you wear a tie.

Bars that serve serious food are detailed along with restaurant **listings** later in this chapter, as are some sources of hot hors d'oeuvres. For convenience in locating a nearby place on a walk around the city, they are also cross-referenced by area in the Manhattan and Outer Boroughs chapters.

Coffee, tea, soft drinks

Coffee is drunk widely in New York and is usually fresh and good, served black or "regular" (with cream or milk, though in other parts of the States "regular" coffee is black coffee); *Sanka* is the most popular type of decaffeinated. You can get coffee "to go" in most delis, and in restaurants coffee is often served "ad lib", ie you can keep asking for refills at no extra charge. **Tea** is becoming more popular, and will normally be served straight or with lemon; if you want milk request it, and specify whether you want it hot or cold.

Soft drinks (sodas) come in caffeine-free versions as well. Watch out for **root beer**, a rather nasty concoction not unlike drinking bubble gum, and rainbow varieties of **coke**. These are drunk in three sizes: small (large), regular (bigger), and large (practically a bucket).

Restaurants

What follows is simply an introduction to the food you're likely to eat, and to peculiarly New York/American procedures of eating and paying for it. Specific **restaurant recommendations** start on p.269.

American food and ethnic cuisines

American cooking, as served by New York restaurants, tends to be of consistently good quality and served in huge portions. Salads are frequently eaten with meals, not as a main course but as a starter, and ordering one entails fielding more rapid questions as to the kind of dressing you want. Italian (more like European "French"), French (nothing like European "French"), thousand island and blue cheese are the usual alternatives. Some restaurants have a salad bar from which you can help yourself to as much as you can eat while waiting for the main course. Main dishes include steaks and burgers (which are near ubiquitous) and a good choice of fish and seafood. Vegetables will almost certainly include french fries and baked potato. Ordering a burger may be more complicated than you're used to: they're treated like regular steaks and you'll be asked how you want them cooked – rare, medium or well-done.

In New York City, at least, so-called American food inevitably fades into the background when you're confronted with the startling variety of different **ethnic cuisines**. Among them, none has had so dominant an effect as **Jewish** food, to the extent that many Jewish specialities – bagels, pastrami, lox and cream cheese – are now considered archetypal New York. Others retain more specific identities. **Chinese** food, available not just in Chinatown but all over Manhattan, is most frequently (and familiarly) Cantonese, though many restaurants serve the spicier Szechuan and Hunan dishes. Chinese prices are usually among the city's lowest. **Japanese** food is generally expensive – the Eighties craze and still plentiful, in particular *sushi* (raw fish), served as much for the aesthetic arrangement as for the taste, which you'll either love or hate. Other Asian cuisines include **Indian**, becoming more widespread though still nothing like as ubiquitous – or as good – as their British counterparts, and a broad and increasing sprinkling of **Thai**, **Korean** and **Indonesian** restaurants, all of which tend to be pricier than Chinese but not prohibitively so.

Closer to home, **Irish** food dominates the city's bars, with corned beef (more like salt beef than the tinned British bully), shepherd's pie and Irish stew. **Italian** cooking is also widespread, and not terribly expensive, especially if you stick to pizza; as is **Spanish**, whose huge seafood dishes can make an economical night out for those in a group. **French** restaurants are fairly expensive on the whole, particularly so of late with the cultish popularity of *nouvelle cuisine*, although there are an increasing number of bistros and brasseries turning out authentic and reliable French nosh for very attractive prices.

Drinking and Eating

Drinking and Eating

Glossary of American food terms for foreign visitors

A la mode	With ice cream
Au jus	Meat served with a gravy made from its own juices
BLT	Bacon, lettuce and tomato toasted sandwich
Broiled	Grilled
Brownie	A gooey biscuit of chocolate and fudge
Brunch	Originally a meal between breakfast and lunch; now a midday meal at weekends
Caesar salad	Cos lettuce in egg dressing with anchovy paste, olives and lemon served with garlic croutons and parmesan cheese
Check	Bill
Clam chowder	A thick soup made with clams and other seafood. Very tasty, and with bread almost a meal in itself
Club sandwich	Traditionally, a triple-decker sandwich with various combinations of meats, cheese, lettuce and tomato
Doggy bag	Not a bag but a stylish wrapping-up of your leftovers for reheating later at home
Egg cream	Neither eggs nor cream but a drink containing milk, chocolate or vanilla syrup and seltzer
Eggplant	Aubergine
English muffin	Toasted bread roll, similar to a crumpet
Hash browns	Mashed potato shaped into cubes and fried in fat
Hero	Sandwich made with French bread
Home fries	Thick-cut fried potatoes, often cooked with onions and spiced with pepper
Jello	Jelly
Jelly	Jam
Maitre'd	Head waiter
Muffin	Leavened cake made with bran, blueberry, etc
Pecan pie	Desert dish made of pastry, pecan nuts and caramel syrup
Popsicle	Ice lolly
Potato chips	Crisps
Pretzels	Savoury circles of glazed pastry
Seltzer	Fizzy/soda water
Scrod	Young Atlantic cod
Sherbet	Sorbet
Shrimp	Prawns
Soda	Generic term for any soft drink
Soft-shell crab	A kind of crab with a soft edible shell. Eating an entire crab shell and all may be a bit hard to get used to, but persevere – it's rightly considered a delicacy on the East Coast
Squash	Marrow
Tab	Bill
Teriyaki	Chicken or beef, marinated in soy sauce and grilled
Waffles	Like pancakes but thicker and crispier; egg batter cooked in an iron and served with maple syrup or honey and butter
Waldorf salad	Celery, chopped apple and walnuts served on lettuce leaves with a mayonnaise dressing
Zucchini	Courgettes
Fillet	The same as in England but pronounced "fillay"
Frank	Frankfurter (hot dog)
(French) fries	Chips
Half-and-half	Half cream, half milk

Glossary of ethnic food terms

Jewish

The Jewish faith allows two types of restaurant: those in which meat can be eaten and those where dairy products can be consumed. The two types of cooking can't be mixed. This section includes some Russian and Ukrainian dishes, which, though occasionally spelt differently on menus, are often much the same.

Bagel	Hard bread roll, in the shape of a ring, often toasted
Blintz	Crépe filled with cheese or fruit and eaten with sour cream
Borscht	Beetroot soup
Challah	Egg-bread, eaten traditionally as part of the Friday evening Sabbath meal
Falafel	(Middle Eastern) Deep-fried spiced chick pea balls
Glatt kosher	Type of cuisine and restaurant catering to the diet of ultra-orthodox Jews
Kasha	Cracked buckwheat cooked until tender and served with soup or as a side dish
Knaidel	Flour dumpling. Also known as *matzo balls*
Knish	Pastry filled with cheese, meat, potato, fruit or anything else that comes to hand
Kreplach	Noodle-dough shells filled with *kasha*, meat, potato, etc
Kugel	Potato or noodle pudding
Lox	Smoked salmon
Matzo	Flat unleavened bread eaten all year round but particularly at Passover
Pareve	Term for "neutral", ie something which can be eaten with meat or dairy food
Pirogen	Baked envelopes of dough filled with potato, meat or cheese
Schmaltz	Chicken fat
Tzimmes	Literally "a mixture". Casserole of meat, vegetables and fruit

Italian

Cacciatore	"Hunter's style" – cooked with tomatoes, mushrooms, herbs and wine
Calzone	Pizza folded in half so the topping is inside
Alla carbonara	Sauce made with bacon and egg
Alla Veneziana	Cooked with onions and white wine
Alfredo	Tossed with cream, butter and cheese
Al forno	Cooked in the oven
Posillipo	Tomato cooked with garlic, Neapolitan style
Puttanesca	Literally "whore style", cooked with tomato, garlic, olives, capers and anchovies
Zabaglione	Dessert of whipped egg yolks, sugar and marsala

Pasta

Cannelloni	Large pasta tubes, stuffed with minced meat and tomato and baked
Cappelleti	"Little hats" stuffed with chicken, cheese and egg
Cappelli d'angeli	"Angel's hair", very fine pasta strands
Fettucini	Flat ribbons of pasta
Fusilli	Pasta spiral
Gnocchi	Pasta and cheese dumplings
Linguine	Flat pasta noodles, like *fettucini*
Manicotti	Squares stuffed with cheese; ravioli are the same only with meat
Tortellini	Rings of pasta stuffed with either spiced meat or cheese
Vermicelli	Very thin spaghetti
Ziti	Small tubes of pasta, often baked with tomato sauce

Drinking and Eating

Drinking and Eating

Japanese

California roll	Mild-tasting sushi with a slice of avocado
Gyoza	Meat and vegetable dumplings
Karagei	Fried chicken
Larmen	Noodles in spicy broth
Negimayaki	Sliced beef with scallions
Okonomi	Literally "as you like it", used with regard to sushi when choosing the topping
Sake	Strong rice wine, drunk hot
Sashimi	Thinly sliced raw fish eaten with soy sauce or *Wasabi*
Sushi	Raw fish wrapped up in rice in seaweed. See below
Tempura	Seafood and vegetables deep-fried in batter
Tonkatsu	Deep-fried pork with rice
Wasabi	Hot green horseradish sauce

Sushi/sashimi

Anago	Sea eel
Chirashi	Mixed fish on rice
Ebi	Shrimp
Ikura	Salmon roe
Kappa (maki)	Cucumber with rice and seaweed
Maguro	Tuna
Nigiri	Rice topped with fish
Tai	Red snapper
Tekka (maki)	Tuna with rice rolled in seaweed (nori)
Toro	Extra meaty part of the tuna

Chinese

Cantonese	Szechuan/Hunan	
Chow	Chao	Stir-fried
Daofu	Doufu	Bean curd
Fun, fon	Fun	Rice
Gai, gee	Ji	Chicken
Har, ha	Xia	Shrimp (prawns)
Siu	Shao	Roasted
Jyu yuk	Zhu rou	Pork
Ngow yuk	Niu rou	Beef
Opp, opp	Ya	Duck
Ow	Zha	Deep-fried
Yu	Yu	Fish

Dim Sum (Cantonese)

Bao, bau	Bun (generally steamed)
Cha Siu Bao	Steamed bun filled with sweet cubes of roast pork
Chow fun	Fried flat rice noodles
Chow mai fun	Fried rice vermicelli
Har Gow	Steamed shrimp dumplings
Jook	Congee, or rice gruel
Kow, gow	Dumplings
Lo mein	Stir-fried noodles
Mai fun	Rice noodles
Tong mein	Soup noodles
Wonton, won ton	Thin-skinned dumplings filled with fish, usually served in broth

Greek

Baklava	Very sweet, flaky pastry with nuts and honey
Dolmades	Vine leaves stuffed with rice and meat
Feta	Crumbly white cheese made with goat's milk
Gyro	Minced lamb
Horta	Greens, often dandelion leaves
Kasseri	Rubbery cheese made with sheep's milk
Kokeretsi	Grilled lamb innards
Moussaka	Baked aubergine pie, topped with cheese sauce
Pastitsio	Lamb pie topped with macaroni
Souvlaki	Shish kebab
Spanakopita	Spinach pie
Stifado	Lamb stew
Taramasalata	Paste made of cod's roe, olive oil and lemon juice
Tiropita	Cheese pie
Tzatziki	Yoghurt with garlic and cucumber

Mexican

Arroz	Rice, usually prepared in tomato sauce
Burritos	Folded tortillas stuffed with refried beans or beef, and grated cheese

Chiles rellenos	Green chillies stuffed with cheese and fried in egg batter	*Mariscos*	Seafood
		Menudo	Soup made from a cow's stomach, said to be a cure for hangovers
Enchiladas	Soft tortillas filled with meat and cheese or chilli and baked	*Nachos*	Tortilla chips topped with melted cheese
Fajitas	Soft flour tortillas served with a prawn, chicken or beef dish to wrap inside	*Salsa*	Chillies, tomato, onion and cilantro, served in varying degrees of spiciness
Frijoles	Refried beans, ie mashed fried beans	*Tacos*	Folded, fried tortillas, stuffed with chicken, beef or (occasionally) cow's brains
Guacamole	A thick sauce made from avocado, garlic, onion, and chilli, and used as a topping	*Tamales*	Corn mill dough with meat and chilli, wrapped in a corn husk and baked
Margarita	*The* cocktail to drink in a Mexican restaurant, made with tequila, triple sec, lime juice and limes, and blended with ice to make slush. Served with or without salt	*Tortillas*	Maize dough pancakes used in most dishes
		Tostada	Fried, flat tortillas, smothered with meat and vegetables
		Quesadilla	Folded soft tortilla containing melted cheese

Drinking and Eating

More realistically, a whole range of **eastern European** restaurants – Russian, Ukrainian, Polish and Hungarian – serve well-priced filling fare. **Greek** food is easy to find in most parts of the city (especially, of course, in the Greeks' own quarters) and is usually edible and affordable. Finally, you'll also find **Tex-Mex** restaurants everywhere, a common hybrid all over America (though not at its best in New York City); it's honest stodge by any standards, and as variable as you might expect, although you always get plenty and there are no extras to push up the bill.

Other sundry places include **Cuban-Chinese** and **Kosher-Chinese** hybrids, and any number of **vegetarian** and **wholefood** eateries to cater for any taste or fad. The key is to keep your eyes peeled and not be afraid to be adventurous. Eating is *the* great joy of being in New York, and it would be a shame to waste it on the familiar.

Brunch

Brunch can also be a good-value deal, and is something of a New York institution, usually served at weekends between noon and 4pm, and sometimes including a free cocktail with your meal – though generally speaking the places that offer this often serve the worst food. Lox and cream cheese on a bagel, steak and eggs and eggs benedict are favourite brunch items. See p.268 for specific brunch venue recommendations.

Service, tipping . . . and home deliveries

Whatever you eat, **service** everywhere will be excellent, since not only is the notion of customer service deeply engrained into the American psyche, but the system of **tipping**, whereby (in New York) you double the figure on the bill for tax (just over 8 percent) to work out the minimum tip, can make the staff almost irritatingly attentive. There's no way round this: if you either refuse or forget to tip there's little point in going back to that restaurant. As far as actual **payment** is concerned, many – although by no means all – restaurants take credit/charge cards (if you use one you'll find a space left for you to write in the appropriate tip); travellers' cheques are also widely accepted (see *Basics,* "Money and Banks").

Drinking and Eating

If you're not in the mood to get dressed up or fight the crowds, you might consider having **food delivered** to your hotel or host's home. Many pizza and most Chinese places offer this service for free if the order exceeds a given minimum and you're within a reasonable distance – though you should, of course, tip the bearer.

Drinking

Bars generally open from mid-morning (around 10am) to the early hours – 4am at the latest, when they have to close by law. As for prices, in a basic bar you'll be paying $2–2.50 for a glass of draught beer (a little over a half-pint), $3–4 a bottle, although in a swankier and/or more fashionable environment, or in a singles joint, this may go up to $4–5 a glass or more. Detailed **listings** and recommendations on p.258.

Specific **savings on drinking** can often be made in the larger bars by ordering quart or half-gallon pitchers of beer, which represent a considerable discount on the price per glass. Look out, too, for "Happy Hour" bargains (usually 60 minutes stretched somewhere between 5 and 7pm) and two-for-the-price-of-one deals. Also, avoid bars or clubs that offer "free drinks for ladies" – they tend to be cattle markets or worse.

What to drink

When you've made your choice of bar, the problem is deciding **what to drink**. Despite its successful incursion into the British market over recent years, American **beer** enjoys something of a reputation in Europe for being fizzy, tasteless, and with virtually no alcoholic content at all. This may be slightly over-stated, but even Americans don't make much of a spirited defence of the brew; for them it's not a drink to get drunk on, more to quench your thirst, and it's normally served so chilled that the taste barely matters anyway. The major brands you'll see are, of course, *Budweiser*, *Miller* and *Michelob*, of which the last is by far the nicest. If you do care, imported beers like Canadian *Molsen*, Mexican *Dos Equis* and the familiar European varieties are widely available, though also substantially more expensive. If price is a problem, then bear in mind you can walk into any supermarket and buy beer at around $1 a can.

Don't be afraid to try Californian **wine**, since not only can it be very good, it's also fairly inexpensive at around $7–8 for a bottle in a liquor store, less than this if you buy a so-called "jug wine" – basically the rawest, lowest quality wine there is. If you're keen to sample something reasonably decent, try the varieties from the Napa or Sonoma valleys, just north of San Francisco, which between them produce some of the best quality wines in the country. New York State also produces wine, though of a lesser quality than California. French and Italian wines come more expensive, but they're still by no means costly. In all cases, however, wine does demand a better-filled wallet when in a restaurant or bar: expect 100 percent mark-up on the bottle.

As for the **hard stuff**, there are a number of points of potential confusion. First bear in mind that whether you ask for a drink "on the rocks" or not, you'll most likely get it poured into a glass full to the brim with ice; if you don't want it like this ask for it "straight up". Don't forget either that if you ask for *whisky* you'll be given the American kind, *bourbon*, of which the most common brands are *Old Grandad* and *Jim Beam* (*Jack Daniels* isn't technically bourbon since it's not made in Tennessee). If you want Scotch or Irish whisky you have to ask for them by nationality or brand name. Neither should you ask for *Martini* if you want the herby drink drunk by beautiful people: to Americans a martini is a mixture of gin and vermouth – vermouth (pronounced "vermooth") to an American being what the British would call Martini.

Cocktails are popular all over the States, especially during happy hours and weekend brunch (see p.255). The standards are listed opposite, but really varieties are innumerable, sometimes specific to a single bar. With any names you come across, experiment – that's half the fun. Look out too for something called **jello-**

shots: they're served in the livelier bars and restaurants and are a gelatinous sort of jam, only made with vodka instead of water, and thus something of a peculiar way to get drunk.

Buying your own alcohol, you need to find a liquor store – supermarkets only have beer, just one of New York State's complex **licensing laws**. Other regulations worth keeping in mind are that you have to be over 21 to buy or consume alcohol in a bar or restaurant (and you'll be asked to provide evidence if there's any dispute); that it's against the law to drink alcohol on the street (which is why you see so many people furtively swigging from brown paper bags); and that you can't buy off-licence booze, other than beer, anywhere on a Sunday.

Bars

It's in **Manhattan** – and more specifically Lower Manhattan (ie below about 23rd Street) – that you're likely to spend most time **drinking and eating**. Many of the city's better bars are situated in this part of town, as well the majority of the cheaper (and ethnic) restaurants. We've

divided Manhattan into four main sections – "Bars", "Cafés and Tea Rooms", "Budget eats" and "Restaurants" – although you can generally eat in any of these, including most bars. For drinking only, you'll find some of the bars listed here (music and gay-orientated places, most obviously) cross over into the "Nightlife" chapter that follows, both in terms of feel and often escalating prices. Just in case you have a sudden 4am urge for bagels and cream cheese, **24-hour** eateries, coffee shops and delis are also detailed at the end of this section.

The bar scene
The **bar scene** in New York City is a varied one, with a broader range of places to drink than in most American cities, and prices to suit most pockets. At the bottom end of the scale, the cheapest watering-holes you'll find, all over the city, are roughish places, sometimes Irish in name and ownership – convivial enough, though difficult ground for women on their own. In addition to these, there are more mixed hang-outs, varying from some of the long-established haunts in Greenwich Village to newer, louder and

Drinking and Eating

Cocktails			
Bacardi	white rum, lime and grenadine – not the brand name drink	Manhattan	vermouth, whisky, lemon juice and soda
Black Russian	vodka with coffee liqueur, brown cacao and coke	Margarita	tequila, triple sec and lime (or strawberry) juice
Bloody Mary	vodka, tomato juice, tabasco, worcester sauce, salt and pepper	Mimosa	champagne and orange juice
		Mint Julep	bourbon, mint and sugar
Daquiri	dark rum, light rum and lime, often with fruit such as banana or strawberry	Pina Colada	dark rum, light rum, coconut, cream and pineapple juice
		Screwdriver	vodka and orange juice
Harvey Wallbanger	vodka, galliano, orange juice	Tequila Sunrise	tequila, orange juice and grenadine
Highball	any spirit plus a soda, water or ginger ale	Tom Collins	gin, lemon juice, soda and sugar
Kir Royale	champagne, cassis	Vodka Collins	vodka, lemon juice, soda and sugar
Long Island Iced Tea	gin, vodka, white rum, tequila, lemon juice and coke	Whisky Sour	bourbon, lemon juice and sugar
		White Russian	vodka, white cacao and cream

Drinking and Eating

more deliberately stylish places that spring up – and die out – all the time in the downtown neighbourhoods. Bars with some kind of theme are particularly big right now. Finally there are also bars, known as "singles bars", many of which concentrate around midtown on the east side, which New Yorkers tend to use to pick up a member of the opposite (or same) sex. Expect prices to be hiked up greatly anywhere like this.

Selections that follow are personal favourites. The potential choice, obviously, is a lot wider – below 14th Street it's hard to walk more than a block without finding a bar – and takes in the whole range of taste, budget and purpose. (Bear in mind that many places double as bar and restaurant, and you may therefore find them listed not here but under "Budget eats" or "American restaurants".) The best hunting grounds are, in Lower Manhattan, Greenwich Village, the East Village and SoHo; there's a good choice of bars in midtown – though here bars tend to be geared to an after-hours office crowd and (with a few notable exceptions) can consequently be pricey and rather dull; uptown, the Upper West Side, between 60th and 85th streets along Amsterdam and Columbus, has a good array of bars and restaurants.

Hours of opening are generally mid-morning through to 1am or 2am; some stay open later but by law all must close by 4am. Bar kitchens usually stop operating around midnight or a little before. Wherever you go, even if you just have a drink you'll be expected to **tip**: the going rate is roughly ten percent of the bill or 50¢ for a single drink.

Groupings – as with the restaurant reviews that follow – are by the three main chapter divisions (Lower, Midtown and Upper). For ease of reference, however, all specifically **gay and lesbian** bars are gathered together in a single section on p.262.

Almost everywhere

Blarney Stone. Chain of Irish (and essentially male-only) bars with branches all over Manhattan. Nothing too wild, and

often filled with downbeat drunks slumped into their bourbon, but with the city's cheapest drinks and some decent value food.

McAnn's. Another Irish chain serving affordable booze and a broad selection of food. Their biggest, best (and for women most accessible) branch is the E 45th St basement, between Fifth Ave and Madison.

Lower Manhattan

Broome Street Bar, 363 West Broadway ☎925-2086. A popular and long-established local haunt, these days more restaurant than bar, serving reasonably priced burgers and salads in a dimly lit setting. A nice place just to nurse a beer too, especially when footsore from SoHo's shops and galleries.

Cedar Tavern, 82 University Place ☎929-9089. Legendary beat and artists' meeting-point in the 1950s and now a cosy bar with food – burgers for around $4 and other entrées $6 and up – and well-priced drinks. Summertime you can sit and eat in their covered roof garden.

Chelsea Commons, 242 Tenth Ave at 24th St ☎929-9424. Not only a personable bar but a great place to eat – outside meals for under $8. Very much a local hang-out.

Chumley's, 86 Bedford St ☎675-4449. Not easy to find, and with good reason – this place used to be a speakeasy and is obviously so well known now it doesn't need to advertise its presence. High on atmosphere and with a good choice of beers and food from around $8. Best arrive before 8pm if you want to eat at one of the battered tables – at which, incidentally, James Joyce put the finishing touches to *Ulysses*.

Continental Divide, 25 Third Ave ☎529-6924. Casual bar with a Western theme. Occasional live bands.

Downtown Beirut, 158 First Ave ☎777-9011. Mega-sleaze East Village punk bar with music, live and recorded. Jukebox vintage 1977–79. Another branch – *Downtown Beirut II* – at 157 Houston ☎614-9040, which repeats much the same formula.

Fanelli, 94 Prince St ☎226-9412. SoHo's oldest established bar, cosy and informal. Food – homecooked, unpretentious fare – weighs in at $5–7.

Fifty Five, 55 Christopher St ☎929-9883. Almost next door to the more renowned *Lion's Head*, but cheaper, and with a great jazz jukebox and regular performances of live jazz.

Grassroots Tavern, 20 St Mark's Place ☎475-9443. Basement bar at the centre of the East Village hum: not expensive, and with a good oldies jukebox and two dartboards.

Holiday Cocktail Lounge, 75 St Mark's Place ☎777-9637. Offbeat Village Bar that attracts a mixed bag of customers. Quite safe, but Bohemia with an edge nonetheless.

Jeremy's Alehouse, 254 Front St ☎964-3537. Earthy bar near the South Street Seaport, and one of the best in an otherwise bland area; see "Fish and seafood" restaurants, p.284.

Jekyll and Hyde, 91 Seventh Ave South ☎989-7701. Novelty pub with a haunted house theme that appeals to a mainly under-25 crowd.

Joes, E 6th St between aves A & B (no phone). Cheap beer and pool table in a tatty East Village setting.

La Jumelle, 55 Grand St ☎941-9651. Just down from the *Lucky Strike* in SoHo (see below), and similar in many ways, though perhaps a tad trendier at the moment, and used by a younger crowd. Popular with Europeans.

Lion's Head, 59 Christopher St ☎929-0670. Small bar in the heart of the Village, traditionally patronised by a literary clientele that has plastered its book covers all over the walls. Nothing too alternative, but a lively place for a drink, especially at weekends. Food too – burgers, steaks, etc; on busier evenings you might find you need to eat to get a table.

Lucky Strike, 59 Grand St ☎941-0479. Convivial bar/bistro patronised by a mixed bunch of young and middle-aged SoHoites. Food served out back (nothing

special and not cheap), and DJs on Friday, Saturday and Sunday nights, when the scene can be buzzing – though it's really best at lunchtime, when it's less frenetic.

Manhattan Brewery Company, 42 Thompson St ☎219-9250. Started by an Englishman with an eye to a money-spinner, this cavernous bar-restaurant brews and sells its own English-style beer and doles out simple food at okay prices. A hectic, crowded place, patronised by the after-hours office bunch.

McSorley's, 15 E 7th St ☎473-9148. New York City's longest-established watering-hole, or so it claims, and a male-only bar until just over a decade ago. These days it retains a saloon look, with a youthful gang indulging themselves on the cheap strong ale. There's no trouble deciding what to drink – you can have beer, and you can have it dark or lite.

NoHo Star, 330 Lafayette St ☎925-0070. Laid-back NoHo ("North of Houston") bar decorated by its artist clientele and serving a mix of Chinese and American food.

Peculier Pub, 145 Bleecker St ☎353-1327. Popular local bar whose main claim to fame is the number of beers it sells – over 300 in all and examples from any country you care to mention.

Puffy's, 95 Hudson St ☎766-9159. Small, funky TriBeCa bar with lunchtime food, very cheap booze, and a great jukebox.

Scrap Bar, 130 W 3rd St (no phone). Built on the site of the folk club where Bob Dylan had his first residency, a small punky bar with loud music.

Sophie's, E 5th St at Ave A (no phone). Beers for a dollar make this East Village bar popular, especially with ex-pat Brits.

Sporting Club, 99 Hudson St ☎219-0900. Sports-orientated bar with a large electronic screen to keep up with the action.

Sugar Reef, 93 Second Ave ☎477-8427. High-spirited East Village bar with flaming tropical decor, forty different varieties of rum and bopping waiters that's among Manhattan's hottest spots. You should expect to wait if you want to sample the Caribbean food, which goes for $10–15.

Drinking and Eating

Drinking and Eating

Temple Bar, 332 Lafayette St ☎ 925-4242. Small, dark, elegant bar serving champagne and, some claim, Manhattan's best martinis to a self-consciously Beautiful Bunch. A place to people-watch.

Vazac's, 108 Ave B ☎ 473-8840. Known as "Seven and B" for its location on the corner of Tompkins Square, this is a popular East Village hang-out, with an extremely mixed crowd, that's often used as a sleazy set in films and commercials – perhaps most famously in the film *Crocodile Dundee*.

White Horse Tavern, 567 Hudson St ☎ 243-9260. Convivial and inexpensive Village bar where Dylan Thomas supped his last before being carted off to hospital with alcoholic poisoning, and where today you can buy burgers, chilli and the like for around $5. Bareboards Bohemia, little changed, apart from the excellent jukebox, since Dylan fell off his barstool.

Midtown Manhattan

The Coffee Shop, 29 Union Square West ☎ 243-7969. A former coffee shop turned trendy bar and restaurant that at time of writing was very much *the* place to be seen. Still with the curvy counter and barstools of the old coffee shop, the bar is a nice place to hang out at any time; the noisy adjacent restaurant, complete with booths, serves vaguely Caribbean-style food – a little overpriced at around $12 a main course but not half bad, and there's cheaper stuff as well, making it a decent alternative for lunch.

Costello's, 225 E 44th St ☎ 599-9614. Journalists' bar once, legend has it, frequented by Ernest Hemingway. Busy early evening. Food in the restaurant out back starts at around $10.

Green Derby, 978 Second Ave ☎ 688-1250. Just opposite *Murphy's*, this tries hard to be Irish through and through. Basically, though, a singles hang-out, convivial if not especially cheap.

Irish Pub, 839 Seventh Ave ☎ 664-9364. As the name suggests, a straightforward, no-nonsense boozer with a long bar in a neighbourhood that needs just that.

Live Bait, 14 E 23rd St ☎ 353-2400. Cajun bar/restaurant run by the same people as *The Coffee Shop* (see above), and popular with the after-office crowd. Not the place for a quiet drink.

McHales 8th Ave and 46th St. Cosy Bar with a small restaurant attached serving well-priced burgers, pasta and chicken dishes. A reassuringly comfortable option in the hotel ghetto around Times Square.

Mickey Mantle's, 42 Central Park South ☎ 688-7777. Bar that's entirely given over to sport, with numerous TV screens showing different events, and even a video library of sports tapes. Decent food – burgers, squid and good desserts.

Molly Malone's, 287 Third Ave ☎ 725-8375. Comfortable Irish bar with solid, if unexciting, food.

Mulligan's Grill, 857 Seventh Ave ☎ 246-8840. There's nothing particularly stunning about this place, except that it offers a welcome and affordable escape from the costlier reaches of theatreland, both for drink and food.

Mumbles, 603 Second Ave ☎ 889-0750; 1491 Second Ave; 1622 Third Ave. Casual, friendly and cosy bars in which people gather to watch the seasonal sport. Mixed, neighbourhood crowd.

Murphy's, 977 Second Ave ☎ 751-5400. Irish bar which attracts the midtown singles set. Drinks are costly but food less so – a rare and useful standby in this part of town.

Old Town Bar and Restaurant, 45 E 18th St ☎ 473-8874. One of the oldest bars in the city, and a favourite with publishing types, artists, models and photographers from the surrounding Flatiron district. High on atmosphere, and with an excellent, if standard, menu of chilli, burgers and the like. Occasionally features in the *David Letterman Show*.

Pete's Tavern, 129 E 18th St ☎ 473-7676. Convivial watering-hole and former speakeasy that claims to be the oldest bar in New York, opened in 1864 – though these days it inevitably trades somewhat on its history. The restaurant serves American-Italian food, but the burgers are reputedly excellent.

P.J. Clarke's, 915 Third Ave ☎759-1650. One of the city's most famous watering-holes, this is a spit-and-sawdust alehouse with a not-so-cheap restaurant out the back. You may recognise it as the location of the film *The Lost Weekend*.

Ye Olde Tripple Inn, 263 W 54th St ☎245-9849. Basic Irish bar that serves inexpensive food at lunchtimes and early evening. A useful place to know about if you're after affordable food in this part of town.

Upper Manhattan

Augie's, 2751 Broadway ☎864-9834. One of the more interesting places on this stretch of Broadway, downbeat and unpretentious, and favoured by local jazz fans for its live music from 10pm onwards. Also has inexpensive snacks and food.

Border Café, 244 E 79th St ☎535-4347. Friendly neighbourhood hang-out good for satisfying cravings for frozen margaritas. A down-to-earth place despite its upscale location. Also at 2637 Broadway, though not as lively.

Buckaroo's Bar & Rotisserie, First Ave and 74th St ☎861-8844. *The* place to mingle with thirtysomethingish Upper East Siders, with a good selection of fruit-based drinks, including jello-shots, and a pool table out back where you can lounge for hours. The food is pretty decent as well – great chicken wings for under $4 and fine burgers for around $7.

Cannon's Pub, Broadway and 108th St (no phone). Big, brash and above all loud bar that is a getaway spot for rock freaks and serious drinkers on this corner of the Upper West Side. Unvarying selections of West Coast soft rock make it the antithesis of the East Village.

The Clubhouse, 1586 Yorke Ave ☎288-3218. Sports bar on the Upper East Side.

Drake's Drum, 1629 Second Ave ☎988-2826. Easy-going pub selling burgers, fish and chips, etc, for under $10.

Dublin House, 225 W 79th St ☎874-9528. Brash Irish bar with a young crowd, good jukebox and inexpensive drinks. Recommended if you're up this way.

Emerald Inn, Columbus Ave between 69th St and 70th St ☎874-8840. Amiable pub with food.

Hudson Bay Firm, 1454 Second Ave ☎861-5683. Neighbourhood bar that offers occasional all-you-can-eat specials.

KCOU, 430 Amsterdam Ave ☎580-0556. Straightforward upmarket bar with jukebox. Not expensive, despite appearances.

Lucy's Retired Surfers, 503 Columbus Ave ☎787-3009. Day-glo painted, surfboard-decorated bar with killer cocktails. Inevitably popular with Upper West Side yuppies, and with a restaurant out back.

Jim McMullen, 1341 Third Ave ☎861-4700. Upper East Side bar usually crammed with the Beautiful People of the neighbourhood.

Oscar and Toni's, 2662 Broadway at 101st St ☎222-0242. A neighbourhood bar that's popular with locals, especially students from nearby Columbia University.

Outback, 1668 Third Ave ☎996-8117. Bar with an Aussie theme. Always hopping.

Racoon Lodge, 480 Amsterdam Ave ☎874-9984. Simple bar with cheap drinks. Also on the East Side at 1439 York Ave ☎650-1775.

Ruby's River Road Cafe & Bar, 1754 Second Ave ☎348-2328. Home of the famous jello-shots (shots of liquor made with different coloured jellies), and a fun bar with a Cajun café in the back.

Rusty's, 1271 Third Ave ☎861-4518. Small bar, good for burgers and brew, that's run by an ex Mets baseball player and has the sporting paraphernalia to match – including a big screen TV to watch the action. Another branch – known as *Rusty Staub's* – is at 575 Fifth Ave in a shopping mall (☎682-1000), where the food is probably better.

The Saloon, 1920 Broadway ☎874-1500. Large bar/restaurant with a vast menu. Bonuses include outside seating and waiters on roller skates. Good for brunch.

Drinking and Eating

Drinking and Eating

Gay and lesbian bars

New York's **gay men's** bars cover the spectrum: from relaxed, mainstream cafés to some very heavy numbers indeed, although the scene has quietened down a lot since the early 1980s; the recommendations below are geared firmly towards the former. Most of the better established places are in **Greenwich Village**, with the **East Village** and **Murray Hill-Gramercy Park** areas (the east 20s and 30s) up-and-coming, the East Village having a more lesbian – and more political – identity. Things tend to get raunchier further west as you reach the bars and cruisers of the West Side Highway and meat-packing (literally – this is not gay slang) districts, both of which are hard-line and, at times, dangerous. For further listings and details, see the weekly *Outweek*.

Lesbian and **women-only** bars are, in comparison, thin on the ground, often operating only on one or two nights a week at one of the gay men's bars. *Womanews*, as well as *Outweek*, can be a useful supplement for listings and events.

Mainly for men

The Bar, 68 Second Ave ☎674-9714. Neighbourhood bar for the East Village. Relaxed, pool table.

Boots and Saddle, 76 Christopher St ☎929-9684. Middle-of-the-road leather action. A little sleazy.

Keller's, 384 West St ☎243-1907. Lively West Village bar that draws a mostly black male crowd.

Marie's Crisis, 59 Grove St ☎243-9323. Well-known cabaret/piano bar popular with gay men, and featuring old-time singing sessions on Friday and Saturday nights. Often packed, always fun.

The Monster, 80 Grove St ☎924-3558. Large, campy bar with a drag cabaret, piano and video.

South Dakota, 405 Third Ave ☎684-8376. One of the friendliest spots in the city, and with excellent food. Recommended.

Spike, 120 Eleventh Ave ☎243-9688. Another very popular leather bar.

Star Sapphire, 400 E 59th St ☎688-4710. New York's only gay Asian bar; gets going late on weekend nights.

Town and Country, 656 Ninth Ave ☎307-1503. Clientele reflects the neighbourhood – Hispanic/Irish. Unpretentious and downmarket.

The Tunnel Bar, 116 First Ave ☎777-9232. Formerly a leather bar, this establishment increasingly caters to a younger, more activist-orientated gay male crowd.

Ty's, 114 Christopher St ☎741-9641. Relaxed but convivial.

Uncle Charlie's, 56 Greenwich Ave ☎255-8787. Bar attracting a young, mainstream gay crowd.

The Works, 428 Columbus Ave ☎799-7365. Laid-back theme bar. Cool and pleasant and about the only option for this part of town.

Mainly for women

Crazy Nanny's, 21 Seventh Avenue ☎366-6312. Yuppie-orientated, rather stylish lesbian bar.

Pandora's, 70 Grove St ☎242-1408. Formerly known as the *Grove Club*, this legendary lesbian dive is small, tacky and overpriced, but has a devoted following.

Cafés and tea rooms

In addition to regular bars, New York has a number of **cafés and tea rooms**, which don't always serve alcohol but concentrate instead on providing fresh coffee and tea, fruit juices and pastries and light snacks, and sometimes full meals. Many of the more long-established cafés are downtown, congenial places with a European emphasis; indeed they're often determinedly Left Bank in feel (like the grouping at the junction of Bleecker and Macdougal Street) and perfect for lingering or just resting up between sights. The posher midtown **hotels** are good places to stop for tea too, if you can afford the prices they charge for the fake English country house atmosphere they often try to contrive. Failing that, if all you want is a cup of something hot and a pastry, most of the larger **department stores** have coffee shops.

Algonquin Oak Room, 59 W 44th St ☎840-6800. The archetypal American interpretation of the English drawing room. Good for afternoon teas.

Anglers & Writers, 420 Hudson St ☎675-0810. Village café serving a daily afternoon tea between 3pm and 6pm, as well as decent American fare – soups and puddings are a speciality. A good place to just have a coffee, a snack or a full meal.

Au Café, 1700 Broadway ☎757-2233. Rare in being a midtown place where you can linger over coffee. Outdoor seating.

Boathouse Café, Central Park Boating Lake – 72nd St entrance ☎517-2233. Peaceful retreat from a hard day's trudging around the Fifth Avenue museums, and with great views of the famous Central Park skyline.

La Boulangere, 49 E 21st St ☎475-8582. Good for a midday pick-me-up, with a menu of breads and pastries.

Café Calo, 201 W 83rd St ☎496-6031. A West Side coffee house with scrumptious desserts.

Caffé Biondo, 141 Mulberry St ☎226-9285. A little brick-walled cappuccino shop with excellent Italian desserts.

Caffé Dante, 79 Macdougal St ☎982-5275. A morning stopoff for many locals since 1915. Good cappuccino, double espresso and caffé alfredo with ice cream. Often jammed with NYU students and teachers.

Café Le Figaro, 184 Bleecker St ☎677-1100. Former Beat hang-out during the 1950s and the ersatz Left Bank at its finest. Good views of the Bleecker Street hubbub, and excellent snacks and sandwiches too.

Caffé Reggio, 119 Macdougal St ☎475-9557. One of the first Village coffee houses, dating back to the 1920s, usually crowded and with tables outside for people-watching.

Caffé Vivaldi, 32 Jones St ☎929-9384. An old-fashioned Viennese-style coffee house with fireside cosiness.

Café Roma, 385 Broome St ☎226-8413. Old Little Italy *pasticceria*, ideal for a drawn-out coffee and pastry. Try the homemade Italian cookies, and the gelato counter out the back.

Citicorp Atrium, Lexington Ave and 53rd St. Again, a good place to stoke up after a hard morning's tramp around the midtown sights.

Ferrara, 195 Grand St ☎226-6150. The oldest and best-known of all the Little Italy coffee houses, also with outside seating in summer.

Les Friandises, 922 Lexington Ave ☎988-1616. A paradise for pastries on the Upper East Side.

Peacock Caffé, 24 Greenwich Ave ☎242-9395. Puccini arias as background music to accompany rich desserts and *Café Royale* – coffee with whipped cream.

Tea and Sympathy, 108 Greenwich Ave ☎807-8329. Self-consciously British tea room, serving an afternoon High Tea full of traditional Brit staples like jam roly-poly and treacle pud, along with shepherd's pie, fish cakes, etc. Perfect if you're feeling homesick.

Veniero's, 342 E 11th St ☎674-4415. East Village bakery and almost century-old institution that sells wonderful pastries and has some seating in the back.

Drinking and Eating

Budget eats

Bars are often the cheapest places to eat in New York, but they're by no means the only budget option. Any number of **diners**, **coffee shops** and **burger joints** will serve you straight American food for $5–7, and many **delis** do hot takeaway meals as well as snacks and bumper sandwiches. We've also included here the New York institution of **happy hour hors d'oeuvres**, one of the city's best scams if you're on a tight budget, when hors d'oeuvres are laid out around 5–7pm in numerous midtown bars and restaurants, all consumable for the cost of a drink. There is also a list of places to eat **brunch**, where many restaurants compete for custom by laying on a special well-priced brunch menu – sometimes including a free cocktail or even unlimited champagne thrown in with the cost of your meal.

Drinking and Eating

For **further cheap eating options**, be sure to look also at the places detailed in the following "Restaurants" section. Although Chinese and East European food, and of course pizza, are perhaps the only cuisines that are reliably cheap pretty much everywhere, there are some good bargains to be had in every category.

Burgers, delis and diners

Most of the listings that follow are for **diners** or basic **café-restaurants**, many of which tend to serve standard American dishes (burgers, steak and seafood) for around $10, plus drinks and tip, as well as a selection of the more interesting **delis** that offer sit-down meals.

Lower Manhattan

Around the Clock, 8 Stuyvesant St ☎598-0402. Centrally situated East Village restaurant serving crepes, omelettes, burgers and pasta at reasonable prices. Open 24 hours.

Astor Riviera, 452 Lafayette St ☎677-4461. Inexpensive East Village 24-hour restaurant serving a broad coffee shop menu.

Bagel Buffet, Sixth Ave at 8th St ☎477-0448. Wide selection of fillings and good value bagel salad platters for around $5. Open 24 hours.

Bendit Diner, 219 Eighth Ave at 21st St ☎366-0560. Typical diner, but with an usually large menu.

Boxer's, 190 W 4th St ☎929-8942. Dimly lit bar-restaurant serving some of the most inexpensive food and drink in the city – solid American fare for under $10.

Brother's Bar-B-Q, 228 W Houston St ☎727-2775. Downbeat SoHo diner serving some of the best barbecue food east of the Mississippi. The mashed potatoes and collard greens are not to be missed. Cheap too – two people can eat handsomely for around $20.

Campus Coffee Shop, 31 W 4th St ☎228-1460. Old-established café usually packed with students from the nearby NYU. Excellent breakfast bargains before 11am.

Carmella's Village Garden, 49 Charles St ☎242-2155. Cheap café serving omelettes, pasta and the like for $5 up.

Corner Bistro, 331 W 4th St ☎242-9502. Somewhat dark and dingy pub with cavernous cubicles and healthy servings of burgers, beer and desserts for reasonable prices. Long-standing haunt of West Village literary and arty types.

Dave's Pot Belly, 98 Christopher St ☎243-9614. Friendly all-night restaurant with inexpensive American food in very large helpings. The desserts are easily enough for two.

Ear Inn, 326 Spring St ☎226-9060. Arty kind of place, with cheap food (all under $10) and a good jukebox. Live folk and country music on Tuesday nights.

Elephant and Castle, 68 Greenwich Ave ☎243-1400. Old Village favourite serving well-priced food and drink. Also another location at 183 Prince St ☎260-3600.

Empire Diner, 210 Tenth Ave ☎243-2736. With its gleaming chrome-ribbed Art Deco interior this is one of Manhattan's original diners, still open 24 hours and still serving up plates of simple American food. The food is very average, but the place is a beauty.

Fuddrucker's, 87 Seventh Ave South ☎255-9349. Burger restaurant imported from Texas, and serving suitably giant-size burgers and other down-home American food. Outdoor seating when it's warm enough.

Harry's at Hanover Square, 1 Hanover Square ☎425-3412. Bar that gets into its stride when the floor traders come in after work. Great burgers.

Khan's, 23 Third Ave (no phone). A Mongolian barbecue restaurant (sic) which offers lunch specials for $4.50 and all-you-can-eat dinner deals for a mere $8.95. Strictly carnivores only.

Life Café, 343 E 10th St ☎477-8791. Peaceful and long-established East Village haunt right on Tompkins Square that hosts sporadic classical and other music concerts. Food is sandwiches, Tex-Mex or vegetarian – plates all around $6–8.

Little Mushroom Café, 183 W 10th ☎ 242-1058. Fish, pasta and omelettes at $5–12. One of the cheaper places along this stretch of the Village, catering to a mixed gay/straight crowd. Bring your own booze from the deli opposite. Also with an uptown location at 1439 Second Ave ☎ 988-9006.

Nick and Eddie, 203 Spring St ☎ 219-9090. Great home-cooked American food at modest prices. Has a pleasant outdoor garden.

Phebe's, 361 Bowery ☎ 473-9008. Good value food – including weekend brunch and a three-hour "happy hour" during the week. Opening hours till 4am make it a regular off-off Broadway hang-out.

Prince Street Bar, 125 Prince St ☎ 228-8130. SoHo bar and restaurant used by the local arthouse clique. Broad array of different foods, and, for the area, not terribly expensive.

Riviera Café, 225 W 4th St ☎ 242-8732. Central Village restaurant serving acceptable food at low prices. In the 1960s this was very much the place to be seen.

Second Avenue Deli, 156 Second Ave ☎ 677-0606. The East Village rival to *Katz's* (see p.283), serving up marvellous burgers, pastrami sandwiches and other deli goodies in ebullient, snap-happy style.

South Street Seaport Market, east end of Fulton St. The market's second-floor selection of fast-food chains are among the least expensive places to eat in the area.

Spring Street Market, 111 Spring St ☎ 226-4410. Wonderful deli. The best sandwiches downtown.

Stromboli Pizzeria, 112 University Place ☎ 255-0812. Excellent thin crust pizzas – a good place for a quick slice.

Violet Café, 80 Washington Square East ☎ 529-5428. Coffee shop-cum-restaurant popular with NYU students. Best for inexpensive sandwiches and breakfasts.

Wolf's Delicatessen, 42 Broadway ☎ 422-4141. Classic New York deli that is a good stop for lunch in between seeing the sights of the Financial District.

Midtown Manhattan

J. J. Applebaum's Deli, 34th St at Seventh Ave ☎ 563-6200. Huge and excellent deli with two sit-down floors. Good for refortifying after *Macy's*.

Bagel Palace, 36 Union Square ☎ 673-0452. Bagels topped with just about anything, plus a hundred different omelettes.

Boogies Diner, 711 Lexington Ave ☎ 355-1001. A funky clothing store downstairs and a fun, casual, 1950s-style luncheonette upstairs. Great place for kids.

Broadway Diner, 570 Lexington Ave ☎ 486-8838, and 1724 Broadway ☎ 765-0909. An upscale coffee shop with 1950s-style ambience.

Carnegie Deli, 854 Seventh Ave ☎ 757-2245. This place is known for the size of its sandwiches – by popular consent the most generously stuffed in the city, and a full meal in themselves. The chicken noodle soup is good, too. Not cheap, however, and the waiters are among New York's rudest.

Chez Laurence, 245 Madison Ave ☎ 683-0284. Well-placed little patisserie that makes cheap breakfasts, decent lunches – and good coffee at any time of the day.

Ellen's Stardust Diner, 1377 Sixth Ave ☎ 307-7575. Another 1950s-style diner serving traditional American food and built around the "missed my subway home" theme.

Hamburger Harry's, 145 W 45th St ☎ 840-0566. Handy diner just off Times Square; cousin to its downtown location but more refined. Some claim its burgers are the best in town.

Hard Rock Café, 221 W 57th St ☎ 489-6565. Burger restaurant that for some reason continues to pull in celebrity New York, or at least the odd rock star. Full to bursting most nights, especially at weekends, but only the famous can book ahead – everyone else stands in line outside. The food isn't bad, but only really worth it if you've a teenager in tow.

Drinking and Eating

Drinking and Eating

Harold's, 150 E 34th St at Lexington and Third Ave ☎684-7761. Decent American food that's reasonably priced – quite a find for this part of town. Has outdoor seating in summer.

Houlihan's. Many midtown locations. 380 Lexington ☎922-5660, 729 Seventh Ave ☎626-7312, 677 Lexington ☎339-8858, 350 Fifth Ave ☎630-0036, 767 Fifth Ave ☎339-8850. Very American-style restaurant with decent food at good prices.

Jackson Hole Wyoming, 521 Third Ave ☎679-3264; 1633 Second Ave ☎737-8788. Midtown burger chain with a reputation for obscenely large burgers. Good value for dyed-in-the-wool carnivores.

Jerry's Metro Delicatessen, 790 Eighth Ave ☎581-9100. Large deli restaurant with a huge choice of sandwiches, omelettes and burgers, etc. Good breakfasts, too, which is handy given the Times Square vicinity location.

Landmark Tavern, 626 Eleventh Ave ☎757-8595. Long-established Irish bar/restaurant popular with the midtown yuppie crowd. Good food, and huge portions.

Market Diner, 572 Eleventh Ave ☎244-6033. The ultimate 24-hour diner, chrome-furnished and usually full of weary clubbers filling up on breakfast. A good place to refuel early evening too.

New York No.1 Delicatessen, 104 57th St ☎541-8320. Enormous art deco restaurant, renowned for its pastrami and corned beef, and handily situated for those suffering from midtown shopping fatigue. Good breakfasts too.

Planet Hollywood, 140 W 57th St ☎333-7827. A tourist trap similar to other European branches. In the *Hard Rock Café* vein, but with movie rather than music memorabilia.

O'Reilly's, 56 W 31st St ☎684-4244. Posh Irish pub/restaurant with standard American dishes at $6-12. Good value.

Reuben's, 244 Madison Ave ☎867-7800. Busy midtown diner that makes a fine and filling haven in between the sights and shops of Fifth Avenue.

Sarge's, 548 Third Ave ☎679-0442. Large coffee shop serving enormous portions of deli grub. Open 24 hours a day.

Scotty's Diner, 336 Lexington Ave ☎986-1520. Conveniently placed midtown diner, close to Grand Central and the Empire State. Solid diner food, good breakfasts until 11am and a friendly Spanish owner.

Stage Deli, 834 Seventh Ave ☎245-7850. Another reliable all-night standby, and long-time rival to the *Carnegie Deli*, p.265.

Taste of the Apple, 1000 Second Ave ☎751-1445. Home of the over half-pound burger, and very fair prices for this part of town; also serves Mexican food. Also at 283 Columbus Ave ☎873-8892.

Wine and Apples, 117 W 57th St ☎246-9009. A kind of hybrid Greek-Hungarian diner with meals priced from $5-8 and inexpensive booze. A life-saver in this part of midtown.

Upper Manhattan

Amsterdam's, 428 Amsterdam Ave ☎874-1377. Bar-restaurant serving burgers, chicken and pasta and the like for $12-15. Downtown branch at 454 Broadway ☎925-6166.

BBQ, 27 W 72nd St ☎873-2004; 1265 Third Ave ☎772-9393; 21 University Place ☎674-4450; 132 Second Ave ☎777-5574. A real-value budget option for this part of town, just off Central Park, though the Upper East Side branch has a better reputation. Excellent barbecue chicken and burgers for $5-8, chilli for less. Whichever branch you try it'll be crowded, however, and the service can be poor, to say the least.

Diane's Uptown, 249 Columbus Ave ☎799-6750. Fast, quick hearty burgers, and handy for *Ben & Jerry's* ice cream next door.

E.A.T., 1064 Madison Ave ☎772-0022. Expensive but excellent food – especially the breads.

EJ's Luncheonette, 433 Amsterdam Ave ☎873-3444. Newly opened diner that does its best to look old, with mirrors, booths upholstered in turquoise vinyl and walls adorned with Fifties photographs.

Breakfast: coffee shops and diners

You rarely have to walk more than a block or two in Manhattan to find somewhere that serves **breakfast**: there are coffee shops and diners all over town serving up much the same array of discounted specials before 11am. But when you're desperate for a shot of early morning coffee, the following checklist should help you avoid traipsing too far from wherever you happen to be staying. You'll find full reviews, where appropriate, elsewhere in this chapter; otherwise just expect a regular Greek-run coffee shop.

Drinking and Eating

Lower

Astor Riviera, 452 Lafayette St ☎677-4461.

Bendit Diner, 219 Eighth Ave at 21st St ☎366-0560.

Campus Coffee Shop, 31 W 4th St ☎228-1460.

Life Café, 343 E 10th St ☎477-8791.

Odessa, 117 Ave A ☎473-8916.

Triumph, 148 Bleecker St ☎228-3070.

Village Inn, 169 Bleecker St ☎533-0823.

Violet Café, 80 Washington Square East ☎529-5428.

Waverley, 385 Sixth Ave ☎675-3181.

ZZZ, 60 University Place ☎777-7370.

Midtown

Astro, 101 W 55th St ☎489-6284.

Broadway Diner, 590 Lexington Ave ☎486-8838 and 1724 Broadway ☎765-0909 .

Brooks, 330 Fifth Ave ☎997-1030.

Chez Laurence, 245 Madison Ave ☎683-0284.

Ellen's Stardust Diner, 1377 Sixth Ave ☎307-7575.

Grand Central, Grand Central Terminal, 42nd St ☎883-0009.

Jerry's Metro Delicatessen, 790 Eighth Ave ☎581-9100.

Lantern, 209 E 42nd St ☎867-2760.

New York No.1 Deli, 104 57th St ☎541-8320.

Penn Garden, 150 W 31st St ☎736-0293.

Red Flame, 67 W 44th St ☎869-3965.

Upper

Googies Diner, 1491 Second Ave ☎717-1122.

New Wave, 937 Madison Ave ☎734-2467.

Tramway Coffee Shop, 1143 Second Ave ☎758-7017.

Utopia, 267 Amsterdam Ave ☎873-6233.

Venus Coffee Shop, 1051 Second Ave ☎759-5597.

Unpretentious American food which includes pancakes in many guises and banana splits to die for. Expect long lines for the brunch served on Sunday.

Googies Diner, 1491 Second Ave ☎717-1122. Arty diner with funky decor and Italian-influenced American food.

Gray's Papaya, Broadway at 72nd St (no phone). Two all-beef frankfurters and a papaya juice for just $1.65. A New York experience. No ambience, no seats, just good cheap grub.

Hi-Life Bar and Grill, 477 Amsterdam Ave ☎787-7199; also 1340 First Ave ☎249-3600. An in spot for Upper West and East Siders for basic American fare and good people-watching.

Madhatter, 1485 Second Ave ☎628-4917. Casual pub serving decent burgers and other simple food.

Madison Ave Café, 937 Madison Ave ☎734-2467. A fairly standard coffee shop handily situated for the museums, especially the Whitney. It's also a nice cheap option for those who have just blitzed with their credit card in the nearby Madison Avenue designer clothing emporia.

Nectar, 1090 Madison Ave ☎734-9395. Good coffee shop with daily specials. Very handy for the Met.

Papaya King, 179 E 86th St ☎369-0648. By general – and *New York Times* – consent, the best hot dogs in the city.

Drinking and Eating

Rathbones, 1702 Second Ave ☎369-7361. Opposite *Elaine's* (see "Expense account", p.287) and an excellent alternative for ordinary humans. Take a window seat and watch the stars arrive, and eat for a fraction of the price. Burgers, steak, fish for under $10 – and a wide choice of beers.

Serendipity 3, 225 E 60th St ☎838-3531. Cheap long-established daytime eatery and ice cream parlour. The frozen hot chocolate is out of this world.

Happy hours and free food

Happy hour hors d'oeuvres are essentially a midtown phenomenon –and the hour(s) in question are generally 5 to 7pm, Monday to Friday only. Since the idea is to draw in well-heeled clientele,

just out from their offices, you'll do well to dress in similar fashion, though the places listed below are all pretty accessible as long as you perform with confidence and don't too obviously clear the tables. The cost of a regular drink or cocktail at any should work out around $3. For happy hour devotees, there are additional possibilities in addition to those below: just check out the more upmarket midtown bars and hotels.

The Champion, Marriott Hotel, 525 Lexington Ave ☎755-4000. One of the most popular happy hours, with excellent hors d'oeuvres disappearing rather quickly. Don't arrive much after 6pm.

Charley O's, 218 W 45th St ☎626-7300. Burger place that's best for drinks only.

Giggles, 115 W 40th St ☎840-1900. Good for munching free food while mingling with the "garmentos" as those in the garment industry like to be called.

Ryan McFadden's, 800 Second Ave ☎599-2226. A long-established hang-out of *Daily News* reporters and ex-pats. Always crowded and fun.

Sfuzzi, 58 W 65th St ☎385-8080. Swinging bar scene and lots of Italian hors d'oeuvres – easily enough to make yourself a mini dinner.

Top of the Sixes, 666 Fifth Ave ☎757-6662. No better place to freeload really. Hot hors d'oeuvres every evening, Monday to Friday, and some great views over Manhattan.

Trattoria, ground floor of the Pan Am (Met Life) Building, E 45th St ☎661-3090. Pasta, pizzas and Italian dainties in relatively unintimidating surroundings. Recommended.

Whaler Bar, Madison Towers Hotel, 22 E 38th St ☎685-3700. Casual atmosphere and choice of cheese and veggie dishes.

Restaurants

New York's ethnic make-up is at its most obvious and accessible in the city's **restaurants**. Somewhere in Manhattan you can eat just about any world cuisine – and often a lot better than you'd find in its natural habitat. Don't, however, make the mistake of assuming ethnic food is necessarily inexpensive. Often it's not. You pay Manhattan's highest prices for the better Italian, French and Japanese eateries; Greek and Spanish food, too, often works out expensive, and really only Chinese, Jewish and East European (and sometimes Mexican) are dependably low-budget. (One other thing to bear in mind is that these days many of New York's better ethnic restaurants are in the Outer Boroughs.) **Selections** below shouldn't break the bank – most serve entrées at $10 or under (some well under) and at lunchtime you'll often find special deals or set menus – though we have tried to include the *best* of Manhattan's restaurants as well as the cheapest. The listings which follow are by country of origin, with closing sections on *Fish and seafood, Vegetarian and wholefood* and last (and in many cases least) *Expense account.*

American, Latin and South American

Grouped together for simplicity, these are all filling and good-value options. Regional **American** restaurants can be fairly sedate but will always be generous, and some serve interesting regional variations; similarly with **Mexicans** and **Tex-Mex** restaurants – though they're usually livelier hang-outs serving cocktails. Watch out for Manhattan's **Brazilian** restaurants, which are gaining in popularity – and numbers.

Lower Manhattan

Bayamo, 704 Broadway ☎475-5151. Chino-Latino food, served in vast portions at moderate prices – around $15 for a main course. Try the stir-fried duck with chilli and beans.

Bay-O, 103 Greenwich Ave ☎924-3161. A young crowd enjoys the grub at this funky downtown Caribbean/Southern joint. Deadly tropical drinks too.

Benny's Burritos, 113 Greenwich Ave ☎633-9210. Huge burritos with all kinds of fillings, and speedy, amiable service. Cheap too. Now with a branch in the East Village at 4th St and Avenue A.

Caliente Cab Co, 61 Seventh Ave at Bleeker St ☎243-8517. Average Tex-Mex food but with some good bargains: Mon–Fri happy hour (4.30–7pm) has free bar food; weekend brunch buffet (Sat & Sun noon–3pm) comes with as many margaritas mimosas, or screwdrivers as you can drink.

Caribe, 117 Perry St ☎255-9191. A funky Caribbean restaurant filled with a leafy jungle decor and blasted with reggae music. Fairly spicy food, washed down with wild tropical cocktails, make it the place for a fun night out. Cash only.

Casa Mexico, 557 Hudson St ☎366-4893. Village restaurant serving solid Tex-Mex grub for $6 upwards. Firmly average food, but on a Saturday night it may be the only place to get a table around these parts if you haven't booked.

Drinking and Eating

Drinking and Eating

Cottonwood Café, 415 Bleecker St ☎924-6271. Noisy Village restaurant with almost exclusively young custom, mainly NYU students. Texan cuisine (chicken, chops, okra and mash) – good, filling and not too expensive at $6 up. Live music every night (except Sunday) from 10.30pm.

Cowgirl Hall of Fame, 519 Hudson St ☎633-1133. Down-home Texan-style barbecue. Try the fried chicken.

El Coyote, 774 Broadway ☎ 677-4291. Texas-style food at low prices.

The Cupping Room Café, 359 W Broadway ☎925-2898. Absurdly quaint American restaurant that serves good wholesome food to occasional jazz and the odd tarot or palm reader on selected evenings. Brunches are excellent, with freshly baked breads and muffins, though you'll probably need to wait. Recommended.

Flying Fish, 395 West St ☎924-5050. Crowded Caribbean West Village place selling cheap Jamaican food.

Friend of a Farmer, 77 Irving Place ☎477-2188. Rustic Gramercy café serving homey "comfort meals".

Great Jones Café, 54 Great Jones St ☎674-9304. Blackened redfish, great burgers, molasses cornbread, beer and Cajun martinis in an intentionally anonymous-looking neighbourhood restaurant.

Jerry's Restaurant, 101 Prince St ☎966-9464. American-French restaurant with an upscale diner-type atmosphere that's become one of SoHo's trendier spots of late. Casual and good for people-watching. Moderate prices. Another branch – *Jerry's 103* – in the East Village at 103 Second Ave ☎777-4120.

Lupe's East LA Diner, 110 Sixth Ave ☎966-1326. Very laid-back, hole-in-the-wall restaurant serving great beer and burritos. Good fun, and cheap.

Mary Ann's, 116 Eighth Ave ☎633-0877. Good-value Tex-Mex food, most for under $10, also available from a branch in the East Village at 300 E 5th St ☎475-5939.

Mesa Grill, 102 Fifth Ave ☎807-7400. One of Lower Manhattan's more fashionable eateries, serving unique and eclectic Southern fare at highish prices. Full of publishing and advertising types doing lunch.

Mi Cucina, 57 Jane St ☎627-8273. Authentic Mexican food (but without the grease) in a simple setting. Good prices.

Miracle Grill, 112 First Ave ☎254-2353. A southwestern restaurant with interesting taste combinations and an attractive garden at the back.

Moondance Diner, 80 Sixth Ave ☎226-1191. Flashy and loud, popular with a would-be Bohemian crowd. Burgers, sandwiches, and great apple pancakes.

The Pink Teacup, 42 Grove St ☎807-6755. Soul-food restaurant in the heart of the Village. Cheap and filling.

Royal Canadian Pancake Restaurant, 145 Hudson St ☎219-3038. A memorable restaurant serving numerous kinds of vast – and delicious – pancakes, with fillings ranging from lager to white chocolate and almond to berries and bananas. Come hungry. A perfect venue for Sunday brunch, though come later (after 3pm) when the crowds have gone.

SoHo Kitchen and Bar, 103 Greene St ☎925-1866. Smart burger-pizza-pasta place frequented by local gallery-goers. Average food, moderately priced, and supplemented, if you so wish, by a fine list of wines and beers – though experimenting with this inevitably makes it less of a reasonable option.

El Teddy's, 219 W Broadway ☎941-7070. Eccentrically decorated restaurant that serves good Mexican food and superb margaritas. Try fried tortillas wrapped around spicy chicken for starters. Entrees run $10–15.

Tennessee Mountain, 143 Spring St ☎431-3993. Though situated in the heart of SoHo, this is a very un-SoHo-like restaurant, serving huge portions of barbecued meat and fish for $10–15. Good value if you're hungry.

Time Café, 380 Lafayette St ☎533-7000. Happening restaurant with an eclectic

Americanish menu. A place just to drink too, with regular live jazz, usually on Wednesdays.

Tortilla Flats, 767 Washington St ☎ 243-1053. Cheap Tex-Mex Village dive with great margaritas and a loud jukebox.

TriBeCa Grill, 375 Greenwich St ☎ 941-3900. Part-owned by Robert de Niro, so people come here for a glimpse of the actor when they should really be concentrating on the food – fine, French-American cooking at around $30 a main course. The setting is nice too, a large airy eating area around a central Tiffany bar (rescued from the legendary Upper East Side singles' hang-out, *Maxwell's Plum*). Well worth the money.

Two Boots, 37 Avenue A ☎ 505-5450. East Village restaurant serving pizzas with a Cajun flavour – crawfish and jalapeño peppers are common toppings. Main dishes, too, follow the same bias, spicy pasta and seafood options mainly. Not at all expensive.

Zoe, 90 Prince St ☎ 966-6722. Currently one of SoHo's trendier places to eat, with a California-style setting and menu packed full of the intriguing and often delicious combinations for which the state's cuisine is famous. Not cheap, but highly popular.

Midtown Manhattan

America, 9 E 18th St ☎ 505-2110. Enormous restaurant with menu to match. Very yuppie, very New York; have a drink at the bar and watch the scene.

American Festival Café, Rockefeller Plaza, Fifth Ave at 50th St ☎ 246-6699. For the views, at least, there's no better place to sample regional American cooking – everything from Louisiana catfish to Mississippi mud pie. A nice place to warm up after a spin on the Rockefeller rink, immediately outside – though it doesn't come at all cheap.

Arriba Arriba, 762 Ninth Ave at 51st St ☎ 489-0810. Boozy Tex-Mex place, popular with the after-work crowd for the margaritas as much as the meals.

Banana Café, 111 E 22nd St ☎ 995-8500. Excellent Brazilian food served up in great surroundings. Expensive, but worth shelling out a few more bucks for.

Blue Moon Café, 150 Eighth Ave ☎ 463-0560. Standard Mexican food at moderate prices. Hockey fans may be interested to know the restaurant is owned by the NY Rangers.

Brazilian Pavillion, 316 E 53rd St ☎ 758-8129. Decent, simple Brazilian fare in lurid green-tiled surroundings.

Drinking and Eating

Restaurants with views

This is a brief checklist of – mainly Manhattan – restaurants that draw many people just for their views or location. Some of the restaurants are covered in more detail in other sections (primarily "Expense account"); where they're not, it's worth bearing in mind that the quality of the views will almost invariably be reflected in the size of your bill.

Hudson River Club, 250 Vesey St ☎ 786-1500.

Marriot Marquis, 1535 Broadway ☎ 398-1900.

Nirvana, 30 Central Park South, 15th floor ☎ 486-5700.

The Rainbow Room, RCA Building, 65th floor ☎ 632-5100.

River Café, 1 Water St, Brooklyn ☎ 718/522-5200.

Tavern on the Green, Central Park West and 67th St ☎ 873-3200.

Top of the Sixes, 666 Fifth Ave, 39th floor ☎ 757-6662.

The Water Club, 500 E 30th St ☎ 683-3333.

Windows on the World (and City Lights Bar), 1 World Trade Center, 107th floor ☎ 938-1111. *Closed until 1994.*

World Yacht Cruises, Pier 62, W 23rd St ☎ 929-7090.

Drinking and Eating

Cabana Carioca, 123 W 45th St ☎581-8088. Fun, colourfully decorated Brazilian restaurant that's a great place to try out Brazilian specialities, like *fejioda* (black bean and meat stew), washed down with fiery *caipirinhas*. And portions large enough for two make it reasonably inexpensive too.

Chefs' and Cuisiniers Club', 36 E 22nd St ☎228-4399. An eclectic American menu has won this place rave reviews from the critics. If you have the cash, it's certainly an excellent place to explore regional American cooking.

Joe Allen's, 326 W 46th St ☎581-6464. Tried and tested formula of chequered tablecloths, cosy bar-room feel and reliable American food.

Mike's American Bar & Grill, 650 10th Ave ☎246-4155. Funky "downtown" bar in midtown west (aka "Hell's Kitchen"). The decor changes each season, but the menu stays basic: burgers, nachos and the like for under $25.

El Rio Grande, 160 E 38th St ☎867-0922. Long-established Murray Hill Tex-Mex place with a gimmick: you can eat Mexican, or if you prefer, Texan, by simply crossing the "border" and walking through the kitchen. Personable and fun – and the margaritas are earth (and brain) shattering.

Symphony Café, 950 Eighth Ave ☎397-9595. Situated between Carnegie Hall and Lincoln Center, it's not surprising to find a restaurant with a "symphony" theme. The food is nouvelle American, the surroundings pleasant, and in summer you can sit outside; moderately priced too.

Union Square Café, 21 E 16th St ☎243-4020. A relatively new addition to the Manhattan quality dining scene, but a successful one, notching one of the city's best reputations for modern American food in no time. Not at all cheap – prices average $100 for two – but the Californian menu, not to mention the stylish, bustling environment, is a treat.

Via Brasil, 34 W 46th St ☎997-1158. Excellent, though pricey, Brazilian food. Not much for under $10.

Zarela, 953 Second Ave ☎644-6740. A reaction against the "nachos with everything, washed down with tequila" philosophy of most Tex-Mex restaurants, the food here is fresh and endeavours to be authentic: if you've ever wondered what Mexican food really tastes like, this is the place to go. It's noticeably more expensive than most regular places.

Upper Manhattan

All State Café, 250 W 72nd St ☎874-7883. An interesting mixture of American and French food from $7 to $15 makes this a popular Upper West Side hang-out. Seating is limited, and it closes at 11.30pm; get here early to be sure of a place.

Arizona 206, 206 E 60th St ☎838-0440. Intriguing southwestern decor and food, though it doesn't come cheap, and the service is variable. The next-door café section is cheaper, serving essentially the same food in smaller portions.

Bahama Mama, 2628 Broadway ☎866-7760. Caribbean food in a soulful atmosphere. Fish and beef predominate and there's a wide array of cocktails. Meals run $13–16.

Bertha's, 2160 Broadway at 76th St ☎362-2500. Sister to the *Benny's Burritos* chain (p.269): hearty, low-priced Cal-Mex food.

Brother Jimmy's BBQ, 1461 First Ave ☎545-RIBS. Casual, fun barbecue restaurant whose motto is "Pig Out!". Quite a happening bar scene too.

Canyon Road, 1470 First Ave ☎734-1600. Upper East Side place affecting a Santa Fe atmosphere. Inexpensive.

La Caridad, 2199 Broadway ☎874-2780. Something of an Upper West Side institution, a tacky little hole-in-the-wall doling out plentiful and cheap Cuban-Chinese food to hungry and (usually) queuing punters. Bring your own beer, and don't expect polite service.

Caridad Restaurant, 4311 Broadway ☎928-4645. Not to be confused with the Upper West Side restaurant of (almost) the same name, this places serves mountains of Dominican food at cheap prices. Try the *mariscos* or seafood, speciality of the house and eaten with lots of *pan y ajo*, thick slices of French bread, grilled with olive oil and plenty of garlic. Be sure to go feeling hungry.

City Café, 1481 York Ave ☎570-9810. Attractive American-style café, included here because of its great and not too expensive food.

Flor de Mayo, 2651 Broadway ☎630-5520 and 171 Third Ave ☎472-0600. Very cheap, very popular Cuban-Chinese restaurant with coffee shop decor and lots of food, though not much for vegetarians – spicy chicken, Cuban-style steaks, etc. You can eat well for around $12.

Josephina, 1900 Broadway (across from Lincoln Center) ☎799 1000. Large airy restaurant painted with colonial murals serving American-Italian food – good salads, soups and suchlike – for moderate prices.

Los Panchos, 71 W 71st St ☎874-7336. Moderate Tex-Mex restaurant serving a good-value weekend brunch. Tables outdoors in summer.

Main Street, 446 Columbus Ave ☎873-5025. Homestyle American restaurant lauded for its meatloaf and sweet potato fries in particular. In a city where even the most average portions tend to the large, *Main Street* has a reputation for serving vast plates – usually enough to feed two at least.

El Pollo, 1746 First Ave ☎996-7810. Fast-food Peruvian-style chicken restaurant, serving rotisserie chicken flavoured with a variety of spices to eat in or take out. Delicious – and very cheap.

Popovers, 551 Amsterdam Ave ☎595-8555. Excellent uptown eatery whose dishes (American/wholefood) come served with a popover – a sort of dyspeptic brioche from the Midwest.

Positively 104th St, 2725 Broadway ☎316-0372. Basic but good American food, with excellent steaks, and a friendly atmosphere make this a good choice for this part of town. Reasonably priced too.

Sylvia's Restaurant, 328 Lenox Ave at 125th St ☎996-0660. Legendary southern soul-food restaurant in Harlem. Go early on a Wednesday night and get free tickets for amateur night at the *Apollo*.

Teacher's, 2271 Broadway ☎362-4900. Pasta and fish from $6. Nice atmosphere and a useful noticeboard. Good brunch.

Third World Café, 700 W 125th St ☎749-8199. If Paul Simon's *Rhythm of the Saints* were a restaurant, it would be this one – a fantasy jumble of Cajun, Indian and Caribbean spices. It serves sweet potato fries and black-eyed peas, Brazilian *picadillo* and southern barbecue, in main dishes running about $8 each, to a background plump with the music of Bob Marley and Hugh Masekela. Not the best neighbourhood late at night, especially if you're alone, but worth it for the fun atmosphere and fantastic food.

USA Border Café, 2637 Broadway ☎749-8888. A good Tex-Mex menu with meals for $9–13 and regular live music. Can be good later on when the going gets lively.

Victor's Café, 240 Columbus Ave ☎595-8599. Cuban food at moderate prices on Columbus's central restaurant strip.

Vince & Eddie's, 70 W 68th St ☎721-0068. Slightly pseudo country-style American restaurant serving grub like American grannies supposedly used to make – hearty, wholesome, and delicious. Moderately priced.

West Side Storey, 700 Columbus Ave ☎749-1900. A wide range of American-style food, and ultra-friendly management, although the white tiled booths take some getting used to. But at $8–12 for a main course, there's little to complain about.

Yellow Rose Café, 450 Amsterdam Ave ☎595-8760. As the name suggests, meaty Texan food. Burgers, ribs and steaks from $5–15.

Chinese, Thai and Vietnamese

Chinese cuisine provides one of the city's best bargains, particularly if you pick up *dim sum* and other lunchtime specials. As far as areas go, Chinatown not surprisingly has the highest restaurant concen-

Drinking and Eating

Drinking and Eating

tration, but there's another good contingent in the Upper West Side 90s. More expensively, **Thai** food has become more prevalent of late, and you'll find Thai restaurants springing up all over Manhattan, not to mention an increasing number of **Vietnamese** restaurants.

Lower Manhattan

Bo Ky, 80 Bayard St ☎ 406-2292. Cramped Chinese-Vietnamese serving very inexpensive noodle and seafood dishes.

Canton, 45 Division St ☎ 226-4441. Fairly upmarket compared to other Chinatown restaurants in terms of style and service, and only marginally more expensive. Seafood is the speciality here; bring your own booze

Indochine, 430 Lafayette St ☎ 505-5111. Not the kind of place you go to save money, more to lap up the elegant surroundings and authentic Vietnamese food . . . and maybe spot a minor celebrity or two.

Mon Bo, 65 Mott St ☎ 964-6480. Bright, cheery Cantonese serving incapacitating rice and noodle dishes for around $5, more exotic fare for just a little more.

Oriental Pearl, 103 Mott St ☎ 219-8388. Great *dim sum* served in a vast Chinatown warehouse of a restaurant.

New Lin Heong, 69 Bayard St ☎ 233-0485. *Mon Bo*'s sister restaurant – and similarly substantial.

Nice Restaurant, 35 E Broadway ☎ 406-9776. Vast restaurant especially good for *dim sum*. Usually crowded, particularly on Sundays.

Nom-Wah, 13 Doyers St ☎ 962-6047. Reliable Cantonese restaurant, good for *dim sum*.

Phoenix Garden, 46 Bowery Arcade ☎ 233-6017. Tucked away from the tourists but well known to New Yorkers for the quality and authenticity of its (Cantonese) food. Great value.

Pongsri, 106 Bayard St ☎ 349-3132. Thai restaurant popular at lunchtime with local businesspeople for its extensive and good-value lunch menu – rice and noodle combos a speciality. A massive menu in

the evenings, and Thai beer. A second branch at 244 W 48th St ☎ 582-3392.

Say Eng Look, 5 E Broadway ☎ 732-0796. Good-value Shanghai restaurant that'll tailor your meal to fit your budget. Just tell them how much you can afford and they'll do the rest. They rarely miss.

Siam Square, 92 Second Ave ☎ 505-1240. Small restaurant serving excellent Thai food for very reasonable prices. Fine service, tacky decor.

Silver Palace, 50 Bowery ☎ 964-1204. Predominantly *dim sum* restaurant.

Sun Say Gay, 220 Canal St ☎ 964-7256. An obvious Chinatown lunchtime choice, serving up huge plates of meat and rice for around $3.

Thai House Café, 151 Hudson St ☎ 334-1085. Small, friendly TriBeCa Thai restaurant, popular for its well-priced and authentic food. Beer and wine only.

Toons, 417 Bleecker St ☎ 924-6420. Higher prices than the *Thai House Café*, but with a lower-lit, more intimate atmosphere. A Thai community favourite.

Vegetarian Paradise, 48 Bowery ☎ 571-1535. Delicious vegetarian Chinese food at low prices. $5 buys enough for two.

Wo Hop, 17 Mott St ☎ 962-8617. Noodle shop used by local Chinese. Inexpensive.

Wong Kee, 113 & 117 Mott St ☎ 226-9018/966-1160. Good cheap, reliable Cantonese.

Wonton Garden, 52 Mott St ☎ 966-4886. Chinatown's cheapest noodles. Good for a quick lunch stopover.

Midtown Manhattan

Chop Suey Looey's Litchi Lounge, 1345 6th Ave ☎ 262-2020. Original dishes (and drinks) in a wild setting. Good fun.

Fortune Garden, 209 E 49th St ☎ 753-0101. Unusual combination of Chinese food and live jazz, though you come more for the music and ambience than the food, which isn't cheap.

Siam Inn, 916 Eighth Ave ☎ 489-5237; 854 Eighth Ave ☎ 757-4006. Unpretentious restaurant serving averagely priced spicy Thai fare. Try the masaman curry or the chilli and garlic fried sea bass.

Tina, 249 Park Ave South ☎477-1761; also uptown at 117 W 70th ☎724-2031. Good Chinese in an area not known for its Chinese restaurants.

Upper Manhattan

Bangkok House, 1485 First Ave ☎249-5700. Terrific Thai food, fairly priced.

BTI, 1712 Second Ave ☎427-1488; also 250 W 86th St ☎875-0460. Burmese, Thai and Indian make up the initials of the name, and you can combine the different cuisines here at reasonable cost. Ideal if you can't make up your mind between the three styles.

Empire Szechuan, 2581 Broadway ☎666-0555; 193 Columbus Ave ☎496-8778. Szechuan food from $6.

Hunan Balcony, 2596 Broadway ☎865-0400. Hunan-style food from $6.

Ollie's, 2315 Broadway ☎362-3712; 2957 Broadway ☎932-3300; and 200 W 44th St ☎921-5988. Downscale Chinese fast-food noodle shop that serves marvellous noodles. Not, however, a place to hang about.

Pig Heaven, 1540 Second Ave ☎744-4333. Good-value Chinese restaurant decorated with images of pigs. Not surprisingly, the accent is on pork.

Sala Thai, 1718 Second Ave ☎410-5557. Restaurant serving lots of hot and spicy Thai food for under $15 a head.

French

French restaurants tend to trade on their names in New York: those that are good know it and make you pay accordingly, although a handful have slipped through with value-for-money intact. Since *nouvelle cuisine* reached its peak popularity in the late 1980s there's been something of a return both to more complex *haute cuisine* and to rural cooking. Simple creperies are also popular, and almost all restaurants and bistros go out of their way to frenchify the surroundings in a mock-Parisienne style. Beware the wine list: prices for French vintages can be considerably more than Californian wines of comparable quality.

Lower Manhattan

La Boheme, 24 Minetta Lane ☎473-6447. Bright and amiable, if cramped, restaurant in the heart of the Village with pasta, pizza and meat and fish dishes for $12–15. Good food, and nice in the summer when they open the big French doors to the street.

Café de Bruxelles, 118 Greenwich Ave ☎206-1830. *Not* French, but a very authentic – and popular – Belgian restaurant in Greenwich Village. Moderately priced, interesting food – try the *Waterzooi*, a rich and creamy chicken stew.

Capsuto Frères, 451 Washington St ☎966-4900. A wonderful French Bistro with a TriBeCa lofty feel.

Chez Brigitte, 77 Greenwich Ave ☎929-6736. Tiny restaurant that fits only eleven, but with an all-day roast meat dinner for under $10 as well as other bargains from a simple menu.

Chez Ma Tante, 189 W 120th St ☎620-0223. A tiny French bistro that's most fun in summer, when the doors open out onto the street. NYC rustic, but charming nevertheless.

Chez Michallet, 90 Bedford St ☎242-8309. A Village version of a French country inn. Moderate to expensive.

Florent, 69 Gansevoort St ☎989-5779. Ultra-fashionable bistro on the edge of the meat-packing district that serves good French food, either à la carte or from a *prix fixe* menu ($16.95, $14.95 before 7.30pm). Coffee shop decor; excellent food and decent service; always busy. They also serve weekend brunch.

French Coast, 458 Sixth Ave ☎533-2233. A smart café where you can while away hours reading the newspapers and magazines while drinking café au lait. Decent food and snacks; open 24 hours.

La Luncheonette, 130 Tenth Ave ☎675-0342. Parisian-style bistro serving good quality French food, though in an unfortunately downbeat and out-of-the-way location. Don't go too late at night.

Drinking and Eating

Drinking and Eating

La Metairie, 189 W 10th St ☎989-0343. Charming West Village bistro serving excellent French country fare.

Montrachet, 239 W Broadway ☎219-2777. *Nouvelle cuisine* food in a relaxed unpretentious setting.

Odeon, 145 W Broadway ☎233-0507. Very long-established restaurant serving Mediterranean-style food to a still largely chic clientele. Entrees go for around $20, and on the whole are well worth it.

Paris Commune, 411 Bleeker St ☎929-0509. Cosily intimate West Village bistro with reliable French home cooking. Moderate prices.

Provence, 38 Macdougal St ☎475-7500. Very popular SoHo bistro that serves excellent food but – at around $16 up for a main course – ain't that cheap. A nice place for a special occasion, though, with a lovely airy eating area and a garden for the summer.

Raoul's, 180 Prince St ☎966-3518. French bistro seemingly lifted from Paris. The food and service are wonderful – as you'd expect at these prices. Expensive ($36–60).

Steak Frites, 9 E 16th St ☎463-7101. As the name suggests, great steak and chips, at fair prices.

Au Troquet, 328 W 12th St ☎924-3413. Romantic Village haunt that has an authentic Parisian feel. Good food, moderately priced.

Midtown Manhattan

Bellevue, 496 Ninth Ave ☎967-7850. French bistro with upscale coffee shop decor and good food. The neighbourhood, however, isn't great – don't go too late.

Brasserie, 100 E 53rd St ☎751-4840. Always more highly regarded for its 24-hour opening policy than its food, and perhaps rightly so, although its hearty French staples have improved of late, if the atmosphere hasn't.

Café Un, Deux, Trois, 123 W 44th St ☎354-4148. French brasserie-style restaurant close to Times Square serving fair-to-middling food. Crayons for table-top doodling while you wait for your order. $10–20.

Chantal Café, 257 W 55th St ☎246-7076. Homely little bistro.

La Cité, 120 W 51st St ☎956-7100. A handsome midtown French steakhouse.

Hourglass Tavern, 373 W 46th St ☎265-2060. Tiny midtown French restaurant – around eight tables in all – which serves an excellent-value two-course *prix fixe* menu for just $11.50. Choose between two starters and half a dozen or so main courses – a small range that guarantees good cooking. The gimmick is the hourglass above each table, the emptying of which means you're supposed to leave and make way for someone else; in reality they seem to last more than an hour, and they only enforce it if there's a queue.

La Bonne Soupe, 48 W 55th St ☎586-7650. Traditional French food at reasonable prices. Steaks, omelettes, snails and fondues from $6.

La Fondue, 43 W 55th St ☎581-0820. Fondues for under $10.

Les Halles, 411 Park Ave South ☎679-4111. Noisy, bustling bistro with the carcasses dangling in a butcher's shop in the front. Very pseudo rive gauche, very expensive. Not recommended for veggies.

Le Madeleine, 403 W 43rd St ☎246-2993. Pretty midtown French bistro with modest prices. Try and get a seat in the outdoor garden.

Man Ray, 169 Eighth Ave ☎627-4220. Affordably priced French food in a sleek setting.

Park Bistro, 414 Park Ave South ☎689-1360. Sister to *Les Halles* (see above) and similar in prices and style, though a little less hectic.

Prix-Fixe, 18 W 18th St ☎675-6777. A relative newcomer to the New York restaurant scene, but another that has fast established a reputation for good food. Its *prix fixe* menu for just over $20 a head is excellent value.

Les Sans-Culottes, 1085 Second Ave ☎838-6660. Wonderful food served in massive portions. One of the best deals in town.

West Bank Café, 407 W 42nd, Manhattan Plaza ☎695-6909. Some French, some American, all delicious and not as expensive as you'd think – upwards of $7.

Upper Manhattan

Bistro du Nord, 1312 Madison Ave ☎289-0997. A cosy bistro with excellent Parisian fare. Very stylish atmosphere; moderate to expensive.

La Boite en Bois, 75 W 68th St ☎874-2705. Rustic, moderately priced Lincoln Center bistro that has good country French food.

Café Luxembourg, 200 W 70th St ☎873-7411. Trendy Lincoln Center area bistro that packs in (literally, some say) a self-consciously hip crowd to enjoy its first-rate

contemporary French food. Not too pricey – two people can eat for $50 or so.

Mme Romaine de Lyon, 29 E 61st St ☎758-2422. The best place for omelettes: they've got 550 on the lunch menu and dinner features an expanded non-omelette menu.

Poiret, 474 Columbus Ave ☎724-6880. A trendy and fun – and reasonably inexpensive – French bistro with excellent food and outside seating in summer. A nice place for brunch too.

Le Refuge, 166 E 82nd St ☎661-4505. Intimate and deliberately romantic old-style French restaurant situated in an old city brownstone. Expensive; save for special occasions.

Le Steak, 1069 Second Ave ☎421-9072. Choose between steak-frites or swordfish-frites at this Upper East Side bistro – beautifully cooked and moderately priced. Dinner only.

Voulez Vous, 1462 First Ave ☎249-1776. Decently priced Upper East Side French bistro.

Greek, Middle Eastern and Turkish

While **Greek** restaurants are plentiful, few make it onto anyone's list of top ten places to eat: vegetarians in particular may be faced with few options, and for the best Greek cooking you should head for Astoria in Queens, home turf of most of the city's Greek population. Greek tends to be pricey for what you get, as do the city's **Turkish** restaurants. Other than a handful of places serving pitta-related snacks, **Middle Eastern** food is rather thin on the ground in Manhattan.

Lower Manhattan

Ariana, 787 Ninth Avenue ☎262-2323. Fine and inexpensive kebab and vegetarian Afghan restaurant, albeit in a rather dour neighbourhood.

Delphi, 109 West Broadway ☎227-6322. Accommodating Greek restaurant with good menu, great portions and unbeatable prices. The antipasti and fish are excellent value at $5–10 or there's kebabs and the like from $2.50. Best Manhattan choice for bargain Greek eating.

Drinking and Eating

Drinking and Eating

Khyber Pass, 34 St Mark's Place ☎473-0989. Afghan food, which if you're unfamiliar is filling and has plenty to offer vegetarians (pulses, rice, aubergines are frequent ingredients). Excellent value for around $7. No liquor licence.

Mamun's, 119 Macdougal St ☎674-9246. Inexpensive snack bar and takeaway serving felafel, kebabs and suchlike.

Midtown Manhattan

Afghan Kebab, 764 Ninth Ave ☎307-1612. A casual neighbourhood restaurant with little decor and few tables, but excellent and inexpensive chicken, lamb and beef kebabs. Bring your own beer or wine. Another branch across the street on the corner of Ninth Avenue and 50th St; also at 1345 Second Ave ☎517-2776 and 155 W 46th St ☎768-3875.

Lofti's Couscous, 145 W 45th St, between Broadway & Sixth Ave ☎768-8738. Moderately priced Moroccan hidden away on the second floor. Lots of spicy dishes, vegetarian options, and inexpensive salads.

Upper Manhattan

At Our Place, 2485 Broadway ☎864-1410. Middle Eastern cuisine at its best and least expensive, and including an extensive vegetarian menu. Most dishes around the $6 mark.

Istanbul Cuisine, 303 E 80th St ☎744-6903. Canteen-style restaurant where you can eat home-style Turkish food at what must be close to Turkish prices. Crowded, but great value.

Periyali, 35 W 20th St ☎463-7890. Greek food that's a cut above the average in a cheerful Mediterranean setting.

Symposium, 544 W 113rd St ☎865-1011. Neighbourhood restaurant near Columbia University serving favourite Greek dishes in a relaxed, studenty atmosphere.

Uskudar, 1405 Second Ave ☎988-2641. Authentic Turkish cuisine at a rather spartan Upper East Side venue. Great prices – reckon on $25 or so for two.

Indian, Pakistani, African

Two good places to look for **Indian** food in New York are in midtown Manhattan, along Lexington Avenue between 28th and 30th streets, and (much cheaper) in the East Village, on the block-long stretch of 6th Street between First and Second avenues – the latter one of the city's best budget eating options. Budget **African** restaurants are becoming increasingly common, their pulse-based meals almost always including vegetarian options.

Lower Manhattan

Abyssinia, 35 Grand St ☎226-5959. Ethiopian restaurant, ethnically furnished and popular with a youthful crowd. A good array of vegetarian dishes.

Ghandhi, 345 E 6th St ☎614-9718. One of the best and least expensive of the E 6th Street Indian restaurants.

Mingala Burmese, 21 E 7th and uptown at 325 Amsterdam ☎873-0787. Indian and Chinese cuisines combine in these bargain Burmese kitchens. Try the Tousand Layer Pancakes.

Mitali, 334 E 6th St ☎533-2508. Though more expensive than the other 6th Street Indians, this one is well worth it, and still at half the price of spots further uptown. Another branch across town, **Mitali West**, at 296 Bleecker St ☎989-1367.

Passage to India, 308 E 6th St ☎529-5770. Tasty Tandoori dishes and breads, very cheap prices.

Sonali, 324 E 6th St ☎505-7517. Good cheap, substantial Indian food.

Midtown Manhattan

Annapurna, 108 Lexington Ave ☎679-1284. Good-value northern Indian restaurant.

Curry in a Hurry, 130 E 29th St ☎889-1159. Fast and inexpensive Indian café – eat for around $5.

Darbar, 432 W 56th St ☎432-7227. One of the best and most reasonable Indian restaurants in town.

Madras Palace, 104 Lexington Ave ☎532-3314. One of few places serving South Indian cuisine. Around $10.

Shaheen, 99 Lexington Ave ☎683-2139. Good, cafeteria-style Pakistani meals for around $5.

Upper Manhattan

Asmara, 951 Amsterdam Ave ☎749-9614. African restaurant serving a variety of curried meat dishes, along with a few vegetarian alternatives, eaten with chapati-like *injera* bread. Very cheap, and, although rather gloomy, the neighbourhood is quite safe.

Blue Nile, 103 W 77th St ☎580-3232. Ethiopian restaurant, where the food is served on a communal tray at low tables. Eat with your fingers using soft, flat *injera* bread. The food consists of rich meat stews and lentil and vegetable concoctions washed down with sharp African beer. Main dishes priced around $10.

Mughlai, 320 Columbus Ave ☎724-6363. Uptown, upmarket Indian with prices about the going rate for this strip: $10–15.

Zula, 1260 Amsterdam Ave ☎663-1670. High quality and inexpensive ($7 up) Ethiopian food that's popular with the folk from Columbia. Spicy chicken, beef and lamb dishes mainly, though a few veggie plates too.

Italian . . . and pizzas

Little Italy is the most obvious location for **Italian** food, though much of the area is geared towards tourists these days and consequently can be pricey: pick with care. For the real thing it's again best to head out to the Outer Boroughs – Belmont in the Bronx or Carroll Gardens in Brooklyn – or content yourself with pizza, either from *Ray's* (or a similar snack joint), or a regular sit-down restaurant.

Everywhere

Ray's Pizza. The city's most ubiquitous pizza chain, with branches all over midtown (and other districts) of Manhattan. Reckon on $1.50 or so for a slice, $10–12 upwards for the whole thing.

Lower Manhattan

Arturo's Pizza, 106 W Houston St ☎475-9828. Excellent entrées around $10, coal-oven pizzas big enough to share for a little less. While-you-eat entertainment includes live music. Convivial, if not the cheapest feed in town.

Benito I, 174 Mulberry St ☎226-9171; **Beniti II**, 163 Mulberry St ☎226-9012. The smell of garlic lures you in to these two homey little Italian spots that serve simple Sicilian fare.

Cent' Anni, 50 Carmine St ☎989-9494. Small Village restaurant serving delicious, and not overpriced, Florentine food.

Cucina della Fontana, 368 Bleecker St ☎242-0636. From the outside this place looks like a normal bar, but out the back there's a plant-filled atrium where you can eat fine Italian food. Mussels, fish, pasta all excellent.

Cucina di Pesce, 87 E 4th St ☎260-6800. Excellent East Village Italian seafood restaurant.

Cucina Stagionale, 275 Bleecker St ☎924-2707. Enormously popular restaurant, sister to *Cucina di Pesce*, with most dishes at around $6. Expect to queue, and bring your own wine – there's no licence.

Ennio and Michael, 539 La Guardia Place ☎677-8577. Old-fashioned Italian bistro, intimate and homey.

Il Fornaio, 132a Mulberry St ☎226-8306. Smart, bright tiled Italian restaurant with good lunch deals – fine calzone and pizza for $4. Affordable and decent southern Italian cooking, too – Italian stews and the like. Recommended.

Grotta Azzurra, 387 Broome St ☎925-8784. Bustling Little Italy institution that serves hearty homecooked southern Italian food.

John's of 12th Street, 302 E 12th St ☎475-9531. Heaped portions of southern Italian food – including good brick oven pizza – in a dark, candle-lit room. Great value.

John's Pizzeria, 278 Bleecker St ☎243-1680. No slices, no takeaways, but one of the city's best (thin crust) pizzas. Be prepared to queue. Uptown branches at 408 E 64th St ☎935-2895 and 48 W 65th St ☎721-7001.

Drinking and Eating

Drinking and Eating

La Luna, 112 Mulberry St ☎226-8657. Surrounded by the valet-parked limos and eating palaces of Little Italy, this must be one of the city's cheapest Italian restaurants: honest and unassuming in every way, from the vast peasant portions of pasta they serve to the gruff Brooklyn manner of the waiters and the fact that you have to walk through the kitchen to sit down.

Le Madri, 168 W 18th St ☎727-8022. Elegant eatery whose marvellous food and wine is only slightly marred by the snooty service.

La Mela, 167 Mulberry St ☎431-9433. Old-established Little Italy restaurant serving food in huge portions.

Mezzogiorno, 195 Spring St ☎334-2112. Bright, trendy SoHo Italian restaurant that's as much a place to people-watch as eat. A little overpriced, but a good and inventive menu, including excellent pizzas for around $12 (in the evening only available after 9pm), great salads and carpaccio – thinly sliced raw beef served in various ways. Sister restaurant is *Mezzaluna* – see p.281.

Minetta Tavern, 113 Macdougal St ☎475-3850. One of the oldest bars in New York, decorated with murals showing Greenwich Village as it was in the 1930s, and with a restaurant out back turning out Italian food that's worth the splurge.

Pellegrino, 138 Mulberry St ☎226-3177. Pleasant and pretty Italian food in the heart of Little Italy.

Puglia, 189 Hester St ☎226-8912. One of Little Italy's more affordable restaurants, where they cut costs and sharpen the atmosphere by sitting everyone at the same long trestle tables. Consistently good food, consumed loudly and raucously.

Pizza Piazza, Broadway at W 10th St ☎505-0977. Generously filled deep pan pizzas in various sizes on wholewheat crusts. Good desserts too.

Pizzeria Uno, 391 Sixth Ave ☎242-5230. Solid value pizzas but again frequent queues. It's a good idea to book. Also at 432 Columbus Ave ☎595-4700.

Ray's Pizza, 465 Sixth Ave ☎243-2253. Long-time rival to *John's*, and not to be confused with the chain you see all over the city. Thick crusts.

Midtown Manhattan

Becco, 355 W 46th St ☎397-7597. A fairly recent addition to "Restaurant Row", where you get huge amounts of antipasto and pasta for $19.

Chelsea Trattoria, 108 Eighth Ave ☎924-7786. A brick-lined northern Italian restaurant that's cosy and enjoyable for the ambience as much as the moderately priced food.

Frank's, 431 W 14th St ☎243-1349. Long-established Italian-American restaurant with pasta dishes from $5 up.

Lamarca, 161 E 22nd St ☎674-6363. Fresh pasta in a cafeteria-style setting. Bring your own booze. Cheap.

Le Madri, 168 W 18th St ☎727-8022. Named after the Italian "mothers" who work in the kitchen, this Tuscan restaurant has taken its place among the city's very best Italians since its opening in 1989. On the pricey side, but worth it. Try and get a table in the patio out back – if you can get one at all.

Pasta Presto, 613 Second Ave ☎889-4131. Fast-paced inexpensive pasta joint. Other branches at 93 Macdougal St ☎260-5679; 37 Barrow St ☎691-0480; 959 Second Ave ☎754-4880.

Prego, 1365 Sixth Ave ☎307-5775. Pasta joint with a wide choice of generously spooned dishes for about $7 but an off-puttingly bathroom-like interior. Not for the hungover – and no liquor licence either. Fill up and move on.

Rocky Lee, 987 Second Ave ☎753-4858. Not the most ambient environment, but the thin crust pizzas here get rave reviews.

Supreme Macaroni Co., 511 Ninth Ave ☎502-4842. A macaroni shop with a small restaurant attached.

Trattoria, Met Life (formerly Pan Am) Building, 200 Park Ave ☎661-3090. Slightly characterless midtown Italian whose rather average food is best appre-

ciated at lunchtime or during its regular
evening happy hour.

Trattoria dell'Arte, 900 Seventh Ave
☎245-9800. Unusually nice restaurant for
this rather tame stretch of midtown, with
a lovely airy interior, excellent service and
good food. Great, wafer-thin crispy pizzas,
decent and imaginative pasta dishes for
around $15 and a mouth-watering anti-
pasto bar – all eagerly patronised by an
elegant out-to-be-seen crowd. Best book.

Upper Manhattan

Antico Café, 1477 Second Ave ☎879-
4824. Part of the East 77th Street corner
of restaurants, this has good Italian food
at reasonable prices, and hence is
extremely popular.

Bella Donna, 307 E 77th St ☎535-2866.
Quaint Italian storefront restaurant with
home-made pastas, low prices and long
waits for a table.

Caffé Buon Gusto, 243 E 77th St ☎535-
6884. This stretch of the Upper East Side
has plenty of cool, Italian joints: what
Buon Gusto lacks in style it makes up for
in taste and prices. A real find.

Carino, 1710 Second Ave ☎860-0566.
Family-run Upper East Side Italian, with
low prices, friendly service and good food.
Two can eat for under $25.

Carmine's, 2450 Broadway ☎362-2200;
also in midtown at 200 W 44th St ☎221-
3800. The original large Upper West Side
restaurant justifiably made a name for
itself for its combination of decent (and
decently priced) home-style Southern
Italian food, in mountainous portions (be
careful not to over-order), and the noisy,
convivial atmosphere in which it's served.
If you're in a group of six or more you can
book; otherwise be prepared to queue for
at least thirty minutes – it's very popular.

Contrapunto, 200 E 60th St ☎751-8616.
More than twenty fresh pastas daily at
this friendly, shopping neighbourhood
Italian restaurant. Reasonably priced as
well.

Corrado, 1373 Sixth Ave ☎333-3133.
Northern Italian eatery with a breezy
decor and great pasta. Moderately priced.

Ecco-la, 1660 Third Ave ☎860-5609.
Unique pasta combinations at very moderate prices make this place one of the
Upper East Side's most popular Italians. If
you don't mind waiting, though, a real
find.

Ernie's, 2150 Broadway ☎496-1588.
Casual, extra-large Upper West Side
Italian, serving staple, affordable Italian
food.

Genoa, 271 Amsterdam Ave ☎787-1094.
Very small, very authentic Italian restau-
rant. Cheap, dark and always crowded.
Expect to queue for a table.

Mezzaluna, 1295 Third Ave ☎535-9600.
Sister restaurant to the SoHo eatery,
Mezzogiorno, this claims to be the place
that introduced carpaccio to Manhattan.
Whatever the truth of that, the food here
is fine (great pizzas, inventive pastas),
though the environment doesn't really
justify the moderate-to-high prices.

Perretti, 270 Columbus Ave ☎362-3939.
Neighbourhood Italian with below-
average prices.

Presto, 2770 Broadway ☎222-1760. An
inexpensive Italian that's not bad for its
pasta dishes – huge platefuls for around
$9.

Sambuco, 20 W 72nd ☎787-5656. Best
described as *Carmine's* without the super-
ior attitude, noise and long queues, this
serves up great portions of good food at
excellent prices.

Café Trevi, 1570 First Ave ☎249-0040.
Casual Italian restaurant serving good
food that doesn't cost the earth.

V&T Pizzeria, 1024 Amsterdam Ave
☎663-1708. Chequered tableclothed
pizzeria near Columbia that draws a
predictably college-aged crowd. Good,
though, and very inexpensive.

Il Vagabondo, 351 E 62nd St ☎832-
9221. Southern Italian food in a casual
setting that includes the restaurant's own
bocci court.

Valones, 1234 Third Ave ☎288-0202. A
sort of second rate, East Side version of
Carmine's, but enjoyable nonetheless.

Drinking and
Eating

Drinking and Eating

Via Via, 1294 Third Ave ☎535-9600. Popular Upper East Side Italian, with a wide choice of brick-oven pizzas, decent stand-by pasta dishes and carpaccios. A downtown branch at 560 Third Ave ☎573-6093.

Vinnie's Pizza, 285 Amsterdam Ave ☎874-4332. Some say the best, cheesiest pizzas on the Upper West Side. Cheap too.

Japanese

When sushi arrived on the scene in the 1980s, **Japanese** food took off in a big way, and it's still one of the city's most popular cuisines. It tends to be expensive, however, with many of the restaurants in the pricier reaches of midtown Manhattan. But if you know where to go it is possible to experiment reasonably cheaply.

Everywhere

Dosanko. Chain of fast-food restaurants serving Japanese food at prices that most can afford. The food isn't the best in the city, and the surroundings are pure *McDonald's*, but there's no better way to try Japanese food if you're on a shoestring.

Lower Manhattan

Dojo, 24 St Mark's Place ☎674-9821. Popular East Village hang-out, with reasonably priced vegetarian and Japanese food in a brash, fun environment. One of the best value restaurants in the city, and certainly one of the cheapest Japanese menus you'll find.

Iso, 175 Second Ave ☎777-0361. Not your ordinary Japanese fare – this creative restaurant offers a funky downtown setting and intriguing variations on sushi at moderate prices. Especially good for sushi and seafood.

Japonica, 90 University Place ☎243-7752. Some of the freshest sushi in the city, at some of the most reasonable prices. Saturday and Sunday brunch deals are excellent – big plates of sushi or sahimi (teriaki too), with salad and beer or plum wine for around $12 a head. Be prepared to queue after 7pm.

Omen, 113 Thompson St ☎925-8923. Zen-inspired SoHo spot featuring authentic Kyoto flavours and flair.

Shabu Tatsu, 216 E 10th St ☎477-2972. Great Japanese barbecue and $3 soups – some of the best buys around.

Midtown Manhattan

Asia, 1155 Third Ave ☎879-5846. Pan-Asian cuisine in a handsome wood-panelled setting.

Choshi, 77 Irving Place ☎420-1419. Modestly priced Gramercy Japanese.

Genroku Sushi, 365 Fifth Ave ☎947-7940. Sushi and other Japanese-Chinese food. You pick what you fancy off a moving conveyor belt.

Hatsuhana, 17 E 48th St ☎355-3345; 237 Park Ave ☎661-3400. Every sushi lover's favourite sushi restaurant, now with two branches. Not at all cheap.

Meri Ken, 189 Seventh Ave ☎620-9684. Art Deco style sushi place.

Yoshi, 9 E 17th St ☎989-2938. Reasonably cheap Japanese restaurant. Good tempura and huge bottles of Sapporo.

Upper Manhattan

Fujiama Mama, 467 Columbus Ave ☎769-1144. The West Side's best – and most boisterous – sushi bar, with hi-tech decor and loud music.

Lenge, 200 Columbus Ave ☎799-9188. Decent Japanese restaurant, averagely priced.

Rikyu, 210 Columbus Ave ☎799-7847. A wide selection of Japanese food, including sushi made to order. Inexpensive lunches and early-bird specials make this place a bargain.

Sakura, 2298 Broadway ☎769-1003. Another highly elegant sushi bar.

Jewish, east European and German

The city's large **Jewish** community, most of whom originated in eastern Europe, means that kosher restaurants (serving dairy and non-dairy menus) are found all over town, with Manhattan's highest concentration on the Lower East Side.

They cover all price ranges, but usually represent good, and very filling, value – as do the various and consistently delicious **Polish**, **Hungarian**, and other **central European** restaurants.

Lower Manhattan

Bernstein-on-Essex, 135 Essex St ☎473-3900. Small Jewish restaurant serving orthodox menu and (believe it or not) kosher-Chinese food.

Christine's, 208 First Ave ☎505-0376. Long-standing Polish coffee shop, one of several such places in the area – great soups, blintzes and pirogi.

Grand Dairy Restaurant, 341 Grand St ☎673-1904. Unpretentious restaurant with well-priced kosher food.

Katz's Deli, 205 E Houston St ☎254-2246. Cafeteria-style or sit down and be served. The pastrami or corned beef sandwiches, doused with mustard and with a side pile of pickles, should keep you going for about a week. If you've seen the movie *When Harry Met Sally*, you may recognise this as the place of the famous "fake orgasm" scene.

Kiev, 117 Second Ave ☎674-4040. Eastern European dishes and burgers. Great and affordable food at any time of the day or night.

Odessa, 117 Ave A at Tompkins Square ☎473-8916. The scramble for a seat may put you off, but the food here – a filling array of dishes from the Caucasus – and prices (under $5 for a meal) are impressive. Coffee shop decor, loud, plastic and brightly lit – not the sort of place to chew the fat.

Ratner's, 138 Delancey St ☎677-5588. Massive dairy restaurant, crowded at all times of the day. High on atmosphere though on the pricey side. Recently re-opened after renovation.

Sammy's Roumanian Restaurant, 157 Chrystie St ☎673-0330. Surrounded by the boarded-up shopfronts of Chrystie Street, *Sammy's* is some indication of just how far the Upper East Side is swayed by a restaurant's reputation. The food, if you've $25 or so to burn for a full meal, is undeniably a treat, though most people come for the raucous live music.

Triplet's Roumanian, 11–17 Grand St ☎925-9303. Noisy neighbourhood restaurant that's like crashing a loud Jewish wedding. A guaranteed blast.

Ukrainian Restaurant, 140 Second Ave ☎529-5024. An East Village institution, still serving staggering portions of Slav fare for under $10. Very popular, though large enough to cope.

Veselka, 144 Second Ave ☎228-9682. Ukrainian-Polish eatery that offers fine homemade borscht for $3.

Yonah Schimmel's, 137 E Houston St ☎477-2858. Knishes, baked on the premises, and some wonderful bagels. Unpretentious and patronised by a mixture of wrinkled old men wisecracking in Yiddish and – on Sundays especially – young uptowners slumming it while they wade through the *New York Times*.

Midtown Manhattan

Lox Around the Clock, 676 Sixth Ave ☎691-3535. Blintzes, bagels and, of course, lox, in a trendy, noisy environment. Good for brunch. Open 24 hours.

Uncle Vanya, 315 W 54th St ☎262-0542. White Russian delicacies, including more than just the obligatory borscht and caviar. Moderately priced; closed Sunday.

Upper Manhattan

Barney Greengrass, 541 Amsterdam Ave ☎724-4707. A West Side deli that's been around since time began. The smoked salmon section is a particular treat.

Café Geiger, 208 E 86th St ☎734-4428. Famed German eatery in Yorkville. Around $7–14.

Fine & Schapiro, 138 W 72nd St ☎877-2721. Long-standing Jewish deli that's open for lunch and dinner and serves delicious old-fashioned kosher fare – an experience that's getting harder to find in New York. See *Shops and Markets*.

Ideal Restaurant, 238 E 86th St ☎535-0950. The genuine Germanic item: a small luncheonette serving wursts and sauerkraut in huge portions for paltry prices.

Drinking and Eating

Drinking and Eating

Kleine Konditorei, 234 E 86th St ☎737-7130. German patisserie and restaurant serving all manner of Teutonic stodge.

Mocca Hungarian, 1588 Second Ave ☎734-6470. Homely restaurant serving hearty portions of Hungarian comfort food – schnitzel, goulash and chicken paprikash, among others. Moderately priced, but be sure to come hungry.

Spanish

Downtown, in Greenwich Village especially, are a number of enjoyable **Spanish** restaurants, mostly not too pricey, and certainly nowhere near as expensive as their French counterparts. Paellas, often intended to be eaten by two, will cut costs, and house wines are affordable.

Lower Manhattan

Café Español, 172 Bleecker St ☎353-2317. Hole-in-the-wall restaurant serving sumptuous Spanish fare for $10–15 a plate. Try the *Mariscada* – a filling seafood dish that can easily feed two.

El Faro, 823 Greenwich St ☎929-8210. A dark, lively restaurant, where garlic smells from the kitchen and the look of the food at the next table (it's that cramped!) are guaranteed to stir any appetite. You can't go wrong with the paella or the seafood in green sauce. Moderate prices too, and you can share most main dishes.

Rio Mar, 7 Ninth Ave ☎243-9015. A welcoming Spanish restaurant that serves low-priced and authentic food, albeit in a fairly downbeat setting. Recommended.

Spain, 113 W 13th St ☎929-9580. Budget prices and large portions are the prime attractions of this cosy Spanish restaurant. Order the paella and split it with a friend.

Midtown Manhattan

The Ballroom, 253 W 28th St ☎244-3005. Long-established Chelsea tapas bar that's good both for snacks and for a full feed. Also one of the city's classiest cabaret and comedy spots; see Chapter 10, *The Performing Arts and Film*.

Solera, 216 E 53rd St ☎644-1166. Spanish food in a stylish townhouse

setting. As you'd expect from the surroundings and the ambience, it can be expensive.

Upper Manhattan

Alcala, 349 Amsterdam Ave ☎769-9600. Upper West Side Spanish bar-restaurant where you can either enjoy the terrific tapas and wine at the bar or splurge on the more pricey restaurant.

Café San Martin, 1458 First Ave ☎288-0470. One of the city's best Spanish restaurants at very affordable prices.

Malaga, 406 E 73rd St ☎737-7659. Intimate Spanish restaurant frequented by locals. Good, wholesome food at decent prices.

Fish and seafood

Budget **fish restaurants** are a rarity in the city, especially since the area around the downtown fish market was dolled up into the South Street Seaport. However, fish and particularly seafood remain something New York does extremely well, and a couple of the places listed below are among its most unmissable culinary treats – though, with a couple of notable exceptions, they rarely come at all cheap.

Lower Manhattan

Jeremy's Alehouse, 254 Front St ☎964-3537. Once a waterside sleaze bar in the shadow of the Brooklyn Bridge, *Jeremy's* fortunes changed with the aggrandisement of the nearby South Street Seaport. However, it still serves well-priced pint mugs of beer and excellent fish fresh from the adjacent Fulton St Market, as well as burgers. Expect to spend $10, all told. Try the $1 Oyster Shots – a giant raw oyster with tabasco, tomato sauce and topped up with beer – if you dare.

Jane Street Seafood Café, 31 Eighth Ave ☎242-9237. A cosy New England-style seafood restaurant with moderate prices and friendly service. Something of a neighbourhood favourite.

Le Pescador, 18 King St (off Sixth Ave, south of West Houston St) ☎924-3434. A trendy seafood bistro in a charming French setting. Moderate prices.

Drinking and Eating

24-hour eats

This is simply a checklist for **late night** – and mainly budget-constrained – hunger. For details, either check the listings in the "Budget eats" and "Restaurants" sections, or assume they serve a straight coffee shop menu.

If you're nowhere near any of the addresses below, don't despair. There are numerous additional all-night delis (for takeaway food), and in most neighbourhoods of the city you'll also find at least one 24-hour Korean greengrocer – good for most food supplies.

Lower

Around the Clock, 8 Stuyvesant St ☎598-0402.

Astor Riviera, 454 Lafayette St ☎677-4461.

Bagel Buffet, Sixth Ave at 8th St ☎477-0448.

Dave's Pot Belly, 98 Christopher St ☎243-9614.

Empire Diner, 210 Tenth Ave ☎243-2736.

Florent, 69 Gansevoort St ☎989-5779.

French Toast, 458 Sixth ave ☎533-2233.

Kiev, 117 Second Ave ☎674-4040.

Triumph Restaurant, 148 Bleecker St ☎228-3070.

Waverley Restaurant, 385 Sixth Ave ☎675-3181.

West Side Diner, W 31st and Ninth Ave ☎560-8407.

Midtown

Brasserie, 100 E 53rd St ☎751-4840.

Gemini Diner, 641 Second Ave ☎532-2143.

Lox Around the Clock, 676 Sixth Ave ☎691-3535.

Sarge's Deli, 548 Third Ave ☎679-0442.

Stage Deli, 834 Third Ave ☎245-7850.

Market Diner, 411 Ninth Ave ☎695-6844; 572 Eleventh Ave ☎244-6033.

Uptown

Gray's Papaya, 2090 Broadway ☎799-0243.

Green Kitchen, 1477 First Ave ☎988-4163.

H&H Bagels, 2239 Broadway ☎595-8000.

Tramway Coffee Shop, 1143 Second Ave ☎758-7017.

Pier Nine, 215 Second Ave ☎673-9263. Good, reasonably priced fish and shellfish dishes, many with an oriental flavour.

Umberto's Clam House, 129 Mulberry St ☎431-7545. As renowned for its role as famous Mafia execution spot as for the food. Cooking, though, is good – seafood, hot, medium or mild, and always delicious. See Chapter 2, *Lower Manhattan*, for more.

Vincent's Clam Bar, 119 Mott St ☎226-8133. Little Italy restaurant serving cheap seafood dishes – clams, mussels and squid.

Midtown Manhattan

Goldwater's, 988 Second Ave ☎888-2122. Fish dishes in huge portions for $10–15 a head.

Hobeau's, 882 First Ave ☎421-2888. Fresh fish and seafood for very reasonable prices – $8 and up.

Oyster Bar, Grand Central Terminal ☎490-6650. Wonderfully atmospheric old place, down in the vaulted dungeons of Grand Central, where midtown office workers break for lunch. Fish, seafood, and of course oysters, though none of it exactly budget rated – reckon on $20 upwards. If you're hard up, settle for the clam chowder with bread – delicious, quite ample and around $3 – or great creamy bowls of pan roast oysters or clams for around $10.

Upper Manhattan

Coastal, 300 Amsterdam Ave ☎769-3988. Fresh fish and a yuppie to-the-max crowd eating it. Good and moderately priced nonetheless. Dinner only.

Drinking and Eating

Dock's Oyster Bar, 2427 Broadway ☎724-5588; 633 Third Ave ☎986-8080. Some of the freshest seafood in town at these popular uptown restaurants. The Upper West Side is the original and tends to have the homelier atmosphere – though both can be noisy.

Fishin' Eddie, 73 W 71st St ☎874-3474. Fresh fish in a homey New England-style setting.

Vegetarian and wholefood

Surprisingly, exclusively **vegetarian** restaurants are a rarity in New York, although most places serve fish and poultry along with meatless dishes, and unless you're in a real carnivore's haven it's unusual to find a menu that doesn't have something completely meat-free.

Lower Manhattan

Anjelica Kitchen, 300 E 12th St ☎228-2909. Good quality vegetarian with various daily specials. Cheap, too. Patronised by an artistic and fashion crowd.

Bell Caffé, 310 Spring St ☎334-BELL. Cheap crunchy granola-style fare in an unhurried atmosphere.

Boostan, 85 Macdougal St ☎533-9561. Intimate Village vegetarian: good food, and you can take your own booze. Inexpensive.

Bubby's, 120 Hudson St ☎219-0666. TriBeCa dive serving health-aware food.

Eva's, 11 W 8th St ☎677-3496. Healthy food in a coffee shop setting. Nice grub, speedily served, and very cheap.

Souen, 210 Sixth Ave ☎807-7421; E 13th St ☎627-7150. Politically correct vegetarian seafood.

Spring Street Natural Restaurant, 62 Spring St ☎966-0290. Pricier and not wholly vegetarian but very good. From $9.

Vegetarians' Paradise, 48 Bowery ☎571-1535. East Village vegetarian Chinese – pricier than ordinary downtown Chinese restaurants but still pretty reasonable. Another location at 144 W 4th St ☎260-7049, near Washington Square.

Whole Wheat 'n' Wild Berries, 57 W 10th St ☎677-3410. Gourmet health food and vegetarian specials, including fresh fish, pasta dishes, salads and homemade soups.

Midtown Manhattan

Everything Yoghurt, 954 Third Ave ☎688-5757. Much as the name suggests, and with branches at 11 Fulton St and 1 Herald Square.

The Great American Health Bar, 35 W 57th St ☎ 355-5177; 2 Park Ave ☎685-7117; 55 John St ☎227-6100. This Manhattan chain comes well praised, but in reality the food can be rather bland and uninviting. Committed veggies only.

Health Pub, 371 Second Ave ☎529-9200. Vegetarian restaurant in light, airy café setting. Not especially cheap, but the food will appeal to veggies and meat-eaters alike.

Tibetan Kitchen, 444 Third Ave ☎679-6286. Vegetarian food from the Himalayas – at just $3 up. Bring your own drink. Closed Sundays.

Vegetable Garden, 15 E 40th St ☎532-3232. Vegetarian snacks and light meals.

Zen Palate, 663 Ninth Ave ☎582-1669. Stylish and modern, with what it calls a "Zen atmosphere", this serves up health-conscious vegetarian Chinese food.

Upper Manhattan

Living Springs, 116 E 60th St ☎319-7850. All-you-can-eat lunch buffet for $7. Vegetarian entrées, salads, wholegrains, steamed vegetables and fruit. Takeout too.

Zucchini, 1336 First Ave ☎249-0559. Reliable and healthy vegetarian restaurant.

Expense account

Should you win the lottery or have rich relatives, New York has some superb restaurants to choose from, most of them serving **French** or French-tinged **American** food, or in some cases variations on **California-style** cuisine. Go expecting to pay upwards of $75 a head, dress up, and phone first.

Arcadia, 21 E 62nd St ☎223-2900. Small, beautifully decorated restaurant serving French-accented American food cooked up by one of America's leading young chefs.

Aquavit, 13 W 54th St ☎307-7311. Superb Scandinavian food – pickled herrings, salmon, even reindeer – in a lovely atrium restaurant. A real treat.

Aureole, 34 E 61st St ☎319-1660. Magical French-accented American food in a gorgeous old brownstone setting. The prix fixe options should bring the cost down to $70 per head.

Le Bernadin, 155 W 51st St ☎489-1515. Renowned as perhaps the best place in New York to eat fish, for which the chef has received rave reviews. However, to enjoy both that and the clubby teak decor of this place you have to book months in advance. And it's one of the city's most expensive restaurants, of any kind. Not for the dilettante eater.

Bouley, 165 Duane St ☎608-3852. One of New York's best French restaurants, serving modern French food made from the freshest ingredients under the eye of chef David Bouley. Popular with city celebrities, costs for the magnificent meals can be softened by opting for the prix fixe lunch and dinner options.

Le Cirque, 58 E 65th St ☎794-9292. This place is widely thought of as the city's top-rated restaurant. Very orchestrated, *very* expensive, and honoured by such names as Liza Minelli, Richard Nixon and Ronald Reagan. Not for the likes of us.

Elaine's, 1703 Second Ave ☎534-8103. Remember the opening shots of Woody Allen's *Manhattan*? That was Elaine's, and today her restaurant is still something of a favourite with New York celebrities – though it's hard to see why. If you want to star-gaze there's no better place to come; if you're hungry or watching the pennies, best go somewhere else.

Four Seasons, 99 E 52nd St ☎754-9494. Housed in Mies van der Rohe's Seagram Building, this is one of the city's most noted restaurants, not least for the decor, which includes murals by Picasso, sculp-

tures by Richard Lippold and interior design by Philip Johnson. The food isn't at all bad either, and there's a relatively inexpensive pre-theatre menu – around $40 – if you want to try it.

Gotham Bar & Grill, 12 E 12th St ☎620-4020. This restaurant serves marvellous American fare in an airy, trendy setting. Generally reckoned to be one of the city's truly best restaurants; and it's at least worth a drink in the bar to see the city's beautiful people drift in.

Hudson River Club, 4 World Financial Center, 250 Vesey St ☎786-1500. Worth the $70 or so per head for the view over the harbour to the Statue of Liberty, especially until *Windows on the World* reopens. Food is American, with special emphasis on New England/New York State cooking.

Lutece, 249 E 50th Street ☎752-2225. Once rated as the best restaurant in the country, and still well up there with the best of the places that New Yorkers (those that can afford it) will kill to get a table at. Again, big bucks and best dress.

The Rainbow Room, RCA Building, 65th floor ☎632-5100. The city's best views, most overpriced food, and tackiest entertainment. Early evening, though, you might find it worth the price of a cocktail to take in the city skyline in comfort. Once again, Sunday best only.

River Café, 1 Water St, Brooklyn ☎718/522-5200. You probably won't be able to afford the food, but for the price of a drink you can enjoy the best view of the Lower Manhattan skyline there is. Try brunch – it's the best bargain.

Russian Tea Room, 150 W 57th Street ☎265-0947. There's hardly a better place to eat in the city if you want to spot a celebrity, and rates are perhaps not as high as in the city's top French dining spots; plus it's easier to get a table at short notice. The wonderfully garish interior makes eating here a real occasion, too, though choose carefully on the rather over-rated menu, and stick to the old favourites – the blinis are among the city's best, as is the chicken kiev.

Drinking and Eating

Drinking and Eating

21 Club, 21 W 52nd St ☎ 582-7200. Though its days when the likes of Dorothy Parker regularly dined here are over, this remains a stylish, power-broking restaurant, enormously popular despite its high (some might say through the roof) prices.

Windows on the World, World Trade Center, 107th floor ☎ 938-1111. The views, obviously, are the main attraction. But if you've money to burn the food's good too, and the wine cellar is said to be among the best in New York. A nice venue for Sunday brunch; during weekdays though, lunch is only served to lunch club members. *Windows on the World is closed until early 1994 for renovation.*

The Outer Boroughs

If you decide to explore the **Outer Boroughs**, food could be as good a motivation as any. The ethnic communities here have for the most part retained close character – and their restaurants are similarly authentic, generally run by and for the locals. All of New York's ethnic groups are well represented, and you can eat more or less anything: **Brooklyn** has some of New York's best West Indian and Italian food, not to mention its most authentic Russian restaurants; **Queens** holds the city's biggest Greek and South American communities; while Belmont in the **Bronx** is one of the best places in the city to eat authentic Italian cuisine.

Brooklyn

Downtown Brooklyn, Brooklyn Heights and Atlantic Avenue

Frost Restaurant, 193 Frost St ☎ 718/389-3347. Williamsburg neighbourhood Italian serving moderately priced food.

Gage & Tollner, 372 Fulton St ☎ 718/875-5181. Old-fashioned seafood restaurant that's long been part of the downtown Brooklyn eating scene. Not as expensive as it looks, and serving great crab cakes.

Henry's End, 44 Henry St ☎ 718/834-1776. Varied menu with a wide selection of seasonal dishes, appetisers and desserts. Popular with Brooklyn Heights locals, and normally crowded. Don't expect it to be all that cheap either.

Leaf 'n' Bean, 136 Montague St ☎ 718/855-7978. Exotic coffees and teas plus excellent homemade soups, and, on weekends, brunch for about $10. Outdoor seating when it's fine.

Montague Street Saloon, 122 Montague St ☎ 718/522-6770. Burgers and salads for under $10.

Moroccan Star, 205 Atlantic Ave ☎ 718/643-0800. Perhaps New York's best Moroccan restaurant, with wonderful tajines alongside western food. The chef once worked at the *Four Seasons*, and the quality of his cooking remains undiminished.

Pete Luger's Steak House, 178 Broadway ☎ 718/387-7400. Pricey ($40 a head) place, but reckoned by aficionados to have the best steaks in the city – which is quite a claim. Good service and pleasant ambience make it a great place to eat.

Promenade, 101 Montague St ☎ 718/237-9796. Greek diner in the heart of Brooklyn Heights with a massive menu and good lunch specials for $5–7.

Slade's, 107 Montague St ☎ 718/858-1200. Moderately priced burgers, salads and Sunday brunch specials – and a big-screen TV.

Teresa's, 80 Montague St ☎ 718/797-3996. Large portions of Polish homecooking – blintzes, pirogi and the like – make this a good lunchtime stopoff for those on tours of Brooklyn Heights.

Tripoli, 160 Atlantic Ave ☎ 718/596-5800. Lebanese restaurant serving fish, lamb and vegetarian dishes for a low $8 or so.

Central Brooklyn

Aunt Sonia's, 1123 Eighth Ave at 12th St ☎ 718/965-9526. Eclectic menu featuring everything from Caribbean to Thai to Italian to traditional American. Main courses for around $10.

Aunt Suzie's, 247 Fifth Ave, Park Slope ☎ 718/788-3377. Neighbourhood Italian serving decent food for as little as $10 a person. Not a restaurant to drive from Manhattan for, but if you happen to be in the area, it's one of the best-value places around.

Cucina, 256 Fifth Ave ☎718/230-0711. Homely Italian restaurant serving fine food for affordable prices.

Once Upon a Sundae, 7702 Third Ave ☎718/748-3412. Turn-of-the-century ice cream parlour.

101, 101 Fourth Ave ☎718/833-1313. Eclectic Italian restaurant with a lively bar. A great neighbourhood haunt.

Sam's, 238 Court St, Cobble Hill ☎718/596-3458. Long-established restaurant serving standard Italian fare at reasonable prices.

Tutta Pasta, 160 Seventh Ave ☎718/788-9500 and 8901 Third Ave ☎718/238-6066. Better-than-average pasta at low prices.

Coney Island and Brighton Beach

Carolina, 1409 Mermaid Ave, Coney Island ☎718/714-1294. Inexpensive, family-run Italian restaurant that's been around forever. Great food, great prices.

Gargiulo's, 2911 West 15th St ☎718/266-4891. Large, noisy family-run Coney Island restaurant famed for its large portions of hearty Neapolitan grub. Cheap.

Jean's Clam Bar, 2123 Emmons Ave ☎718/646-9285. Inexpensive and lively seafood restaurant on Sheepshead Bay's main drag.

Joe's, 2009 Emmons Ave ☎718/646-9375. Medium-priced Sheepshead Bay restaurant that's well worth the trip from Manhattan to sample.

Nathan's Famous, Surf and Stillwell Ave ☎718/266-3161. New York's most famous hot dogs (and most other American snacks). Not the ultimate in gastronomy but legend nonetheless.

Odessa, 1113 Brighton Beach Ave ☎718/769-2869. Excellent and varied Russian menu at unbeatable prices.

Primorski, 282 Brighton Beach Ave ☎718/891-3111. Perhaps the best of Brighton Beach's Russian hang-outs, serving up a huge menu of authentic Russian dishes at absurdly cheap prices – main courses around $5 – though you may have problems communicating with the waiting staff, most of whom barely speak English. Live music in the evening.

Mrs Stahl's, 1001 Brighton Beach Ave ☎718/648-0210. Long-standing Brighton Beach knishery.

Star of China, 2901 Bragg St ☎718/615-2080. Reliable Chinese alternative to Sheepshead Bay's seafood.

The Bronx

Belmont

Ann and Tony's, 2407 Arthur Ave, corner of 187th St ☎364-8250. Good pizzas.

Il Boschetto, 1660 E Gun Hill Rd ☎379-9335. Pricey, but the entrées and fresh pasta are worth it.

Dominick's, 2356 Westchester Ave ☎822-8810. All you could hope for in a Belmont Italian: great atmosphere, wonderful food and low(ish) prices.

Mario's, 2342 Arthur Ave ☎584-1188. Pricey but impressive cooking, enticing even die-hard Manhattanites to the Bronx.

Queens

Astoria

Cyprus Taverna, 29-19 23rd Ave ☎718/728-9561. Authentic Greek neighbourhood restaurant.

Omonia Café, 32-20 Broadway ☎718/274-6650. Good, affordable Greek food .

Roumeli, 33-04 Broadway, between 33rd and 34th sts ☎718/278- 7533. Excellent Greek – a little upmarket but popular.

Jackson Heights

Inti-Raymi, 86-14 37th Ave ☎718/424-1938. Unpretentious restaurant serving substantial low-priced Peruvian food.

Las Americas, 93-09 37th Ave at 90th St ☎718/458-1638. Columbian cakes, pastries and full meals. Good for inexpensive lunches.

La Pequena Columbia, 83-27 Roosevelt Ave ☎718/478-6528. Literally "Little Columbia", this place doles out heaped portions of seafood casserole, pork and tortillas. Try the fruit drinks too, *maracuay* (passion fruit) or *guanabana* (soursoup).

Drinking and Eating

Drinking and Eating

Tierras Columbianas, 82-18 Roosevelt Ave ☎718/426-8868. One of the most popular of the Jackson Heights Columbians – great food (wonderful soups, and spicy meat dishes), decently priced and in large portions.

Victor's, 6909 Roosevelt Blvd ☎718/651-9474. Filipino restaurant serving up huge portions of rice, beans, chicken and beef for upwards of $6 a main course.

Forest Hills, Jamaica, Bayside

Carmichael's Diner & Cocktail Lounge, 117-08 Gut R. Brewer Blvd ☎718/723-6908. Fried chicken, chopped barbecue and black-eyed peas for around $10.

Chalet Alpina, 98-35 Metropolitan Ave ☎718/793-3774. Reasonably priced, strong on meat and potato dishes.

Eddie's Sweet Shop, 105–29 Metropolitan Ave, Forest Hills ☎718/520-8514. An old-fashioned candy store with fantastic ice creams.

Suzu, 39-32 Bell Blvd ☎718/224-5622. Invent your own sushi for about $15.

Staten Island

Basilio Inn, 2-6 Galesville Court ☎718/720-6835. Homestyle Italian with a *bocci* court out the back.

Bella Mama, 266 Morning Star Rd ☎718/891-0545. Huge portions of southern Italian food.

La Fosse aux Loups, 11 Schuyler St ☎718/442-9111. Once an inexpensive Mexican eatery, now a fairly expensive Belgian restaurant – though still, oddly enough, serves inexpensive Mexican food.

Lido's, 37 Victory Blvd ☎718/447-1137. Old-style family restaurant with American-Italian cooking and moderate prices.

Tug's, 1115 Richmond Terrace ☎718/447-6369. Good for watching the water while you eat, and, on Sundays, a nice place for brunch.

Chapter 9

Nightlife

Considering New York's everyday energy and diversity, its **music scene** can be disappointing. There is excellent **jazz**, traditional and contemporary and still concentrated in Greenwich Village, and around the venues – and to a greater extent in the Outer Boroughs – you'll find a scattering of blues, Latin American and hip-hop. But straight **rock music** is currently something of a write-off – at least as far as originality goes. Although there has been something of a rock revival of late, if you see anyone interesting, they're often likely to be a British import.

With **nightclubs**, New York is more in its element, though the trend towards so-called "supper clubs", where the emphasis is more on style and comfort than light shows and dancing, has deprived the city of some of its more spectacular places. That said, New York is as hung up on fashion as it ever was, and the scene just as capricious, with clubs still furnished for a year or so of fame on multimillion-dollar budgets, and often with sound and light systems that are nowhere rivalled. Some of the more interesting places are still by definition the most exclusive, their doors guarded against the unhip by fashion-wary bouncers. But if you just want to dance, there are any number of places to do so, many charging prices that, while never cheap, won't break the bank.

The **sections** that follow give accounts of the best of current venues, though you should keep in mind that the music – and especially the club – scenes change continually; for the current **background**, check out *The Paper*, New York's "style"

barometer for the trendier club listings. And for adequate, though sometimes confusing listings, pick up the *Village Voice* – rather better for venues than clubs – or the more mainstream *New York Magazine*. Also worth checking out is *Homo Xtra* and its sister magazine *It* for detailed listings of clubs, theatre and venues for both the gay *and* straight scenes. And remember to take some **ID** with you wherever you go: venues have been forced to be more observant of laws on entry and under-age drinking (ie under 21). Look anything around the magic age and you may well not get in at all.

Rock music

New York's **rock music scene** has changed quite radically recently. It's more diffused now, and rising rents and closing venues have (as in just about every other field) forced many musicians out of Manhattan and into the Outer Boroughs and New Jersey: if there is a scene at all nowadays, it's one that has no clear centre. That said, there are still plenty of bands around, playing many different kinds of music: there's an exciting off-Manhattan hub in Hoboken, New Jersey, centring on *Maxwell's* (see overleaf); rap and hip hop, including acid and house, are still big, both in the streets and the recording studios, which put out a regular diet of 12-inch singles; and, in Brooklyn and Queens at least, there's a huge Latin/South American and reggae contingent – though the venues themselves are way off the average tourist circuit.

Nightlife

In Manhattan itself – principally in the East Village and Lower East Side – most of the energy is provided by a growing assortment of neighbourhood bars which host a variety of new wave and (often) blues talent. Basically the listings below should point you to the more major venues; if you want to get more involved or listen to something more obscure, the *Village Voice*, or a gaggle of free publications, the best being the *New York Press*, which you can pick up in most downtown stores and bars, should more than suffice.

The big performance venues

Madison Square Garden, Seventh and Eighth aves, W 31st–33rd sts ☎465-6741. New York's principal large stage, hosting not only hockey and basketball but also a large proportion of the really big rock acts that visit the city. The arena, seating 20,000-plus, is not the most soulful place to see a band, but it may be the only chance you get.

Meadowlands Stadium, East Rutherford, New Jersey ☎201/935-3900. The city's other really big venue, again with room for around 20,000.

Radio City Music Hall, Sixth Ave and 50th St ☎247-4777. Not the prime venue it once was; most of the acts that play here now are firmly of the mainstream – although the building itself has as great a sense of occasion as it ever did.

Smaller venues

Apollo Theater, 253 W 125th St ☎749-5838. Regular black acts, as well as amateur nights (Wednesdays) and the odd dog show. $5–30.

Beacon Theater, 2124 Broadway ☎496-7070. Live bands, including occasional big names, at $20–40.

The Bitter End, 147 Bleecker St ☎673-7030. Young, fairly mainstream bands in an intimate cabaret club setting. Don't expect to see anyone famous. Cover around $5.

The Bottom Line, 15 W 4th St ☎228-6300. Not New York's most adventurous venue but one of the better known – and the place where you're most likely to see

established name bands. Cabaret setup, with tables crowding out any suggestion of a dance floor. Claim to fame: Bruce Springsteen is said to have first turned heads here. Entrance $15–25.

CBGB (and OMFUG), 315 Bowery ☎982-4052. Deliberately sleazy, and despite a relative demise in influence still a great place to see (if not actually listen to) a band. Shows at 9.30pm (Fri/Sat 10.30pm); admission $5–10.

China Club, 2130 Broadway ☎877-1166. Music-industry venue peopled by celebs and ageing rockers. Open nightly until 4am, $10–20.

Continental Club, 25 Third Ave ☎529-6924. Home to beer blasts (very cheap beer specials) and the loudest alternative rock this side of punk. A platform for local talent. $3 and up.

Dan Lynch's, 221 Second Ave ☎677-0911. Blues and R&B bands nightly from 10pm. Free entrance Sun–Thurs; Fri & Sat $5.

The Grand, 76 E 13th St ☎777-0600. Long-established club and venue with a minimalist interior and live bands most nights of the week. Consisting of a large dance floor surrounded by tables, it's one of the city's nicest live venues; admission $15+.

Irving Plaza, 17 Irving Place ☎249-8870. Once a great rock venue, then home to an off-Broadway musical, hence the ornate decor, *Irving Plaza* has returned to its former glory, showcasing rock, jazz, folk and rap. An excellent, intimate venue. $10–25.

Lauterbach's, 335 Prospect Ave, Brooklyn ☎718/788-9140. A place to hear rock 'n' rollers destined for stardom, or the proverbial dumpster. Cheap beer, nice atmosphere, laid-back service. $3 Fri–Sun.

Lone Star Café Roadhouse, 240 W 52nd St ☎245-2950. The uptown outpost of the now defunct downtown rock'n'roll bastion, with a good variety of nightly acts, though fewer big names. Cheap drinks, good food (burgers, chicken, etc); still one of the city's better live venues. Entrance around $5–25.

Manny's Car Wash, 1558 Third Ave ☎ 369-2583. Smoky, Chicago-style blues bar with a small dance floor and reasonable prices. Shows from 9.15pm. No cover Sundays for blues jams; Mondays women get in free. Otherwise, covers range from $3 to $25.

Marquee, 547 W 21st St ☎ 929-3257. Supposedly a sister club to its London namesake, the *Marquee* presents a mixture of blues, rock and, especially, new British bands – if you're hoping to see *Blur* or *Jesus Jones*, this could be the place. Admission $10–25.

Maxwell's, Washington and 11th St, Hoboken, New Jersey ☎ 201/798-4064. Neighbourhood club hosting up to a dozen bands a week: some big names but really one of the best places to check out the current tri-state scene. Admission $6–10.

New World, 254 E 2nd St ☎ 677-5200. Venue for visiting bands and host space to a broad array of specialised club nights, from the Rock 'n' Roll Fag Bar (go-go boys and drag queens) to Sunday night's Girl World.

Nightingale Bar, Second Ave at 13th St ☎ 473-9398. Bar with blues and new wave bands nightly.

North River Bar, 145 Hudson St ☎ 226-9411. Down-to-earth TriBeCa bar that books regular live – mostly rock – bands. Try the shots served in test tubes.

The Pyramid Club, 101 Avenue A ☎ 420-1590. After a long hiatus, one of NYC's best clubs is back on the scene, serving up a tasty smorgasbord of industrial and dance music. Also home to *Fuck!*, Sunday night's gay extravaganza. $3–10.

The Ritz, W 54th St at Eighth Ave ☎ 541-8900. Now in a new location in the old *Studio 54* building, this is the *Bottom Line*'s main rival for name acts. Limited seating; music at 9pm and 11pm most nights; admission $5–25.

SOB's ("Sounds of Brazil"), 204 Varick St ☎ 243-4940. Disco/club/restaurant, with regular jazz, salsa-tinged and World Music acts. Lively and fun, popular with a predominantly yuppie crowd. Two performances a night. Admission $5–20.

Sweetwater's, 170 Amsterdam Ave ☎ 873-4100. Restaurant with R&B, jazz and rock bands nightly. Cover $20.

Tilt, 179 Varick St ☎ 463-0509. Themed live shows with at least three bands on the bill nightly. Also a mecca for the house and hip-hop generation. Free draught beer on Thursday nights. $8–10.

Tramps, 54 W 21st St ☎ 727-7788. Blues and new wave bands almost nightly, from 9pm (weekends additional show at midnight). Entrance $5–20.

Wetlands, 161 Hudson St ☎ 966-4225. A self-proclaimed "ecosaloon" that books regular live bands – particularly reggae – and circulates petitions among the punters. Very 1960s. Admission $6–15.

Jazz and folk

There are few cities anywhere that are home to quite so many **jazz** clubs, festivals, jazz-related organisations or, indeed, musicians – and if you're serious about jazz then this itself could be a good reason for visiting (even moving to) Manhattan.

There are around forty places in Manhattan presenting jazz nightly or at least regularly. Most clubs are located downtown, most often in **Greenwich Village** or **SoHo**; midtown clubs tend on the whole to be slick dinner-dance joints for businesspeople and as such are expensive and largely unexciting. The usual sources (notably the *Voice*) have listings of what's on. There's also *Hothouse*, a free monthly magazine that you can sometimes pick up from the venues themselves, and the jazz **monthly** *Downbeat*. Or simple listen to some of the city's jazz-orientated **radio stations**. Two of the best of these are *WBGO* (88.5 FM), a 24-hour jazz station, and *WKCR* (98.7 FM) – Columbia University's radio station. Failing that, phone **Jazz Line** (☎ 718/465-7500), for recorded information detailing the night's events.

Price policies vary from club to club, but at most there's a hefty **cover** ($10–12.50) and always a **minimum** charge for food and drinks. An evening out at a major club will set you back at least $15 per

Nightlife

Nightlife

person, $25–30 if you want to eat. **Piano bars** – usually small and atmospheric – come cheaper with neither admission fee nor a minimum, though drinks are obviously still hiked up.

Jazz venues

Arthur's BeBop Cafe, 1 Charles St ☎989-2339. Live weekend jazz. No credit cards.

Arthur's Tavern, 57 Grove St ☎675-6879. Small, amiable piano bar with some inspired performers and no cover or minimum – though drinks are predictably pricey. A good place for a night out as long as you're not into getting wrecked.

Birdland, 2745 Broadway ☎749-2228. Not the original place where Charlie Parker played, but an Upper West Side venue with live jazz seven nights of the week. Music from 9pm (from 6pm on Sunday); cover $5–7 – big names at weekends.

The Blue Note, 131 W 3rd St ☎475-8592. Big names mainly and with high prices – but good music and atmosphere. For all shows there's a $5 drinks minimum per person plus anything between $15 and $45 cover charge per table, depending on who's playing. $10 if you sit at the bar. Late-night shows – until 4am – are free if you've seen the previous set, $5 if you haven't.

Bradley's, 70 University Place ☎228-6440. Neighbourhood bar that features well-known bass/piano duos and acts as meeting point of local jazz musicians. A good place to catch big names jamming with people they wouldn't normally play with. Best to arrive late, as early evening the bar is too crowded with locals to actually hear anything. $8 minimum per person at the tables; $5–10 cover except Monday and Tuesday when it's free.

Condon's, 117 E 15th St ☎254-0960. A relatively new, small, intimate venue close to Union Square that stages big names. Cover $12.50, and a two-drink minimum; there's a cover at the bar but no minimum but – although the sound is good – the view is very restricted. Sets at 9/10pm and 11pm/midnight. If they're not too busy (most likely on Tuesday or Wednesday) they'll let you stay for the second set with-

out paying again. *Closed for refurbishment until spring 1994.*

Fat Tuesday's, 190 Third Ave ☎533-7902. Another of New York's principal jazz venues, small and atmospheric in a mirrored basement with low ceilings. Prices vary according to who's on, but generally hover around the $12.50 cover, $7.50 minimum mark. Sets at 8pm and 10pm, so a better choice for early risers than some of the other venues.

Fifty Five, 55 Christopher St ☎929-9883. See "Bars" in Chapter 8, *Drinking and Eating.*

Fortune Garden Pavillion, 209 E 49th St ☎753-0101. They call it "Dim sum and Jazz", and the music lives up to the food. $20 first set, $15 second set.

Greene Street Café, 101 Greene St ☎925-2415. Huge converted warehouse, split between two levels and with dreadful acoustics. The music is generally excellent but views from the bar are so restricted you'll need either to pay for a balcony seat ($5 cover plus $5 minimum) or splash out on a dinner table.

J's, 2581 Broadway ☎666-3600. Intensely swinging jazz. Cover $5–10.

Knickerbocker's, 9th St and University Place ☎228-8490. Just down the street from *Bradley's*, this is an excellent restaurant with high-calibre bass/piano duos. $7 minimum at the tables – nothing at the bar (which has a better view of the performers); no cover.

The Knitting Factory, 47 E Houston St ☎219-3055. Small, vibrant club hosting live jazz and avant-garde rock. Shows at 9pm and 11pm. Entrance $5–10.

Michael's Pub, 211 E 55th St ☎758-2272. This slick midtown bar isn't so much known for the quality of its jazz as for the fact that Woody Allen plays clarinet here on occasional Monday nights. From all accounts, that's its only recommendation, as service is surly and the outrageous $15–35 cover (plus a two-drink minimum) doesn't give you much for your money.

Sweet Basil, 88 Seventh Ave ☎242-1785. One of New York's major – and most crowded – jazz spots, particularly at weekends, when there's brunch and free jazz through the afternoon. For the best of the music, though, stick to weekday evenings. Shows usually start at 9pm. $15 cover and a $6 minimum at the tables, per set ($12 at the bar including a drink).

Village Gate, Bleecker St at Thompson ☎475-5120. One of New York's oldest and largest surviving jazz clubs and still one of the best. Monday salsa nights are the current highlight, well worth the $10 entrance; other times, you can cut costs by taking a seat in the downstairs sidewalk café and listening to regular bass/piano duos for a $5 minimum.

Village Vanguard, 178 Seventh Ave ☎255-4037. An NYC jazz landmark that celebrated its fiftieth anniversary a few years back and still lays on a regular diet of big names. Admission around $10; $5 drink minimum at weekends.

Visiones, 125 Macdougal St ☎673-5576. Spanish restaurant four doors down from *The Blue Note* that hosts a wide, more contemporary array of different acts. Two shows nightly, at 9.30pm and 11.30pm. Often no cover charge, otherwise $5.

Wonderland Blues Bar, 519 Second Ave ☎213-5098. Cosy jazz bar which caters to the after-midnight crowd. No cover during the week, $5 weekends.

Zanzibar & Grill, 550 Third Ave ☎779-0606. Restaurant (serving regional American food) and jazz club. Sets start at 9pm, Monday to Saturday, and on Sundays at 8pm.

Folk venues

Eagle Tavern, 355 W 14th St ☎924-0275. Local and imported Irish folk and occasional poetry on selected weeknights. $7–12 cover.

O'Lunney's, 12 W 44th St ☎840-6688. Restaurant serving steaks, hamburgers and the like to traditional country 'n' western live sounds. $3 cover at the tables.

The Speakeasy, 107 Macdougal St ☎598-9670. The only folk club in NYC with music seven nights a week. Something of a hang-out for musicians and folkies. $5–10 cover; bland health-food menu.

Nightclubs and discos

Like its London counterpart, New York – and especially Manhattan – **club life** is a rapidly evolving creature. While many of the name DJs remain the same, venues shift around and open and close according to the whims of fashion. Musically, garage and house holds sway at the moment – with the emphasis on the deep, vocal style that's always been popular in the city – but Latin Freestyle, dancehall reggae and rap all retain interest.

That said, the rundown below would be a fun one right now, but within weeks it's bound to have serious omissions. Always check, ask contacts for information, look in *The Paper*, *It* or *Homo Xtra* and hunt down flyers that advertise venues and one-off events: you'll find them in bars and restaurants, record and clothes shops, even telephone booths. Many offer substantial discounts on the cover charge, especially if you're prepared to turn up unfashionably early.

The hipness quotient of a club can go up or down at the drop of a hat, and that clubs can (and must if they want to survive) change rapidly. Many of the hipper clubs follow a pattern whereby the trendy, dressed-up and predominantly white downtown crowd is targeted at the opening, waiting for the name to get established before letting the Spanish and black kids in from Uptown – the people who prefer dancing to showing off.

The **procedure** of clubbing in New York is less likely to change its ways. Assuming you're curious (and in many cases rich) enough, these are the main points:

• Hippest (and cheapest) time to club is during the week. Weekends are favoured by out-of-towners and so shunned by serious nightpeople. Admission to clubs at weekends is in any case invariably more expensive than during the week.

• Style is vital: don't expect to get into some of the more exclusive places just because you can afford to.

• Nothing gets going much before midnight. Don't go before this. When you eventually stagger out (most clubs close around 4am), keep your wits about you.

Nightlife

Nightlife

• Don't reckon to beat bar prices by smuggling in a hip flask – the mixers are the same price as everything else: around $5. A night at any NYC club needs money.

Au Bar, 41 E 58th St ☎308-9455. "Supper club" full of European ex-pats and would-be American aristocrats. Best dress. Sunday–Thursday admission $10, Friday and Saturday $15.

Baja, 246A Columbus Ave at 71st St ☎724-8890. Yuppie Upper West Side club playing standard dance music to a fairly safe, smartly dressed clientele. $5 weeknights, $10+ weekends.

Bank, 225 E Houston St ☎505-5033. An eclectic mix of East Village bohoes, Brits and Hispanics makes for some interesting clubbing. Wednesday is Ward 6 - punk and goth night. $5–12.

Cave Canem, 24 First Avenue ☎529-9665. Restaurant/dance club housed on two floors of a former bathhouse that's decked out in decadent Roman style and serves food based on Imperial Roman cuisine. Main dishes in the restaurant run at $13–20. A wide range of music, no cover charge during the week, $5 at weekends.

The Crane Club, 201 W 79th St ☎877-3097. An upscale bar that plays loud contemporary rock and charges around $5 cover. Preppies galore.

Danceteria, 29 E 29th St ☎683-1046. Once one of NYC's great clubs, offering several floors of dancing. It also hosts *Rocketeria* (Thursdays) and *Technoteria* (Saturdays). $5–15.

Delia's, 197 E 3rd St ☎254-9184. Another supper club whose sleazy location satisfies Upper East Side desires to slum it downtown. And inside is anything but sleazy, the formidable Delia presiding over a plush environment designed to cater to the needs of leisurely diners and dancers alike. If the neighbourhood doesn't appeal, Delia will book a car to take you home.

Giant Step at Metropolis, 31 Union Square West ☎675-2300. Taking its cue from London's *Talking Loud, Saying Something*, this excellent club features

live jamming over rap and jazz classics. Well worth the queueing. $10.

Island Club, 285 W Broadway ☎226-4598. Wednesday, Thursday and Sunday hard-core reggae music, Fridays and Saturdays salsa and Latin-edged sounds. Admission $5–10.

Jackie 60 at Bar Room 432, 432 W 14th St ☎366-5680. Pseudo-intellectuals, artists and cross-dressers cavort to the beats provided by Johnny Dynell and occasionally David Morales. Poetry readings at 1am every fortnight. $5.

KI-OM at the Ukrainian Center, 140–142 Second Avenue. This Friday-only club offers a great mixture of ragga, roots and dancehall. $10.

Limelight, 660 Sixth Ave ☎807-7850. Housed in a converted Gothic church, this caused a storm of outrage when it opened, and is enjoying something of a renaissance after a lean period, particularly for its UK-influenced Thursday night sessions. Though still streets ahead of its dull London clone, it's no longer the exclusive hang-out it was. Admission $12+.

The Living Room, 154 E 79th St ☎772-8488. A preppy club with an attitude. Wear black and look suitably cool and you'll have no problem getting in.

Mission, 531 E 5th St, between aves A and B ☎473-9096. East Village club specialising in goth, punk and new wave music – Jesus and Mary Chain, Psychedelic Furs, Sisters of Mercy, Cure, etc – and apparently a hang-out of various members of the aforementioned groups. Open Thurs–Sat from 10pm; admission is $6 and drinks are cheap.

Mr Fuji's Tropicana, 61 Fifth Avenue, ☎243-7900. By day an eatery, by night a clubbing hot spot. Thursdays is rock'n'roll night. $10 after 10pm.

Muse, 28-30 Tenth Avenue ☎691-6262. One of the safest, professionally run hip-hop clubs in NYC, unlike its predecessor, the sadly missed *Mars*. Mainly black and Hispanic, with a sprinkling of white folks, all congregating on four pulsating floors of hip-hop, old skool and ragga. $8–15.

NASA, 157 Hudson St ☎ 330-8233. DJs Keoki, DB and Jason Jinx provide the soundtrack for the NYC rave generation. As close to a rave as you'll get in an intimate club situation. Standard club fare – smart bar, condoms and potato chips – should see you through the night. $14.

Nell's, 246 W 14th St ☎ 675-1567. First of the so-called "supper clubs" and still going strong, although its reputation for the city's most exclusive establishment has some-what waned of late. Admission Mon–Wed $7; Thurs $20; Fri–Sat $15; Sun $12.

Nick's Grove, 209 E 84th St ☎ 744-5003. *Baja*-like dance place for the East Side. Cover $5.

Palladium, 126 E 14th St ☎ 473-7171. Biggest and for some still among the best of New York clubs – though *Palladium*'s initial exclusivity was deliberately short-lived, and it now caters for a fairly mixed custom. Housed in an enormous old thea-tre, the dance floor, light and sound system take some beating, as does the music, especially midweek. For no-nonsense dancing without the posing, still one of the best. Admission $15–20.

Peggy Sue's, 121 University Place, ☎ 260-4095. Wednesday night is classic rock *and* funk night courtesy of DJ Alberto for the 20- to 30-something generation. Saturdays is disco night, where admission is a mere $5 if you sport disco couture. $5–10.

Private Eye's, 12 W 21st St ☎ 206-7770. Nowadays the city's premiere gay club, with a tiny dance floor, video screens and some of the most spirited carousing you'll find. $15.

Red Zone, 440 W 54th St ☎ 582-2222. Popular with a young, mainly Latin crowd. David Morales plays on Saturdays; open Tues–Sun.

Roseland, 239 W 52nd St ☎ 247-0200. Ballroom dancing from lunchtime to midnight, Thursday to Sunday, just as it's been for the last 65 years. $15+ admission.

Roxy, 515 W 18th ☎ 645-5157. Dance music with the emphasis on garage.

Rotating DJs, including Frankie Knuckles once a month. Drag queens and gay roller skating are the order of the day. 100 percent kitsch, 100 percent fun. $17; $15 before midnight.

Save the Robots, on Avenue C. East Village club that gets going when the other nightspots are winding down. Open Thurs, Fri, Sat from 4am until 8am, entrance $10. Can be difficult to get into . . ..

Shelter, 157 Hudson St ☎ 677-2582. Expect a lethal mixture of deep house and disco classics played over an awesome sound system to a mainly black crowd. Great atmosphere, with the emphasis on serious dancing. Saturday night is gay night.

Soul Kitchen at the Supper Club, 240 W 47th St ☎ 921-1940; *Soul Kitchen* hotline ☎ 481-8030. Frankie Jackson spins classic funk and soul, while the slew of babes bat their lashes. Unaccompanied men are barred. $10 men; $5 women.

Sound Factory, 530 W 27th St ☎ 643-0728. It is, without any reservations, the best clubbing experience in NYC, though not for the faint of heart. DJ Junior Vasquez spins the deepest house, the hardest garage and a bit of Bette Midler for extra flavour. Awesome. $20. No alcohol.

20 West, 27 W 20th St ☎ 924-0205. Fifties- and Sixties-style dance club complete with dancing DJs, waiters and bartenders. No cover Tuesdays, Wednesday and Thursday $5, Friday and Saturday $10.

USA, 218 W 47th St ☎ 869-6103. With rooms by Gaultier and Mugler, neon signs and kitsch Japanese art, *USA* was designed for success. Mainstream house and a fairly average mix of trendies, suits and bridge-and-tunnel warriors. $15.

Webster Hall, 125 E 11th St ☎ 353-1600. A cavernous place that is home to *The Make Up Room* - very gay and very decadent, and also *Paradise*, a club night with S/M overtones and "chemical" house tunes provided by DJ George Briceno. $15.

Nightlife

Chapter 10

The Performing Arts and Film

With Broadway, the Met and the New York Philharmonic, New York City can still supply glittering venues and glamorous events – but you may need to take out a mortgage to attend. **Theatre** is fabulous, and fabulously expensive, with Broadway prices crippling and even Off-Broadway seats going for well over London's West End prices. If you know where to look, though, there are a variety of ways to get tickets cheaper, and on the fringe prices approach the realistic. The best of these options are detailed below. **Dance**, **music** and **opera** are also superbly catered for: again the big mainstream events are extremely expensive; smaller ones are often equally as interesting as well as far cheaper. As for **cinema**, New York gets the first-run of most American films and many foreign ones – you can see movies here long before they reach Europe, and although queues can be long, prices can be cheaper than in London.

What's on listings can be found in a number of places. Perhaps the most useful source, clear and comprehensive, is *New York Magazine*, though the *Village Voice* is better for things downtown and anything vaguely "alternative". The Sunday *New York Times Weekly Guide* is also good, especially for mainstream events: the paper's *Weekend* section, on Fridays, lists "ticket availability" of the major shows not sold out for the weekend. *Critics' Choice*, a glossy, free magazine also

published by the *New York Times*, lists recent film and theatre openings, previews, Broadway and Off-Broadway productions and performance art in its *Arts and Leisure Guide*. Pick it up at any of the more expensive hotels or from the distributors outside Grand Central. Specific Broadway listings can be found in the free *Official Broadway Theatre Guide*, available from theatre and hotel lobbies or the New York Convention and Visitors' Bureau (see "Information, Maps and Tours" in *Basics*.

Theatre

New York is one of the great **theatre** centres of the world. You can find just about any kind of production here, from lavish, over-the-top musicals to experimental productions in converted garages: the variety is endless. But it's not cheap. Indeed, the big-budget Broadway blockbusters seem to be pricing themselves out of existence – with prices steadily spiralling and audience levels dropping, theatreland is in trouble. The good news for Broadway, though, is that the stars are temporarily leaving Hollywood to do some "serious" work on the East Coast. Jessica Lange, Alec Baldwin and Al Pacino have all recently trod the Great White Way, bringing in a few more bums on seats and showing that audiences will go for big names rather than fresh writing talent. What follows is a guide to where to find the various types of production –

and how to avoid paying the earth for them.

Venues in the city are referred to as **Broadway**, **Off-Broadway**, or **Off-Off-Broadway**, groupings which represent a descending order of ticket price, production polish, elegance and comfort (but don't necessarily have much to do with the address). They also represent an ascending order of innovation, experimentation, and theatre for the sake of art rather than cash. **Broadway** offerings consist primarily of large-scale musicals, comedies and dramas with big-name actors, with the occasional classic and one-person show. **Off-Broadway** theatres also tend to provide polished production qualities, but combine them with a greater willingness to experiment. It's in Off-Broadway you'll find social and political drama, satire, ethnic plays and repertory: in short, anything that Broadway wouldn't consider a surefire money-spinner. Lower operating costs also mean that Off-Broadway often serves as a forum to try out what sometimes ends up as big Broadway productions. **Off-Off Broadway** is the fringe – drama on a shoestring, sometimes on subjects other theatres find too sensitive or not profitable enough to mount. Unlike Off-Broadway, Off-Off doesn't have to use professional actors.

For the record, it's the size of the theatre that technically determines the category it falls into: under 100 seats and a theatre is Off-Off; 100 to 500 and it's Off. Most Broadway theatres are located in the blocks just east or west of Broadway between 40th and 52nd streets; Off and Off-Off-Broadway theatres are sprinkled throughout Manhattan, with a concentration in the east and west Villages, Chelsea, and several in the 40s and 50s west of the Broadway theatre district.

Tickets

Nowhere are regular **tickets** cheap on Broadway – a couple of orchestra seats for something like *Les Miserables* will set you back a cool $100. Off-Broadway prices have risen recently too, to as much as $40 in some cases, though most seats remain cheaper than anything you'll find

along the Great White Way: in general, expect to pay upwards of $15 Off-Broadway and $10 Off-Off. If you know where and how to look, even these prices can be cut considerably. Basically there are two straightforward and well-practised methods of **cutting costs**, the first of which requires a little patience.

• Queue up on the day of the performance at the **TKTS booth** at Times Square, where at least one pair of tickets for every performance of every Broadway and Off-Broadway show is available at half price (plus a $2.50 ticket service charge – altogether around $15–20). There's a single queue for all shows, and the most popular sell out soonest: get here early if you're after the hit of the month. TKTS hours are Monday to Saturday 3 to 8pm, 10am to 2pm for Wednesday and Saturday matinees, and for all Sunday performances from noon until closing (7pm or so), but the booth opens as early as 10.30am if a long line forms; on Sunday, matinee and evening performance tickets are on sale from noon until they run out. There's another TKTS booth in the lobby of 2 World Trade Center (useful to know if it's raining, and even more useful in that certain matinee tickets are sold here on the day *before* the performance) and one at Court and Montague streets near Borough Hall in Brooklyn (Tues–Fri 11am–5.30pm, Sat 11am-3.30pm), closed on Mondays but reputedly with the shortest queues of all, and which also sells tickets for matinees the following day on Tuesdays, Fridays and Saturdays. All three booths take cash or traveller's cheques only; best days for availability and short queues are Tuesday, Wednesday and Thursday.

• Look for **twofer discount coupons** in either of the New York Convention and Visitors' bureaux and many shops, banks, restaurants and hotel lobbies. These entitle two people to a hefty discount (though the days when they really offered two-for-the-price-of-one are long gone) and unlike TKTS it's possible to book ahead, though don't expect to find coupons for the latest shows. If you can't find a coupon for the production you want, the *Hit Show Club*

The
Performing
Arts and
Film

The Performing Arts and Film

(630 Ninth Ave, NY 10036) will send a pair of discount slips for every Broadway show going on receipt of a stamped addressed envelope – useful if you're around for any length of time.

• If you're prepared to pay **full price** you can, of course, go directly to the theatre, but rather easier *Tickets Central*, 406 West 42nd St (☎279-4200), sell tickets for fifty Off and Off-Off-Broadway theatres from 1 to 8pm daily: expect to pay upwards of $15 Off-Broadway, $6 Off-Off. Finally, if queuing for tickets is below your dignity and your credit rating, *Ticketron* (☎1-800/ SOLD OUT) will book seats for those with credit cards; they will fax a seating chart to your hotel and deliver your tickets overnight. A charge of $2.50 is added to the top-whack ticket price you'll pay.

Off-Off Broadway and repertory

American Jewish Theater, 307 W 26th St ☎633-9797. Classical and contemporary plays in English on Jewish themes.

American Place Theater, 111 W 46th St ☎840-2960. New works by living Americans.

Astor Place Theater, 434 Lafayette St ☎254-4370. Showcase for some exciting work since the 1960s, when Sam Shepard's *The Unseen Hand* and *Forensic and the Navigators* had the playwright on drums in the lobby. The current long-running show *Tubes by the* Blue Man Group is one of the best things on stage at the time of writing.

Circle In The Square Uptown, 1633 Broadway ☎307-2700. Classics and "potential classics".

Circle Repertory Company, 99 Seventh Ave South ☎924-7100. Contemporary: has premiered many award winners.

Dixon Place, 258 Bowery between Prince and Houston ☎219-3088. Small venue dedicated to experimental theatre and works in progress.

Jean Cocteau Repertory, Bouwerie Lane Theater, 330 Bowery ☎677-0060. Aims at "dramatic poem" production style. Genet, Sophocles, Shaw, Strindberg, Sartre, Wilde, Williams, etc, along with unknowns.

Hudson Guild Theater, 441 W 26th St ☎760-9800. Introduces new American and European playwrights.

The Kitchen, 519 W 19th St between Tenth and Eleventh aves ☎255-5793. Well-established venue for avant-garde performance art, theatre and music.

Steve McGraw's, 158 W 72nd St ☎595-7400. Cabaret satire and spoofs of Broadway hits.

Negro Ensemble Company, 155 W 46th St ☎575-5860. Plays about the black experience.

New Federal Theater, Henry Street Settlement, 466 Grand St ☎598-0400. Outlet for minority playwrights, performers and production staff. Has premiered some award winners.

The Public Theater, 425 Lafayette St ☎598-7100. Year-round, six performing areas stage new American plays and accommodate visiting artists and companies. In summer the **Shakespeare Festival** takes off at the open-air Delacorte Theater in Central Park (☎861-7277). Performances are free but come early for the best places.

Ontological-Hysteric Theater Company at St Marks in the Bowery ☎533-4650. Avant-garde/destructionist productions.

Playwrights Horizons, 416 W 42nd St ☎279-4200 and 564-1235. New works and new writers. Originated the controversial "Sister Mary Ignatius Explains It All to You", as well as "Sunday In The Park With George".

Theater For the New City, 155 First Ave ☎254-1109. Known for following the development of new playwrights and presenting integration of dance, music, and poetry with drama.

West Side Repertory, 407 W 43rd St ☎315-2244. Small basement theatre that puts on four productions a year: Shaw, Wilde, Pirandello. Professional producer-director; performers and staff are pros and talented amateurs.

The Wooster Group (Performing Garage), 33 Wooster St ☎966-3651. Experimental/multimedia/abstract.

WPA Theater, 519 W 23rd St ☎206-0523 and ☎691-2274. Neglected American classics and American Realist plays, acted in a style described as "derived from Stanislavski".

Off-Broadway

Worth checking out for interesting productions are:

American Theater of Actors, 314 W 54th St ☎581-3044.

Vivian Beaumont Theater, Lincoln Center, 150 W 65th ☎239-6200.

Cherry Lane Theater, 38 Commerce St ☎989-2020.

Chicago City Limits Improvisational Theater, 351 E 74th St ☎772-8707.

Circle Repertory, 99 Seventh Ave South at Sheridan Square ☎924-7100.

Douglas Fairbanks Theater, 432 W 42nd St ☎532-8038.

Jan Hus Theater Company, 351 E 74th St ☎288-6743.

La Mama Experimental Theater Club, 74A E 4th St ☎475-7710.

Lucille Lortel Theater, 121 Christopher St ☎924-8782.

Manhattan Theater Club, 131 W 55th St ☎581-1212.

Minetta Lane, 18 Minetta Lane between Bleeker and W 3rd sts ☎420-8000.

Off Center Theater, no permanent location ☎768-3277.

Orpheum Theater, 126 Second Ave ☎477-2477.

Promenade Theater, 216 Broadway ☎580-1313.

Provincetown Playhouse, 133 Macdougal St ☎477-5048.

Ridiculous Theater Company, 1 Sheridan Square ☎691-2271.

Roundabout Theater Company, 1530 Broadway at 45th St ☎869-8400.

Samuel Beckett Theater, 410 W 42nd St ☎594-2826.

Second Stage Theater, 2162 Broadway ☎787-8302.

SoHo Repertory Company, 46 Walker St ☎941-1949.

St Clements Theater, 423 W 46th St ☎246-7277.

Theater at St Peter's Church, Lexington Ave and 54th St ☎935-2200.

Theater East, 211 E 60th ☎838-9090.

13th St Theater, 50 W 13th St ☎675-6677.

Westbeth Theater Center, 151 Bank St ☎691-2272.

Dance

New York has five major ballet companies, dozens of modern troupes and untold thousands of soloists. You would have to be very particular indeed in your tastes not to find something of interest. Events are listed in broadly the same places as for music and theatre − if this is your particular interest, though, you might want also to pick up *Dance Magazine*. Half-price tickets, on a day-to-day basis only, are available from **The Music & Dance Booth** in Bryant Park (42nd St between Fifth and Sixth avenues). This is open Tuesday to Sunday noon to 3pm and 4pm to 7pm; call ☎382-2323 for details of ticket availability. The **dance season** runs from September to January, and April to June.

Venues and companies

American Ballet Theater, 890 Broadway ☎477-3030. Formerly under the direction of Mikhail Baryshnikov, the ABT is big, glamorous and the epitome of the standard idea of ballet. The company has its studios and offices downtown near Union Square but performs at the Metropolitan Opera House (in Lincoln Center) from early May into July. Dogged by financial and leadership problems in recent years, (in 1992 the company had a $5.7 million debt and had gone through three artistic directors in four years), the ABT is slowly pulling through. Under artistic director Kevin McKenzie the company has found firm ground again with strong individual performances from the likes of Julio Bocca, Julie Kent, Elizabeth Ferrell, Jeremy Collins and the young Paloma Herrera, and has reportedly paid back $2 million of bank debts and raised $1 million toward a new "Nutcracker".

The Performing Arts and Film

The Performing Arts and Film

Brooklyn Academy of Music, 30 Lafayette St, Brooklyn ☎718/636-4100. Universally known as BAM, this is America's oldest performing arts academy and one of the busiest and most daring producers in New York. In the autumn, BAM's *Next Wave* festival showcases the hottest international attractions in avant-garde dance and music; in winter visiting artists appear, and each spring there's a *Festival of Black Dance* – everything from ethnic authenticity to tap and body-popping. A great venue and one definitely worth crossing the river for.

City Center, 131 W 55th St ☎581-1212 and ☎581-7907. Rivalling Radio City Music Hall for tinges of exotic kitsch, five resident dance troupes hold seasons here from two weeks to a month. Companies include modern ensembles led by America's two undisputed choreographic giants, the *Merce Cunningham Dance Company* and the *Paul Taylor Dance Company*. Also here are the *Alvin Ailey American Dance Theater* (glossy contemporary pizzazz with an emphasis on black dance), the *Joffrey* and *Dance Theater of Harlem* (see below), and occasionally the *Martha Graham Dance Company*. What's left of the year is devoted to a mix of visiting artists from the USA and abroad.

The Cunningham Studio, 11th floor, Westbeth, 463 West St ☎691-9751. The home of the *Merce Cunningham Dance Company*, this rooftop studio is used as an evening performance space by young choreographers. The night-time views of the Manhattan skyline provide a stunning backdrop to performances.

Dance Theater of Harlem. The mostly black ensemble founded in 1971 has rapidly developed into a company of major standing. They perform annually at *City Center* (see above) and at the *New York State Theater* at Lincoln Center (☎870-5570) in a mixed repertory that includes many classics along with short works devised specifically for their own company. The ensemble are based at 247 W 30th St, and for one day each month keep an open house (admission $5; ☎967-3470 for details).

Dance Theater Workshop, down the block and around the corner from the *Joyce* at 219 W 19th St ☎924-0077. Alternative dance is king at DTW, with varied programmes featuring the broadest range of the newest and brightest. The small space is located on the second floor of a former warehouse, has an unintimidating relaxed atmosphere, low ticket prices and performances virtually every night of the year.

Dancespace Project, St Mark's-in-the-Bowery Church, 10th St and Second Ave ☎674-8194. Experimental contemporary dance with a season running from September to June, in a beautiful performance space.

Emanu-El Midtown YM/YWHA, 344 E 14th St ☎674-7200. Has been presenting dance for decades. The facility is actually a gymnasium and can be stifling on even moderate days. Still, the range of talents seen here (and the budget-priced admission) make it a space to know about.

The Joffrey Ballet, at the *City Center* (see above). Famed for its interpretations of twentieth-century classics and contemporary works by the likes of Twyla Tharp and resident choreographer Gerald Arpino, the *Joffrey* divides its time between New York and Los Angeles.

The Joyce Theater, 175 Eighth Ave ☎242-0800. Probably the most important middle-sized dance space in Manhattan, the *Joyce* has the *Eliot Feld Ballet* in residence plus short seasons of other top-notch companies.

New York City Ballet. Performs for six months of the year at Lincoln Center's *New York State Theater* (see opposite) and is considered by many to be the greatest dance company in existence.

PS 122, 150 First Ave at 9th St ☎228-4249. A converted school in the East Village: tends to the radical and the new, with dance bordering on performance art.

Riverside Church. This has a small theatre in its complex on Riverside Drive at 122nd St ☎864-2929. The annual *Riverside Dance Festival* (phone for dates) presents both ethnic and traditional modern dance.

Classical music and opera

New Yorkers take serious music seriously. Long queues form for anything popular, many concerts sell out, and summer evenings can see a quarter of a million people turning up in Central Park for free performances by the New York Philharmonic. The range of what's on offer is wide, but it's big names at big venues that pull the crowds, leaving you with a good number of easily attended selections. **Tickets** for these are available half price (on the day) from the *Music & Dance Booth* in Bryant Park (see p.301 for details).

Opera venues

The **Lincoln Center** (Broadway at 64th St; see Chapter 4, *Upper Manhattan*), New York's powerhouse of highbrow art, very much dominates the city's operatic scene. Its star turn is **The Metropolitan Opera House**, usually known as "The Met" (box office Mon–Fri 10am–8pm, Sun noon–6pm; ☎362-6000), with the *Metropolitan Opera Company* playing from September to late April and the *American Ballet Theater* (see "Dance") taking over in the spring. Tickets are outrageously expensive and difficult to get hold of, and while last-

minute cancellations and standing-room tickets *can* be picked up from the box office, a line is likely to form the night before if the performance is a popular one. A much better option, still in the Lincoln Center, is **The New York State Theater** (box office Mon 10am–7.30pm, Tue–Sat 10am–8.30pm, Sun 11.30am–7.30pm; ☎870-5770) where Beverley Sills' *New York City Opera* plays David to the Met's Goliath. Its wide and adventurous programme varies wildly in quality – sometimes startlingly innovative, occasionally failing totally. Seats go for less than half the Met's prices, and standing room tickets are available if a performance sells out. Occasionally the students of the **Juilliard School** (☎799-5000) take on opera productions under the control of a famous conductor, usually for low ticket prices.

Away from Lincoln Center productions come on a smaller scale with ticket prices to match. Quality will vary wildly from production to production, but companies are all pretty good and, importantly, often schedule works which are neglected in the Met's roster of familiar "top-of-the-charts" classics.

The Performing Arts and Film

Free summer concerts

In the light of high concert ticket prices, it's surprising that so many events in the city, especially in summer, are **free**. The *Summerstage Festival* in **Central Park** puts on an impressive range of free concerts, performances and readings every Wednesday to Sunday throughout July, and on weekends in the last half of June and the first half of August. Performances take place at Rumsey Playfield (by the 72nd St and Fifth Ave entrance). Pick up a calendar of events from *Tower Records* (4th St and Broadway) or look in the *Village Voice* or *New York Press* for details. Recent performers have included Los Lobos, Patti Smith, Joan Baez, Thomas Mapfumo and the New York Grand Opera. Central Park is also the venue for huge free concerts – such as those by

Simon and Garfunkel and Pavarotti – and the almost equally popular performances by the New York Philharmonic. Check the *New York Times'* "Arts and Leisure Guide" for news and details. Downtown, the **World Financial Center's** Winter Garden and outdoor Plaza are venue for free concerts – encompassing jazz, ballet and orchestral works as well as World Music. Performances take place at lunchtimes and evenings from late June to early September (☎945-0505 for details). On July and August weekends the **Prospect Park Bandshell** is venue for the *Celebrate Brooklyn* festival (☎718/768-0699); recent attractions have included artists as diverse as Hugh Masakela, the Piccolo Teatro dell' Opera performing *Otello*, and the Brooklyn Gospel Festival.

The
Performing
Arts and
Film

Amato Opera Theater, 319 Bowery
☎228-8200. This downtown group
presents an ambitious and varied repertory of classics. Singers, designers and
conductors are young professionals on
the way up. Weekends only.

Concert halls

The Avery Fisher Hall, in Lincoln Center
☎875-5030. Permanent home of the
New York Philharmonic under Zubin
Mehta, and temporary one to visiting
orchestras and soloists. Ticket prices for
the Philharmonic range from $12 to $50.
An often fascinating bargain are the **NYP
open rehearsals** at 9.45am on concert
days. Tickets for these, non-reservable,
cost just $6.

The Alice Tully Hall ☎875-5050; for tickets call *Centercharge* ☎721-6500 Mon–
Sat 10am–8pm, Sun noon–8pm, also in
Lincoln Center, is a smaller venue for
chamber orchestras, string quartets and
instrumentalists. Prices similar to those in
the Avery Fisher Hall.

Brooklyn Academy of Music, 30 Lafayette
St, Brooklyn ☎718/636-4100. See
"Dance".

Bargemusic, Fulton Ferry Landing,
Brooklyn ☎718/624-4061. Chamber
music at 7.30pm on Thursday ($20), 4pm
Sunday ($23); students $15 either day.

Carnegie Hall, 154 W 57th St ☎247-
7800. The greatest names from all
schools of music performed here in the
past, from Tchaikovsky and Toscanini to
Gershwin and Billie Holiday. The acoustics
remain superb, and a patching-up operation is under way to amend years of
structural neglect and restore the place to
former glories. Expect music of just about
any sort, and low to moderate prices.

Kaufman Concert Hall, in the 92nd Street
Y at Lexington Avenue ☎996-1100.

Lehman Center for the Performing Arts,
Bedford Park Boulevard, the Bronx
☎718/960-8232. First-class concert hall
drawing the world's top performers.

Merkin Concert Hall, Abraham Goodman
House, 129 W 67th St ☎362-8719.

Town Hall, 123 W 43rd St ☎840-2824.

Cabaret and comedy

Comedy clubs and **cabaret spots** are rife
in New York and often of an extraordinarily high standard. The shows vary from
stand-up comics and improvised comedy
(amazing if you've never been before –
quick-fire wit is part of the city psyche) to
singing waiters and waitresses, many of
whom are professional performers waiting
for their big break. Most clubs have shows
every night, with two at weekends (at
about 8.30pm and 11pm) and charge a
cover ($5 up) and a minimum that works
out about equivalent to a couple of drinks.
Those below are usually worth trying, but
check *New York Magazine* for the fullest
and most up-to-date listings.

Asti, 13 E 12th St ☎741-9105. Actually a
restaurant, though it's not worth coming
here just to eat – or outside a large
group. Live entertainment daily includes
opera stars and singing waiters. A rowdy,
fun night out. No cover.

The Ballroom, 253 W 28th St ☎244-
3005. One of the largest stages around,
with some of the city's most ambitious
singers and comedians. Cover $15–25,
two-drink minimum. The bar and dining
area also double as New York's best
tapas bar; see Chapter 8, *Drinking and
Eating*, for details.

Brandy's Piano Bar, 235 E 84th St
☎650-1944. Small, neighbourhood bar
featuring bar staff and waitresses who
sing popular Broadway show hits as well
as old theme tunes from TV shows like
Mary Tyler Moore, even the Flintstones.
No cover charge, though there's a two-
drink minimum charge at the tables.

Cafe Wha ? Comedy Cellar, 115
MacDougal St ☎254-3630. Music
upstairs, comedy below ground in this
popular club that opens nightly. Saturday
shows usually present seven or eight acts.
$10 plus $5 minimum food and drinks.

Caroline's Comedy Club, 1626 Broadway
at 49th St ☎757-4100. Moved from its
old location at the Seaport, *Caroline's* still
books some of the best acts in town. $2–
$17.50 cover during the week, $5 or
$17.50 at weekends, plus two-drink
minimum.

Catch a Rising Star, 1487 First Ave ☎794-1906. New talent showcase running twice nightly, three times on Saturday. Alumni include Pat Benatar. Cover varies from $6 to $12; two-drink minimum.

Chicago City Limits, 351 E 74th St ☎772-8707. Improvisation club playing one show nightly, two at weekends. 8.30pm and 10.30pm. Ticket price $10/$15/$20.

Coldwater Gladys' Comedy Room Upstairs, 988 Second Ave near 52nd St ☎888-2122. Gladys Simon presents various comics at 9.30pm on Thurs, Fri and Sat. $8 plus a $7 minimum food/drink charge.

Comedy Cellar, 117 Macdougal St ☎254-3630. Comedy club with nightly shows and two or three at weekends. Cover around $10.

Comic Strip, 1568 Second Ave ☎861-9386. Famed showcase for stand-up comics and young singers going for the big time. Cover $8–12. Phone for performance times.

Dangerfield's, 1118 First Ave ☎593-1650. New talent showcase run by the established comedian Rodney Dangerfield. Cover $12–15, no minimum drinks charge.

Don't Tell Mama, 343 W 46th St ☎757-0788. Lively, convivial piano bar and cabaret featuring rising stars. Shows at 8pm and 10pm. Cover $6–15, two-drink minimum.

Duplex, 61 Christopher St ☎255-5438. Village cabaret popular with gays; it was here too that Joan Rivers was discovered. Two shows a night at 8pm and 10pm (Friday and Saturday 10pm and midnight), mainly comedy, previewing yet more up-and-coming New York talent. Cover $12, two-drink minimum. The rowdy piano bar downstairs is worth catching.

Eighty Eight's, 228 W 10th St ☎924-0088. New addition to the local cabaret scene, owned by comedians and entertainers who have been playing the circuit for years. Cabaret upstairs, piano bar down; cover $10–15. Friday and Saturday are the best nights.

5 and 10 No Exaggeration, 77 Greene St between Spring and Broome ☎925-7414. An antiques shop and bar in front; a cabaret and supper club in the back.

Flannery's, 205 W 14th St ☎929-9589. Thursday open mike, sign up at 5.30pm for 6.30 show.

Improvisation, 358 W 44th St ☎765-8268. Nightly new comic and singing talent – most, as the name suggests, improvised. Cover $11. Shows at 9pm during the week; two shows on Friday, three on Saturday.

Lost Footage, National Improv Theater, 233 Eighth Ave ☎243-7224. Improvisational comedy, usually Thursdays and Fridays, but phone to check (and reserve). $12, students $6.

NY Comedy Club, 915 Second Ave ☎714-8275. Major New York club with shows daily (two at weekends). $10 and two-drink minimum.

Stand Up New York, 236 W 78th St ☎595-0850. Upper West Side club that's not so much a showcase as a forum for established acts. Nightly shows, two sometimes three at weekends. Weekdays $7 cover plus two-drink minimum, Fri and Sat $12.

Stone Street Café, 6 Stone St ☎425-1700. Top acts from NYC and LA. $7.

The Performing Arts and Film

Film

New Yorkers treat **film** with an enthusiasm which borders on obsession: people queue hours to see obscure foreign movies; being literate in movie trivia is taken as a sure sign of cultured sophistication; and revival cinemas do brisk business. Talk to a New Yorker and sooner or later the conversation will get around to their favourite line from a favourite scene of a favourite movie. Fortunately it's not difficult to get wise to the flavour of the month, since the city catches the **latest releases** way before London. If you want to be ahead of the crowds back home, flip though any newspaper (most critically Georgia Brown, J. Hoberman and Manohla Dargis in the *Village Voice* or Anthony Lane in the *New*

The Performing Arts and Film

Yorker) for details of which film is showing where, and be warned that for the newest movies you'll need to queue up to an hour just to buy your ticket, usually some time before the film starts. Be sure you're in the right queue for the showing you want, and expect to pay around $7.

If you're here mid-September to early October the **New York Film Festival** at the Alice Tully Hall, Lincoln Center, is well worth catching: a showcase of serious cinema from around the world. Otherwise there are far fewer specialist movie theatres than you might expect, though at those which do exist the choice is good. Bills change daily, so you'll need a keen eye to spot a favourite from what's on offer. The following regularly feature **revival and art movies**.

Angelika Film Center, corner of Houston and Mercer sts ☎ 995-2000. Shows the latest non-Hollywood offerings, including European art house movies. The air-conditioned coffee shop is a good place to meet.

Anthology Film Archives, 32–34 Second Ave ☎ 505-5181. Shows many films you thought you'd never have the chance to see again.

Biograph, 225 W 57th St ☎ 582-4582. Revival house featuring all your favourite movie classics.

Cinema Village, 22 E 12th St ☎ 924-3363. Modern films (1950 onwards) are the standard bill here, plus the occasional festival.

Eighth Street Playhouse, 52 W 8th St ☎ 674-6515. Shows the *Rocky Horror Picture Show* Fridays and Saturdays at midnight, with cast performing in front of the screen and full participation by the audience. A hoot.

Film Forum, 209 West Houston, near Varick St ☎ 727-8110. Selection of independent American and foreign films along with lesser known works by big-name film makers.

Gramercy, 127 E 23rd St ☎ 475-1660. A good selection of classic art house movies.

The Museum of Modern Art, 11 W 53rd St ☎ 708-9490. Two new theatres devoted to a vast array of classic films. Archival material is available in MoMA's film library.

Museum of the Moving Image, 35th Ave and 36th St, Queens ☎ 718/784-0077. Foreign and avant-garde films.

Theatre 80 St Marks, 80 St Mark's Place ☎ 254-7400. Also schedules classics. Don't miss the mini-Grauman's Chinese Theater collection of star footprints and autographs in the pavement outside.

Walter Reade Theater, 65th St between Broadway and Amsterdam ☎ 875-5600. Rapid turnover of classic and rarely seen films.

Chapter 11

Sport and Outdoor Activities

Sport in America is big business, which is to say that for all spectator sports financial considerations come first. The Brooklyn Dodgers, New York's official baseball team, upped and left (for LA) as long ago as 1957, and every other professional team intermittently threatens to do the same. Yet New Yorkers are themselves highly sports-conscious: the city's newspapers devote a great many pages to the subject, as do the TV stations, which cover most of the regular season games and all of the post-season matches in the big four American team sports – **football**, **baseball**, **basketball** and **ice hockey** (known simply as hockey). If you want to watch a game, bear in mind that tickets can be hard to come by and don't come that cheap. Remember, also, that bars – like, for example, the *McCann* chain – are a good alternative to actually being there, especially those (often known as sports bars) with a special king-size screen.

Participation sport isn't cheap either – unless you're prepared to **swim** (either at the local pools or the borough beaches) or **jog**, still one of the city's main obsessions. If you fancy a game of soccer there are generally lots of pick-up games on the Great Lawn in Central Park on summer Sundays. Other participatory sports, and all **fitness** fads, cost a lot of money, and many New Yorkers are members of private health clubs in order to cut costs. For anyone interested, these places fill sizeable sections of the city's Yellow Pages.

Watching

In this section we've included details of each of the main **spectator sports** in New York – including a run-through of the rules, where necessary – followed by a section detailing the venues and ticket prices.

Baseball

Baseball is America's game. No other sport generates as much interest in the US over the whole season, and nothing else compares with the tradition and mystique that surround this still essentially parochial and small-town game (see overleaf).

American football

If you're a foreign visitor and haven't seen an **American football** game before you arrive in New York you won't have long to wait. All big matches feature on TV and they're a major slot in most neighbourhood bars. For the uninitiated, the spectacle of all-American razzmatazz is probably novelty enough, though the game does get more interesting if you can pick up at least some of the rules (see box).

The **season** stretches from September to the end of December, when the playoffs take place to decide who goes to the

SPORT AND OUTDOOR ACTIVITIES

307

Sport and Outdoor Activities

The game of baseball: an explanation for foreign visitors

As with cricket, baseball has a complex set of rules that only a true aficionado completely understands. Games are played (162 each season) all over the US close on every day from April until September, with the season culminating in the modestly titled World Series in October – the final best-of-seven play-off between the champions of the two leagues, the National and the American. Watching a game, even if you don't understand what's going on, can at least be a pleasant day out, drinking beer and eating hot dogs in the sun: tickets are not too expensive and the crowds usually friendly and sociable.

New York has two baseball teams, the **Yankees** and the **Mets**. The Yankees, who play at Yankee Stadium in the Bronx, are the oldest side (alumni include Joe di Maggio and Babe Ruth), but they have experienced something of a decline over recent years, their place at the top usurped by the Mets – a relatively young team, launched in 1962 to compensate for the loss of the Brooklyn Dodgers. They play at Shea Stadium in Flushing, Queens, and last won the World Series back in 1986. **Tickets** for both venues are around $10, though *bleacher* seats – on the unshaded area behind the home run, and site of the most raucous scenes and high-volume beer consumption – are about half that.

The rules

The basic set-up looks like the English game of rounders, with four **bases** set at the corners of a 90-foot square **diamond**; at the bottom corner the base is called **home plate** and serves much the same purpose as do the stumps in cricket. Play begins when the **pitcher**, standing on a low **pitcher's mound** in the middle of the diamond, throws a ball at upwards

of 100 mph, making it curve and bend as it travels towards the **catcher**, who crouches behind home plate; seven other defensive players take up **positions**, one at each base and the others spread out around the field of play. A **batter** from the opposing team stands beside home plate and tries to hit the ball with a tapered, cylindrical wooden bat. If the batter swings and misses, or if the pitched ball crosses the plate above the batter's knees and below his chest, it counts as a **strike**; if he doesn't swing and the ball passes outside of this **strike zone**, it counts as a **ball**. If the batter gets **three strikes** against him he is **out**; **four balls** and he gets a free **walk**, and takes his place as a **runner** on first base.

If he succeeds in hitting the pitched ball into **fair territory**, the wedge between the first and third bases, the batter runs towards first base; if the opposing players catch the ball before it hits the ground, the batter is **out**. Otherwise they field the ball and attempt to relay it to first base before the batter gets there; if they do he is **out**, if they don't the batter is **safe** – and stays there, being moved along by subsequent batters until he makes a complete circuit of the bases and scores a **run**. The most exciting moment is the **home run**, when a batter hits the ball over the outfield fences, a boundary 400 feet away from home plate; he and any runners on base when he hits the ball each score a run. If there are runners on all three bases it's a **grand slam**, and earns four runs.

Games take up to three hours to play and each side – made up of nine players – bats through nine innings; each side gets **three outs** per **inning**. Games are normally held at night. There are no tied games; the teams play **extra innings** until one side pulls ahead and wins.

Superbowl – America's version of the FA Cup final, played on the third Sunday of January. New York's teams are the **NY Jets** and the **NY Giants**, both of whom

play at the Meadowlands Sports Complex in New Jersey. On recent form, there is no contest between the two teams: the Giants are the 1991 Superbowl champi-

The rules of American football

Basically, American football is like rugby. The aim is to reach the end zone with the ball and score a **touchdown** (though players don't actually have to place the ball on the ground). The action is organised into a series of **plays** and each time the player with the ball is tackled to the ground or the ball goes off the pitch, that play is concluded. Only one forward pass per play is allowed – a climax with the players allowed to stop, block or push over their opponents even if they're not in possession of the ball.

The other main unit of the game is a **down**, an attempt to move the ball forward two lines (ten yards) of the pitch. A team gets four attempts to achieve a down – then another four if they succeed. If they fail, possession of the ball goes to the opposing team. In the rambling mysteries of the commentary "second and 4" means the game is

on the second down and four more yards are needed. If it seems unlikely that the offensive team will get the yards required (eg at "fourth and 9") a **kicker** will attempt to secure a **field goal** by beating the ball between the posts; if the ball is far from the opposition's goal a **punter** comes on to drop kick the ball as far down the field as possible. The opposing team will then take possession and try to run back up the field before being stopped by tackles.

The game lasts for one hour of play, divided into four **quarters** with a break after the second quarter. However the clock only runs when the game is in progress, which means that it can run for three hours or more – more than enough time to master the complexities if you're prepared to sit back and listen, since on TV every moment is analysed and re-analysed ad nauseam.

Sport and
Outdoor
Activities

---

ons; the Jets haven't won anything in years. The cheapest tickets can be tough to get. If you don't manage to get any, don't worry too much: at least two games are shown on TV every Sunday afternoon, with another on Monday night during the regular season.

Basketball

Basketball is perhaps the most popular American game to be played outside the US; it's also by far the most athletic of American team sports, and the most graceful to watch. Played over an hour, the game is non-stop action conducted at a blistering pace. Until the 1950s the sport was all-white: in the last thirty years or so, however, it has been dominated by a succession of black athletes – Dr J, "Magic" Johnson, Kareem Abdul Jabbar, and, currently, Michael Jordan, all of whom have proved big crowd-pullers across the country.

The basketball season begins in October and runs until the first week of July, when the championships take place. The two New York professional teams are

the **NY Knickerbockers** (Knicks), who play at Madison Square Garden, and the **Nets**, whose venue is the Meadowlands Sports Complex in New Jersey. Tickets are scarce and as a result expensive: for a popular game you might have to pay upwards of $50 to an agency. College basketball is also hugely popular, and worth watching if you can catch it on TV. The college season culminates in the divisional play-offs and final in the first two weeks of March – aptly titled "March Madness".

Ice hockey

To someone who isn't familiar with the game, **hockey**, as it is called in the US, might seem a very odd excuse for getting a bunch of guys to beat the hell out of each other for the benefit of the paying public. However, this would be a serious misrepresentation of one of the country's best-loved – and patronised – games. It is a violent sport, certainly, and some players are without doubt chosen mainly for their punching ability. But there's a fair amount of skill involved too, even if it does take some watching to work out

Sport and Outdoor Activities

where the puck is – the speed the action takes place at is, without question, phenomenal. The two New York teams are the Rangers, who play at Madison Square Garden, and the less purely New York Islanders, whose venue is out at the Nassau Coliseum on Long Island. There's also a local New Jersey side, the Devils, who play at Meadowlands.

Tennis

The **American Open Championships**, held in Queens each September at the National Tennis Center, Flushing Meadows (☎718/592-8000), is the top tennis event of the year. The Flushing complex is perhaps most renowned for the at times excruciating noise of jets taking off and landing at nearby La Guardia Airport, although this is set to be less of a problem in years to come since Mayor Dinkins, an avowed tennis fan, has ordered the planes to be rerouted during the championships. Ticket prices for the big matches are, however, astronomical and you need to book them well in advance. Madison Square Garden also boasts annual international tennis matches in the form of the Virginia Slims Tournament, held each year at the end of November.

Soccer

Thanks mainly to the South and Latin American communities of Queens, and the Italian areas of the Outer Boroughs and New Jersey, **soccer** is enormously popular in New York. However, apart from the occasional British game shown on the sports cable channels, most of the soccer shown on TV is confined to the Spanish-language stations – usually every Sunday on channels 31 and 41. No professional soccer is actually played in the New York area, though if you're desperate to see a game, decent quality college matches are played out at Rutgers University in New Jersey.

Plans have been made for New York to be one of the host cities of the 1994 World Cup, but it seems likely that games will actually be played in New Haven, Connecticut.

Cricket

Bizarre though it may seem, there is a thriving and long-established **cricket** community in the New York area, dating back to the late nineteenth century and the formation of the Staten Island Cricket Club – where, on summer Sunday afternoons, the sound of leather upon willow can still be enjoyed. Likewise Van Cortlandt Park in the Bronx is the weekly setting for the New York Cricket League, which is particularly popular with the Indian, Pakistani and West Indian populations here. It is claimed, in fact, that there are around a million cricket players in the US, and American enthusiasts are trying hard to expand the game's popularity: a match in New York in September 1990, when an England XI played the West Indies, drew some 15,000 supporters.

Horse racing

There are two major **race tracks** in the New York area, the **Aqueduct Race Track** ("The Big A") in Rockaway, Queens, and **Belmont**, Long Island – home to the Belmont Stakes, which, along with the Kentucky Derby and Preakness, is one of the big three American races of the year (the "Triple Crown").

Meetings take place at the Aqueduct between January and May, and in June and July. It is possible to get there on a special A train from 42nd St with a ticket that includes grandstand admission. More details on ☎718/330-1234. Belmont can be reached on similar all-inclusive tickets from Penn Station on the Long Island Railroad. Details on ☎516/739-4200. It's open May to June and August to October. The **Meadowlands Complex** also has races from January to August, starting at 8pm in an enclosed stadium.

To **place a bet** anywhere other than the race track itself you'll need to find an **OTB – Off Track Betting** – office. There's one at Grand Central, plus a pamphlet explaining the laws and complications of the American betting system. Otherwise there are plenty of others around the city – see the Yellow Pages for specific addresses. Opening hours are Monday to Friday 9am–5pm, Saturday 9am–3pm.

Wrestling

Wrestling, held regularly at Madison Square Garden, is perhaps the least "sporting" of all the sports you can watch in New York, more of a theatrical event really, with a patriotically charged, almost salivating crowd cheering on all-American superheroes against evil and distinctly un-American foes. Bouts start with a rendition of the "Star-spangled Banner", after which the action – a stagey affair between wrestlers with names like Hulk Hogan and the Red Devil – takes place to a background of jingoistic roars, the true-blue US spirit invariably winning the day. For details of bouts, call Madison Square Garden direct.

Tickets and venues

Tickets for most events can be booked ahead with a credit card, through the *Ticketmaster, Chargit* or *Teletron* numbers, and collected at the gate, though it's cheaper – and of course riskier for popular events – to pick up tickets on the night. If all else fails, try *Mackey's* at 234 W 44th St (☎840-2800), a ticket agency for all sporting events, or simply catch the action on the big screen in a sports bar.

Madison Square Garden Center, W 33rd St and Seventh Ave ☎465-5000; credit card bookings on ☎465-6741 or ☎516/888-9000 or ☎201/507-8900. Subway #1, #2, #3 to 34th Street Penn Station. Box office open Sept–June Mon–Sat 10am–8pm, Sun 11am–7pm.

Meadowlands Sports Complex, off routes 3, 17, and Turnpike exit 16, East Rutherford, New Jersey ☎201/935-3900; credit card bookings on ☎201/507-8900 or ☎307-7171. Regular buses from Port Authority Bus Terminal on 42nd Street and Eighth Avenue. Box office open for all arenas Mon–Sat 10am–6pm, Sun noon–5pm.

Nassau Coliseum, Hempstead Turnpike, Uniondale, New York ☎516/794-9300; credit card bookings on ☎307-7171 or ☎516/888-9000. Long Island Railroad to Hempstead, then bus N70, N71 or N72 from Hempstead bus terminal, one block away. Box office open daily 10.30am–5.45pm.

Sports Bars

Mickey Mantle's, 42 Central Park South ☎688-7777.

Rusty Staub's, 575 Fifth Ave ☎682-1000.

Sporting Club, 99 Hudson St ☎219-0900.

Shea Stadium, 126th Street at Roosevelt Avenue, Queens ☎718/507-8499; credit card bookings on ☎307-7171. Subway #7, direct to Willets Point/Shea Stadium Station. Box office open Mon–Fri 8am–6pm, Sat & Sun 9am–5pm. Dress warmly in autumn and winter as Shea is a windy icebox.

Yankee Stadium, 161st St and River Ave, the Bronx ☎718/293-6000; credit card bookings on ☎307-7171 or ☎516/888-9000; subway C, D or #4 direct to 161st St Station. Huddle in with the crowds when you leave – it's not a nice neighbourhood. Box office open Mon–Fri 9.30am–5pm and during evening games.

Participating

For those energetic enough to try them, the following section details most of the **sports-related activities** possible within the city limits, along with listings of **beaches** for less athletic types.

Jogging

Jogging is still very much number one fitness pursuit: the number of yearly coronaries in Central Park, the most popular venue, probably runs well into double figures. A favourite circuit in the park is around the Receiving Reservoir; just make sure you jog in the right direction – anticlockwise. The East River Promenade and almost any other stretch of open space long enough to get up speed are also well jogged.

If, rather than bust your own guts, you'd prefer to see thousands of others do so, the **New York Marathon** takes place on the first Sunday of November. Two million people turn out each year to watch the 16,000 runners complete the

Sport and Outdoor Activities

Sport and Outdoor Activities

26-mile course, which starts in Staten Island, crosses the Verrazano Narrows Bridge and passes through all the other boroughs before ending up at the *Tavern on the Green* in Central Park. To take part you need to apply for an entry form from the *New York Road Runners Club*, 9 E 89th St ☎860-4455.

Roller and ice-skating . . . and tobogganing

In winter, the freezing weather makes for good **ice-skating**, while in summer **roller-skating** is a popular activity, on the paths in Central Park and specifically the north-west corner of the Sheep Meadow; also at Riverside Park and even the smaller open spaces. **Tobogganing** is another popular winter activity, up on the slopes of Van Cortlandt Park in the Bronx; phone ☎718/543-4595 to see if the snow's thick enough.

Lasker Rink, 110th St, Central Park ☎996-1184. The lesser-known ice rink in Central Park, way up towards the Harlem end. Much cheaper than the Wollman Rink, though less accessible, and the neighbourhood isn't great. Avoid at night. Open Mon–Thurs 10am–9.30pm, Fri & Sat 10am–11pm. Admission $2.50 plus $2 for skate rentals.

Rockefeller Center Ice Rink ☎757-5730. Without doubt the slickest place to skate, though you may have to queue and it's pricier than anywhere else. Open Mon–Thurs 9am–10pm, Fri & Sat 9am–midnight, Sun 9am–10pm. Admission $8 plus $4 for skate rentals.

Skyrink, 450 W 33rd St ☎695-6555. Centrally situated indoor rink, high up a midtown skyscraper. Mon–Thurs 8.30am–10.15pm, Fri–Sat 8am–11pm. Admission $6.50 plus $2.50 for skate rentals.

Wollman Rink, 64th St, Central Park ☎517-4800. Lovely rink, where you can skate to the marvellous, inspiring back-drop of the lower Central Park skyline – incredibly impressive at night. Open Mon 9am–5pm, Tues–Thurs 10am–9.30pm, Fri–Sun 10am–11pm. Admission $5 plus $2.50 for skate rentals.

Pool and snooker

Aside from bars and nightclubs, the new thing to do of an evening in Manhattan is play **pool**, not in dingy halls but in gleam-ing bars where well-heeled yuppies mix with the regulars. **Snooker** fans will also find a few tables.

The Billiard Club, 220 W 19th St ☎206-7665. A pool club with a nice, vaguely European atmosphere and a small bar serving soft drinks and cappuccinos.

Chelsea Billiards, 54 W 21st St ☎989-0096. A casual place with both snooker and pool tables. Refreshments from machines.

Sharkey's Billiards, 10 E 21st St ☎529-8600. More of a bar than a straight pool hall, but fun nonetheless.

Horse riding and carriage rides

Carriage Rides, Central Park South, between Fifth and Sixth Ave. For some, the ideal way to see Central Park, and some carriages are willing – with a little persuasion – to take you further afield. Not cheap, though – around $30 for half an hour – and bear in mind the warning on p.138. Every day, all day, until the late evening.

Claremont Riding Academy, 175 W 89th St ☎724-5100. For riding in Central Park, this place hires out ponies by the hour for $33. Saddles are English-style; lessons $35 per half-hour.

Jamaica Bay Riding Academy, 7000 Shore Parkway, Brooklyn ☎718/531-8949. Trail riding, with western-style saddles, around the eerie landscape of Jamaica Bay. Very much the more atmospheric riding alternative, and a little less expensive than Claremont at $20 for 45 minutes' ride; lessons $40 an hour.

Tenpin bowling

Bowlmor Lanes, 110 University Place ☎255-8188. Long-established and large bowling alley with a bar and shop. Open Sun–Thurs 10–1am, Fri & Sat 10–4am. Price $3 per game per person, plus 75¢ shoe-hire.

Health and fitness: pools, gyms and baths

Carmine St Pool, Clarkson St and Seventh Ave ☎242-5228. You have to be a member to use this pool and gym; it costs $25 if you're over 18, $10 under, but you need to prove you're living in New York, and provide a passport-sized photo. Mon–Fri evenings only.

East 54th St Pool, 342 E 54th St ☎397-3154. Good-sized indoor pool; annual membership just $2. Exercise classes too. Open afternoons and evenings only Mon–Fri, all day until 5pm Sat & Sun.

Sutton Gymnastics and Fitness Center, 20 Cooper Union ☎533-9390. One of the few gyms in New York where you don't have to be a member to use the facilities. Gymnastic and exercise classes for around $20. Open Mon–Fri all day, for adults, and at weekends for kids.

Tenth Street Turkish Baths, 268 E 10th St ☎674-9250. An ancient place, something of a neighbourhood landmark and still going, with steam baths, sauna and pool, as well as exercise rooms, whirlpool, massage, etc. A restaurant too. Admission $15, access to the various facilities extra. Open daily 9am–10pm; men only Sun & Thurs; women only Wed; co-ed Mon, Tues, Fri & Sat.

West 59th St Pool, 533 W 59th St and West End Ave ☎397-3159. Two pools, one indoor and another outdoor. Open Mon–Sat, afternoons and evenings only; admission free.

Boating

Loeb Boathouse, Central Park ☎517-4723. Rowing boats for hire between April and October, daily 9am–6pm. Rates are $10 an hour plus $20 deposit.

Beaches

Few visitors come to New York for the **beaches**, and those New Yorkers with money tend to turn their noses up at the city strands, preferring to move further afield to Long Island, just a couple of hours away and much better. But the city's beaches, though often crowded, *are* a cool summer escape from Manhattan and most are also just a subway token away.

Brooklyn

Coney Island Beach, at the end of half a dozen subway lines: fastest is the D train to Stillwell Avenue. After Rockaway (see below), NYC's most popular bathing spot, jam-packed on summer weekends. The Atlantic here is only moderately dirty and there's a good, reliable onshore breeze.

Brighton Beach, D train to Brighton Beach. Technically the same stretch as Coney, but less crowded and given colour by the local Russian community (pick up ethnic snacks from the boardwalk vendors).

Manhattan Beach, D train to Sheepshead Bay Road, walk to Ocean Avenue and cross the bridge. Small beach much used by locals.

Queens

Rockaway Beach, A and C trains to any stop along the beach. Forget California: this seven-mile strip is where New Yorkers – up to three-quarters of a million daily in summer – come to get the best surf around. Best beaches are at 9th St, 23rd St, and 80–118th sts.

Jacob Riis Park, IRT #2 train to Flatbush Avenue, then Q35 bus. Good sandy stretches, the western ones used almost exclusively by a gay male crowd.

The Bronx

Orchard Beach, subway train #6 local to Pelham Bay Park, then Bx12 bus. Lovingly known as "Horseshit Beach" – and in any case less easy to get to than the rest.

Staten Island

Great Kills Park, bus 103 from Staten Island Ferry Terminal. Quiet and used by locals.

Wolfe's Pond Park, bus 103 to Main Street Tottenville, at Hylan and Cornelia. Packs in the crowds from New Jersey.

Sport and Outdoor Activities

Chapter 12

Parades and Festivals

The other big day-time activities in New York, and often worth timing your visit around, are its **parades** and street **festivals**. The city takes these, especially the **parades**, very seriously. Almost every large ethnic group in the city holds an annual get-together, often using Fifth Avenue as the main drag; the events are often political or religious in origin, though now are just as much an excuse for music, food and dance. Chances are your stay will coincide with at least one: the following list is roughly chronological – for more details and exact dates of parades, phone ☎ 397-8222. As you might expect, New York's **festivals** are concentrated in the spring and summer, tending to tie in with ethnic holidays and religious observances. We've included those that take place in Manhattan: for further details, exact dates and lists of events in other boroughs, phone ☎ 755-4100.

Parades

The big celebration – and undoubtedly New York City's most famous – is the **St Patrick's Day Parade**, held on the weekend nearest March 17. Celebrating an impromptu march through the streets by Irish militiamen on St Patrick's Day 1762, it has become a draw for every Irish band and organisation in the US and Ireland, which in recent years has meant increasing political overtones, with Noraid and Sinn Fein out in full force. Much of the city lines the route up Fifth Avenue from 44th to 86th streets, and general dementia runs especially high in Irish bars – should you

find yourself in one, steer clear of politics. A good vantage point is St Patrick's Cathedral, where the Bishop of New York greets the marching pipes and bands.

The **Greek Independence Day Parade** (March 25) isn't as long or as boozy, more a patriotic nod to the old country from floats of pseudo-classically dressed Hellenes. When Independence Day falls in the Orthodox Lent, the parade is shifted to April or May. It kicks off from Fifth Avenue to 49th Street. Also in April is the **Easter Parade** (Fifth Avenue between 49th and 59th streets), an opportunity for New Yorkers to dress up in outrageous Easter bonnets.

Martin Luther King Jr Memorial Day (May 17) is marked by a procession along Fifth Avenue from 44th to 86th streets to celebrate his work for equal rights for blacks. Of several Puerto Rican celebrations in the city, the largest is the **Puerto Rican Day Parade** (first Sunday of June), three hours of bands and baton twirling from 44th to 86th streets on Fifth Avenue, then across to Third. July 4 sees nationwide celebration of **American Independence Day**, and in New York **Macy's firework display** – visible all over lower Manhattan but best seen from Battery Park from around 9.30pm on. More local shindigs can be found just about everywhere else.

The **Gay Pride March** on the last Sunday in June commemorates the Stonewall riots of 1969 (see Chapter 2) – a well-attended celebration of gay rights running south from Columbus Circle. The

Steuben Day Parade is the biggest German-American event, taking place on the third weekend of September. Baron von Steuben was a Prussian general who fought with Washington at the battle of Valley Forge, which is as good an excuse as any for a costumed parade in his honour from 61st to 86th streets and Fifth Avenue. The **Columbus Day Parade** on or around October 12 is, after St Patrick's Day, the city's largest binge, commemorating the day America was put on the map. **Halloween** is celebrated on October 31 in a chase through Greenwich Village culminating at Washington Square. On the last Thursday in November, **Macy's Thanksgiving Parade** runs from 77th Street down Central Park West to Columbus Circle, afterwards down Broadway to Herald Square, with lots of bands, celebrities and giant balloons.

Fifth Avenue gets seasonal trimming at **Christmas**, especially in the last two Sundays before Christmas week: Rockefeller Center lights up its Christmas tree in the first week of December and decorates Channel Gardens, so beginning the festivities. On the two Sundays before Christmas, Fifth Avenue is closed to traffic, with entertainment on the streets. **New Year's Eve** is traditionally marked by a mass gathering on Times Square where the last seconds of the year signal drunken but good-natured revelry in the snow.

Festivals

The festival year kicks off with **Chinese New Year**, a noisy, colourful occasion celebrated around Mott Street in Chinatown on the first full moon after January 21. Dragons dance in the street, firecrackers chase away evil spirits and the chances of getting a meal anywhere in Chinatown are slim; phone ☎267-5780 for further details.

In May the **Ukrainian Festival** fills a weekend on East 7th Street between Second and Third avenues: marvellous Ukrainian costume, folk music and dance plus authentic foods. At the Ukrainian Museum (Twelfth Ave and 2nd St) there's a special exhibition of *pysanky* – tradi-

tional hand-painted eggs; ☎228-0110 for festival details. The same area witnesses some celebrations of a rather different sort on Labor Day, in the first week of September, when **Wigstock** takes place in Tompkins Square Park – an essentially transvestite festival, with many different singing and dancing acts performing on the bandstand throughout the day.

The high spot of May is the **Ninth Avenue Festival** which closes the avenue between 34th and 57th for the weekend, giving you the chance to snack your way along the strip of delis and restaurants that come out on to the street with their wares. Smaller, though perhaps more interesting, are the **Fiestas de Loiza Aldea** on the second weekend of July, miniature versions of the great Fiestas de Santiago Apostol (Festival of St James the Apostle) in the town of Loiza Aldea, Puerto Rico. Following mass at the Church of San Pueblo at Lexington and 117th, separate processions of women, men and children each carry a statue of the apostle to the footbridge at 102nd St and East River Drive to Ward's Island. Look out for the *Vejigante*, the animal-headed creature covered with horns who symbolises the devil, and *Caballero*, a sixteenth-century Spanish nobleman. After the procession there's a festival of Latin music, dance and salsa on Ward's Island, with plenty of Puerto Rican food: try the *pasteles* (spicy meat pies wrapped in a plantain), washed down with *coquito*, a drink made from eggs, coconut cream and rum. Also, check out the **Fiesta Folklorica**, an all-singing, all-dancing spectacle that fills Central Park on the last Sunday in August, and the Lower East Side's **Loisada Street Fair**, traditionally held on the last weekend in May.

The city's two Italian festivals are well publicised: the **Festival of St Anthony**, held in early June, is a two-week celebration on Sullivan Street from Spring to West Houston Street, culminating in a procession of Italian bands, led by a life-size statue of the saint carried on the shoulders of four men. More popular, and with great street stalls, is the **Festival San Gennaro**, patron saint of Naples, held

Parades and Festivals

Parades and Festivals

along Mulberry Street in Little Italy for ten days during the week of September 19. High spot is a procession of the saint's statue through the streets, donations of dollar bills pinned to his cloak.

From early July to late August the **Summer Festival** has outdoor concerts and plays in Central Park, Rockefeller Center and the South Street Seaport, many of which are free: phone ☎669-9430 for a daily round-up. Also running

from mid-July to August is Lincoln Center's **Mostly Mozart** festival, which starts with a free outdoor performance and continues in a series of cut-price concerts in Avery Fisher Hall: phone ☎875-5030 for more details. One of the most popular summer events is the series of **concerts** given by the New York Philharmonic in **Central Park** and other parks throughout the boroughs, all for free: ☎875-5079 for a schedule of times and places.

New York's parades and festivals

Jan	*Chinese New Year*	Chinatown
March 17	*St Patrick's Day Parade*	Fifth Ave
25	*Greek Independence Day Parade*	Fifth Ave
April	*Easter Day Parade*	Fifth Ave
May	*Ninth Avenue Food Festival*	34th to 57th
	Ukrainian Festival	East 7th St
17	*Martin Luther King Jr Memorial Day Parade*	Fifth Ave
last weekend	*Loisada Street Fair*	
June	*Puerto Rican Day Parade*	Fifth Ave
	Festival of St Anthony	Sullivan St
	Indian Festival	Central Park
	Lower East Side Jewish Spring Festival	East Broadway
	Tompkins Square Art Festival	
last Sunday	*Gay Pride March*	from Columbus Circle
July 4	*Independence Day Celebrations*	
	New York Summer Festival of Theater & Music	
	Mostly Mozart Music Festival	Lincoln Center
	Japanese Oban Festival	Riverside Park
	Fiestas de Loiza Aldea	Lexington Ave
August	*Fiesta Folklorica*	Central Park
September	*Steuben Day Parade*	Fifth Ave
	Festival of San Gennaro	Little Italy
October 4	*Pulaski Day Parade*	Fifth Ave
12	*Columbus Day Parade*	Fifth Ave
31	*Halloween*	Greenwich Village
November	*Macy's Thanksgiving Day Parade*	Broadway
December	*Rockefeller Center Christmas Tree Celebrations*	
31	*New Year's Eve*	Times Square

Central Park Mall (72nd St entrance) sees the **Indian Festival** in June or July: Indian music and dance, sari stalls and lots of Indian snacks. The biggest of the Jewish festivals is the **Lower East Side Jewish Spring Festival** (second Sunday in June) on East Broadway between Rutgers and Montgomery streets, featuring *glatt kosher* foods, Yiddish and Hebrew folk singing and guided tours of Jewish Lower East Side. Another religious-based occasion – and one of New York's prettiest – is the **Japanese Oban Festival**, which takes place at Riverside Park Mall at West 103rd Street in the early evening of the Saturday nearest to July 15. Slow, simple dancing in the lantern-hung park make this well worth catching.

Parades and Festivals

Chapter 13

Kids' New York

Believe it or not, New York can be a great place to visit with **children**. It's a visual, noisy, friendly place, and while the physical environment can be trying on the nerves of parents, chances are the kids will love it. Just walking around the streets, watching the buskers, climbing the skyscrapers, taking a helicopter ride or a trip on the Circle Line ferry may be entertainment enough – and you should certainly do at least some of these things, both for your own entertainment and theirs. But as a supplement to the many and varied attractions that will appeal to kids and grown-ups alike, we've detailed below a number of ideas that are especially useful if you're travelling with children – listings of the best **museums** (together with a checklist of others that may be of interest, detailed in the *Museums and Galleries* chapter); **shops** catering specifically for kids; as well as details of visiting **circuses**, **puppet shows** and **children's theatres**. We've also given addresses of **babysitters** for when you fancy some time to yourself. For further listings of a "What's on this week" type, see "Activities for Children' in *New York Magazine*.

Remember that children under 44 inches (112cm) tall ride free on the subway and buses when accompanied by an adult.

Museums, galleries and other sights

Though the majority of New York **museums and galleries** have at least something of interest to kids, the following places boast attractions that will probably evoke more than dutiful enthusiasm.

Aunt Len's Doll and Toy Museum

6 Hamilton Terrace at 141st St ☎ 281-4143. Phone first for an appointment; donation appreciated.

"Aunt Len" is Mrs Lennon Holder Hoyte, a scholarly and charming retired schoolteacher whose collection of 3000-plus dolls and teddy bears is amusing and interesting – and made all the more so by her infectious enthusiasm. Call and arrange a time for a visit before turning up.

Brooklyn Children's Museum

145 Brooklyn Ave. Subway #3 to Kingston Ave–Eastern Parkway. Wed–Fri 2–5pm, Sat–Sun 10am–5pm, closed Mon & Tues; $3.

Participatory museum stacked full of scientific and natural artefacts with which to play. Fun for both children and adults.

Children's Museum of the Arts

72 Spring St between Broadway and Lafayettes St ☎ 941-9198. Tues–Sun 11am–5pm, Thurs until 7pm. $4, free Thurs 4–7pm.

Art gallery of works by and /or for children which holds weekend workshops for kids over the age of four. Children are encouraged to look at different types of art and then create their own, with paints, clay, plaster of Paris and any other simple medium. Can be great fun.

Children's Museum of Manhattan

212 W 83rd St. Subway B or C to 80th St. Wed–Mon 10am–5pm; children and adults $5.

Other museums kids might like

The following **museums**, at least in part, will also appeal to kids. For detailed accounts of them, see Chapter 6, *Museums and Galleries*.

Abigail Adams Smith Museum, 421 E 61st St. #4, #5, or #6 subway trains to 59th St/Lexington Avenue. $3, children under 13 free.

American Museum of Natural History/ Hayden Planetarium, Central Park West at 79th St. Subway C to 81st St–Central Park West. Mon, Tue, Thur, Sun 10am–5.45pm, Wed, Fri, Sat 10am–9pm; free 10am–9pm Fri and Sat: otherwise suggested donation $5, Planetarium $5.

Liberty Science Center, Liberty State Park, Jersey City, New Jersey. PATH train from Port Authority to Grove Street/Journal Square and catch Central Avenue Bus Company service: ☎201/201-1000 for details. At weekends there's a ferry from the World Financial Center: ☎800/53-FERRY for details.

Museum of Television and Radio, 25 W 52nd St. Subway E or F to Fifth Ave–53rd St. Tues noon–8pm, Wed & Thurs noon–5pm, Fri noon–9pm, Sat noon–6pm; suggested donation $4, children $3. Tues noon–8pm; pay what you wish. Phone ☎621-6600 or 621-6800 for details of lectures by artists and directors.

Museum of the American Indian, Audubon Terrace, 3753 Broadway at 155th St. Subway #1 to 157th St–Broadway. Tues–Sat 10am–5pm, Sun 1–5pm. $3, children $2.

Museum of the City of New York, Fifth Ave at 103rd St. Subway #6 to 103rd St–Lexington Ave. Wed–Sat 10am–5pm, Sun 1–5pm; suggested donation $4, children $2, families $8.

Museum of the Moving Image, 35th Ave at 36th St, Astoria, Queens. Subway R to Steinway St. Tues–Fri noon–4pm, Sat & Sun noon–6pm; $5, students $2.50; film and exhibition information ☎718/784-0077 or ☎718/784-4520. See overleaf.

New York City Transit Exhibit, Old subway entrance at Schermerhorn St and Boerum Place, Brooklyn. Nearest subway Borough Hall. Tues–Fri 10am–4pm, Sat & Sun 11am–4pm; $3, children $1.50.

Queens Museum, Flushing Meadows–Corona Park. Subway #7 to Willets Point–Shea Stadium. Tues–Fri 10am–5pm, Sat & Sun noon–5pm; $3, students and children $2.

South Street Seaport Children's Center and Museum, 165 & 171 John St. Subway #2, #3, #4, #5 to Fulton St. Daily 10am–6pm; $6, children $3.

Kids' New York

See also Bronx Zoo, detailed on p.179, and Central Park Zoo, p.138.

Another participatory museum centring on science and nature exhibits. Primarily directed at ages up to 12 years. Guest performers and storytellers at weekends.

Fire Museum

278 Spring St. Subway C or E to Spring St. Tues–Sat 10am–4pm; $3, kids 50¢.

An unspectacular but pleasing homage to New York City's firefighters, and indeed firepeople everywhere. On display are fire engines from the last century (hand-drawn, horse-drawn and steam-powered), helmets, dog-eared photos and a host of motley objects on three floors of a disused fire station. A neat and endearing display.

Intrepid Sea-Air-Space Museum

Far western end of 46th St at Pier 86. M42 crosstown bus. Mon–Fri 10am–5pm; $7, children $4.

This worn-out aircraft carrier had a distinguished history, including hauling Neil Armstrong and Co. out of the ocean following the Apollo 11 moonshot. Today it holds a celebration of the nation's military might of the very worst kind – fighter planes clustered with bombs and emblazoned with "World's Greatest Dad" stickers, prototype models for the evil-looking B-1B fighter-bomber housed in a cavernous ship that reeks of gunmetal and regimented sweat.

Kids' New York

New York Aquarium

W 8th St and Surf Ave, Coney Island. Subway D, N or R. Daily 10am–4.45pm; summer weekends 10am–7pm; $5.75, children $2.

First opened in 1896, the aquarium in Coney Island is the kind of place your New York friends used to be taken when they were kids, and it's still going strong, with fish and invertebrates from the world over. Mostly it's a series of darkened halls full of tanks containing creatures of various sizes from the deep, but there are also open-air shows of marine mammals several times daily, as well as a new educational hall, with crashing waves, a mock-up of a salt marsh and other marine environments, tanks of baby sharks and turtles, not to mention a (rather sad) whale exhibit. There's also a soon-to-be-opened sea cliff exhibition, with basking walruses and seals.

New York Hall of Science

47–01 111th St, Corona, Queens. Subway #7 to 111th St. Wed–Sun 10am–5pm; $3.50 adults, kids $2.50.

This relatively new museum has the latest in technological displays, with hands-on exhibits that make it more fun for kids. Not worth a special trip in itself, but certainly meriting a visit on the way out to nearby Shea Stadium.

Staten Island Children's Museum

Snug Harbor, 1000 Richmond Terrace, Staten Island ☎ 718/273-2060. Tues–Sun 10am–5pm, closed Mon; $3.

Part of the Snug Harbor Cultural Center development, this is a good way to round off a trip on the Staten Island ferry; it's reachable on a trolley bus from the ferry terminal. There are many hands-on exhibits, covering subjects like the environment and technology, puppets and toys. Phone for details of special weekend activities.

Shops: toys, books and clothes

Big City Kites, 1201 Lexington Ave ☎ 472-2623. Manhattan's largest and best kite store, with a huge range.

Bodyscapes, 20 W 22nd St ☎ 243-2414. One-off designer jumpsuits and the like for kids – which sounds expensive but prices are in fact quite reasonable.

Books of Wonder, 132 Seventh Ave at 18th St ☎ 989-3270. Excellent kids' bookstore, with a great story-hour too.

Citykids, 130 Seventh Ave ☎ 620-0906. A tiny store that sells clothes to the "discerning child", alongside toys and other kiddy-related items.

Dinosaur Hill, 302 E 9th St ☎ 473-5850. Small downtown store selling a range of handmade toys, as well as clothes up to age five.

Dolls and Dreams, 19 W 24th St ☎ 876-2434. All kinds of dolly paraphernalia, from antiques to modern, from around the world.

Eeyore's Books for Children, 2212 Broadway at 76th St ☎ 362-0634. Not the only specialist children's bookshop in Manhattan but easily the best, with a broad selection of titles and storytelling sessions on Sunday mornings and Monday afternoons.

Enchanted Forest, 85 Mercer St ☎ 925-6677. A marvellous shop that hides its merchandise – stuffed animals, puppets, masks and the like – partly in the branches of its mock forest.

Kids Kids Kids, 44 Greenwich Ave ☎ 366-0809. Small but original and friendly children's clothes store – quite affordably priced.

The Last Wound Up, 1595 Second Ave, ☎ 288-7585. Huge collection of wacky, off-the-wall wind-up toys, some at pocket money prices.

Monkeys and Bears, 506 Amsterdam Ave ☎ 873-2673. Upscale, funky clothes for kids. Can be pricey, but good value.

Penny Whistle Toys, 1283 Madison Ave ☎ 369-3868; 448 Columbus Ave ☎ 873-9090; 132 Spring St ☎ 925-2088. Shop selling a fun, imaginative range of toys that deliberately eschews guns and war accessories.

Red Caboose, 16 W 45th St ☎ 575-0155. Another shop specialising in models, but concentrating on trains and train sets.

F.A.O. Schwarz, 767 Fifth Ave ☎644-9400. Showpiece of a nationwide chain sporting three floors of everything a child could want. Fans of Barbie will want to check out the new Barbie store, in the back of F.A.O. Schwarz on Madison Ave.

Second Childhood, 283 Bleecker St ☎989-6140. Toys dating back to 1850, with a wide assortment of miniatures, soldiers and lead animals.

Storyland, 1369 Third Ave ☎517-6951. Small but well-stocked kids' bookstore. Readings and other events on Sunday lunchtimes.

Toy Park, 112 E 86th St ☎427-6611. Well-stocked general toy shop that's a possible alternative to F.A.O. Schwarz – though not nearly as much fun.

Theatre, puppet shows, circuses and others

The following is a highly selective round-up of other activities, particularly cultural ones, that might be of interest to young children. Bear in mind that you can – as always – find out more by checking the pages of Friday's *Daily News* or *New York Times*; or take a look at *New York Magazine* or the *Village Voice*, which also sometime list children-orientated events. Note too that stores like *Macy's* and *F.A.O. Schwarz* often have events for children – puppet shows, story-hours and the like –

Babysitting

All of the following offer **babysitting services**, with approved sitters. Fees range between $6 and $12 an hour, depending on the age of your child (kids under a year old generally cost more), plus a sum to cover transportation. As always, call for the full picture. Be sure, in all cases, to book well in advance – at the latest the day before you need the sitter, if possible.

Babysitters Guild, 60 E 42nd St ☎682-0227.

Babysitters Association, 610 Cathedral Parkway ☎222-9884.

Gilbert Childcare Agency, 115 W 57th St ☎757-7900.

---

not to mention the better children's bookstores, most of whom regularly have storytelling sessions (see above).

Barnum & Bailey Circus, Madison Square Garden ☎465-6000. This large touring circus is usually in New York between April and June.

Big Apple Circus, Lincoln Center ☎875-5400. Small circus which performs in a tent behind Lincoln Center, from late October to early January. Tickets $10–45.

Hans Christian Andersen statue, Central Park, 72nd St entrance. Regular storytelling sessions, appropriately held next to the figure of the Danish writer. Saturdays 11am–noon, June to September.

Manhattan Raceway, 15 Waverly Place ☎673-4100. The largest Scalextric track in America, apparently, where slot-cars are manipulated around the track. Open Mon–Fri 3–11pm, Sat & Sun 11am–11pm; prices around $5 for half an hour.

Museum of the Moving Image, 35th Ave at 36th St, Astoria, Queens ☎718/784-0077 or ☎718/784-4520. Showings of kids' films and TV classics in a marvellously over-the-top old-style movie palace, decorated in fancy pseudo-Egyptian style. Showings are usually held Tues to Fri at lunchtime, and lunchtimes and afternoons on Sat and Sun. Call for details.

On Stage Children, 413 W 46th St ☎666-1716. Children's theatre company that mounts around four productions a year, between autumn and early May. Performances take place at weekends, usually Saturday; phone for details.

Puppet Playhouse, 555 E 90th St ☎369-8890. Puppet theatre that puts on shows at weekends. Seasons run October to May – call for a schedule; reservations only.

Swedish Marionette Theater, Central Park, 79th St entrance ☎988-9093. Another puppet theatre, housed in a former Swedish school building that was brought to New York in the last century, and putting on regular performances between late September and early June. Again, tickets must be reserved in advance, and again performances usually take place on weekends.

Kids' New York

For sporting items see Chapter 14, Shops and Markets.

Shops and Markets

New York is consumer capital of the world. Its **shops** cater for every possible taste, preference, creed or perversity, in any combination and in many cases at any time of day or night – and, as such, they're as good a reason as any for visiting the city. To enjoy them to the full you obviously have to have money, and lots of it, but even if you can't afford to buy, the city's shop windows, department stores, gourmet grocers, ethnic and oddity stores are still there for the browsing.

As in most large cities, New York stores are concentrated in specific neighbourhoods, so if you want something particular you invariably know exactly where to head. The most mainstream shopping territory is **Midtown Manhattan**, where you'll find department stores, big-name clothes designers and branches of the larger chains. **Downtown Manhattan** plays host to a wide variety of more offbeat stores: small boutiques, second-hand bookshops and almost pedantically specialised stores, selling nothing but candles or a hundred different types of caviar. **Uptown**, the Upper East Side is an upmarket continuation of midtown Manhattan, with, on Madison especially, a greater concentration of exclusive clothiers and antique and art dealers – a concentration that doesn't extend to the other side of the park, where the **Upper West Side** has a quite different personality and an array of off-the-wall stores that can compare to anything in SoHo or the Village. Bear in mind, too, that New York's **ethnic** enclaves have some of the city's

most exciting and colourful places to shop, and – the Outer Boroughs included – some of its most specialised. For details on specific shopping neighbourhoods, see the relevant sections of this chapter.

When to shop, how to pay

Most parts of the city are at their least oppressive for shopping early weekday mornings, and at their worst around lunchtimes and on Saturdays. There are few days of the year when everything closes (really only Thanksgiving, Christmas and New Year's Day) and many shops, including the big midtown department stores, regularly open on Sundays. Remember, however, that certain (usually ethnic) communities close their shops in accordance with religious and other holidays: don't bother to shop on the Lower East Side on Friday afternoon or on Saturday, for example, though places there are open on Sunday. By contrast, Chinatown is open all day every day, while the stores of the Financial District follow the area's nine-to-five routine and for the most part are shut all weekend.

Opening hours in midtown Manhattan are roughly Monday–Saturday 9am–6pm, with late closing on – usually – Thursdays; downtown shops tend to stay open later, at least until 8pm and sometimes until about midnight; bookstores especially are often open late. Unless we've stated otherwise the stores listed follow broadly these hours.

As far as **payment** goes, credit cards are as widely accepted as you'd expect:

even the smallest of shops will take *Visa*, *American Express*, *MasterCard* (*Access*) and *Diners Club*; many department stores also run their own credit schemes. Travellers' cheques are a valid currency too, though they must be in US dollars and you may have to provide ID. Finally, wherever you're shopping, be careful. Manhattan's stores, crowded frenzied places that they are, are ripe territory for **pickpockets and bag-snatchers**.

Department stores and malls

In *Saks*, *Bloomingdale's* and *Macy's*, New York has some of the great **department stores** of the world. However, the last few years have seen a number of the better established stores close down, while others have gone upmarket, making them less places to stock up on essentials and more outlets for designer clothes and chi-chi accessories, full of concessions on the top-line names. If you want to buy something in a hurry without turning it into a major New York shopping experience, you'd often do better to use a more specialised shop; if, on the other hand, you are on the look-out for a specific item, especially clothes, a department store might be a good first stop. With the exchange rate reasonable for most European visitors, prices are not too prohibitive, and during sale-times you may well find some excellent bargains; visit on and around holiday periods and watch the newspapers for timings.

Manhattan also has a number of **shopping malls**: shopping precincts basically, housed in purpose-built locations or in conversions of older premises, whose anodyne locations are on occasion reasonable places to browse – though they're not at all what New York does best. The larger and more important ones are listed below.

Department stores

Barney's, 142 W 17th St ☎929-9000. Though a proper department store, Barney's actually concentrates on clothes, particularly men's, with the emphasis on high-flying, up-to-the-minute designer

garments, alongside a relatively new womenswear department. If you've the money, there's no better place in the city to look for clothes. There's also a branch at Madison and 61st St ☎883-2277, and a smaller one at 225 Liberty St in the World Financial Center mall ☎945-1600.

Bergdorf Goodman, 754 Fifth Ave ☎753-7300. The name, the location, the thick pile carpets and discreetly hidden escalators – everything about Bergdorf's speaks of its attempt to be New York City's most gracious department store. Lucky that most of the folk who shop here have purses stacked with charge cards – the rustle of money would utterly ruin the feel. Recently restored to its former glories with many new contemporary designers.

Bloomingdale's, 1000 Third Ave ☎355-5900. New Yorkers are proud of *Bloomingdale's*: somehow it's an affirmation of their status, their sense of style, and they not surprisingly flock here in droves. You may not be so impressed. *Bloomingdale's* has the atmosphere of a large, bustling bazaar, packed full with concessions to perfumiers and designer clothes. It's certain, though, that whatever you want, Bloomies – as the store is popularly known – is likely to stock it.

Henri Bendel, 712 Fifth Avenue ☎247-1100. *Bendel's* is and always has been deliberately more gentle in its approach than the biggies, with a name for exclusivity and top-line modern designers. One of Manhattan's most refined shopping experiences.

Lord & Taylor, 424 Fifth Ave ☎391-3344. The most establishment of the New York stores, and to some extent its most pleasant, with a more traditional feel than *Macy's* or *Bloomingdale's*. Though no longer at the forefront of New York fashion, it's still good for classic designer fashions, household goods and accessories, and the more basic items.

Macy's, Broadway at 34th St ☎695-4400. Quite simply, the largest department store in the world, with two buildings, two million square feet of floor space, ten

Shops and Markets

Shops and Markets

floors (four for women's garments alone) and around $5m gross turnover every day. It's also these days a serious designer fashion rival to *Saks* and *Bloomingdale's*. Wander around even if you don't want to buy: you'll be sprayed with the latest fragrances from France or Beverly Hills, smeared with virulent lipsticks and fed on tasters in the cellar food hall. If you see only one of the city's large department stores, it should really be this.

Saks Fifth Avenue, 611 Fifth Ave ☎753-4000. The name is virtually synonymous with style, and, although *Saks* has retained its name for quality, it has also updated itself to carry the merchandise of all the big designers. In any case, with the glittering array of celebrities that use the place regularly, *Saks* can't fail.

Shopping malls

A&S Plaza/Herald Center, Sixth Ave and 33rd St. Perhaps because of its location right opposite *Macy's*, this large, mirror-fronted and rather glitzy shopping centre has never really been a success, a humdrum string of mainstream stores in what resembles nothing so much as a provincial shopping precinct. Unless there's a specific shop you want, or you want to pig out at the various ethnic nosh counters in the food hall, you'd be better off in *Macy's*.

Pier 17, South Street Seaport. Again, not quite the shopping experience it has been cracked up to be, although it has a more interesting selection of shops than the chain stores of A&S Plaza, in a more sensitively converted location.

Trump Tower, Fifth Ave and 56th St. The gaudiest and most expensively meretricious of the Manhattan malls, with a range of exclusive boutiques set around a deep, marbled atrium that mark it out as a tourist attraction in itself.

World Financial Center, Battery Park City. Centring on the huge, greenhouse-like Winter Garden, this is worth a visit just for a look at the development as a whole, and it has a handful of intriguing stores. On the other hand, it's rather out of the way just for a spot of shopping.

Pharmacies and drugstores

There's a **pharmacy or drugstore** on every corner in New York, and during the day at least it shouldn't be too difficult to find one. If you can't, the Yellow Pages has complete listings of places selling medicines and toiletries, listed under "pharmacies". Most pharmacies are open roughly Monday to Saturday 9am to 6pm, though many also open on Sunday in busy shopping or residential neighbourhoods. Some of the better or more specialised pharmacies are listed below, along with a selection of those that stay open longer hours in case of need.

Everywhere

Duane Reed. A chain of drugstores which has cornered the market on discount medicines, toiletries, cigarettes and basic stationery over much of Manhattan, especially midtown. Check the phone book for the nearest location.

Lovels. Another chain with locations all over Manhattan. Prices rival *Duane Reed*.

McKay. A drugstore chain, though with far fewer branches than *Duane Reed*. Again, exact locations in the phone book.

Lower Manhattan

Bigelow Pharmacy, 414 Sixth Ave ☎533-2700. Established in 1832, this is one of the oldest chemists in the city – and that's exactly how it looks, with the original Victorian shopfittings still in place. Open seven days a week.

Kiehl Pharmacy, 109 Third Ave ☎475-3400. Another ancient pharmacy but with a stock more in keeping with its age, including herbs, roots, dried flowers and spices.

Tak Sun Tong, 11 Mott St ☎374-1183. Herbal Chinese remedies: snake skin, shark's teeth and the like.

Midtown Manhattan

Caswell-Massey Ltd, 518 Lexington Ave ☎755-2254; 21 Fulton St ☎608-5401. The oldest pharmacy in America, and a national chain, selling a shaving cream created for George Washington and a cologne blended for his wife, as well as more mainstream items.

Edward's Drug Store, 225 E 57th St ☎753-2830. General pharmacy open seven days a week.

Freeda Pharmacy, 36 E 41st St ☎685-4980. Kosher drugs. Closed weekends.

Westerly Pharmacy, 911 Eighth Ave ☎247-1096. Open seven days.

Upper Manhattan

Alexander Pharmacy, 1751 Second Ave ☎410-0060. Open seven days.

Arnowitz Pharmacy, 1551 York Ave ☎737-3305. Open seven days.

Jaros Drug Inc., 25 Central Park West ☎247-8080. Open seven days.

Plaza Pharmacy, 251 E 86th St ☎427-6940. Open daily until midnight.

Star Pharmacy, 1540 First Ave ☎737-4324. Open seven days.

Tower Chemist Inc., 1257 Second Ave ☎838-1490. Open seven days.

Windsor Pharmacy, 1419 Sixth Ave ☎247-1538. Open until midnight seven days a week.

Food and drink

Food – the buying as much as consuming of it – is a New York obsession. Nowhere do people take eating more seriously than Manhattan, and there's no better place to shop for food. Where to buy the best bagels, who stocks the widest – and weirdest – range of cheeses, are questions that occupy New Yorkers a disproportionate amount of time. The shops themselves are mouth-watering, and even the simplest street-corner deli should be enough to get your tastebuds jumping; more sophisticated places, gourmet or speciality shops for example, will be enough to make you swoon.

The listings below, while comprehensive, are by no means exhaustive. Wander the streets and you'll no doubt uncover plenty more besides. If you're after **drink**, remember that you can only buy liquor – ie wines, spirits or anything else stronger than beer – at a specialist liquor store, and that you need to be 21 or over to do so.

Supermarkets, delis and greengrocers

For the most **general food requirements**, there are a number of **supermarket** chains which pop up all over the city. *Big Apple*, *Sloan's* and *Grand Union* you'll find pretty much everywhere; *D'Agostino* and *Gristedes* tend to appear in the smarter neighbourhoods. In addition, many of the **department stores** listed above – principally *Macy's* and *Bloomingdale's* – have food halls. **At night**, there's the *Food Emporium*, which opens 24 hours a day at most of its Manhattan branches (see the phone book for locations).

On a smaller scale, there are **delis and greengrocers** – the latter usually run by Koreans – which sell basic food and drink items, as well as sandwiches and coffee to take away, and sometimes hot ready meals and the chance to dip into a copiously provided salad bar. You should never have to walk more than a couple of blocks to find one, and most, especially those owned by Korean shopkeepers, are open late or all night.

Gourmet shops

Gourmet shops are essentially a step up from delis and are gloriously stocked places, selling all manner of edible items in a super-abundant environment that will make your taste buds jump. In general – though not exclusively – they supply the more gentrified neighbourhoods with their most obscure (and more mainstream) objects of desire.

Adriana's Bazaar, 2152 Broadway ☎877-5757. A collection of exotic and Middle Eastern foods.

Balducci's, 424 Sixth Ave ☎673-2600. This is the long-term, non-Jewish, downtown rival of *Zabar's* (see overleaf), a family-run store that's no less appetising – though some say it's slightly pricier.

Dean & Delucca, 560 Broadway ☎431-1691. One of the original big neighbourhood food emporia. Very chic, very SoHo and not at all cheap.

EAT Gourmet Foods, 403 E 91 ☎831-4800 and 1064 Madison Ave ☎772-0022. A brother to *Zabar's*, primarily based

Shops and Markets

Shops and Markets

in the East Side and packed with gourmet delights. Try the wonderful *Eli's* bread.

Faicco's, 260 Bleecker St ☎243-1974. Long established, very authentic Italian deli.

Fairway, 2127 Broadway ☎595-1888. Long-established Upper West Side grocery store that for many locals is the better value alternative to *Zabar's*. They have their own farm on Long Island, so the produce is always fresh, and their range in some items is enormous.

Fine & Schapiro, 138 W 72nd St ☎877-2874. Long established, with excellent, principally kosher meals to go and renowned sandwiches and cold meats. Also a restaurant – see Chapter 8.

Grace's Marketplace, 1237 Third Ave ☎737-0600. Gourmet deli offspring of *Balducci's* that is a welcome addition to the Upper East Side food scene. An excellent selection of just about everything.

Russ & Daughters, 179 E Houston St ☎475-4880. Technically, this store is known as an *appetizing* – the original Manhattan gourmet shop, set up at the turn of the century to sate the homesick appetites of immigrant Jews, selling smoked fish, caviar, pickled vegetables, cheese and bagels. This is one of the oldest.

Schaller & Weber, 1654 Second Ave ☎879-3047 and other stores in the Outer Boroughs. Culinary heart of the Upper East Side's now sadly diminished German-Hungarian district of Yorkville, this shop is a riot of cold cuts, salami and smoked meats. Not for vegetarians.

Silver Palate, 274 Columbus Ave ☎799-6340. Tiny gourmet shop whose products and recipe books helped revolutionise New York's takeout food business. If you can afford it, there's no better place for a ready-made exotic picnic.

Zabar's, 2245 Broadway ☎787-2000. The apotheosis of New York food-fever, *Zabar's* is still the city's most eminent foodstore. Choose from an astonishing variety of cheeses, cooked meats and salads, fresh baked bread and croissants, excellent bagels, and cooked dishes to go.

Upstairs stocks implements to help you put it all together at home. Not to be missed.

Bakeries and patisseries

Damascus Bakery, 56 Gold St, Brooklyn ☎718/855-1456. Syrian bakery, long established, with the city's best supply of different pitta breads, as well as a dazzling array of pastries.

The Erotic Baker, 582 Amsterdam Ave ☎362-7557. The name says it all really, and if you're imagining all kinds of crusty phalluses and full frontal crotch arrangements, you'd be absolutely right. If you've got something special in mind you'll need to order it a day or two in advance.

Ferrara, 195 Grand St ☎226-6150. Little Italy café-patisserie with branches in Milan and Montreal.

Fung Wong, 30 Mott St ☎267-4037. Chinese pastries.

HBH Pastry Shop, 29–28 30th Ave, Astoria, Queens ☎718/274-1609. Greek pastry shop selling *baklava* plus numerous less well-known Balkan sweetmeats. Sit-down café too.

H&H Bagels, 2239 Broadway & 1551 Second Ave ☎595-8000. Open 24 hours, seven days a week, this is the reputed home of New York's finest bagel.

Hungarian Pastry Shop, 1030 Amsterdam Ave ☎866-4230. Though a long way from Yorkville, and not actually run by Hungarians, this place is good either for an afternoon snack or to round off a meal nearby. Popular with Columbia students.

Kleine Konditorei, 234 E 86th St ☎737-7130. Yorkville German patisserie with a restaurant serving up all manner of honest Teutonic stodge.

Kossar's, 367 Grand St ☎473-4810. Jewish baker specialising in *bialys*.

Little Pie Company, 424 W 43rd St ☎736-4780. Specialises in pies and cakes, some of which are out of this world.

Moishe's, 181 E Houston St ☎475-9624; 115 Second Ave ☎505-8555. New York's most authentic Jewish bakery.

Orwasher's, 308 E 78th St ☎248-6569. Handmade breads and rolls, all certified kosher.

Veniero's, 342 E 11th St ☎674-7264. Century-old Italian style patisserie.

Vesuvio, 160 Prince St ☎925-8248. SoHo's most famous Italian bakery.

Yonah Schimmel's, 137 E Houston St ☎477-2858. Specialists in home-made *knishes*, with a variety of fillings (kasha, potato, cheese, etc), which you can take away or consume on the premises. Even if you've tried the *knishes* sold by street vendors and didn't like them, it's worth giving this place a go. Yonah's *knishes* taste nothing like the mass-produced kind.

Zaro's, Grand Central Station. Croissants, bagels, and all good things. Good place to stop off for a breakfast on your feet.

Zito's, 259 Bleecker St ☎929-6139. Long-established downtown Italian baker, renowned for its fine round *pane di casa*. Open every day.

Cheese and dairy

Alleva Latticini, 188 Grand St ☎226-7990. Italian cheesery and grocers.

Ben's Cheese Shop, 181 E Houston St ☎254-8290. Next door, and a nice complement to *Russ & Daughters* on the Lower East Side. Most of the cheese sold here is still made on the premises.

Cheese of all Nations, 153 Chambers St ☎732-0752. Cheese from all over the world. Upstairs, a small restaurant serves substantial cheesy lunches for around $5, and there's a plentifully stocked wine cellar to help wash it all down.

Cheese Unlimited, 240 Ninth Ave ☎691-1512. The name says it all . . . a huge variety of cheeses.

Di Paolo, 226 Grand St ☎206-1033. A wide array of different cheeses, including fresh varieties made on the premises.

Joe's Dairy, 156 Sullivan St ☎677-8780. Family store that's the best bet for fresh mozzarella.

Ideal Cheese Shop, 1205 Second Ave ☎688-7579. A fine cheese emporium.

Murray's Cheese Shop, 257 Bleecker St ☎243-3289. A variety of fresh cheeses.

Fish and seafood

Caviarteria, 29 E 60th St ☎759-7410. Mainly caviar – over a dozen varieties – and a stock of smoked fish and patés.

Citarella, 2135 Broadway ☎874-0383. Upper West Side store selling a huge variety of fish and seafood, and with a wonderful bar serving prepared oysters, clams and the like to take away. Great, artistic window displays, too.

Murray's Sturgeon Shop, 2429 Broadway ☎724-2650. Another popular Upper West Side haunt, this place specialises in smoked fish and caviar.

Petrossian, 182 W 58th St ☎245-2214. This well-known shop imports only the finest Russian caviar, alongside a range of other gourmet products – smoked salmon and other fish mainly – as well as pricey implements to eat it all with. Quite the most exclusive place to shop for food in town, and with a restaurant attached to complete the experience.

Health food, vegetarian and spice shops

Aphrodisia, 282 Bleecker St ☎989-6440. For herbs and spices only, this place is hard to beat.

Brownies, 91 Fifth Ave ☎242-2199. New York's first health food store and still one of the best in town.

Commodities, 117 Hudson St ☎334-8330. Huge new health food store.

General Nutrition Center. The city's largest health food chain (check the phone book for addresses), though often the one-off downtown health shops are rather better.

Good Earth Foods, 1334 First Ave ☎472-9055; 167 Amsterdam Ave ☎496-1616. Not cheap but one of the best-equipped health food outlets in the city. Has a worthy juice and food café.

Gramercy Natural Food Center, 427 Second Ave ☎725-1651. Best known for its fish, poultry and organic dairy products.

The Health Nut, 2611 Broadway ☎678-0054 and other Manhattan locations. Good general health food and macrobiotic chain.

Shops and Markets

Shops and Markets

Nature Food Center, 348 W 57th ☎757-4180 and locations across Manhattan. The "department store" of natural foods – an excellent selection.

Pete's Spice, 174 First Ave ☎254-8773. Speciality herbs and spices for the serious cook.

Prana, 125 First Ave ☎982-7306. Wholefood shop, again pricey.

Vitamin Quota, 1039 Second Ave ☎751-3920 and 1645 Second Ave ☎734-0333. Health food supermarket. Many other locations across town.

Whole Foods in SoHo, 117 Prince St ☎673-5388 and 2421 Broadway ☎874-4000. Health food supermarket, open daily with a very wide selection.

Ethnic foods

Not surprisingly, you'll find the best ethnic foodstores in the areas where those communities live. Try the following:

British

Myers of Keswick, 634 Hudson St ☎691-4194, is the place to go if you're pining for Marmite, pork pies and the like.

Chinese

The best Chinese supermarket in Chinatown is *Kam-Man*, 200 Canal St ☎571-0330. A marginally cheaper alternative, though with a greatly reduced selection, is *Chinese American Trading*, 91 Mulberry St ☎267-5224.

Greek

Astoria in Queens is the best source of Greek specialities – try *Kalamata Foods*, 38-01 Ditmars Boulevard ☎718/626-1250, or *Titan Foods*, 25–50 31st St ☎718/626-7771.

Indian

Kalustyan's, 123 Lexington Ave ☎685-3451, is the best of the small gang of fooderies that make up the tiny Little India district of Manhattan. Failing that, *Spice and Sweet* is just up the block at no. 135 ☎683-0900, *Foods of India* across the road at 121 Lexington Ave ☎683-4419.

Italian

Carroll Gardens in Brooklyn or the Italian district of Belmont in the Bronx have many authentic Italian stores. More accessibly, you could visit the *Alleva Latticini* or *Di Paolo* (see above under "Cheese and dairy"), or the *Italian Food Center*, 186 Grand St ☎925-2954 – all in Little Italy.

Jewish

There are still many places down on the Lower East Side that specialise in Jewish and kosher foods, although Jewish cuisine tends to appear all over the city. See the "Gourmet shops" listings for some suggestions.

Middle Eastern

Although much depleted, there are still a handful of Middle Eastern stores on Atlantic Avenue in Brooklyn, not least the *Damascus Bakery* (see p.326). In Manhattan, try *Tashjian*, 123 Lexington Ave ☎685-8458.

Latin/South American

The best neighbourhoods to try are East Harlem (El Barrio), where *La Marqueta* (see p.331) is a riot of good things, and Jackson Heights in Queens, where you could try *La Constancia*, 95-05 Roosevelt Ave ☎718/476-1876.

Ice cream

Two chains have largely carved up the city's appetite for ice cream between them: **Baskin-Robbins**, who have about half a dozen outlets spread between Wall St and Harlem, and the considerably better **Haagen-Dazs**, who trade from about ten locations across Manhattan; again, the phone book has details.

While their ice cream is excellent, and comes in myriad different flavours, there are a few smaller operators which die-hard New York ice cream freaks swear by. Of these **Steve's** (444 Sixth Ave; 145 Second Ave; 286 Columbus Ave), **Ben & Jerry's** (1 Herald Square; 327 Sixth Ave; 41 Third Ave) and **Frusen Gladje** (29 E 8th St; 349 Sixth Ave; 170 Spring St) all have their vehement defenders; and the **Chinatown Ice Cream Factory**, 65 Bayard

St ☎608-4170, incurs the most bemused reactions, since it's the only place that serves up mango, green tea and lychee flavours.

Sweets, nuts and chocolates

Bazzini, 339 Greenwich St ☎227-6241. Fabulous selection of nuts in all shapes and sizes. A wide selection of sweets, too.

David's Cookies. A chain with numerous branches all over the city (see the phone book for exact locations) selling excellent cookies.

Economy Candy, 131 Essex St ☎254-1531. Best of a bunch of unpretentious Lower East Side stores selling tubs of sweets, nuts and dried fruit. Another branch at 108 Rivington St.

Elk, 240 E 86th St ☎650-1177. A Yorkville candy store selling Yorkville-style candies – rich and marzipaned.

Godiva, 701 Fifth Ave ☎593-2845. This renowned Belgian chocolatier has branches all over Manhattan – unbeatable for satisfying anyone's chocolate craving.

Li-Lac, 120 Christopher St ☎242-7374. Delicious chocolates hand-made on the premises since 1923. One of the city's best treats for sweet teeth.

Mutual, 127 Ludlow St ☎673-3489. Another Lower East Side candy store, this time specialising in dried fruit.

Teuscher, 620 Fifth Ave ☎246-4416; 251 E 61st St ☎751-8482. The truffles of this Upper East Side store are renowned.

Treat Boutique, 200 E 86th St ☎737-6619. Six different kinds of home-made fudge and a broad selection of dried fruit and nuts.

Tea and coffee

Gillies 1840, 160 Bleecker St ☎614-0900. America's oldest coffee shop.

McNulty's, 109 Christopher St ☎242-5351 and 247 Columbus Ave ☎362-4700. Coffee, and a wide selection of teas.

Porto Rico, 201 Bleecker St ☎477-5421. Best for coffee, and with a bar for tasting.

The Sensuous Bean, 68 W 70th St ☎724-7725. Mostly coffee, with some tea.

Liquor stores

Prices for all kinds of **liquor** are controlled in New York State and vary little from one shop to another. There are, however, a number of places which either have a particularly good selection or where things tend to be a touch less expensive. It's those which are listed here. Bear in mind there's a state law forbidding the sale of strong drink on Sundays, a day on which all liquor stores are closed.

Manhattan liquor stores

Acker Merrall & Condit, 160 W 72nd St ☎787-1700. Holds a very wide selection of wine from the USA, especially California. Open until 11.30pm.

Astor Wines and Spirits, 12 Astor Place ☎674-7500. Manhattan's best selection and most competitive prices.

Beekman Liquor Store, 500 Lexington Ave ☎759-5857. Good, well-priced midtown alternative to *Astor*.

Columbus Circle Liquor Store, 1780 Broadway ☎247-0764. Ditto for uptown.

Cork & Bottle, 1158 First Ave ☎838-5300. Excellent selection; deliveries too.

Garnett Wine & Liquor, 929 Lexington Ave ☎772-3211. Another good-value liquor store.

Maxwell Wine & Spirits, 1657 First Avenue ☎289-9595. Upper East Side liquor store that opens until midnight at weekends.

Morrell & Co, 535 Madison Ave ☎688-9370. One of the best selections of good-value wine in town.

Schapiro's, 126 Rivington St ☎674-4404. Kosher wines made on the premises. Free tours of the cellars, with wine tasting, Sunday 11am–4pm on the hour.

Schumer's, 59 E 54th St ☎355-0940. Stays open until midnight Friday and Saturday, and will also deliver.

Sherry-Lehman, 679 Madison Ave ☎838-7500. New York's foremost wine merchant.

Spring Street Wines, 187 Spring St ☎219-0521. Well-stocked SoHo liquor store.

Shops and Markets

Shops and Markets

Markets

New York doesn't really go in for **markets** in a big way: those that exist are mostly highly organised, wholesale-only affairs with retail stores attached, or simply neighbourhoods devoted to specific items. Street markets, on the other hand, can't compare with those in Europe.

Flea markets, junk and bargains

Flea markets have yet to catch on in the States, though New York has more outlets than most American cities for old clothes, antiques and suchlike, as well as any number of odd places – parking lots, playgrounds, or maybe just an extra-wide bit of sidewalk – where people set up to sell their wares, and groupings of streets where stores and stalls devoted to specific items sell at discount rates. Below is a rundown of likely locations, but bear in mind that it's illegal to sell anything in the street without a licence, so the more impromptu affairs may have disappeared by the time you read this.

Lower

Greenwich Village Flea Market, PS 41, Greenwich Ave at Charles St. About seventy outdoor booths full of everything you've ever needed. Saturday noon–7pm.

Canal West Flea Market, 370 Canal Street. The bargain basement of New York flea markets, with clothing for as little as $1.50 an item. Open Saturdays and Sundays 7am–6pm.

Tower Market, Broadway between W 4th St and Great Jones St. Lots of new, craftsy stalls, selling woven goods from South America, New Age paraphernalia and the like. Saturdays and Sundays 10am–7pm.

Midtown

Bryant Park Crafts Show, 42nd St between Fifth and Sixth Ave. Crafts market with antique jewellery and the usual range of collectibles. Friday noon–7pm.

Upper

Antique Flea and Farmers Market, PS 183, E 67th St between First and York Ave. Usually about 150 stalls of fresh food, odd antiques and needlework. Saturday 10am–6pm.

Yorkville Flea Market, 351 E 74th St. Just a small market, with a regular location in the Jan Hus Presbyterian church. Saturday 9am–4pm, June to August.

Local specialities

Besides regular organised markets, there are a number of Manhattan neighbourhoods which are worth visiting simply for the specialities they are devoted to, usually sold at discount prices, not to mention the odd impromptu sidewalk market. **Orchard Street**, main artery of the Jewish Lower East Side, is worth a trip for its cheap clothes stores, especially on Sunday when it's pedestrianised. Lively, vibrant and stacked full of bargains, it attracts people from all over the city. The rest of the **Lower East Side** is similarly well stocked with discount items all week: **Allen Street**, just below Houston, is good for shirts and, especially, ties; sections of **Grand Street** are given over to hosiery, underwear, fabrics and bed linen; while the shops on **Bowery** below Houston sell mainly lamps and lighting fixtures – above Houston, catering and kitchen items. Across town, **14th Street** is a good place to pick up discount household wares; the stores of **Canal Street** between Sixth Avenue and Lafayette Street, further south, are stacked high with obscure electrical items, fake designer watches, pirate tapes and cassette recorders.

On a less organised basis, **Cooper Square**, in summer at least, is usually lined with people squatting in front of pieces of old carpet piled high with junk and the clutter of various Manhattan attics and wardrobes. Nearby, on and around St Mark's Place and on **First Avenue** from around 12th Street down to Houston, there are numerous secondhand clothing stores. Across in SoHo the emphasis is more upmarket, with small markets selling new woollens and handmade jewellery, like those on the corners of **Spring and Wooster Street** and of **Prince and Greene Street**.

Finally, the **Flower District**, in west Manhattan on Sixth Avenue between 26th and 30th streets, has the city's largest concentration of plants and flowers. If you can't find what you want here, be it houseplant, tree, dried, cut or artificial flower, then it's a fair bet it's not available anywhere else in New York.

Block fairs

Look out, too, for neighbourhood **block fairs**. Organised by the local tenants' association, these are like urban village fêtes, cropping up most frequently in midsummer and giving residents the chance to turn out their unwanted junk. They're advertised locally, on noticeboards and in newspapers, and depending on the neighbourhood it can be well worth going along. The kind of thing that counts as unwanted junk on Madison Avenue might be someone else's idea of treasure. More significantly, block fairs are a good way of getting a taste of real, neighbourhood New York, beyond the sirens and skyscrapers.

Food markets

Perhaps the best market in Manhattan dedicated specifically to food is **La Marqueta**, on Park Avenue between 111th and 116th streets in the heart of El Barrio, which sells sweets, spices, vegetables, fruits and all things Latin American. The few ranks of stalls along **Ninth Avenue** between 37th and 42nd streets sell foods from just about every country that has any kind of ethnic representation in New York, however small – a market in that in mid-May blossoms into the **Ninth Avenue Festival**, in which the length and breadth of the avenue is taken up with foodstalls; see *Parades and Festivals*, Chapter 12. You can buy most types of food at the **Essex St Covered Market**, as well as gaudy jewellery, cheap lace and wigs, though the market has hit hard times of late and is now more a refuge for down-and-outs than a serious place to shop. If you're up early enough (5am – see "Information, Maps and Tours" in *Basics*) the daily **Fulton fish market** is a lively affair; for New York's freshest fish at any time of day (though of course the earlier the better), use the market's retail store at 18 Fulton St ☎952-9658.

Greenmarkets

Early risers might also want to visit one of the city's **greenmarkets**, which open early morning on a couple of days a week at about a dozen locations over Manhattan principally to sell fruit and vegetables. These are run by the city authorities, roughly between June and November, and act as a forum for market gardeners and small farmers from Long Island or the Hudson Valley who come into New York to sell their produce direct. Many of them close down at lunchtime (though the Union Square market continues all day), so get there in the morning to be sure of seeing anything.

Shops and Markets

Where to find greenmarkets

Greenmarket locations vary, but you should find one at the following places on at least one day a week. Further information on ☎566-0990.

World Trade Center Tuesday and Thursday.

Southbridge Towers between Beekman and Pearl St Saturday.

City Hall Friday.

Independence Plaza at Greenwich and Harrison St Wednesday and Saturday.

St Mark's-in-the-Bowerie Tuesday.

Tompkins Square Saturday.

Union Square Wednesday, Friday and Saturday.

57th St and Ninth Ave Wednesday and Saturday.

67th St between First and Second Ave Saturday.

87th St between First and Second Ave Saturday.

102nd St at Amsterdam Ave Friday.

Shops and Markets

Clothes and fashion

Dressing right is important to many in Manhattan, and fashion is a key reference point, though you may find that clothes are more about status here than setting trail-blazing trends. Although New York may be streets in front of the rest of the country fashion-wise, compared to Europe it can sometimes seem pretty staid. If you are prepared to search the city with sufficient dedication you can find just about anything, but it's **designer clothes** and the snob values that go with them that predominate. **Secondhand clothes**, of the "vintage" or "antique" variety, have caught on of late but never seem to have developed the chic they picked up in Britain; plus, the "vintage" or "antique" label tends to make them ridiculously overpriced. Basically, if you want *real* secondhand stuff go to a thrift shop, roughly akin to a charity shop in Britain and more reasonably priced.

For secondhand and/or trendy clothes the best **place to look** is downtown, and particularly the East Village and parts of SoHo; for American jeans, especially Levis, Orchard Street is as good a place as any. Designer items, from the better known international designers, can be found on Fifth Avenue, in the larger and more reputed department stores and along Madison Avenue in the 60s and 70s. The Garment District – basically the blocks between Sixth and Seventh avenues in the 30s – can be a good place for picking up designer clothes at a discount. There's an office here for every women's garment retailer and manufacturer in the country, and though some are wary of selling to one-off, non-wholesale customers, you can pick up some enviable bargains if

Clothing and shoe sizes

Women's dresses and skirts

American	4	6	8	10	12	14	16	18
British	6	8	10	12	14	16	18	20
Continental	38	40	42	44	46	48	50	52

Women's blouses and sweaters

American	6	8	10	12	14	16	18
British	30	32	34	36	38	40	42
Continental	40	42	44	46	48	50	52

Women's shoes

American	5	6	7	8	9	10	11
British	3	4	5	6	7	8	9
Continental	36	37	38	39	40	41	42

Men's suits

American	34	36	38	40	42	44	46	48
British	34	36	38	40	42	44	46	48
Continental	44	46	48	50	52	54	56	58

Men's shirts

American	14	15	15½	16	16½	17	17½	18
British	14	15	15½	16	16½	17	17½	18
Continental	36	38	39	41	42	43	44	45

Men's shoes

American	7	7½	8	8½	9½	10	10½	11	11½
British	6	7	7½	8	9	9½	10	11	12
Continental	39	40	41	42	43	44	44	45	46

you have enough front, carry cash and are not prepared to take no for an answer; again, check the phone book for possibilities. Bear in mind, too, that many **department stores** stock as good a selection of the (more mainstream) designer fashions as you're likely to find.

New and designer clothes

Agnes B, 116 Prince St ☎925-4649; 1063 Madison Ave ☎570-9333. Great designs, now at two Manhattan branches.

Banana Republic, 205 Bleecker St ☎473-9570; and branches at Lexington Ave and 59th St, Broadway and 87th St and South Street Seaport. Expensive clobber for the chic traveller: boots, bags, designer safari suits, etc.

Betsey Johnson, 130 Thompson St ☎420-0169. SoHo outlet of the New York designer. Functional clothes at almost affordable prices.

Brooks Brothers, 346 Madison Ave ☎682-8800. Something of an institution in New York, priding itself on its non-observance of fashion and still selling the same tweeds, gaberdines and quietly striped shirts and ties it did fifty years ago. It's a formula that seems to work.

Burberry's, 9 E 57th St ☎371-5010. If you're still not sure how to identify a yuppie, take a look at the clothes they sell here.

Canal Jean Co., 504 Broadway ☎226-1130. Enormous warehousey store sporting a prodigious array of jeans, jackets, t-shirts, hats and more, new and second-hand. Young, fun and reasonably cheap.

Capezio, 1650 Broadway ☎245-2140; 136 E 61st St ☎758-8833; 177 Macdougal St ☎477-5634. Basically a dancewear outfitters, although the Village branch now sells a range of New York's best designers. Not especially cheap, but some nice stuff.

Charivari. The city's fastest-growing designer fashion empire. Branches for men at 2339 Broadway at 85th St ☎873-7242; for women at 2315 Broadway at 83rd St ☎873-1424; for all at 257 Columbus Ave ☎787-7272 and 18 W 57th St ☎333-4040.

Cignal, 79 Fifth Ave ☎645-4330. Trendy, moderately pricey garments for men and women. Another branch at the World Trade Center.

Comme des Garçons, 116 Wooster St ☎219-0660. Manhattan shop of the pricey Japanese designer.

Dave's Army & Navy Store, 779 Sixth Ave ☎989-6444. Good place to buy Levis; prices from $25.

Patricia Field, 10 E 8th St ☎254-1699. Touted as Manhattan's most inventive clothes store, Pat Field's was one of the first NYC vendors of "punk chic", and has since blossomed into one of the few downtown emporia that yuppie uptowners will actually visit.

Gucci, 685 Fifth Ave ☎826-2600. Manhattan's snootiest clothes store.

Tommy Hilfinger, 284 Columbus Ave ☎769-4910. Brand-new fashions for the yuppie man-about-town. Expensive.

Paul Smith, 108 Fifth Ave ☎627-9770. New Manhattan branch of the stylish British menswear designer.

Paul Stuart, Madison Ave at 45th St ☎682-0320. Classic men's garb, not unlike *Brooks Brothers* but more stylish.

Trash 'n' Vaudeville, 4 St Mark's Place ☎982-3590. Famous to the extent that it advertises its wares in British magazines like *ID*. Great clothes, new and "antique", in the true East Village spirit.

Urban Outfitters, 628 Broadway ☎475-0009, at Waverly Place ☎677-9350 and 127 E 59th St ☎688-1200. A good range of stylish clothing at reasonable prices.

Antique and secondhand clothes

Antique Boutique, 712 Broadway ☎460-8830. Self-proclaimed "largest and best vintage clothing store in the world".

Cheap Jack's, 841 Broadway ☎777-9564. Large vintage clothing store.

Exchange Unlimited, 563 Second Ave ☎889-3229. Thrift shop that puts up-to-the-minute style within most budgets.

Love Saves the Day, 119 Second Ave ☎228-3802. Probably the only one of Manhattan's vintage clothes shops that could be described as anything like cheap.

Shops and Markets

Shops and Markets

Memorial Sloan Kettering Thrift Shop, 1440 Third Avenue ☎535-1250. Good thrift store with a fairly contemporary selection of clothes and tons of other bits and pieces.

Reminiscence, 74 Fifth Ave ☎243-2292. Funky secondhand clothes for men and women. Quite inexpensive.

Discount clothing

Bolton's. Designer clothes at vast reductions. Locations include: 19 E 8th St ☎475-9457; 53 W 23rd St ☎924-9547; 1180 Madison Ave ☎722-4419; 225 E 57th St ☎755-2527; 27 W 57th St ☎935-4431; 2251 Broadway ☎873-8545.

Century 21, 12 Cortlandt St ☎227-9092. A department store with designer brands for half the cost, a favourite among budget yet label-conscious New Yorkers. Only snag – no dressing rooms.

Dave's A & C Jeans, 779 Sixth Ave ☎989-6444. Comes recommended as the best place to buy jeans in Manhattan. Helpful assistants, no blaring music, and brands other than just Levis.

J. Crew, 203 Front St ☎385-3500. South Street Seaport discount store housed in a former waterfront labourers' hostel and selling subtly updated classic garments in a rainbow of colours at easy-to-pay prices.

Daffy's, 111 Fifth Ave ☎529-4477. A funkier version of *Loehmann's* (see below).

Gabay's, 225 First Ave ☎254-3180. Overordered, flawed or returned goods from the upmarket midtown department stores. Well worth a rummage.

Orva, 166 E 86th St ☎369-3448. Discount fashion clothing and shoes for women. Great bargains.

Labels for Less. The name says it all – a chain selling discount designer labels for women. Branches at 639 Third Ave ☎682-3330; 130 W 48th St ☎997-1032; 130 E 34th St ☎689-3455; 1302 First Ave ☎249-4800.

Loehmann's. New York's best-known store for designer clothes at knockdown prices. No frills, no refunds, no exchanges, but people still flock here with almost religious fervour. Next time you're deep in designer labels on Fifth Ave in the 50s, bear in mind that most of the garments probably came from *Loehmann's*. Branches at: 19 Duryea Place, Brooklyn ☎718/469-9800; 60-06 99th St, Rego Park, Queens ☎718/271-4000; 5746 Broadway, the Bronx ☎718/543-6420.

S&W, 165 W 26th St ☎924-6656. American designer sportswear at considerable discounts.

Finishing touches: shoes, hair, specs

The best place to go for a bargain **haircut** in New York City is the *Astor Place Haircutters* at 2 Astor Place ☎475-9854, where people queue six deep on the pavement outside while a doorman calls names from a clipboard. It's by no means Vidal Sassoon, but they'll do any kind of style, and, most importantly, don't cost the earth – around $10 (plus tip) for a straight cut, which by NYC standards is extremely cheap. Give your name to the doorman on arrival and however long the queue seems you should be seen in under half an hour. If you don't fancy *Astor* bear in mind that hairdos elsewhere cost upwards of $25.

As for **shoes**, for bargains the greatest concentration of shops is on West 8th Street between Fifth and Sixth avenues in the Village. If it's designer labels you're after you'll have to head way uptown – on and around Fifth Avenue in the 50s.

Glasses are considerably cheaper here than in Europe. If you break yours, or simply need a new pair to go with the new Armani outfit, try taking a look at the vast array at *Cohen's Optical*, 117 Orchard Street ☎674-1986. Nicaragua's Daniel Ortega supposedly spent $3000 here on a pair of bulletproof ones.

Books

There's a fantastic selection of **books** in New York. New or secondhand, US or foreign, there's little that isn't available somewhere. If there's a particular book you want to look at, but not buy, don't forget the New York Public Library at 42nd Street and Fifth Avenue.

General interest and new books

B. Dalton. A nationwide chain (now owned by *Barnes & Noble* – see below), and overall the city's best-stocked and most reliable bookstore for general titles, with a main branch in Manhattan at 666 Fifth Ave ☎247-1740 and 396 Sixth Ave ☎674-8780.

Barnes & Noble. New Yorkers feel cheated if they pay full price for anything: here they can pick up new hardbacks and paperbacks for a fraction of their published price. Branches at 105 Fifth Ave ☎807-0099; their sale annexe opposite; a "superstore" at 82nd and Broadway, designed like a library with its own café; Rockefeller Center; 56 W 8th St; Third Ave and 47th St; 57th St and Seventh Ave; Third Ave and 59th St; Broadway at 73rd St; 45th St and Broadway; 86th St near Lexington Ave; and at Penn Plaza. Many more in the Outer Boroughs.

Book Forum, 2955 Broadway ☎749-5535. Good on politics, poetry and academic subjects.

Books and Co., 939 Madison Ave ☎737-1450. Delightful bookshop with a literary bias and information on readings, events, etc.

Brentano's, 597 Fifth Ave ☎826-2450. Housed in the fine old Scribner's bookstore, and continuing that shop's tradition of good service and stock in elegant surroundings.

Coliseum Books, 1771 Broadway ☎757-8381. Large store, good on paperbacks and academic books.

Doubleday. The American arm of *W.H. Smith*, and an excellent general bookstore. Main branches at 245 Park Ave ☎984-7561, and, larger, at 724 Fifth Ave ☎397-0550.

Endicott Booksellers, 450 Columbus Ave ☎787-6300. Believe it or not, this place was here before the arthouse gang colonised Columbus, and certainly it tries hard to give the impression it has been here since the city began, providing helpful service and a wonderful range of titles.

Gotham Book Mart, 41 W 47th St ☎719-4448. The former owner of this store, Frances Stelloff, who died a few years back, made her name as patron of authors like Henry Miller, James Joyce and Gertrude Stein in the 1920s, and needless to say, the shop still enjoys a legendary reputation. Good on drama and theatre publications, and excellent for the more obscure literary stuff. A noticeboard downstairs advertises readings and literary functions, and a gallery has sporadic exhibitions.

Papyrus, 2915 Broadway ☎222-3350. New and used titles, especially good on political and radical literature.

Shakespeare & Co., 2259 Broadway ☎580-7800. New and used books, paper and hardcover, neatly placed to capture the Upper West Side yuppie trade.

Spring Street Books, 169 Spring St ☎219-3033. SoHo's most wide-ranging and pleasant bookshop, good on paperbacks, magazines and newspapers from home and abroad, as well as books.

Three Lives, 154 W 10th St ☎741-2069. Excellent, consciously literary bookstore that has an especially good selection of books for and by women, as well as general titles.

Secondhand books

Argosy Bookstore, 116 E 59th St ☎753-4455. Unbeatable for rare books, and also sells clearance books and titles of all kinds, though the shop's reputation means you may well find mainstream works cheaper elsewhere.

Bryant Park. Secondhand bookstalls Monday–Friday whenever the temperature hits 40°F or more. Excellent bargains if you're prepared to rummage.

Burlington Bookshop, 1082 Madison Ave ☎288-7420. Secondhand and new books.

Gryphon Bookshop, 2246 Broadway ☎362-0706. Used and out of print books, records, CDs.

Pageant Book & Print Shop, 109 E 9th St ☎674-5296. Large selection of secondhand books and prints.

Shops and Markets

Shops and Markets

Ruby's Book Sale, 119 Chambers St ☎732-8676. Civic Center's other used bookstore, dealing especially in paperbacks and ancient dog-eared magazines. Excellent value.

Strand Bookstore, 828 Broadway ☎473-1452. With around eight miles of books and a stock of over two million, this is the largest book operation in the city – and one of few survivors in an area once rife with secondhand book stores. As far as recent titles go, you can pick up review copies for half price; more ancient books go for anything from 50¢ up.

Special interest bookstores

Like most large cities, New York has a good number of stores **specialising** in books on one particular area, from travel and art to more arcane subjects. The following is a fairly selective list.

Travel

The Complete Traveller, 199 Madison Ave ☎679-4339. Manhattan's premier travel bookshop, excellently stocked, secondhand and new.

The Civilized Traveler, 2003 Broadway 875-0306; 1072 Third Ave ☎758-8305; Two World Trade Center ☎786-3301. Similar to *The Complete Traveller*, though perhaps not as well stocked.

Travellers Bookstore, 22 W 52nd St ☎664-0995. Small but well-stocked store that's a serious and friendly rival to *The Complete Traveller*.

New York Bound Bookshop, 50 Rockefeller Plaza ☎245-8503. Most city bookshops are copiously stacked with books about New York, but this one specialises in them, especially rare and out-of-print editions, alongside maps, photographs and memorabilia.

Rand McNally Map and Travel Store, 150 E 52nd St ☎758-7488. As much a map shop as a place for guide books, with maps of all the world and specialist ones of New York State and City.

Art and architecture

Rizzoli Bookstore, 31 W 57th St ☎759-2424; 200 Vesey St ☎385-1400; 454

West Broadway ☎674-1616. Latest titles in sophisticated settings.

Urban Center Books, 457 Madison Ave ☎935-3592. Architectural book specialists.

Photography, cinema and the theatre

A Photographer's Place, 133 Mercer St ☎431-9358. Lovingly run bookshop specialising in all aspects of photography.

Applause Cinema Books, 100 W 67th St ☎787-8858. Books on all aspects of the cinema, including screenplays, biographies etc.

Applause Theater Books, 211 W 71st St ☎496-7511. Books on all aspects of the theatre.

Drama Bookshop, 723 Seventh Ave ☎944-0595. Theatre books, scripts and publications on all manner of drama-related subjects.

Crime

Foul Play, 10 Eighth Ave ☎675-5115. Books for mystery and detective buffs.

Murder Ink, 2486 Broadway ☎362-8905. The first bookstore to specialise in mystery and detective fiction in the city, it's still the best, billed as stocking every murder, mystery or suspense title in print, and plenty out.

Mysterious Bookshop, 129 W 56th St ☎765-0900. Run by a columnist from *Ellery Queen* magazine; especially good on used and out-of-print titles.

Sci-fi and comics

Forbidden Planet, 821 Broadway ☎473-1576. Science fiction, fantasy and horror fiction and comics.

Science Fiction Shop, 163 Bleecker St ☎473-3010. New and used science fiction records and books.

Science Fiction Mysteries and More, 140 Chambers St ☎385-8798. Basic sci-fi bookstore.

Language and foreign

Liberation Bookstore, 421 Lenox Ave ☎281-4615. Works from Africa and the Caribbean.

**Librairie de France/Libreria Hispanica/
The Dictionary Store**, 115 Fifth Ave
☎673-7400. Massive complex housing
New York's French and Spanish bookshops, a dictionary store with over 8000
dictionaries of more than 100 languages,
and a department of teach-yourself
language books, records and tapes.

Rizzoli, 31 W 57th St ☎759 2424; 454a
W Broadway ☎674-1616. Manhattan
branches of the prestigious Italian bookstore chain and publisher, specialising in
European publications, with a selection of
foreign newspapers and magazines.

Mind and body

East West Books, 78 Fifth Ave ☎243-
5994. Bookshop with a mind, body and
spirit slant.

Esoterica, 61 Fourth Ave ☎529-9808.
New Age Californiana (but not
psychedelia).

Quest, 240 E 53rd St ☎ 758-5521. New
Age books.

Samuel Weiser Inc., 132 E 24th St
☎777-6363. Occult and oriental books:
witchcraft, eastern religions, satanism and
spiritualism.

Radical, feminist and gay

Revolution Books, 13 E 16th St ☎691-
3345. New York's major left-wing bookshop and contact point. Books, pamph-
lets, periodicals and information on
current action and events.

St Mark's Bookshop, 12 St Mark's Place
☎260-7853. Probably the largest and
best-known "alternative" bookstore in the
city, with a good array of titles on politics,
feminism and the environment, literary criticism and journals, as well as more
obscure subjects. Good postcards too, and
one of the best places to buy radical and
art New York magazines. Open late.

A Different Light, 548 Hudson St ☎989-
4850. Excellent gay/lesbian bookstore, as
well as a centre for contacts and further
information.

Oscar Wilde Memorial Bookshop, 15
Christopher St ☎255-8097. Principally a
gay men's bookstore.

Miscellaneous

The things listed below fit easily into
none of the previous categories. They're
either shops which might be interesting
to visit simply for themselves; or they sell
items which are cheaper in New York
than in Britain; or they're places which
deserve a mention just because they're
weird.

Antiques

You'd be pretty crazy to come to New
York to buy **antiques** – prices are outrageous. But if you do, much the cheapest
place to browse is in Brooklyn, along
Atlantic Avenue between Hoyt and Third
Street. For just looking, there are any
number of snooty antique stores on
Madison Avenue in the 60s and 70s.
What follows is a highly selective
rundown of the most interesting shopping
places in the city.

American Hurrah, 766 Madison Ave
☎535-1930. Aged Americana mainly:
furniture, quilts, paintings and bric-a-brac.
A wonderful selection but prohibitive
prices.

Annex Antiques Fair, Sixth Ave at 26th St
☎243-5343. A huge range of stalls set
up here at weekends, 9am to 5pm, to
sell a range of antiques and memorabilia.
Good for browsing, even if you're not
looking for anything in particular.
Admission $1.

Antique Arts & Ends, 83 Wooster St
☎925-9470. Antique Wurlitzer jukeboxes,
one-armed bandits, roulette wheels and
neon signs.

Darrow's Fun Antiques, 309 E 61st St
☎838-0730. Animation art, and a wide
variety of fun whimsical antiques.

Depression Modern, 150 Sullivan St
☎982-5699. A lesson in how to make
money out of things people previously
discarded as junk.

Manhattan Art and Antiques Center,
1050 Second Ave ☎355-4400. Around
seventy shops and stalls in all, ranged
over three floors and stocking a vast
assortment – everything from American
quilts to Oriental ceramics.

**Shops and
Markets**

*For listings of
children's
bookstores, see
Chapter 13,,
Kids' New York.*

Shops and Markets

Urban Archeology, 285 Lafayette St ☎431-6969. Large-scale accessories and furniture, mainly American turn-of-the-century, so authentic that the shop rents them out for film sets.

Art supplies

Arthur Brown Inc., 2 W 46th St ☎575-5555. America's largest art suppliers, with a pen department that claims to stock every pen in the known universe.

Lee's Art Shop, 220 W 57th St ☎247-0110. All the artist's needs under one roof. Framing, too.

New York Central Art Supply, 62 Third Ave ☎473-7705. Suppliers to New York artists for four generations.

Pearl Paint Company, 308 Canal St ☎431-7932. Five floors of artist supplies including one for house painting. Another contender for title of the country's largest art shop.

Sam Flax. Artists' supplies store with branches at 15 Park Row ☎620-3040; 25 E 28th St ☎620-3040; 55 E 55th St ☎620-3060; 747 Third Ave ☎620-3050; and 12 W 20th St ☎620-3038.

Ethnic crafts

General

The *United Nations Gift Center*, in the basement of the UN Building on First Avenue ☎754-7700, and the excellent *Brooklyn Museum shop* (see p.216), both sell crafts from different nations.

American

The *Museum of American Folk Art* on Lincoln Square ☎496-2966, stocks American crafts and applied arts, though little that can't be found cheaper elsewhere. For Native American crafts, try *The Common Ground*, 50 Greenwich Ave ☎989-4178, which has jewellery, rugs, pottery and sculpture, and the *Alaska Shop/Gallery of Eskimo Art*, 31 E 74th St ☎879-1782.

Chinese

There are numerous places in Chinatown to buy Chinese and Oriental knick-knacks;

try *Orienthouse*, 242 Broadway ☎431-8060, or *Quons, Yuen, Shing and Co.* on Mott St.

Irish

The *Irish Pavilion*, 130 E 57th St ☎759-9040, stocks all manner of things made in Ireland, especially knitwear. *Shamrock Imports*, Level 5, A&S Plaza, 901 Sixth Ave, ☎564-7474 is similar.

Japanese

The *Japanese Craft Shop* at E 6th St and Second Avenue, and *Things Japanese*, 127 E 60th St ☎371-4661, both have exquisite gifts.

Mexican/Latin American

Buena Dia, 108 W Houston St ☎673-1910; *Putumayo*, 857 Lexington Ave ☎734-3111; 341 Columbus Ave ☎595-3441; 141 Spring St ☎966-4458. More clothes than crafts. *Back From Guatemala*, 306 E 6th St ☎260-7010, sells jewellery and knick-knacks from Central America.

Music, records and electrical equipment

All kinds of **electrical equipment** are cheaper in New York than in Europe and some parts of America, not least **cameras**, which work out very inexpensive. **Records and CDs**, too, can be quite a lot cheaper, with chart CDs retailing at $10–12, records for even less.

Record shops

If you're after anything fairly mainstream, branches of the **Sam Goody** chain (motto "Goody's got it") make a good first stop; addresses in the phone book. **Tower Records**, too, at 692 Broadway and 1965 Broadway, is great for most new records, tapes, CDs and videos. For anything more specialised, or if you're just into browsing, try the selections below.

Bleecker Bob's, 118 W 3rd St ☎475-9677. Long-established record store specialising in punk and new wave that has sadly of late become something of a tourist rip-off. Best avoid.

CBGB Record Canteen, 313 Bowery ☎677-0455. New wave and alternative music.

Colony Record & Tape Center, 1619 Broadway ☎265-2050. Printed sheet music and hard-to-find records.

Dayton's, 799 Broadway ☎254-5084. Rare records, old reviewer's copies and deleted show and film soundtracks.

Finyl Vinyl, 89 Second Ave ☎533-8007. Specialises in records from the 1930s to the 1970s.

Footlight Records, 113 E 12th St ☎533-1572. The place for show music – everything from Broadway to Big Band, Sinatra to Mermand. A must for record collectors.

The Golden Disc, 239 Bleecker St ☎255-7899. Jazz, rock oldies, blues and gospel.

Gryphon Record Shop, 251 W 72nd St ☎874-1588. Specialises in deleted and rare LPs.

House of Oldies, 35 Carmine St ☎243-0500. Just what the name says – oldies but goldies of all kinds. Vinyl only.

HMV, 2081 Broadway, at 72nd St ☎721-5900. Manhattan branch of the newly arrived British chain. Also at 86th St and Lexington Ave.

J&R Music World, 23 Park Row ☎732-8600. Good discounts; J&R's jazz and classical section is a few doors along at no. 33.

Rebel Rebel, 319 Bleecker St ☎989-0770. Good supply of old and new vinyl and CDs.

Record Mart in the Subway, near the N train in the Times Square subway station, 1470 Broadway ☎840-0580. One of the best places in the city to find Caribbean – not to mention Central and South American – music. A knowledgeable staff too; good browsing for the enthusiast.

Second Coming, 235 Sullivan St ☎228-1313. The place to come for heavy metal and hard-core punk.

Sounds, 16 St Mark's Place ☎677-2727. New and used records.

Vinyl Mania, 41 Carmine St ☎463-7120. This, and two other branches in Carmine St, is where DJs come for the newest, rarest releases, especially of dance music. Hard-to-find imports too, as well as home-made dance tapes.

Musical instruments

New York's heaviest concentration of musical instrument stores is located on one block of W 48th St between Sixth and Seventh Ave: **Manny's**, at 156 ☎819-0576, **Rudy's** at 169 ☎391-1699, and **Alex** at 164 ☎765-7738, are the best known in a row of many. A treat for guitar lovers, though harder to get to, is **Mandolin Brothers** at 629a Forest Ave on Staten Island ☎718/981-8585, which has one of the world's best collections of vintage guitars.

Electrical equipment and cameras: bargains for overseas visitors

Given even a reasonable exchange rate, **electrical goods** of almost any description are extremely cheap in America when compared to prices in Europe. The best place for discount shopping is on Seventh Avenue a little north of Times Square in the 50s, where there are any number of stores selling cameras, stereo equipment, radios and the like; for **cameras**, especially anywhere in midtown from 30th and 50th streets between Park and Seventh avenues is the patch. You'll be offered different prices depending on whether you buy the equipment with or without a guarantee (ask for the price with to prevent any misunderstanding), and it's no use going into a shop without an exact idea of the model you want.

In all cases the best advice is to shop around, as prices vary wildly – extremely hard-nosed bargaining is the order of the day, and you should be prepared for rudeness followed by a rapid drop in price when you walk out on someone's "best offer". Remember too that you'll usually get a better price for cash than if you use a credit or charge card. You could also simply try one of the chains, among the best of which are *47th St Photo*, at 67 W 47th St ☎398-1410 (and other branches around Manhattan) and, while never the cheapest, *The Wiz*, 12 W 45th St ☎302-2000 and many other

Shops and Markets

Retailers of electrical and photo equipment are usually rude to the point of nastiness; don't expect any niceties.

Shops and Markets

For toy shops, both new and antique, see Chapter 13, Kids' New York.

locations. Don't be tempted by American TVs or videos – they won't work on the British or most European systems – and make sure that anything you buy is dual voltage if you want it to work in a country with 240 volts, like Britain.

Provided the voltage matches and the machine is pulse/tone dial switchable (and you change the plug for a BT one), most **phones** and answering machines will work in the UK – though neither we nor the shops will guarantee that.

Computers and computer peripherals are also particularly cheap, but again you'll be faced with the voltage compatibility problem – and the fact that a bulky machine is hard for customs officials to miss. Laptops and palmtops, however, usually have an external power supply which you can replace with a 240v model when you return to Britain, and are much less obvious when carried.

Prints, posters and cards

Eurotrash, 301 Columbus Ave ☎787-9119. Great selection of posters, old and new.

The Fourth Street Card Shop, 177 W 4th St ☎675-5465. Marvellous collection of postcards and greetings cards.

Postermat, 37 W 8th St ☎228-4027. Reproduction posters.

Poster Originals, 924 Madison Ave ☎620-0522. Original (and as such expensive) prints from the States and Europe.

Metropolitan Museum of Art, Fifth Ave ☎570-3726. Considering the size and breadth of the museum, its shop is disappointing: a fair selection of mainstream

art books, posters, cards and general paraphernalia.

Museum of Modern Art Shop, 11 W 53rd St ☎708-9700. Large collection of modern art books, cards and posters.

Untitled, 159 Prince St ☎982-2088. Art books, posters and the world's largest selection of postcards.

Sports, games and outdoors

Athlete's Foot, 149 W 72nd St ☎874-1003 and many other Manhattan locations. Jogging gear at affordable prices.

Herman's, 135 W 42nd St ☎730-7400; 845 Third Ave ☎688-4603; 110 Nassau St ☎233-0703; 39 W 34th St ☎279-8900. Sporting goods chain that has an excellent range of equipment, clothing and footwear.

Modell's, 200 Broadway, 280 Broadway, 243 W 42nd St and 111 E 42nd St ☎962-6200. Army surplus and outdoor equipment plus straight sporting items.

Paragon, 867 Broadway ☎255-8036. Giant bargain-priced sports good store.

Tents and Trails, 21 Park Place ☎227-1760. Three floors of camping and hiking equipment.

Village Chess Shop, 230 Thompson St ☎475-9580. Every kind of chess set for every kind of pocket. Usually packed with people playing. Open until midnight.

Trivia and oddities

Dapy Inc., 232 Columbus Ave ☎877-4710. Assorted gadgets, novelties and other useless gifts. Second location at 431 West Broadway ☎925-5082.

Hammacher Schlemmer, 147 E 57th St ☎421-9000. Established in 1848, and probably New York's longest-running trivia store. Unique items, both practical and whimsical. Claims to be the first store to sell the pop-up toaster.

J&R Tobacco Corp., 11 E 45th St ☎983-4160. Self-proclaimed largest cigar store in the world, with an enormous – and affordably priced – range including all the best-known (and some not so known) brands.

The Last Wound-Up, 5095 Second Ave ☎288-7585. Wind-up toys of every shape and size.

Little Rickie, 49 1/2 First Ave at 3rd St, ☎505-6467. A selection of kitsch 24-hour Church of Elvis fridge magnets, plastic nativity scenes for the dashboard, etc.

Maxilla & Mandible, 451–5 Columbus Ave ☎724-6173. Animal and human bones for collectors, scientists or the curious. Worth a visit even if you're not in the market for a perfectly preserved male skeleton.

Merrimack Publishing Corp., 85 Fifth Ave ☎989-5162. Victorian repro toys, decorations, greetings cards, etc, as well as all manner of useless and trivial items – wind-up toys, yo-yos and the like.

Only Hearts, 386 Columbus Ave ☎724-5608. Everything heart-shaped.

Pipeworks & Wilke, 16 W 55th St ☎956-4820. Specialists in all kinds of pipe, including hand-made and antique versions.

The Sharper Image, 4 W 57th St ☎265-2550. Novelty items for yuppies – talking alarm clocks, massage devices and the sort of stuff you find in little catalogues that drop out of Sunday newspaper supplements.

Star Magic, 745 Broadway ☎228-7770. Out of this world space-age gifts – crystals, celestial maps, books, cards and records.

Think Big!, 390 West Broadway ☎925-7300. Oversized everyday items for the giant in your life.

Shops and Markets

Contexts

The historical framework

To Europe she was America, to America she was the gateway of the earth. But to tell the story of New York would be to write a social history of the world.

H.G. Wells

Early days and colonial rule

In the earliest times the area that is today New York City was populated by Native Americans. Each tribe had its own territory and lived a settled existence in villages of bark huts, gaining a livelihood from crop planting, hunting, trapping and fishing. In the New York area the Algonquin tribe was the most populous. Survivors of this and other tribes can still be seen at Long Island's **Shinnecook reservation** – as well as remnants of native culture at the upstate Turtle Center for the Native American Indian.

The native lifestyle represented a continuum of several thousand years, one that was to end with the arrival of European explorers. In 1524 **Giovanni da Verrazano**, an Italian in the service of the French King Francis I, arrived, following in the footsteps of Christopher Columbus 32 years earlier. On his ship, the *Dauphane*, Verrazano had set out to find the legendary Northwest Passage to the Pacific; instead he discovered **Manhattan**. "We found a very agreeable situation located within two small prominent hills, in the midst of which flowed to the sea a very great river, which

was deep within the mouth; and from the sea to the hills, with the rising of the tide, which we found eight feet, any laden ship might have passed." Verrazano returned, "leaving the said land with much regret because of its commodiousness and beauty, thinking it was not without some properties of value", to woo the court with tales of fertile lands and friendly natives, but oddly enough it was nearly a century before the powers of Europe were tempted to follow him.

In 1609 **Hendrik Hudson**, employed by the **Dutch East India Company**, landed at Manhattan and sailed his ship, the *Half-Moone*, as far as Albany. Hudson found that the river did not lead to the Northwest Passage he had been commissioned to discover – but in charting its course for the first time gave his name to the mighty river. "This is a very good land to fall with", noted the ship's mate, "and a pleasant land to see." In a series of skirmishes Hudson's men gave the native people a foretaste of what to expect from future adventurers. Hudson sailed home to England, where he was promptly ticked off for working for the Dutch and sent on another expedition under the British flag: arriving in Hudson Bay, the temperature falling and the mutinous crew doubting his ability as a navigator, Hudson, his son and several others were set adrift in a small boat on the icy waters where, presumably, they froze to death.

The British fear that the Dutch had gained the upper hand in the newfound land proved well justified, for they had the commercial advantage and wasted no time in making the most of it. In the next few years the Dutch established a trading post at the most northerly point Hudson had reached, **Fort Nassau**. In 1624, four years after the Pilgrim Fathers had sailed to Massachusetts, thirty families left Holland to become New York's first European settlers, most sailing up to Fort Nassau but a handful – eight families in all – staying behind on a small island they called Nut Island because of the many walnut trees there; today's Governor's Island. Slowly the community grew as more settlers arrived, and the little island became crowded; the decision was made to move to the limitless spaces across the water, and **the settlement of Manhattan**, an Indian word whose meaning is uncertain, began.

The Dutch gave their new outpost the name **New Amsterdam** and in 1626 **Peter Minuit** was sent out to govern the small community of just over three hundred. Among his first, and certainly more politically adroit, moves was to buy the whole of Manhattan Island from the Indians for trinkets worth 60 guilders (about $25 today); though the other side of the anecdote is even better – for the Indians Minuit dealt with didn't even come from Manhattan, let alone own it. As the colony slowly grew, a string of governors succeeded Minuit, the most famous of them **Peter Stuyvesant** – "Peg Leg Pete", a seasoned colonialist from the Dutch West Indies who'd lost his leg in a scrap with the Portuguese. Under his leadership New Amsterdam doubled in size and population, protected from British settlers to the north by an encircling wall (**Wall Street** today follows its course) and defended by a rough-hewn fort on what is now the site of the Customs House. Stuyvesant also built himself a farm (a *bowerie* in Dutch) a little to the north, that gave its name to the **Bowery**.

Meanwhile the **British** were steadily and stealthily building up their presence to the north. Though initially preoccupied by Civil War at home, they maintained their claim that all of America's East Coast, from New England to Virginia, was theirs, and in 1664 sent a Colonel Richard Nicholls to claim the lands around the Hudson that King Charles II had granted to his brother, the Duke of York. To reinforce his sovereignty Charles sent along four warships and landed troops on Nut Island and Long Island. The Dutch settlers had by then had enough of Stuyvesant's increasingly dictatorial rule, especially the high taxation demanded by the nominal owners of the colony, the Dutch West India Company, and so refused to defend Dutch rule against the British. Captain Nicholls' men took New Amsterdam, renamed it **New York** in honour of the Duke and settled down to a hundred-odd years of British rule, interrupted but briefly in 1673 when the Dutch once more managed to gain the upper hand.

During this period not all was plain sailing. When King James II was forced to abdicate and flee Britain in 1689, a German merchant called **James Leisler** led a revolt against British rule. Unfortunately for Leisler it mustered little sympa-

thy, and he was hanged for treason. Also, by now black slaves constituted a major part of New York's population, and though laws denied them weapons and the right of assembly, in 1712 a number of slaves set fire to a building near Maiden Lane and killed nine people who attempted to stop the blaze. When soldiers arrived, six of the incendiaries committed suicide and twenty-one others were captured and executed. In other areas primitive civil rights were slowly being established: in 1734 **John Peter Zenger**, publisher of the *New York Weekly Journal*, was tried and acquitted of libelling the British government, establishing freedom for the press that would later bring about the First Amendment to the Constitution.

Revolution

By the 1750s the city had reached a population of 16,000, spread roughly as far north as Chambers Street. As the new community became more confident, so it realised that it could exist independently of the government in Britain. But in 1763 the **Treaty of Paris** concluded the Seven Years' War with France, and sovereignty over most of explored North America was conceded to England. British rule was thus consolidated and the government decided to try throwing its weight about. Within a year, discontent over British rule escalated with the passage of the punitive **Sugar**, **Stamp and Colonial Currency Acts**. Further resentment erupted over the **Quartering Act**, which permitted British troops to requisition private dwellings and inns, their rent to be paid by the colonies themselves. Ill-feeling steadily mounted and skirmishes between soldiers and the insurrectionist **Sons of Liberty** culminated in January 1770 with the killing of a colonist and the wounding of several others. **The Boston Massacre**, in which British troops fired upon taunting protestors, occurred a few weeks later and helped formulate the embryonic feelings of the Revolution.

In a way, New York's role during the **War of Independence** was not crucial, for all the battles fought in and around the city were generally won by the side that lost the war. But they were the first military engagements between the British and American forces after the **Declaration of Independence**, proclaimed to the cheering crowds outside the site of today's **City Hall Park**, who then went off to tear down the statue of George III that stood on the Bowling Green. The

British, driven from Boston the previous winter, resolved that New York should be the place where they would reassert their authority over the rebels, and in June and July of 1776 some two hundred ships under the command of **Lord Howe** arrived in New York harbour. The troops made camp on Staten Island while the commander of the American forces, **George Washington**, consolidated his men, in the hope that the mouth of the harbour was sufficiently well defended to stop British ships from entering it and encircling his troops. But Howe managed to slip two frigates past Washington to moor north of the city and decided to make his assault on the city by land. On August 22 he landed 15,000 men, mainly Hessian mercenaries, on the southwest corner of Brooklyn. His plan was to occupy Brooklyn and launch an attack on Manhattan from there. In the **Battle of Long Island**, Howe's men penetrated the American forward lines at a number of points, the most important engagement taking place at what is today Prospect Park.

The Americans fell back to their positions and as the British made preparations to attack the fortifications, Washington could see that his garrison would be easily defeated. On the night of August 29, under cover of rain and fog, he evacuated his men safely to Manhattan from the ferry slip beneath where the Brooklyn Bridge now stands, preserving the bulk of his forces. A few days later Howe's army set out in boats from Green Point and Newtown Creek in Brooklyn to land at what is now the 34th Street heliport site. The defenders of the city retreated north to make a stand at Harlem Heights, but were pushed back again to eventual defeat at the **Battle of White Plains** in Westchester County (the Bronx), where Washington lost 1400 of his 4000 men. More tragic still was the defence of **Fort Washington**, perched on a rocky cliff 230 feet above the Hudson, near today's George Washington Bridge. Here, rather than evacuate the troops, the local commander made a decision to stand and fight: trapped by the Hudson to the west it was a fatal mistake, and upwards of 3000 men were killed or taken prisoner. Gathering more forces, Washington retreated, and for the next seven years New York was occupied by the British as a garrison town. During this period many of the remaining inhabitants and most of the prisoners taken by the British slowly starved to death.

Lord Cornwallis's **surrender** to the Americans in October 1783 marked the end of the War of Independence, and a month later New York was finally relieved. Washington, the man who had held the American army together by sheer will-power, was there to celebrate, riding in triumphal procession down Canal Street and saying farewell to his officers at **Fraunces Tavern**, a building that still stands at the end of Pearl Street. It was a tearful occasion for men who had fought through the worst of the war years together: "I am not only retiring from all public employments," he declared, "but am retiring within myself."

But that was not to be. New York was now the fledgling nation's **capital** and, as Thomas Jefferson et al framed the Constitution and the role of President of the United States, it became increasingly clear that there was only one candidate for the position. On April 30, 1789, Washington took the oath of President at the site of the **Federal Hall National Memorial** on Wall Street. The federal government was transferred to Philadelphia a year later.

Immigration and Civil War

In 1790 the first official census of Manhattan put the population at around 33,000: business and trade were on the increase, with the market under a buttonwood tree on Wall Street being a forerunner to the New York Stock Exchange. A few years later, in 1807, **Robert Fulton** launched the *Clermont*, a steamboat that managed to splutter its way up the Hudson River from New York to Albany, pioneering trade with upstate areas. A year before his death in 1814 Fulton also started a ferry service between Manhattan and Brooklyn, and the dock at which it moored became a focus of trade and eventually a maritime centre, taking its name from the inventor.

But it was the opening of the **Erie Canal** in 1825 that really allowed New York to develop as a port. The Great Lakes were suddenly opened to New York, and with them the rest of the country; goods manufactured in the city could be taken easily and cheaply to the American heartlands. It was on this prosperity, and the mass of **cheap labour** that flooded in throughout the nineteenth and early twentieth centuries, that New York – and to an extent the nation – became wealthy. The first waves of **immigrants**, mainly **German** and **Irish**, began to arrive in the mid-nineteenth century, the latter forced out by the Potato Famine of 1846, the former by the failed Revolution of

1848–49, which had left many German liberals, labourers, intellectuals and businessmen dispossessed by political machinations. The city could not handle people arriving in such great numbers and epidemics of yellow fever and cholera were common, exacerbated by poor water supplies, insanitary conditions and the poverty of most of the newcomers. But in the 1880s large-scale **Italian** immigration began, mainly of labourers and peasants from southern Italy and Sicily, whilst at the same time refugees from **eastern Europe** started to arrive – many of them Jewish. The two communities shared a home on the **Lower East Side**, which became one of the worst slum areas of its day. On the eve of the Civil War the majority of New York's 750,000 population were immigrants; in 1890 one in four alone of the city's inhabitants was Irish.

During this period life for the well-off was fairly pleasant and development in the city proceeded apace. Despite a great fire in 1835 that destroyed most of the business district downtown, trade boomed and was celebrated in the opening of the **World's Fair** of 1835 at the Crystal Palace on the site of Bryant Park – an iron and glass building that fared no better than its London namesake, burning down in 1858. In the same year work began on clearing the shanty-towns in the centre of the island to make way for a newly landscaped open space – a marvellous design by Frederick Law Olmsted and Calvert Vaux that became **Central Park**.

Two years later the **Civil War** broke out, caused by growing differences between the northern and southern states, notably on the issue of slavery. New York sided with the Union (north) against the Confederates (south), but had little experience of the hand-to-hand fighting that ravaged the rest of the country. It did, however, form a focus for much of the radical thinking behind the war, particularly with **Abraham Lincoln**'s influential "Might makes Right" speech from the **Cooper Union Building** in 1860. In 1863 a **conscription law** was passed that allowed the rich to buy themselves out of military service. Not surprisingly this was deeply unpopular, and New Yorkers rioted, burning buildings and looting shops: over a thousand people were killed in these **Draft Riots**. A sad addendum to the war was the assassination of Lincoln in 1865: when his body lay in state in New York's City Hall, 120,000 people filed past to pay last respects.

The late nineteenth century

The end of the Civil War saw much of the country devastated but New York intact, and it was fairly predictable that the city would soon become the wealthiest and most influential in the nation. Broadway developed into the main thoroughfare, with grand hotels, restaurants and shops catering for the rich; newspaper editors **William Cullen Bryant** and **Horace Greeley** respectively founded the *Evening Post* and the *Tribune*; and the city became a magnet for writers and intellectuals, with **Washington Irving** and **James Fenimore Cooper** among notable residents. By dint of its skilled immigrant workers, its facilities for marketing goods, and the wealth to build factories, New York was also the greatest business, commercial and manufacturing centre in the country. **Cornelius Vanderbilt** controlled a vast shipping and railroad empire, and **J.P. Morgan**, the banking and investment wizard, was instrumental in organising financial mergers that led to the formation of prototype corporate business. But even bigger in a way was a character who was not a businessman but a politician: **William Marcy Tweed**. From lowly origins Tweed worked his way up the Democratic Party ladder to the position of alderman at the age of 21, eventually becoming chairman of the party's State Central Committee. Surrounded by his own men – the **Tweed Ring** – and aided by a paid-off mayor, "Boss" Tweed took total control of the city's government and finances. Anyone in a position to endanger his money-making schemes was bought off by cash extorted from the huge bribes given by contractors eager to carry out municipal services. In this way $160 million found its way into Tweed's and his friends' pockets. Tweed stayed in power by organising the speedy naturalisation of aliens, who, in repayment, were expected to vote in Tweed and his sidekicks every so often. For his part, Tweed gave generously to the poor, who knew he was swindling the rich but saw him as a Robin Hood figure. As a contemporary observer remarked, "The government of the rich by the manipulation of the poor is a new phenomenon in the world." Tweed's swindles grew in audacity and greed until a determined campaign by **George Jones**, editor of the *New York Times*, and **Thomas Nast**, whose vicious portrayals of Tweed and his henchmen appeared in *Harper's Weekly*, brought him down. The people who kept Tweed in power may not have been able to read or write, but they could understand a cartoon – and Tweed's heyday was over. A committee was established to investigate corruption in City Hall and Tweed found himself in court. Despite a temporary escape to Spain he was returned to the US, and died in Ludlow Street jail – by pleasing irony a building he had commissioned as Chief of Works.

The latter part of the nineteenth century, however, was for some the city's golden age: elevated railways (the **Els**) sprung up to ferry people quickly and cheaply across the city, **Thomas Edison** lit the streets with his new electric light bulb, powered from the first electricity plant on Pearl Street, and in 1883, to the wonderment of New Yorkers, the **Brooklyn Bridge** was opened, Brooklyn itself along with Staten Island, Queens and the part of Westchester that became the Bronx, becoming part of the city in 1898. All this commercial expansion stimulated the city's cultural growth; **Walt Whitman** eulogised the city in his poems, and **Henry James** recorded its manners and mores in novels like *Washington Square*. **Richard Morris Hunt** built palaces for the wealthy robber barons along Fifth Avenue, who plundered Europe to assemble art collections to furnish them – collections that would eventually find their way into the newly opened Metropolitan Museum. For the "Four Hundred", the wealthy élite that revelled in and owned the city, New York in the "gay nineties" was a constant string of lavish balls and dinners that vied with each other until opulence became obscenity. At one banquet the millionaire guests arrived on horseback and ate their meals in the saddle; afterwards the horses were fed gourmet-prepared fodder.

Further immigration and building

At the same time, emigration of Europe's impoverished peoples continued unabated, and in 1884 new immigrants from the Orient settled in what became known as **Chinatown**; the following year saw a huge influx of southern Italians to the city. As the Vanderbilts, Astors and Rockefellers lorded it over the mansions uptown, overcrowded tenements led to terrible living standards for the poor. Working conditions were little better, and were compassionately described by police reporter and photographer **Jacob Riis**, whose book *How the Other Half Lives* detailed the long working hours, exploitation and child labour that kept the city's coffers full.

More Jewish immigrants arrived to cram the Lower East Side, and in 1898 the population of New York amounted to over 3 million – the largest city in the world. Twelve years earlier Augustus Bartholdi's **Statue of Liberty** had been finished, holding a symbolic torch to guide the huddled masses; now pressure grew to limit immigration, but still people flooded in. **Ellis Island**, the depot which processed arrivals, was handling 2000 people a day, a total of 10 million by 1929, when laws were passed to curtail immigration. By the turn of the century, around half of the city's peoples were foreign-born, and a quarter of the population was made up of German and Irish migrants, most of them people living in slums. The section of Manhattan bounded by the East River, East 14th Street and Third Avenue, the Bowery and Catherine Street was probably the most densely populated area on earth, inhabited by a poor who lived under worse conditions and paid more rent than the inhabitants of any other big city in the world. Yet, in 1900, J.P. Morgan's United States Steel Company became the first billion-dollar corporation.

The early 1900s saw some of this wealth going into adventurous new architecture. SoHo had already utilised the **cast iron building** to mass produce classical facades, and the **Flatiron Building** of 1902 announced the arrival of what was to become the city's trade mark – the skyscraper. On the arts front **Stephen Crane**, **Theodore Dreiser** and **Edith Wharton** used New York as the subject for their writing, **George M. Cohan** was the Bright Young Man of Broadway, and in 1913 the **Armory exhibition** of Modernist painting by Picasso, Duchamp and others caused a sensation. Meantime the skyscrapers were pushing higher and higher, and in the same year a building that many consider the *ne plus ultra* of the genre, the **Woolworth Building**, was opened. Also that year **Grand Central Terminal** celebrated New York as the gateway to the continent.

The first two decades of the century saw a further wave of immigration, made up chiefly of Jews. In that period one-third of all the Jews in eastern Europe arrived in New York and upwards of 1.5 million of them settled in New York City, primarily in the Lower East Side. Despite advances in public building, caused by the outcry that followed Jacob Riis's reports, the area could not cope with a population density of 640,000 per square mile, and the poverty and inhuman conditions reached their worst as people strove to better themselves by working in the sweat-shops of Hester Street. Workers, especially those in trades dominated by Jewish immigrants from socialist backgrounds, began to strike to demand better wages and working conditions. Most of the garment manufacturers, for example, charged women workers for their needles and the hire of lockers, and handed out swingeing fines for spoilage of fabrics. Strikes of 1910–11 achieved only limited success, and it took disaster to rouse public and civic conscience. On March 25, 1911, just before the **Triangle Shirtwaist Factory** at Washington Place was about to finish work for the day, a fire broke out. The workers were trapped on the tenth floor and 146 of them died (125 were women), mostly by leaping from the blazing building. Within months the state had passed 56 factory reform measures, and unioni-sation spread through the city.

The war years: 1914–1945

With America's entry into World War I in 1917 New York benefited from wartime trade and commerce. At home, perhaps surprisingly, there was little conflict between the various European communities crammed into the city. Although Germans comprised roughly one-fifth of the city's population, there were few of the attacks on their lives or property that occurred elsewhere in the country.

The post-war years saw one law and one character dominating the New York scene: the law was **Prohibition**, passed in 1920 in an attempt to sober up the nation; the character was **Jimmy Walker**, elected mayor in 1925 and who led a far from sober lifestyle. "No civilised man", said Walker, "goes to bed the same day he wakes up", and during his flamboyant career the Jazz Age came to the city. In speakeasies all over town the bootleg liquor flowed and writers as diverse as **Damon Runyon**, **F. Scott Fitzgerald** and **Ernest Hemingway** portrayed the excite-ment of the times. With the **Wall Street** crash of 1929 (see "The Financial District" in Chapter 2, *Lower Manhattan*), however, the party came to an abrupt end. The Depression began and Mayor Walker was flushed away with the torrent of civic corruption and malpractice that the changing times had uncovered and unleashed.

By 1932 approximately one in four New Yorkers was unemployed, and shantytowns, blackly known as "Hoovervilles" after the then President, had sprung up in Central Park to house

the workless and homeless. Yet during this period three of New York's most opulent – and most beautiful – skyscrapers were topped out: the **Chrysler Building** in 1930, the **Empire State** in 1931 (though it was to stand near-empty for years) and in 1932 the **Rockefeller Center** – all very impressive, but of little immediate help to those in Hooverville, Harlem or other depressed parts of the city. It fell to **Fiorello LaGuardia**, Jimmy Walker's successor as mayor, to take over the running of the crisis-strewn city. He did so with ruthless tax and rationalisation programmes that, surprisingly, won him the approval of the people in the street: Walker's good living had got the city into trouble, reasoned voters; hard-headed, straight-talking LaGuardia would get it out. Moreover President Roosevelt's **New Deal** supplied funds for roads, housing and parks, the latter undertaken by the controversial Parks Commissioner **Robert Moses**. Under LaGuardia and Moses, the most extensive public housing programme in the country was undertaken; the Triborough, Whitestone and Henry Hudson bridges completed; 50 miles of new expressway and 5000 acres of new parks opened. And, in 1939, Mayor LaGuardia opened the airport that carries his name.

LaGuardia ran three terms as mayor, taking the city into the **war years**. The country's entry into World War II in 1941 had few direct effects on New York City: lights were dimmed, 200 Japanese were interned on Ellis Island and guards placed on bridges and tunnels. But, more importantly, behind the scenes experiments taking place at Columbia University split the uranium atom, giving a name to the **Manhattan Project** – the creation of the first atomic weapon.

The Post-war years

Though the beleaguered black community of Harlem erupted into looting and violence in 1943, the city maintained its pre-eminent position in the fields of finance, art and communications, both in America and the world, its intellectual and creative community swollen by refugees escaping the Nazi threat to Europe. When the **United Nations Organisation** was seeking a permanent home, New York was the obvious choice: lured by Rockefeller-donated land, the UN began the build-ing of the Secretariat in 1947.

The building of the United Nations, along with the boost in the economy that followed the war, brought about the development of midtown

Manhattan. First off in the race to fill the once-residential Park Avenue with offices was the **Lever House** of 1952, quickly followed by skyscrapers like the **Seagram Building** that give the area its distinctive look. Downtown, the **Stuyvesant Town** and **Peter Cooper Village** housing projects went ahead, along with many others all over the city. As ever, there were plentiful scandals over the financing of the building, most famously concerning the **Manhattan Urban Renewal Project** on the Upper East Side.

A further scandal, this time concerning organised crime, ousted Mayor **William O'Dwyer** in 1950: he was replaced by a series of uneventful characters who did little to stop the gradual **decline** that had begun in the early 1950s as a general stagnation set in among the country's urban centres. New York fared worst: immigration from Puerto Rico had once more crammed East Harlem and the Lower East Side, and the nationwide trend of black migration from poorer rural areas was also magnified here. Both groups were forced into the ghetto area of Harlem, unable to get a slice of the city's wealth. Racial disturbances and riots occurred in what had for two hundred years been one of the more liberal of American cities. One response to the problem was a general exodus of the white middle classes – the **Great White Flight** as the media gleefully labelled it – out of New York. Between 1950 and 1970 over a million families left the city. Things went from bad to worse during the 1960s with **race riots** in Harlem, Bedford-Stuyvesant and East Harlem.

The **World's Fair** of 1964 was a white elephant to boost the city's credit in the financial world, but on the streets the call for civil liberties for blacks and protest against US involvement in Vietnam were, if anything, stronger than in the rest of the country. What little new building went up during this period seemed wilfully to destroy much of the best of earlier traditions: a new **Madison Square Garden** was built on the site of the grandly neoclassical **Pennsylvania Station**, and the **Singer Building** in the Financial District was demolished for an ugly skyscraper. In Harlem municipal investment stopped altogether and the community stagnated.

The 1970s and 1980s

Manhattan reached **crisis point** in 1975. By now the city was spending more than it received in taxes – billions of dollars more. In part, this could be attributed to the effects of the White Flight: companies closed their headquarters in the city when offered lucrative relocation deals elsewhere, and their white-collar employees were usually glad to go with them, thus doubly eroding the city's tax base. Even after municipal securities were sold, New York ran up a debt of $13,000 million. Essential services, long shaky through underfunding, were ready to collapse. The mayor who oversaw this farrago, **Abraham Beame**, was an accountant.

Three things saved the city: the **Municipal Assistance Corporation** (aka the **Big Mac**), which was formed to borrow the money the city could no longer get its hands on; the election of **Edward I. Koch** as mayor in 1978; and, in a roundabout way, the plummeting of the dollar on the world currency market following the oil price rises of the 1970s. This last effect, combined with cheap transatlantic airfares, brought European tourists into the city *en masse* for the first time, and with them came money for the city's hotels and service industries. Mayor Koch, cheerfully saying "Isn't it terrible?" to whatever he could not immediately put right, and asking "How am I doing?" each time he scored a success, gained the appreciation of New Yorkers, ever eager to look to their civic leaders for help or blame.

The slow reversal of fortunes coincided with the completion of two face-saving building projects: though, like the Empire State Building it long remained half empty, the **World Trade Center** was a gesture of confidence by the Port Authority of New York and New Jersey, which financed it; and in 1977 the **Citicorp Center** added modernity and prestige to its environs on Third Avenue.

Since the mid-1970s slump the city in some respects went from strength to strength. Ed Koch managed simultaneously to offend liberal groups and win the electoral support of ethnic groups, and despite the death of his friend and supporter Queens borough president **Donald Manes**, (who committed suicide when an investigation into the city's various debt collecting agencies was announced) he was probably the most popular mayor since LaGuardia – some measure of his adroitness as a politician.

Into the 1990s

A spate of building gave the city yet more fabulous architecture, notably **Battery City Park** downtown, while master builder Donald Trump provided housing for the super-wealthy. But the popularity of Ed Koch waned. Many middle-class constituents considered Koch to have only rich property-barons' interests at heart; he also alienated a number of minorities – particularly blacks – with off-the-cuff statements that he was unable to bluff away. And although he was not directly implicated, the scandals in his administration, beginning with the suicide of Donald Manes and continuing with the indictment (although she was acquitted) for bribery of another prominent friend, former Arts Commissioner Bess Myerson, took their political toll.

In 1989, Koch lost the Democratic nomination for the mayoral elections to **David Dinkins**, a 61-year old, black ex-marine and borough president of Manhattan. In a toughly fought election the same year, Dinkins beat Republican Rudolph Giuliani, a hard-nosed US attorney (whose role as leader of the prosecution in a police corruption case was made into the film *Prince of the City*). But even before the votes were counted, pundits were forecasting that the condition of the city was beyond any mayoral healing.

By the end of the 1980s New York was slipping hard and fast into a **massive recession**: in 1989 the city's budget deficit ran at $500 million; of the 92 companies that had made the city their base in 1980, only 53 were left, the others having moved to cheaper pastures; one in four New Yorkers was officially classed as poor – a figure unequalled since the Depression. The first black to hold the office, David Dinkins oversaw his first year as mayor reasonably well: the city's **Board of Estimate** had been declared unconstitutional by the Supreme Court (it violated the one person, one vote principle), and was abolished and replaced by a beefier City Council. Dinkins used his powers to quell racial unrest that had seemed about to explode in the spring, and skilfully passed a complex budget through the Council.

The date from which Dinkins's – and to some extent the city's – slide commenced was during the first week of the US open tennis tournament in summer 1990. On his way to the match, Brian Watkins, a tennis fan from Utah, was stabbed to death in a subway station by a group of muggers while trying to protect his mother.

Instead of holding a Koch-style "what is this city coming to?" press conference, Dinkins issued a statement saying that the media were exaggerating the importance of the murder – and then boarded a police helicopter to fly to the tennis event. As was predictable, the press latched onto this immediately, and Dinkins fell swiftly, and seemingly irrevocably, from popular favour, becoming known as the man "to whom everything sticks but praise".

From the summer on, the city's fortunes went into freefall. The unions went on the offensive when it was learned the city intended to lay off 15,000 workers; crime – especially related to the sale of crack (a cheap, cocaine-derived stimulant) – escalated; business failed. By the end of the year the city's budget deficit had reached $1.5 billion and city creditors were threatening to remove support for municipal borrowing unless the figure was reduced drastically.

Throughout 1991 the previous year's financial disasters started to have the knock-on effect on the city's **ordinary people**: homelessness increased as city aid was cut back, schools became no-go zones with armed police and metal detectors at the gates (less than half of high school kids in the city graduate, a far smaller proportion than elsewhere in the United States), and a garbage workers' strike in May left piles of rubbish rotting on the streets. Once again, New York seemed to have hit bottom, and this time there was no obvious solution. Unlike in 1976, the state government refused to bail the city out with aid loans; and, as far as the federal government were concerned, the coffers ran out for New York long ago. Neither does the new Clinton administration promise much for the city, other than the indirect hope that Hillary Clinton's much-vaunted shake-up of the health system will help the city's socially disadvantaged, especially in the light of the 1993 mayoral elections, in which the beleagured Democrat, David Dinkins, lost narrowly to the brash ex-lawyer, Rudy Giuliani – making him the city's first Republican mayor for 28 years. With New York now something like $3 billion in the red, and a mayor who certainly won't find any cooperation among the city's traditionally Democrat administrators, the future for New York can't help but look bleak.

Architectural chronology

1625	First permanent **Dutch settlement** on Manhattan.	No buildings remain of the period. **Wall Street** marks the settlement's defensive northern boundary in 1653.
Late 18th c.	New York under **British colonial rule**.	**St Paul's Chapel** (1766) built in Georgian style.
1812	British blockade of Manhattan.	**City Hall** built.
1825	Opening of **Erie Canal** increases New York's wealth.	**Fulton Street** dock and market area built. Greek Revival row houses popular – eg **Schermerhorn Row**, **Colonnade Row**, **St Mark's Place**, **Chelsea**. Of much Federal-style building, few examples remain: The **Abigail Adams Smith House**, the **Morris-Jumel Mansion** and **Gracie Mansion** the most notable.
1830–50	First wave of **immigration**, principally German and Irish.	The **Lower East Side** developed. **Trinity Church** built (1846) in English Gothic style, **Federal Hall** (1842) in Greek Revival.
1850–1900	**More immigrants** (more Irish and Germans, later Italians and east European Jews) settle in Manhattan. **Industrial development** brings extreme wealth to individuals. The **Civil War** (1861–65) has little effect on the city.	Cast iron architecture enables buildings to mimic grand Classical designs cheaply. Highly popular in SoHo, eg the **Haughwout Building** (1859). Large, elaborate mansions built along Fifth Avenue for America's new millionaires. **Central Park** opened (1876). The **Brooklyn Bridge** (1883) links Gothic with industrial strength; **St Patrick's Cathedral** (1879) and **Grace Church** (1846) show it at its most delicate. **Statue of Liberty** unveiled (1886).
Early 20th c.		The **Flatiron Building** (1902) is the first skyscraper. Much civic architecture in the Beaux Arts neoclassical style: **Grand Central Terminal** (1919), **New York Public Library** (1911), **US Customs House** (1907), **General Post Office** (1913) and the **Municipal Building** (1914) are the finest examples. The **Woolworth Building** (1913) becomes Manhattan's "Cathedral of Commerce".
1915		The **Equitable Building** fills every square inch of its site on Broadway, causing the first zoning ordinances to ensure a degree of setback and allow light to reach the streets.
1920	**Prohibition** law passed. Economic confidence of the 1920s brings the **Jazz Age**.	Art Deco influences show in the **American Standard Building** (1927) and the **Fuller Building** (1929).
1929	**Wall Street Crash**. America enters the **Great Depression**.	Many of the lavish buildings commissioned and begun in the 1920s reach completion. Skyscrapers combine the monumental with the decorative: **Chrysler Building** (1930), **Empire State Building** (1930), **Waldorf Astoria Hotel** (1931) and the **General Electric Building** (1931). The **Rockefeller Center**, the first exponent of the idea of a city-within-a-city, is built through the decade. The **McGraw-Hill Building** (1931) is self-consciously modern.

Architectural chronology continued

| 1930s | The **New Deal** and **WPA** schemes attempt to reduce unemployment. | Little new building other than housing estates. WPA murals decorate buildings around town, notably in the **New York Public Library** and **County Courthouse**. |

1941   America enters the **war**.   New zoning regulations encourage the development of the setback skyscraper: but little is built during the war years.

1950   **United Nations Organisation** established.   The **UN Secretariat** (1950) introduces the glass curtain wall to Manhattan. Similar Corbusier-influenced buildings include the **Lever House** (1952) and, most impressively, the **Seagram Building** (1958), whose plaza causes the zoning regulations to be changed in an attempt to encourage similar public spaces. The **Guggenheim Museum** (1959) opens.

1960s   **Protest movement** stages demonstrations against US involvement in Vietnam.   Much early-1960s building pallidly imitates the glass box skyscraper. The **Pan Am** (1963) building attempts something different, but more successful is the **Ford Foundation** (1967). In the hands of lesser architects, the plaza becomes a liability. New **Madison Square Garden** (1968) is built on the site of the old Penn Station. The minimalist **Verrazano-Narrows Bridge** (1964) links Brooklyn to Staten Island .

1970s   Mayor Abraham Beame presides over **New York's decline**. City financing reaches **crisis point** as businesses leave Manhattan.   The **World Trade Center Towers** (1970) add a soaring landmark to the lower Manhattan skyline. **The Rockefeller Center Extensions** (1973–4) clone the glass box skyscraper. Virtually no new corporate development until the **Citicorp Center** (1977) adds new textures and profile to the city's skyline. Its popular atrium is adopted by later buildings.

1975   Investment in the city increases.   **One UN Plaza** adapts the glass curtain wall to skilled ends.

1978   **Corporate wealth returns** to Manhattan. **Ed Koch elected mayor**.   The **IBM Building** (1982) shows the conservative side of modern architecture; post-modernist designs like the **AT&T Building** (1983) and **Federal Reserve Plaza** (1985) mix historical styles in the same building.

1980s   **Ed Koch returned as mayor**.   **Statue of Liberty** restoration completed. The mixed-use **Battery City Park** opens to wide acclaim.

1986   Wall Street **crashes;** Dow Jones index plunges 500 points in a day.   Property market takes a dive. **Equitable Building** on Seventh Ave opens.

1989   **Ed Koch** loses Democratic nomination to **David Dinkins**, who goes on to become NYC's first black mayor.   **Rockefeller Center** sold to Japanese. **RCA Building** renamed **General Electric Building**.

1990   Major **recession** hits New York.   **Ellis Island** museum of immigration opens to public.

1991   NYC's **budget deficit** reaches record proportions.   **Guggenheim** Museum reopens with new extension.

Twentieth-century American art

This is no more than a brief introduction to a handful of American painters; for more detailed appraisals, both of the century's major movements and specific painters, see "Books".

Twentieth-century American art begins with **The Eight**, otherwise known as the **Ashcan School**, a group of artists who were painting in New York in the first decade of this century. Led by Robert Henri, many of them worked as illustrators for city newspapers, and they tried to depict modern American urban life – principally in New York City – as honestly and realistically as possible, in much the same way as earlier painters had depicted nature. Their exhibitions, in 1908 and 1910, were, however, badly received, and most of their work was scorned for representing subjects not seen as fit for painting. Paralleling the work of the Ashcan School was that of the group that met at the **Photo-Secession Gallery** of the photographer Alfred Stieglitz on Fifth Avenue. They were more individual, less concerned with social themes than expressing their own individual styles, but were equally unappreciated. Art, for Americans, even for American critics, was something that came from Europe, and in the early years of the twentieth century attempts to Americanise it were regarded with suspicion.

Change came with the **Armory Show** of 1913: an exhibition, set up by the remaining Ashcan artists (members of the new *Association of American Painters and Sculptors*), to bring more than 1800 European works together and show them to the American public for the first time. The whole of the French nineteenth century was represented at the show, together with Cubist and Expressionist painters, and, from New York, the work of the Ashcan painters and the Stieglitz circle. It was visited by over 85,000 people in its month-long run in New York, and plenty more caught it as it toured America. The immediate effect was uproar. Americans panned the European paintings, partly because they resented their influence but also since they weren't quite sure how to react; the indigenous American artists were criticised for being afraid to adopt a native style; and the press fanned the flames by playing up to public anxieties about the subversive nature of modern art. But there was a positive effect: the modern art of both Europe and America became known all over the continent, particularly abstract painting. From now on American artists were free to develop their own approach.

The paintings that followed were, however, far from abstract in style. The Great Crash of 1929 and subsequent Depression led to the school of **Social Realism** and paintings like **Thomas Hart Benton**'s *America Today* sequence (now in the Equitable Center at 757 Seventh Ave): a vast mural that covered, in realistic style, every aspect of contemporary American life. The New Deal and the resultant **Federal Art Project** of the WPA supported many artists through the lean years of the 1930s by commissioning them to decorate public buildings, and it became widely acknowledged that not only were work, workers and public life fit subjects for art, but also that artists had some responsibility to push for social change. Artists like **Edward Hopper** and **Charles Burchfield** sought to re-create, in as precise a way as possible, American contemporary life, making the particular (in Hopper's case empty streets, lone buildings, solitary figures in diners) "epic and universal". Yet while Hopper and Burchfield can be called great artists in their own right, much of the work of the time, particularly that commissioned as public works, was inevitably dull and conformist, and it wasn't long before movements were afoot to inject new life into American painting. It was the beginning of abstraction.

With these ideas so the centre of the visual art world gradually began to shift. The founding of the **Museum of Modern Art**, and also of the **Guggenheim Museum** some years later, combined with the arrival of many European artists throughout the 1930s (Gropius, Hans Hofmann, the Surrealists) to make New York a serious rival to Paris in terms of influence. **Hans Hofmann** in particular was to have considerable influence on New York painters, both through his art school and his own boldly Expressionistic works. Also, the many American artists who had lived abroad came back armed with a set of European experiences which they could couple with their native spirit to produce a new, indigenous and wholly original style. First and most prominent of these was **Arshile Gorky**, a European-born painter who had imbibed the influences of Cézanne and Picasso – and, more so, the Surrealists. His technique, however, was different: not cold and dispassionate like the Europeans but expressive, his paintings textured and more vital. **Stuart Davis**, too, once a prominent member of the Ashcan School, was an important figure, his paintings using everyday objects as subject matter but jumbling them into abstract form – as in works like *Lucky Strike*, which hangs in the Museum of Modern Art. Another artist experimenting with abstract forms was **Georgia O'Keefe**, best known for her depictions of flowers, toned in pastelly pinks and powder blues. These she magnified so they became no more than unidentified shapes, in their curves and ovular forms curiously erotic and suggestive of fertility and growth. The Whitney Museum holds a good stock of her work.

The **Abstract Expressionists** – or **The New York School** as they came to be known – were a fairly loose movement, and one which splits broadly into two groups: the first created abstractions with increasing gusto and seemingly endless supplies of paint, while the rest employed a more ordered approach to their work. Best known among the first group is **Jackson Pollock**,

a farmer's son from Wyoming who had studied under Thomas Hart Benton in New York and in the 1930s was painting Cubist works reminiscent of Picasso. Pollock considered the American art scene to be still under the thumb of Europe, and he deliberately set about creating canvases that bore little relation to anything that had gone before. For a start his paintings were huge, and it was difficult to tell where they ended; in fact Pollock would simply determine the edge of a composition by cutting the canvas wherever he happened to feel was appropriate at the time – a large-scale approach that was much imitated and in part determined by the large factory spaces and lofts where American artists worked. Also, it was a reaction against bourgeois (and therefore essentially European) notions of what a painting should be: the average Abstract Expressionist painting simply couldn't be contained in the normal collector's home, and as such was at the time impossible to classify. Often Pollock would paint on the floor, adding layers of paint apparently at random, building up a dense composition that said more about the action of painting than any specific subject matter: hence the term "action painting" which is invariably used to describe this technique. As a contemporary critic said: with Pollock the canvas became "an arena in which to act – rather than as a space in which to reproduce . . .".

Similar to Pollock in technique, but less abstract in subject matter, was the Dutch-born artist **Willem de Kooning**, whose *Women* series clearly attempts to be figurative – as do a number of his other paintings, especially the earlier ones, many of which are in the Museum of Modern Art. Where he and Pollock are alike is in their exuberant use of paint and colour, painted, splashed, dripped or scraped on to the canvas with a palette knife. **Franz Kline** was also of this "gestural" school, though he cut down on colour and instead covered his canvas with giant black shapes against a stark white background: bold images reminiscent of Chinese ideograms and Oriental calligraphy. **Robert Motherwell**, who some have called the leading light of the Abstract Expressionist movement (in so far as it had one), created a similar effect in his *Elegies to the Spanish Republic*, only here his symbols are drawn from Europe not the East – and unlike Abstract Expressionist paintings they gain their inspiration from actual events. Again, for his work the Whitney and MoMA are good sources.

Foremost among the second group of Abstract Expressionists was **Mark Rothko**, a Russian-born artist whose work is easy to recognise by its broad rectangles of colour against a single-hued background. Rothko's paintings are more controlled than Pollock's, less concerned with exuding their own painterliness than with expressing, as Rothko put it, "a single tragic idea". Some have called his work mystic, religious even, and his paintings are imbued with a deep melancholy, their fuzzy-edged blocks of colour radiating light and, in spite of an increasingly lightened palette, a potent sense of despair. Rothko, a deeply unhappy man, committed suicide in 1970, and it was left to one of his closest friends, **Adolf Gottlieb**, to carry on where he left off. With his "pictographs" Gottlieb spontaneously explored deep psychological states, covering his canvases with "Native" American signs. He also used a unique set of symbols of cosmos and chaos – discs of colour above a blotchy earth – as in his *Frozen Sounds* series of the early 1950s, currently in the Whitney collection.

The Abstract Expressionists gave native American art stature worldwide and helped consolidate New York's position as centre of the art world. But other painters weren't content to follow the emotional painting of Pollock and Rothko *et al*, and toned down the technique of excessive and frenzied brushwork into impersonal representations of shapes within clearly defined borders – **Kenneth Noland**'s *Target* and the geometric (and later three-dimensional) shapes of **Frank Stella** being good examples. **Ad Reinhardt**, too, honed down his style until he was using only different shades of the same colour, taking this to its logical extreme by ultimately covering canvases with differing densities of black.

Barnett Newman is harder to classify, though he is usually associated with the Abstract Expressionists, not least because of the similarities to Rothko of his bold "fields" of colour. But his controlled use of one striking tone, painted with only tiny variations in shade, and cut (horizontally or vertically) by only a single contrasting strip, give him more in common with the trends in art that followed. **Helen Frankenthaler** (and later **Morris Louis**) took this one stage further with pictures like *Mountains and Sea*, which by staining the canvas rather than painting it lends blank areas the same importance as coloured ones, making the painting as if created by a single stroke. With these two artists, colour was the most important aspect of painting, and the canvas and the colour were absorbed as one. In his mature period Louis began – in the words of a contemporary critic – "to think, feel and conceive almost exclusively in terms of open colour". And as if in rejection of any other method, he destroyed most of his work of the previous two decades.

With the 1960s came **Pop Art**, which turned to America's popular media for subject – its films, TV, advertisements and magazines – and depicted it in heightened tones and colours. **Jasper Johns**' *Flag* bridges the gap, cunningly transforming the Stars and Stripes into little more than a collection of painted shapes, but most Pop Art was more concerned with monumentalising the tackier side of American culture: **Andy Warhol** did it with Marilyn Monroe and Campbell's Soup; **Claes Oldenburg** by re-creating everyday objects (notably food) in soft fabrics and blowing them up to giant size; **Robert Rauschenberg** by making collages or "assemblages" of ordinary objects; **Roy Lichtenstein** by imitating the screen process of newspapers and cartoon strips; and **Ed Kienholz** through realistic tableaux of the sad, shabby or just plain weird aspects of modern life. But what Pop Art really did was to make art accessible and fun. With it the commonplace became acceptable material for the twentieth-century artist, and as such paved the way for what was to follow. **Graffiti** has since been elevated to the status of art form, and New York painters like **Keith Haring** (who died in 1990) and **Kenny Scharf** were celebrities in their own right, regularly called in to decorate Manhattan nightclubs.

Ironically, over the last decade or so there has been a return to straight figurative depictions, either supra-realistically as in the poignant acetate figures of **Duane Hanson** and the more conventional nude studies of **Philip Pearlstein**, or in a minimal way as with the quasi-abstractions of **Robert Moskowitz**. There has even been a return by some artists to the conventions of nineteenth-century portraiture and history painting, seen in the work of **Mark Tansey** and **Robert Arneson**. Most exciting is the work of the KOS group, from the South Bronx. As for the future, things have never been more fluid. But New York remains, at least in terms of the marketplace, centre of art worldwide – and the city to which everyone continues to look for inspiration.

Writers on New York City

GARRISON KEILLOR

■

New York City is about reaction: its devotees are committed; so are its critics. Below are three pieces on the city: the first by Midwesterner **Garrison Keillor**; the second by resident New Yorker **Quentin Crisp**; the third by **David Widgery**, who lived in London.

Garrison Keillor

Garrison Keillor was born in Minnesota in 1942. From the mid-1970s to the late 1980s he hosted the live radio show A Prairie Home Companion, *but his chief fame lies in creating Lake Wobegon, a small Midwestern town where, as he puts it, "all the women are strong and all the men are beautiful". His books are humorous, often autobiographical, collections of stories of characters from Lake Wobegon.*

Keillor now spends much of his time in New York City: the contrast between Manhattan and his native Midwest comes over clearly in his thoughts on a subject that has inspired numerous writers over the years – the New York subway.

Solidarity Forever

When I moved from Minnesota to New York, so many New Yorkers warned me against setting foot in the subway that I naturally headed there first, and I've been riding it daily ever since. It's dirty, plagued with beggars, sometimes miserably slow, and yet, it's a *train* and that gives it grandeur, even with homeless people sleeping across the seats. When you grow up in a little town like Wobegon, next to a deserted railroad track rusting in the weeds, and you imagine a shiny train chugging in and carrying you away, it marks you for the rest of your life. When I stand in my dreary station on West 68th Street and see the C train's lights come around the tunnel bend and feel the rails shake, my heart smiles. I feel fulfilled.

You can tell I'm not a real New Yorker, by the way, when I call it the C train. The subway is such a part of the soul of the city, the mark of a native New Yorker is the way he refers to the subway lines by their antique names – the BMT, the IRT, and the IND – the initials of transit companies dead 60 years or more. To us immigrants, they are the A train or the No 1, known by the letter or number on the sign in the train window.

The pace of life in New York tends to be stately, and tourists think of it as fast only because they're here at weekends, when there's less traffic. During the week, especially in Manhattan, the pace is so slow, you often feel that any mode of transportation might be as fast as any other – you could walk, drive, take a cab, or ride the subway, and get there about the same time – so we choose our transport more on aesthetic grounds. Like most older American men, I'm sentimental about trains, but my real love is the automobile. In a car, you can sing along with the Temptations or interview yourself ("Gar, you're 48 years old and yet you're the leading pitcher in the National League, what's your secret?"), or yell at your boss. The subway forces you to act reasonable and wear a public face. The automobile is the sweetest privacy a person gets in a day. But in New York, having a car of your own is a handicap, like having a hump of your own. At parties, you sometimes see clumps of car owners comparing costs of garage space, the merits of various routes out of town, discussing the hump. Taxis aren't much better. Traffic in New York ebbs more than it flows, and the narrow cross-streets go into coronary occlusion regularly. Sitting motionless in a cab for 15 minutes as pedestrians flow by, you feel a vibration from deep below. It is the subway. You should get out and go down and take it.

Life in New York is slow, but I feel my steps quicken when I take the handrail and climb down the steps to the subway station. The beggar who sits on the top step never gets a nickel from me. I hurry down and when I go through the turnstile I break into a slow trot down the next flight to the platform. I hurry because I don't want barely to miss a train, which feels logical, but of course, by hurrying, I sometimes barely miss a train that if I had walked slowly I wouldn't have been aware of. If I find the platform crowded, I'm happy. It means that some of the job of waiting has been done by others. If I find a train pulling out, its red lights disappearing into the dark, it's a sad moment, in a place that is forlorn already: water dripping, garbage on the tracks, a raggedy man asleep on a bench. I stand and think of all the things I could have done differently this morning and shaved faster or toasted the bagel lighter. I could've skipped the editorial page of the *New York Times*. Once every few weeks, I come to the platform as the train is rolling in. It stops and I board it, as if it were my private subway. This is a great day, always.

A speed merchant it isn't, though the view from the front window of the Broadway Express as it races downtown from 96th Street, zooming through the turns at 40 miles an hour, is as exciting as the Coney Island roller coaster. Elegant it ain't either. In the stations and cars, none of the ads are for BMWs or ski resorts, they're for haemorrhoids and sore feet, bunions, bad skin, bad teeth, drug treatment. The movie ads show glamorous stars but subway riders like to draw on them, give them warts and pimples, black eyes, make them cry, make stuff come out of their noses and draw big balloons overhead where the stars confess their homosexuality, their drug habits.

It takes a strong person to pursue elegance at street level in New York. A new sidewalk café, Chinese-Mexican, with six tables, opened in my neighbourhood this summer, and every night I walked by and saw people eating Szechuan *tostados* and drinking Dos Equis or Tsing-tao beer, truck exhaust swirling around them, panhandlers leaning over their table, a homeless man curled up in the doorway, and the diners looked as cool as if they were at the Ballroom. I admire the resolution of people who can look reality in the face and deny it. People who are drawn to the romance of the subway, for example.

The subway is where you can study people, through discreet glances, and ponder their histories. The man in the expensive suit with the *Wall Street Journal* tucked under his arm: who he? A young black woman sits reading Thoreau's *Walden*, a woman who, if I saw her on the street, I'd never associate with Thoreau. Thoreau was a surburban guy who walked to work at his pond and who wrote, "Simplicity simplicity, simplicity! Our life is frittered away by detail. Let your affairs be as two or three, and keep your accounts on your thumbnail. In the midst of this chopping sea of civilised life, a man must live by dead reckoning if he would not founder and go

to the bottom. Simplify, simplify." Thoreau never lived in New York. He did not envision the subway.

The subway is where I stand, studying Spanish from the advertising placards such as the ad for Tide *detergente* with the phrase *blanquier tan blanco*, as a young man in a dark suit and a narrow black tie stands in the middle of the car, swaying and preaching the Gospel. I don't imagine that the Spanish for "whiter than white" is a particularly useful phrase in New York but it describes how I feel sometimes: *too damn white*. But this is what the man is preaching, that ye must be washed in the blood of the lamb and be made spotless, whiter than snow. This is a message I grew up hearing, and I look at him and smile to show my agreement, but he reads something else in my expression, like spiritual need. He zeroes in on me. "There are two trains in this life and only two. One train to heaven and the other to hell. Which train are you on, brother?" he asks. His judgement is fierce, like my father's. Across the aisle is a young black woman wearing the biggest hair comb ever seen, with her name spelled out in rhinestones: MICHELLE. As if life is a show and here is her marquee. She needs the Gospel more than I do, but he comes and preaches it to me. I avoid his eyes. I study the Spanish, such a graceful language. The phrase *No se apoye contra la puerta* (Don't lean against the door) sounds like an invitation to dance, compared to what they said where I come from ("What's the matter with you? For crying out loud. Quit leaning against the door!"). Spanish is the loving tongue, like the song says. My dad told me, "Get a job," *Aprenda una vocacion*, says the ad. He said, "Listen to what I'm telling you!" *Este atento a los instrucciones*. If my old man spoke Spanish, maybe I'd have listened to him. The preacher closes up his Bible and gets off at 14th Street. My stop, too, but I ride on to West 4th. I'll walk back.

The subway is a great cultural institution. It makes us New Yorkers stand close to each other, which we imagine we don't want to do, but really we want to be *made* to. We need an institution to bring us together and the subway does that in a big way. Life is constantly spinning, you see, and a powerful centrifugal force wants to hurl us apart, alone, into the darkness, to become recluses in cabins in Vermont. We need to get in a crowd now and then to experience the pleasure of the city, a painful pleasure at first for those of us from the provinces – in the Midwest, a comfortable conversational distance is about four feet, and the first time a Midwesterner boards the subway, he reaches critical mass and implodes – but you get used to it. And then it seems lovely, like when we were kids, and were jammed together in a car. My aunts and uncles produced flocks of kids and believed that, no matter how many were in the back seat, you could always get one more in. If we could exhale enough to whisper, then there was room for another one. The subway operates on a similar principle. At Times Square, they pack into the cars and then more people get on. The train is so packed, you don't even need to hang on, you just ride in a loose human gel.

When people are squeezed tight, they become extremely courteous. No eye contact. No sudden moves. Nothing sudden. Nothing loud or rude. Ten of us stand in 12 square feet at the end of the car, ten people carefully balanced as the train starts, ten arms holding on to a bar so we don't lurch into each other, ten people trying to maintain a half-inch space between each other. Of the nine people around me, five are black, which is more black people than have come through Lake Wobegon in 20 years. To be packed in so close to black men and women seems like a privilege, if you consider that all systems of oppression and cruelty require distance to be maintained. Segregation means exactly that, and so does apartheid. So, to stand inches away from each other is liberating. I wouldn't say this to the woman standing next to me, whose hip I feel against the side of my leg, but it's true.

It occurs to me, riding the subway, that the Golden Rule is a matter of great practicality, reminding you to look at every situation from both sides because the person you are doing it to today can do it to you tomorrow: count on it. Our situations are easily reversed. The Rule means: whatever you do, don't be too arrogant – the person you sack today is the person you'll need tomorrow, the man you put in prison will someday be the warden, so resist the temptation to moral grandeur, because the world does turn. The people crowded around me, whose bodies touch mine, are the broadest slice of New York I'll see today and the closest neighbours I have. I am stunned by their civility. I think of the Rule here because there is no place in New York where it is so assiduously applied. Packed in

tight, you *feel* the social contract and sense its fragility. The train lurches and instantly we each rebalance so as not to break it. Solidarity forever, as the old song says, the subway makes us strong.

© Garrison Keillor 1991

This article was originally published in the Independent Magazine. *Garrison Keillor's books include* Lake Wobegon Days, Leaving Home, Happy to Be Here *and* We are Still Married.

Quentin Crisp

There are few more active devotees of New York City than **Quentin Crisp**. *He has lived here – in a seedy boarding house in the East Village – for five years, making a living from writing and reviewing films and filling up on peanuts and champagne at literary launches, lunches and previews across America: all part of what he calls the smiling and nodding racket. He's a well-known figure in his neighbourhood, and he recently achieved his greatest ambition – to be given full American citizenship after four years as a "resident alien". "Now", says Crisp, "I am beyond deportation and able to commit my first murder." Though in his eighties, he has no desire to return to Britain: he would, he claims, rather live in New York than anywhere else in the world. What follows is a brief personal view of the city, specially written for this book, by one of its most diehard fans.*

I am now a twilight American.

In the days when I was only English, a full-time American, curling his lip as he spoke, said to me, "You British think that where the suburbs of New York end, the suburbs of Los Angeles begin." Actually our ignorance is even more profound than that. When we say "America" we mean New York and when we say "New York", we are referring not to the state nor even to the Bronx or Brooklyn but only to Manhattan. Furthermore, if shown a map of the United States, we mistake Long Island for Manhattan whereas in fact the latter is merely a tiny rock, the shape of a date stone, crushed between Long Island and the rest of the continent. Nevertheless, in spite of its cramped situation and its relatively limited size, it cannot be denied that, when you are in this city, you feel you are at the heart of the world.

At a time when most people who crossed the Atlantic Ocean did so by boat, it was the skyline of New York that made the deepest impression. Returning home, the first things a traveller mentioned were the skyscrapers. They are still spectacular but nowadays, when most capital cities bristle with very tall buildings, this aspect of New York is no longer so remarkable. Indeed it would not be difficult to photograph London or Sydney to look like any American metropolis. For an English person, though not necessarily for an Australian, the uniqueness of New York lies not in its architecture nor in its climate but in its people.

Everybody here is your instant friend.

Strange to relate, it is the natives themselves who issue dire warnings concerning the coldness and the dangers of the place. Ignore what they say. Take exactly the same safety precautions that you would use as a visitor to any big modern city. Do not stroll, swaddled in furs and bristling with diamonds, along dim side streets after midnight. At all other times, wander whither you please. Even those denizens who wish to praise their habitat misguidedly tell you that you will love the bustle of New York. In truth, except during rush hours, it is a leisurely city in which anything goes. I have seen elderly gentlemen meandering through mid-Manhattan wearing nothing but their running shorts. In fact there is almost nothing that anyone could wear or say or do here that would cause anything like the shocked reaction that in England greets the slightest deviation from traditional dress or behaviour.

See the sights if you must; go to the top of the Empire State Building or the World Trade Center if you are a born tourist, but spend most of your time in the streets where you will find you are perpetually welcome as though this teeming city were a village. It is not a good idea to travel on the subway. The system is very complicated and the situation is made worse by the fact that all maps have been disfigured beyond recognition. Moreover, the stations are bleak and the trains so noisy that conversation of any kind is impossible. Unless you are desperate, try not to take taxis. They are amazingly plentiful but the drivers, though friendly, have no more idea of the whereabouts of your destination than you do. English cabbies, if you try to give them instructions, interrupt you angrily with the words, "D'yer wanna drive the damn thing yerself?" Their American counterparts expect a guided tour and, to complicate matters further, may not understand anything you say. As you look through the thick pane of glass that separates you from them, you will see they have names like Ascencio or Rodriguez so, if communications break down, try Spanish.

When your feet give out, take buses. They are frequent, air cooled in summer and warm in winter but unfortunately you must pay your fare (a dollar at the moment) in exactly the right amount of silver coinage. Bus drivers give no change. This is almost the only annoying quirk that mars the joy of metropolitan life.

Feel free to ask for street directions from anybody; you will get their life story. And though they look like gangsters, even the policemen are cozy.

New York is one vast carnival. The splendour and the squalor are woven together more closely and more conspicuously than in any other city that I, at any rate, have ever visited. At one moment you are treading sidewalks paved with the names of famous people; the next you are bouncing down avenues in such a state of disrepair that, if you are in a fast-moving vehicle, your head hits the roof. It is also a gloriously noisy place in which ambulances, police cars and fire engines never seem to sleep. Being in New York is like taking part in a Frank Capra movie – crazy, human, beautiful. You will notice as soon as you arrive that everyone is handsome, probably because of the dazzling mixtures of races that have made their homes here.

If there are any drawbacks to this earthly paradise, they are climatic and financial.

At a distance most parts of the world seem to have a climate; when you are in them, they only have weather. This is true of New York. Occasionally the seasons are as unpredictable as those of Southern England but I am happy to tell you that they are never as dreary. Speaking generally, the winters are short, as bright and bitter as one of Dorothy Parker's epigrams, but the summers seem long because they are so hot. Some years for most of July and all of August the temperature hovers at ninety degrees. If, during this time, there is a thunderstorm, do not expect any relief. Hot water pours from the sky, a torrid wind blows through the concrete canyons and the next day is as humid as the one before. To enjoy the city at its best, come in the autumn – like Mr. Columbus. This time of year is almost always clear, beautiful and dry.

The rigours of the financial climate are harder to evade. When you visit America, stay with friends however much you may come to dislike them before the end of your stay. Hotels are staffed by very obliging people and their managers make a great fuss of you but accommodation is far from cheap. All this happiness has to be paid for.

However, do not allow these minor disadvantages to deter you for a moment. Pack tonight; leave home tomorrow.

Books by Quentin Crisp include The Naked Civil Servant; How to Become a Virgin; *and* Manners from Heaven.

David Widgery

David Widgery *combined a career as a general practitioner in London's East End with that of a writer and critic. He was a great fan of New York, and regarded "riding the Circle Line, sunbathing on top of the World Trade Center and eating in Little Italy during the San Gennaro Festival as among the greatest pleasures of civilised life". In a letter to the authors of this book he wrote his own introduction to the piece that follows: "I love the United States, but it's the America of radicalism, muckraking and rhythm and blues which the establishment is at present so keen to deny." David Widgery died in 1992, aged 46.*

I first went to Manhattan twenty years ago; a terrified teenager clutching a "99 Day, $99" coach ticket. America seemed to be curling open like an old tin can before my eyes, the civil rights movement was spilling into the northern city ghettoes, the Berkeley students were discovering pot and "organising within the knowledge factory" and a huge plume of smoke hung above Los Angeles from the gleeful riot in Watts. Sixties New York was fast, belligerent and scared. My strongest memories were the poster over the Students for a Democratic Society's HQ saying "No Vietnamese ever called me Nigger"; the smell of hot oil and rubber inside Greyhound Stations and queues of poor people with their parcels wrapped up with infinite patience and newly achieved dignity.

Back again in 1974, New York still felt, to a European, a radical city, a place of imminence, a mix of the older 1960s possibilities and the new spirit of the women's and gay movement which still meant change. The Watergate Tapes were

on sale in supermarket checkouts, Vietnam was in every other sentence and the Movement was still moving. Political optimism was only temporarily stalled, the Empire was uneasy.

So the first shock of New York deep into the Reign of Reagan is its platitudinous self-confidence, its intellectual conformism and a social conservatism so profound it has ceased to be a cosmetic and has been absorbed into the very civic skin. Never mind the homeless sleeping out in the public parks, subways unfit for cattle, the poor hawking secondhand goods on the street corners and the plummeting stock exchange; there is a tennis clip on every mountain bike, a new restaurant on every intersection and if you don't *enjoy*, it's your own damn fault.

Typical is what's happened to the poor old Statue of Liberty, spruced up for its Centennial as the new brand image of capitalism, another product from the people who gave you freedom. The statue was a democratic gesture, its catchline was written by the socialist poet Emma Lazarus, and the French fund-raising effort was an act of defiance against absolutism. But its incessantly produced image now beams benignly over the aerial bombardment of Tripoli and the rolling up of the Contras, or whatever wheeze comes next from the patriots who now direct US foreign policy.

Inside Liberty's tower, a Museum of Immigration is now housed* (rather tough on Black Americans, who mostly arrived in shackles at the plantation posts), which even includes Samuel Gompers, George Grosz and Helen Keller. But the Museum is deserted while thousands stand in a queue to photograph themselves looking out from Liberty's flame. While I read a panel on the rise of the No-Nothing-Party before the First World War and its campaign against dope fiends and alien gunmen, someone strides past in a studied "Don't Mess with the US" T-shirt shouting "All this history bores me". Indeed.

History is now New York's enemy and if you enquire about Watergate, let alone Stonewall, people brought up on TV and leisure magazines look back with alarm. Being a European sentimentalist, I trot off to the usual shrines, eating a cold turkey sandwich on the spot John Lennon got shot; gawping at the Apollo and the Cedar Bar and visiting Trotsky's old print shop in St

---

*Now moved to Ellis Island

Mark's Place. While wading through throngs of New Yorkers queuing for "Vienna 1900" (a kind of Habitat catalogue for the Franz-Josef era) at the Museum of Modern Art to see the Pollocks and De Koonings I hear the gallery guide announcing that "the Post-Impressionists were like the European Romantics. That is they were alcoholics and committed suicide." But the real New York is a another time-space continuum. Now.

As a city it has lost none of its architectural exuberance and manic energy. The taxis still swerve rather than drive, the sign language is still imperative and muscular ("Don't block the box", "Touchbank Here", "Stop Cheap Steaks") and people throw frisbees as if their life depended on it. There is less English spoken, more babies with bald fathers and a lot more purple prose in the delis which now stick reviews over their midget vegetables and lake sturgeons and offer varietal grape juices. *Enjoy* is the supreme injunction.

If you think gentrification is people sticking brass door knockers on their Stoke Newington front doors, you should see the gentry in operation in New York. There a neighbourhood can be razed, and replaced by yuppie lego in a matter of months and gourmetified and art-galleried in the process.

Which is not to say all the cultural landmarks have been built over by sushi bars and designer bike shops. Despite AIDS, people still strip for charity, organise telephone sex link-ups which are shown on your telephone bill as long distance calls, and queue to see "My Beautiful Launderette" which, along with Laura Ashley, muffins and antique clocks, was one of the few signs that the United Kingdom exists.

The US labour movement, once mighty but now organising only 17 per cent of the workforce, soldiers on, thank God, and the best day I spent in New York was being shown around the back of a power plant, Mafia-disposed toxic waste and all, by a rank and file organiser. And there is a Left, although in comparison with the movement of the 1960s and 1970s it is microscopic.

So I was delighted to meet Victor Navasky, the editor of the *Nation*, an organ of sensible liberalism which, in current circumstances, seems crypto-Bolshevik; to come across writers for the post-Murdoch *Village Voice* who are as appalled by Reaganism as most Europeans; and to meet people who are, ahem, Marxists.

What is surprising is the degree of self-delusion among those tyros of empiricism, the bankers themselves. Banker availability is a New York speciality, they are young, they are noisy and they are everywhere: restaurants, gallery openings, night clubs and all younger than oneself. I interrupt one who is discussing the investment potential of a Jamie Reid Sex Pistols daub at Reid's New York opening at the Josh Bauer Gallery.

"Does it matter to you that since Reaganomics, the USA is not only a net debtor, but the biggest debtor in the world? And why are all the farms going bust?"

He isn't worried, his art collection will see him through; if the Exchange busts, he has a Schnabel under the table.

Steve Mass, founder of the Mudd Club, is also delighted by the ironies of yuppies shelling out for Situationist off-cuts, but equally off-beam. "What we really needed in New York was someone like David Hebridge to tell us what it all *meant*." Hmmm. Was it like this in 1928, I wonder?

At the Palladium, which has less style than Stoke Newington's Three Crowns on Friday night, more bankers are waiting to meet the Eurythmics, whose co-leader's birthday we are celebrating. "Do you know any good bands in Britain? Up and coming and with investment potential?" asks one. I take a deep breath, "Well, there's this group called the Redskins. You seem to have plenty of statues that need kicking down."

This article was originally published in City Limits *Magazine in October 1986; thanks to them for letting us reprint. David Widgery's works include* Beating Hearts, *a study of racism and anti-racism centring on the East London Bangladeshi community where he practiced, and the introduction to the photobook* A Day in the Life of London.

Books

Publishers are given in the order British/American; where a book is published only in one country, it is designated UK or US; o/p indicates a book out of print.

Travel and impressions

Mike Marqusee and Bill Harris (eds) *New York: an Anthology* (Cadogan/Salem House). Pricey, but the best and most neatly packaged collection of writings on New York – from Walt Whitman to Kathy Acker – that you'll find.

B. Cohen, S. Chwast and S. Heller (eds) *New York Observed* (Abrams). An anthology of writings on and illustrations of the city from 1650 to the present: a good alternative to the more literary Marqusee/Harris book.

Stephen Brook *New York Days, New York Nights* (Picador/Atheneum). A witty and fairly penetrating account of the city, marred only by some remarkably sexist passages.

Jan Morris *Manhattan '45* (Faber/OUP). Morris's latest, and best, writings on Manhattan, reconstructing New York as it greeted returning GIs in 1945. Effortlessly written, fascinatingly anecdotal, marvellously warm about the city. See also *The Great Port* (OUP).

Brendan Behan *Brendan Behan's New York* (Hutchinson/Geis). Behan's journey through the underbelly of New York City in the early 1960s, readably recounted in anecdotal style – and with some characterful sketches by Paul Hogarth.

Jerome Charyn *Metropolis* (Abacus/Avon). A native of the Bronx, Charyn dives into current-day New York from every angle and comes up with a book that's sharp, sensitive and refreshingly real:

one of the best things you can read on the city, from one of its better contemporary writers. See "New York in fiction", overleaf.

Florence Turner *At the Chelsea* (Hamish Hamilton/Harcourt Brace Jovanovich). 1960s memoir of the famed hotel and its various arty (and artless) transients, by a woman who lived there for a decade.

Edmund White *States of Desire: Travels in Gay America* (Picador/NAL-Dutton). A revealing account of life in gay communities across America, containing an informed if dispassionate chapter on New York. Good on Fire Island and the more lurid aspects of NYC gay bars.

Geoffrey Moorhouse *Imperial City: the Rise and Fall of New York* (Sceptre/H. Holt). Though not exactly packed full of penetrating insights, this has reasonably entertaining background on the Big Apple. Nice for dipping into on the plane over.

Bernard Levin *A Walk up Fifth Avenue* (Sceptre UK). Pompous, rather banal account of Levin's self-congratulatory meander up NYC's greatest street, from the TV series of the same name.

Henry James *Lake George to Burlington* (Tragara Press UK). Travels through the peaceful and often wild backwaters of New York State in the late 1800s. As ever, elegantly written.

Frederico Garcia Lorca *Poet in New York* (Penguin/Grove Weidenfeld). The Andalusian poet and dramatist spent nine months in the city around the time of the Wall Street Crash. This collection of over thirty poems reveals his feelings on the brutality, loneliness, greed, corruption racism and mistreatment of the poor.

History, politics and society

Oliver E. Allen *New York New York* (Macmillan). Entertaining anecdotal illustrated history with good accounts of the robber barons and other eminent New Yorkers, along with a deft appraisal of the Koch era.

Edward Robb Ellis *The Epic of New York City* (Coward-McCann o/p/Mabaro). Popularised history of the city in which its major historical figures – Peter Stuyvesant, William Tweed and the rest – become a cast of characters as colourful as any historical novel. Interesting, but you sometimes wonder where Ellis gets his facts from.

Hugh Brogan *Penguin History of the United States* (Penguin/Viking Penguin). Good, up-to-date and very complete general history of America.

Ron Rosenbaum *Manhattan Passions* (Penguin/Viking Penguin). Rosenbaum lunches with the rich and powerful in New York – and writes about it with wit, style and sometimes hardbitten contempt. Pieces on Donald Trump, Ed Koch and the late Malcolm Forbes to name just a few.

Art, architecture and photography

Paul Goldberger *The City Observed: A Guide to the Architecture of Manhattan* (Penguin/Random). If you need an up-to-date, well-written and erudite rundown on New York's premier buildings look no further. Goldberger's book is hard to fault.

Gerard R. Wolfe *New York: A Guide to the Metropolis* (McGraw-Hill US). Only available in the States, this is more academic – and less opinionated – than Goldberger's book, but it does include some good stuff on the Outer Boroughs. Also informed historical background.

N. White and E. Willensky (eds.) *AIA Guide to New York* (Macmillan/Harcourt Brace Jovanovich). Standard guide to the city's architecture, more interesting than it sounds.

Richard Berenhurst *Manhattan Architecture* (Prentice Hall). Magnificent coffee-table tome of lavish photos with an informed introductory essay on Manhattan's skyscrapers and other buildings.

H. Klotz (ed.) *New York Architecture 1970–1990* (Prestel/Rizzoli). Extremely well illustrated account of the shift from Modernism to post-modernism and beyond.

Margot Gayle and Michele Cohen *Guide to Manhattan's Sculpture* (Prentice Hall). The Art Commission and Municipal Art Society's very thorough illustrated guide to more or less every piece of standing sculpture on the island. Accessibly laid-out and written.

W. Brown *American Art* (Abrams). Encyclopedic account of movements in the visual and applied arts in America from colonial times to the present day.

Les Krantz *American Artists* (Phaidon/Facts on File). An attractive and indispensable alphabetical guide to American art after World War I.

Barbara Rose *American Twentieth-century Painting* (Skira/Rizzoli). Full and readable, with prints that more than justify the price.

Jacob Riis *How the Other Half Lives* (Dover/Hill & Wang). Republished photojournalism reporting life in the Lower East Side at the end of the nineteenth century. The original awakened many to the plight of New York's poor.

Philip S. Foner and Reinhard Schultz *The Other America* (Journeyman/Unwin Hyman). Art and images of poverty and the labour movement in the USA. Includes photographs of early twentieth-century New York by Jacob Riis (see above) and Lewis W. Hine.

Specific guides

Toby and Gene Glickman *The New York Red Pages* (Praeger US). Radical guide to the city taking in politically significant sites and points of interest. Covering Lower Manhattan only, and again solely available in America; if you can get hold of it it's an informing read.

Mark Leeds *Ethnic New York* (Passport Books US). A guide to the city that details its major ethnic neighbourhoods, with descriptions of restaurants, shops and festivals. Though its maps are terrible, it's an excellent introduction to the city's ethnic locales, especially outside Manhattan.

Myer Alperson and Mark Clifford *The Food Lover's Guide to the Real New York* (Prentice Hall US). Complete illustrated guide to the edible ethnic delights of all five boroughs.

Deborah Jane Gardner *New York Art Guide* (Art Guide Pubs). Pocket book detailing city galleries, museums, performance spaces, art and architectural associations and much more. Useful if you're touring private galleries.

Richard Alleman *The Movie Lover's Guide to New York* (Harper & Row US). Over two hundred listings of corners of the city with cinematic associations. Interestingly written, painstakingly researched and indispensable to anyone with even a remote interest in either New York or film history.

Bubbles Fisher *The Candy Apple: New York for Kids* (Prentice Hall). Written by a quintessentially New York grandmother, this guide is fun for adults to read, and offers lots of good ideas about what to do with kids in the city.

James Stevenson *Uptown Local, Downtown Express* (Viking US). Line drawings and droll commentary on some of the minutiae of New York's urban landscape by the *New Yorker* writer and cartoonist.

Judi Culbertson and Tom Randall *Permanent New Yorkers* (Chelsea Green US). This unique guide to the cemeteries of New York includes the final resting-places of such notables as Herman Melville, Duke Ellington, Billie Holliday, Horace Greeley, Mae West, Judy Garland and 350 others.

R. and P. Albright *Short Walks on Long Island* and **Phil Angellino** *Short Bike Rides on Long Island* (Globe-Pequot US). Apart from the *Rough Guide to the USA*, much the best books to buy if you're spending any length of time on Long Island.

New York in fiction

Martin Amis *Money* (Penguin/Viking Penguin). Following the wayward moments of degenerate film director John Self between London and New York, a weirdly scatological novel that's a striking evocation of 1980s excess.

Paul Auster *The New York Trilogy: City of Glass, Ghosts* and *The Locked Room* (Faber/Viking Penguin). Three Borgesian investigations into the mystery, madness and murders of contemporary NYC. Using the conventions of the crime thriller, Auster unfolds a disturbed and disturbing picture of the city.

James Baldwin *Another Country* (Penguin/Dell). Baldwin's best-known novel, tracking the feverish search for meaningful relationships among a group of 1960s New York bohemians. The so-called liberated era in the city has never been more vividly documented – nor its knee-jerk racism.

John Franklin Bardin *The Deadly Percheron; The Last of Philip Banter; Devil Take the Blue-Tail Fly* (Penguin/Viking Penguin). These three unique tales are the only work by Bardin, who disappeared from literary life in 1948; paranoid, almost surreal mysteries that use 1940s New York as a vivid backdrop for intricate storylines.

Wilton Barnhardt *Emma Who Saved My Life* (Futura/St Martin). Warm and witty novel about making it in New York in the 1970s. Full of sharply observed, satirical detail on city characters, locations, dilemmas and situations, and funny enough to make you laugh out loud, it's perhaps the most perfect thing to take with you on a visit.

Madison S. Bell *The Year of Silence* (Abacus/Viking Penguin). The story of an Upper West Side suicide, and the effects it has on everyone connected, from the woman's lover to the Broadway panhandler who discovers the body. Controlled, delicately paced writing, structured (almost) as a set of separate stories, and unsentimentally revealing the city and its people. See also Bell's collection of short stories, *Zero db* (Abacus), and his *Waiting for the End of the World* (Abacus), an earlier novel about a terrorist plot to plant a nuclear device in the subway tunnels under Times Square.

William Boyd *Stars and Bars* (Penguin/Viking Penguin). Set partly in New York, part in the deep South, a well-observed novel that tells despairingly and hilariously of the unbridgeable gap between the British and Americans. Full of ringing home truths for the first-time visitor to the States.

Peter Cameron *Leap Year* (Hamish Hamilton/HarperCollins). A delightful comic novel, somewhat in the mould of Armistead Maupin, set in New York and taking a gently satirical look at the lives of a number of interconnected Manhattanites in the late 1980s. Entertaining and perceptive.

Jerome Charyn *War Cries over Avenue C* (Abacus/Viking Penguin). Alphabet City is the derelict backdrop for this novel of gang warfare among the Vietnam-crazed coke barons of New York City. An offbeat tale of conspiracy and suspense. His latest book, *Paradise Man* (Abacus), is the violent story of a New York hit man.

John Cheever *The Stories of John Cheever* (Vintage/Ballantine). These marvellous stories have a warmth, depth of understanding and a narrative tension that makes utterly compelling reading. And they are also a superb evocation of New York (city and state) in the 1950s and 1960s.

James Cochrane (ed.) *The Penguin Book of American Short Stories* (Penguin UK). Lead story in this is Washington Irving's classic *Legend of Sleepy Hollow*, set in the Catskills and the Hudson Valley.

E.L. Doctorow *Ragtime* (Picador/Bantam). America, and particularly New York, before World War One: Doctorow cleverly weaves together fact and fiction, historical figures and invented characters, to create what ranks as biting indictment of the country and its racism. See also the earlier and equally skilful *Book of Daniel; World's Fair* –

a beautiful evocation of a Bronx boyhood in the 1930s; *Loon Lake*, much of which is set in the Adirondacks; and his latest, *Billy Bathgate*. All are available in Picador.

J.P. Donleavy *A Fairy Tale of New York* (Penguin/ Atlantic Monthly). Comic antics through the streets of New York in the well-worn Donleavy tradition.

Andrea Dworkin *Ice and Fire* (Secker & Warburg/ Grove Weidenfeld). An unpleasant and disturbing romp through the East Village by one of America's leading feminist writers.

Brett Easton Ellis *American Psycho* (Picador/ Vintage). Arriving in a blaze of hype, Easton Ellis's profoundly unpleasant book studies the life of Patrick Bateman, who works on Wall Street by day and tortures women to death for sexual pleasure by night. As in his previous book, *Less than Zero* (set in LA), the protagonist's world is a vapid one where designer labels are more important signifiers than people's names. Reviled by critics, *Psycho* is, in the final analysis, not a profound enough literary vessel for the disturbing ideas it contains.

Ralph Ellison *Invisible Man* (Penguin/Random). The definitive if sometimes long-winded novel of what it's like to be black and American, using Harlem and the 1950s race riots as a background.

F. Scott Fitzgerald *The Great Gatsby* (Penguin/ Collier Macmillan). Fitzgerald's best and best-known novel, set among the estates, the parties and hedonism of Long Island's Gold Coast in the Twenties. Stylishly written detail on the city too.

Helen Hanff *Apple of My Eye* (Futura o/p/Moyer Bell). Deliberately ironic look at the city by a native New Yorker who found fame as the author of *84 Charing Cross Road*. At times irritatingly naive, but often insightful and gently penetrating.

Oscar Hijuelos *Our House in the Last World* (Serpent's Tail/Pocket Books). A warmly evocative novel of immigrant Cuban life in New York from before the war to the present day.

Chester Himes *The Crazy Kill* (Alison & Busby/ Random). Himes writes violent, fast-moving and funny thrillers set in Harlem, of which this is just one.

Andrew Holleran *Dancer from the Dance* (Penguin/NAL Dutton). Enjoyable account of the embryonic gay disco scene of the early 1970s. Interesting locational detail of Manhattan haunts and Fire Island, but suffers from over-exaltation of the central character.

Henry James *Washington Square* (Penguin/Viking Penguin). Skilful examination of the codes and dilemmas of New York genteel society in the nineteenth century.

Tama Janowitz *Slaves of New York* (Picador/ Pocket Books). Written by one of the so-called "brat-pack" of young American writers, this collection of short stories pokes gentle fun at New York in the 1980s. Janowitz's recurring cast of characters is colourful, shocking, sad and endearing. Her most recent novel, *A Cannibal in Manhattan* (Picador), is a far less fresh or original work.

Joyce Johnson *Minor Characters* (Picador/Pocket Books). Women were never a prominent feature of the Beat generation; its literature examined a male world through strictly male eyes. This book, written by the woman who lived for a short time with Jack Kerouac, redresses the balance superbly well. And there's no better novel available on the Beats in New York. See also her *In the Night Café* (Flamingo), a novel which charts – again in part autobiographically – the relationship between a young woman and a struggling New York artist in the 1960s.

Stephen Koch *The Bachelor's Bride* (Marion Boyars). Readable if slightly affected novel of art society in 1960s New York.

Joseph Koenig *Little Odessa* (Penguin/Ballantine). An ingenious, twisting thriller set in Manhattan and Brooklyn's Russian community in Brighton Beach. A seriously readable, exciting novel, and a good contemporary view of New York City.

Larry Kramer *Faggots* (Mandarin/NAL Dutton). Parody of the NYC gay scene, lewdly honest and raucously funny, by the author of the AIDS play *The Normal Heart*.

Mary McCarthy *The Group* (Penguin/Avon). Eight Vassar graduates making their way in the New York of the Thirties. Sad, funny and satirical.

Jay McInerney *Bright Lights, Big City* (Flamingo/ Vintage). A cult book, and one which made first-time novelist McInerney a mint, following a struggling New York yuppie from one cocaine-sozzled nightclub to another. See also McInerney's latest novel, *Story of My Life* (Penguin/Vintage): easily his best work to date, a superbly observed social satire in which the heroine weaves her way through a Manhattan that's disturbingly (and sometimes hilariously) superficial, self-indulgent and exhausted.

Henry Miller *Crazy Cock* (HarperCollins/Grove Weidenfeld). Semi-autobiographical work of love, sex and angst in Greenwich Village in the 1920s.

Ann Petry *The Street* (Virago/Houghton Mifflin). The story of a black woman's struggle to rise from the slums of Harlem in the 1940s. Convincingly bleak.

Marge Piercy *Braided Lives* (Penguin/Fawcett). More a novel of Detroit than New York but an excellent one, and with much 1950s detail on the city, its neighbourhoods and embryonic movements.

Thomas Pynchon *V* (Picador/HarperCollins). First novel by one of America's greatest living writers. The settings shift from Valletta to Namibia, but New York's Lower East Side is a key reference point. And there's a fantastic crocodile-hunt through the city sewers. Recommended.

Judith Rossner *Looking for Mr Goodbar* (Cape/Pocket Books). A disquieting book, tracing the progress – and eventual demise – of a woman teacher through volatile and permissive New York in the 1960s. Good on evoking the feel of the city in the 1960s era, but on the whole a depressing read.

Henry Roth *Call It Sleep* (Penguin/Avon). Roth's only work of any real note traces – presumably autobiographically – the awakening of a small immigrant child to the realities of life among the slums of the Jewish Lower East Side. Read more for the evocations of childhood than the social comment.

Paul Rudnick *Social Disease* (Penguin/Ballantine). Hilarious, often incredible, send-up of Manhattan night-owls. Very New York, *very* funny.

Damon Runyon *First to Last* and *On Broadway* (Penguin); in the US *Guys and Dolls* (River City). Collections of short stories drawn from the chatter of *Lindy's Bar* on Broadway and since made into the successful musical *Guys 'n' Dolls*.

J.D. Salinger *The Catcher in the Rye* (Penguin/Bantam). Salinger's brilliant novel of adolescence, following Holden Caulfield's sardonic journey of discovery through the streets of New York. Essential reading.

Sarah Schulman *The Sophie Horowitz Story* (Naiad Press US) and *After Dolores* (Plume US). Lesbian detective stories set in contemporary New York: dry, downbeat and very funny. See also *Girls, Visions and Everything* (Seal Press US), a stylish and, again, humorous study of the lives of Lower East Side lesbians.

Hubert Selby Jr. *Last Exit to Brooklyn* (Paladin/Grove Weidenfeld). When first published in Britain in 1966 this novel was tried on charges of obscenity and even now it's a disturbing read, evoking the sex, the immorality, the drugs, the violence of downtown Brooklyn in the 1960s with fearsome clarity. An important book, but to use the words of David Shepherd at the obscenity trial, you will not be unscathed.

Dyan Sheldon *Dreams of an Average Man* (Penguin o/p/Crown). Dense, typically mordant novel of deceit, social manners and mid-life crises among NYC yuppies. An insightful and frequently scary read.

Isaac Bashevis Singer *Enemies* (Penguin/Farrar Straus & Giroux). A Polish Jew settles in New York following the war and marries the woman who helped him escape the Nazis, only to find the wife he thought was dead has managed to escape too. A bleak tale, suffused with guilt and regret, set in a Manhattan haunted by the horrific and seemingly everlasting shadow of the holocaust.

Betty Smith *A Tree Grows in Brooklyn* (Pan/HarperCollins). Something of a classic, and rightly so, in which a courageous Irish girl makes good against a vivid pre-war Brooklyn backdrop. Totally absorbing.

Rex Stout *The Doorbell Rang* (Fontana/Viking). Stout's Nero Wolfe is perhaps the most intrinsically "New York" of all the literary detectives based in the city, a larger-than-life character who, with the help of his dashing assistant, Archie Goodwin, solves crimes – in this story and others published by Fontana – from the comfort of his sumptuous midtown Manhattan brownstone. Compulsive reading, and wonderfully evocative of the city in the 1940s and 1950s.

Lee Tulloch *Fabulous Nobodies* (Picador/HarperCollins). Latest in a line of novels simultaneously satirising and celebrating New York's obsession with style. Tulloch writes with some wit, but the endless lists of designer labels in lieu of any real plot is wearying.

Edith Wharton *Old New York* (Virago/Scribner o/p). A collection of short novels on the manners and mores of New York in the mid-nineteenth century, written with Jamesian clarity and precision. Virago/Scribner also publish her *Hudson River Bracketed* and *The Mother's Recompense*, both of which centre around the lives of women in nineteenth-century New York.

Tom Wolfe *The Bonfire of the Vanities* (Picador/Bantam). Wolfe's first novel, and one which uses his skills of social observation to the full. Sherman McCoy is a Wall Street bond dealer who finds he can't live on $1 million a year, and meets his match when, while swooning at the monied spires of Manhattan, he inadvertently drives his Mercedes into the South Bronx. The best top-to-toe revelation of New York in the late 1980s you could wish for – and a fine racy read to boot, despite its recent appearance as a much criticised film (see "New York on film" overleaf).

New York on film

"There are eight million stories in the Naked City." So goes the line in the 1948 movie of the same name. Ever since the silent era, film makers have been mining some of those stories, hoping to turn them into cinematic gold. What follows is a selection, biased by our own tastes, of some of the more representative films set and/or shot in the city and its environs. For more details of the city in film, get hold of *The Movie Lover's Guide to New York* by Richard Alleman (see "Books").

After Hours (Martin Scorsese: 1985). Feverish nightmare comedy of young computer programmer's overnight descent into hell – downtown New York. Lightweight but entertaining, thanks to game cast and Scorsese's at-his-fingertips technique.

All About Eve (Joseph L. Mankiewicz: 1950). Terrifically talky, overripe egos in Manhattan theatre world. A script peppered with brilliantly artificial dialogue, delivered from the guts by Bette Davis as ageing Broadway star Margo Channing.

All That Jazz (Bob Fosse: 1979). Broadway choreographer Roy Scheider's life and death viewed as a running, Felliniesque production number in Fosse's autobiographical ego-trip. What can be said about a musical whose high point is an open-heart surgery extravaganza?

Angel Heart (Alan Parker: 1987). Mickey Rourke runs up against destiny and one Louis Cyphre (Robert de Niro) in the New York of the 1950s: atmospheric shots of Harlem and Coney Island add to the ambience of evil, violence and guilt.

Angels with Dirty Faces (Michael Curtiz: 1938). Action, comedy and sentimentality expertly whipped up by Warner Brothers. Archetypal role for James Cagney as gangster who goes to the chair pretending to be a coward for the sake of idolising slum boys (The Dead End Kids).

Angelo My Love (Robert Duvall: 1983). Actor-turned-director Duvall's neo-realist portrait of young city gypsy (a motion picture natural) and his milieu.

Annie Hall (Woody Allen: 1977). Oscar-winning autobiographical comic romance between neurotic Allen and scatty Diane Keaton is a Valentine to her and to the city. Simultaneously clever, bourgeois and very winning. For place-spotters, Annie's apartment was on 70th Street between Lexington and Park avenues.

Batman (Tim Burton: 1989). After the campy tongue-in-cheek TV series of the 1960s, the celluloid Batman returns to his comic-strip origins, battling villains in a sombre, psychologically intense Gotham City. Jack Nicholson steals the show as The Joker.

Blackboard Jungle (Richard Brooks: 1955). Idealistic teacher Glenn Ford tames violent young thugs in studio-bound NYC high school. Watchable, even though it's largely contrived Hollywood social realism. The sensation it caused had something to do with the use of Bill Haley and the Comets' song "Rock Around the Clock".

Bonfire of the Vanities (Brian de Palma: 1990). Disappointingly miscast version of Tom Wolfe's bestseller (see "Books") with Tom Hanks as Wall Street dealer Sherman McCoy driving to disaster. Much use of Bronx/Brooklyn locations can't enhance an ill-starred big-budget attempt.

Breakfast at Tiffany's (Blake Edwards: 1961). Truman Capote's sophisticated novella somewhat softened to accommodate Audrey Hepburn as charmingly loose Manhattanite Holly Golightly.

Bright Lights, Big City (James Bridges: 1988). Adaptation of Jay McInerney's cult novel (see "Books") about a coked-out yuppie whose life disintegrates as he stumbles from club to club. Michael J. Fox does his best in the lead role, but fails to bring across the feverish cynicism of the character or the book.

Broadway Danny Rose (Woody Allen: 1974). Warm, engaging little showbiz fable with Allen as good-hearted, small-time agent on the run from loony Mafia family. Mia Farrow is the blond floozie catalyst. Scenes shot at Carnegie Deli, 55th and Broadway.

Crimes and Misdemeanors (Woody Allen: 1989). Two stories about guilt, only slightly linked thematically, and with Allen in his pessimistic mode, depite the second story's comedy. Not a laugh a minute.

Coogan's Bluff (Don Siegel: 1968). First teaming of *Dirty Harry* director and Clint Eastwood, as upright Arizona lawman showing NY's Finest how to corral criminals. Siegel's **Madigan**, made the same year, contrasts detective Richard Widmark's routine with police commissioner Henry Fonda's problems. Both pictures are stylish, tough character studies.

The Cool World (Shirley Clarke: 1964). This arty documentary-style scan of a Harlem teenager who longs to be a gun-toting gang member doesn't coalesce, despite grippingly "real" moments. Three years earlier Clarke experimented with film forms in **The Connection**, in which a group of addicts awaiting their pusher are recorded by docu-film maker. Three years later she trained her camera on a monologuing black hustler in **Portrait of Jason**.

The Cotton Club (Francis Ford Coppola: 1984). Jazz and gangsters in costly, overplotted musical melodrama starring Richard Gere.

Crossing Delancey (Joan Micklin Silver: 1989). Lovely if overdramatised story of a Jewish woman (Amy Irving) who lives uptown but visits her grandmother south of Delancey each week. The matchmaking scenes between the grandmother and the local *yenta* steal the show. An engaging view of contemporary life in the Jewish Lower East Side.

The Crowd (King Vidor: 1928). Downbeat, influential silent study of day-to-day lives of hard-luck office worker and wife. Mixes pathos, realism and humour in just the right amounts.

Cruising (William Friedkin: 1980). Cop Al Pacino goes underground to ferret out killer of gays in tasteless, unbalanced thriller filmed on location. Salaciously stylised "realism".

Cry of the City (Robert Siodmak: 1948). Ruthless gangster Richard Conte pursued by boyhood friend turned cop Victor Mature. Made at a time when police sirens and rain-soaked sidewalks were the stuff of poetry.

Dead End (William Wyler: 1937). Highly entertaining, stage-derived tragedy of the East Side's teeming poor, set on an impressive studio-built street set. With Humphrey Bogart as a mother-obsessed small-time gangster, and a pack of lippy adolescents who earned their own movie series as *The Dead End Kids*.

Desperately Seeking Susan (Susan Seidelman: 1985). Bored suburban housewife Rosanna Arquette becomes obsessed with mysterious Madonna in off-the-wall comedy. Effervescent and unpretentious with a feel for modern New York.

Dog Day Afternoon (Sidney Lumet: 1975). Outlandish but true story of a man (Al Pacino, perfect) robbing a bank so his lover (Chris Sarandon, ditto) can have a sex change.

Do the Right Thing (Spike Lee: 1989). Set over 24 hours in and around an Italian-owned pizza joint in Bedford-Stuyvesant, Brooklyn, Lee's best film to date skilfully moves from comedy to an adept exploration of the racial problems of that neighbourhood and the city itself. Realistic, stylish and with a great soundtrack.

Easter Parade (Charles Walters: 1948). Fred Astaire came out of retirement to partner Judy Garland in a musical festooned with 17 Irving Berlin songs. The title tune – featuring a stroll on Fifth Avenue – was, like everything else, shot on a Hollywood backlot.

Escape from New York (John Carpenter: 1981). In 1997 Manhattan has become a maximum security prison from which anti-hero Kurt Russell has to rescue the hijacked US President. Visually explosive thriller which promises more than it delivers.

Eyes of Laura Mars (Irvin Kershner: 1978). Chic terror in surprisingly effective pulp thriller that uses NY locations cannily. Faye Dunaway is riveting as vulnerable fashion photographer with psychic vision.

Eyewitness (Peter Yates: 1981). Unsuccessfully updated 1940s-style melodrama benefits from Manhattan setting and comic-romantic by-play between janitor William Hurt and Sigourney Weaver as TV reporter investigating a murder he supposedly saw.

Fame (Alan Parker: 1980). Collective, contemporary puttin'-on-a-show sort of musical-drama set against the background of Manhattan's High School for the Performing Arts. Some good scenes and acting, but end result is neither fish nor fowl.

Fort Apache, The Bronx (Daniel Petrie: 1981). Paul Newman in handsome form as veteran cop based in the city's most crime-infested and corrupt precinct. Tense, entertaining and totally unbelievable.

42nd Street (Lloyd Bacon: 1933). Milestone backstage musical from Warner Bros, starring Ruby Keeler as the young chorine who has to replace the ailing leading lady: she goes out onstage as an unknown and, guess what, comes back a star. Corny and cheerful.

The French Connection (William Friedkin: 1971). Plenty of juicy atmosphere in extremely tense, sensationally made Oscar-winning cop thriller starring Gene Hackman, whose classic car chase takes place under the Bensonhurst Elevated Railroad.

The Godfather (Francis Ford Coppola: 1972). Oscar-winning epic about Mafia family, friends and enemies is superb movie opera. **Part Two**, two years later, developed and deepened its predecessor's themes and strengths. **Part Three** (1990) concluded the story, but was a disappointment to fans. A great triple bill.

Ghostbusters (Ivan Reitman: 1985). A trio of flaky paranormal investigators – Dan Ackroyd, Bill Murray and Harold Rami – go into business flushing out the spooks and spirits of Manhattan. Some genuinely funny moments in the Public Library and the Upper West Side.

Green Card (Peter Weir: 1990). Gerard Dépardieu (in his first big English-speaking role) marries Andy MacDowell, he to get a coveted Green Card, she to get an apartment. Months later, the authorities investigate and the two have to ensure their stories match. An obvious plot, but the capable hands of director Weir (who also made *Witness*, *Picnic at Hanging Rock*, *Gallipoli*, etc) mold the scenes into near poetic vision of the great city.

Goodfellas (Martin Scorsese: 1990). A swift, stylish excercise in violence from Scorsese, detailing the decline into organised crime of one Henry Hill. If you can stand the gore, a brilliant movie.

Gremlins II (Joe Dante: 1990). Hilarious sequel sees thousands of gremlins taking over a prestigious skyscraper, a move which threatens to ruin the business empire of a Trump-like figure. Worth seeing if only for the rendition of "New York, New York" by thousands of the little reptiles.

The Group (Sidney Lumet: 1966). A bevy of fine acting talent on display in ambitious, episodic adaptation of Mary McCarthy's novel about the personal/professional careers of a 1930s Vassar College clique. See "Books".

Guys and Dolls (Joseph L. Mankiewicz: 1955). Marlon Brando sings and dances in this over-blown version of Broadway musical about Damon Runyon-derived low-lifes. Jean Simmons is fetching as Salvation Army woman he woos, while Frank Sinatra walks amiably through.

Hannah and Her Sisters (Woody Allen: 1986). Allen in mellowed, Chekhovian mood. The human comedy on view is exceptionally well played and wryly observed, but it lacks depth.

Hello Dolly! (Gene Kelly: 1969). This elephantine nail in the movie musical's coffin was an extravagant showcase for Barbra Streisand, too young but dynamic anyway as widowed matchmaker Dolly Levi.

Hester Street (Joan Micklin Silver: 1975). Young, tradition-bound Russian-Jewish immigrant Carol Kane joins her husband in turn-of-the-century Lower East Side to find he's cast off Old World ways. Simple but appealing tale with splendid period feeling.

Insignificance (Nicholas Roeg: 1985). Marilyn Monroe, Albert Einstein and Eugene McCarthy lookalikes play stagey games in the Roosevelt Hotel. Essentially empty, Roeg's movie is worth watching for Tony Curtis's boozy senator and the lyrical, terrifying last few minutes.

Ironweed (Hector Babenco: 1987). Based on William Kennedy's *Albany Trilogy*, this is a convincingly sombre re-creation of the depression years, with Meryl Streep and Jack Nicholson in top form as the drink-sodden lovers. To capture the feeling of Albany in the 1930s, scenes were shot in upstate Hudson.

It's Always Fair Weather (Gene Kelly, Stanley Donen: 1955). *On the Town* gone sour. Trio of wartime buddies reunite ten years later to discover they loathe one other and themselves. Smart, cynical, satirical musical that was – undeservedly but unsurprisingly – a box office flop.

King Kong (Merian C. Cooper/Ernest B. Schoedsack: 1933). A giant ape runs amok when taken from his jungle home to far less respectful New York by a film producer. The scene where King Kong stands astride the Empire State Building, swatting passing planes while tending Fay Wray, has become part of the city myth.

King of Comedy (Martin Scorsese: 1983). Quirky, biting satire set on the fringes of the New York entertainment world mixes the familiar with the bizarre in the tale of talentless autograph hound Rupert Pupkin (Robert de Niro) who wants to be a celebrity on a par with his Johnny Carson-like idol Jerry Lewis.

Klute (Alan J. Pakula: 1971). Oscar-winner Jane Fonda as Manhattan call-girl Bree Daniel, ably supported by titular detective Donald Sutherland, in taut, well-above-average damsel-in-distress thriller with modern twists.

Last Exit to Brooklyn (Uli Edel: 1989). As films-of-the-books go, not a bad version of Hubert Selby's *succès de scandale* (see "Books"). Partly set in Red Hook (see Chapter 5), the film is strong on period detail and just as shocking in its portrayal of sex and violence as the novel.

Looking for Mr Goodbar (Richard Brooks: 1977). Diane Keaton plays Upper West Side schoolteacher by day, promiscuous coke-sniffing clubgoer by night, until she winds up in the evil hands of Richard Gere. Violent and frightening – even more so once you know it was based on a true story. See "Books".

The Lost Weekend (Billy Wilder: 1945). Strong, enduring drama about dipso writer Ray Milland's delirium tremens-strewn path to Bellevue. One of the most famous scenes is his long trek down Third Avenue trying to sell his typewriter. Shot on location, including *P.J. Clarke's* bar (for more on which see Chapter 8, *Drinking and Eating*).

The Manchurian Candidate (John Frankenheimer: 1962). Enormously skilful critique of American politics (from Richard Condon's novel) culminates with brainwashed Laurence Harvey turning assassin in Madison Square Garden. With Frank Sinatra, Angela Lansbury and Janet Leigh.

Manhattan (Woody Allen: 1979). A black-and-white masterpiece of middle-class intellectuals' self-absorptions, lifestyles and romances, cued by a Gershwin soundtrack in what is probably the greatest eulogy to the city ever made. Essential viewing.

Manhattan Melodrama (W.S. Van Dyke: 1934). Clark Gable and William Powell as boyhood pals from the slums who grow up on opposite sides of the law. Mickey Rooney plays Gable aged 12, Myrna Loy is the love interest. The movie earned notoriety when Public Enemy Number 1 John Dillinger was shot down as he emerged from seeing it in a Chicago cinema.

Marathon Man (John Schlesinger: 1976). Ex-Nazi deathcamp doctor Laurence Olivier goes after student Dustin Hoffman's teeth – and life – in incredible, botched-up and brutal thriller.

Marty (Delbert Mann: 1955). Modest Oscar winner from Paddy Chayefsky's teleplay about fat, mother-dominated Bronx butcher Ernest Borgnine meeting equally shy schoolteacher Betsy Blair in a Brooklyn dance hall. Hailed as a breakthrough in the way in which it focused on "real" people, it looks rather tame today.

Mean Streets (Martin Scorsese: 1973). Scorsese's breakthrough film breathlessly follows small-time hood Harvey Keitel and his volatile, harum-scarum buddy Robert de Niro around Little Italy (actually Belmont in the Bronx) before reaching the inevitably violent climax.

Midnight Cowboy (John Schlesinger:1969). The love story between Jon Voight's naive hustler Joe Buck and Dustin Hoffman's touching city creep Ratso Rizzo is the core of this ground-breaking Oscar winner. The pair are superlative. Much of the rest of the picture is empty, flashy aggression.

Miracle on 34th Street (George Seaton: 1947). Macy's Santa Claus Edmund Gwenn tries to prove he's the genuine item to young Natalie Wood and the courtroom.

Mixed Blood (Paul Morrisey: 1984). Blithely amoral comedy about flamboyant drug-pushing "Godmother" Marilia Pera and her Alphabet City brood. Bloody cartoon action peppered with a hot salsa soundtrack.

Moonstruck (Norman Jewison: 1987). Romantic comedy with Cher in good form as a Brooklyn Italian princess finding love and excitement with a Brandoesque Nicolas Cage. Good views of Brooklyn Heights and the Metropolitan Opera.

Moscow on the Hudson (Paul Mazursky: 1984). Robin Williams as a Russian circus saxophonist who defects in this witty, sentimental comedy on the East/West divide. More schmaltzy propaganda for the US.

My Dinner with André (Louis Malle: 1981). Chamber version of the ultimate New York movie. It's all talk, analysis, philosophy, as playwright-actor Wallace Shawn and former *avant-garde* theatre director André Gregory play scripted (by Shawn) versions of themselves. Unique.

My Favourite Year (Richard Benjamin: 1984). The year is 1954 and the film is based on Mel Brooks's real life, when as a rookie writer for Sid Caesar's *Your Show of Shows*, he had to keep Errol Flynn sober for a live TV broadcast. Locations include Radio City Music Hall, Central Park and parts of Brooklyn.

New York, New York (Martin Scorsese: 1977). Intense performances from Robert de Niro and Liza Minelli in moody, impressive attempt to sour and splinter 1940s movie-musical conventions. The tone is dark, the narrative unbalanced, but occasionally it all really works. NY imaginatively re-created on studio soundstages.

New York Stories (Martin Scorsese/Francis Ford Coppola/Woody Allen: 1989). A trilogy of stories, of which the Coppola is a mess, the Scorsese pretentious and the Allen, *Oedipus Wrecks*, hilarious. A good idea which should have brought better work from Allen's chums.

Next Stop, Greenwich Village (Paul Mazursky: 1974). Brooklyn boy heads to the Village in 1953, hoping to become actor in endearing autobiographical comedy. Shelley Winters is outstandingly funny as his smothering, over-the-top mother.

On the Town (Gene Kelly, Stanley Donen: 1949). Exhilarating, landmark musical, ballet-inspired, about three sailors' romantic adventures on 24-hour leave in NYC. With Gene Kelly, Frank Sinatra, and Ann Miller flashing her gams in the Museum of Natural History. Partly shot on location (from Brooklyn Navy Yard to the top of the Empire State), it's as much New York travelogue as musical.

On the Waterfront (Elia Kazan: 1954). Oscar winner contains what is arguably Marlon Brando's greatest performance as anti-hero Terry Malloy, an inarticulate longshoreman reluctantly caught up in union racketeering. Superb location shooting. With Eva Marie Saint, Karl Malden and Rod Steiger.

Once Upon a Time in America (Sergio Leone: 1984). Sprawling, self-indulgent, but often brilliantly atmospheric saga starring Robert de Niro. Spanning decades, it comes close to capturing some of the pulp pleasures of 1930s and 1940s movies.

The Out of Towners (Arthur Hiller: 1970). From the moment they set foot in the city, everything that can go wrong for Jack Lemmon and Sandy Dennis does in Neil Simon's fraught and rather unsympathetic comedy.

Panic in Needle Park (Jerry Schatzberg: 1971). Al Pacino and Kitty Winn give dedicated performances as pair of druggies in authentic-seeming downer.

The Pope of Greenwich Village (Stuart Rosenberg: 1984). Thin, shaky-footed retread of *Mean Streets* with Mickey Rourke and Eric Roberts as small-time thieves falling foul of the Mafia.

Radio Days (Woody Allen: 1987). Mia Farrow rises from cigarette girl to Manhattan personality in Allen's slender collection of vignettes from the days of 1930s radio. Some location shooting in Brooklyn and Times Square, but not a film to compare with his best work.

Ragtime (Milos Forman: 1981). Miscalculated adaptation of E.L. Doctorow's novel nevertheless has a fresh performance from Elizabeth McGovern as Evelyn Nesbit and an amusing one from James Cagney as the wily old police commissioner. See "Books".

Rear Window (Alfred Hitchcock: 1954). Broken-legged photographer James Stewart plays Peeping Tom and discovers one of his neighbours is a killer. Peerless Hitchcock comedy-thriller, notable for its backlot re-creation of a NYC courtyard, and the sexual chemistry between Stewart and Grace Kelly.

The Roaring Twenties (Raoul Walsh; 1939). World War I veteran gets involved with NY bootleggers. James Cagney supported by Humphrey Bogart. Definitive Warner's gangster formula, and crackling entertainment.

Rosemary's Baby (Roman Polanski: 1968). Seminal urban Gothic from Ira Levin's best-seller, about pregnant young married Mia Farrow plagued by satanic cult. The building she lives in is the famed Dakota, 72nd Street and Central Park West (for more on which, see "The Upper West Side" in Chapter 4).

Saturday Night Fever (John Badham: 1977). Crudely scripted, shrewdly marketed flick that was a massive youth cult hit, with John Travolta as a sensitive stud using disco as his escape route over the Brooklyn Bridge to Manhattan. Not totally bad, unlike the 1983 sequel **Staying Alive**.

The Secret of my Success (Herbert Ross: 1987). Michael J. Fox plays the hick come to New York to make it whatever the costs, and becomes the bemused target of his boss's wife's advances. Scatty, funny and with some great shots of NYC.

Serpico (Sidney Lumet: 1973). Al Pacino is on target as real-life NYC cop, atypically cultured and incorruptible, in fast-paced tribute to loner righteousness that teems with atmosphere.

The Seven Year Itch (Billy Wilder: 1955). When his wife and kid vacate humid Manhattan, Mitty-like pulp editor Tom Ewell is left guiltily leching over the innocent TV-toothpaste temptress upstairs – Marilyn Monroe, at her most wistfully comic. The sight of her pushing down her billowing skirt as she stands on a subway grating (at Lexington Avenue and 52nd St) is one of the era's most resonant movie images.

Sid and Nancy (Alex Cox: 1986). The Chelsea Hotel is setting for the final scenes in the lives of punk's *enfants terribles*, Sid Vicious and Nancy Spungen. Their sad, shabby and often sick story is handled with warmth and humour.

Skyline (Fernando Colomo: 1980). Warm and gentle comedy about a young Spanish photographer coping with culture shock in NYC.

Smithereens (Susan Seidelman: 1982). Cheaply and roughly made story of city's punks and dispossessed that has its moments. Very obviously a springboard for the same director's *Desperately Seeking Susan*.

Sophie's Choice (Alan J. Pakula: 1982). Meryl Streep sports a Polish accent as Jewish biologist Kevin Kline's mistress in this glum but honourable adaptation of William Styron's novel set in 1947 Flatbush Brooklyn. Guilt and retribution stirred with romantic melodrama.

Something Wild (Jonathan Demme: 1986). About the best of the yuppie-in-peril nouvelle vogue with Melanie Griffith hijacking mild Manhattan businessman Jeff Daniels for a ride into New Jersey and her colourful past. The skill of the film is its ability to change gear several times – from screwball comedy to high school nostalgia to something very wild and very nasty indeed.

The Sweet Smell of Success (Alexander Mackendrick: 1957). Broadway gossip columnist Burt Lancaster and sleazy press agent Tony Curtis are a great team in this biting study of showbiz corruption. British director Mackendrick handles the juicy on-location, night-time milieu with real flair.

Superman (Richard Donner: 1978). Chris Reeve struggles for Truth, Justice and the American Way in contemporary Manhattan by way of the Planet Krypton and a lovingly filmed Midwest. Alter ego Clark Kent's offices are the *Daily News* building on 42nd Street. The sequel **Superman 2** has stunning night-time vistas from atop the Verrazano Narrows Bridge.

Taxi Driver (Martin Scorsese: 1976). Superbly unsettling study of obsessive outsider Robert de Niro, with Jodie Foster as the pubescent hooker he tries to "save" in horrifying gory climax. Scorsese's NYC is hallucinatorily seductive, yet thoroughly repellent.

Tootsie (Sydney Pollack: 1982). Dustin Hoffman's performance as an intense, out-of-work New York actor who dons female drag and becomes a soap opera celebrity is a work of masterful comic talent.

A Tree Grows in Brooklyn (Elia Kazan: 1945). This touching working-class family saga, from a bestseller set in the earlier years of this century, was Kazan's directorial debut. See "Books".

Up the Down Staircase (Robert Mulligan: 1967). Harren High School is the setting for screen version of Bel Kaufman's bestseller about beleaguered teacher Sandy Dennis. *Blackboard Jungle* with a sex-change.

Wall Street (Oliver Stone: 1987). Facile tale of good versus evil in the wheeler-dealer corporate jungle of the late 1980s. Michael Douglas is convincingly wicked, and the views out of his office window are terrific. But as a movie it's almost laughably shallow.

West Side Story (Robert Wise, Jerome Robbins: 1961). Sex, Shakespeare and singing in an overlauded, hypercinematic Oscar-winning musical (via Broadway) about rival street gangs. Certainly it's excitingly assembled and impressively packaged.

Wolfen (Michael Wadleigh: 1981). A skilful and very scary werewolf tale, contrasting the amoral, big business side of the city with the social wasteland of the suburbs. One of the first films to use the Steadicam, giving a terrifying view of the action from the eyes of the Wolfen.

Yankee Doodle Dandy (Michael Curtiz: 1942). James Cagney's Oscar-winning performance as showbiz Renaissance man George M. Cohan is a big, spirited bio-pic with music. Of its kind, probably the best ever.

Year of the Dragon (Michael Cimino: 1985). Mickey Rourke is a racist Vietnam-veteran cop setting out to clean up Chinatown from newly appointed smack baron John Lone. Ostensibly anti-racist, but in fact falling into standard traps with glamourised violence and the condoning of its hero.

A glossary of New York terms and people

New York has a jargon all its own – often unintelligible to non-natives. A guide to New York language appears in the next section. What follows here is a selection of words basic to an understanding of the city, a scattering of art/architecture terms used in the guide and, lastly, a roll call of New York names, past and present.

New York terms and acronyms

Art Deco Style of decoration popular in the 1930s, characterised by geometrical shape and pattern.

Art Nouveau Art, architecture and design of the 1890s typified by stylised vegetable and plant forms.

Atrium Enclosed, covered pedestrian space usually forming the lobby of a corporate building.

Avenue of the Americas Recent and little-used name for Sixth Avenue.

Bag Lady Homeless woman who carries her possessions around in a bag.

Bathroom/Restroom/Washroom/Comfort Station Euphemisms for a toilet.

Beaux Arts Style of neoclassical architecture taught at the Ecole des Beaux Arts in Paris at the end of the last century and widely adopted in New York City.

Big Apple New York City. Possibly from the slang of jazz musicians who referred to anything large as a "big apple" – and, for them, New York was the biggest apple of all.

Brownstone Originally a nineteenth-century terraced house with a facade of brownstone (a kind of sandstone): now any row or townhouse.

Clapboard House covered with overlapping timber boards.

Colonial Style of neoclassical architecture popular in the seventeenth and eighteenth centuries.

Colonial Dames Of America Patriotic organisation of women descended from worthy ancestors who became American residents before 1750.

Condo Short for condominium, an individually owned apartment within a building.

Co-op The most popular form of apartment ownership in the city. A co-op differs from a condo in that you buy shares in the building in which the apartment is sited, rather than the apartment itself.

CUNY City Universtiy of New York.

Federal Hybrid of French and Roman domestic architecture common in the late eighteenth century and early nineteenth century.

Greek Revival Style of architecture that mimicked that of classical Greece. Highly popular for banks and larger houses in the early nineteenth century.

Gridlock Traffic freeze – when cars get trapped in street and avenue intersections, preventing traffic on the cross streets passing through.

Historical District Official label for an area considered of historic interest or importance.

Lex Conversational shorthand for *Lexington Avenue*.

Loft Large open space at the top of an apartment block, popular with artists because of the direct lighting.

MTA (*Metropolitan Transit Authority*) Runs the city's buses and subway lines: the *IND* (Independent), *BMT* (Brooklyn-Manhattan Transit) and *IRT* (Interborough Rapid Transit).

PATH (*Port Authority Trans Hudson*) The agency that operates the commuter train, also known as the PATH, between Manhattan and New Jersey.

Plaza Wide, open space that acts as a pedestrian forecourt to a skyscraper – and which gives it a prestigious address (One So-and-So Plaza) that can lead to much confusion when you try and work out just where the building actually *is*. See also **Zoning Ordinances.**

Port Authority Conversational shorthand for the Port Authority Bus Terminal on Eighth Avenue and 41st St.

Robber Barons Nineteenth-century magnates who made their fortunes at the expense and to the detriment of ordinary Americans.

Skyscraper The word comes from the highest sail on a sailing ship, and hence refers to any high building.

SRO Single room occupancy hotel – most often lived in long term by those on welfare (state benefit).

Stoop Open platform, with steps leading up to it, at the entrance to a house.

SUNY State University of New York.

Tenement Large, nowadays often slummy, building divided into apartments.

Tri-State Area All-encompassing term for New York, New Jersey and Connecticut states.

Vest Pocket Park Tiny park or open space.

WPA *(Works Project Administration)* Agency begun by Roosevelt in 1935 to create employment. As well as construction work the **WPA** art projects produced many murals in public buildings and a renowned set of guidebooks to the country.

Zoning Ordinances Series of building regulations. The first, passed in 1915, stated that the floor space of a building could not be more than twelve times the area of its site, discouraging giant monoliths and leading to the setback or wedding cake style of skyscraper. A later ordinance allowed developers to build higher provided they supplied a public space at the foot of the building. Hence the **Plaza**.

New York people

ALLEN Woody Writer, director, comedian. Many people's clichéd idea of the neurotic Jewish Upper East Side Manhattanite, his clever, crafted films *Annie Hall*, *Manhattan*, *Broadway Danny Rose*, *Hannah and Her Sisters*, *Radio Days* and *Crimes and Misdemeanors* comment on, and have become part of, the New York myth. His fall from grace in 1993, accused of child abuse by Mia Farrow after he left her for his adopted daughter, caused the biggest storm of publicity seen in the city in years.

ASTOR John Jacob (1822–1890) Robber baron, slum landlord and, when he died, the richest man in the world. Astor made his packet from exacting swingeing rents from those living in abject squalor in his many tenement blocks. By all accounts, a right bastard.

BEECHER Henry Ward (1813–1887) Revivalist preacher famed for his support of women's suffrage, the abolition of slavery – and as the victim of a scandalous accusation of adultery that rocked nineteenth-century New York. His sister, Harriet Beecher Stowe, wrote the best-selling novel *Uncle Tom's Cabin*, which contributed greatly to the anti-slavery cause.

BRADY James ("Diamond Jim") (1856–1917) Financier, wide boy and bon vivant of the Gay Nineties. Famed for bespattering himself with diamonds – hence the nickname. One of the good guys of the era, he gave much money to philanthropic causes.

BRESLIN Jimmy Bitter, Brit-hating but often brilliant columnist for *New York Newsday*. Once ran for mayor on a Secessionist ticket (declaring New York independent from the state) with Norman Mailer as running mate.

BRILL Diane Doyenne of the nightclub hangers-out and hangers-on.

BRYANT William Cullen (1794–1878) Poet, newspaper editor and main mover for Central Park and the Metropolitan Museum. The small park that bears his name at 42nd St and Fifth Ave is a semi-seedy and ill-fitting memorial to a nineteenth-century Wunderkind.

BURR Aaron (1756–1836) Fascinating politician whose action-packed career included a stint as vice-president, a trial and acquittal for treason, and, most famously, the murder of Alexander Hamilton (qv) in a duel. His house, the Morris-Jumel Mansion, still stands.

CARNEGIE Andrew (1835–1919) Emigré Scottish industrialist who spent most of his life amassing a vast fortune and his final years giving it all away. Unlike most of his wealthy contemporaries he was not an ostentatious man – as his house, now the Cooper-Hewitt Museum, shows.

COHAN George M. (1878–1942) If you've seen the illustrious bio-pic *Yankee Doodle Dandy* you probably think this actor, dancer, composer, playwright and Broadway producer was a wonderful chap; in reality Cohan was a dislikeable and disreputable wheeler-dealer who ruined others for his success.

CRISP Quentin Writer (*The Naked Civil Servant*) and celebrated apologist for NYC, living in self-imposed exile from his native England. Frequently to be found giving readings.

CUOMO Mario Governor of New York State and often suggested contender for the Democratic Party presidential nomination. A liberalish politician whose main problem in achieving greater things will probably be his Italian ancestry.

DINKINS, David First black mayor of New York City. Elected in 1989 after a hard, mud-slinging mayoral battle against Republican Rudolph Giuliani, his term in office has so far left him seeming ineffectual and weak: "Everything sticks to him" said a pundit "– but praise".

FRICK Henry Clay (1849–1919) John Jacob Astor minus the likeable side. Frick's single contribution to civilisation was to use his inestimable wealth to plunder some of the finest art treasures of Europe, now on show at his erstwhile home on Fifth Avenue.

FULTON Robert (1765–1815) Engineer, inventor and painter who got surburban commuting going with his ferry service to Brooklyn. The point where it landed now marks the beginning of Fulton St. He did not, as you'll read everywhere else, invent the steamboat.

GARVEY Marcus (1887–1940) Activist who did much to raise the consciousness of blacks in the early part of the century (and is now a Rasta myth). When he started to become a credible political threat to the white-controlled government he was thrown in prison for fraud; pardoned but deported, he spent his last years in London.

GILBERT Cass (1859–1934) Architect of two of the city's most beguiling landmarks – the Woolworth Building and the Customs House.

GOULD Jay (1836–1892) Robber baron extraordinaire. Using the telegraph network to be the first person in the know, Gould made his fortune during the Civil War, and went on to manipulate the stock market and make millions more. His most spectacular swindle cornered the gold market, netted him $11 million in a fortnight and provoked the "Black Friday" crash of 1869.

GREELEY Horace (1811–1872) Campaigning founder-editor of the *New Yorker* magazine and *Tribune* newspaper who said but never did "Go West, young man!". An advocate of women's rights, union rights, the abolition of slavery and other worthy, liberal matters.

HAMILL, Pete Newspaper editor, writer, broadcaster and expert on Manhattan and – especially – the Outer Boroughs. One of the best no-bullshit commentators around today.

HAMILTON Alexander (1755–1804) Brilliant Revolutionary propagandist, fighter (battlefield aide to Washington), political thinker (drafted sections of the Constitution) and statesman (first Secretary to the Treasury). Shot and killed in a duel by Aaron Burr (qv). His house, Hamilton Grange, is preserved at the edge of Harlem.

HARING Keith Big-name artist who used crude animal forms for decoration/patterning. Designed bits of *Palladium* nightclub, sleeve to Malcolm McLaren's *Buffalo Girls*, etc. His early death prematurely removed one of America's most promising artists and designers.

HELMSLEY Harry Property-owning tycoon who, like Donald Trump (qv), had a penchant for slapping his name on all that fell into his grasp. Hence many old hotels are now Helmsley Hotels, and, more offendingly, the New York Central Building on Park Avenue has become the Helmsley Building. Since the trial of his wife Leona, Harry has apparently gone senile.

HELMSLEY Leona Wife of Harry, self-styled "Queen of New York" and majordomo of the *Helmsley Palace Hotel*. To the delight of many, the shit hit the fan for Leona in 1989, when she was found guilty of million-dollar tax evasion.

IRVING Washington (1783–1859) Satirist, biographer, short story writer (*The Legend of Sleepy Hollow*, *Rip Van Winkle*) and diplomat. His house, just outside the city at Tarrytown, is worth a visit.

JOHNSON Philip Architect. As henchman to Ludwig Mies Van der Rohe, high priest of the International Style glass box skyscraper, he designed the Seagram Building on Park Avenue. In later years he has moved from Modernism to postmodernism, with the AT&T Building on Third Avenue (passable), the Federal Reserve Plaza on Liberty Street (puerile) and the thing at 53rd Street and Third (unspeakable). Other claims to fame: a brief stint as token intellectual for quasi-fascist senator Huey Long in the 1930s, and his personal founding of the thoroughly fascist *Youth and The Nation* organisation.

KOCH Ed The most popular mayor of New York since Fiorello LaGuardia (qv). Elected by a slender majority in 1978, Koch won New Yorkers over by his straight-talking, no-bullshit approach – and by moving to appease the loudest liberal/ethnic groups when, and only when, it became politically necessary. After three terms in office, he lost the Democratic nomination in 1990 to David

Dinkins (qv) following scandals involving other council officils and his insensitive handling of black social problems.

LAGUARDIA Fiorello (1882–1947) NYC mayor who replaced Jimmy Walker (qv) and who gained great popularity with his honest and down-to-earth administration.

MAILER Norman The old sexist slugger still breezes in from Brooklyn between novels.

MORGAN J. Pierpont (1837–1913) Top-of-the-pile industrialist and financier who bailed the country out of impending doom in 1907 and used a little of his spare cash to build the Morgan Library on Third Avenue. He created a financial empire that was bigger than the Gettys' and that enabled him to buy out Andrew Carnegie and Henry Frick.

MOSES Robert (1889–1981) Moses is perhaps more than anyone responsible for the way the city looks today. Holder of all the key planning and building posts from the 1930s to the 1960s, his philosophy of urban development was to tear down whatever was old and in the way, and slap concrete over the green bits in between.

OLMSTED Fredrick (1822–1903) Landscape designer and writer. Central Park and many others were the fruits of his partnership with architect Calvert Vaux.

O'NEILL Eugene (1888–1953) NYC's (and America's) most influential playwright. Many of the characters from plays like *Mourning Becomes Electra, The Iceman Cometh* and *Long Day's Journey into Night* are based on his drinking companions in *The Golden Swan* bar.

PARKER Dorothy (1893–1967) Playwright, essayist and acid wit. A founder member of the Round Table group.

RIIS Jacob (1849–1914) Photo-journalist. His compassionate account of the poor and the horrors of slum dwelling, *How the Other Half Lives*, was instrumental in hastening the destruction of the worst tenements.

ROCKEFELLER John D. (1839–1937) Multi-millionaire oil magnate and founder of the dynasty.

ROCKEFELLER John D. Jr (1874–1960) Unlike his tight-fisted dad, Rockefeller Junior gave away tidy sums for philanthropic ventures in New York. The Cloisters Museum, The Museum of Modern Art, Lincoln Center, Riverside Church and most famously the Rockefeller Center were all (or mainly all) his doing.

ROCKEFELLER Nelson (1908–1979) Politician son of John D. Jr. Elected governor of New York State in 1958 he held on to the post until 1974, when he turned to greater things and sought the Republican Party presidential nomination. He didn't get it, but before his death served briefly as vice-president under Gerald Ford.

RUBELL Steve (1946–1989) Entrepreneur. Founder and former owner of *Studio 54*, his last venture (with business partner Ian Shrager) was *The Royalton* hotel, the last word in with-it luxury.

SABAN Steven Nightperson and writer. Chronicler of the after-hours in-crowd, Saban's column in *Details* magazine should be read by those who have to be in bed by midnight.

SIMON Neil Playwright. With a record of Broadway/film hits as big as his bank balance (*Brighton Beach Memoirs* the latest), Simon can lay claim to being the most popular MOR playwright today.

TRUMP Donald Property tycoon. When you shell out $70 for your shoebox room, reflect that Donald sits on top of a real estate empire worth, at its peak, $1300 million. His creations include the glammed-out Trump Tower on Fifth Avenue, Trump Plaza near Bloomingdale's and Trump's Casino in Atlantic City, NJ. In 1990 his financial empire took a massive drumming and his personal life collapsed with a much-publicised divorce from his wife Ivana.

TWEED William Marcy "Boss" (1823–1878) Top banana of the NY Democratic Party who fiddled city funds to the tune of $200 million and gave Democratic Party headquarters Tammanny Hall its bad name.

VANDERBILT Cornelius "Commodore" (1794–1877) Builder and owner of much of the nation's railroads in the nineteenth century. At his death he was the wealthiest-ever American.

VANDERBILT Cornelius (1843–1899) Commodore's son and another hard-nosed capitalist. He doubled the family wealth between his father's death and his own – a fortune that kept (and keeps) successive generations of Vanderbilts in spare change.

WALKER Jimmy (1881–1946) Professional songwriter who turned politician and was elected NYC mayor at the height of the jazz age. As a dapper-dressed man-about-town he reflected much of its fizz, but with the Depression he lost popularity and office.

WARHOL Andy (?–1987) Artist and media manoeuvrist. Instigator of Pop Art, The Velvet Underground, The Factory, *Interview* magazine and *Empire* – a 24-hour movie of the Empire State Building (no commentary, no gorillas, nothing but the building). Died, oddly enough, after a routine gallstone operation.

WHITE Stanford (1853–1906) Partner of the architectural firm McKim, Mead and White, which designed such neoclassical piles as the General Post Office, Washington Square Arch, the Municipal Building and bits of Columbia University. Something of a *roué*, White's days were brought to an abrupt end with a bullet through the head from the gun of a cuckolded husband.

New York slang

New York City slang is essentially a kind of quickspeak, a shorthand which reflects the pace of the place, spat out brusquely (though never rudely) and without affectation. It's a language with its own variations – the corporate-based jargon of Madison Avenue is far from the street slang of the Lower East Side – but its roots, like so much else here, lie with New York's development as a city of immigrants. Yiddish words, in particular, now have currency as regular city slang; so too, though with narrower effect, do Italian. More recently, the Spanish spoken by New York's rapidly swelling Puerto Rican community has come close to making English the city's second language: adverts on the subway are in Spanish (significantly only those obviously directed at low-income brackets); there are specifically Spanish schools and TV stations; and there are parts of the city where you will not hear English spoken at all. What follows are a few of the most widely used New York phrases. Most of them were originally specific to the city, though several have spread through the US, and a few, over recent years, across the Atlantic.

Airhead A stupid, ignorant person.

Attitude adjustment What you do during Happy Hour.

AWOL Mentally unbalanced.

B'n'Ts Bridge and Tunnel people, ie those unfortunate enough to live outside of Manhattan.

BBQ Acronym for the Outer Boroughs: Brooklyn, the Bronx and Queens.

Catch the rays Sunbathe.

Cheap Tacky.

Chill out Cool off, relax.

Chutzpah Playful arrogance.

Clover hole An Irish bar.

Crack A highly addictive smokable derivative of cocaine.

Crucial Excellent, highly admirable.

Cute When used to describe a person: attractive, engaging. For things: nice, dinky – more like the British meaning.

Ditsy Silly, inconsequential, frivolous.

Flaky Odd, whacky, eccentric.

Funky With no pretensions, Bohemian.

Gross Revolting.

Grungy Grotty, tatty, dirty.

Jappie Pertaining to a Jewish American Princess, ie young, beautiful and rich.

Kvetch Complain.

Maven Buff, expert. As in movie maven.

MIA Missing In Action, ie not all there mentally. Similar to **AWOL**

Off the wall Odd, out of the ordinary.

Party pooper One who sneaks off home early.

Pig out To stuff one's face.

Pissed Pissed off, annoyed.

Preppie The predecessor of the yuppie, ie someone who went to an Ivy League University, buys clothes from Brooks Bros, etc.

Ritzy/glitzy Swish, ostentatious.

Schlep To move around or carry out a task lazily or with difficulty.

Schlock Cheap, inferior or tacky goods.

Schlong Penis.

Schlmiel Person, for example, who spills soup on someone.

Schmozel The person he or she spills the soup on.

Schmuck Person who laughs at both of them.

Schmeck A small amount.

Scuzzy Grotty – like **Grungy.**

Sens Sensimillia, a particularly potent type of marijuana.

Smart Clever.

Space cadet A stupid, sometimes scatty person.

Stressed out Suffering from extreme anxiety.

SOL Shit Out of Luck.

Talk Turkey To speak plainly, clearly and honestly.

Veg out Switch off your brain, perhaps in front of "Dallas" or "Lifestyles of the Rich and Famous".

WASP White Anglo-Saxon Protestant.

"What can I tell you?" Not really a question, more of an intensifier of what's just been said, eg: "this guy is a real asshole, what can I tell you?"

Yo! Hey you! The usual way of attracting someone's attention.

Yuppie Young Urban Professional. A person of either sex who lives in a major city, is between the ages of 25 and 35 and lives for personal prestige, money and power. Alternatively known as "Baby Boomers" and "Fast Trackers". Once a great catch-all term, "Yuppie" now seems a somewhat dated leftover of the last decade.

Zoned/phased/paced (out) Blitzed, worn out, knackered.

Index

Help Us Update

We've gone to a lot of effort to ensure that this edition of the *Rough Guide to New York* is completely up-to-date and accurate. However, things do change – in New York more rapidly than anywhere – and if you feel that there's something we've missed, or that you'd like to see included, please write and let us know. We'll credit all contributions, and send a copy of the new book (or any other *Rough Guide*, if you prefer) for the best letters. Please mark letters "Rough Guide New York Update", and send to: The Rough Guides, 1 Mercer Street, London WC2H 9QJ, or The Rough Guides, 375 Hudson Street, 4th Floor, New York NY 10014.

DIRECT ORDERS IN THE USA

Title	ISBN	Price			
Able to Travel	1858281105	$19.95	Italy	1858280311	$17.9
Australia	1858280354	$18.95	Kenya	1858280435	$15.9
Berlin	1858280338	$13.99	Mediterranean Wildlife	1858280699	$15.9
Brittany & Normandy	1858280192	$14.95	Morocco	1858280400	$16.9
Bulgaria	1858280478	$14.99	Nepal	185828046X	$13.9
Canada	185828001X	$14.95	New York	1858280583	$13.9
Crete	1858280494	$14.95	Paris	1858280389	$13.9
Cyprus	185828032X	$13.99	Poland	1858280346	$16.9
Czech & Slovak Republics	185828029X	$14.95	Portugal	1858280842	$15.9
Egypt	1858280753	$17.95	Prague	185828015X	$14.9
England	1858280788	$16.95	Provence & the Côte d'Azur	1858280230	$14.9
Europe	185828077X	$18.95	St Petersburg	1858280303	$14.9
Florida	1858280109	$14.95	San Francisco	1858280826	$13.9
France	1858280508	$16.95	Scandinavia	1858280397	$16.9
Germany	1858280257	$17.95	Scotland	1858280834	$14.9
Greece	1858280206	$16.95	Sicily	1858280370	$14.9
Guatemala & Belize	1858280451	$14.95	Thailand	1858280168	$15.9
Holland, Belgium & Luxembourg	1858280877	$15.95	Tunisia	1858280656	$15.9
Hong Kong & Macau	1858280664	$13.95	USA	185828080X	$18.9
Hungary	1858280214	$13.95	Venice	1858280362	$13.9
			Women Travel	1858280710	$12.9
			Zimbabwe & Botswana	1858280419	$16.9

Rough Guides are available from all good bookstores, but can be obtained directly in the USA and Worldwide (except the UK*) from Penguin:

Charge your order by Master Card or Visa (US$15.00 minimum order): call 1-800-255-6476; or send orders, with complete name, address and zip code, and list price, plus $2.00 shipping and handling per order to: Consumer Sales Penguin USA, PO Box 999 – Dept #17109, Bergenfield, NJ 07621. No COD. Prepay foreign orders by international money order, a cheque drawn on a US bank, or US currency. No postage stamps are accepted. All orders are subject to stock availability at the time they are processed. Refunds will be made for books not available at that time. Please allow a minimum of four weeks for delivery.

The availability and published prices quoted are correct at the time of going to press but are subject to alteration without prior notice. Titles currently not available outside the UK will be available by January 1995. Call to check.

* For UK orders, see separate price list

DIRECT ORDERS IN THE UK

Title	ISBN	Price			
...sterdam	1858280184	£6.99	Mediterranean Wildlife	0747100993	£7.95
...stralia	1858280354	£12.99	Morocco	1858280400	£9.99
...rcelona & Catalunya	1858280486	£7.99	Nepal	185828046X	£8.99
...rlin	1858280338	£8.99	New York	1858280583	£8.99
...azil	0747101272	£7.95	Nothing Ventured	0747102082	£7.99
...ttany & Normandy	1858280192	£7.99	Paris	1858280389	£7.99
...lgaria	1858280478	£8.99	Peru	0747102546	£7.95
...lifornia	1858280575	£9.99	Poland	1858280346	£9.99
...nada	185828001X	£10.99	Portugal	1858280842	£9.99
...ete	1858280494	£6.99	Prague	185828015X	£7.99
...prus	185828032X	£8.99	Provence & the	1858280230	£8.99
...ech & Slovak	185828029X	£8.99	Côte d'Azur		
...epublics			Pyrenees	1858280524	£7.99
...ypt	1858280753	£10.99	St Petersburg	1858280303	£8.99
...gland	1858280788	£9.99	San Francisco	1858280826	£8.99
...rope	185828077X	£14.99	Scandinavia	1858280397	£10.99
...orida	1858280109	£8.99	Scotland	1858280834	£8.99
...ance	1858280508	£9.99	Sicily	1858280370	£8.99
...ermany	1858280257	£11.99	Spain	1858280079	£8.99
...reece	1858280206	£9.99	Thailand	1858280168	£8.99
...uatemala & Belize	1858280451	£9.99	Tunisia	1858280656	£8.99
...olland, Belgium	1858280036	£8.99	Turkey	1858280133	£8.99
...& Luxembourg			Tuscany & Umbria	1858280559	£8.99
...ong Kong & Macau	1858280664	£8.99	USA	185828080X	£12.99
...ungary	1858280214	£7.99	Venice	1858280362	£8.99
...eland	1858280516	£8.99	West Africa	1858280141	£12.99
...aly	1858280311	£12.99	Women Travel	1858280710	£7.99
...enya	1858280435	£9.99	Zimbabwe & Botswana	1858280419	£10.99

...ough Guides are available from all good bookstores, but can be obtained
...rectly in the UK* from Penguin by contacting:

...enguin Direct, Penguin Books Ltd, Bath Road, Harmondsworth, West
...rayton, Middlesex UB7 0DA; or telephone our credit line on 081-899 4036
...9am–5pm) and ask for Penguin Direct. Visa, Access and Amex accepted.
...elivery will normally be within 14 working days. Penguin Direct ordering
...cilities are only available in the UK.

...he availability and published prices quoted are correct at the time
...f going to press but are subject to alteration without prior notice.

...For USA and international orders, see separate price list.

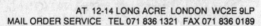